Imposing Data Sharing among Private Actors

Information Law Series (INFO)

VOLUME 48

Editor

Prof. P. Bernt Hugenholtz, Institute for Information Law, University of Amsterdam.

Objective & Readership

Publications in the Information Law Series focus on current legal issues of information law and are aimed at scholars, practitioners, and policy makers who are active in the rapidly expanding area of information law and policy.

Introduction & Contents

The advent of the information society has put the field of information law squarely on the map. Information law is the law relating to the production, marketing, distribution, and use of information goods and services. The field of information law therefore cuts across traditional legal boundaries, and encompasses a wide set of legal issues at the crossroads of intellectual property, media law, telecommunications law, freedom of expression, and right to privacy. Recent volumes in the Information Law Series deal with copyright enforcement on the Internet, interoperability among computer programs, harmonization of copyright at the European level, intellectual property and human rights, public broadcasting in Europe, the future of the public domain, conditional access in digital broadcasting, and the "three-step test" in copyright.

The titles published in this series are listed at the back of this volume.

Imposing Data Sharing among Private Actors

A Tale of Evolving Balances

Thomas Tombal

Wolters Kluwer

Published by:
Kluwer Law International B.V.
PO Box 316
2400 AH Alphen aan den Rijn
The Netherlands
E-mail: international-sales@wolterskluwer.com
Website: www.wolterskluwer.com/en/solutions/kluwerlawinternational

Sold and distributed by:
Wolters Kluwer Legal & Regulatory U.S.
7201 McKinney Circle
Frederick, MD 21704
United States of America
E-mail: customer.service@wolterskluwer.com

Printed on acid-free paper.

ISBN 978-94-035-4160-0

e-Book: ISBN 978-94-035-4165-5
web-PDF: ISBN 978-94-035-4170-9

Printed and bound by CPI Group (UK) Ltd, Croydon, CR0 4YY

About the Author

Thomas Tombal is Post-Doctoral Researcher at Tilburg University. He is affiliated to the Tilburg Institute for Law, Technology, and Society (TILT) and the Tilburg Law and Economics Center (TILEC). He holds expertise in ICT law, and more specifically in the areas of competition law, platform regulation, data sharing, data governance and data protection issues linked to the data economy.

Before joining Tilburg University, Thomas worked for five years as a researcher at the CRIDS (Centre de Recherche Information, Droit et Société) of the University of Namur (Belgium), where he obtained his PhD in September 2021.

In addition to his research activities at Tilburg University, Thomas has teaching appointments at the University of Namur, where he teach the classes 'ICT Law', 'Comparative Law and English Legal Terminology', and 'Environmental Law'.

Thomas obtained a Master's in Law (Université Catholique de Louvain) – during which he carried out an Erasmus at Trinity College in Dublin – and a Complementary Master's in ICT Law (University of Namur).

Table of Contents

Acknowledgements

This book, which has lastly been updated on 30 November 2021, is the result of five years of doctoral research and is based on my PhD dissertation. Before delving into its subject matter, I would like to take a moment to thank all the people that have either helped or supported me in my endeavours. While the PhD process might sometimes be described as a solitary adventure, the truth is that without the help of all of these formidable people, the road would have been much more complicated. As so many of them have, each in their own way, helped me to carry this project over the line, I apologise in advance for anyone that I might have forgotten.

First, I would like to thank all the people that directly assisted me in improving this manuscript.

In this regard, I would like to thank Prof. Dr Heike Schweitzer and Prof. Dr Giorgio Monti for giving me the honour of accepting to be part of my jury and for taking the time to read my work. Your fresh look at the manuscript and the insightful remarks that you have provided to me have pushed me to challenge myself and to go the extra mile, in order to improve my text. The same goes for Prof. Dr Benoît Michaux, whose role has evolved during the process of the research, but who has always been supportive and available when I needed his enlightened opinion, which also contributed to the enrichment of my findings.

I would also like to thank my two promoters, Prof. Dr Cécile de Terwangne and Prof. Dr Alexandre de Streel, as the lively and enriching exchanges that we have had during the whole doctoral process have shaped the final result of my research, which you undeniably contributed to improve, as you never stopped pushing me to refine my text. I would also like to thank you for all the precious professional and personal advices that you have provided to me over the years.

More generally, I would like to thank Prof. Dr Séverine Dusollier, Prof. Dr Michal Gal, Prof. Dr Reto Hilty, Prof. Dr Ioannis Lianos, Prof Dr Yves Poullet, Dr Inge Graef, Bertin Martens, Nestor Duch-Brown; Dr Luc Desaunettes, Dr Heiko Richter and the other people I met at the Max Planck Institute for Innovation and Competition in Munich; and all the other people that I have had the pleasure to exchange opinions with about my doctoral research, and whose advice has helped me to better shape my ideas.

Finally, I would like to thank the editing teams at Kluwer Law International and at Newgen, in particular Mr Simon Bellamy, Ms Sudha and Ms Pritha, for their precious assistance in the editing and publication of this manuscript.

Second, I would like to thank all of the people that I have had the chance to collaborate with during the last five years, as the pleasure of working with them has given me the motivation to push forward and to reach my goals.

In this regard, I would like to thank Prof. Dr Marc Nihoul and Prof. Dr Hervé Jacquemin for all the support that they have provided to me in their respective roles, which enabled me to complete my doctoral journey with serenity. Your availability to answer all the questions I had has been precious.

I would also like to thank my partners on the FLEXPUB and DIGI4FED research projects, which were conducted in parallel to this doctoral research, for the fascinating interdisciplinary exchanges that we have had.

I thank my colleagues and friends from the Law Faculty of the University of Namur and from the Centre de Recherche Information, Droit et Société (CRIDS), for their camaraderie and the countless laughs and good moments that we have shared, and which allowed me to enjoy writing this dissertation in a convivial environment.

I also thank the support staff of the Faculty and of the CRIDS, whose assistance has been vital not only for the different steps of the doctoral research but also in my daily life as a researcher.

Third, I would like to thank my family and my friends for providing me with the love and affection that I needed to see the finish line.

In particular, I would like to thank my sister, Marie, and my brother, Martin, for always being there for me when I needed them. I am truly blessed that you are not only my siblings but also two friends for life.

I would also like to thank my parents, Anne and Bertrand, for their unconditional support and for all of the sacrifices that you have made, each in your own way, in order to give us the best life possible. I know that we are not the most expressive people when it comes to sharing our feelings, but you have always made me feel loved and protected. I can never thank you enough for that.

Last but not least, I would like to thank my partner in life and my best friend, Cecilia. Without this doctoral research, I would not have met you, and without you I would have struggled a lot more to finalise this dissertation. You calm me down when I am stressed, you cheer me up when I am down, you give me faith when I doubt myself and you always push me to do more and to get out of my comfort zone. In short, you make me a better man, and having you in my life makes me the luckiest man on earth.

Introduction

1. Data is often presented as the new oil of our modern economy. It is the fuel of information and knowledge creation in an increasingly connected world. In the context of this book, 'data' is defined in a broad sense, on the basis of the definitions provided in the European Commission's proposals for a Data Governance Act and for a Digital Markets Act, and means 'any digital representation of acts, facts or information and any compilation of such acts, facts or information, including in the form of sound, visual or audiovisual recording'.[1]

The European economy runs on data, which has become an essential resource for economic growth, job creation and societal progress,[2] and the value of the data market is expected to reach between EUR 432 and EUR 827 billion by 2025.[3] Such numbers do not come as a surprise, given that the amount of data generated increases exponentially. Indeed, our increased reliance on electronic networks generates troves of data, as every action taken on these networks leaves 'footprints' in the shape of data. This growth will not slow down any time soon, as the emergence of the 'Internet of Things' (IoT)[4] will contribute to the increase of this phenomenon. One might simply think of data that is (or will be) generated by smart cars, smart houses, smart farming, etc.

---

1. Article 2.1 of the Proposal for a Regulation of the European Parliament and of the Council on European data governance (Data Governance Act), 25 November 2020, COM(2020) 767 final; Article 2.19 of the Proposal for a Regulation of the European Parliament and of the Council on contestable and fair markets in the digital sector (Digital Markets Act), 15 December 2020, COM(2020) 842 final.
2. Communication from the Commission to the European Parliament, the Council, the European Economic and Social Committee and the Committee of the Regions, '*Building a European Data Economy*', Brussels, 10 January 2017, COM(2017) 9 final, p. 2.
3. International Data Corporation and the Lisbon Council, 'The European Data Market Study Monitoring Tool – Final Study Report', June 2020, SMART 2016/0063, available at http://datalandscape.eu/, p. 9.
4. 'The Internet of things (IoT) is the inter-networking of physical devices, vehicles (also referred to as "connected devices" and "smart devices"), buildings, and other items—embedded with electronics, software, sensors, actuators, and network connectivity that enable these objects to collect and exchange data' (https://en.wikipedia.org/wiki/Internet_of_things).

While the economic value deriving from the processing of these data seems obvious, determining the legal framework to be applied to it is, on the contrary, a complex task. This stems from the fact that data is a complex good, towards which many natural or legal persons can potentially claim a right or interest. For instance, the data generated by an autonomous vehicle is relevant for multiple categories of stakeholders, such as vehicle manufacturers, car dealers, spare parts manufacturers, authorised and independent garages and repairers, developers of infotainment software used in vehicles, vehicle users, and possibly also public authorities for the optimisation of road traffic management. This example illustrates the inherent complexity of this resource, which will often be at the crossroads of multiple claims and rights aimed at controlling, accessing, or benefiting from the data processing.

2. This highlights the need for a clear legal framework, especially as the data markets are still emerging.[5] Moreover, the lack of a clear legal environment may contribute to insufficient data sharing, possibly stifling innovation and creating entry barriers for new market entrants,[6] and possibly impairing access to information or our societies' ability to tackle environmental, health or mobility challenges.[7] In the context of this book, 'data sharing' is defined in a broad sense, on the basis of the definition provided in the European Commission's proposal for a Data Governance Act.[8] Namely, it is the act through which one or several data holder(s)[9] provide(s) access to its(their) data to one or several data recipient(s), directly or through an intermediary, for the purpose of joint or individual use of the shared data, on the basis of voluntary agreements or of compulsory rules.

---

5. M. Barbero, et al., 'Study on Emerging Issues of Data Ownership, Interoperability, (Re-)Usability and Access to Data, and Liability', 25 April 2018, available at https://ec.europa.eu/digital-single-market/en/news/study-emerging-issues-data-ownership-interoperability-re-usability-and-access-data-and, p. 31.
6. Communication from Commission, '*Building a European Data Economy*', *supra*, p. 3.
7. Communication from the Commission to the European Parliament, the Council, the European Economic and Social Committee and the Committee of the Regions, '*A European Strategy for Data*', 19 February 2020, COM(2020) 66, p. 3. *See also* J. Drexl, 'Data Access and Control in the Era of Connected Devices', *Study on Behalf of the European Consumer Organisation (BEUC)*, 2019, available at https://www.beuc.eu/publications/beuc-x-2018 121_data_access_and_control_in_the_area_of _connected_devices.pdf, pp. 6-8; P. Picht, 'Towards an Access Regime for Mobility Data', *International Review of Intellectual Property and Competition Law*, 2020, Vol. 51(8), p. 942.
8. 'Data sharing means the provision by a data holder of data to a data user for the purpose of joint or individual use of the shared data, based on voluntary agreements, directly or through an intermediary' (Article 2.7 of the Proposal for a Data Governance Act).
9. The more generic term of 'data holder' is used in the context of this analysis, rather than 'data owner', as the issue of data 'ownership' is widely debated (*see* Part I, Chapter 2, Section 2.2.2). For a proposed definition of a 'data holder', *see* Article 2.5 of the Proposal for a Data Governance Act: 'a legal person or data subject who, in accordance with applicable Union or national law, has the right to grant access to or to share certain personal or non-personal data under its control'.

3. It should be outlined from the outset that the legal framework pertaining to (compulsory) data sharing is clearer when it comes to the sharing of data between governments and businesses ('G2B data sharing'). Indeed, in 2003, the European legislator adopted the Public Sector Information (PSI) Directive, which invited public sector bodies to open their PSI for reuse.[10] However, given that the public sector bodies had the choice, rather than the obligation, to open their data, only few of them did so. To remedy that weakness, the PSI Directive was amended in 2013 to force public sector bodies to make their PSI reusable for commercial or non-commercial purposes, for free or with charges limited to the marginal costs incurred for their reproduction, provision and dissemination.[11] More recently, in June 2019, the European legislator adopted a recast version of the PSI Directive, which had to be transposed in all Member States by July 2021.[12] Finally, in November 2020, the European Commission also proposed a Data Governance Act, which notably aims at laying down the conditions for the reuse of certain categories of data held by public sector bodies.[13] This string of legislations is motivated by the fact that public sector data are highly valuable resources that can be used to foster accountability and transparency, and to foster the European economy by generating digital innovation and preventing the distortion of competition in the internal market.[14]

4. Contrary to G2B data sharing, the field of (compulsory) business-to-business data sharing ('B2B data sharing') is still in the early phases of its construction. In the context of this book, the term 'business' should be understood broadly, and is not limited to undertakings pursuing profit. It also covers, for instance, data sharing with non-profits pursuing societal goals.[15] Rather, it should be understood as being distinct from business-to-government (B2G) data sharing.[16] In this regard, B2B data sharing can pursue not only economic goals but also societal and 'empowerment' goals.[17]

As underlined by the European Commission, 'data sharing between companies has not taken off at sufficient scale. This is due to a lack of

10. Directive 2003/98/EC of the European Parliament and of the Council of 17 November 2003 on the re-use of public sector information, *OJ L 345/90*, 31 December 2003.
11. Directive 2013/37/EU of the European Parliament and of the Council of 26 June 2013 amending Directive 2003/98/EC on the re-use of public sector information, *OJ L 175/1*, 27 June 2013, Articles 3.1 and 6.1.
12. Directive (EU) 2019/1024 of the European Parliament and of the Council of 20 June 2019 on open data and the re-use of public sector information, *OJ L 172/56*, 26 June 2019.
13. Articles 1.1.a) and 3-8 of the Proposal for a Data Governance Act.
14. *See* Recitals, 3, 7, and 11 of Directive (EU) 2019/1024 of the European Parliament and of the Council of 20 June 2019 on open data and the re-use of public sector information, *OJ L 172/56*, 26 June 2019.
15. On these societal goals, *see* Part I, Chapter 2, Section 2.3.1.
16. I will therefore not focus on the data sharing obligations that are imposed on businesses to the benefit of the public sector (e.g., banks are compelled to share financial information with public authorities in the context of the fight against money laundering).
17. *See* Part I, Chapter 2, Section 2.2.3 and Section 2.3.

economic incentives (including the fear of losing a competitive edge), lack of trust between economic operators that the data will be used in line with contractual agreements, imbalances in negotiating power, the fear of misappropriation of the data by third parties, and a lack of legal clarity on who can do what with the data'.[18] These factors can lead to market failures, such as the lack of incentives to collect data, uncertainties in terms of risks, high transaction costs for sharing and missing markets, and asymmetries of information distorting decision-making.[19]

One way to address these market failures is through the adoption of legal instruments promoting *voluntary* data sharing, which will tend to focus more on data governance and technical issues (standardisation, interoperability,[20] etc.), in order to create more favourable conditions for the market actors to remedy, or at least reduce, these market failures themselves.[21] For instance, the European Commission has adopted a Communication 'Towards a common European data space', containing key principles for *voluntary* B2B data sharing.[22] It has also created a 'Support Centre for Data

18. Communication from the Commission, '*A European Strategy for Data*', *supra*, p. 7.
19. *See* point 78. For a broader analysis of all of the potential types of data market failures, *see* M. Stucke and A. Grunes, *Big Data and Competition Policy*, Oxford, Oxford University Press, 2016; J. Krämer, D. Schnurr and S. Broughton Micova, 'The Role of Data for Digital Markets Contestability: Case Studies and Data Access Remedies', *CERRE Report*, September 2020, available at https://cerre.eu/publications/data-digital-markets-contestability-case-studies-and-data-access-remedies/; J. Crémer, Y.-A. de Montjoye and H. Schweitzer, 'Competition Policy for the Digital Era: Final Report', 2019, available at http://ec.europa.eu/competition/publications/reports/ kd0419345enn.pdf; B. Martens, et al., 'Business to Business Data Sharing: An Economic and Legal Analysis', *EU Science Hub*, 2020, available at https://ssrn.com/abstract=3658100; M. Bourreau and A. de Streel, 'Digital Conglomerates and EU Competition Policy', *CERRE Report*, March 2019, available at http://www.crid.be/pdf/public/8377.pdf; B. Martens, 'An Economic Perspective on Data and Platform Market Power', *JRC Digital Economy Working Paper 2020-09*, February 2021, available at https://www.researchgate.net/publication/3491 79464.
20. Interoperability is defined as 'the ability of disparate and diverse organisations to interact towards mutually beneficial and agreed common goals, involving the sharing of information and knowledge between the organisations, through the business processes they support, by means of the exchange of data between their respective ICT systems' (Decision 2015/2240 of the European Parliament and of the Council of 25 November 2015 establishing a programme on interoperability solutions and common frameworks for European public administrations, businesses and citizens (ISA2 programme) as a means for modernising the public sector, *OJ L 318/1*, 4 December 2015, Article 2.1).
21. B. Martens, et al., 'Business to Business Data Sharing', *supra*, p. 28. *See also* R. Feasey and A. de Streel, 'Data Sharing for Digital Market Contestability: Towards a Governance Framework', *CERRE Report*, September 2020, available at https://cerre.eu/publications/ data-sharing-digital-markets-competition-governance/.
22. *See* point 64. Communication from the Commission to the European Parliament, the Council, the European Economic and Social Committee and the Committee of the Regions, '*Towards a Common European Data Space*', Brussels, 25 April 2018, COM(2018) 232 final, p. 10. *See also* Commission Staff Working Document establishing

Sharing',[23] with the aim of putting in place a series of measures facilitating (voluntary) data sharing, in particular by providing examples of good practice, standard contractual clauses or existing contract models.[24] More recently, it has adopted a proposal for a Data Governance Act that notably aims at promoting *voluntary* data sharing services by intermediaries,[25] as well as *voluntary* data sharing in the common good ('data altruism').[26] The underlying idea behind all these instruments is that, in light of the proportionality principle,[27] it is preferable to first attempt to create a clear framework to incentivise the market actors to share data on their own initiative, rather than to compel them to do so. In this perspective, the European Commission seems to repeat the approach that it adopted for G2B data sharing, as the PSI Directive did not contain any *compulsory* G2B data sharing obligation either in its first version of 2003.[28]

Yet, such *voluntary* data sharing initiatives may not always be sufficient to address the above-mentioned issues, and legislators could be tempted to go a step further by imposing *compulsory* B2B data sharing in some 'specific circumstances'.[29] These specific circumstances can either be economic or societal.[30] For example, they might be justified if, as it is currently the case, a small number of large firms hold a significant part of the world's data, as this might diminish the incentives of smaller data-driven firms to emerge, grow and innovate, due to high entry barriers.[31] The high degree of market power deriving from this 'data advantage' could also affect the contestability of some markets.[32] Moreover, some platforms have acquired significant

---

a guidance on sharing private sector data in the European data economy accompanying the Communication '*Towards a Common European Data Space*', Brussels, 25 April 2018, SWD(2018) 125 final.

23. *See* https://eudatasharing.eu/homepage.
24. *See* point 65. Commission Staff Working Document establishing a guidance on sharing private sector data, *supra*, p. 6.
25. *See* point 78. *See* Articles 9-14 of the Proposal for a Data Governance Act. *See also* Commission Staff Working Document, Impact assessment report accompanying the Data Governance Act, *supra*, pp. 11-12.
26. *See* point 93. *See* Articles 15-22 of the Proposal for a Data Governance Act.
27. Article 5.4 of the Treaty on European Union, *OJ C 326/13*, 26 October 2012; Protocol (No. 2) on the application of the principles of subsidiarity and proportionality, *OJ C 326/206*, 26 October 2012.
28. *See* point 3.
29. *See*, *inter alia*, M. Stucke and A. Grunes, *Big Data and Competition Policy*, *supra*; J. Krämer, D. Schnurr and S. Broughton Micova, 'The Role of Data for Digital Markets Contestability', *supra*; J. Crémer, Y.-A. de Montjoye and H. Schweitzer, 'Competition Policy for the Digital Era', *supra*; R. Feasey and A. de Streel, 'Data Sharing for Digital Market Contestability', *supra*.
30. *See infra* Part I, Chapter 2, Section 2.2.3 and Section 2.3.
31. *See* Part I, Chapter 2, Section 2.2.3.3 Communication from the Commission, '*A European Strategy for Data*', *supra*, p. 3.
32. *Ibid.*, p. 8.

scale, effectively allowing them to act as 'private gatekeepers', and *compulsory* B2B data sharing is being discussed as a potential remedy to ensure that their systemic role will not endanger the fairness and openness of the markets.[33] On the other hand, this data concentration phenomenon[34] could also possibly impair access to information and our societies' ability to tackle environmental, health or mobility challenges.[35] In this regard, the European Commission has suggested that it would explore legislative options in order to promote a wider (compulsory) sharing and availability of data, in order to ensure 'contestability, fairness and innovation and the possibility of market entry, as well as public interests that go beyond competition or economic considerations'.[36]

It must nevertheless be outlined here that *voluntary* and *compulsory* data sharing should not be seen as two extremes on the regulatory intervention scale. Rather, there are links to be made between these two approaches, which complement each other. Indeed, if the step has to be taken from *voluntary* to *compulsory* data sharing regulatory initiatives, the latter should not reinvent the wheel and should build on the former. Indeed, the data governance principles and the technical provisions contained in *voluntary* initiatives are equally relevant for, and should support, these *compulsory* initiatives. For instance, the key principles for *voluntary* B2B data sharing contained in the Communication 'Towards a common European data space' could be integrated, in the future, in *compulsory* B2B data sharing instruments. Moreover, the national authorities that the European Commission's proposal for a Data Governance Act suggests to appoint, in order to supervise *voluntary* B2B data sharing with trusted data intermediaries, could also be appointed as the regulatory authorities for (some) *compulsory* data sharing regulatory initiatives.[37] This is because these national authorities will arguably have expertise with the governance, pricing and technical mechanisms used for *voluntary* data sharing, which are, in essence, the same as those that could be used for *compulsory* data sharing. Furthermore, the work made by the 'Support Centre for Data Sharing', mentioned above, and the European Data Innovation Board – which is a formal expert group that

---

33. Communication from the Commission to the European Parliament, the Council, the European Economic and Social Committee and the Committee of the Regions, '*Shaping Europe's Digital Future*', Brussels, 19 February 2020, COM(2020) 67, p. 8.
34. *See* Part I, Chapter 2, Section 2.2.3.3.
35. *See* footnote 7.
36. Communication from the Commission, '*Shaping Europe's Digital Future*', *supra*, p. 9; Communication from the Commission, '*A European Strategy for Data*', *supra*, pp. 5 and 14.
37. *See* points 217 and 403. *See* Recitals 22-34 and Articles 13 and 23-25 of the Proposal for a Data Governance Act.

should support the European Commission's work on technical standardisation and interoperability to facilitate *voluntary* data sharing –[38] would also be a precious resource for *compulsory* data sharing initiatives.

5. Despite this complementarity, I have chosen to focus on *compulsory* B2B data sharing regulatory initiatives because if the legislator decides to take this step forward in the degree of its intervention, this will require the prior consideration of a certain number of fundamental economic and societal balancing exercises. My focus will be to highlight the nature of these balancing exercises and to provide insights on how they could potentially be addressed. This contribution will thus be structured around the following research question: '***What are the economic and societal balancing exercises underlying compulsory B2B data sharing?***'

More concretely, and without entering into too much detail at this stage, I will focus on three balancing exercises, namely the need to balance the benefits stemming from compulsory B2B data sharing initiatives with: (i) the economic interests of the data holder;[39] (ii) personal data protection considerations;[40] (iii) and the long-term and collective costs that (some of) these initiatives could entail in terms of individual autonomy.[41] This focus can be explained by the evolution of my research, which has paralleled the evolution of the policy discussions on compulsory B2B data sharing since 2016.

Indeed, while the focus of the research and of these policy discussions was originally set on whether it would be relevant to create an intellectual property (IP)-like 'data producer's right',[42] both have shifted away from developments pertaining to 'property' on data, towards legal reflections revolving around notions of data 'control' and 'access'.[43] However, as will be outlined throughout the book, what has remained constant in the policy discussions is the large emphasis on the need to ensure that these initiatives do not excessively distort the economic interests of the data holders, whether in the context of competition law remedies or of *ex ante* legislations imposing data sharing, as their incentives to collect and process data must be preserved. Accordingly, my first ambition was to adopt an analytical approach, in order to shed more light on how these economic interests of the data holders are factored in the existing compulsory B2B data sharing

38. *See* point 307. *See* Recitals 40 and 41 and Articles 26 and 27 of the Proposal for a Data Governance Act. *See also* Commission Staff Working Document, Impact assessment report accompanying the Data Governance Act, *supra*, p. 54.
39. *See*, *inter alia*, Part I, Chapter 2, Section 2.2.3.5; Part II, Chapter 5, Section 5.1.1; Part II, Chapter 5, Section 5.3; Part III, Chapter 6; Part III, Chapter 8, Section 8.2; and Part III, Chapter 9, Section 9.1.
40. *See*, *inter alia*, Part II, Chapter 5, Section 5.1.2; Part II, Chapter 5, Section 5.3; Part III, Chapter 7; Part III, Chapter 8, Section 8.2; and Part III, Chapter 9, Section 9.1.
41. *See*, *inter alia*, Part I, Chapter 2, Section 2.3.2; and Part II, Chapter 5, Section 5.1.3.
42. *See* Part I, Chapter 2, Section 2.2.2.2.
43. *See* Part I, Chapter 2, Section 2.2.2.3.

initiatives, and to provide some insights on how these interests could be factored in future initiatives.

Then, it quickly became apparent that, as many of the data that would be shared in the context of these initiatives could be deemed as being personal data,[44] it is essential for these compulsory B2B data sharing initiatives to factor personal data protection considerations. However, it is striking that while legislators and policymakers seem to be aware of the necessity to consider this issue, they usually simply indicate that 'where data qualifies as personal data, the data protection framework, in particular the [General Data Protection Regulation (GDPR)[45]], will apply',[46] without providing detailed indications on how this could be articulated in practice. Accordingly, my second ambition was to adopt a normative approach in order to fill this gap, by attempting to clarify the core elements that must be factored in this balancing exercise, and by attempting to provide insights on how this delicate articulation can be solved.

Finally, as will be outlined below,[47] I observed that, up to now, the European legislator seemed to favour (some forms of) data portability models when adopting compulsory B2B data sharing initiatives. Yet, while legislators and policymakers heavily focus on the positive aspects of these types of initiatives, they seem to completely overlook the long-term and collective costs that they could entail in terms of personal autonomy and informational self-determination. Accordingly, my third ambition was, once again, to adopt a normative approach in order to fill this gap, by attempting to raise awareness about the crucial need to take these risks into consideration, and by attempting to provide insights on how this delicate balance between short-term individual benefits, on the one hand, and long-term and collective risks, on the other hand, can be addressed.

6. In order to answer the above-mentioned research question, it is first necessary to explain the fundaments of (data) sharing, which will be the aim

44. 'Any information relating to an identified or identifiable natural person (data subject)' (Article 4.1 of Regulation (EU) 2016/679 of the European Parliament and of the Council of 27 April 2016 on the protection of natural persons with regard to the processing of personal data and on the free movement of such data, and repealing Directive 95/46/EC (General Data Protection Regulation), *OJ L 119*, 4 May 2016).
45. *Ibid.*
46. Communication from Commission, '*Building a European Data Economy*', *supra*, p. 9. *See also* Recital 28 of the Proposal for a Digital Governance Act: 'This Regulation should be without prejudice to the obligation of providers of data sharing services to comply with Regulation (EU) 2016/679 and the responsibility of supervisory authorities to ensure compliance with that Regulation. Where the data sharing service providers are data controllers or processors in the sense of Regulation (EU) 2016/679 they are bound by the rules of that Regulation'; and Article 7.1 of the proposal for a Digital Markets Act: 'The gatekeeper shall ensure that these measures are implemented in compliance with Regulation (EU) 2016/679 and Directive 2002/58/EC, and with legislation on cyber security, consumer protection and product safety.'
47. *See* Part I, Chapter 3, Section 3.1.3 and Part II.

of **Part I**. To do so, the concept of *data* (what?) will first be specified and **Chapter 1** will suggest a data typology. Then, the rationale for (data) sharing (why?) will be analysed. In this regard, **Chapter 2** will first revert to the more standard discussions on whether a resource should be shared. Then, it will be questioned whether the findings made in the realm of (in)tangible resources can be translated to the realm of data. It will be outlined that the rationale for data sharing can be economic, societal or based on 'empowerment' considerations. **Chapter 3** will then present a typology of data sharing models and initiatives (how?). To this end, this chapter will first take a more practical approach, and will present the most common *conceptual models of data sharing*. Then, it will take a more abstract approach, by focusing on the underlying objectives pursued by *compulsory B2B data sharing initiatives*. Indeed, it would be ill-advised to consider *compulsory* data sharing as a goal in itself.[48] Rather, it should only be used as a means to achieve determined objectives. In this regard, while the debates at the European level usually crystallise around economic objectives (contestability of data markets, social welfare deriving from data sharing and reuse, etc.), societal objectives could also be pursued through the imposition of compulsory B2B data sharing (tackling environmental challenges, contributing to healthier and more sustainable societies, improving mobility, etc.).[49] Moreover, compulsory B2B data sharing can also be used as a means to empower individuals,[50] as illustrated by the personal data portability right granted by Article 20 of the GDPR.[51] Considering these distinct objectives will lead to the identification of two main categories of compulsory B2B data sharing initiatives, which will guide the rest of the analysis. These are ***empowerment initiatives imposing B2B data sharing***, on the one hand, and ***economic or societal initiatives imposing B2B data sharing***, on the other hand. Importantly, it must be clarified from the outset that while these two main categories of compulsory B2B data sharing initiatives pursue different objectives, synergies can be found between these two types of initiatives, which explains why they are both addressed in this book.[52]

7. Part II will be devoted **to *empowerment initiatives imposing B2B data sharing*. Chapter 4** will first present the main data sharing initiatives aiming at empowering individuals, which are essentially structured around (some forms of) data portability rights.[53] In this regard, it will be outlined that these empowerment initiatives can pursue two different types of sub-objectives. On the one hand, empowerment initiatives can pursue the objective of allowing the exercise of fundamental rights, such as the right to personal data

48. B. Martens, et al., 'Business to Business Data Sharing', *supra*, p. 5.
49. *See* footnote 7.
50. Communication from the Commission, '*A European Strategy for Data*', *supra*, p. 10.
51. *See* Part II.
52. *See* point 128.
53. *See* Part II, Chapter 4, Sections 4.1 and 4.2.

protection and informational self-determination.[54] On the other hand, empowerment initiatives can be adopted to address specific market failures, through the strengthening of the individuals' control on their data.[55] However, the effectiveness of these data sharing initiatives is being criticised,[56] leading to a growing call for the introduction of a 'continuous portability' right.[57] Moreover, a brief digression will be made about a more recent phenomenon, namely the adoption of several regulatory initiatives aiming at 'empowering' specific (small) business users.[58]

Chapter 5 will focus on the key balancing exercises for these types of initiatives. First, there is a need to balance the benefits that the specific individual will derive from the data sharing, on the one hand, and the potential effects that this might entail on the rights and freedoms of third parties, on the other hand. More concretely, a balance must be found between the benefits of the data sharing for the specific individual and the business interests of the data holder, and the data sharing must comply with the other data subjects' right to personal data protection.[59] Second, there is a need to balance the potential short-term gains that are promised to individuals via these 'empowerment' initiatives with the potential long-term costs for these individuals in terms of control, autonomy and self-determination; and to balance the individual's potential gains from data sharing with the potential collective costs for other individuals.[60] Moreover, the matter of the competitive effects of these types of initiatives will also be addressed. On that basis, some insights on how these types of initiatives could be constructed will be formulated.

8. Part III will be devoted to ***economic or societal initiatives imposing B2B data sharing***. In this Part, several key balancing exercises will also be discussed. The first three Chapters will be dedicated *to economic initiatives imposing B2B data sharing*. **Chapter 6** will first analyse whether the existing competition law balances pertaining to refusals to share a resource (essential facilities doctrine, abuse of economic dependence and input foreclosure),

---

54. *See* Part II, Chapter 4, Section 4.1.
55. *See* Part II, Chapter 4, Section 4.2.
56. *See* J. Krämer, P. Senellart and A. de Streel, 'Making Data Portability More Effective for the Digital Economy', *CERRE Report*, 2020, available at https://www.cerre.eu/publications/report-making-data-portability-more-effective-digital-economy.
57. *Ibid.*; Communication from the Commission, '*A European Strategy for Data*', *supra*, p. 20. *See* Part II, Chapter 4, Section 4.3.
58. *See* Part II, Chapter 4, Section 4.4. *See* Regulation (EU) 2018/1807 of the European Parliament and of the Council of 14 November 2018 on a framework for the free flow of non-personal data in the European Union, *OJ L 303/59*, 28 November 2018; Regulation (EU) 2019/1150 of the European Parliament and of the Council of 20 June 2019 on promoting fairness and transparency for business users of online intermediation services, *OJ L 186/57*, 11 July 2019.
59. Article 29 Working Party, *Guidelines on the right to data portability*, WP 242 rev.01, 13 April 2017, pp. 11-12.
60. *See* Part I, Chapter 2, Section 2.3.2 and Part II, Chapter 5, Section 5.1.3.

aiming at finding a balance between the benefits and costs of access/sharing in terms of incentives for each of the parties,[61] remain appropriate in light of data's characteristics, or whether the results of these balancing exercises need to be adapted in order to better fit the characteristics of the data markets. This fits in a broader discussion pertaining to whether competition law needs to be adapted in order to better fit the digital environment.[62]

Then, **Chapter 7** will discuss another balancing exercise entailing stronger societal considerations, namely the articulation between competition law and data protection law. In fact, it will be outlined that this articulation generates two core issues. First, there are growing concerns that the GDPR might limit competition and increase concentration in personal data and

---

61. P. Larouche, 'The European Microsoft Case at the Crossroads of Competition Policy and Innovation', *Antitrust Law Journal*, 2008, Vol. 75(3), pp. 933-937.
62. *See* (EU) J. Crémer, Y.-A. de Montjoye and H. Schweitzer, 'Competition Policy for the Digital Era', *supra*; (Germany) H. Schweitzer, et al., 'A New Competition Framework for the Digital Economy', *Report by the Commission 'Competition Law 4.0' for the German Federal Ministry for Economic Affairs and Energy*, 2019, available at https://www.bmwi.de/Redaktion/EN/Downloads/a/a-new-competitionframework.pdf?__blob=publicationFile&v=2; H. Schweitzer, et al., *Modernisierung der Missbrauchsaufsicht für marktmächtige Unternehmen*, Baden-Baden, Nomos, 2018 (also available at https://www.bmwi.de/Redaktion/DE/Publikationen/Wirtschaft/modernisierung-der-missbrauchsaufsicht-fuer-marktmaechtigeunternehmen.html (an executive summary in English is available at https://ssrn.com/abstract=3250742)); (France) Autorité de la concurrence, 'Contribution de l'Autorité de la concurrence au débat sur la politique de concurrence et les enjeux numériques', 19 February 2020, available at https://www.autoritedelaconcurrence.fr/sites/default/files/2020-02/2020.02.19_contribution_adlc_enjeux_numeriques_vf.pdf; (BeNeLux) J. Steenbergen, M. Snoep and P. Barthelmé, 'Joint Memorandum of the Belgian, Dutch and Luxembourg Competition Authorities on Challenges Faced by Competition Authorities in a Digital World', 2 October 2019, available at https://www.belgiancompetition.be/en/about-us/publications/joint-memorandum-belgian-dutch-and-luxembourg-competition-authorities; (UK) J. Furman, et al., 'Unlocking Digital Competition', *Report of the Digital Competition Expert Panel for the British Chancellor of the Exchequer and Secretary of State for Business, Energy and Industrial Strategy*, 2019, available at https://www.gov.uk/government/publications/unlocking-digital-competition-report-of-the-digital-competition-expert-panel; UK Competition & Markets Authority, 'Online Platforms and Digital Advertising: Market Study Final Report', 1 July 2020, available at https://www.gov.uk/cma-cases/online-platforms-and-digital-advertising-market-study; (USA) Stigler Committee on Digital Platforms, 'Final Report', September 2019, available at https://research.chicagobooth.edu/stigler/media/news/committee-on-digital-platforms-final-report; (Australia) Australian Competition and Consumer Commission, 'Digital Platforms Inquiry – Final Report', 26 July 2019, available at https://www.accc.gov.au/publications/digital-platforms-inquiry-final-report. For a comparative analysis of some of these reports, *see* W. Kerber, 'Updating Competition Policy for the Digital Economy? An Analysis of Recent Reports in Germany, UK, EU, and Australia', September 2019, available at https://ssrn.com/abstract=3469624; and S. Ennis and A. Fletcher, 'Developing International Perspectives on Digital Competition Policy', 31 March 2020, available at https://ssrn.com/abstract=3565491.

data-related markets.[63] Second, the GDPR must also be taken into consideration by a competition authority wishing to impose a data sharing remedy when (some of) the data at hand is personal data.[64]

Because of the complexity to solve the balancing exercises outlined in Chapters 6 and 7, growing discussions have emerged about alternative solutions than resorting to competition law for imposing B2B data sharing.[65] Accordingly, **Chapter 8** will discuss the creation of potential *ex ante* legislations imposing B2B data sharing for economic purposes. In essence, such *ex ante* legislations could be sectoral or could have a more general horizontal scope. Each of these options, which are not necessarily exclusive from one another, entail their own balancing exercises, which will need to be considered by the European legislator.

While the policy discussions pertaining to these economic initiatives are quite advanced, the reflections around the creation of *societal initiatives imposing B2B data sharing* are, on the other hand, still scarce. Yet, as they could have a significant role to play in achieving societal goals,[66] they will be addressed in a shorter **Chapter 9**, which will not aim for exhaustivity on this growingly important topic, but will rather have as main objective to launch avenues of exploration on why such initiatives could be envisaged and on how they could be constructed in the future.

9. Finally, the **Conclusion** will come back on the fundaments of data sharing outlined in Part I, before synthesising the key balancing exercises that will have been emphasised in Parts II and III, as well as the insights made throughout this contribution in order to address them.

---

63. M. Gal and O. Aviv, 'The Competitive Effects of the GDPR', *Journal of Competition Law and Economics*, September 2020, Vol. 16(3), pp. 349-391; T. Zarsky, 'Incompatible: The GDPR in the Age of Big Data', *Seton Hall Law Review*, 2017, Vol. 47, No. 4(2), pp. 995-1020; T. Zarsky, 'The Privacy–Innovation Conundrum', *Lewis & Clark Law Review*, 2015, Vol. 19(1), pp. 115-168; D. Geradin, T. Karanikioti and D. Katsifis, 'GDPR Myopia: How a Well-Intended Regulation Ended Up Favoring Google in Ad Tech', *TILEC Discussion Paper DP 2020-012*, May 2020, available at https://ssrn.com/abstract=3598130; G. Johnson and S. Shriver, 'Privacy & Market Concentration: Intended & Unintended Consequences of the GDPR', March 2020, available at https://ssrn.com/abstract=3477686.
64. T. Tombal, 'The GDPR: A Shield to a Competition Authority's Data Sharing Remedy?', *Deep Diving into Data Protection*, J. Herveg (coord.), Bruxelles, Larcier, 2021, pp. 67-94.
65. *See* Part III, Chapter 6, Section 6.5.2. *See* Communication from the Commission, '*Shaping Europe's Digital Future*', *supra*, p. 9; Communication from the Commission, '*A European Strategy for Data*', *supra*, pp. 3, 5 and 14.
66. *See* Part I, Chapter 2, Section 2.3.1.

Part I

The Fundaments of (Data) Sharing: What, Why and How?

10. As outlined in the introduction, the main research question underlying this contribution is '***What are the economic and societal balancing exercises underlying compulsory B2B data sharing?***' In the context of my analysis, 'data sharing' is defined as the act through which one or several data holder(s) provide(s) access to its(their) data to one or several data recipient(s), directly or through an intermediary, for the purpose of joint or individual use of the shared data, on the basis of voluntary agreements or of compulsory rules.[67] It covers not only transfers of data from one party to another but also data pooling initiatives, where different parties aggregate their data together in order to extract (economic and/or societal) value from the access to increased resources. A more extensive list of the various models of data sharing is presented in Chapter 3, Section 3.1.

To answer this main research question, the concept of *data* first needs to be specified (**what?**). This will be done in **Chapter 1**, where a data typology, to be used for the remainder of the analysis, will be proposed. Then, the rationale for (data) sharing will be analysed (**why?**). In this regard, **Chapter 2** will first look back at the rationale for sharing 'traditional' tangible or intangible resources, before turning to the same question for data. Finally, **Chapter 3** will present a typology of data sharing models and initiatives (**how?**). Here, two main categories of *compulsory B2B data sharing initiatives* will be identified on the basis of the rationale for data sharing that will have been outlined in the previous Chapter, namely, *empowerment initiatives imposing B2B data sharing*, on the one hand, and *economic or societal initiatives imposing B2B data sharing*, on the other hand.

---

67. This definition is based on Article 2.7 of the Proposal for a Data Governance Act; and Article 2.19 of the Proposal for a Digital Markets Act.

Chapter 1
Sharing What? A Typology of Data

11. Data is not a homogeneous good. It can be described on the basis of numerous typologies (*public sector data v. private sector data*; *proprietary data v. public domain data*; *closed data v. open data, etc.*).[68] As, for the sake of concision, it would not be possible to delve into all of the possible typologies of data, I will focus on two fundamental typologies. The first one pertains to the form of the data along the value chain (Section 1.1). The second one pertains to the classic dichotomy between personal and non-personal data, which is broadly relied upon in the European legal framework (Section 1.2).[69] On the basis of this analysis, a data typology will be suggested, which will be relied upon in the remainder of the analysis (Section 1.3).

1.1 FORM OF THE DATA ALONG THE VALUE CHAIN

12. Data comes in multiple forms and shapes, which evolve along the data value chain.[70] First, data is collected from users, extracted from

---

68. *See,* for instance, OECD, *Enhancing Access to and Sharing of Data: Reconciling Risks and Benefits for Data Re-use across Societies*, OECD Publishing, Paris, 2019, available at https://www.oecd.org/publications/enhancing-access-to-and-sharing-of-data-276aaca8-en.htm, pp. 25-31.
69. For a criticism of this broad reliance on the personal versus non-personal data dichotomy, *see*: I. Graef, R. Gellert and M. Husovec, 'Towards a Holistic Regulatory Approach for the European Data Economy: Why the Illusive Notion of Non-personal Data Is Counterproductive to Data Innovation', *TILEC Discussion Paper No. 2018-028*, September 2018, available at http://ssrn.com/abstract=3256189.
70. On the steps of this data value chain, *see* M. Gal and D. Rubinfeld, 'Data Standardization', *New York University Law Review*, 2019, Vol. 94(4), pp. 746-747. *See also* OECD, *Consumer Data Rights and Competition – Background Note*, June 2020, DAF/COMP(2020)1, available at http://www.oecd.org/daf/competition/consumer-data-rights-and-competition.htm, pp. 14-15; OECD, *Data-Driven Innovation: Big Data for Growth and Well-Being*, OECD Publications, 2015, available at https://www.oecd.org/sti/data-driven-innovation-9789264229358-en.htm, p. 32.

sensors,[71] or generated by the data holder itself (e.g., a football match calendar or a television programme). At this stage, it is considered as raw (or unstructured) data. This raw data can be collected/extracted/generated either as the object of the data collector's core economic activity (e.g., data collected by Facebook about its users in order to finance its activity by making profit through the sale of (personalised) advertising space) or as a by-product of this activity (e.g., data generated by sensors in a car assembly line).[72] This is also described as active or passive data collection/extraction/generation.[73] In many cases, firms will first start to collect/extract/generate data passively, as a by-product of their core economic activity, but once they realise the value that such data can have, they will tend to move towards more active approaches.[74]

Accordingly, in practice, it might be extremely difficult to determine whether a specific data set has been collected/extracted/generated as a by-product or as the object of the data collector's core economic activity. Indeed, this notion of 'core economic activity' is evolutive. For instance, Bayer-Monsanto, historically considered as an agriculture and bioengineering firm, seems to be 'heading towards becoming an information broker'.[75] Therefore, while the data sets generated through the use of its agricultural and bioengineering products would have likely been considered, in the past, as by-products of its core economic activity, the same conclusion might not necessarily be reached today. In fact, it could maybe even be argued that generating this agricultural data is part of its new core economic activity, which is to become a major agricultural data broker, and that it only sells agricultural and bioengineering products in order to generate more data. In the same vein, car manufacturers might attempt to argue that, in the near future, with the advent of autonomous cars, they will strive towards becoming 'mobility data companies' rather than simple 'car builders'. Accordingly, data generated by these autonomous cars might no longer be considered as by-products generated by these car manufacturers' core economic activity (building and selling cars), but might rather be considered as part of their new core economic activity (becoming leading mobility data companies that only sell cars in order to generate more data).

---

71. M. Gal and D. Rubinfeld, 'Data Standardization', *supra*, p. 746.
72. *Ibid.*; D. Rubinfeld and M. Gal, 'Access Barriers to Big Data', *Arizona Law Review*, 2017, Vol. 59, p. 357; OECD, *Consumer Data Rights and Competition*, *supra*, p. 15.
73. OECD, *Consumer Data Rights and Competition*, *supra*, p. 15.
74. *Ibid.*, pp. 15-16. For an example in the retail business, *see* J. Turow, *The Aisles Have Eyes: How Retailers Track Your Shopping, Strip Your Privacy, and Define Your Power*, New Haven, Yale University Press, 2017.
75. I. Carbonell, 'The Ethics of Big Data in Big Agriculture', *Internet Policy Review*, 2016, Vol. 5(1), available at https://policyreview.info/articles/analysis/ethics-big-data-big-agriculture, p. 5.

13. Second, this raw (unstructured) data is structured, interpreted and organised, transforming it into information (structured data).[76] In a joint study, the French and German competition authorities (the *Autorité de la Concurrence* and the *Bundeskartellamt*) distinguish between structured and semi-structured data.[77] The former follow 'a model that defines a number of fields, what type of data these fields contain and how they relate to each other', while the latter 'does not conform to a predefined model but certain elements or fields therein can be identified through a marker-type system'.[78] This structuration of data increases the possibilities to extract value from the data, as they can more easily be processed and used than raw (unstructured) data.[79]

14. Third, this information (structured data) is analysed, transforming it into knowledge (analysed data) which can be used for prediction or decision-making.[80] To conduct these analyses, *Big Data*[81] analytics are increasingly called upon. They are characterised by the *four Vs*, namely 'the **V**olume of data collected, the **V**ariety of sources, the **V**elocity with which the analysis of the data can unfold, and the **V**eracity of the data which could (arguably) be achieved through the analytical process' (emphasis in the text).[82] These *four Vs* subsequently increase the **V**alue that can be derived from the data analysis.[83] According to the Organisation for Economic Co-operation and Development (OECD), 'the value of data is mainly reaped at two moments: first when data are transformed into knowledge (gaining insights), and then when they are used for decision-making (taking action). Decisions taken can

76. M. Gal and D. Rubinfeld, 'Data Standardization', *supra*, p. 746; R. Kitchin, *The Data Revolution: Big Data, Open Data, Data Infrastructures & Their Consequences*, London, Sage Publications, 2014, pp. 10 et seq.; M.J. Adler, *A Guidebook to Learning: For a Lifelong Pursuit of Wisdom*, London, Macmillan, 1986; L. Floridi, *Information: A Very Short Guide*, Oxford, Oxford University Press, 2010; H. von Baeyer, *Information: The New Language of Science*, Cambridge, Harvard University Press, 2003; D. Weinberger, *Too Big to Know*, New York, Basic Books, 2011; D. McCandless, 'Data, Information, Knowledge, Wisdom', 29 November 2010, available at http://www.informationisbeautiful.net/2010/data-information-knowledge-wisdom/.
77. Autorité de la concurrence and Bundeskartellamt, 'Competition Law and Data', 10 May 2016, available at http://www.autoritedelaconcurrence.fr/doc/reportcompetitionlawanddatafinal.pdf, p. 6.
78. *Ibid.*
79. *Ibid.*
80. *See* footnote 76.
81. '"Big data" is a field that treats ways to analyze, systematically extract information from, or otherwise deal with data sets that are too large or complex to be dealt with by traditional data-processing application software' (https://en.wikipedia.org/wiki/Big_data).
82. T. Zarsky, 'Incompatible: The GDPR in the Age of Big Data', *Seton Hall Law Review*, 2017, Vol. 47, No. 4(2), pp. 998-999.
83. M. Gal and D. Rubinfeld, 'Data Standardization', *supra*, p. 744; OECD, *Consumer Data Rights and Competition*, *supra*, p. 10.

in turn lead to more or different data generated and thus trigger a new data value cycle'.[84]

Naturally, some data holders can skip the above-mentioned data value chain by directly acquiring structured or analysed data from third parties, such as data brokers. In that case, they directly acquire information (structured data) or knowledge (analysed data) rather than raw (unstructured) data.

15. While it might seem somewhat artificial, the above-mentioned typology based on the form of the data along the value chain has an importance in practice because the true value of data does not generally derive from the raw data as such, but rather from the information and knowledge that can be extracted from it.[85] Indeed, as elegantly put by Mayer-Schönberger and Padova, data 'is like a single puzzle piece that taken by itself offers little value, but when combined with others to complete an image is turned into something precious'.[86]

1.2 PERSONAL AND NON-PERSONAL DATA: A POROUS BOUNDARY

16. Data can also be classified as personal or non-personal. Personal data are defined in the 'GDPR' as 'any information relating to an identified or identifiable natural person (data subject)'.[87] Information can relate to an identified or identifiable natural person, whether in content, purpose, result or impact.[88] According to the GDPR, an identifiable natural person is one who can be identified, directly or indirectly, in particular by reference to an

84. OECD, *Data-Driven Innovation: Big Data for Growth and Well-Being*, *supra*, p. 32.
85. D. Rubinfeld and M. Gal, 'Access Barriers to Big Data', *supra*, p. 342. However, this does not mean that raw data does not have any value at all, as a third party may prefer to have access to raw data, in order to create its own structured data (information) that better corresponds to its needs, rather than to information that has been structured differently by the data holder.
86. V. Mayer-Schönberger and Y. Padova, 'Regime Change? Enabling Big Data Through Europe's New Data Protection Regulation', *Columbia Science & Technology Law Review*, Vol. XVII, 2016, p. 320.
87. Regulation (EU) 2016/679 of the European Parliament and of the Council of 27 April 2016 on the protection of natural persons with regard to the processing of personal data and on the free movement of such data, and repealing Directive 95/46/EC (General Data Protection Regulation), *OJ L 119*, 4 May 2016, Article 4.1. *See also* Modernised Convention for the Protection of Individuals with Regard to the Processing of Personal Data, 17-18 May 2018, CM/Inf(2018)15-final, Article 2.a.
88. Article 29 Working Party, *Opinion 4/2007 on the concept of personal data*, WP 136, 20 June 2007, available at https://ec.europa.eu/justice/article-29/documentation/opinion-recommendation/files/2007/wp136_en.pdf, pp. 9-12; I. Graef, R. Gellert and M. Husovec, 'Towards a Holistic Regulatory Approach for the European Data Economy' *supra*, p. 5.

identifier.[89] In order to determine whether a person is identifiable, account must be taken of all the reasonable means likely to be used, either by the data controller[90] or by a third party, to identify, directly or indirectly, the person.[91] In other words, a person is identifiable if it can be singled out.[92] To ascertain the likeliness of the reidentification of the person, account must be taken of a series of objective factors, such as the costs of, and the amount of time required for, the reidentification, in light of the available technology and technological developments at the time of the processing.[93]

17. In the context of its guidelines on the right to data portability enshrined in Article 20 of the GDPR,[94] the Article 29 Working Party (today the European Data Protection Board – EDPB) has identified three categories of personal data.[95]

The first category of personal data is 'data actively and knowingly provided by the data subject'.[96] This includes, but is not limited to, any information provided by completing an online registration form, posts on social media, etc. This category is also sometimes referred to as 'volunteered data'.[97] Yet, this latter terminology can be somewhat misleading, as it seems to imply that the data subject has always taken the initiative to provide the data 'willingly'. However, in some cases, the data subject has no other choice than to actively provide the data, even if she is not 'willing' to do so (e.g., bank customers are legally obliged to disclose some information to their bank). Accordingly, a less ambiguous term such as 'actively provided data' is preferable to describe this first category.

The second category of personal data is 'observed data provided by the data subject by virtue of the use of the service or the device'.[98] Examples include the search history of a data subject, the history of the websites she

89. Article 4.1 of the GDPR.
90. 'The natural or legal person, public authority, agency or other body which, alone or jointly with others, determines the purposes and means of the processing of personal data' (Article 4.7 of the GDPR).
91. Recital 26 of the GDPR.
92. Article 29 Working Party, *Opinion 4/2007 on the concept of personal data*, *supra*, pp. 12-15; Article 29 Working Party, *Guidelines on Automated individual decision-making and Profiling for the purposes of Regulation 2016/679*, WP 251 rev.01, 6 February 2018, available at https://ec.europa.eu/newsroom/article29/item-detail.cfm?item_id=612053, pp. 6-8; I. Graef, R. Gellert and M. Husovec, 'Towards a Holistic Regulatory Approach for the European Data Economy', *supra*, p. 5.
93. Recital 26 of the GDPR.
94. On this right, *see* Part II, Chapter 4, Section 4.1.
95. Article 29 Working Party, *Guidelines on the right to data portability*, WP 242 rev.01, 5 April 2017, available at https://ec.europa.eu/newsroom/article29/item-detail.cfm?item_id=611233, pp. 9-11.
96. *Ibid.*, p. 10.
97. OECD, *Enhancing Access to and Sharing of Data, supra*, p. 30.
98. Article 29 Working Party, *Guidelines on the right to data portability*, WP 242 rev.01, 13 April 2017, p. 10.

has visited, traffic and location data generated by the use of a mobile application, or other types of data, such as the average pulse rate or the number of steps taken by a data subject, which would be collected by a connected watch. For these observed data, a further distinction can be made between first-party and third-party observed data.[99] First-party observed data are data collected directly by the controller from its users, on the basis of their use of the controller's product or service (e.g., the search queries typed by users and collected by Google).[100] Third-party observed data, on the other hand, are data collected indirectly from the users, on the basis of their use of the product or service of a third party, via a range of different technologies such as 'cookies' (e.g., the data collected by Google through third-party tracking cookies on a range of websites not operated by Google).[101]

The third category of personal data is 'inferred data and derived data created by the data controller on the basis of the data "provided by the data subject."'[102] This refers to data resulting from a subsequent analysis carried out by the controller on the basis of data provided (actively or observed) by the data subject. Examples are user profiles created by the controller on the basis of the analysis of data provided by the data subjects, or the results of an assessment of the data subject's health based on the health data collected by her smart watch.[103] This is also sometimes presented as 'second generation data', which is created, inferred or derived from 'first generation data'.[104] These types of data will often be the most valuable for data holders, as this is where the real added-value of their service must be found.[105] The difference between derived and inferred data relies on the type of analytics used to generate them. Indeed, according to the United Kingdom's Information Commissioner's Office (the UK's data protection authority), derived data 'is produced from other data in a relatively simple and straightforward fashion, e.g. calculating customer profitability from the number of visits to a store and items bought', while inferred data 'is produced by using a more complex method of analytics to find correlations between data sets and using these to categorise or profile people, e.g. calculating credit scores or

99. OECD, *Consumer Data Rights and Competition*, *supra*, pp. 16-18.

100. *Ibid.*, p. 16.

101. *Ibid. See also* V. Robertson, 'Excessive Data Collection: Privacy Considerations and Abuse of Dominance in the Era of Big Data', *Common Market Law Review*, 2020, Vol. 57, p. 162.

102. Article 29 Working Party, *Guidelines on the right to data portability*, WP 242 rev.01, 13 April 2017, p. 10.

103. *Ibid.*

104. R. Kemp, 'Legal Aspects of Managing Data (White Paper)', October 2019, available at http://www.kempitlaw.com/legal-aspects-of-managing-data/, p. 8.

105. Primary and observed data can, however, also be of great value, especially when the costs of data collection are very high and/or when the data is difficult to collect (e.g., satellite imagery). On this point, *see also* points 301 and 302.

predicting future health outcomes. Inferred data is based on probabilities and can thus be said to be less "certain" than derived data'.[106]

A fourth category of personal data can be added, namely 'acquired data', which is personal data obtained from third parties on the basis of a voluntary data sharing mechanism (e.g., data acquired from data brokers),[107] or on the basis of a compulsory data sharing mechanism. Indeed, as it will be outlined further below, some well-identified data recipients have a right to acquire some data from well-identified data holders, provided that certain specific conditions are met. For instance, the revised Directive on payment services in the internal market (PSD2)[108] grants to the providers of payment initiation service and the providers of account information service[109] the right to acquire the payment account information[110] of the users of their services (the consumers), if the latter have explicitly consented to it.[111]

Distinguishing between these categories of personal data is relevant, as the individuals' level of awareness about the processing of their personal data will be different for each category, which in turn has an impact on the control they have on 'their' personal data.[112] Indeed, individuals will likely be aware of, and more comfortable with, the processing of actively provided or first-party observed data. On the other hand, the collection of third-party observed data, the generation of inferred or derived data and the acquisition of personal data will be more obscure to them, and will affect the sense of control that they have on the types of data processing for which they are used.[113]

---

106. Information Commissioner's Office, 'Big Data, artificial intelligence, machine learning and data protection', 4 September 2017, available at https://ico.org.uk/media/for-organisations/documents/2013559/big-data-ai-ml-and-data-protection.pdf, pp. 12-13.
107. OECD, *Enhancing Access to and Sharing of Data, supra*, p. 31. *See* Part I, Chapter 3, Section 3.1 for a presentation of the most common conceptual models that can be used for such voluntary data sharing.
108. Directive (EU) 2015/2366 of the European Parliament and of the Council of 25 November 2015 on payment services in the internal market, amending Directives 2002/65/EC, 2009/110/EC and 2013/36/EU and Regulation (EU) No. 1093/2010, and repealing Directive 2007/64/EC, *OJ L 337/35*, 23 December 2015. *See* Part II, Chapter 4, Section 4.2.2.
109. Respectively defined as 'a service to initiate a payment order at the request of the payment service user with respect to a payment account held at another payment service provider' and as 'an online service to provide consolidated information on one or more payment accounts held by the payment service user with either another payment service provider or with more than one payment service provider' (Directive 2015/2366, Articles 4.15 and 4.16).
110. Defined as 'account held in the name of one or more payment service users which is used for the execution of payment transactions' (Directive 2015/2366, Article 4.12).
111. Directive 2015/2366, Articles 64-67.
112. OECD, *Consumer Data Rights and Competition, supra*, p. 17.
113. *Ibid.*

18. Non-personal data, on the other hand, are usually residually defined as all data other than personal data,[114] either because they have never been personal data in the first place (such as industrial data generated by the 'IoT',[115] e.g., sensors installed on industrial machines that provide data on maintenance needs), or because they have been anonymised[116] (e.g., through mathematical and statistical operations) and therefore no longer qualify as personal data because the data subject is no longer identifiable.[117] In this regard, anonymised data should not be confused with pseudonymised data, which remain personal data subject to the GDPR, given that the data subject can still be re-identified by using additional information.[118] Importantly, determining whether specific data should be considered as anonymised or pseudonymised will always be a function of the specific circumstances of each individual case.[119]

19. This choice of a residual definition for non-personal data has been criticised, as it presumes that the scope of what constitutes personal data can be clearly defined.[120] Yet, in practice, it might not be easy to determine whether specific data should be considered as personal or not. This is due to the broad definition of personal data, making it a dynamic, fluid and open-ended concept, as the possibilities of reidentification evolve with the technology, increasing over time the scope of what should be considered as

114. *See*, for instance, Regulation (EU) 2018/1807 of the European Parliament and of the Council of 14 November 2018 on a framework for the free flow of non-personal data in the European Union, *OJ L 303/59*, 28 November 2018, Article 1.
115. *See* footnote 4.
116. The ISO 29100 standard defines anonymisation as the: 'process by which personally identifiable information (PII) is irreversibly altered in such a way that a PII principal can no longer be identified directly or indirectly, either by the PII controller alone or in collaboration with any other party' (ISO 29100:2011, point 2.2, available at https://www.iso.org/obp/ui/#iso:std:iso-iec:29100:ed-1:v1:en).
117. Recital 26 of the GDPR; Communication from the Commission to the European Parliament and the Council, '*Guidance on the Regulation on a Framework for the Free Flow of Non-personal Data in the European Union*', Brussels, 29 May 2019, COM(2019) 250 final, p. 6. On anonymisation, *see* Article 29 Working Party, *Opinion 05/2014 on Anonymisation Techniques*, WP 216, 10 April 2014, available at https://www.pdpjournals.com/docs/88197.pdf, pp. 5-11.
118. Recital 26 and Article 4.5 of the GDPR. On pseudonymisation, *see* Article 29 Working Party, *Opinion 05/2014 on Anonymisation Techniques*, *supra*, pp. 10-11 and 20-23.
119. Communication from the Commission, '*Guidance on the Regulation on a Framework for the Free Flow of Non-personal Data in the European Union*', *supra*, p. 6.
120. L. Somaini, 'Regulating the Dynamic Concept of Non-personal Data in the EU: From Ownership to Portability', *European Data Protection Law Review*, 2020/1, pp. 88-89; I. Graef, R. Gellert and M. Husovec, 'Towards a Holistic Regulatory Approach for the European Data Economy', *supra*, pp. 4-6.

personal data.[121] Indeed, 'technological and other developments may change what constitutes "unreasonable time, effort or other resources" (…) to re-identify the data subject'.[122]

This has led some authors to call for a new taxonomy of data because it is impossible to govern and regulate personal data and non-personal data separately, in light of the constant flow between each category.[123] Moreover, the above dichotomy is also complex to apply in practice because, in most cases, data sets will be 'mixed', i.e., composed of both personal and non-personal data, in light of technological developments such as the *IoT* or *Big Data* analytics.[124] Additionally, if these mixed data sets are 'inextricably linked', the GDPR will have to be applied to the entirety of the data set, even if personal data only represent a small part of it.[125] Although this concept of 'inextricably linked' is not defined, it should be understood as encompassing situations where it would be impossible, economically inefficient, or technically infeasible to separate the personal data from the non-personal data in the set.[126] The changing nature of the data and a significant decrease in the value of the data set, if separated, could lead to such situations.[127] In sum, because most of the data sets are mixed and 'inextricably linked', there is a risk that 'in the near future everything will be or will contain personal data, leading to the application of data protection to everything'.[128]

---

121. OECD, *Enhancing Access to and Sharing of Data, supra*, p. 26; L. Somaini, 'Regulating the Dynamic Concept of Non-personal Data in the EU', *supra*, pp. 88-90; I. Graef, R. Gellert and M. Husovec, 'Towards a Holistic Regulatory Approach for the European Data Economy', *supra*, p. 4.
122. Council of Europe, 'Explanatory Report to the Protocol amending the Convention for the Protection of Individuals with regard to Automatic Processing of Personal Data', *Council of Europe Treaty Series No. 223*, Strasbourg, 10 October 2018, available at https://rm.coe.int/cets-223-explanatory-report-to-the-protocol-amending-the-convention-fo/16808ac91a, p. 4.
123. L. Taylor, 'Hacking a Path Through the Personal Data Ecosystem', December 2013, available at https://linnettaylor.wordpress.com/2013/12/12/hacking-a-path-through-the-personal-data-ecosystem/. *See also* I. Graef, R. Gellert and M. Husovec, 'Towards a Holistic Regulatory Approach for the European Data Economy', *supra*.
124. Communication from the Commission to the European Parliament, the Council, the European Economic and Social Committee and the Committee of the Regions, '*Guidance on the Regulation on a Framework for the Free Flow of Non-personal Data in the European Union*', *supra*, pp. 4 and 7; I. Graef, R. Gellert and M. Husovec, 'Towards a Holistic Regulatory Approach for the European Data Economy', *supra*, p. 6.
125. Regulation (EU) 2018/1807 of the European Parliament and of the Council of 14 November 2018 on a framework for the free flow of non-personal data in the European Union, *OJ L 303/59*, 28 November 2018, Article 2.2; Communication from the Commission, '*Guidance on the Regulation on a Framework for the Free Flow of Non-personal Data in the European Union*', *supra*, p. 9.
126. Communication from the Commission, '*Guidance on the Regulation on a Framework for the Free Flow of Non-personal Data in the European Union*', *supra*, p. 10.
127. *Ibid.*
128. N. Purtova, 'The Law of Everything: Broad Concept of Personal Data and Future of EU Data Protection Law', *Law, Innovation and Technology*, 2018, Vol. 10(1), p. 40.

20. This is even more so if one considers the constant development of *Big Data* analytics. Indeed, *Big Data* analytics allow the gathering of data at an unprecedented scale, as the time and cost required to do so have been drastically reduced by technological evolutions.[129] In turn, this increases the possibility to do cross-analysis on multiple data sets, to which it was previously more difficult to have access. This consequently exacerbates the risk of direct or indirect reidentification of a data subject on the basis of these data, whether by the controller or by a third party. In doing so, data considered at a time 'T' as non-personal may thus, on the basis of technological developments in data analytics capabilities, become personal data at time 'T+1'.

For example, at the end of the 1990s, a researcher in the United States (US) managed to reidentify more than 80% of the people whose data were contained in a database of a private company operating in the health sector, even though these data were supposed to be anonymised.[130] In fact, while the names of these people had been deleted, the database still contained medical information as well as the postal code, gender, and full date of birth. Yet, the latter three pieces of information were also included in the registers of electoral lists, which were accessible to the public, enabling the researcher to cross-reference these data, to identify 80% of the persons contained in the file and to obtain information on their health status. This example illustrates that the risk of reidentification increases with the development of new technologies and increasing access to large data sets.[131] Therefore, what is presented as anonymisation techniques are, in fact, often merely pseudonymisation techniques.[132] Yet, as already outlined, pseudonymised data remain personal

129. V. Mayer-Schönberger and Y. Padova, 'Regime Change? Enabling Big Data Through Europe's New Data Protection Regulation', *supra*, pp. 317-318.
130. L. Sweeney, 'Weaving Technology and Policy Together to Maintain Confidentiality', *Journal of Law, Medicine & Ethics*, 1997, Vol. 25(2 & 3), pp. 98-110; Article 29 Working Party, *Opinion 05/2014 on Anonymisation Techniques*, *supra*, pp. 33-34.
131. For other examples, *see* M. Barbaro and T. Zeller, 'A Face Is Exposed for AOL Searcher No. 4417749', *The New York Times*, 9 August 2006, available at https://www.nytimes.com/2006/08/09/technology/09aol.html; P. Ohm, 'Broken Promises of Privacy: Responding to the Surprising Failure of Anonymization', *UCLA Law Review*, 2010, Vol. 57, pp. 1716-1722; J. Pearson, 'Yahoo's Gigantic "Anonymized" User Dataset Isn't All That Anonymous', 14 January 2016, available at https://www.vice.com/en/article/yp3d8v/yahoos-gigantic-anonymized-user-dataset-isnt-all-that-anonymous; L. Rocher, J. Hendrickx and Y.-A. de Montjoye, 'Estimating the Success of Re-identifications in Incomplete Datasets Using Generative Models', *Nature Communications*, 2019, Vol. 10, No. 3069, available at https://www.nature.com/articles/s41467-019-10933-3.
132. 'The processing of personal data in such a manner that the personal data can no longer be attributed to a specific data subject without the use of additional information, provided that such additional information is kept separately and is subject to technical and organisational measures to ensure that the personal data are not attributed to an identified or identifiable natural person' (Article 4.5 of the GDPR). *See also* Article 29 Working Party, *Opinion 8/2014 on the Recent Developments on the Internet of Things*,

data subject to the GDPR, given that the data subject can still be re-identified.[133]

1.3 PROPOSED DATA TYPOLOGY

21. Because this boundary between personal and non-personal data is porous and often difficult to establish in practice, I will suggest an alternative data typology, following a common holistic approach for both personal and non-personal data,[134] which will nevertheless take personal data protection considerations into account when relevant.[135] This proposed typology will then be relied upon in the remainder of the analysis.

Indeed, when looking at the four categories of personal data presented above (actively provided, observed, inferred/derived, and acquired data),[136] these categories can also be applied to non-personal data. Indeed, while objects cannot 'knowingly' provide data about themselves, as they have no conscience (e.g., a machine in an assembly line does not decide to provide data about its wear and tear to the manufacturer), non-personal data can be actively and knowingly provided by an anonymous person (e.g., votes in an election, answers to a survey, etc.). It can also be actively created by the data holder itself (e.g., a football match calendar or a television programme). Furthermore, non-personal data collected via *IoT* sensors or via the observation of electronic operations can be considered as 'observed data' (e.g., weather, humidity or pesticides level data collected by 'smart tractors'; or wear and tear data collected by a sensor on an industrial machine in a car assembly line). Moreover, 'inferred/derived non-personal data' can be generated on the basis of these actively provided and observed data, as insights are drawn from their analysis (e.g., the weather/humidity data can be analysed to infer when it will be optimal to plant a specific type of seed; or the wear and tear data of the assembly line machine can be analysed in order to derive when the next maintenance operation will need to be planned). In this regard, personal data that has become non-personal because it has been anonymised shall be considered as derived data, as it is a second generation of data that derives from mathematical operations conducted on the first generation of personal data. Additionally, non-personal data can also be

---

WP 223, 16 September 2014, available at https://ec.europa.eu/justice/article-29/documentation/opinion-recommendation/files/2014/wp223_en.pdf, p. 8.

133. Recital 26 of the GDPR.
134. For a call to follow such a holistic approach *see* I. Graef, R. Gellert and M. Husovec, 'Towards a Holistic Regulatory Approach for the European Data Economy' *supra*, pp. 14-18.
135. *See*, for instance, Part III, Chapter 7 'Articulation Between Data Protection and Competition Law'.
136. *See* point 17.

acquired from third parties (acquired data), such as data brokers (e.g., farmers could acquire, from agriculture data brokers, data about the level of efficiency of specific pesticides against specific diseases or insects).

These four categories of data (actively provided, observed, inferred/derived, and acquired data) can in fact be classified in three broader categories of data, namely: (i) 'primary data', (ii) 'inferred/derived data', and (iii) 'acquired data'. Indeed, actively provided and observed data can be classified in a common group of 'primary data'. Inferred/derived data are a second generation of data drawn, by the data holder itself, from the analysis of this first generation of primary data. The data holder could also opt to acquire primary or inferred/derived from third parties, such as data brokers ('acquired data'). The distinction between these three broader categories of data (primary data, inferred/derived data and acquired data) will be relevant when considering (future) data sharing obligations imposed by the European Union (EU) legal framework.

22. When integrating the forms of data along the value chain in the equation, it can be assumed that primary data (actively provided and observed) will generally be raw (unstructured), semi-structured or structured data (information). This will notably be the case for personal data collected through an online form or through the observation of individuals' behaviour on the internet, and for non-personal IoT data collected by sensors on 'smart' agricultural or industrial machinery. Moreover, depending on the circumstances of the case, this primary data can either be the object of the data collector's core economic activity or a by-product of this activity.[137] Taking the non-personal IoT data examples mentioned above, it could be argued that collecting weather, humidity or pesticides level data may constitute the core economic activity of the provider of smart farming equipment, while the wear and tear data collected by a sensor on an industrial machine in a car assembly line could be considered as a by-product of the data collector's core activity, which is to manufacture cars.

Inferred/derived data, on the other hand, will generally be considered as analysed data (knowledge), as it is a second generation of data drawn from the analysis of the first generation of primary data. For instance, data collectors will be able to draw profiles of individuals and to infer knowledge about their preferences, on the basis of the primary personal data that has been collected about them (their age, sex or country of residence; the websites they have visited; the music they listen to; the videos they have watched, etc.). Similarly, data collectors will be able to generate knowledge/insights on the basis of the primary non-personal data that they have collected. For instance, the analysis of truck tyres' sensor data and the combination of this information with data about the weight of the loads that have been put in those trucks could allow transport service providers to infer

137. *See* point 12.

knowledge about the optimal load weight for a specific type of truck, in order to reduce tyre degradation and to increase the durability of those tyres. Finally, 'acquired data' could be raw (unstructured) data, information (structured data) or knowledge (analysed data).

23. Although this suggested typology follows a common holistic approach for both personal and non-personal data, it must be outlined from the outset that the remainder of the analysis will focus more on behavioural or consumer data than on non-personal IoT data. This is mainly because the two gaps that this contribution aims to fill through a normative approach precisely pertain to such behavioural/consumer data.[138] Moreover, most of the European policy discussions pertaining to compulsory B2B data sharing relate to large data actors that draw a 'data advantage' from their privileged access to, and control of, consumer/behavioural data.[139] In fact, even the European policy discussions on IoT data mostly focus on consumer/behavioural data, rather than on purely industrial non-personal IoT data, as illustrated by the recent preliminary report of the European Commission on its 'Consumer Internet of Things sector inquiry'.[140] Indeed, this sector enquiry focuses on four consumer IoT segments, namely the manufacture of smart home devices and of wearable devices, and the provision of voice assistants and of consumer IoT services (such as search or health services). This focus can be explained by the fact that consumer/behavioural data are at the core of certain online markets such as search, social networks or e-commerce, and constitute a fundamental resource to compete on these markets. Accordingly, the issue of the (lack of) access to such data is particularly sensitive.

On the other hand, IoT non-personal data have received much less policy attention, especially since the option to create a 'data producers right' on non-personal machine generated data has been abandoned.[141] A potential explanation for this is that such data is often generated as a by-product of other industrial activities, and that, as a result, they might not be perceived as creating as many data access issues. While this could change in the future with the growth of the IoT, notably in the context of societal initiatives imposing B2B data sharing,[142] this also explains why I mostly focus on consumer/behavioural data, rather than on IoT non-personal data.

138. *See* point 5.
139. *See* Part I, Chapter 2, Section 2.2.3; Part II, Chapter 4; Part III, Chapters 6 and 8. *See*, for instance, the Proposal for a Regulation of the European Parliament and of the Council on contestable and fair markets in the digital sector (Digital Markets Act), 15 December 2020, COM(2020) 842 final.
140. Commission Staff Working Document, Preliminary Report – Sector inquiry into consumer internet of things, Brussels, 9 June 2021, SWD(2021) 144 final.
141. On this topic, *see* Part I, Chapter 2, Section 2.2.2.2.
142. *See* Part I, Chapter 2, Section 2.3.1; and Part III, Chapter 9.

24. Finally, it must be admitted that the classification suggested above may not always be perfectly applicable. Nevertheless, this simplified classification has the merit to offer a clear data typology for the remainder of the analysis. For clarity purposes, this typology is summarised in Figure 1.1.

Figure 1.1 Proposed Data Typology

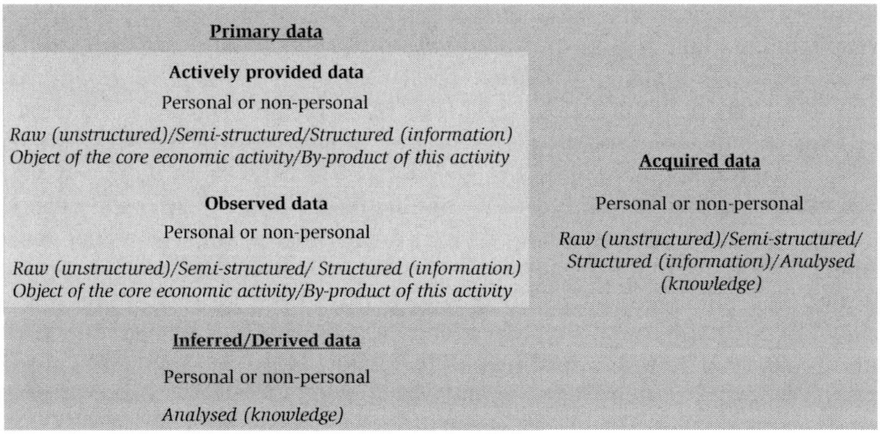

Chapter 2

Why Sharing? The Rationale for (Data) Sharing

25. In order to answer the main research question underlying this contribution (‘***What are the economic and societal balancing exercises underlying compulsory B2B data sharing?***’), it is necessary to focus on fundamental considerations pertaining to the rationale for data sharing. Said otherwise, what could justify the imposition of data sharing obligations?

Before attempting to answer this question, it is worth reverting to more classical discussions on whether a resource should be shared. Indeed, such types of discussions have not emerged with data. Finding a balance between granting exclusive ownership/property rights to the few, on the one hand, and providing access to and sharing resources with the many, on the other hand, has also always been a challenge, whether this related to tangible or intangible resources. Therefore, Section 2.1 will shed light on the **balance between the exclusive use of, and the access to/sharing of, tangible and intangible resources,** and on the various critics pertaining to how it has been addressed. On that basis, the **economic and societal rationale for sharing intangible resources** will be presented. I will solely focus on intangible resources for this last aspect because they share a key characteristic with data, namely their non-rivalrous nature, while tangible resources, on the other hand, are rivalrous.[143]

Then, I will turn, in Sections 2.2 and 2.3**,** towards the analysis of the same **balance in the realm of data**. Section 2.2 will focus on the **economic rationale for data sharing**. To do so, **data's characteristics** will first be presented. Moreover, the question of **whether data are subject to (intellectual) property rights** will be tackled. Afterwards, I will dive deeper in the analysis of the **economic rationale for data sharing**, as it is not a goal in itself and as a balance must be found between exclusive use of and access to/sharing of data.[144]

---

143. *See* points 33 and 52.
144. B. Martens, et al., ‘Business to Business Data Sharing: An Economic and Legal Analysis’, *EU Science Hub*, 2020, available at https://ssrn.com/abstract=3658100, p. 5.

Section 2.3 will be dedicated to **the societal and the empowerment rationale** for data sharing. On the one hand, data sharing could support **broader societal objectives.**[145] On the other hand, data sharing is increasingly presented as a **way to empower individuals**, by giving them more control on 'their' data.[146] Regarding these **empowerment initiatives**, it will be outlined that one should not be blinded by their benefits and that great attention should also be paid to the **long-term and collective risks that they could entail in terms of personal autonomy and (informational) self-determination**.

2.1 TO SHARE OR NOT TO SHARE RESOURCES: A BALANCE BETWEEN EXCLUSIVE USE AND ACCESS/SHARING

26. Since the dawn of humanity, dividing resources between the various members of a group has always been a challenge. This Section will first address the debates pertaining to the sharing of tangible resources, before moving on to intangible resources. Then, an attempt at the identification of some rationales for sharing resources will be made.

2.1.1 Balance Between Exclusive Use of and Access to/Sharing of Tangible Resources

2.1.1.1 The Tragedy of the Commons

27. In the realm of tangible resources, exclusive property has, for centuries, been invoked as an efficient solution to avoid overuse of resources leading to their depletion.[147] One of the most emblematic pleas in this regard is

145. *See* Communication from the Commission to the European Parliament, the Council, the European Economic and Social Committee and the Committee of the Regions, '*A European Strategy for Data*', 19 February 2020, COM(2020) 66.
146. *Ibid.*, p. 10. *See also* pp. 20-21.
147. W. Blackstone, *Commentaries on the Laws of England*, Book 2, Chapter 1, Oxford, Oxford University Press, 1771, available at https://avalon.law.yale.edu/18th_century/blackstone_bk2ch1.asp; R.-J. Pothier, 'Traité de la propriété', *Œuvres de R.-J. Pothier*, D. Ainé (ed.), tome V, Bruxelles, Tarlier, 1831; B. Windscheid, *Lehrbuch des Pandektenrechts*, 3 volumes, Frankfurt am Mein, Rutten & Loening, 1891; J. Bonnecase, *Précis de droit civil*, 2e éd., Paris, Rousseau, 1938, t. I; R. Schlatter, *Private Property: The History of an Idea*, New Brunswick, Rutgers University Press, 1951; G. Hardin, 'The Tragedy of the Commons', *Science*, December 1968, Vol. 162(3859), pp. 1243-1248; P. Ehrlich, *The Population Bomb*, New York, Ballantine Books, 1968; D. Feeny, et al., 'The Tragedy of the Commons. Twenty-Two Years Later', *Human Ecology*, 1990, Vol. 18(1), pp. 1-19; M. Kramer, *John Locke and the Origins of Private Property*,

Hardin's paper in *Science* titled 'The Tragedy of the Commons'.[148] Hardin's starting point, as a biologist working on the issue of Earth's 'population problem' (i.e., overpopulation), is that, because the population naturally tends to grow exponentially, while the amount of tangible resources in a specific territorial area is finite,[149] the per capita share of the available resources will necessarily steadily decrease.[150]

Questioning Adam Smith's theory of the 'invisible hand', following which decisions taken individually by people having their own interest and gain in mind actually lead to benefits for the whole society,[151] Hardin argues that allowing people to act as they please and to consume freely commonly shared tangible resources would inevitably lead to a 'tragedy of the commons'.[152] In perhaps the most notorious extract of his paper, Hardin explains how, according to him, this 'tragedy' unfolds:

> Picture a pasture open to all. It is to be expected that each herdsman will try to keep as many cattle as possible on the commons. Such an arrangement may work reasonably satisfactorily for centuries because tribal wars, poaching, and disease keep the numbers of both man and beast well below the carrying capacity of the land. Finally, however, comes the day of reckoning, that is, the day when the long-desired goal of social stability becomes a reality. At this point, the inherent logic of the commons remorselessly generates tragedy.
> As a rational being, each herdsman seeks to maximise his gain. Explicitly or implicitly, more or less consciously, he asks, 'What is the utility to me of adding one more animal to my herd?' This utility has one negative and one positive component.
>
> 1) The positive component is a function of the increment of one animal. Since the herdsman receives all the proceeds from the sale of the additional animal, the positive utility is nearly +1.
> 2) The negative component is a function of the additional overgrazing created by one more animal. Since, however, the effects of

---

Cambridge, Cambridge University Press, 1997; T. Merrill, 'Property and the Right to Exclude', *Nebraska Law Review*, Vol. 77(4), 1998, pp. 730-755; P. Gansey, *Thinking about Property: From Antiquity to the Age of Revolution*, Cambridge, Cambridge University Press, 2007; B. Frischmann, A. Marciano and G. Ramello, 'Retrospectives: Tragedy of the Commons after 50 Years', *Journal of Economic Perspectives*, 2019, Vol. 33(4), pp. 211-228.

148. G. Hardin, 'The Tragedy of the Commons', *supra*, pp. 1243-1248.
149. It must be outlined from the outset that Hardin's starting point focuses on depletable finite resources and that, accordingly, his reasoning cannot be translated to the use of non-depletable tangible resources such as the energy that can be derived from the sun or the wind.
150. G. Hardin, 'The Tragedy of the Commons', *supra*, p. 1243.
151. A. Smith, *An Inquiry into the Nature and Causes of the Wealth of Nations*, London, Longman and Co., 1776.
152. G. Hardin, 'The Tragedy of the Commons', *supra*, p. 1244.

> overgrazing are shared by all the herdsmen, the negative utility for any particular decision-making herdsman is only a fraction of -1. Adding together the component partial utilities, the rational herdsman concludes that the only sensible course for him to pursue is to add another animal to his herd. And another; and another ... But this is the conclusion reached by each and every rational herdsman sharing a commons. Therein is the tragedy. Each man is locked into a system that compels him to increase his herd without limit in a world that is limited. Ruin is the destination toward which all men rush, each pursuing his own best interest in a society that believes in the freedom of the commons. Freedom in a commons brings ruin to all.[153]

Moving away from this bucolic narrative, Hardin outlines that the tragedy of the commons equally applies to more contemporary issues such as overfishing or pollution.[154] For him, such a scenario could only be averted by granting private property rights or through governmental regulation, even if such a legal system is itself not perfect and potentially unjust.[155] This is because, for him, '[t]he alternative of the commons is too horrifying to contemplate. Injustice is preferable to total ruin'.[156]

28. Hardin's paper had a huge impact as it became *Science*'s most-cited article ever, and his depiction of the 'tragedy of the commons' was relayed by numerous economists, social scientists and politicians in order to justify the need for strong private property.[157] In fact, it has been reformulated by some as a prisoner's dilemma game,[158] outlining 'the paradox that individually rational strategies lead to collectively irrational outcomes'.[159] Moreover, a closely related view was developed by Olson in his book *The Logic of Collective Action*.[160] He indicated that 'unless there is coercion or some other special device to make individuals act in their common interest, rational, self-interested individuals will not act to achieve their common or group interests'.[161] According to Ostrom, these three models (the tragedy of the commons, the prisoner's dilemma and the logic of collective action) are closely related because the free-rider problem lies at the heart of each of

153. *Ibid.*
154. *Ibid.*, p. 1245.
155. *Ibid.*, pp. 1245-1247.
156. *Ibid.*, p. 1247.
157. D. Bollier and S. Helfrich, *Free, Fair and Alive: The Insurgent Power of the Commons*, Gabriola Island, New Society Publishers, 2019, p. 16.
158. *See* R.M. Dawes, 'The Commons Dilemma Game: An N-person Mixed Motive Game with a Dominating Strategy for Defection', *Oregon Research Institute Research Bulletin*, 1973, Vol. 13(2), pp. 1-12.
159. E. Ostrom, *Governing the Commons: The Evolution of Institutions for Collective Action*, Cambridge, Cambridge University Press, 1990, p. 5.
160. *Ibid.*
161. M. Olson, *The Logic of Collective Action: Public Goods and the Theory of Groups*, Cambridge, Harvard University Press, 1965, p. 2.

them.[162] As she explains, 'whenever one person cannot be excluded from the benefits that others provide, each person is motivated not to contribute to the joint effort but to free-ride on the efforts of others. If all participants choose to free ride, the collective benefit will not be produced'.[163] As will be outlined below, this free-rider problem is also a key concern raised in the debates pertaining to compulsory B2B data sharing.[164]

29. As a result of these three models, the decline of the commons and the evergrowing importance of private property have led to a steep increase in the quantity and concentration of capital.[165] To some extent, this is not surprising because, in our Western societies, 'the right to exclude is the essential feature of owning property, and every limit is at most exceptional and temporary'.[166] This paradigm of modern private property finds its roots in our history, going back to the concept of *dominium* in Roman law and culminating in the definition of property in the Napoleonic Code of 1804[167] and in the German private law Code of 1896.[168] Its justification is traditionally rooted in the pursuit of social stability (Grotius[169] and Hobbes[170]) and of individual liberty (Locke[171]), and, more recently, in the pursuit of wealth maximisation through an efficient allocation of resources (Posner[172]).[173] In this regard, the Napoleonic Code understands property above all as an individual relationship to goods, and regimes of collective property are only considered as temporary and marginal situations.[174] The essence of the property right as enshrined in the Code is thus the power to exclude.[175]

---

162. E. Ostrom, *Governing the Commons, supra*, p. 6.
163. *Ibid.*
164. *See* below point 55.
165. U. Mattei and A. Quarta, *The Turning Point in Private Law: Ecology, Technology and the Commons*, Cheltenham, Edward Elgar, 2019, p. 3.
166. *Ibid.*, p. 12.
167. 'Property is the right to enjoy and dispose of things in the most absolute manner, as long as one does not make use of them in a manner prohibited by laws or regulations' (author's own translation from Article 544 of the Belgian Civil Code of 21 March 1804).
168. U. Mattei and A. Quarta, *The Turning Point in Private Law, supra*, pp. 14, 21.
169. H. Grotius, *De Iure Belli ac Pacis*, 1625.
170. T. Hobbes, *Leviathan or The Matter, Forme and Power of a Commonwealth Ecclesiasticall and Civil*, London, George Routledge and Sons, 1651.
171. J. Locke, *Two Treatises of Government*, London, Awnsham Churchill, 1690.
172. R. Posner, *Economic Analysis of Law*, Boston, Little Brown, 1973.
173. B. Lomfeld, 'Fondements de la propriété (Théories de la propriété)', *Dictionnaire des biens communs*, M. Cornu, F. Orsi et J. Rochfeld (dir.), Paris, Presses universitaires de France, 2017, pp. 566-569.
174. A. Chaigneau, 'Propriété collective', *Dictionnaire des biens communs*, M. Cornu, F. Orsi et J. Rochfeld (dir.), Paris, Presses universitaires de France, 2017, p. 955.
175. G. Salord, 'Propriété commune', *Dictionnaire des biens communs*, M. Cornu, F. Orsi et J. Rochfeld (dir.), Paris, Presses universitaires de France, 2017, p. 961; Y. Emerich, 'Propriété exclusive ou exclusivité', *Dictionnaire des biens communs*, M. Cornu, F. Orsi et J. Rochfeld (dir.), Paris, Presses universitaires de France, 2017, pp. 980-981.

This dominant legal approach to the idea of 'property as exclusion' has a significant political impact, as it determines the default rules of our legal system, namely that the exclusive property model should be the norm, unless there are legally established reasons to depart from it.[176] Such departure from the 'exclusivity norm' can, for instance, be observed for *res nullius*, which are goods that are not owned by anyone,[177] or for *res communes omnium*, which belong to everyone because it is not necessary to appropriate them in order to be able to use them (e.g., air or light).[178] Consequently, this dominant legal approach also has an impact on the rationale for sharing because, in our social construct, 'exclusive ownership' or 'exclusive property' is generally the default model, while models based on sharing/access are less common.

2.1.1.2 Reconsidering (the Tragedy of) the Commons

30. While Hardin's analysis has had a tremendous impact, it is, to some extent, flawed.[179] This is because what Hardin depicts as a commons is in fact not a commons, but 'a free-for-all in which nothing is owned and everything is free for the taking'.[180] Rather, the notion of 'commons' refers to 'a form of community management or governance of a shared resource [i.e. one that is produced, used, and/or consumed by multiple actors, either concurrently or sequentially].[181] Governance involves a group or community of people who share access to and/or use of the resource and who manage their behaviour via an established set of formal and informal rules and norms'.[182]

The same argument is made by Ostrom, whose body of work has shed a whole new light on the commons.[183] She points out that the world is more complex than the presentation that is made of it by the three models

176. U. Mattei and A. Quarta, *The Turning Point in Private Law, supra*, p. 13.
177. *Res nullius* are however 'open to exclusive rights' and are thus a 'property-to-be and anyone who uses it first, by taking hold thereof will thereby gain an exclusive right of property' (S. Dusollier, 'The Commons as a Reverse Intellectual Property: From Exclusivity to Inclusivity', *Concepts of Property in Intellectual Property Law*, H.R. Howe and J. Griffiths (eds.), Cambridge, Cambridge University Press, 2013, p. 266).
178. J. Bart, 'Res communes omnium, res nullius, res publicae, res universatis', *Dictionnaire des biens communs*, M. Cornu, F. Orsi et J. Rochfeld (dir.), Paris, Presses universitaires de France, 2017, p. 1052; I. Durant, *Droit des biens*, Bruxelles, Larcier, 2017, pp. 20-21 and 180; Article 714 of the Napoleonic Code.
179. D. Bollier and S. Helfrich, *Free, Fair and Alive, supra*, p. 16.
180. *Ibid.*
181. M. Madison, 'Tools for Data Governance', *Technology and Regulation*, Vol. 1, 2020, p. 33, fn 32.
182. M. Madison, K. Strandburg and B. Frischmann, 'Knowledge Commons', *Legal Studies Research Paper Series: Working Paper No. 2018-39*, December 2018, available at http://ssrn.com/abstract=3300348, p. 3.
183. E. Ostrom, *Governing the Commons, supra.*

mentioned above (the tragedy of the commons, the prisoner's dilemma and the logic of collective action[184]).[185] Admittedly, these models could be true in certain scenarios, namely 'when conditions in the world approximate the conditions assumed in the models, observed behaviours and outcomes can be expected to approximate predicted behaviours and outcomes'.[186] However, without being inherently wrong, these models rely on extreme assumptions rather than on general theories.[187] Ostrom, in fact, goes on to demonstrate that some groups of individuals can break free from the commons dilemma when managing 'common-pool resources' (hereinafter 'CPR').[188]

In her work, Ostrom defines a CPR as 'a natural or man-made *resource system* that is sufficiently large as to make it costly (but not impossible) to exclude potential beneficiaries from obtaining benefits from its use' (emphasis added).[189] Resource systems are 'stock variables that are capable, under favourable conditions, of producing a maximum quantity of flow variable without harming the stock or the resource system itself'.[190] It is crucial to distinguish these resource systems from the *resource units*, which are 'what individuals appropriate or use from resource systems'.[191] The process of withdrawing resource units from a resource system is called 'appropriation', and 'as long as the average rate of withdrawal does not exceed the average rate of replenishment, a renewable resource is sustainable over time'.[192]

31. This concept of 'appropriation' is fundamental to understand, as it distinguishes a CPR from a public good, which nobody is prevented from using.[193] Indeed, it is only the resource system, and not the resource units withdrawn from the system that are jointly used (everyone is free to fish, but once a fish is caught, it is appropriated by that person).[194] This is an important finding because it contrasts with the classic 'open/closed binary', which limits individuals to two choices: either they retain private ownership or they give it away.[195] As pointed out by Bollier and Helfrish:

> Given this binary, it is not surprising that many people conflate 'openness' with the commons, and conclude that its general, defining feature is that everything is free for the taking, at no cost. This is absolutely not true. The point of a commons is to maximize shared control and benefits, a goal that requires thoughtful rules for access and use. Openness can work only when the resource

184. *See* point 28.
185. E. Ostrom, *Governing the Commons, supra.*, p. 183.
186. *Ibid.*
187. *Ibid.*
188. *Ibid.*, p. 21.
189. *Ibid.*, p. 30.
190. *Ibid.*
191. *Ibid.*
192. *Ibid.*
193. *Ibid.*, p. 32.
194. *Ibid.*, p. 31.
195. D. Bollier and S. Helfrich, *Free, Fair and Alive, supra*, p. 71.

> being used is nonrivalrous – i.e., it is not depleted when used and shared, such as digital information. (…) But for rivalrous natural resources that can be used up, successful commons set limits on usage, restrict access at certain periods of time, or for certain people, etc.[196]

Therefore, sharing should not be confused with absolute openness. Rather, 'open' and 'closed' are merely two extremes of a wider spectrum of possible sharing and access rules.[197] This is clearly outlined in Ostrom's design principles of enduring and self-governing CPR institutions, which notably rely on clearly defined boundaries and on appropriation rules.[198]

32. In light of the above, it becomes clear that concepts such as 'property' or 'ownership', on the one hand, and 'sharing' or 'commons', on the other hand, should not be opposed so strongly. Indeed, commons can be subject to ownership and can thus be subject to a form of appropriation or reservation, but, importantly, this does not lead to the exclusion of others.[199] Rather, commons are a form of ownership that organise the collective and shared use of a resource.[200] To some extent, they reflect a form of 'inclusive property', as opposed to 'exclusive property', which can be defined as a 'legal relationship between a person and a good, which is characterised, on the one hand, by the absence of a power to exclude – numerous people being included in the use of the good – and, on the other hand, by the necessarily collective use of the good, as opposed to the individualism of use generally permitted by exclusive property'.[201] Commons, and other forms of sharing, are thus situated somewhere along a continuum between absolute exclusive property/ownership, on the one hand, and the absence of any form of property/ownership (public good/free-for-all), on the other hand.

Without entering into too much detail, as this is not the core focus of my analysis, it is worth mentioning several forms of property/ownership that can be found along this continuum. One example is collective property, where individuals having exclusive property over a specific good are required to cooperate in order to preserve and maintain a resource of which their good is a subpart (e.g., an apartment in a building), or where separate individuals

196. *Ibid.*, p. 71.
197. *Ibid.*, p. 69.
198. E. Ostrom, *Governing the Commons, supra*, p. 90.
199. S. Dusollier, 'Du commun de l'intelligence artificielle', *Penser le droit de la pensée. Mélanges en l'honneur de Michel Vivant*, Paris, Dalloz, 2020, p. 116.
200. *Ibid.*
201. S. Dusollier et J. Rochfeld, 'Propriété inclusive ou inclusivité', *Dictionnaire des biens communs*, M. Cornu, F. Orsi et J. Rochfeld (dir.), Paris, Presses universitaires de France, 2017, p. 986 (author's own translation). On this concept of 'inclusive property', *see also* S. Dusollier, 'The Commons as a Reverse Intellectual Property: From Exclusivity to Inclusivity', *supra*, pp. 258-281; and G. Van Overwalle, 'Inventing Inclusive Patents: From Old to New Open Innovation', *Kritika: Essays on Intellectual Property*, Volume 1, P. Drahos, G. Ghidini and H. Ullrich (eds.), Cheltenham, Edward Elgar, 2015, pp. 206-277.

having exclusive property over goods decide to group them together in order to pursue a common goal through the collective management of the grouped goods.[202] Another example is common property, where a plurality of people shares an ownership right on a resource.[203] The difference between common and collective property is that, in the former case, a same right on a resource is shared between multiple individuals, while in the latter case, each individual has its own exclusive right on a good that forms a subpart of a resource managed collectively.[204] Importantly, such common property does not prevent the possibility to exclude third parties from using the resource, but the difference with exclusive property, as it is traditionally conceived, is that in this case, the power to exclude belongs to a group of people and not to a single individual (exclusivity must not be confused with individuality).[205] However, in its most extreme form, collective property belongs to everyone (*res communes omnium*), in which case no one can be excluded from the use of the resource (e.g., air or light).[206] A last interesting example is the concept of 'Common goods' (*beni comuni*) in Italy, which has been developed by Mattei, Reviglio and Rodotà.[207] These are 'things that are functional to the exercise of fundamental rights and to a free development of human beings (…) [such as] rivers, streams, spring waters, lakes and other waters; the air; national parks as defined by the law; forests and wooden areas; mountain areas at a high altitude, glaciers and perpetual snows; seashores and coasts established as natural reserves; protected wildlife; archaeological, cultural and environmental goods'.[208] According to these authors, the legal system should safeguard these resources, should guarantee their collective fruition to benefit future generations, and should ensure that everyone is entitled to the jurisdictional protection of these resources.[209]

---

202. *See* A. Chaigneau, 'Propriété collective', *supra*, pp. 954-957.
203. *See* G. Salord, 'Propriété commune', *supra*, pp. 960-964.
204. *Ibid.*, p. 961.
205. *Ibid.*, pp. 962-964.
206. J. Bart, 'Res communes omnium, res nullius, res publicae, res universatis', *supra*, p. 1052; I. Durant, *Droit des biens*, *supra*, pp. 20-21.
207. U. Mattei, E. Reviglio and S. Rodotà (eds.), *Invertire la rotta. Idee per una riforma della proprietà pubblica*, Bologna, Il Mulino, 2007; U. Mattei, E. Reviglio and S. Rodotà (eds), *I beni pubblici. Dal governo democratico dell'economia alla riforma del codice civile*, Rome, Accademia Nazionale dei Lincei, 2010.
208. F. Cortese, 'What Are Common Goods (Beni Comuni)? Pictures from the Italian Debate', *Revista da Faculdade de Direito da UFMG – N° Especial 2nd Conference Brazil-Italy*, 2017, pp. 125-126.
209. *Ibid.*, p. 126.

2.1.2 Balance Between Exclusive Use of and Access to/Sharing of Intangible Resources (Information and Knowledge)

33. In transitioning from considerations on sharing *tangible* resources to considerations pertaining to the sharing of *intangible* resources, it is important to point out that a large share of Ostrom's research on the commons focused on *tangible* (natural/biophysical) resources, which fit Ostrom's definition of a CPR.[210] *Intangible* resources, such as information and knowledge, on the other hand, do not fit this definition because, by essence, they are non-rivalrous, non-excludable and non-depletable.[211] This has led to the development of 'knowledge commons', which are 'an institutional approach (commons) to governing the production, use, management, and/or preservation of a particular type of resource (knowledge)'.[212]

Intangible resources are non-rivalrous because their consumption by one person does not diminish the amount of the resource that can be consumed by others (multiple people can use the resource at the same time).[213] Tangible resources, on the contrary, are rival because their use by one person prevents others from using them at the same time (if a person drives a car, nobody else can drive that car at the same time). Moreover, intangible resources are, by essence, non-excludable because 'it is either impossible to exclude non-payers (free-riders) from using the [resource], or the costs for such exclusion are so high that it would be inefficient to exclude'.[214] Indeed, in light of their intangible nature, information and knowledge do not have physical boundaries and their duplication can be made at very low cost, having as a consequence that the 'marginal costs of exclusion are often greater than the marginal costs of provision, so it is inefficient to spend resources to exclude non-payers'.[215] Finally, intangible resources are non-depletable because their use does not affect their existence, although it may affect their value.[216]

---

210. M. Madison, 'Tools for Data Governance', *supra*, p. 35.
211. *Ibid.*
212. M. Madison, K. Strandburg and B. Frischmann, 'Knowledge Commons', *supra*, p. 2.
213. M.A. Carrier, 'Limiting Copyright Through Property', *Concepts of Property in Intellectual Property Law*, H.R. Howe and J. Griffiths (eds), Cambridge, Cambridge University Press, 2013, p. 196.
214. N. Elkin-Koren and E. Salzberger, *The Law and Economics of Intellectual Property in the Digital Age: The Limits of the Analysis*, London, Routledge, 2013, p. 59.
215. *Ibid.* It is key to mention here that in some cases the costs of exclusion may be lower than the costs of provision, making the access to the information excludable. *See* point 41.
216. M. Madison, 'Tools for Data Governance', *supra*, p. 34.

2.1.2.1 The Underproduction Problem

34. Although intangible resources have different characteristics than tangible resources,[217] legal scholars have often assimilated the above-described 'tragedy of the commons' metaphor to problems pertaining to the creation and circulation of intangible resources such as information and knowledge.[218] This is because intangible resources are conventionally conceived as (free-for-all) public goods, due to their non-excludable and non-rivalrous nature.[219] Yet, assimilating such a metaphor to the realm of intangible goods presents an inherent problem, as it pertains to depletable resources, while, as indicated above, information and knowledge are non-depletable.[220]

Therefore, the basic social dilemma to be solved will not be a classic 'tragedy of the commons' overconsumption problem.[221] Rather, it is a free-rider dilemma leading to an underproduction problem, as the prospect of free-riders may discourage the creators from producing intangible resources, in light of their potential inability to generate returns on investments.[222] As will be outlined below, this free-rider problem is also a key concern raised in the debates pertaining to compulsory B2B data sharing.[223]

Because this leads to an underproduction – rather than an overconsumption – issue, the key concern is not to regulate the use of the resource, but rather to ensure that it is created in the first place.[224] Legal scholars' solution to this problem has been the creation and assignment of marketable exclusive property rights on these intangible resources, namely IP rights such as patents or copyright.[225]

35. Naturally, one might question whether it makes sense to apply the concept of 'property' to both tangible and intangible resources, notably in light of the non-rivalrous and non-depletable nature of intangible resources, which is an essential difference with tangible resources.[226] In this regard, it should be reminded here that the dominant legal paradigm for tangible goods

---

217. It should however be noted that some tangible resources, such as the energy that can be derived from the sun or the wind, are non-depletable and, therefore, have similar characteristics than intangible resources (non-excludable and non-rivalrous).
218. M. Madison, 'Tools for Data Governance', *supra*, p. 34.
219. M. Madison, K. Strandburg and B. Frischmann, 'Knowledge Commons', *supra*, p. 5.
220. M. Madison, 'Tools for Data Governance', *supra*, p. 34.
221. M. Madison, K. Strandburg and B. Frischmann, 'Knowledge Commons', *supra*, pp. 9-10.
222. *Ibid.*; N. Elkin-Koren and E. Salzberger, *The Law and Economics of Intellectual Property in the Digital Age, supra*, p. 60.
223. *See* below point 55.
224. M. Madison, 'Tools for Data Governance', *supra*, p. 34.
225. M. Madison, K. Strandburg and B. Frischmann, 'Knowledge Commons', *supra*, p. 5.
226. T. Dreier, 'How Much "Property" Is There in Intellectual Property? The German Civil Law Perspective', *Concepts of Property in Intellectual Property Law*, H.R. Howe and J. Griffiths (eds), Cambridge, Cambridge University Press, 2013, p. 127.

is the idea of 'property as exclusion'.[227] Such a paradigm can indeed, as a matter of legal technique, be translated to intangible goods through the assignment of exclusive (intellectual) property rights. As summarised by Dreier, the common point between 'property' on tangible and intangible resources 'is the aim of providing the legal basis to enable the right holder to exclude others from using the particular [resource] in question. (…) In other words, if any similarity attaches, it is only at the level of the formulation of the exclusivity of rights'.[228] Whether this importation of the 'property as exclusion' paradigm from tangible to intangible goods is justified is another question, to which I now turn.

2.1.2.2 The Advent of IP Rights as a Solution to the Underproduction Problem

36. As outlined above, the allocation of exclusive (intellectual) property (IP) rights has been the legal scholars' response to the underproduction problem of intangible resources. Such a response did not emerge out of the bloom. It is the result of a balancing exercise between the need to incentivise the creation of intangible goods in order to avoid the underproduction problem, on the one hand, and the importance of ensuring the largest dissemination of information and knowledge for the benefit of society, on the other hand.[229] Indeed, the non-rivalrous nature of information and knowledge implies that there is no social loss associated with their usage because others are not deprived of using them as well.[230] Because everyone can use information and knowledge simultaneously, it is in the general interest to ensure that it is used by as many people as possible, as this will nurture the human capital that will subsequently contribute to the production of more information and knowledge.[231] In more economic terms, the consumption of information and knowledge generates positive externalities, and 'there is a benefit in their widest possible usage in order to maximize welfare in society and as a basis for further innovation'.[232]

One important aspect of this balancing exercise must be underlined from the outset, namely that exclusive IP rights are not granted on

227. *See* point 29.
228. T. Dreier, 'How Much "Property" Is There in Intellectual Property?', *supra*, p. 127.
229. *See* N. Elkin-Koren and E. Salzberger, *The Law and Economics of Intellectual Property in the Digital Age, supra*; B. Martens, 'An Economic Perspective on Data and Platform Market Power', *supra*.
230. N. Elkin-Koren and E. Salzberger, *The Law and Economics of Intellectual Property in the Digital Age, supra*, p. 61.
231. *Ibid.*
232. *Ibid. See also* P. Régibeau and K. Rockett, 'The Relationship Between Intellectual Property Law and Competition Law: An Economic Approach', *The Interface Between Intellectual Property Rights and Competition Policy*, S. Anderman (ed.), Cambridge, Cambridge University Press, 2007, p. 509.

information/knowledge as such, but rather solely on the concrete way in which they have been expressed by the IP right holder. For instance, a copyright holder is only granted exclusive rights pertaining to the specific material form in which the work has been fixed.[233] The ideas underlying the work, on the other hand, are not protected.[234] This idea/expression dichotomy is fundamental and well established.[235] Similarly, a patent holder is only granted exclusive rights on the concrete product or process that she has invented, which must be specified in the forms of 'claims' that define the invention for which the patent is sought and determine the scope of the exclusive rights, and not on the idea(s) underlying the invention.[236] This balance is fundamental, as it does not prevent the wide dissemination of information and knowledge as such, which is in the general interest and generates positive externalities. Accordingly, when, in the following lines, I refer to IP rights on information and knowledge, this must be understood within the limits formulated in this paragraph.

37. The paragraphs above reflect the dominant approach to the justification of the creation and allocation of IP rights, namely the *incentive theory*.[237] This economic discourse of the *incentive theory* became globally dominant over the years as it was perceived as more objective than alternative theories, such as the *natural rights* theory[238] (human beings have an unconditional 'ownership' right on the result of their labour and there is a moral duty to

233. Berne Convention for the Protection of Literary and Artistic Works, 9 September 1886, as amended on 28 September 1979, Article 2.2. *See also* Council Directive 91/250/EEC of 14 May 1991 on the legal protection of computer programs, *OJ L 122/42*, 15 May 1991, Article 1.2.
234. Agreement on Trade-Related Aspects of Intellectual Property Rights, contained in Annex 1C to the Agreement establishing the World Trade Organisation (WTO), Marrakesh, 15 April 1994, Article 9.2; *See also* Council Directive 91/250/EEC of 14 May 1991 on the legal protection of computer programs, *OJ L 122/42*, 15 May 1991, Article 1.2.
235. *See*, *inter alia*, E. Derclaye, 'Introduction', *Research Handbook on the Future of EU Copyright*, E. Derclaye (ed.), Cheltenham, Edward Elgar, 2009, p. 3; T. Aplin, 'Subject Matter', *Research Handbook on the Future of EU Copyright*, E. Derclaye (ed.), Cheltenham, Edward Elgar, 2009, pp. 50, 59 and 64.
236. Agreement on Trade-Related Aspects of Intellectual Property Rights, contained in Annex 1C to the Agreement establishing the World Trade Organisation (WTO), Marrakesh, 15 April 1994, Article 27.1; Code de droit économique, Article XI.3; M. Fisher, *Fundamentals of Patent Law: Interpretation and Scope of Protection*, Oxford, Hart Publishing, 2007, p. 1.
237. A. Flanagan and M. Montagnani, 'Intellectual Property Law: Economic and Social Justice Perspectives: Introduction', *Intellectual Property Law: Economic and Social Justice Perspectives*, A. Flanagan and M. Montagnani (eds), Cheltenham, Edward Elgar, 2010, p. xi.
238. *See* J. Locke, *Two Treatises of Government, supra*; P. and W. Prinz zu Waldeck und Pyrmont, 'Introduction', *Intellectual Property and Competition Law*, P. Chrocziel, M. Lorenz and W. Prinz zu Waldeck und Pyrmont (eds), Alphen aan den Rijn, Kluwer, 2016,

protect their creations) and the *reward* theory[239] (a creator/inventor should be rewarded for contributing to the public knowledge by disclosing a creation/invention). Indeed, the latter theories were seen as more relativist due to their reliance on moral considerations.[240] On the contrary, the incentive theory is not concerned with the more ethical question of whether 'the scope of the granted rights is "just" in respect of the contribution made by the [creator/inventor]'.[241] Rather, the incentive theory is purely utilitarian in the sense that it provides that IP rights are granted 'to incentive certain desirable behaviour that would otherwise not occur'.[242]

This theory is the direct result of the 'underproduction' problem presented above,[243] as it alleges that without (intellectual) 'property' rights, information and knowledge would not be produced, due to the fear of free-riding.[244] As explained by Elkin-Koren and Salzberger, this theory 'views information [and knowledge] as public goods that bring about a market failure, and thus require central intervention by granting IP rights. The goal, according to this approach, is to design laws, which will maximize society's welfare or wellbeing'.[245]

38. One of the core assertions behind the incentive theory is that IP rights are the cheapest and most effective way for society to incentivise these desired behaviours of creation/invention.[246] Yet, IP rights come at a cost, as they create monopolies on, and barriers to, access to pre-existing creations/inventions, which can themselves stifle future creation and innovation.[247] In a way, the 'public good' market failure is thus replaced by a 'monopoly' market failure.[248] This creates an inherent paradox because, in order to generate more knowledge for the public good, which is the ultimate goal of IP rights, exclusive rights are allocated to generate incentives to create/invent, but these rights limit the access to existing knowledge.[249]

IP policies thus struggle with a balancing act between 'the social welfare costs of monopolistic exclusive rights and the social welfare gains

pp. 3-4; G. Spina Ali, 'Intellectual Property and Human Rights: A Taxonomy of Their Interactions', *International Review of Intellectual Property and Competition Law*, 2020, Vol. 51(4), p. 417.

239. *See* P. Chrocziel and W. Prinz zu Waldeck und Pyrmont, 'Introduction', *supra*, p. 4.
240. P. Chrocziel and W. Prinz zu Waldeck und Pyrmont, 'Introduction', *supra*, p. 4.
241. *Ibid.*, p. 5.
242. *Ibid.*
243. *See* point 34.
244. *See*, in this regard, N. Elkin-Koren and E. Salzberger, *The Law and Economics of Intellectual Property in the Digital Age, supra*, pp. 59-60.
245. *Ibid.*, p. 11.
246. *Ibid.*, p. 57.
247. *Ibid.*
248. *Ibid.*, p. 88.
249. *Ibid.*, pp. 87-88.

from the innovation incentive effects'.[250] Accordingly, the incentive theory treats IP rights 'as an inevitable evil that must be limited to the scope [and length] necessary for serving its goal'.[251] Indeed, if the incentivising regime is misconstrued and does not limit sufficiently the scope and length of these IP rights, this might inflate the price of future creations/inventions, or may even prevent their creation altogether, as it will be too costly to build on this pre-existing material and knowledge protected by IP rights.[252] In such a scenario, the benefits derived from the incentive effects might even be discounted by the increase in the information/knowledge production costs.[253]

39. This creates a challenge, for legislators, to find the right balance between these various competing interests in order to maximise the public good through a broad access to information and knowledge, while protecting the incentives of the creators/inventors, through the appropriate determination of the subject matter, the scope, the length of and the limitations to IP rights.[254] This inherent tension between incentivising creation and granting the widest possible public access to information and knowledge is reflected in the various international and European instruments where IP is enshrined as a human right.[255] Indeed, these instruments aim at protecting the creators'/inventors' fundamental rights over their creations/inventions and at providing the necessary economic incentives for a thriving cultural diversity and scientific innovation while primarily recognising the general public's right to benefit from cultural and scientific progress.[256] In this regard, the European Court of Human Rights has outlined in two judgments of 2013[257] that the application and enforcement of IP rights had to be balanced with the right to

---

250. B. Martens, 'An Economic Perspective on Data and Platform Market Power', *supra*, p. 23.
251. N. Elkin-Koren and E. Salzberger, *The Law and Economics of Intellectual Property in the Digital Age, supra*, p. 61.
252. *Ibid.*, p. 62.
253. G. Ramello, 'Intellectual Property, Social Justice and Economic Efficiency: Insights from Law and Economics', *Intellectual Property Law: Economic and Social Justice Perspectives*, A. Flanagan and M. Montagnani (eds), Cheltenham, Edward Elgar, 2010, p. 13.
254. P. Chrocziel and W. Prinz zu Waldeck und Pyrmont, 'Introduction', *supra*, p. 8.
255. Article 27 of the Universal Declaration of Human Rights, signed in Paris on 10 December 1948; Article 15.1.b) and c) of the International Covenant on Economic, Social and Cultural Rights, 16 December 1966; Article 1 of Protocol n° 1 to the European Convention for the Protection of Human Rights and Fundamental Freedoms, signed in Paris on 20 March 1952; Article 17.2 of the Charter of Fundamental Rights of the European Union, *OJ C 326/391*, 26 October 2012. *See* G. Spina Ali, 'Intellectual Property and Human Rights', *supra*, pp. 411-445.
256. G. Spina Ali, 'Intellectual Property and Human Rights', *supra*, pp. 414-417. *See also* L. Helfer, 'Mapping the Interface Between Human Rights and Intellectual Property', *Research Handbook on Human Rights and Intellectual Property*, C. Geiger (ed.), Cheltenham, Edward Elgar, 2015, pp. 12-13.
257. ECtHR, *Ashby Donald and Others v. France*, 10 January 2013, App. No. 36769/08; ECtHR, *Neij and Kolmisoppi v. Sweden*, 19 February 2013, App. No. 40397/12.

freedom of information enshrined in Article 10 of the European Convention on Human Rights,[258] which also encompasses a right of access to information.[259]

2.1.2.3 Questioning the Underproduction Problem and the IP Answer to It

40. IP rights have thus been created in order to solve the alleged 'underproduction' problem of intangible goods presented above,[260] according to which information and knowledge would not be produced, due to the fear of free-riding, unless exclusive (intellectual) 'property' rights are granted on these intangible resources in order to incentivise their creation.[261] However, the existence of this 'underproduction problem', and/or of the appropriateness of the IP answer to it, is being questioned.

2.1.2.3.1. Is There Really an Underproduction Problem?

41. The rationale behind the underproduction problem is the 'public good market failure', namely that, because intangible goods are non-rivalrous and non-excludable, this will lead to their underproduction. However, as pointed out by Madison et al., 'knowledge-generating institutions based on successful coordination and collaboration among knowledge producers and users have existed for centuries, often despite the absence of IP rights owned by individual creators or inventors'.[262] For instance, they outline that 'universities have long served as knowledge-generating and knowledge-sustaining institutions despite faculty researchers often exercising few conventional market-based IP interests'.[263]

In spite of this finding, the narrative of the underproduction problem remains strongly used by right holders as a rhetorical justification for the superiority of the rationale of exclusion over the rationale of access/sharing,

258. D. Voorhoof, 'Freedom of Expression and the Right to Information: Implications for Copyright', *Research Handbook on Human Rights and Intellectual Property*, C. Geiger (ed.), Cheltenham, Edward Elgar, 2015, p. 331; L. Helfer, 'Mapping the Interface Between Human Rights and Intellectual Property', *supra*, p. 7.
259. ECtHR, *Youth Initiative for Human Rights v. Serbia*, 25 June 2013, App. No. 48135/06, §§ 20 and 24; D. Voorhoof, 'Freedom of Expression and the Right to Information', *supra*, p. 337. *See also* C. de Terwangne, 'Droit à la vie privée: un droit sur l'information et un droit à l'information', *Law, Norms and Freedoms in Cyberspace / Droit, normes et libertés dans le cybermonde: Liber Amicorum Yves Poullet*, E. Degrave, C. de Terwangne, S. Dusollier et R. Queck (dir.), Bruxelles, Larcier, 2018, pp. 555-579.
260. *See* point 34.
261. *See*, in this regard, N. Elkin-Koren and E. Salzberger, *The Law and Economics of Intellectual Property in the Digital Age, supra*, pp. 59-60.
262. M. Madison, K. Strandburg and B. Frischmann, 'Knowledge Commons', *supra*, p. 5.
263. *Ibid.*

especially in the advent of digital technologies that facilitate the reproduction and dissemination of their creations/inventions.[264] Yet, these technological changes that have occurred, mostly in the digital environment, could actually be used to formulate a contradictory argument to that of the right holders. Indeed, although these evolutions enable easier reproduction and dissemination of creations/inventions, they also enable much easier and cheaper technical exclusion of the access to them, which could thus question the 'public good market failure' premise, as large fractions of information and knowledge may now be made excludable through technical, as well as contractual, means.[265] This could be especially problematic if the access to information or knowledge that is not covered by exclusive IP rights is technically or contractually excluded (e.g., information and knowledge falling out of the scope of these rights;[266] or information and knowledge falling within the scope of the exceptions to these rights).[267]

42. Alternatively, even if these technological developments were not deemed to be sufficient to tackle the non-excludability issue, some authors have outlined that monetary incentives, deriving from the granting of exclusive IP rights, are not the only way to stimulate creation/innovation.[268] For them, the assumption that monetary incentives are necessary to induce creation/innovation relies on shaky grounds, as there is limited empirical evidence to support the claim that people will not create/invent if they are not promised some financial profits in return.[269] In fact, some empirical evidence suggests that monetary incentives may actually sometimes undermine people's motivation to create/invent.[270] Such studies show that offering monetary rewards may make people less creative as their free-choice is undermined due to performance constraints,[271] or could reduce the quality of their

264. T. Dreier, 'How much "Property" Is There in Intellectual Property?', *supra*, p. 132; J. Waldron, 'From Authors to Copiers: Individual Rights and Social Values in Intellectual Property', *Chicago-Kent Law Review*, 1993, Vol. 68, p. 851.
265. N. Elkin-Koren and E. Salzberger, *The Law and Economics of Intellectual Property in the Digital Age, supra*, p. 77.
266. On this limit, *see* point 36.
267. On this issue for the sui generis database right, *see* points 58-60.
268. N. Elkin-Koren and E. Salzberger, *The Law and Economics of Intellectual Property in the Digital Age, supra*, p. 11; *see also* A. Flanagan and M. Montagnani, 'Intellectual Property Law: Economic and Social Justice Perspectives', *supra*, pp. x-xviii.
269. N. Elkin-Koren and E. Salzberger, *The Law and Economics of Intellectual Property in the Digital Age, supra*, p. 65.
270. *Ibid.*, p. 66.
271. E. Deci, R. Koestner and R. Ryan, 'A Meta-Analytic Review of Experiments Examining the Effects of Extrinsic Rewards on Intrinsic Motivation', *Psychological Bulletin*, 1999, Vol. 125(6), pp. 627-668.

work.[272,273] Moreover, it is practically impossible to determine the desirable or optimal level of incentives that should be aimed for, and, consequently, it is extremely complex to tailor IP rights perfectly (in terms of scope, duration, exceptions, etc.) in order to achieve this optimum.[274]

Rather, these authors outline that there are also many non-monetary motivations that incentivise people to create/invent, such as the natural drive to create/invent, the need to express ideas or talents and to be acknowledged for it, or the wish to gain recognition among peers or the general public.[275] These can be intrinsic (self-oriented) motivations and/or social motivations (other-oriented).[276] To give a famous example, when Dr Jonas Salk was asked in 1955 who owned the patent to the polio vaccine that he had just co-created, he answered: 'Well, the people I would say. There is no patent. Could you patent the sun?'[277,278]

To conclude on this critique, it can also be added that some argue that creation and innovation are, in any case, profitable even without the granting of exclusive (intellectual) 'property' rights, as first-mover advantages and 'lead time' (although this lead time might be short-lived in the digital age) are alternative considerations that offset the lower production costs of free-riders.[279]

2.1.2.3.2 Even If There Is an Underproduction Problem, Are IP Rights the Adequate Solution?

43. Even if the dominant assumption that intangible goods face an underproduction problem was deemed to be correct,[280] some have questioned whether exclusive (intellectual) 'property' rights are the adequate solution to tackle it. Or rather, they question whether the balance struck in the past by IP rights is still optimal today, as our society increasingly relies on

272. A. Kohn, *Punished by Rewards: The Trouble with Gold Stars, Incentive Plans, A's, Praise, and Other Bribes*, Boston, Houghton Mifflin, 1999, pp. 136-138.
273. N. Elkin-Koren and E. Salzberger, *The Law and Economics of Intellectual Property in the Digital Age, supra*, p. 66.
274. *Ibid.*, p. 101.
275. *Ibid.*, p. 66. On these motivational factors, *see also* S. Sandeen, 'The Value of Irrationality in the IP Equation', *Intellectual Property Law: Economic and Social Justice Perspectives*, A. Flanagan and M. Montagnani (eds), Cheltenham, Edward Elgar, 2010, pp. 44-65.
276. N. Elkin-Koren and E. Salzberger, *The Law and Economics of Intellectual Property in the Digital Age, supra*, pp. 66-67.
277. CBS Television interview with Salk, *See It Now*, 12 April 1955, quoted in J. Cohen, *Shots in the Dark: The Wayward Search for an AIDS Vaccine*, New York, W.W. Norton, 2001.
278. D. Bollier and S. Helfrich, *Free, Fair and Alive, supra*, p. 227.
279. *Ibid.*, pp. 62 and 69.
280. For the purpose of my analysis, I do not believe that it is necessary to take a definitive stance on this issue.

information and knowledge, which might entail the need to review the existing balance in favour of more access than what is currently allowed under the IP rights system.[281]

To support their argument, these authors allege that IP rights have enabled right holders to exclude the use of information and knowledge far beyond the economic incentive purposes that they were designed to serve, and that these rights have actually become a major tool to expand market power, reduce competition and concentrate the control over the production and distribution of information and knowledge.[282] Taking the example of copyright, Halbert argues that it is 'a socially constructed discourse that has become a powerful social myth'.[283]

Moreover, because knowledge heavily relies on sharing processes, overly extensive appropriation of it through strong IP rights will inexorably reduce the amount of access to it and will produce an adverse outcome for overall efficiency.[284] On the contrary, a weaker form of appropriation generates positive effects on knowledge production, as it will imply 'lower productive costs for follow-on creators, wider access to knowledge, and the possibility of free-riding, understood as unpaid access to knowledge for a considerable amount of individuals. Stated differently, *efficiency in the knowledge domain requires the preservation of broad access*' (emphasis added).[285] In fact, some argue that the benefits from information and knowledge disclosure should be more strongly seen as important values in their own right, rather than merely as counterweights to the granting of appropriation rights.[286] Taking the example of copyright, Morando argues that weaker forms of appropriation, such as the Creative Commons licences, are preferable default rules in terms of efficiency, fairness and social justice than the current copyright 'default rule' (e.g., full protection – 'All rights reserved').[287]

To summarise these authors' positions, they invite to reconsider the existing balance at the basis of exclusive (intellectual) 'property' rights, because the costs, for society, of exclusion of information and knowledge through IP rights have grown, while society increasingly depends on the access to it. As outlined above, this notably derives from the fact that the

281. N. Elkin-Koren and E. Salzberger, *The Law and Economics of Intellectual Property in the Digital Age, supra*, p. 58.
282. *Ibid.*, p. 90. *See also* P. Régibeau and K. Rockett, 'The Relationship Between Intellectual Property Law and Competition Law', *supra*, 2007, pp. 505-552.
283. D. Halbert, *Intellectual Property in the Information Age: The Politics of Expanding Ownership Rights*, Westport, Quorum books, 1999, p. 2. *See also* pp. xi and xv.
284. G. Ramello, 'Intellectual Property, Social Justice and Economic Efficiency', *supra*, pp. 2-3.
285. *Ibid.*, p. 17.
286. S. Sandeen, 'The Value of Irrationality in the IP Equation', *supra*, p. 57.
287. F. Morando, 'Copyright Default Rule: Reconciling Efficiency and Fairness', *Intellectual Property Law: Economic and Social Justice Perspectives*, A. Flanagan and M. Montagnani (eds), Cheltenham, Edward Elgar, 2010, pp. 25-27.

access to large fractions of information and knowledge that are not covered by exclusive IP rights may now be technically or contractually excluded.[288]

2.1.3 The Rationale for Sharing Intangible Resources

44. In light of the above, it is apparent that the classic solution to the 'exclusion v. access/sharing balance' is increasingly challenged, mainly for intangible resources.[289] Indeed, growing calls for a wider sharing of information and knowledge are being made, notably on the grounds of their non-rivalrous nature.[290] In fact, two types of rationale are called upon to support this reconsideration of the classic balance, namely economic considerations on the one hand, and more societal considerations, on the other hand. Because data are also non-rivalrous and non-depletable,[291] the rest of this Section will focus on the rationale for sharing intangible resources, as these might suffer (like data) from an underproduction problem, rather than from the overconsumption problem of tangible goods.[292]

2.1.3.1 Economic Rationale for Sharing Intangible Resources

45. To a large extent, the economic rationale for sharing intangible resources has already been outlined above, in the discussion pertaining to the existence of the 'underproduction problem' and of the appropriateness of the IP answer to it.[293] The key argument is that there is no social loss incurred by to the use of intangible resources, in light of their non-rivalrous character.[294] As outlined by Ramello, 'efficiency in the knowledge domain requires the preservation of broad access', as it will lower the production costs for follow-on creation/innovation, while overly extensive exclusive rights will reduce the access to it and will produce an adverse outcome for overall efficiency.[295] This economic rationale has also been brilliantly explained in Benkler's work on the 'networked information economy',[296] which will be briefly summarised here.

288. *See* point 41.
289. *See* Part I, Chapter 2, Section 2.1.2.3.
290. N. Elkin-Koren and E. Salzberger, *The Law and Economics of Intellectual Property in the Digital Age, supra*, p. 61.
291. *See* point 52.
292. *See* point 34.
293. *See* Part I, Chapter 2, Section 2.1.2.3.
294. N. Elkin-Koren and E. Salzberger, *The Law and Economics of Intellectual Property in the Digital Age, supra*, p. 61.
295. G. Ramello, 'Intellectual Property, Social Justice and Economic Efficiency', *supra*, pp. 2-3; 17.
296. Y. Benkler, *The Wealth of Networks: How Social Production Transforms Markets and Freedom*, New Haven, Yale University Press, 2003.

46. The more widely information and knowledge are diffused and shared, the more benefits it will generate for society. This has led to the establishment of a balance between static and dynamic efficiency.[297] Indeed, from a static perspective, the most efficient approach for society's overall welfare would be to ensure the broadest access to/sharing of information and knowledge possible, by limiting exclusive rights on it.[298] However, from a dynamic perspective, creators/innovators may refrain from generating this information/knowledge if they know that they will have to share it freely with anyone.[299] Therefore, under the classic approach, some static inefficiency is traded off to achieve dynamic efficiency; i.e., exclusive rights are granted to creators/inventors so they can charge positive prices for resources that have a zero marginal cost,[300] in order to incentivise them to create/invent.[301] Allegedly, the result of this balance will be to generate more information and knowledge over time, which will 'outweigh the inefficiency at any given moment caused by selling the information at above its marginal cost'.[302]

47. Yet, Benkler points out that there is in fact remarkably little support, both in theory and in empirical evidence, for such an approach of the information and knowledge production.[303] On the contrary, because information is non-rivalrous and because it is both an input and an output of its own production process, it is economically detrimental to excessively exclude the access to / sharing of it.[304] Indeed, because any new informational resource builds on pre-existing information and knowledge, granting strong exclusive rights on this prior information and knowledge will increase the price of new information production, which can lead to both static *and* dynamic inefficiency, as 'we will not only have too little consumption of information today, but also too little production of new information for tomorrow'.[305] Moreover, the high price for new information production deriving from strong exclusive rights will also drive concentration in the information production process.[306]

48. In light of the above, Benkler argues that it is more efficient for information and knowledge to be shared, and that the costs to do so have dramatically declined with the advent of the 'networked information economy'.[307] Indeed, the 'networked information economy' has widely

297. *Ibid.*, p. 36.
298. *Ibid.*, p. 37.
299. *Ibid.*
300. The cost of reproducing and sharing the resource is zero.
301. Y. Benkler, *The Wealth of Networks, supra*, p. 37.
302. *Ibid.*
303. *Ibid.*, p. 39.
304. *Ibid.*, pp. 37-38.
305. *Ibid.*, p. 38.
306. *Ibid.*, p. 50.
307. *Ibid.*, p. 56.

distributed the high-capital costs that were necessary for information production and sharing, which, in turn, has reduced the access barriers to information and allows for much more non-market decentralised models of information production and sharing that do not depend on proprietary strategies.[308]

While peer production of information, like Wikipedia, and peer-to-peer exchange platforms are good examples of this, the paramount example of this new paradigm is free software (or 'freeware').[309] This freeware movement relies on licensing constraints, originally designed by Richard Stallman and Eben Moglen through the *Free Software Foundation*,[310] which allow anyone to use the freeware on the condition that any modification of it must be distributed under the same licensing terms as the original freeware.[311] It can be seen as a formalised example of 'inclusive property', as opposed to 'exclusive property', as mentioned above.[312] The most well-known licence in this regard is the *GNU General Public License*.[313] As the outputs of these processes are non-rivalrous resources (information and knowledge), sharing them freely is more efficient, all other things being equal, than if they were produced and shared under the classic proprietary model.[314] To summarise, the economic rationale for sharing intangible resources derives from two of their characteristics, namely that they are non-rivalrous and that they are both an input and an output of their own production process.

2.1.3.2 Societal Rationale for Sharing Intangible Resources

49. Next to the economic considerations outlined above, there are also more societal considerations that can justify sharing intangible resources. Once again, this mainly flows from these resources' non-rivalrous nature. Because everyone can use information and knowledge simultaneously, it is in the general interest to ensure that it is used by as many people as possible, as this will nurture the human capital that will subsequently contribute to the production of more information and knowledge.[315] This also flows from the fact that intangible resources are both an input and an output of their own production process.[316] Indeed, because the production of new information

308. *Ibid.*, pp. 32-33. This might however not be true for all kinds of information, as there are still high costs associated with some types of information collection (e.g., satellite imagery).
309. *Ibid.*, p. 60.
310. https://fr.wikipedia.org/wiki/Free_Software_Foundation.
311. Y. Benkler, *The Wealth of Networks, supra*, p. 63.
312. *See* point 32.
313. *See* https://www.gnu.org/licenses/gpl-3.0.en.html.
314. Y. Benkler, *The Wealth of Networks, supra*, p. 107.
315. N. Elkin-Koren and E. Salzberger, *The Law and Economics of Intellectual Property in the Digital Age, supra*, p. 61.
316. Y. Benkler, *The Wealth of Networks, supra*, pp. 37-38.

and knowledge depends on the broadest access possible to existing information and knowledge, sharing intangible resources is crucial for societal progress in all fields, whether it pertains to the preservation of human's health or living environment, to the understanding of the infinitely big or the infinitely small, or to the pursuit of other societal goals (better health, cleaner environment, etc.).

50. Yet, in practice, information and knowledge are increasingly concentrated in the hands of a few very large actors, who thus benefit from tremendous economic, political and technological power.[317] For Bollier and Helfrish, this is the natural result of a society built around capitalist markets and the narrative of individual freedom and property ownership developed by philosophers such as Descartes, Hobbes and Locke.[318] Indeed, if access to intangible resources is regulated by the market via a 'pay for access' model, this will automatically have as a consequence to provide greater access to, and control of, intangible resources to wealthier people, as their large financial means will allow them not only to pay for broader access to them but also to invest more heavily in their creation/invention and management.[319]

Accordingly, Bollier and Helfrish call for an ontological shift (an 'OntoShift' as they call it) from exclusion towards more access/sharing.[320] The rationale behind such increased sharing is that this would considerably diminish the access barriers to information and would improve everyone's equality of opportunity of access to information.[321] This fits into broader social justice and human rights considerations, as everyone has a right of access to information, which is important because it enables individuals to fully enjoy and exercise a variety of other rights (right to privacy, to education, to culture or to move freely) and to take fundamental decisions.[322] For instance, access to relevant health and environmental information has an impact on the individuals' right to privacy as it allows them to take informed decisions regarding the place where they want to live.[323] Moreover, access to mobility information such as information about public transportation schedules or traffic jams enables individuals to move freely in the most optimal way. Furthermore, broader access to/sharing of information and knowledge 'creates the opportunities for greater autonomous action, a more critical

317. U. Mattei and A. Quarta, *The Turning Point in Private Law, supra*, pp. ix and 3.
318. D. Bollier and S. Helfrich, *Free, Fair and Alive, supra*, pp. 34, 88, 211.
319. *Ibid.*, p. 72.
320. *Ibid.*, pp. 29 and 72.
321. Y. Benkler, *The Wealth of Networks, supra*, pp. 13-14.
322. *See* C. de Terwangne, 'Droit à la vie privée: un droit sur l'information et un droit à l'information', *supra*, pp. 555-579.
323. *Ibid.*, pp. 573-576; ECtHR, *Guerra et al. v. Italy*, 19 February 1998, App. No. 14967/89, § 60; ECtHR, *McGinley and Egan v. United Kingdom*, 9 June 1998, App. No. 21825/93 and 23414/94, §§ 97 and 101; ECtHR, *Roche v. United Kingdom*, 19 October 2005, App. No. 32555/96, §§ 162 and 165.

culture, a more discursively engaged and better informed republic, and perhaps a more equitable global community'.[324]

Once again, open-source software production or peer production of knowledge can be cited as socially beneficial initiatives aiming at providing the largest access possible to information and knowledge.[325] Indeed, wide access to information through websites like Wikipedia can contribute to the individuals' right to education and culture, as they can easily obtain information about historical events, about fundamental rules and principles in all fields of social and natural sciences, about the functioning of mechanical objects and technologies, about works of arts (books, theatre plays, movies, paintings, music, etc.), etc.

2.2 ECONOMIC RATIONALE FOR DATA SHARING

51. After having presented the classic balance between exclusive use of and access to/sharing of tangible and intangible resources, and the various critics pertaining to how it has been addressed, it is now time to turn towards the analysis of the same balance for data. In fact, most of the developments pertaining to intangible resources are equally applicable to data, which are also, by essence, intangible resources. Much like information and knowledge, data's value emerges when it is shared and aggregated.[326] This Section will focus on the economic rationale for data sharing, while Section 2.3 will be dedicated to the societal and 'empowerment' rationale for data sharing.

2.2.1 Data's Characteristics

52. Data is often presented in the policy debates as the 'new oil' of our modern economy. Yet, this broadly used catchphrase is somewhat misleading as oil is both tangible and depletable, which is not the case of data, which is intangible and non-depletable, as its use does not affect its existence, although it may affect its value.[327] However, this metaphor does make some sense if one considers oil's '"infrastructural" qualities, in that it can be directed to numerous applications, with diverse values'.[328] In this sense, data, much like oil, is an important component of a great number of technical and

324. Y. Benkler, *The Wealth of Networks, supra*, p. 92.
325. *Ibid.*, pp. 32-33; D. Bollier and S. Helfrich, *Free, Fair and Alive, supra*, p. 259; M. Madison, K. Strandburg and B. Frischmann, 'Knowledge Commons', *supra*, p. 4.
326. M. Madison, 'Tools for Data Governance', *supra*, p. 29.
327. M. Madison, 'Tools for Data Governance', *supra*, pp. 31 and 34; M. Stucke and A. Grunes, *Big Data and Competition Policy*, *supra*, pp. 44-45.
328. M. Madison, 'Tools for Data Governance', *supra*, p. 31.

commercial applications and it 'lubricates social and technical processes'.[329] This is why data is, itself, sometimes characterised as an 'infrastructural resource' because its use creates spill overs in multiple fields across society.[330]

According to Frischmann, infrastructural resources 'are "shared means to many ends", which satisfy the non-rivalrous, the capital good and the general-purpose criteria'.[331] First, data are a non-rivalrous resource that can be replicated and consumed by an unlimited number of actors – even simultaneously – and 'maximising access to the non-rivalrous [resource] will in theory maximise social welfare, as every additional private benefit comes at no additional cost'.[332] Second, data is often a capital resource, which means that it is used as an input for goods or services rather than as an end it itself. This is because data often has no intrinsic value, as the value will derive from the use made of this data in order to extract information or knowledge. As data are a non-rival capital resource that 'can in theory be used (simultaneously) by multiple users for multiple purposes as an input to produce an unlimited number of goods and services',[333] data access and sharing are highly valuable. Third, data may be described as a general-purpose resource. Indeed, data could, in theory, be used for an unlimited number of purposes, including not only economic but also public and social purposes, and additionally, the use of data for one purpose can provide valuable insights for uses in other domains, thus having significant spill over effects.[334]

53. On the other hand, whether data should be considered as an excludable or non-excludable resource is less clear.[335] Indeed, even if data is arguably non-excludable by nature,[336] in practice, data is both technically and contractually excludable.[337] Regarding technical excludability, it has already

329. *Ibid.*
330. *Ibid.*, p. 40.
331. B. Frischmann, *Infrastructure: The Social Value of Shared Resources*, Oxford, Oxford University Press, 2012, cited in OECD, *Data-Driven Innovation: Big Data for Growth and Well-Being*, OECD Publications, 2015, available at https://www.oecd.org/sti/data-driven-innovation-9789264229358-en.htm, p. 179.
332. OECD, *Data-Driven Innovation: Big Data for Growth and Well-Being*, *supra*, pp. 179-180. *See also* N. Elkin-Koren and E. Salzberger, *The Law and Economics of Intellectual Property in the Digital Age, supra*, p. 61.
333. OECD, *Data-Driven Innovation: Big Data for Growth and Well-Being*, *supra*, pp. 180-181.
334. *Ibid.*, pp. 181-182.
335. *See also* point 41 where some doubts are cast on the non-excludable nature of intangible resources such as information or knowledge.
336. B. Martens, et al., 'Business to Business Data Sharing', *supra*, p. 4.
337. W. Kerber, 'Rights on Data: The EU Communication "Building a European Data Economy" from an Economic Perspective', *Trading Data in the Digital Economy: Legal Concepts and Tools*, S. Lohsse, R. Schulze and D. Staudenmayer (eds), Baden-Baden, Nomos, 2017, p. 118.

been outlined that technological changes in the digital environment enable much easier and cheaper technical exclusion of the access to intangible resources such as information and knowledge,[338] and this equally applies to data. Data holders can set technical safeguards in order to ensure that third parties will not be able to access their data. They can also technically ensure that the data they hold remains secret in order, for instance, to benefit from the protection granted to trade secrets.[339] Moreover, data holders can contractually exclude the access to (some of) their data. In fact, as pointed out by Stucke and Grunes, 'data's competitive significance (and value) arise in part from the ability of firms to exclude others from access and analysing it as quickly'.[340]

54. Therefore, in light of data's potentially excludable character, it can be argued that data is not a public good, which is non-rivalrous and non-excludable, but is better depicted as a 'club good', which is non-rivalrous but excludable.[341] This is an important finding because it means that the 'public good market failure', that is at the basis of the justification of the creation of exclusive (intellectual) 'property' rights to avoid the 'underproduction problem' of intangible resources (such as information and knowledge), cannot simply be transposed to the realm of data. As will be outlined below, this has had an impact in the discussions pertaining to the creation of an 'IP-like' data producer's right.[342]

55. That being said, if data holders are not able to exclude the access to their data (for instance, because of data sharing obligations), the free-rider dilemma allegedly leading to the 'public good market failure' and the 'underproduction problem' for intangible resources (i.e., the prospect of free-riders may discourage the creators from producing intangible resources, in light of their potential inability to generate returns on investments)[343] may also surface for data. Indeed, data collection and processing, and consequently data sharing, entails costs for the data holder, and data sharing obligations might create disincentives for data collection and processing.[344] Accordingly, a balance must be found between the benefits and costs of data

338. *See* point 41.
339. *See* Directive (EU) 2016/943 of the European Parliament and of the Council of 8 June 2016 on the protection of undisclosed know-how and business information (trade secrets) against their unlawful acquisition, use and disclosure, *OJ L 157*, 15 June 2016. *See* point 183.
340. M. Stucke and A. Grunes, *Big Data and Competition Policy*, *supra*, p. 46.
341. M. Madison, 'Tools for Data Governance', *supra*, p. 34; M. Stucke and A. Grunes, *Big Data and Competition Policy*, *supra*, p. 45.
342. *See* point 63.
343. *See* point 34.
344. J. Crémer, Y.-A. de Montjoye and H. Schweitzer, 'Competition Policy for the Digital Era: Final Report', 2019, pp. 76-77, available at http://ec.europa.eu/competition/publications/reports/ kd0419345enn.pdf.

sharing.[345] As such balance had been solved, for intangible resources, through the means of IP rights, the question naturally emerged of whether the same balance, for data, could also be solved through (intellectual) 'property' rights.

2.2.2 Are Data Subject to (Intellectual) Property Rights?

56. Unsurprisingly, the strong establishment of (intellectual) property rights in our society has led to discussions on whether data should also be subject to some form of exclusive (intellectual) 'property' right.[346]

2.2.2.1 Evolution of the Debates on (Intellectual) Property over Information Towards Discussions on (Intellectual) Property over Data

57. In fact, these discussions build on older debates pertaining to 'property' on information. Indeed, at the beginning of the 21st century, information, much like data today, was considered as an essential strategic resource because it was the 'raw material' for important products such as databases or software, and this generated boiling discussions on the legal stakes of its potential 'appropriation' by firms or people.[347] For instance, several French authors like Leclercq and Catala proposed, in the early 1980s, a theory according to which information, as such, should be considered as a good that can be subject to legal 'appropriation'.[348] The concept of 'appropriation' is understood as another way of formulating the concept of 'property', as it covers all exclusive rights on a good.[349] Indeed, according to Leclercq and Catala's theory, the 'creator' of information must be considered as the owner of absolute exclusive rights on it, and should be able to exclude others from using it unduly.[350] On the contrary, others argued that there is no such

345. P. Larouche, 'The European Microsoft Case at the Crossroads of Competition Policy and Innovation', *Antitrust Law Journal*, 2008, Vol. 75(3), pp. 933-937. For a more extensive analysis of this balance *see* points 89 and 90 below.
346. Communication from the Commission to the European Parliament, the Council, the European Economic and Social Committee and the Committee of the Regions, '*Building a European Data Economy*', *supra*, p. 13.
347. F. Dubuisson, *Existe-t-il un principe general d'appriopriation de l'information?*, Thèse de doctorat, Université Libre de Bruxelles, 2005, pp. 1-2.
348. P. Leclercq, 'Essai sur le statut juridique des informations', *Les flux transfrontières de données: vers une économie internationale de l'information ?*, A. Madec (ed.), Paris, La Documentation française, 1982, pp. 119-150; P. Catala, *Le droit à l'épreuve du numérique. Jus ex machina*, Paris, PUF, 1998, pp. 224-263; F. Dubuisson, *Existe-t-il un principe general d'appriopriation de l'information?*, *supra*, p. 2.
349. F. Dubuisson, *Existe-t-il un principe general d'appriopriation de l'information?*, *supra*, p. 14.
350. *Ibid.*

principle of 'appropriation/property' on information, and that this notably stems from the fact that IP rights such as copyright[351] and the sui generis database right[352] do not protect the information as such.[353]

58. Although this debate on the 'property' of information will not be further analysed here in light of the scope of my contribution,[354] it is worth underlining that IP rights such as copyright and the sui generis database right similarly do not erect a principle of 'appropriation/property' on individual data either.[355] Indeed, data, as such, cannot be protected by copyright.[356] Only the particular expression of a semantic content extracted from data could be protected by copyright if the conditions for the benefit of this protection are met, such as originality.

That being said, data will rarely be apprehended as an isolated good and will often be included in databases,[357] which benefit, in the EU, from the protection of two distinct IP rights, both contained in the Directive on the legal protection of databases.[358]

On the one hand, this Directive provides that databases which, by reason of the selection or arrangement of their contents, constitute the author's own intellectual creation shall be protected as such by copyright.[359] This copyright protection is however limited, as it is only granted to the structure of the database, not to its content.[360] On the other hand, a so-called

351. *See* Directive 2001/29/EC of the European Parliament and of the Council of 22 May 2001 on the harmonisation of certain aspects of copyright and related rights in the information society, *OJ L 167/10*, 22 June 2001; Directive (EU) 2019/790 of the European Parliament and of the Council of 17 April 2019 on copyright and related rights in the Digital Single Market and amending Directives 96/9/EC and 2001/29/EC, *OJ L 130/92*, 17 May 2019.
352. *See* Directive 96/9/EC of the European Parliament and of the Council of 11 March 1996 on the legal protection of databases, *OJ L 77/20*, 27 March 1996.
353. *See* point 36.
354. For an extensive analysis, *see* F. Dubuisson, *Existe-t-il un principe general d'appriopriation de l'information?, supra*.
355. On this point, *see* M. Knockaert et T. Tombal, 'Quels droits sur les données?', *Actualités en droit du numérique*, H. Jacquemin et B. Michaux (eds), Limal, Anthémis, 2019, pp. 58-68.
356. N. Duch-Brown, B. Martens and F. Mueller-Langer, 'The Economics of Ownership, Access and Trade in Digital Data', *Digital Economy Working Paper 2016-10*, JRC Technical Reports, 2016, available at https://papers.ssrn.com/sol3/papers.cfm?abstract_id=2914144, p. 7.
357. 'A collection of independent works, data or other materials arranged in a systematic or methodical way and individually accessible by electronic or other means' (Article 1.2 of Directive 96/9/EC).
358. Directive 96/9/EC of the European Parliament and of the Council of 11 March 1996 on the legal protection of databases, *OJ L 77/20*, 27 March 1996.
359. Article 3.1 of Directive 96/9/EC.
360. Article 3.2 of Directive 96/9/EC.

sui generis right is granted to the maker[361] on the content of the database.[362] Its aim is to grant to the maker some form of control on the extraction, by third parties, of data from the database, as a reward for the investment it has made in building this database.[363] However, the scope of this sui generis right is also limited, as it is only granted to the maker of the database if there has been a qualitatively and/or quantitatively substantial investment in either the obtaining, verification or presentation of the contents.[364] Inversely, a substantial investment in the creation of the data will not induce protection under the Directive.[365] Moreover, this sui generis right allows the maker to prevent extraction and/or reutilisation of the whole or of a qualitatively and/or quantitatively substantial part of the contents of that database.[366] Thus, this sui generis right only 'protects the database as a whole and not specific data in the set'.[367]

The maker of the database is thus only protected against the extraction and/or reutilisation of substantial parts of the database, which implies that third parties can access the database in order to extract and reuse insubstantial parts of it. Nevertheless, the repeated and systematic extraction and/or reuse of insubstantial parts of the contents of the database will also be forbidden if it implies acts which conflict with a normal exploitation of that database or which unreasonably prejudice the legitimate interests of the database maker.[368] To evaluate this 'substantial' nature of the extracted or reused data, the economic value of the data also has to be taken into consideration.[369] Here, it is important to point out that what should be evaluated is not the intrinsic value of the data as such, but rather the amount of the human, technical or financial investments that were made by the maker to obtain, verify or present the data.[370]

---

361. 'The person who takes the initiative and the risk of investing' (Recital 41 of Directive 96/9/EC).
362. Articles 7-11 of Directive 96/9/EC.
363. Recital 12 of Directive 96/9/EC.
364. Article 7.1 of Directive 96/9/EC. *See also* ECJ, *The British Horseracing Board e.a.*, 9 November 2004, C-203/02, EU:C:2004:695, §§ 31-36.
365. ECJ, *The British Horseracing Board e.a.*, §§ 35-40. *See also* ECJ, *Football Dataco e.a.*, 1 March 2012, C-604/10, EU:C:2012:115, § 36. This distinction between unprotected creation and protected obtention can create some uncertainties in practice. On this issue, *see* A. Masson, 'Creation of Database or Creation of Data: Crucial Choices in the Matter of Database Protection', *European Intellectual Property Review*, 2006, Vol. 28(5), pp. 261-267.
366. Article 7.1 of Directive 96/9/EC. *See also* ECJ, *Innoweb*, 19 December 2013, C-202/12, EU:C:2013:850, §§ 34-37.
367. N. Duch-Brown, B. Martens and F. Mueller-Langer, 'The Economics of Ownership, Access and Trade in Digital Data', *supra*, p. 14.
368. Article 1.2 of Directive 96/9/EC.
369. M. Knockaert et T. Tombal, 'Quels droits sur les données?', *supra*, p. 62.
370. ECJ, *The British Horseracing Board e.a.*, §§ 70-72.

59. While the text of the Database Directive can be relied upon to refute the idea of (intellectual) 'property' on data, because the sui generis database right merely protects the contents of the database as a whole and not the individual data in the set, the evolution of the European Court of Justice's case law has arguably slipped towards the protection of some 'independent materials' (e.g., some of the data) in the set,[371] and this may revive the debate on the 'appropriation/property' of data.

This is notably apparent from the *Verlag Esterbauer* case, where the European Court of Justice was asked whether topographic maps can be defined as a database, and more specifically whether the data describing the nature of specific points on the maps constituted 'independent materials' within the meaning of Article 1.2 of Directive.[372] The Court first reminded that, under the Directive, a database is the collection of 'independent elements', which are defined as materials that retain their autonomous informative value after having been separated from one another.[373] It added that the Directive does not preclude the combination of two or more pieces of information from being held to be 'independent materials', provided, however, that the extraction of that information from the database does not affect their autonomous informative value.[374] This implies that even if the value of these materials declines after their extraction from the database, they should still be considered as 'independent materials' benefitting from the protection granted by Article 1.2 of the Directive, provided that they retain an autonomous informative value after the extraction.[375] Accordingly, following the Court's reasoning, the Directive protects (a combination of) some 'independent materials' (e.g., some of the data) from this database, namely those that retain an autonomous informative value for the recipients after their extraction.[376] Nevertheless, in order to establish an infringement, the database maker will still have to demonstrate that the third party has extracted or reused (a combination of) individual data that constitutes a qualitatively substantial part of the maker's database, in light of the human, technical or financial investments that were made by the maker to obtain, verify or present that data.[377]

371. *See* J. Drexl, 'Data Access and Control in the Era of Connected Devices', *supra*, pp. 74-75. *See also* M. Knockaert et T. Tombal, 'Quels droits sur les données?', *supra*, pp. 62-64.
372. ECJ, *Verlag Esterbauer*, 29 October 2015, C-490/14, EU:C:2015:735, § 9. On this case, *see* B. Michaux, 'La Cour de justice favorise-t-elle l'appropriation des données par celui qui les a traitées ?', note sous C.J.U.E., 29 octobre 2015, C-490/14, *Auteurs et Média*, 2017, Issue 1, pp. 28-34.
373. ECJ, *Verlag Esterbauer*, § 17; ECJ, *Fixtures Marketing*, 9 November 2004, C-444/02, EU:C:2004:697, § 29.
374. ECJ, *Verlag Esterbauer*, §§ 21-22.
375. *Ibid.*, §§ 23-24.
376. *Ibid.*, § 27.
377. *See* J. Drexl, 'Data Access and Control in the Era of Connected Devices', *supra*, p. 78.

However, this means that the database maker could prevent the extraction of (a combination of) a small number of these individual data, namely those which required a substantial investment to obtain.[378] In fact, in the case at hand, the extracted data (the geographical coordinates point of the map and the 'signature', which is the numbered code used by the map producer to designate a unique feature, such as a church)[379] only represented an infinitesimally small part, and a very specific subcategory, of the total data set.[380] As outlined by Michaux, 'this phenomenon of fragmentation, or even atomisation, contributes to the impression that there is an *evolution towards the protection of data as such*, which seems to run counter to the legislator's initial objectives',[381] and 'this movement towards an ever finer granularity could, if proven, be likely to *bring about a subtle gradual shift towards a protection of the data constituting the database*, rather than a protection of the database as a whole (taken in its entirety) or of its main subsets' (emphasis added).[382]

60. Another relevant decision of the European Court of Justice is the *Ryanair* case, where it held that the exceptions granted by the Directive to the lawful users of databases are not applicable to a database which is not protected by the Directive,[383] and that, in those cases, the database maker is not prevented from adopting stricter contractual clauses concerning the conditions of use of such a database.[384] This leads to the peculiar consequence that the database maker can more strongly restrict the access to its database, via contractual clauses if the latter is not covered by the Directive than if it is protected under the Directive. Indeed, these contractual clauses could go so far as to protect each individual data in the set from any kind of extraction or reuse, without granting any exceptions to third parties, through the self-proclamation of 'ownership/property' rights on the data at hand.[385] This seriously endangers the balance between exclusive use of and access to/sharing of data that had been achieved by the European legislator in the Directive, notably through the limitations of the sui generis right and the provision of exceptions for lawful users, which define the circumstances in which the contents of the database can be accessed, extracted and/or reused by third parties.

---

378. B. Michaux, 'La Cour de justice favorise-t-elle l'appropriation des données par celui qui les a traitées ?', *supra*, p. 32.
379. ECJ, *Verlag Esterbauer*, § 18.
380. B. Michaux, 'La Cour de justice favorise-t-elle l'appropriation des données par celui qui les a traitées ?', *supra*, p. 32.
381. *Ibid.* Author's own translation.
382. *Ibid.*, p. 33. Author's own translation.
383. In casu, the Court of Appeal of Amsterdam had ruled that Ryanair had failed to establish the existence of a 'substantial' investment in the obtaining, verification or presentation of the contents of its database, i.e., its website (ECJ, *Ryanair*, 15 January 2015, C-30/14, EU:C:2015:10, § 22).
384. ECJ, *Ryanair*, § 39.
385. On these 'ownership/property' rights on data, *see* Part I, Chapter 2, Section 2.2.2.2.

This is especially worrying when one considers that the Directive might allegedly not apply to data generated by connected devices and sensors, as these data could be considered as being created, rather than collected.[386] Indeed, and according to the *Ryanair* case, the maker of a database not covered by the Directive has the right to restrict more strongly the access to its database, via contractual clauses. This can be highly problematic if this database is the sole source of a specific type of data,[387] although the refusal to provide access to a sole source of data might be considered as an abuse of dominant position according to the essential facilities doctrine, as will be outlined below.[388] It should however be noted that Drexl argues that the recognition of a sui generis database right to such sole sources of data might also potentially create additional barriers to data access, and that, as a consequence, some call for the introduction of a compulsory licensing system, as originally included in the Commission's proposal[389] for the Directive.[390]

In fact, the European Commission's inception impact assessment on its future 'Data Act' seems to suggest that the Database Directive might need to be reviewed as it might constitute an obstacle to data sharing, which could lead to the introduction of a compulsory licensing scheme on fair, reasonable, proportionate, transparent and non-discriminatory terms.[391] Interestingly, this suggestion by the European Commission coincides with a recent decision by the European Court of Justice, which acknowledges that 'it is necessary to strike a fair balance between, on the one hand, the legitimate interest of the makers of databases in being able to redeem their substantial investment and, on the other hand, that of users and competitors of those makers in having

386. J. Drexl, 'Data Access and Control in the Era of Connected Devices', *supra*, p. 70.
387. *Ibid.*, p. 68.
388. *See* Part III, Chapter 6, Section 6.1.
389. Proposal by the Commission of the European Communities for a Council Directive on the legal protection of databases, Brussels, 13 May 1992, COM(92) 24 final, Article 8.
390. J. Drexl, 'Data Access and Control in the Era of Connected Devices', *supra*, pp. 73 and 81-83. The pros and cons of such a compulsory licensing were extensively discussed in the final evaluation report of the Database Directive, but it has not led to any modification (*see* Jiip, Technopolis, L. Bently and E. Derclaye, 'Study in Support of the Evaluation of Directive 96/9/EC on the Legal Protection of Databases – Final Report', 2018, available at https://ec.europa.eu/digital-single-market/en/news/study-support-evaluation-database-directive, pp. 34-44; J. Drexl, 'Data Access and Control in the Era of Connected Devices', *supra*, p. 81). Drexl is not in favour of such a compulsory licensing system, but rather supports the creation of a new exception in the Directive 'that gives precedence to any existing and future data access regimes over the *sui generis* database right' (p. 85).
391. European Commission, Inception Impact Assessment: '*Data Act (including the review of the Directive 96/9/EC on the legal protection of databases)*', May 2021, Ares (2021)3527151, pp. 2-6.

access to the information contained in those databases and the possibility of creating innovative products based on that information'.[392]

2.2.2.2 Creation of a New 'Property-Like' Right over Data?

61. The European Court of Justice is not the only institution that has revived the debate on the 'appropriation/property' of data, as the European Commission also explored the potential creation of a new 'data producer's right', establishing a form of ownership over non-personal data.[393] In doing so, the Commission was actually echoing a request originally stemming from the German automotive industry, as car manufacturers were seeking to appropriate exclusive rights on data generated by the cars they produce.[394] This is because such data is becoming more and more attractive for third parties such as car dealers, spare parts manufacturers, authorised and independent garages and repairers, developers of infotainment software used in vehicles, insurers, vehicle users, and possibly also public authorities. Taking a more general perspective, the Commission's underlying idea was that such a right would generate more data sharing by clarifying the situation for the data holders, while giving third parties the possibility to use the data in certain specific cases. The Commission's endeavour was thus in line with the default model of 'exclusive property'.[395]

2.2.2.2.1 Data Producer's Right

62. Under this new 'data producer's right', the producer, defined as the long-term owner or user of the machine creating the data, would have been granted a right to use and authorise the use of non-personal data.[396] However, the development of such a right was a source of uncertainty on four levels, namely the nature of the right, the scope of the data covered, the attribution of ownership of the right and the determination of exceptions to the right.

---

392. ECJ, *CV-Online Latvia*, 3 June 2021, C-762/19, EU:C:2021:434, § 41. For a brief comment of this decision, *see* Z. Aszendorf and G. Pratt, 'CJEU Narrows Protection Afforded to Database Right in the EU', 9 June 2021, available at https://www.lexology.com/library/detail.aspx?g=f399c5bb-58ac-4162-b2c8-b8a53297f800&utm_source=Lexology+Daily+Newsfeed&utm_medium=HTML+email+-+Body+-+General+section&utm_campaign=Lexology+subscriber+daily+feed&utm_content=Lexology+Daily+Newsfeed+2021-06-11&utm_term=.
393. Communication from Commission, '*Building a European Data Economy*', *supra*, p. 13.
394. T. Hoeren and P. Bitter, 'Data Ownership Is Dead: Long Live Data Ownership', *European Intellectual Property Review*, 2018, 40(6), pp. 347-348; T. Hoeren, 'A New Approach to Data Property?', *Tijdschrift voor Auteurs-, Media- en Informatierecht*, 2018/2, p. 58.
395. *See* point 29.
396. Communication from Commission, '*Building a European Data Economy*', *supra*, p. 13.

With regard to the nature of the right, the Commission considered two options. The first was the creation of a new right in rem enforceable *erga omnes*, conferring an exclusive right to use non-personal or anonymised machine-generated data.[397] In such perspective, this right would have allowed the holder to object to the use of these data by third parties, regardless of any contractual relationship, and to claim damages for any unauthorised access or use of the data. However, the Commission did not fail to point out that such a right could not have concerned personal data, since the right to personal data protection is a fundamental right aimed at ensuring that data subjects retain control on 'their' personal data, which cannot be traded away. Indeed, according to the European Data Protection Supervisor (EDPS), since such data are an integral part of the human being, they must therefore remain non-transferable, similarly to organs.[398] The second option was the creation of a *set of purely defensive rights*, similar to the protection afforded to trade secrets.[399] Unlike the more protective approach of the first option, this second option aimed to increase data sharing while reassuring data owners by granting them a series of rights in the event of illegal use of data by third parties, equating to a protection of de facto possession of data rather than to a protection of ownership of data. Had such an approach been adopted, the question would also have arisen of the need to establish a (restrictive) list of hypotheses of legal and illegal use.

Regarding the scope of the data covered, it would probably have been limited to non-personal or anonymised data not yet structured in a protected database,[400] as well as metadata[401] relating to such data.[402] However, only the syntactic level (data and code), and not the semantic level of the information

---

397. Commission Staff Working Document on the free flow of data and emerging issues of the European data economy accompanying the Communication '*Building a European Data Economy*', Brussels, 10 January 2017, SWD(2017) 2 final, p. 33.
398. European Data Protection Supervisor, *Opinion 4/2017 on the Proposal for a Directive on certain aspects concerning contracts for the supply of digital content*, 14 March 2017, available at https://edps.europa.eu/sites/edp/files/publication/17-03-14_opinion_digital_content_en.pdf, p. 7; European Data Protection Supervisor, *Opinion 8/2018 on the legislative package 'A New Deal for Consumers'*, 5 October 2018, available at https://edps.europa.eu/sites/edp/files/publication/18-10-05_opinion_consumer_law_en.pdf, pp. 16-17. *See also*, S. Gutwirth and G. Gonzalez Fuster, 'L'éternel retour de la propriété des données: de l'insistance d'un mot d'ordre', *Law, norms and freedom in cyberspace – Liber Amicorum Yves Poullet*, E. Degrave, C. de Terwangne, S. Dusollier and R. Queck (eds), Bruxelles, Larcier, 2018, pp. 117-140.
399. *Ibid.*, pp. 33-34. *See* Directive (EU) 2016/943 of the European Parliament and of the Council of 8 June 2016 on the protection of undisclosed know-how and business information (trade secrets) against their unlawful acquisition, use and disclosure, *OJ L 157/1*, 15 June 2016. *See* point 183.
400. Article 1.2 of Directive 96/9/EC. On database protection, *see* points 58-60.
401. 'Metadata is "data information that provides information about other data". Many distinct types of metadata exist, including descriptive metadata, structural metadata, administrative metadata, reference metadata and statistical metadata' (https://en.wikipedia.org/wiki/Metadata).

or ideas expressed by that data, would have been protected, in order to avoid the creation of a 'super IP right'.[403] For example, this right would not have protected the visual rendering of a digital photograph, which is otherwise protected by copyright, but would have conferred certain rights on the data contained in this file.

Allocating the ownership of this right would also have been a thorny issue to be resolved. In the event that the option selected was the creation of a right in rem, the Commission suggested that the right should be allocated on the basis of the investments and resources devoted to the creation of the data.[404] In concrete terms, this would have led to the granting of the right to the manufacturer of the machine generating the data – the latter having invested in this tool – or to the economic operator using this machine. This would have posed practical attribution difficulties, especially since in many situations, several persons or companies jointly invest in such machines, making it virtually impossible to accurately identify one or more holders. On the contrary, if the option selected had been the creation of a series of purely defensive rights, the Commission proposed to grant these rights to the legitimate de facto possessor of these data, subjecting this protection to the condition that the de facto possessor has put in place technical protection measures in order to limit access to its data by third parties.[405]

Finally, as with IP rights, it would also have been required to specify a range of exceptions to the data producer's right. In practice, these exceptions would have taken the form of an obligation to share data in certain situations, for instance, in order to foster scientific research or to achieve public interest purposes (environmental protection, mobility, etc.).[406]

2.2.2.2.2 Criticism in the Literature

63. While some have supported the idea of developing such a right,[407] the large majority of legal scholars have expressed their concern about the

402. Commission Staff Working Document on the free flow of data and emerging issues of the European data economy, *supra*, p. 34.
403. *Ibid.* On this distinction between syntactic and semantic information, which is not always easy to make in practice, *see* H. Zech, 'Data as Tradeable Commodity', *European Contract Law and the Digital Single Market*, A. De Franceschi (ed.), Cambridge, Intersentia, 2016, pp. 51-79.
404. Commission Staff Working Document on the free flow of data and emerging issues of the European data economy, *supra*, pp. 34-35.
405. *Ibid.*, p. 35.
406. *Ibid.*, pp. 35-36. Communication from Commission, '*Building a European Data Economy*', *supra*, p. 13.
407. B. Van Asbroeck, J. Debussche and J. César, 'White Paper – Data Ownership in the Context of the European Data Economy: Proposal for a New Right', 2017, available at https://www.twobirds.com/en/news/articles/2017/global/data-ownership-in-the-context-of-the-european-data-economy. In this White Paper, the authors suggest the creation of a non-exclusive, flexible and extensible ownership right in data(sets).

creation of a 'property-like' right over data, arguing that there was no economic justification to support such a proposal.[408] Indeed, according to the latter, there is no evidence that the absence of such a right creates a lack of incentives for the production, analysis or marketing of data.[409] There is thus no 'underproduction problem'. Moreover, the creation of such a right could lead to disruptive juxtapositions and delimitation problems with existing IP rights,[410] and it could also strengthen entry barriers that, consequently, would increase the market power of large data holders.[411] Additionally, the difficulty in determining the scope of application of such a right and the allocation of its ownership could have led to significant legal uncertainty, entailing high costs and obstacles for future innovation.[412] Furthermore, the reference to the concept of 'property' seems inappropriate in view of the intangible and non-rivalrous nature of data, and, in any case, 'the dependency of data's value on contextualisation contradicts the justification for establishing a hypothetical property right as a one-size-fits-all measure'.[413]

Finally, it is important to remind that data may be technically and contractually excludable.[414] Therefore, data is arguably not a public good, which is non-rivalrous and non-excludable, but rather a 'club good', which

---

408. *See*, *inter alia*, J. Drexl, 'Designing Competitive Markets for Industrial Data: Between Propertisation and Access', *Max Planck Institute for Innovation & Competition Research Paper No. 16-13*, 31 October 2016, available at https://ssrn.com/abstract=2862975, pp. 30-38; A. Weibe, 'Protection of Industrial Data: A New Property Right for the Digital Economy?', *Journal of Intellectual Property Law & Practice*, 2017, Vol. 12(1), pp. 66-71; B. Hugenholtz, 'Data Property in the System of Intellectual Property Law: Welcome Guest or Misfit?', *Trading Data in the Digital Economy: Legal Concepts and Tools*, S. Lohsse, R. Schulze and D. Staudenmayer (eds), Baden-Baden, *Nomos*, 2017, pp. 78-82; W. Kerber, 'Governance of Data: Exclusive Property vs. Access', *International Review of Intellectual Property and Competition Law*, 2016, Vol. 47(7), p. 761; W. Kerber, 'Rights on Data', *supra*, pp. 115-120; H. Zech, 'Data as Tradeable Commodity', *supra*, pp. 51-79; A. Strowel, 'Big Data and Data Appropriation in the EU', *Research Handbook on Intellectual Property and Digital Technologies*, T. Aplin (ed.), Camberley, Edward Elgar, 2020, pp. 107-135; T. Hoeren and P. Bitter, 'Data Ownership Is Dead: Long Live Data Ownership', *supra*, pp. 347-348; T. Hoeren, 'A New Approach to Data Property?', *supra*, pp. 58-60; D. Kim, 'No One's Ownership as the Status Quo and a Possible Way Forward: A Note on the Public Consultation on Building a European Data Economy', *Journal of Intellectual Property Law & Practice*, 2018, Vol. 13(2), pp. 154-165.
409. J. Drexl, 'Designing Competitive Markets for Industrial Data: Between Propertisation and Access', *supra*, pp. 30-34; B. Hugenholtz, 'Data Property in the System of Intellectual Property Law', *supra*, pp. 80-81.
410. B. Hugenholtz, 'Data Property in the System of Intellectual Property Law', *supra*, pp. 89-94.
411. L. Somaini, 'Regulating the Dynamic Concept of Non-personal Data in the EU: From Ownership to Portability', *supra*, p. 86.
412. W. Kerber, 'Governance of Data: Exclusive Property vs. Access', *supra*, p. 761.
413. L. Somaini, 'Regulating the Dynamic Concept of Non-personal Data in the EU', *supra*, p. 86.
414. *See* points 53 and 54.

is non-rivalrous but excludable.[415] Accordingly, the 'public good market failure', on which the justification of IP rights is based, cannot simply be applied by analogy to data. This is an additional reason for excluding the creation of 'property' rights on data.

2.2.2.2.3 Contractual Freedom and Market Self-Regulation Rather than 'Property' Rights

64. In light of this criticism, the European Commission has therefore abandoned the idea of creating a 'property-like' right on data. Rather, the discussions pertaining to 'property' on data have shifted towards legal reflections revolving around notions of data 'control' and 'access'.[416] Nevertheless, as a fall-back solution, the Commission has established, in its Communication 'Towards a common European data space', key principles for *voluntary* data sharing between companies.[417] However, these principles are not binding, in order to respect the contractual freedom of the parties. In addition to these principles, the Commission has also been working on more concrete recommendations as to which contractual provisions should ideally appear in data sharing contracts, in addition to the traditional clauses relating to the duration of the contract, the conditions for the termination of the contract, etc.[418]

65. Moreover, it should be mentioned that the Commission has created a 'Support Centre for Data Sharing',[419] with the aim of putting in place a series of measures facilitating (voluntary) data sharing, in particular by providing examples of good practice, standard contractual clauses or existing contract models.[420] This Support Centre has notably analysed the legal characteristics of a set of existing data sharing contracts, and has developed a standardised set of 'tags', in order to determine which types of clauses are contained in each of the specific contracts, thereby creating a searchable repository of contracts based on a clear and consistent standardised classification system.[421]

---

415. M. Madison, 'Tools for Data Governance', *supra*, p. 34; M. Stucke and A. Grunes, *Big Data and Competition Policy*, *supra*, p. 45.
416. *See* Communication from the Commission to the European Parliament, the Council, the European Economic and Social Committee and the Committee of the Regions, '*Towards a Common European Data Space*', Brussels, 25 April 2018, COM(2018) 232 final, pp. 8-9.
417. *Ibid.*, p. 10.
418. Commission Staff Working Documents, 25 April 2018, SWD(2018) 125 final, pp. 6-8.
419. *See* https://eudatasharing.eu/homepage.
420. Commission Staff Working Document establishing a guidance on sharing private sector data, *supra*, p. 6.
421. Support Centre for Data Sharing, 'B.1 – Report on Collected Model Contract Terms', SMART 2018/2019, 26 July 2019, available at https://eudatasharing.eu/fr/legal-aspects, p. 4. For more information on these tags, *see* pp. 8-17.

2.2.2.3 (Anti-)'Reservation' of Data Rather Than 'Property' on Data

66. There has thus been a shift from discussions pertaining to 'property' on data, towards legal reflections revolving around notions of data 'control' and 'access'.[422] Indeed, independently of any establishment, in law, of a 'property' right on data, the reality of the situation on the field, from a technical and contractual point of view, is that data holders have a de facto exclusive control on their data and can decide on whether, and to whom, they provide access to it.[423] These data holders thus have the ability to 'reserve' their data.

2.2.2.3.1 Data Reservation

67. This concept of 'reservation' has been suggested by Mousseron and Vivant, in order to avoid the complex debates on the 'property' of information.[424] Rather, 'reservation' designates a form of control on this information, which can be not only legal (exclusive rights) but also factual (exclusion through contractual or technical means) or intellectual (trade secrets).[425] As summarised by Mousseron and Vivant, 'it is the fact of being alone on the market that is always sought after in the end: the various paths taken or likely to be taken, which are intertwined, all have the aim, clearly stated or not, of ensuring the economic reservation of information to the one who has control over it'.[426]

This concept can perfectly be translated from the realm of information to the realm of data, as data holders' de facto control on data allows them to economically reserve this data, through technical and contractual exclusion.[427] It also circumvents the issues of 'property' on data. Accordingly, I will refer, in the remainder of my analysis, to the reservation/control on data, rather than to 'property' on data.

Nevertheless, it is relevant to point out that, even if the Commission has moved away from 'property' on data towards data 'reservation', it has not

422. *See* Communication from the Commission, '*Towards a Common European Data Space*', *supra*, pp. 8-9.
423. W. Kerber, 'Data-Sharing in IoT Ecosystems from a Competition Law Perspective: The Example of Connected Cars', 26 August 2019, available at https://ssrn.com/abstract=3445422, p. 32.
424. J.-M. Mousseron et M. Vivant, 'Les mécanismes de réservation et leur dalectique: Le "terrain" occupé par le droit', *Semaine Juridique, Cahiers de Droit de l'Entreprise*, 1989/1, pp. 2-4; S. Dusollier, 'Du commun de l'intelligence artificielle', *Penser le droit de la pensée. Mélanges en l'honneur de Michel Vivant*, Paris, Dalloz, 2020, p. 109.
425. S. Dusollier, 'Du commun de l'intelligence artificielle', *supra*, p. 109.
426. J.-M. Mousseron et M. Vivant, 'Les mécanismes de réservation et leur dalectique', *supra*, p. 3 (author's own translation).
427. S. Dusollier, 'Du commun de l'intelligence artificielle', *supra*, p. 111.

moved away from the dominant model of 'exclusivity' (economic reservation of data through contractual and technical means).[428] In this sense, data are thus commodified, and some authors question whether another avenue, based on an anti-reservation paradigm ('data commons'), could be pursued instead, in order to guarantee a larger collective access to data.[429]

2.2.2.3.2 Data Commons: Anti-reservation of Data

68. According to Dusollier, this anti-reservation paradigm of the 'data commons' implies an impossibility to exert exclusive control on data and a correlative obligation to share it.[430] Instead of thinking in terms of exclusive control on and individual access to data, this paradigm calls for a collective use of this resource because data is a common good and it should therefore be managed in order to produce collective benefits.[431] Such an approach is justified by data's characteristics, as they are non-rivalrous, capital and general-purpose resources,[432] whose use creates multiple spill overs across society.[433]

To give a concrete example, Shkabatur suggests that user-generated data (personal 'primary data' and 'inferred/derived data' in my suggested typology[434]) should be recognised as a 'global commons', and that a wide range of independent stakeholders (researchers, journalists, NGOs, public authorities, etc.) should be granted access to the user-generated data collected, aggregated and processed by any company operating an online platform (and thus not just the GAFAMs), in order to address a variety of public challenges related to transportation, health, agriculture or natural disasters.[435] Importantly, Shkabatur outlined that such a 'global data commons' regime would not imply that these data platforms would have to lose their commercial benefits and decision-making prerogatives, nor that the access to the user-generated data should be free and open to all, independently of any personal data protection and security considerations.[436] Rather, such a regime would need to offer a whole spectrum of data access

---

428. *Ibid.*, p. 113. *See also* point 29.
429. *Ibid.*, pp. 109 and 114. *See also* J. Shkabatur, 'The Global Commons of Data', *Stanford Technology Law Review*, 2019, Vol. 22, pp. 354-411; M. Madison, 'Tools for Data Governance', *supra*, pp. 29-43.
430. S. Dusollier, 'Du commun de l'intelligence artificielle', *supra*, p. 115.
431. *Ibid.*
432. B. Frischmann, *Infrastructure: The Social Value of Shared Resources*, Oxford, Oxford University Press, 2012, cited in OECD, *Data-Driven Innovation: Big Data for Growth and Well-Being*, *supra*, p. 179. *See also* J. Drexl, 'Data Access and Control in the Era of Connected Devices', *supra*, p. 3.
433. M. Madison, 'Tools for Data Governance', *supra*, p. 40. *See* point 52.
434. *See* points 21-24.
435. J. Shkabatur, 'The Global Commons of Data', *supra*, pp. 383 and 389.
436. *Ibid.*, p. 362.

modalities, some more restrictive and some more permissive, which would have to strike a balance between the collective benefits derived from a broader access to data, on the one hand, and the need to protect the user's personal data and the platform's legitimate commercial interests, on the other hand.[437] For instance, the principle of purpose limitation of the GDPR[438] should be kept in mind to restrict the cases in which this user-generated data can be reused, because if a lid is not put on these reuse purposes, data subjects would lose control on 'their' data as they would not know by whom and for which purposes it is processed.[439]

69. Transitioning towards, and establishing, such data commons is a matter of political choice and could be a fertile ground to move away from the classic Western social construct of 'exclusivity as the rule', towards more 'generative' forms of 'rights', based on data sharing and on collective access and usage rights, whose goal is not to lead towards accumulation by the few, but rather towards collective benefits for the many.[440] While this 'data commons' approach is certainly a worthy avenue of exploration for future research, this will not be an exercise conducted here. This is because such an approach requires voluntary efforts, within a diffused community of actors, to govern data and to share it. It thus relies on *voluntary* data sharing in the context of the exercise of collective rights on data as commons. Yet, I focus instead on hypotheses of *compulsory* B2B data sharing,[441] which do not fit in this 'data commons' approach.

2.2.3 The Economic Rationale for Data Sharing

70. In light of data's characteristics, and notably of the fact that data could be considered as an 'infrastructural resource',[442] a growing call for data sharing is being made.[443] As for intangible resources, two types of rationale can be called upon to support data sharing, namely economic considerations on the one hand, which will be addressed here, and more societal and 'empowerment' considerations, on the other hand, which will be addressed in Section 2.3.

---

437. *Ibid.*, pp. 362 and 385. For a complete analysis of this spectrum of modalities, *see* pp. 385-398.
438. Personal data can only be processed for specified, explicit and legitimate purposes, and cannot be further processed in a manner that is incompatible with those purposes (Article 5.1.b) of the GDPR).
439. On this control by individuals, *see* Part I, Chapter 2, Section 2.3.2.
440. S. Dusollier, 'Du commun de l'intelligence artificielle', *supra*, pp. 116-117.
441. *See* points 4 and 5.
442. *See* points 52-55.
443. OECD, *Data-Driven Innovation: Big Data for Growth and Well-Being*, *supra*, p. 179; V. Mayer-Schonberger and T. Ramge, *Re-inventing Capitalism in the Age of Big Data*, New York, Basic Books, 2018.

Importantly, compulsory B2B data sharing is not a goal in itself, and it should only be used, in specific circumstances, as a means to achieve determined objectives.[444] Indeed, a balance must be found between exclusive use of and access to/sharing of data, as an equilibrium must be found between the benefits and costs of data sharing.[445] The aim has never been, and should arguably never be, an unconditional availability of data. Rather, a case-by-case assessment of the necessity of imposing such compulsory sharing legislation will always be required.[446]

71. To get a better grasp of the economic rationale for data sharing, it is first necessary to understand the economics of data in general. Accordingly, the incentives to collect and produce data will first be outlined. Then, it will be outlined that these data collection and production incentives could also create barriers to entry to the data market, and might accordingly entail market failures. These market failures will serve as a rationale for more data sharing, although such sharing should not be absolute, as it should factor the costs and incentives for each of the parties.[447] Naturally, my aim is not to strive for exhaustivity regarding these questions, but rather to provide a sufficient basic understanding of these economic considerations.

2.2.3.1 Data Collection and Production Incentives

72. As outlined above, data's true value does not generally stem from data as such, but rather from the value of the information and knowledge that can be extracted from its combination and aggregation.[448] Indeed, 'the more available and more varied the data, the better the knowledge that can be mined from it'.[449] In economic terms, this means that data is characterised by economies of scope and scale, which provide an advantage to data holders and incentivise them to collect and produce as much data as possible.

To understand the difference between economies of scope and economies of scale, the easiest is to picture a data set 'as a two-dimensional spreadsheet with the number of columns representing the number of variables and the number of rows the number of observations on these variables. (…) Economies of scale refer to increased prediction accuracy due to an increase in the number of rows. Economies of scope refer to increased prediction accuracy due to an increase in the number of columns

---

444. B. Martens, et al., 'Business to Business Data Sharing', *supra*, p. 5.
445. *See* points 90, 91 and 95.
446. Support Centre for Data Sharing, 'B.2 – Analytical report on EU law applicable to sharing of non-personal data', SMART 2018/2019, 24 January 2020, available at https://eudatasharing.eu/fr/legal-aspects, p. 4.
447. P. Larouche, 'The European Microsoft Case at the Crossroads of Competition Policy and Innovation', *supra*, pp. 933-937.
448. *See* point 15.
449. M. Gal and D. Rubinfeld, 'Data Standardization', *supra*, p. 774.

or explanatory variables'.[450] Economies of scale thus pertain to the breadth of the data (e.g., a broad data set has data about more people), while economies of scope pertain to the depth of the data (e.g., a deep data set contains more data about each person).[451] Digital platforms, such as Facebook or Google, are good examples of data aggregators who can realise economies of scope and scale, as their intermediation services allow them to expand both the breadth and depth of their data.[452]

73. Economies of scope in data aggregation generate economic efficiency gains, as more insights and economic value can be extracted from merging two complementary data sets than from keeping them separated in data silos.[453] As a consequence, there are economic efficiencies in concentrating data in large data pools, and there are clear incentives for data-driven firms to expand their activities in as many data-related service markets as possible.[454] Moreover, economies of scale also generate efficiency gains, as having data about more people allows to improve the service offered, which in turn attracts more users, etc.[455]

This is described by Prüfer and Schottmüller as data-driven *indirect* network effects.[456] These *indirect* network effects should not be confused with *direct* network effects, which are completely demand-driven, and which relate to the fact that the utility of a service for a user will be a function of, and will increase with, the number of other users that use the service.[457] For instance, users will only be interested in joining a social network if there are a sufficient number of people already using it with whom they can interact or if their friends are already using it. *Indirect* network effects, on the other hand, are also driven by the number of users, but they generate benefits on the supply-side, as the more users use the service, the more user information will be generated as a costless by-product, which will allow the service provider to better adapt its service or its algorithm to user preferences, which in turn will attract more users, etc.[458] Search engines are a good example of

450. B. Martens, et al., 'Business to Business Data Sharing', *supra,* p. 13.
451. J. Krämer, D. Schnurr and S. Broughton Micova, 'The Role of Data for Digital Markets Contestability', *supra*, p. 7.
452. B. Martens, et al., 'Business to Business Data Sharing', *supra*, p. 15.
453. *Ibid.*, p. 4.
454. *Ibid.*, p. 5.
455. J. Krämer, D. Schnurr and S. Broughton Micova, 'The Role of Data for Digital Markets Contestability', *supra*, p. 7.
456. J. Prüfer and C. Schottmüller, 'Competing with Big Data', *TILEC Discussion Paper No. 2017-006 and CentER Discussion Paper No. 2017-007*, February 2017, available at https://pure.uvt.nl/ws/portalfiles/portal/15514029/2017_007.pdf, p. 1; B. Martens, et al., 'Business to Business Data Sharing', *supra*, p. 15. For a detailed analysis of the various classic and data-driven network effects, *see* M. Stucke and A. Grunes, *Big Data and Competition Policy*, *supra*, pp. 162-216.
457. J. Prüfer and C. Schottmüller, 'Competing with Big Data', *supra*, p. 2.
458. *Ibid.*, pp. 1-2.

this phenomenon.[459] This is also referred to, from a dynamic perspective, as a 'user feedback loop'.[460] It entails decreasing marginal costs of innovation, due to the high consumer demand.[461] Naturally, these two types of network effects are not mutually exclusive, as illustrated by online social networks that are characterised by both.[462]

From a dynamic perspective, these data-driven network effects can also give rise to another self-reinforcing feedback loop, namely a 'monetisation feedback loop', as explained by Krämer et al.[463] Indeed, as these data-driven companies derive a large chunk of their revenues from advertising, collecting more user data enables them to provide more targeted advertising. Because it is more effective, this generates more advertising revenues, which in turn allows them to further invest in the quality of their service, which will attract more users, etc.

74. In light of these economies of scope and scale and of these network effects,[464] data holders are thus incentivised to aggregate data as this provides them with a competitive advantage and generates economic benefits. This is especially true in circumstances where *first-mover advantages* 'can become sustained competitive advantages, because competitors are unable to initiate the same feedback loop'.[465] This will be further developed below when presenting the potential data market failures.[466] That being said, as outlined by Stucke and Grunes, 'while network effects can help insulate the dominant firm from competitive pressure, they do not immunize [it] from competition altogether'.[467]

2.2.3.2 Entry Barriers to Data Markets

75. While economies of scale and scope and data-driven network effects in data aggregation incentivise data collection and data production, the flip side

459. C. Argenton and J. Prüfer, 'Search Engine Competition with Network Externalities', *Journal of Competition Law and Economics*, 2012, Vol. 8(1), pp. 73-105.
460. J. Krämer, D. Schnurr and S. Broughton Micova, 'The Role of Data for Digital Markets Contestability', *supra*, p. 64. *See also* A. Lerner, 'The Role of "Big Data" in Online Platform Competition', 26 August 2014, available at SSRN http://dx.doi.org/10.2139/ssrn.2482780; M. Bourreau, A. de Streel and I. Graef, 'Big Data and Competition Policy: Market Power, Personalised Pricing and Advertising', *CERRE Report*, 2017, available at http://www.cerre.eu/publications/big-data-and-competition-policy.
461. J. Prüfer and C. Schottmüller, 'Competing with Big Data', *supra*, pp. 1-2.
462. *Ibid.*, p. 2.
463. J. Krämer, D. Schnurr and S. Broughton Micova, 'The Role of Data for Digital Markets Contestability', *supra*, p. 64.
464. For a detailed analysis of the various classic and data-driven network effects, *see* M. Stucke and A. Grunes, *Big Data and Competition Policy*, *supra*, pp. 162-216.
465. J. Krämer, D. Schnurr and S. Broughton Micova, 'The Role of Data for Digital Markets Contestability', *supra*, p. 64.
466. *See* points 78-85.
467. M. Stucke and A. Grunes, *Big Data and Competition Policy*, *supra*, p. 214.

of the coin is that these same economic characteristics of data may also raise entry barriers to data markets. These possible entry barriers have been extensively analysed by Rubinfeld and Gal, whose work will be briefly summarised here.[468] Next to the classic legal barriers to data collection (e.g., in circumstances where the data collection is prevented by personal data protection legislation or IP rights such as the sui generis database right),[469] these authors mostly focus on what they describe as technical barriers to data collection. As these technical barriers mainly derive from the economic characteristics of data mentioned above, I will refer to them as techno-economic entry barriers.

76. First, techno-economic entry barriers can arise if incumbent data holders have achieved substantial economies of scope and scale, which allowed them to partially or totally sink their investments.[470] Moreover, they might also take advantage of 'economies of speed' if the velocity of their data collection allows them to discern trends well before others.[471] Google could be such an example in the search market, as its large dominant position allows it to collect much more search data than its competitors and, consequently, to discern new trends faster than others. If the incumbent data holders' economies of scope, scale and speed are sufficiently large, the high fixed costs of data collection for a new entrant might make entry prohibitive.[472]

Second, the data-driven network effects mentioned above could also create techno-economic entry barriers, as new entrants would have to make substantial investments in order to counter, or even merely overcome, the existing network effects benefiting the incumbent data holders.[473] Indeed, the entrant would have to invest to overcome not only the direct network effects (i.e., invest in order to attract a sufficient number of users in order for the service to attain a critical mass and 'take-off') but also the indirect network effects (i.e., because the incumbent has access to more (timely) data about user preferences than the entrant, it can more easily and quickly adapt to the changing demand and it can better target its advertising, which generates more revenue).[474]

Third, techno-economic entry barriers could also emerge due to *lock-in* considerations.[475] Indeed, users could be 'locked into' the service of the incumbent data holder for two reasons. On the one hand, they could be

468. D. Rubinfeld and M. Gal, 'Access Barriers to Big Data', *supra*, pp. 339-381. On these entry barriers, *see* pp. 350-365.
469. *Ibid.*, pp. 359-362.
470. *Ibid.*, p. 352.
471. *Ibid.*, p. 353.
472. *Ibid.*, pp. 352-353.
473. *Ibid.*, p. 355.
474. *Ibid.*, pp. 355-356. *See also* M. Stucke and A. Grunes, *Big Data and Competition Policy*, *supra*, pp. 170 and 189-199.
475. D. Rubinfeld and M. Gal, 'Access Barriers to Big Data', *supra*, p. 364. *See also* M. Stucke and A. Grunes, *Big Data and Competition Policy*, *supra*, p. 159.

locked in because the incumbent's data-driven network effect deters new entrants from developing alternatives. Because no alternative having a minimum scale (i.e., a minimum number of users) exists, the users have nowhere else to go. On the other hand, they could be locked in because the incumbent makes it technically difficult (or even impossible) to extract the data from its service in order to provide it to a new entrant, which then entails high switching costs.[476] This second problem has been tackled, to a certain extent, by data portability rights.[477] Importantly, these two reasons are not mutually exclusive and in fact reinforce each other.

Fourth, techno-economic entry barriers could emerge due to the uniqueness of the data collected by the incumbent data holder, or due to the fact that it is the unique gateway to such data.[478] Indeed, while the non-rivalrous nature of data implies that it can usually be collected from various alternative sources and that, as a consequence, the costs of data collection are usually not prohibitive for new entrants, 'unique access points to unique data may lead to situations in which the data cannot be easily replicated'.[479] This could notably be the case for data created as the result of interactions on a social network, for data pertaining to a very specific event (e.g., data gathered at a specific point in time about a natural disaster) or for data generated as a by-product of a very specific activity conducted by the incumbent data holder (e.g., data about oil-drilling sites).[480] This could also be the case in hypotheses where the incumbent data holder has technically or contractually excluded the access to a unique source of data, or where the access to this unique source is subject to a very high access price and/or to very strict conditions.[481] Pre-installed applications could also act as more subtle gateway barriers to data collection, as it will be difficult for new entrants to replace them, due to the combination of the default option and of users' status quo bias (i.e., users tend to simply use the default options/settings/applications and rarely modify them).[482]

Fifth, techno-economic entry barriers could emerge from the failure to compete for the user's attention, which is mainly captured by several incumbents (Google, Facebook, Netflix, etc.), as new entrants may struggle to collect data if they do not manage to attract users (who only have a finite amount of attention to spend) to their services.[483]

---

476. M. Stucke and A. Grunes, *Big Data and Competition Policy*, *supra*, pp. 291-292.
477. *See* Part II, Chapter 4, Sections 4.1 and 4.2.
478. D. Rubinfeld and M. Gal, 'Access Barriers to Big Data', *supra*, pp. 350-351.
479. *Ibid.*, p. 351.
480. *Ibid.*, pp. 351 and 357.
481. *Ibid.*, p. 362. *See also* B. Lundqvist, 'Regulating Competition and Property in the Digital Economy – The Interface Between Data, Privacy, Intellectual Property, Fairness and Competition Law', *Stockholm Faculty of Law Research Paper Series No. 54*, 2018, available at https://ssrn.com/abstract=3103870, p. 4.
482. D. Rubinfeld and M. Gal, 'Access Barriers to Big Data', *supra*, p. 351.
483. *Ibid.*, p. 357.

Sixth, if the new entrant opts to acquire the data that it needs from third parties, rather than to collect it itself, techno-economic entry barriers could 'arise from limited information on who owns the relevant data, or on the costs of locating and contracting with such data holders'.[484]

77. Naturally, it would be erroneous to say that all of these techno-economic barriers exist in all of the data-driven markets. Rather, these must be understood as a list of potential entry barriers that might occur in these markets. Their existence and magnitude will be a function of the characteristics of each data market, and they should not simply be assumed to exist.[485] A case-by-case analysis is required in order to assess whether these entry barriers exist, and, if they do, the extent to which they prevent market entry.[486] Indeed, even if, in theory, incumbent data holders benefiting from a data advantage (economies of scale, scope and speed and network effects) could be incentivised to engage in exclusionary conduct and to erect techno-economic entry barriers to maintain or strengthen their advantage, 'the mere existence of high entry barriers into these markets, by itself, does not automatically lead to the conclusion that social welfare will be harmed'.[487]

Finally, it is important to point out that, in assessing these entry barriers, the 'capital resource' characteristic of data (i.e., it is used as an input for goods or services rather than as an end in itself[488]) should be factored, having as a consequence that 'the analysis of entry barriers should often extend beyond the specific market under scrutiny to related parts of the data-value chain'.[489] Indeed, as will be developed below, incumbent data holders are rarely present in a single market, but rather build up conglomerates operating across several data-driven markets.[490]

2.2.3.3 Data Market Failures

78. As outlined above, extreme returns to scale, network effects and the prominent role of data (i.e., being able to use data to develop or improve innovative products or services) are incentives for data collection and production and are key competitive parameters. These characteristics lead to strong economies of scope, scale and speed that benefit large incumbent data

484. *Ibid.*, p. 359.
485. *Ibid.*, p. 369.
486. M. Stucke and A. Grunes, *Big Data and Competition Policy*, *supra*, p. 158.
487. D. Rubinfeld and M. Gal, 'Access Barriers to Big Data', *supra*, p. 370.
488. OECD, *Data-Driven Innovation: Big Data for Growth and Well-Being*, *supra*, pp. 180-181.
489. D. Rubinfeld and M. Gal, 'Access Barriers to Big Data', *supra*, p. 375.
490. *See*, *inter alia*, J. Prüfer and C. Schottmüller, 'Competing with Big Data', *supra.*; M. Bourreau and A. de Streel, 'Digital Conglomerates and EU Competition Policy', *CERRE Report*, March 2019, available at http://www.crid.be/pdf/public/8377.pdf.

holders who have access to more (recent) data than their competitors.[491] As summarised by Fast et al., six factors may provide incumbent data holders with a competitive advantage, namely: '(i) exclusive access to data, (ii) exploitative access to data, (iii) economies of scale in data analytics, (iv) platform business models and network effects, (v) data-induced switching costs, and (vi) economies of scope and ecosystem expansion'.[492] Looking at it from the other side of the coin, these characteristics and factors might lead to techno-economic entry barriers (uniqueness of the data collected by the incumbent data holder or unique gateway to it; economies of scale, scope and speed; network effects; lock-in and switching costs),[493] which will make it very difficult to dislodge these incumbent data holders.[494] This is where data market failures might occur. I will focus on the types of market failures that are the most relevant for the topic of compulsory B2B data sharing, namely those that can derive from data concentration on the one hand, and data conglomerates and *domino effects*, on the other hand.

Naturally, other market failures, such as the lack of incentives to collect data, uncertainties in terms of risks, high transaction costs for sharing and missing markets, and asymmetries of information distorting decision-making can also impact the data markets.[495] However, these are, in fact, rather obstacles to *voluntary* data sharing that require other remedies than *compulsory* B2B data sharing. Indeed, the first three of these market failures rather require regulatory interventions in the technical (standardisation, interoperability, etc.) and governance sphere, in order to create more favourable conditions for the emergence of third-party intermediaries that can remedy, or at least reduce, these market failures.[496] This is, for instance, materialised in the European Commission's proposal for a Data Governance Act that notably aims at promoting *voluntary* data sharing services by intermediaries.[497] Asymmetries of information, on the other hand, require transparency interventions, such as provided in Article 9 of the Platform to Business

491. J. Crémer, Y.-A. de Montjoye and H. Schweitzer, 'Competition Policy for the Digital era – Final Report', 2019, available at http://ec.europa.eu/competition/publications/reports/kd0419345enn.pdf, pp. 3 and 19-24.
492. V. Fast, D. Schnurr and M. Wohlfarth, 'Data-Driven Market Power: An Overview of Economic Benefits and Competitive Advantages from Big Data Use', July 2019, available at https://ssrn.com/abstract=3427087, pp. 2 and 19-35.
493. *See* point 76.
494. J. Crémer, Y.-A. de Montjoye and H. Schweitzer, 'Competition Policy for the Digital Era', *supra*, p. 24.
495. For a broader analysis of all of the potential types of data market failures, *see* references in footnote 19.
496. B. Martens, et al., 'Business to Business Data Sharing', *supra*, p. 28.
497. *See* Articles 9-14 of the Proposal for a Regulation of the European Parliament and of the Council on European data governance (Data Governance Act), 25 November 2020, COM(2020) 767 final.

Regulation.[498,499] For the reasons mentioned in the introduction,[500] these other market failure will however not be extensively analysed here. On the other hand, for the types of market failures on which I will focus, namely data concentration on the one hand and data conglomerates and *domino effects* on the other hand, market-based solutions, even if supported by regulatory interventions, may not be sufficient, hence leading to the need for *compulsory* B2B data sharing remedies.[501]

2.2.3.3.1 Data Concentration

79. As data aggregation generates network effects and economies of scope, scale and speed, the economics of data favour concentration.[502] Indeed, due to these factors, data-driven markets have a natural tendency to tip towards monopolisation.[503] Moreover, because such dominance is persistent once the market has tipped, even in dynamic high-tech markets, there is thus 'a strong *first-mover advantage* in data-driven markets, which leads towards monopolization and is built upon data-driven indirect network effects' (emphasis in the text).[504]

Such concentration risks had already been outlined by Benkler at the beginning of the century, who pointed to the fact that the infrastructure of, and the patterns of attention on, the internet may turn out to be much less distributed than what was promised by the decentralised ideology of the internet.[505] Indeed, he outlined that 'a high degree of attention is concentrated on a few top sites – a tiny number of sites are read by the vast majority of readers – while many sites are never visited by anyone',[506] before adding, as a matter of example, in a quasi-prophetic statement that 'Google could

498. Regulation (EU) 2019/1150 of the European Parliament and of the Council of 20 June 2019 on promoting fairness and transparency for business users of online intermediation services, *OJ L 186/57*, 11 July 2019; Expert Group for the Observatory on the Online Platform Economy, 'Work stream on Data: Final Report', 26 February 2021, available at https://ec.europa.eu/digital-single-market/en/news/expert-group-eu-observatory-online-platform-economy-final-reports.
499. *See* below, Part II, Chapter 4, Section 4.4.
500. *See* points 4 and 5.
501. *See, inter alia*, M. Stucke and A. Grunes, *Big Data and Competition Policy, supra.*; J. Krämer, D. Schnurr and S. Broughton Micova, 'The Role of Data for Digital Markets Contestability', *supra*; J. Crémer, Y.-A. de Montjoye and H. Schweitzer, 'Competition Policy for the Digital Era', *supra*; R. Feasey and A. de Streel, 'Data Sharing for Digital Market Contestability', *supra*.
502. M. Stucke and A. Grunes, *Big Data and Competition Policy*, *supra*, p. 336.
503. *See* J. Prüfer, 'Competition Policy and Data Sharing on Data-driven Markets', *Report for the Friedrich-Ebert-Stiftung*, 2020, available at http://library.fes.de/pdf-files/fes/15999.pdf, pp. 6-9; J. Prüfer and C. Schottmüller, 'Competing with Big Data', *supra*, p. 2.
504. J. Prüfer and C. Schottmüller, 'Competing with Big Data', *supra*, p. 2.
505. Y. Benkler, *The Wealth of Networks, supra*, p. 214.
506. *Ibid.*, p. 235.

become so powerful on the desktop, in the e-mail utility, and on the Web, that it will effectively become a supernode.'[507]

80. Due to these first-mover advantage and market tipping dynamics, data concentration might increase entry barriers for new firms and strengthen data aggregators' market power, leading to diminishing incentives for innovation.[508] Moreover, if the market has tipped and if the entry barriers are high, this will drastically reduce the threat of 'creative destruction',[509] and the monopolistic incumbent will thus have fewer incentives to innovate in order to protect its monopoly position from a potential competitor who will be less likely to develop the 'next big thing'.[510] Indeed, as outlined by Prüfer:

> The smaller firms, even if they are equipped with a superior idea/production technology, face higher marginal costs of innovation because they lack access to the large pile of user information that the dominant firm has access to due to its significantly larger user base. Consequently, if a smaller firm were to heavily invest in innovation and roll out its high-quality product, the dominant firm could imitate it quickly – at lower cost of innovation – and regain its quality lead. The smaller firm would find itself once again in the runners-up spot, which entails few users and low revenues, but it would still have to pay the large costs involved in attempting a leap in innovation. Foreseeing this situation, no rational entrepreneur would invest in innovation in a smaller firm. In turn, because the dominant firm knows about the disincentive to innovate among its would-be competitors, it is protected by its large (and constantly renewed) stream of user information and can remain content with a lower level of innovation, too.[511]

81. Such concentration may also establish long-term competitive advantages and this could endanger the contestability of these data-driven markets.[512] This notably derives from the positive feedback loops mentioned above,[513] as 'initially superior access to data may give rise to feedback effects, such that data-driven competitive advantages are magnified over time as improved service quality from data leads to more users and this then turns into access

507. *Ibid.*, p. 261.
508. B. Martens, et al., 'Business to Business Data Sharing', *supra*, p. 24. *See also* J. Prüfer and C. Schottmüller, 'Competing with Big Data', *supra.*; J. Krämer, D. Schnurr and S. Broughton Micova, 'The Role of Data for Digital Markets Contestability', *supra.*
509. *See* J. Schumpeter, *The Theory of Economic Development: An Inquiry into Profits, Capital, Credit, Interest, and the Business Cycle*, Cambridge, Harvard University Press, 1932.
510. J. Krämer, D. Schnurr and S. Broughton Micova, 'The Role of Data for Digital Markets Contestability', *supra*, p. 71. *See also* M. Stucke and A. Grunes, *Big Data and Competition Policy*, *supra*, pp. 281-285.
511. J. Prüfer, 'Competition Policy and Data Sharing on Data-driven Markets', *supra*, p. 6. *See also* J. Prüfer and C. Schottmüller, 'Competing with Big Data', *supra*, p. 2.
512. J. Krämer, D. Schnurr and S. Broughton Micova, 'The Role of Data for Digital Markets Contestability', *supra*, p. 55.
513. *See* point 73.

to even larger data sets'.[514] Because competitors cannot have the same continuous inflow of data as the incumbent data holder – which benefits from self-reinforcing data-driven network effects and economies of scope, scale and speed – it will lack the ability to adapt its good or services to the users changing desires and it will thus struggle to be competitive.[515]

Moreover, the lack of contestability could stem from the fact that incumbent data holders could leverage such data concentration phenomenon to exclude competitors from entering the market.[516] This might especially be the case if the incumbent's first-mover advantage has allowed it to reach a monopolistic market position and that it retains an exclusive access to its data.[517]

Additionally, a lack of contestability could also stem from the fact that data concentration leads to an asymmetry of information between the incumbent data holder and smaller potential competitors, which might distort the latter's efficient decision-making and thus reduce their competitive counterweight.[518] To some extent, this asymmetry of information problem is however tackled by transparency and fairness initiatives such as the Regulation on the Free-Flow of Non-personal Data[519] and the Platform to Business Regulation.[520,521]

82. Finally, it should be added that, more recently, the incumbent data holders have developed an alternative way of aggregating data and reinforcing this concentration phenomenon. They have started to offer ancillary services to third parties, such as identity management services ('Login with Facebook', 'Login with Google', 'Sign in with Microsoft'), payment services ('Pay with Amazon', 'Pay with Apple'), or tracking technologies ('Google Analytics', 'Facebook Pixel'), which act as a new source of data for these incumbents.[522] Indeed, even if offering such ancillary services implies a loss of exclusivity on the incumbents' data as they have to reveal some of it in order for the third parties to be able to use the services, the user data that they obtain in return

---

514. J. Krämer, D. Schnurr and S. Broughton Micova, 'The Role of Data for Digital Markets Contestability', *supra*, p. 56.
515. *Ibid.*, p. 71.
516. B. Martens, et al., 'Business to Business Data Sharing', *supra*, p. 19.
517. *Ibid.*, p. 5.
518. *Ibid.*, p. 27.
519. Regulation (EU) 2018/1807 of the European Parliament and of the Council of 14 November 2018 on a framework for the free flow of non-personal data in the European Union, *OJ L 303/59*, 28 November 2018. *See* in particular Article 6 pertaining to the porting of non-personal data.
520. Regulation (EU) 2019/1150 of the European Parliament and of the Council of 20 June 2019 on promoting fairness and transparency for business users of online intermediation services, *OJ L 186/57*, 11 July 2019; Expert Group for the Observatory on the Online Platform Economy, 'Work stream on Data: Final Report', *supra*.
521. *See* below, Part II, Chapter 4, Section 4.4.
522. J. Krämer, D. Schnurr and S. Broughton Micova, 'The Role of Data for Digital Markets Contestability', *supra*, pp. 72-73.

is far more valuable to them, as it allows them to also track these users, and thus gather more data about them, on websites that are operated by third parties.[523]

This subtler alternative mechanism of data collection thus also reinforces the incumbents' data-driven network effects and also raises entry barriers. More specifically, and as outlined by Krämer et al., in the short run, these third parties are incentivised to adopt these ancillary services in order to gain a competitive advantage over the ones who do not.[524] However, in the medium to long run, as the other third parties also start adopting these ancillary services, none of these third parties manages to gain a truly competitive advantage, and they are actually worse off than if they had refrained from adopting the ancillary service, as they have agreed to broad transfers of data towards the incumbent data holder. As a consequence, and from a dynamic perspective, the incumbents have in fact further strengthened their position through data concentration and competition is weakened.

2.2.3.3.2 Data Conglomerates and Domino Effects

83. These network effects and economies of scope, scale and speed may not only protect incumbent data holders in their core data-driven markets by providing them with a competitive data advantage leading to data concentration but also be leveraged by the incumbent to expand and strengthen its position in adjacent markets.[525] Accordingly, there are clear incentives for data-driven firms to expand their activities in as many markets as possible and to build conglomerates.[526]

Indeed, the dominant position gained in a data-driven market could be leveraged to gain a dominant position in a *connected market*, i.e., another distinct market in which the data gathered in the first market turns out to be a valuable input to improve the goods or services offered.[527] In fact, such expansion to a connected market could even reinforce the incumbent's position in the first market if the data gathered on the second market is a valuable input to improve the goods or services offered on the first market.[528]

---

523. *Ibid.*, p. 73.
524. *Ibid. See also* J. Krämer, D. Schnurr and M. Wohlfarth, 'Winners, Losers, and Facebook: The Role of Social Logins in the Online Advertising Ecosystem', *Management Science*, 2019, Vol. 65(4), pp. 1678-1699.
525. J. Krämer, D. Schnurr and S. Broughton Micova, 'The Role of Data for Digital Markets Contestability', *supra*, p. 56; B. Martens, et al., 'Business to Business Data Sharing', *supra*, p. 19.
526. B. Martens, et al., 'Business to Business Data Sharing', *supra*, p. 5; M. Bourreau and A. de Streel, 'Digital Conglomerates and EU Competition Policy', *supra*.
527. J. Prüfer and C. Schottmüller, 'Competing with Big Data', *supra*, pp. 2-3.
528. *Ibid.*

This is linked to the general-purpose nature of data, which can be reused for a wide variety of goods and services.[529]

If these connected markets' dynamics are combined with the first-mover advantage outlined above, this could lead to a *domino effect*, i.e., 'a first mover in market A can leverage its dominant position, which comes with an advantage on user information, to let connected market B tip, too, even if market B is already served by traditional incumbent firms'.[530] Indeed, once a firm has established a strong data position in one market, 'the marginal costs of expanding into an adjacent complementary data domain are lower than for *de novo* entrants in that domain or incumbents who only cover that specific domain'.[531] The domino effect deriving from this first-mover advantage in an initial market could thus lead to successive market tipping in several connected markets. Indeed, venturing into related markets opens the access to more users, and thus consequently to more data, which will strengthen even more the incumbent data holder's data-driven network effects, and this will, in turn, allow them to venture into further markets.[532] In time, this can lead to the constitution of digital conglomerates. Google, and its ability to leverage its dominant position in the search market to other connected markets (shopping, maps, etc.), is a prime example of such data conglomerate.[533]

84. To constitute these data conglomerates, incumbent data holders either rely on mergers and acquisitions[534] or on *envelopment strategies*, which are summarised in Eisenmann et al.'s seminal paper 'Platform Envelopment':

> Through envelopment, a provider in one platform market can enter another platform market, and combine its own functionality with that of the target in a multi-platform bundle that leverages shared user relationships. Envelopers capture market share by foreclosing an incumbent's access to users; in doing so, they harness the network effects that previously had protected the incumbent.[535]

The target platform can be a complement, a substitute or functionally unrelated to the enveloping platform.[536] In the first case (complementary platform), the enveloper will be the most likely to succeed in situations where both platforms' users overlap significantly.[537] In the second case

529. M. Bourreau and A. de Streel, 'Digital Conglomerates and EU Competition Policy', *supra*, p. 10. On the general-purpose nature of data, *see* point 52.
530. J. Prüfer and C. Schottmüller, 'Competing with Big Data', *supra*, pp. 2-3.
531. B. Martens, et al., 'Business to Business Data Sharing', *supra*, p. 24.
532. J. Krämer, D. Schnurr and S. Broughton Micova, 'The Role of Data for Digital Markets Contestability', *supra*, p. 71.
533. M. Bourreau and A. de Streel, 'Digital Conglomerates and EU Competition Policy', *supra*, p. 11.
534. *Ibid.*, p. 4. For a discussion of the 'killer acquisitions' issue, *see* pp. 21-23.
535. T. Eisenmann, G. Parker and M. Van Alstyne, 'Platform Envelopment', *Strategic Management Journal*, 2011, Vol. 32(12), p. 1270.
536. *Ibid.*, p. 1279.
537. *Ibid.*, p. 1280.

(substitute platform), the enveloper will be the most likely to succeed in situations where bundling leads to significant economies of scope.[538] In the third case (functionally unrelated platform), the enveloper will be the most likely to succeed in situations characterised by both significant users' overlap and high economies of scope deriving from bundling.[539] Additionally, it should be outlined that the envelopment strategy will be especially efficient if the users are unable to multi-home, i.e., to use multiple platforms at the same time.[540] That being said, even if the users multi-home, the enveloper can still gain a competitive advantage over the target platform.[541]

These envelopment strategies are widespread in the data-driven markets, and have notably been used by Microsoft, Google, eBay or LinkedIn.[542] According to Condorelli and Padilla, some of these firms even engage in envelopment strategies through privacy policy tying,[543] which is a strategy through which 'the enveloper requests consumers to grant their consent to combining their data in both [the] origin and target market[s]'.[544] This combination of data allows the enveloper to fund all of its services by monetising data from each of the services in all of the other services, and thus allows the enveloper to entrench its dominant position in the origin market and to expand it in the other markets.[545] This facilitates the domino effect mentioned above.[546]

85. While the constitution of such conglomerates could have procompetitive effects, they might also entail various market failures, such as raising entry barriers for innovative entrants, which could in turn endanger the contestability of these markets on which the conglomerate is active.[547]

Moreover, the conglomerate could also foreclose competition on some of the markets where it is active if these markets depend on the access to an essential resource, such as specific types of data, produced on a primary market where the conglomerate is also active and dominant, and if the

538. *Ibid.*, p. 1281.
539. *Ibid.*, pp. 1281-1282.
540. M. Bourreau and A. de Streel, 'Digital Conglomerates and EU Competition Policy', *supra*, p. 16.
541. *Ibid.*, p. 17.
542. T. Eisenmann, G. Parker and M. Van Alstyne, 'Platform Envelopment', *supra*, p. 1271.
543. D. Condorelli and J. Padilla, 'Harnessing Platform Envelopment Through Privacy Policy Tying', December 2019, available at https://ssrn.com/abstract=3504025. On this specific issue *see* Part III, Chapter 7, Section 7.1.
544. *Ibid.*, p. 1.
545. *Ibid.*, p. 5.
546. J. Krämer, D. Schnurr and S. Broughton Micova, 'The Role of Data for Digital Markets Contestability', *supra*, p. 72.
547. M. Bourreau and A. de Streel, 'Digital Conglomerates and EU Competition Policy', *supra*, p. 14.

conglomerate refuses to provide access to this resource to its competitors and reserves its use for itself.[548]

In the same vein, the combination of conglomeration (through vertical integration) with the occupation of a gatekeeping position could entail market failures. As outlined by Krämer et al., this is especially the case in situations where an incumbent data holder is the gatekeeper of an upstream service and also offers downstream services via this upstream service (e.g., Amazon operates an e-commerce website and also sells goods on it; Google operates a search engine and also offers other services (maps, shopping, etc.) that are findable through that search engine).[549] As this incumbent is the gatekeeper to an important upstream service, third parties operating on downstream markets have to use the upstream service to reach consumers/users, but, in order to do so, they have to reveal key data about their business and their users to the incumbent. Yet, because the incumbent is also active on the downstream markets, these data flows provide it with a great deal of information about these third parties and their users, which seriously hampers their ability to compete with the incumbent on these downstream markets. Moreover, the incumbent's gatekeeper position allows it not only to gain data advantages from its competitors but also to favour its own downstream services, by steering the users towards them rather than towards the ones offered by third parties (self-preferencing).[550]

In this regard, the European Commission imposed, in June 2017, a fine of EUR 2.4 billion on Google for having positioned and displayed more favourably on 'Google Search' its shopping services over those of its competitors.[551] Similarly, the European Commission has opened an investigation in July 2019 against Amazon, which is suspected of using the data it gets from the sellers on its platform to launch competing products and of steering the consumers towards its own products.[552] In November 2020, the Commission sent a Statement of Objections to Amazon in this regard.[553] Unsurprisingly, and from a broader policy perspective, the European Commission wishes to ensure that platforms that have acquired significant scale and a systemic role, effectively allowing them to act as 'private

548. M. Bourreau and A. de Streel, 'Digital Conglomerates and EU Competition Policy', *supra*, pp. 18-19. On these refusals to provide access to data, *see* Part III, Chapter 6.
549. *See* J. Krämer, D. Schnurr and S. Broughton Micova, 'The Role of Data for Digital Markets Contestability', *supra*, pp. 73-74.
550. On this 'frenemy' relationship between the incumbent and these third parties, *see* M. Stucke and A. Grunes, *Big Data and Competition Policy*, *supra*, pp. 293-297.
551. European Commission, *Google Search (Shopping)*, 27 June 2017, AT.39740. This has been upheld by the General Court of the European Union (GC, *Google and Alphabet v Commission (Google Shopping)*, 10 November 2021, T-612/17, EU:T:2021:763).
552. https://ec.europa.eu/commission/presscorner/detail/en/IP_19_4291.
553. *See* https://ec.europa.eu/commission/presscorner/detail/en/ip_20_2077.

gatekeepers', will not endanger the fairness and openness of the markets.[554] In fact, it recently adopted a proposal for a Digital Markets Act,[555] which notably contains a series of obligations and prohibited practices[556] for 'gatekeepers'[557] offering 'core platform services',[558] including the prohibition of some forms of self-preferencing.[559]

2.2.3.4 Benefits from Sharing

86. In order to remedy the market failures deriving from the phenomena of data concentration and data conglomeration presented above, compulsory B2B data sharing is increasingly considered in numerous policy reports across the globe.[560] Indeed, since it reduces the incumbent data holder's data advantage derived from network effects and economies of scope, scale and speed, it is presented by some authors as the best solution to tackle the data concentration problem because, through data sharing, competitors get access to (some of) its data and can thus benefit from those same advantages and compete on the same basis.[561] As a consequence, fair competition would be stimulated.[562]

Similarly, sharing specific types of (essential) data could attenuate the anticompetitive effects of conglomerates by allowing competition to emerge and ensuring market contestability, as 'compulsory access will allow entrants, on the one hand, to enjoy the same economies of scope in product development than the incumbent firm and, on the other hand, to generate

554. Communication from the Commission to the European Parliament, the Council, the European Economic and Social Committee and the Committee of the Regions, '*Shaping Europe's Digital Future*', Brussels, 19 February 2020, COM(2020) 67, p. 8.
555. Proposal for a Regulation of the European Parliament and of the Council on contestable and fair markets in the digital sector (Digital Markets Act), 15 December 2020, COM(2020) 842 final. For more details on this Digital Markets Act, *see* points 317, 380 and 384-385.
556. *See* Articles 5 and 6 of the Proposal for a Digital Markets Act.
557. *See* Articles 2.1 and 3 of the Proposal for a Digital Markets Act. For more details on the designation of these gatekeepers, *see* points 384 and 385.
558. *See* Article 1.2 of the Proposal for a Digital Markets Act. For a definition of these services, *see* Articles 2.2 and 2.5-2.11 of the Proposal.
559. *See* Articles 6.1.a) and d) of the Proposal for a Digital Markets Act.
560. *See* footnote 62 for an overview.
561. J. Prüfer, 'Competition Policy and Data Sharing on Data-driven Markets', *supra*, p. 5. *See also* C. Argenton and J. Prüfer, 'Search Engine Competition with Network Externalities', *supra*, pp. 73-105; J. Prüfer and C. Schottmüller, 'Competing with Big Data', *supra.*; G. Parker, G. Petropoulos and M. Van Alstyne, 'Digital Platforms and Antitrust', May 2020, available at https://ssrn.com/abstract=3608397.
562. Support Centre for Data Sharing, 'B.2 – Analytical Report on EU Law Applicable to Sharing of Non-personal Data', *supra*, p. 4.

demand-side synergies of similar magnitude when integrating the key [data] in their product ecosystems'.[563]

In this regard, the European Commission has notably announced in its *Strategy for data* that it would explore legislative options in order to promote a wider sharing and availability of data, and to ensure that markets stay open and fair.[564] Indeed, the Commission realises that a number of large firms currently hold a significant part of the world's data; that this might diminish the incentives of smaller data-driven firms to emerge, grow and innovate, due to high entry barriers; and that the high degree of market power deriving from this 'data advantage' could also affect the contestability of some markets.[565] In fact, the Commission's proposal for a Digital Markets Act contains several specific data sharing obligations.[566]

Naturally, compulsory B2B data sharing remedies are not the only option to tackle these concentration and conglomeration issues and other avenues are suggested in the legal doctrine, such as the imposition of non-discrimination obligations; structural breakups; preventing incumbent data holders from concentrating more data or forcing them to silo their data, in order to limit the self-reinforcing feedback loops and network effects mentioned above; or preventing 'killer acquisitions' in order to hamper the conglomeration of these incumbent data holders and the domino effect.[567] However, as I focus on compulsory B2B data sharing, these alternatives will not be further detailed here.

---

563. M. Bourreau and A. de Streel, 'Digital Conglomerates and EU Competition Policy', *supra*, p. 30.
564. Communication from the Commission to the European Parliament, the Council, the European Economic and Social Committee and the Committee of the Regions, '*A European Strategy for Data*', Brussels, 19 February 2020, COM(2020) 66, pp. 5 and 14.
565. *Ibid.*, pp. 3 and 8.
566. *See* Recitals 54-56 and Articles 6.1.h) to 6.1.j) of the Proposal for a Digital Markets Act. On these obligations *see* points 167, 180 and 380. For more details on this Digital Markets Act, *see* points 317, 380 and 384-385.
567. On these alternative remedies, *see, inter alia*, J. Crémer, Y.-A. de Montjoye and H. Schweitzer, 'Competition Policy for the Digital Era', *supra*; J. Krämer, D. Schnurr and S. Broughton Micova, 'The Role of Data for Digital Markets Contestability', *supra*; M. Bourreau and A. de Streel, 'Digital Conglomerates and EU Competition Policy', *supra*; United States House of Representatives Committee on the Judiciary, 'Investigation of Competition in Digital Markets – Majority Staff Report and Recommendations', 2020, available at https://judiciary.house.gov/uploadedfiles/competition_in_digital_markets.pdf; J. Hoffmann and G. Johannsen, 'EU-Merger Control & Big Data: On Data-Specific Theories of Harm and Remedies', *Max Planck Institute for Innovation and Competition Research Paper No. 19-05*, 31 May 2019, available at https://ssrn.com/abstract=3364792; OECD, 'Lines of Business Restrictions – Background note', 8 June 2020, DAF/COMP/WP2(2020)1, available at https://one.oecd.org/document/DAF/COMP/WP2(2020)1/en/pdf; S. Besen and P. Verveer, 'Competition and Data: Potential Remedies', *Wake Forest Journal of Business and Intellectual Property Law*, 2021, Vol. 21(2), pp. 103-143. *See also* Articles 3.8, 5 and 6 of the Proposal for a Digital Markets Act.

87. The economic benefits of data sharing are, however, not limited to potentially solving the market failures deriving from the phenomena of data concentration and data conglomeration outlined above. Because data is non-rivalrous and can be used for many different purposes, sharing data entails economic welfare gains.[568] Moreover, data sharing also creates economies of scope in data reuse, as it allows recipients to aggregate various data sets and thus provides them with a wider range of data.[569] Moreover, as outlined by the United Kingdom's Open Data Institute, there are several key business benefits in sharing data, such as 'improving market reach; supporting benchmarking and insights; driving open innovation; driving supply chain optimisation; addressing sector challenges; and building trust'.[570] This perspective of substantial welfare gains deriving from these key business benefits and from the exploitation of the non-rivalrous nature of data is at the core of the data sharing debates.[571]

Indeed, data sharing has a fundamental role to play in the 'European Data Economy'.[572] This is notably apparent from the 'European Data Market Study Monitoring Tool', which identifies three potential scenarios for the evolution of the European Data Market (Baseline, High Growth and Challenge scenarios), and which identifies the amount of data sharing as one of the factors that will influence this concrete evolution (low data sharing will lead towards the Challenge scenario, while high data sharing will lead towards the High Growth scenario).[573] In turn, this will have an impact on the value of the Data Economy, which is expected to reach, by 2025, EUR

---

568. B. Martens, et al., 'Business to Business Data Sharing', *supra*, p. 4. Massive sharing of personal data can however entail long-term losses of control for the individuals (*see* Part I, Chapter 2, Section 2.3.2).
569. B. Martens, et al., 'Business to Business Data Sharing', *supra*, p. 5.
570. Open Data Institute, 'Sharing Data to Create Value in the Private Sector', 2020, available at https://theodi.org/article/report-sharing-data-to-create-value-in-the-private-sector/, p. 4.
571. B. Martens, 'An Economic Perspective on Data and Platform Market Power', *supra*, p. 6.
572. *See* Communication from the Commission to the European Parliament, the Council, the European Economic and Social Committee and the Committee of the Regions, '*Towards a Thriving Data-Driven Economy*', Brussels, 2 July 2014, COM(2014) 442 final; Communication from the Commission to the European Parliament, the Council, the European Economic and Social Committee and the Committee of the Regions, '*A Digital Single Market Strategy for Europe*', Brussels, 6 May 2015, COM(2015) 192 final; Communication from Commission, '*Building a European Data Economy*', *supra*; Communication from the Commission, '*Towards a Common European Data Space*', *supra*; Communication from the Commission, '*A European Strategy for Data*', *supra*; Communication from the Commission, '*Shaping Europe's Digital Future*', *supra*.
573. International Data Corporation and the Lisbon Council, 'The European Data Market Study Monitoring Tool – Final Study Report', June 2020, SMART 2016/0063, available at http://datalandscape.eu/, pp. 8-9.

432 billion in the Challenge scenario, EUR 550 billion in the Baseline scenario and EUR 827 billion in the High Growth scenario.[574]

88. Finally, data sharing is key for the development of a competitive artificial intelligence landscape and is therefore a cornerstone of the European Commission's 'Coordinated Plan on Artificial Intelligence'.[575] Indeed, data is a vital input for the development of machine learning technologies (a form of artificial intelligence), as their learning capabilities are directly a function of the amount of data they can be trained on. Following up on this objective, the Commission has outlined, in its *Strategy for data*, that it will strive for the creation of 'Common European data spaces', in fields such as manufacturing, energy and health, whose aim will be to aggregate public and business data in order to make them accessible to recipients wishing to use these data to train their machine learning technologies.[576] The aim is to facilitate innovation through data reuse and through the fostering of appropriate technical standards and interoperability requirements.[577] These European data spaces should lead to the availability of large pools of data in strategic economic sectors such as the industrial manufacturing and the financial sectors.[578] To support the establishment of these European data spaces, the European Commission has adopted a proposal for a Data Governance Act, which aims at creating an overarching framework encompassing horizontal measures relevant for all Common European data spaces.[579]

2.2.3.5 Need for a Balance Between the Benefits and Costs of Data Sharing

89. While data sharing presents numerous benefits, it does not come without a cost.[580] Indeed, data collection and processing, and consequently data sharing, entail costs for the data holder, and data sharing obligations might create disincentives for data collection and processing.[581] This is because

574. *Ibid.*, p. 9.
575. Communication from the Commission to the European Parliament, the Council, the European Economic and Social Committee and the Committee of the Regions, '*Coordinated Plan on Artificial Intelligence*', Brussels, 7 December 2018, COM(2018) 795 final, pp. 6-7.
576. Communication from the Commission, '*A European Strategy for Data*', *supra*, p. 5; Communication from the Commission, '*Coordinated Plan on Artificial Intelligence*', *supra*, p. 7.
577. Communication from the Commission, '*A European Strategy for Data*', *supra*, p. 12.
578. *Ibid.*, pp. 22-23. These strategic economic sectors are further detailed in the Appendix of the 'European strategy for data' (*see* pp. 26-34).
579. Proposal for a Data Governance Act, p. 6. *See also* Commission Staff Working Document, Impact assessment report accompanying the Data Governance Act, *supra*.
580. B. Martens, et al., 'Business to Business Data Sharing', *supra*, p. 5.
581. J. Crémer, Y.-A. de Montjoye and H. Schweitzer, 'Competition Policy for the Digital Era', *supra*, pp. 76-77.

imposing data sharing might deter innovation by the data holder that is compelled to share its data, as it might no longer want to invest in data collection that used to provide him with a competitive advantage, due to the fear of free-riding that derives from the non-rivalrous nature of data.[582] Moreover, imposing data sharing might also deter innovation by third parties who will no longer see the point in innovating in order to collect the data themselves, as they will receive it from the data holder (expectation to free-ride).

Indeed, while allowing data reuse will not functionally affect the data holder's ability to keep using the data herself, it may have an economic impact on the data holder's business, depending on whether the reuse is complementary or substitutable to it.[583] If the recipient uses the data to develop a substitutable good/service to that of the data holder, this might negatively affect the data holder's business. It will thus not be willing to share the data. On the contrary, if the data recipient uses the data to develop a complementary good/service to that of the data holder, this new good/service might increase the demand for the data holder's good or service and thus positively affect her business. The recipient's good/service could also be purely neutral towards the data holder's good/service, in which case the data holder will have an interest in sharing the data against a price.

While this distinction seems quite straightforward in theory, it will rarely be clear in practice whether the recipient will use the data to develop a substitutable, complementary or neutral good/service.[584] Indeed, a complementary good/service could, in fact, end up becoming a substitute good/service, due to the evolution of the users' needs and expectations.[585] This uncertainty explains why data sharing has not taken off at sufficient scale, as data holders fear to lose the competitive edge they derive from their 'data advantage' because they do not trust the recipients and fear that they might misappropriate 'their' data.[586]

90. Accordingly, any regulatory initiative must consider this balance between the benefits and costs of data sharing.[587] The efficiency gains stemming from sharing (increased competition and innovation from third parties) shall be

582. D. Rubinfeld and M. Gal, 'Access Barriers to Big Data', *supra*, p. 374. Importantly, however, these incentive costs might be quite low if the data has been collected as a by-product of the data holder's core economic activity, rather than as the object its core economic activity. *See* points 12 and 302.
583. B. Martens, et al., 'Business to Business Data Sharing', *supra*, pp. 20-21.
584. *Ibid.*, p. 5.
585. *See* L. Cabral, et al., 'The EU Digital Markets Act: A Report from a Panel of Economic Experts', *EU Science Hub*, 2021, available at https://ec.europa.eu/jrc/en/publication/eu-digital-markets-act, p. 26.
586. Communication from the Commission, '*A European Strategy for Data*', *supra*, p. 7.
587. P. Larouche, 'The European Microsoft Case at the Crossroads of Competition Policy and Innovation', *supra*, pp. 933-937; B. Martens, et al., 'Business to Business Data Sharing', *supra*, p. 5.

carefully weighed against the efficiency gains stemming from the data holder's data-driven network effects and economies of scope, scale and speed.[588] Maximising data sharing should thus not be an objective in its own right, and data sharing obligations should only be imposed if the benefits it creates trump the related costs.[589] This fits in the broader balancing between private and public/social interests and requires a case-by-case analysis.

In evaluating this balance, inspiration can be drawn from the classic balancing exercise, underlying the allocation of IP rights, between the need to incentivise creation/innovation, on the one hand, and the benefits from a large dissemination of these creations/innovations, on the other hand.[590] Indeed, as pointed out by Martens, data economics issues are very similar to the IP rights' law and economics issues, as they struggle with the same balancing act 'between the social welfare costs of monopolistic exclusive rights and the social welfare gains from the innovation incentive effects'.[591]

However, it should be pointed out that, as data are non-rivalrous, capital and general-purpose resources whose use creates spill overs in multiple fields across society,[592] and as data are potentially (technically and contractually) excludable – making them closer to 'club goods' than to 'public goods' –[593] the benefits of data sharing may arguably be greater than the benefits of sharing other resources, and the costs of data sharing may arguably be smaller than the costs of sharing other resources.[594] This serves as an economic rationale for more data sharing.

91. Finally, reaping the potential benefits deriving from data sharing will only be acceptable if this is done in compliance with the right to privacy[595] and to personal data protection[596] of the individuals whose personal data would be

588. J. Krämer, D. Schnurr and S. Broughton Micova, 'The Role of Data for Digital Markets Contestability', *supra*, p. 75.
589. B. Martens, et al., 'Business to Business Data Sharing', *supra*, p. 12.
590. *See supra* points 33-43.
591. B. Martens, 'An Economic Perspective on Data and Platform Market Power', *supra*, p. 23.
592. *See* point 52.
593. M. Madison, 'Tools for Data Governance', *supra*, p. 34; M. Stucke and A. Grunes, *Big Data and Competition Policy*, *supra*, p. 45.
594. M. Bourreau and A. de Streel, 'Digital Conglomerates and EU Competition Policy', *supra*, p. 31; H. Schweitzer, J. Haucap, W. Kerber and R. Welker, 'Modernising the Law on Abuse of Market Power: Executive Summary', *Report for the German Federal Ministry for Economic Affairs and Energy*, 29 August 2018, available at https://ssrn.com/abstract=3250742, p. 10. *See also* J. Prüfer and C. Schottmüller, 'Competing with Big Data', *supra*.
595. Article 7 of the Charter of Fundamental Rights of the European Union, *OJ C 326/391*, 26 October 2012.
596. Article 8 of the Charter of Fundamental Rights of the European Union, *OJ C 326/391*, 26 October 2012.

shared.[597] Indeed, as outlined by the EDPS, a cautious approach should be taken towards initiatives aimed at compulsory access to / sharing of personal data, as such sharing/access must comply with other policy concerns, especially personal data protection.[598]

2.3 THE SOCIETAL AND THE 'EMPOWERMENT' RATIONALE FOR DATA SHARING

92. While the focus, at the European level, is usually set on the economic rationale for data sharing, which was analysed in Section 2.2, data sharing could also be justified by other objectives. On the one hand, it could support broader societal objectives.[599] On the other hand, it could support individual 'empowerment' objectives.[600]

2.3.1 Societal Rationale for Data Sharing

93. As outlined in the European Commission's *Strategy for data,* 'making more data available and improving the way in which data is used is essential for tackling societal, climate and environment-related challenges, contributing to healthier, more prosperous and more sustainable societies'.[601] Indeed, more access to data through data sharing can foster more transparency, more security and it can support research.[602] The underlying idea is that not only public sector data but also private sector data can make a significant contribution to the common good.[603] In this regard, the Commission has set to support the development of a series of 'Common European data spaces', which should lead to the availability of large pools of data in domains of public interest such as environmental protection, health, mobility, energy and agriculture.[604] To support the establishment of these European data spaces, the European Commission has adopted a proposal for a Data Governance Act, which aims at creating an overarching framework encompassing

597. *See* European Data Protection Supervisor, *Opinion 3/2020 on the European strategy for data*, 16 June 2020, available at https://edps.europa.eu/sites/edp/files/publication/20-06-16_opinion_data_strategy_en.pdf, p. 8. *See* Part III, Chapter 7 and Chapter 8, Section 8.2.
598. *Ibid.*, p. 12.
599. *See* Communication from the Commission, '*A European Strategy for Data*', *supra*, p. 3.
600. *Ibid.*, p. 10. *See also* pp. 20-21.
601. *Ibid.*, p. 3.
602. Support Centre for Data Sharing, 'B.2 – Analytical Report on EU Law Applicable to Sharing of Non-personal Data', *supra*, p. 4.
603. *See* Communication from the Commission, '*A European Strategy for Data*', *supra*, p. 6.
604. *Ibid.*, pp. 22-23. These domains of public interest are further detailed in the Appendix of the 'European strategy for data' (*see* pp. 26-34).

horizontal measures relevant for all Common European data spaces.[605] Articles 15-22 of this Data Governance Act notably contain measures aiming at facilitating voluntary data sharing in the common good ('data altruism').

In terms of environmental protection, increased data sharing between businesses would notably allow them to better understand the environmental impact of each step of the supply chain, in order to identify the friction points where they could act in order to reduce the pollution deriving from their activity, thus contributing to Europe's goal to become climate-neutral by 2050.[606] Moreover, increased data sharing, notably with NGOs, could allow the identification of priority actions to be undertaken in order to address fundamental issues such as deforestation, the loss of biodiversity and the management of hazardous waste.[607] In the energy sector, B2B data sharing about the result of innovative experiments aiming at decarbonising the existing energy systems could generate significant environmental benefits by accelerating the transition towards greener energy production.[608] It could also allow undertakings to share information about the energy consumption of certain processes or machines that they use, in order to optimise the efficiency of their energy consumption. Additionally, increased sharing of data about the quality of the air and about the rejection of polluting materials could also enable third parties to develop services recommending, or on the contrary advising against, certain leisure activities for more fragile people in certain specific places.

In terms of mobility, data sharing between navigation technology service providers and freight and logistics businesses can assist the latter in their transition towards more sustainable transport services, as economies of scale can be reached if some travels are rationalised while also making this transport more efficient and secure.[609] Furthermore, data sharing between transport service providers (trains, buses, trams, shared cars, bikes, scooters, etc.) and mobility information service providers could allow the latter to provide suggestions to individuals on how to get the fastest from point A to point B, by relying on multimodal transportation (e.g., taking a train, then a bus, then a shared bike). This could notably take the form of a 'multimodal mobility open data platform', in order to 'facilitate cooperation between different actors involved in mobility issues, establishing the basis for future

605. Proposal for a Data Governance Act, p. 6. *See also* Commission Staff Working Document, Impact assessment report accompanying the Data Governance Act, *supra*.
606. Communication from the Commission, '*A European Strategy for Data*', *supra*, pp. 26-27.
607. *Ibid.*
608. *See* Communication from the Commission, '*A European Strategy for Data*', *supra*, p. 31.
609. Communication from the Commission, '*A European Strategy for Data*', *supra*, p. 28. *See also* https://www.aisin.com/en/product/mobility/cs-s/.

development of Mobility as a Service (MaaS) concepts for citizens'.[610] Such a platform, built on B2B data sharing, would indeed allow the gathering and provision of data from various transport modes, and would notably enable the individuals to opt for the most sustainable ones.

Another interesting example could be the combination of navigation and location data, collected by navigation technology service providers, with data from other sources. This would notably allow the development of ride-sharing services for elderly people who have difficulties moving on their own, such as a shuttle bus service powered by data analytics that calculate and determine the optimal allocation of users between buses and the most efficient routes to bring them to their destination.[611] In fact, such an initiative could even further be combined with the sharing of data with parcel delivery companies, as these shuttle buses could also be used to deliver parcels, for example, if a parcel has to be delivered in the same street as the one where a person is being picked up in the context of the ride-sharing service. This would contribute to two important societal objectives, namely reducing the environmental footprint of transport services, as well as improving mobility by reducing traffic congestion.

Similar objectives could also justify the exchange of data between car manufacturers, navigation system providers, fleet managers and parking operators, in order to develop 'smart parking' services, as 'drivers looking for a parking spot cause about one-third of traffic in city centres'.[612] Through such data exchange, a driver looking for a parking spot could be quickly and efficiently informed about the nearest parking availability and be instantly redirected to it by her navigation system. If deployed at a large scale, this would limit the pollution deriving from CO2 car emissions and would also pursue mobility objectives, by reducing the number of cars on the network.

Regarding healthcare, data sharing can contribute to the prevention, diagnosis and treatment of certain diseases (such as cancer, rare diseases and complex diseases), notably through the sharing of information about the safety and efficacy of medical products and medicines, and can further support research and innovation.[613] In this regard, it is worth mentioning here the Finnish Act on the Secondary Use of Health and Social Data,[614] which compels certain private and public health service providers and social service providers to pool together some of their health and social data, under the

---

610. *See* https://www.bable-smartcities.eu/explore/use-cases/use-case/useCase/open-platform-for-multimodal-mobility-information-and-services.html.
611. *See* https://www.aisin.com/en/product/mobility/cs-s/.
612. *See* https://erticonetwork.com/saving-time-and-reducing-costs-thanks-to-smart-parking/.
613. Communication from the Commission, '*A European Strategy for Data*', *supra*, pp. 29-30.
614. For more information on this Act, *see* https://stm.fi/en/secondary-use-of-health-and-social-data.

supervision of a government agency, in order to make it accessible for research, steering, statistics, supervision and development in the health and social sectors.[615] Moreover, if food and drink companies were to share data about the contents of their products (for instance, whether they contain gluten, lactose or certain allergens), this could allow third parties to offer dietary services to individuals, by recommending to them products that are healthier, that are gluten-free, that do not contain traces of peanuts, etc.

B2B data sharing can also prove to be vital in order to tackle global pandemics, such as the COVID-19 pandemic. For instance, the sharing, between healthcare institutions and emergency services, of data pertaining to the bed occupation rate of the healthcare institutions' intensive care units would allow to better distribute the arrival of new patients in order to ensure that each and every one receives the best care possible in a timely fashion. Similarly, the sharing between pharmaceutical companies, healthcare institutions and research institutions of data pertaining to vaccine/medicine trial results could allow to rapidly abandon trials that lead to unsatisfactory results, or on the contrary to highlight promising results, in order to address such global healthcare challenges caused by pandemics as fast as possible.

In the agricultural sector, sharing production data, supply chain data and other types of data, such as earth observation or meteorological data, would allow the actors of the sector to apply more tailored and precise production approaches.[616] Indeed, farmers increasingly make use of various sensors in order to improve the efficiency of their operations. These can be weather stations, humidity sensors, soil scanners, crop sensors, etc.[617] The latter notably enable the monitoring of the health of crops, as well as to detect plant diseases at an early stage. Accordingly, the sharing of such data pertaining to the apparition of a disease with nearby farmers, which might not be aware of the problem, would contribute to the prevention of food waste, by enabling the farmers to address the issue rapidly and to limit the loss of crops. Similarly, B2B data sharing about the efficiency of a certain type of pesticide and the appropriate dose to be sprayed could reduce the environmental footprint of such practices, by avoiding 'over-spraying'. Furthermore, if 'smart farming' data was shared with NGOs, this could allow the latter to pass on this knowledge to farmers in developing countries and to suggest to them tailored cultivation strategies that are the most efficient for specific climates or soils.

94. As illustrated by the numerous examples mentioned above, which are by no means exhaustive (including in terms of the sectors covered), it is clear

---

615. B. Martens, et al., 'Business to Business Data Sharing', *supra*, p. 33.
616. *Ibid.*
617. Everis, 'Study on data sharing between companies in Europe – Case studies', *Study for the European Commission*, 2018, available at https://publications.europa.eu/en/publication-detail/-/publication/8b8776ff-4834-11e8-be1d-01aa75ed71a1/language-en, p. 43.

that B2B data sharing can significantly contribute to the realisation of several societal objectives. Interestingly, this societal rationale for data sharing seems to receive a large adherence from all categories of actors, as 91.5% of the respondents to the Commission's public consultation on its *Strategy for data* agreed that more data that are useful for the common good (e.g., for improving mobility, delivering personalised medicine, reducing energy consumption and/or contributing to a greener society) should be made accessible.[618] Naturally, such sharing for the common good would have to be respectful of people's privacy and right to personal data protection,[619] and it would have to be ensured that it would not reinforce existing (or create new) situations of data oligopoly by a limited number of large data holders.[620]

95. It is thus clear that data sharing can generate societal benefits. In contrast, this implies that a lack of data sharing, deriving from data concentration and conglomeration, will create not only economic challenges but also societal challenges. Indeed, as outlined by Shkabatur:

> Companies such as Google, Facebook, Apple, and eBay have amassed more data about people and their behavior, health, markets and networks than many governments and organizations around the globe. This data could enlighten us about ourselves, and instruct us on various matters, such as how to improve our health [or] make better informed political decisions.[621]

As the societal value of the data held (exclusively) by some incumbent data holders is enormous, allowing (some) third parties to use this data could generate immense scientific, environmental, health and mobility benefits for our society.[622] Accordingly, for Shkabatur, a just, fair and equal access to (some) of the data that these incumbents hold would be necessary to avoid socio-economic disparities and inequalities of opportunity.[623]

96. Yet, and as for the economic benefits of sharing,[624] these societal benefits would have to be balanced with the corresponding costs for the data holder (notably in terms of incentives for data collection and production), when considering whether to impose B2B data sharing obligations for societal purposes. In this perspective, the requirements of necessity and proportionality entail that such compulsory data sharing should only be imposed if less

---

618. European Commission, 'Summary Report on the open public consultation on the European strategy for data', 24 July 2020, available at https://ec.europa.eu/digital-single-market/en/news/summary-report-public-consultation-european-strategy-data, p. 2.
619. *See* point 91.
620. European Data Protection Supervisor, *Opinion 3/2020 on the European strategy for data*, *supra*, p. 8.
621. J. Shkabatur, 'The Global Commons of Data', *Stanford Technology Law Review*, 2019, Vol. 22, p. 357.
622. *Ibid.*, p. 383. *See* point 93 for some examples.
623. *Ibid.*, pp. 401-402.
624. *See* points 89 and 90.

stringent alternatives, such as *voluntary* data sharing for societal purposes/the common good,[625] turn out to be insufficient to achieve the desired societal objectives, or if it is highly important and/or urgent to achieve these objectives.[626] This will be further analysed below.[627] Nevertheless, it can already be outlined here that if the rationale for data sharing is societal rather than economic, the incumbent data holder's costs may weigh less heavily in the balance, as they are opposed to fundamental societal objectives that could be viewed as superseding 'mere' economic considerations. However, reaping the potential societal benefits deriving from data sharing will only be acceptable if this is done in compliance with the right to privacy and to personal data protection of the individuals whose data would be shared.[628]

2.3.2 The 'Empowerment' Rationale for Data Sharing and Its Impact on Individuals' Autonomy and Self-Determination

97. Data sharing is also increasingly presented as a way to 'empower' individuals, by giving them more control on 'their' data through tools and means allowing them to decide, at a much more granular level, what can be done with it.[629] The underlying idea is that data sharing can optimise the individuals' control over their data by allowing them to securely share it with third parties, in order to be offered better services, more choice and lower prices.[630] As a result, individuals would thus be empowered to compare services, to multi-home and to switch more easily between them, as this would reduce their searching and switching costs.[631] Indeed, it is argued that, at the moment, there is a strong consumer inertia which creates a barrier to entry and expansion for new actors wishing to offer alternative services, as simply providing information about these services (notably about the fact that they are cheaper than the incumbent's service) is not sufficient to

625. *See*, in this regard, Articles 15-22 of the Proposal for a Data Governance Act.
626. H. Richter, 'The Law and Policy of Government Access to Private Sector Data ("B2G Data Sharing")', *Max Planck Institute for Innovation and Competition Research Paper No. 20-06*, 2020, available at https://ssrn.com/abstract=3594109, p. 22.
627. *See* Part III, Chapter 9.
628. *See* point 91 and Part III, Chapter 9.
629. Communication from the Commission, '*A European Strategy for Data*', *supra*, p. 10. *See also* pp. 20-21.
630. *See* point 181.
631. Open Data Institute and Fingleton, 'Open Banking, Preparing for Lift Off: Purpose Progress and Potential', 16 July 2019, available at https://www.openbanking.org.uk/wp-content/uploads/open-banking-report-150719.pdf, p. 4; O. Borgogno and G. Colangelo, 'Consumer Inertia and Competition-Sensitive Data Governance: The Case of Open Banking', 3 January 2020, available at SSRN: https://ssrn.com/abstract=3513514, pp. 4 and 12.

convince the consumers to switch.[632] This is because consumers do not always have the necessary background to understand all of this information. Moreover, 'consumer decision-making can be affected by a range of factors which reinforce inertia, such as high searching and transaction costs (either real or perceived), behavioural biases and contextual factors, but also by firms' strategic conduct aimed at exploiting these biases and poor consumer information by increasing searching and switching costs, thus taking advantage of these demand-side problems in order to weaken competition'.[633]

This individual 'empowerment' is an important policy goal for the European Commission, and it constitutes one of the four pillars of its *Strategy for data*, as 'this promises significant benefits to individuals, including to their health and wellness, better personal finances, reduced environmental footprint, hassle-free access to public and private services and greater oversight and transparency over their personal data'.[634] Indeed, this control that data subjects can (re)claim on their data is fundamental as it will also allow them to exercise a series of other rights, such as their freedom of information,[635] and its deriving right of access to information (covering both personal and non-personal data).[636] Such access to information is important because it can improve the recipients' decision-making and, consequently, their ability to exercise other rights (right to health,[637] right to environmental protection,[638] right to move freely,[639] etc.) and to take fundamental decisions about all aspects of their life.[640] More control on their personal data also

632. *See* point 170. O. Borgogno and G. Colangelo, 'Consumer Inertia and Competition-Sensitive Data Governance', *supra*, pp. 1 and 6.
633. *Ibid.*, p. 2.
634. Communication from the Commission, '*A European Strategy for Data*', *supra*, p. 10.
635. Article 10 of the European Convention for the Protection of Human Rights and Fundamental Freedoms, signed in Rome on 4 November 1950; Article 11 of the Charter of Fundamental Rights of the European Union, *OJ C 326/391*, 26 October 2012.
636. *See* point 39.
637. *See* Article 25 of the Universal Declaration of Human Rights, signed in Paris on 10 December 1948; Article 12 of the International Covenant on Economic, Social and Cultural Rights, 16 December 1966; Article 35 of the Charter of Fundamental Rights of the European Union, *OJ C 326/391*, 26 October 2012.
638. Article 37 of the Charter of Fundamental Rights of the European Union, *OJ C 326/391*, 26 October 2012.
639. *See* Article 5 of the European Convention for the Protection of Human Rights and Fundamental Freedoms, signed in Rome on 4 November 1950; Article 2 of Protocol No. 4 to the European Convention for the Protection of Human Rights and Fundamental Freedoms, securing certain rights and freedoms other than those already included in the Convention and in the first Protocol thereto, as amended by Protocol No. 11, signed in Strasbourg on 16 September 1963; Article 45 of the Charter of Fundamental Rights of the European Union, *OJ C 326/391*, 26 October 2012.
640. *See* C. de Terwangne, 'Droit à la vie privée: un droit sur l'information et un droit à l'information', *supra*, pp. 555-579; ECtHR, *Guerra et al. v. Italy*, 19 February 1998, App. No. 14967/89, § 60; ECtHR, *McGinley and Egan v. United Kingdom*, 9 June 1998,

allows individuals to better understand how they are 'profiled' and why they are offered a specific type of advertisement, search result or content.[641] It should also allow them to understand why they are presented with certain news feed, which may influence their political and democratic choices, as illustrated by the Facebook/Cambridge Analytica scandal. In the same vein, increased access to museum collections via virtual visits through their websites can contribute to the individual's right to culture, and the increased availability of open access lectures by university professors, of recordings of conference presentations, and of open access scientific contributions can all contribute to the individuals' right to education.[642]

Moreover, access to information about a product's environmental footprint (origin, composition, durability, reuse and repair possibilities, recycling at the end-of-life, etc.) allows individuals to make conscious decisions in order to contribute to the protection of the environment by adopting more sustainable habits.[643] For instance, individuals could be inclined to buy food that has been produced in their region, to buy clothes that are made from recycled or second hand materials, or to buy products that are more easily repairable, all of which would contribute to a cleaner environment.

In the field of mobility, access to more information about both the public and private transport operators would enable the offer of more efficient, green and customer friendly multimodal travel options to individuals.[644] Furthermore, information about traffic jams could also enable the individual to better organise her day, by articulating home-office and normal office hours in order to avoid losing too much time during the commute from home to work and vice versa.

Additionally, increasing the individuals' access to health data should 'improve access to and quality of care, cost effectiveness of care delivery and contribute to the modernisation of health systems'.[645] In the same vein, access to information about the most common symptoms of a pathology or about the spread of a new disease can allow the individuals to detect potential issues earlier, in order to improve their chances of being treated in due time and of healing, or to reduce the risks of catching a disease.

App. No. 21825/93 and 23414/94, §§ 97 and 101; ECtHR, *Roche v. United Kingdom*, 19 October 2005, App. No. 32555/96, §§ 162 and 165.

641. *See* Articles 13.2.f) and 14.2.g) of the GDPR, which grant to the data subject the right to receive meaningful information about the logic involved in automated decisions, including profiling, pertaining to her.
642. *See also* the examples mentioned at point 50.
643. Communication from the Commission, '*A European Strategy for Data*', *supra*, p. 27.
644. *Ibid.*, p. 28.
645. *Ibid.*, p. 29.

The main instrument aiming at achieving this 'empowerment' objective is the personal data portability right granted by Article 20 of the 'GDPR',[646] to which I will revert further.[647] However, this objective is being increasingly pursued through several tools – such as consent management tools, personal data spaces / personal information management systems (PIMS)[648] or personal data trusts –[649] and through several initiatives such as the Open Banking,[650] Open Finance[651] and Smart Data[652] initiatives in the UK, which are, however, often still in their infancy.[653]

98. While legislators and policymakers usually heavily focus on the positive aspects of these 'empowerment' tools and initiatives for the individuals,[654] they must be careful not to be blinded by these benefits and should also pay great attention to the risks that they could entail in terms of personal autonomy and informational self-determination.[655]

The first reference to the individuals' right to informational self-determination can be found in a decision of the German Federal Court of December 1983 pertaining to the German Census Act (Volkszählungsurteil),[656] where the Court derived it from Articles 1 and 2 of the German Constitution, protecting human dignity, self-determination and the right to freely develop one's personality, which are foundational to the concept of privacy.[657] The Court defined this right as 'the authority of the individual to decide himself, on the basis of the idea of self-determination, when and within what limits information about private life should be communicated to

646. Regulation (EU) 2016/679 of the European Parliament and of the Council of 27 April 2016 on the protection of natural persons with regard to the processing of personal data and on the free movement of such data, and repealing Directive 95/46 (General Data Protection Regulation), *OJ L 119*, 4 May 2016.
647. *See* Part II, Chapter 4, Section 4.1. *See also* the Digital Content Directive (Part II, Chapter 4, Section 4.2.1), PSD2 (Part II, Chapter 4, Section 4.2.2) and the Electricity Directive (Part II, Chapter 4, Section 4.2.3).
648. *See* points 107 and 172. *See*, for instance, https://www.midata.coop/; https://mydata.org/; http://mesinfos.fing.org/selfdata/; https://solidproject.org/; https://www.decodeproject.eu/.
649. On the concept of data trust, *see* point 110.
650. *See* points 161 and 169.
651. *See* points 163 and 169.
652. *See* points 170 and 171.
653. Communication from the Commission, '*A European Strategy for Data*', *supra*, p. 10.
654. *See* Part II, Chapter 4, Sections 4.1 and 4.2.
655. *See* Preamble of the Modernised Convention for the Protection of Individuals with Regard to the Processing of Personal Data, 17-18 May 2018, CM/Inf(2018)15-final.
656. *See* German Federal Constitutional Court, *Volkszählungsurteil*, 15 December 1983, 1 BvR 209/83 et al., 65 BVerfGE 1.
657. A. Rouvroy and Y. Poullet, 'The Right to Informational Self-Determination and the Value of Self-Development: Reassessing the Importance of Privacy for Democracy', *Reinventing Data Protection: Proceedings of the International Conference (Brussels, 12-13 October 2007)*, Dordrecht, Springer, 2009, pp. 45, 49 and 74.

others'.[658] Self-determination is thus 'an elementary functional condition of a free democratic community based on citizens' capacity to act and collaborate'.[659] It is linked with the autonomic capabilities of individuals, which relate to their capacity to make decisions on all aspects of their life and 'to resist social pressures to conform with dominant views'.[660]

In this regard, the right to personal data protection could, in fact, be seen as an intermediate tool for the preservation and promotion of this more fundamental value of autonomic self-determination.[661] Indeed, the GDPR grants to the data subjects[662] a certain number of rights,[663] which strengthen their informational self-determination.[664] In fact, the aim of these rights is, among other things, to give data subjects a certain form of control[665] over 'their' personal data and to ensure respect for human dignity in an increasingly technological environment. To do so, the data subjects' rights strive to address the information and power asymmetries between the data subjects and the data controllers.[666] First, this right to informational self-determination is at the root of the adaptation of the right of access in the GDPR, which now explicitly provides that the data subject has the right to receive a copy of her personal data undergoing processing.[667] Second, the right to informational self-determination is also the basis of the right of the data subject to receive meaningful information about the logic involved in automated decisions pertaining to her.[668] Third, the right not to be subject to a decision based solely on automated processing is also intended to promote informational self-determination and human dignity.[669] This right indeed echoes the strong desire of human beings not to be completely subjected to the machine since they do not accept the idea that a decision may be imposed on them solely on the basis of conclusions reached by the machine, independently of any human intervention. Fourth, the right of the data subject to object, at any time and on grounds relating to her particular

---

658. *Ibid.*, p. 45.
659. *Ibid.*, p. 47.
660. *Ibid.*, p. 46. *See also* C. Sunstein, *Why Societies Need Dissent*, Cambridge, Harvard University Press, 2003, pp. 157-158.
661. A. Rouvroy and Y. Poullet, 'The Right to Informational Self-Determination and the Value of Self-Development', *supra*, p. 50.
662. '*Any identified or identifiable natural person*' (Article 4.1 of the GDPR).
663. Articles 13-22 of the GDPR.
664. L. Somaini, 'The Right to Data Portability and User Control: Ambitions and Limitations', *MediaLaws – Rivista dir. media*, 2018/3, p. 172.
665. Recital 7 of the GDPR indeed provides that 'natural persons should have control of their own personal data'.
666. L. Somaini, 'The Right to Data Portability and User Control', *supra*, p. 176.
667. Article 15.3 of the GDPR.
668. Articles 13.2.f) and 14.2.g) of the GDPR.
669. Article 22 of the GDPR.

situation, to profiling also promotes her right to informational self-determination.[670] Fifth, the desire to establish a 'right to be forgotten' is also rooted in the broader aim of strengthening the data subject's informational self-determination.[671] This is particularly relevant in light of the specificities of the Internet as, unlike in the physical world, erasure in the digital world will never be automatic and implies voluntary and well-considered action. Finally, the prime example of the promotion of informational self-determination in the GDPR is the right to personal data portability, enshrined in Article 20, which aims at strengthening the power of control that the data subjects have on 'their' personal data.[672] This right to data portability will be further analysed below.[673]

99. This right to informational self-determination has traditionally been interpreted in an individual-centric way, in the sense that 'controlling and manipulating information and data about oneself is an exercise of "self-determination"'.[674] As a result of this traditional interpretation, 'in a context of pervasive possessive individualism and at a time where private property and the laws of the market are perceived as the most efficient ways to allocate rights,[675] the right to "informational self-determination" has increasingly been understood as implying a sort of alienable property right of the individual over his personal data and information'.[676] Yet, for Rouvroy and Poullet, this is a misunderstanding of this concept, as:

> Information and data are not the pre-existing 'elements' or 'building blocks' of an individual's personality or 'self'. Such a conception would be misleading and unduly reductionistic: the 'self' is not merely irreductible but also essentially different from 'data' and 'information' *produced about it*. What the expression 'informational self-determination' means is rather that an individual's control over the data and information produced about him is a (necessary but insufficient) precondition for him to live an existence that may be said 'self-determined'. This is an important thing to recall today, as personal data have become *proxies* for persons (emphasis in the text).[677]

Said otherwise, the individuals' right to informational self-determination should not only be understood as their ability to decide which information/data they share with whom but also, and more fundamentally, as their right to understand and exercise control over who has their data, what

670. Article 21.1 of the GDPR.
671. Article 19 of the GDPR.
672. Recital 68 of the GDPR.
673. *See* Part II, Chapter 4, Section 4.1.
674. A. Rouvroy and Y. Poullet, 'The Right to Informational Self-Determination and the Value of Self-Development', *supra*, p. 51.
675. *See* point 29.
676. A. Rouvroy and Y. Poullet, 'The Right to Informational Self-Determination and the Value of Self-Development', *supra*, p. 51.
677. *Ibid.*

is being done with it and how this impacts their life and their possibility to exercise their autonomy by making their own choices, as opposed to being subject to decisions made about them on the basis of personal data used as proxies and on which they might not have control.[678] Indeed, it is fundamental to take into account the 'individuals' capacity for not doing or wanting everything which they are 'statistically' predisposed to do or want, and to always assert their right to themselves account for their own motivations'.[679] Some forms of opacity are indeed necessary to sustain the individuals' self-determination.[680]

100. Yet, as both public and private actors increasingly rely on evermore invasive observation and monitoring technologies (Big Data, profiling, data mining, machine learning, etc.) as we shift towards a '(capitalism) surveillance society',[681] individuals, who are asked to share more and more data, become increasingly transparent and lose this opacity.[682] As a result, they are increasingly subjected to (semi-)automatic decisions taken on the basis of the constant observation of their choices, behaviours and emotions, and therefore become 'decreasingly capable of living by their fully autonomous choices and behaviours'.[683] This feeling of loss of autonomy and control can be particularly strong when considering the large informational power of a few giant digital actors such as the GAFAM. In this regard, 'empowerment' initiatives such as those mentioned above are sometimes presented as potential avenues to address this loss of autonomy and control, by offering more choices to individuals in the hope that they will get free from the clutches of these giant digital actors.[684]

However, great caution should be applied when considering the adoption of such 'empowerment' initiatives. Indeed, 'empowering' individuals by offering them more choice will not necessarily increase their control, autonomy and (informational) self-determination. In fact, if these 'empowerment' initiatives are not strictly delineated, they might actually entail a high price and a loss of control for the individuals. Indeed, if, in the name of 'empowerment', individuals are asked to divulge large quantities of data

678. *Ibid.*, p. 56.

679. A. Rouvroy, '"Of Data and Men": Fundamental Rights and Liberties in a World of Big Data', *Report for the Consultative Committee of the Convention for the Protection of Individuals with Regard to Automatic Processing of Personal Data (T-PD)*, T-PD-BUR(2015)09REV, Council of Europe, Strasbourg, 11 January 2016, p. 37.

680. A. Rouvroy and Y. Poullet, 'The Right to Informational Self-Determination and the Value of Self-Development', *supra*, p. 58.

681. *See* S. Zuboff, *The Age of Surveillance Capitalism: The Fight for a Human Future at the New Frontier of Power*, New York, PublicAffairs, 2019.

682. A. Rouvroy and Y. Poullet, 'The Right to Informational Self-Determination and the Value of Self-Development', *supra*, pp. 45-46.

683. *Ibid.*, p. 47.

684. Communication from the Commission, '*A European Strategy for Data*', *supra*, p. 10. *See also* pp. 20-21.

about themselves in order to be provided with more personalised choices, there is a risk that those data could be further disseminated with other actors, such as data brokers. This is notably due to the fact that there are strong informational asymmetries, as individuals 'have no direct interaction with these data brokers, [and] they have no way of knowing the extent or nature of the information collected and sold for a multitude of reasons including fraud prevention, marketing and credit scoring'.[685] This is fundamental to keep in mind because, due to these asymmetries of information, 'consumers are rarely (if ever) completely aware about privacy threats and the consequences of sharing and protecting their personal information'.[686] Often, they will not know exactly which data will be used, for which purposes and whether this processing is truly necessary.[687] Moreover, 'personal data may be used to influence individual decision-making in subtle, targeted, and hidden manners,[688] raising questions over the limits of a person's autonomy and self-determination in a world where so much personal data can be gathered and used to influence the individual'.[689]

As a result, an overemphasis on the beneficial aspects of these 'empowerment' initiatives could overshadow these risks, for individuals, of losing control and of becoming decreasingly capable of living by their fully autonomous and self-determined choices and behaviours. Therefore, it will be of paramount importance, when considering the adoption of such 'empowerment initiatives', to exercise caution and to balance the potential short-term gains that are promised to individuals (e.g., getting a more tailored offer from an energy provider based on my exact consumption)[690] with the potential long-term costs for these individuals in terms of control, autonomy and self-determination. Indeed, it must be factored that data that has been shared by these individuals in exchange for these short-term gains might, in the long term, be broadly disseminated and/or be used against them, potentially leading to (price) discrimination, a loss of autonomy and the strengthening of a surveillance society.[691,692] This will be further developed

685. A. Rouvroy, 'Of Data and Men', *supra*, p. 8.
686. A. Acquisti, C. Taylor and L. Wagman, 'The Economics of Privacy', *Sloan Foundation Economics Research Paper No. 2580411*, 8 March 2016, available at https://ssrn.com/abstract=2580411, p. 3.
687. A. Rouvroy and Y. Poullet, 'The Right to Informational Self-Determination and the Value of Self-Development', *supra*, p. 68.
688. *See* R. Calo, 'Digital Market Manipulation', *George Washington Law Review*, 2014, Vol. 82(4), pp. 995-1051.
689. A. Acquisti, C. Taylor and L. Wagman, 'The Economics of Privacy', *supra*, p. 44.
690. *See* point 164.
691. *See* S. Zuboff, *The Age of Surveillance Capitalism, supra.*
692. A. Acquisti, C. Taylor and L. Wagman, 'The Economics of Privacy', *supra*, pp. 6 and 28-31.

below.[693] Moreover, such a large data dissemination would increase risks of potential data breaches, abuses and frauds.[694]

101. In addition to this short-term / long-term balancing exercise, it must also be underlined that protecting an individual's autonomy and self-determination is not only necessary for the individual itself but also, more critically, for the 'collective or societal interest in preserving a free and democratic society: individual autonomy and deliberative democracy pre-suppose a series of rights and liberties allowing individuals to live a life characterized as (partly at least) self-determined, self-authored or self-created, following plans and ideals that they have chosen for themselves'.[695] Accordingly, the individuals' autonomy and their right to (informational) self-determination should not be conceived 'as a liberty held in isolation by an individual living secluded from the rest of society but, on the contrary, as a right enjoyed as member of a free society'.[696]

Therefore, when considering 'empowerment' initiatives such as those mentioned above, it would be ill-advised to solely take an individual approach to the situation (e.g., offering more choice to a specific individual/consumer), without considering this necessary collective approach of autonomy and (informational) self-determination. Indeed, if this collective approach is overlooked:

> The empowerment of individuals with regard to their personal data risks being interpreted as making the satisfaction of individuals' immediate preferences with regard to their personal data, their choice to keep it undisclosed or to commodify personal information a *final value*. It is well-known that those preferences would lead to a large part of the population to waive any protection of their personal data provided they receive immediate gratifications or commercial advantages. What would be lost in such an interpretation is the *intermediate value* of data protection as an instrument aimed at fostering the autonomic capabilities of individuals and therefore not something they may dispose of or trade on the market of personal information (emphasis in the text).[697]

Said otherwise, an individual's decision to share (or not to share) data will have an impact not only on her own autonomy and self-determination but also on those of others. To understand why this is the case, one must first understand how the increasingly sophisticated technologies that are used to

693. *See* Part II, Chapter 5, 5.1.3.
694. O. Borgogno and G. Colangelo, 'Consumer Inertia and Competition-Sensitive Data Governance', *supra*, p. 10.
695. A. Rouvroy and Y. Poullet, 'The Right to Informational Self-Determination and the Value of Self-Development', *supra*, p. 55. *See also* G. Dworkin, *The Theory and Practice of Autonomy*, Cambridge, Cambridge University Press, 1988.
696. A. Rouvroy and Y. Poullet, 'The Right to Informational Self-Determination and the Value of Self-Development', *supra*, p. 57.
697. *Ibid.*, p. 50.

process growing amounts of data operate (e.g., Big Data analytics or artificial intelligence techniques such as machine learning). These technologies exploit the relational and collective nature of data,[698] as the focus is no longer on the individuals as such, but rather on their relations with one another and the profile they correspond to (i.e., their 'statistical doppelganger').[699]

Indeed, when an individual shares data about her own behaviour, habits and preferences, this also reveals significant information about her friends, family, neighbours as well as about any other people having similar characteristics.[700] This can be illustrated by the infamous Cambridge Analytica scandal, where the data disclosed by 270,000 users of the application called 'This is your digital life' allowed Cambridge Analytica to infer detailed information about more than 50 million Facebook users and to use these insights to send targeted political messages to these Facebook users in order to influence the Brexit referendum and the 2016 US presidential election.[701] This illustrative example, which is only the tip of the iceberg, reveals that 'the very nature of predictive big data approaches is to forecast the behaviour or characteristics of groups of individuals from data shared by samples'.[702]

Data sharing by an individual thus creates negative externalities,[703] as it also reveals information about other individuals whose information is correlated with hers, even if they themselves did not share any data.[704] This

---

698. A. Rouvroy, '*Homo juridicus* est-il soluble dans les données ?', *Law, Norms and Freedoms in Cyberspace / Droit, normes et libertés dans le cybermonde: Liber Amicorum Yves Poullet*, E. Degrave, C. de Terwangne, S. Dusollier et R. Queck (dir.), Bruxelles, Larcier, 2018, p. 429.
699. A. Rouvroy et T. Berns, 'Gouvernementalité algorithmique et perspectives d'émancipation. Le disparate comme condition d'individuation par la relation ?', *Réseaux*, 2013, Vol. 177(1), pp. 168, 180 and 184.
700. D. Acemoğlu, et al., 'Too Much Data: Prices and Inefficiencies in Data Markets', *NBER Working Paper No. 26296*, 2019, available at https://www.nber.org/system/files/working_papers/w26296/w26296.pdf, p. 1.
701. D. Acemoğlu, et al., 'Can We Have Too Much Data?', 18 November 2019, available at https://voxeu.org/article/can-we-have-too-much-data; D. Acemoğlu, et al., 'Too Much Data: Prices and Inefficiencies in Data Markets', *supra*, p. 1. *See also* A. Chang, 'The Facebook and Cambridge Analytica Scandal, Explained with a Simple Diagram', 2 May 2018, available at https://www.vox.com/policy-and-politics/2018/3/23/17151916/facebook-cambridge-analytica-trump-diagram; K. Granville, 'Facebook and Cambridge Analytica: What You Need to Know as Fallout Widens', *New York Times*, 19 March 2018, available at https://www.nytimes.com/2018/03/19/technology/facebook-cambridge-analytica-explained.html.
702. D. Acemoğlu, et al., 'Can We Have Too Much Data?', *supra*.
703. On these negative externalities, *see also* J.A. Fairfield and C. Engel, 'Privacy as a Public Good', *Duke Law Journal*, 2015, Vol. 65(3), pp. 385-457; M. MacCarthy, 'New Directions in Privacy: Disclosure, Unfairness and Externalities', *Journal of Law and Policy for the Information Society*, 2011, Vol. 6, pp. 425-512.
704. D. Acemoğlu, et al., 'Can We Have Too Much Data?', *supra*; D. Acemoğlu, et al., 'Too Much Data: Prices and Inefficiencies in Data Markets', *supra*, pp. 3 and 36-37.

is depicted by Ben-Shahar as a phenomenon of 'data pollution'.[705] Therefore, an individual's ability to protect her privacy is influenced by disclosure choices made by others, as 'protecting one's data becomes increasingly costly the more others reveal about themselves'.[706] This can be highly problematic in terms of individual autonomy and (informational) self-determination, as these negative externalities might lead towards excessive data sharing situations, where individuals decide to overlook their own privacy preferences by sharing more data than they would have wanted to because they know that the fact that others have broadly shared their own data will already have revealed much information about them.[707]

It can therefore be concluded, from this relational and collective nature of data,[708] that it will also be fundamental, when considering the adoption of 'empowerment' initiatives, to balance the individual's potential gains from data sharing with the potential collective costs for other individuals in terms of control, autonomy and self-determination. This will be further developed below.[709]

102. To conclude, it must also be added that, as for the economic and broader societal rationale for sharing, the benefits from these 'empowerment' initiatives will have to be balanced with the corresponding costs for the data holder when considering whether to impose B2B data sharing obligations.[710] Additionally, any form of data sharing will have to comply with the personal data protection rights of the (other) individuals whose data would be shared.[711]

705. O. Ben-Shahar, 'Data pollution', *Journal of Legal Analysis*, 2019, Vol. 11, pp. 104-159.
706. A. Acquisti, C. Taylor and L. Wagman, 'The Economics of Privacy', *supra*, p. 5.
707. D. Acemoğlu, et al, 'Too Much Data: Prices and Inefficiencies in Data Markets', *supra*, p. 1.
708. A. Rouvroy, '*Homo juridicus* est-il soluble dans les données ?', *supra*, p. 429.
709. *See* Part II, Chapter 5, Section 5.1.3.
710. *See* points 89, 90, and 96.
711. *See* points 91 and 96 and Part II, Chapter 5, Section 5.1.2.

Chapter 3

Sharing How? A Typology of Data Sharing Models and Initiatives

103. Now that the concept of data has been specified (**what?**) and that the rationale for (data) sharing has been outlined (**why?**), I can turn to the way in which data is shared (**how?**). Accordingly, this chapter will present a **typology of data sharing models and initiatives.** To do so, this chapter will be subdivided into two sections. Section 3.1 will take a more practical approach, and will present the most common *conceptual models of data sharing*. Section 3.2, on the other hand, will take a more abstract approach, by focusing on the underlying objectives pursued by *compulsory B2B data sharing initiatives*. In doing so, two main categories will be established, namely *empowerment initiatives imposing B2B data sharing*, and *economic or societal initiatives imposing B2B data sharing*.

3.1 CONCEPTUAL MODELS OF DATA SHARING

104. As outlined in Chapter 2,[712] the European Commission has abandoned the idea of creating a 'property-like' right on data. Rather, it opted for a form of market self-regulation relying on *voluntary data sharing* and contractual freedom. This approach opens the door for creativity in setting up *conceptual models of data sharing* allowing the data holder and the data recipient, as well as intermediaries in some cases, to extract the most value out of the data. Yet, opting for the 'right' model requires careful consideration and depends on the specific situation of each undertaking. This lack of a 'one-size-fits-all' solution has given rise to a plethora of models. For the sake of concision, all of these models will not be presented,[713] and the focus will be set on the most notorious ones.

---

712. *See* point 64.
713. For an original overview of a wider spectrum of models, in the form of an interactive map, *see* the UK Open Data Institute's 'Data Access Map', available at https://theodi.org/project/the-data-access-map/#1565707571855-6d70b0a0-3243.

3.1.1 Diversity of Conceptual Data Sharing Models

3.1.1.1 Bilateral Contracts

105. The most basic conceptual model of data sharing is bilateral contracts. At first sight, this model is very simple, as illustrated in Figure 3.1: a data holder enters into a contract with a data recipient in order to provide data in exchange of a monetary price, another means of exchange (other data, a service, etc.) or even without any compensation (purely free sharing).

Figure 3.1 Bilateral Contracts

The reality is much more complex, as these contracts can take various forms. Indeed, not all data holders engaging in bilateral contracts operate in the same way, as they can be either considered as data suppliers or data managers, as explained by Thomas and Leiponen.[714] Data suppliers put less effort in providing their data as they typically share unprocessed raw data, for instance, a telecommunication operator sharing customer location data with a recipient providing traffic information, such as Waze. Data managers engage in more preparatory work before sharing the data, as they add value to the raw data by cleaning and structuring it, which converts this raw data into a format that is more interpretable and more efficient to use for the recipient's analysis. Moreover, the object of the contract can differ greatly.[715] However, bilateral contracts not only are used to 'sell' data but can also be used to outsource data analytics of previously gathered data to another undertaking, or to enter into partnerships or joint ventures where two undertakings combine forces to improve their data analytics capabilities. Moreover, they can also be used to sell value-added services that are based on insights generated through data collection, aggregation, repurposing, cross-referencing and contextualisation. Additionally, the concrete output

714. L. Thomas and A. Leiponen, 'Big Data Commercialization', *IEEE Engineering Management Review,* 2016, Vol. 44(2), pp. 74-90.

715. *See* L. Priego, D. Osimo and J. Wareham, 'Data Sharing Practices in Big Data Ecosystems', *ESADE Working Paper 273*, 2019, available at https://ssrn.com/abstract=3355696.

that is shared also varies. In that regard, de Montjoye et al. identify four types of concrete outputs:[716]

- Firstly, the output can simply be a 'copy of (part of) the data holder's dataset' that is shared with the recipient. This is the most intuitive conception of bilateral data sharing. For instance, TomTom sells copies of its navigation and map data to recipients from the automotive and technology sectors, as well as to geographical information system (GIS) providers;[717]
- Secondly, rather than sharing a copy of the data, the data holder can opt to share 'indicators or synthetic data representations' derived from the original data. For example, Telefónica shares aggregated and anonymised insights with recipients, rather than its raw data;[718]
- Thirdly, instead of sharing data as such, the data holder can choose to offer 'remote access to its system', which means that the holder's data is not released but rather stays under its control and that, accordingly, the data analysis conducted by the data recipient takes place within the holder's premises and the data recipient can only extract aggregated data that is the result of this remote analysis. This provides advantages for both the data holder – who can easily supervise by whom the data is accessed, for what purpose, how it is used and can make sure that no data other than aggregated data resulting from the remote analysis leaves the secure area – and the recipient, who gets access to near-real-time data which is highly valuable. This is the model used by Orange, which provides recipients with a remote access to its cloud, where they can analyse some of Orange's anonymised raw data sets (such as call detail records (CDR)) directly on the cloud, but they can only extract the insights derived from their analysis and not any of the underlying raw data;[719]
- Fourthly, the data holder can opt for a 'question-and-answer model', which resembles the remote access model because the data stays within the data holder's system, but differs from it as recipients only access the data through an API and a question-and-answer system (e.g., SafeAnswers or SQL queries). For instance, the data recipient could access the data holder's system and ask 'How many people have participated in the demonstration going from point A to point B on the 20th of September 2020?' and would be provided with the answer '24.672' via the API. This is notably done by Telefónica,

716. Y.-A. de Montjoye, et al., 'Comment: On the Privacy-Conscientious Use of Mobile Phone Data', *Scientific Data*, 2018, Issue 5, available at https://www.nature.com/articles/sdata2018286.
717. Everis, 'Study on data sharing between companies in Europe – Case studies', *supra*, p. 38.
718. *Ibid.*, p. 31.
719. *Ibid.*, p. 25.

which answers, in exchange for a fee, recipients' specific questions in the form of insights.[720]

3.1.1.2 Data Portability

106. In the last decade, another conceptual model of data sharing has gained a lot of attention, notably due to the adoption of the GDPR,[721] namely data portability (*see* Figure 3.2).[722]

Figure 3.2 Data Portability

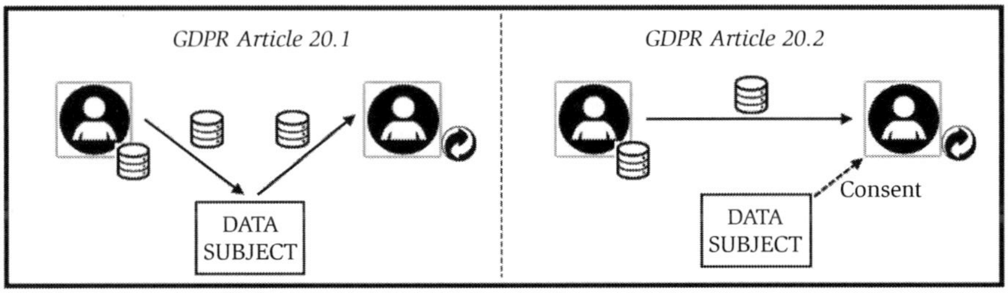

Indeed, Article 20.1 GDPR provides that the data subject has the right to receive the personal data concerning her, which she has provided to a controller, in a structured, commonly used and machine-readable format and have the right to transmit those data to another controller without hindrance from the original controller. For instance, the data subject should have the possibility to extract her list of contacts from her webmail application in order to build a wedding invitation list that she can then share with her wedding planner.[723] If limited to the hypothesis targeted by Article 20.1 of the GDPR, data portability would be a quite cumbersome mechanism of data sharing, as it implies that the data would necessarily have to transit through the data subject's IT system (cloud storage, personal computer, laptop, etc.) before being shared with a recipient. Fortunately, Article 20.2 of the GDPR provides that the data subject also has the right to have the personal data transmitted directly from one controller to another. In essence, this means that a data recipient can port data directly from the data holder's system provided that the data subject has consented to this operation. This

720. *Ibid.*, p. 31.
721. Regulation (EU) 2016/679 of the European Parliament and of the Council of 27 April 2016 on the protection of natural persons with regard to the processing of personal data and on the free movement of such data, and repealing Directive 95/46 (General Data Protection Regulation), *OJ L 119*, 4 May 2016.
722. On the right to data portability, *see infra* Part II, Chapter 4, Section 4.1.
723. Article 29 Working Party, *Guidelines on the right to data portability*, WP 242 rev.01, 5 April 2017, p. 5.

hypothesis is a more effective mechanism of data sharing. However, it only applies 'where technically feasible'. Finally, it should be pointed out that the concept of data portability is not limited to personal data and also has been used for non-personal data.[724]

3.1.1.3 Personal Information Management Systems

107. Data portability can also be used as an instrument to create personal data platforms managed by the data subject or by a trusted third party, from which controllers could access and process such data under the control of the data subject.[725] These are often referred to as (PIMS), the functioning of which is illustrated in Figure 3.3.

Figure 3.3 Personal Information Management System

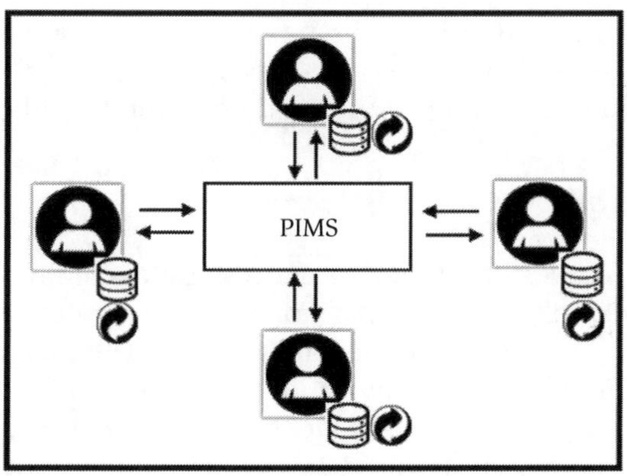

Pilot projects for such PIMS already exist in Europe, such as 'MiData'[726] in the UK and 'MesInfos / SelfData'[727] in France, and at a more global level, with the MyData movement.[728] In practice, the data subjects use trusted third party's services (which may take the form of websites, platforms, applications or personal clouds) on which data controllers who have agreed to

724. *See* Directive 2019/770 of the European Parliament and of the Council of 20 May 2019 on certain aspects concerning contracts for the supply of digital content and digital services, *OJ L 136/1*, 22 May 2019, Article 16.4; Regulation (EU) 2018/1807 of the European Parliament and of the Council of 14 November 2018 on a framework for the free flow of non-personal data in the European Union, *OJ L 303/59*, 28 November 2018, Article 6. For more information, *see* Part II, Chapter 4, Sections 4.2.1 and 4.4.1.
725. Article 29 Working Party, *Guidelines on the right to data portability*, WP 242 rev.01, 5 April 2017, p. 15.
726. *See* https://www.midata.coop/.
727. *See* http://mesinfos.fing.org/selfdata/.
728. *See* L. Langford, et al. (eds), 'Understanding MyData Operators', *MyData Global Report*, 29 April 2020, available at https://mydata.org/wp-content/uploads/sites/5/2020/04/Understanding-Mydata-Operators-pages.pdf.

participate in the project provide, with the consent of the data subject and in accordance with the right to portability, access to the latter's personal data which they process. This type of initiative shows that portability can be an opportunity and not solely a constraint for data controllers.

In the mainstream PIMS models, the person managing and controlling the access rights of data controllers to the personal data is the data subject herself. Another approach is however possible, namely that the PIMS could be managed by an independent intermediary, as explained by Delacroix and Lawrence.[729] This intermediary would exercise the data subject's rights contained in the GDPR on behalf of the data subject and would negotiate data access and use with the data controllers in conformity with the terms of the agreement entered into with the data subject. The long-term objective would be to have a whole ecosystem of such agreements, whether publicly or privately funded, among which the data subjects could choose between different approaches to data governance, and allowing them to switch from one intermediary to another if need be. For this ecosystem to work, the entry barrier for new intermediaries must be low, the security of the data subjects' data must be ensured, and this data must be portable and erasable.

3.1.1.4 Data Clearing Houses

108. The PIMS model described above resembles another conceptual data sharing model, namely data clearing houses. In this model, a clearing house acts as a checkpoint between the data holder and the data recipient, verifying that the recipient has the clearance to access the data holder's data. In essence, this data clearing house model can be divided into two sub-models, as illustrated in Figure 3.4. In the first, the clearing house acts as the gateway through which all recipients have to go in order to access a single database. In the second, the data clearing house is the hub of a peer-to-peer network involving various data holders and recipients.

729. S. Delacroix and N. Lawrence, 'Bottom-Up Data Trusts: Disturbing the "One Size Fits All" Approach to Data Governance', *International Data Privacy Law*, November 2019, Vol. 9(4), pp. 236-252. *See also* C. Wendehorst, 'Of Elephants in the Room and Paper Tigers: How to Reconcile Data Protection and the Data Economy', *Trading Data in the Digital Economy: Legal Concepts and Tools*, S. Lohsse, R. Schulze and D. Staudenmayer (eds), Baden-Baden, Nomos, 2017, pp. 349-353.

Figure 3.4 Data Clearing Houses

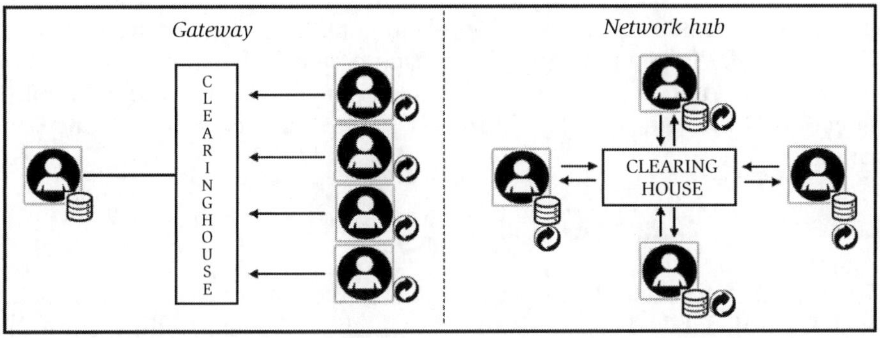

An example of the gateway model can be found in the field of connected cars and the sharing of vehicle data. Indeed, these connected cars generate a huge amount of data that are valuable not only for the car manufacturers (so-called original equipment manufacturers, OEMs) but also for a wide array of stakeholders who have an interest in accessing these data to provide additional services (independent repairers, component suppliers, on-board entertainment service providers, insurers, public authorities, etc.). In the current situation, which raises controversial data sharing questions,[730] the OEMs favour the 'extended vehicle' approach to share car data. Under this approach, all vehicle data are transferred on a single central server outside of the car controlled by the OEM. The recipients access the data on those remote servers (one for each OEM), rather than directly in the car. In this model, the OEMs themselves act as clearing house for their own data, as they decide whether these recipients can get access to their data.[731]

An example of the network hub model is the Belgian Crossroad Bank for Social Security (CBSS).[732] The CBSS acts as the hub of the network of all Belgian social security institutions (SSIs). The CBSS is the core of the network and SSIs are the nodes.[733] While each (or some) of these institutions remain in control of their authoritative sources of social data, the CBSS acts as the central actor for the data sharing between them.[734] Indeed, given the sensitive nature of the personal data at hand, the SSIs can only access the other institutions' data via the CBSS if they have received an authorisation

---

730. *See infra* Part III, Chapter 8, Section 8.1.1 'The Current Strong Reliance on Sectoral Legislations'.
731. *See* W. Kerber and J. Frank, 'Data Governance Regimes in the Digital Economy: The Example of Connected Cars', 3 November 2017, available at https://ssrn.com/abstract=3064794.
732. Loi du 15 janvier 1990 organique de la Banque Carrefour de la sécurité sociale, *M.B.*, 22 février 1990.
733. *See* https://www.ksz-bcss.fgov.be.
734. Loi du 15 janvier 1990, Article 3.

to do so.[735] The CBSS thus does not itself store any data, but rather acts as a 'clearinghouse' that checks that an SSI has the right to access data stored on one of the nodes of the network (another SSI). This distributed model allows for GDPR compliance and for each of the SSIs to remain in control of their authoritative sources of social data while also avoiding multiple collection of the same data by all the SSIs, in accordance with the 'once-only principle'.[736]

3.1.1.5 Data Marketplace

109. A fifth conceptual data sharing model is the data marketplace model, or the 'eBay of data'. This marketplace, which can be an online store or a platform, is set up to act as an intermediary between data holders and data recipients, where the latter can buy the former's data, as illustrated in Figure 3.5. A third party builds up an infrastructure enabling the resale and reuse of data by generating trust for both the data holders and data recipients, thanks to identity management and auditing services that ensure the integrity and the quality of the data on a secure platform.[737] These data marketplaces can also offer a range of additional services such as data storage, enrichment, aggregation, analysis or exchange, and they are usually financed through the collection of a fee for each transaction that occurs on the platform.[738]

---

735. *Ibid.*, Articles 5 and 11.
736. *See* Loi du 5 mai 2014 garantissant le principe de la collecte unique des données dans le fonctionnement des services et instances qui relèvent de ou exécutent certaines missions pour l'autorité et portant simplification et harmonisation des formulaires électroniques et papier, *M.B.*, 4 juin 2014; Tallinn Declaration on eGovernment, 6 October 2017, available at https://ec.europa.eu/digital-single-market/en/news/ministerial-declaration-egovernment-tallinn-declaration; Communication from the Commission to the European Parliament, the Council, the European Economic and Social Committee and the Committee of the Regions, '*EU eGovernment Action Plan 2016-2020 – Accelerating the Digital Transformation of Government*', Brussels, 19 April 2016, COM(2016) 179 final.
737. *See* L. Thomas and A. Leiponen, 'Big Data Commercialization', *supra*, pp. 74-90.
738. Everis, 'Study on data sharing between companies in Europe – Final report', *Study for the European Commission*, 2018, available at https://publications.europa.eu/en/publication-detail/-/publication/8b8776ff-4834-11e8-be1d-01aa75ed71a1/language-en, p. 10.

Figure 3.5 Data Marketplace

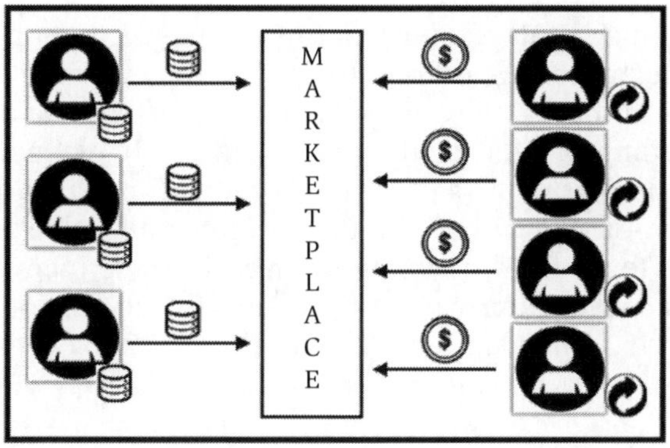

An example of such a data marketplace is Dawex,[739] founded in 2015, that operates an independent online platform allowing data sharing.[740] In order to generate trust and before being allowed to sell/buy data, data holders and data recipients need to subscribe to the platform and outline what their business is. Dawex enables data sharing not only within a sector but also between sectors, and a search tool is embedded in the platform in order to facilitate the identification of potentially interesting data sets. The price of the data set is set by the data holders, who nevertheless have the possibility to ask the platform to help them to value their data set if they are clueless about its worth. Dawex also allows the data holders to specify the conditions and restrictions under which their data can be shared, such as (no) sector-specific limitation; (no) possibility to resell the data; limited geographical scope; (no) purpose limitation. Moreover, Dawex also offers visualisation and sampling tools to data recipients, which allow them to visualise representative samples of the data set generated by algorithms before completing the transaction. This incentivises data recipients to engage in data sharing as it solves the Arrow information paradox, according to which the data recipient does not know the value of the data set until it gets access to it, but if the data set is disclosed then it has in fact acquired it at no cost.[741] Thus, providing the data recipient with a representative sample not only allows it to estimate the value of the whole data set but also benefits the data holder as it preserves the value of the original data set.

739. https://www.dawex.com.
740. *See* Everis, 'Study on data sharing between companies in Europe – Case studies', *supra*, pp. 49-55.
741. K. Arrow, 'Economic Welfare and the Allocation of Resources for Invention', *The Rate and Direction of Inventive Activity: Economic and Social Factors*, National Bureau of Economic Research (ed.), Princeton, Princeton University Press, 1962, pp. 609-626.

3.1.1.6 Data Pools

110. While data marketplaces create a trusted intermediation framework and the necessary technical conditions to enable data sharing and reuse, data pools go a step further as they actively seek to match data holders and data recipients according to their interests and needs.[742] In essence, data pools are a conceptual model of data sharing in which several stakeholders pool their data together, in order to extract more insights and value from the pooled data. This leads to a win-win situation for each of the members of the pool, as they use this data to improve their products or services or to develop new ones. The generic term 'data pool' is used to encompass two data pooling models, namely industrial data platforms and data trusts, which are depicted in Figure 3.6.

Figure 3.6 Data Pools

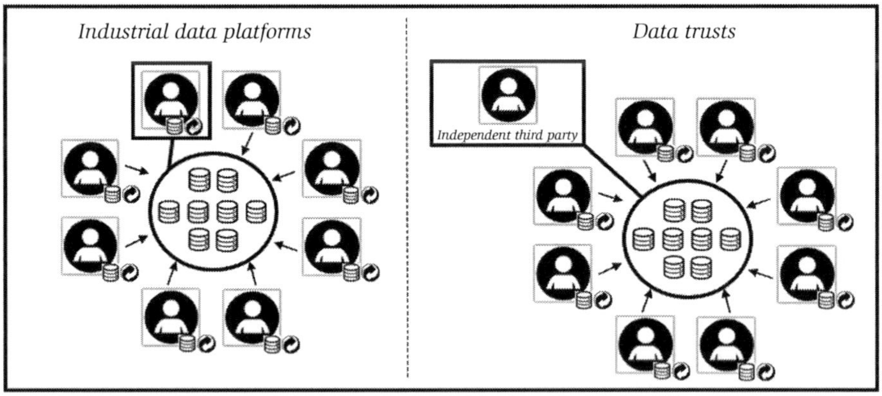

An industrial data platform can be defined as a 'virtual environment enabling the exchange of data among different companies through a shared reference architecture, common governance rules and within a secure business ecosystem'.[743] While these industrial data platforms could, in principle, be open to all, they are often composed of a restricted group of stakeholders who voluntarily join the platform to share some of their data in exchange for the access to some of the other partners' data, in a secure and exclusive environment. They will also usually be sector-specific, though they could also cover different business sectors. Contrary to data marketplaces, the goal is generally not to share data for money, but to share data in exchange for the access to a data pool that is used by each member to enhance its products/services. Such platforms are often managed by a stakeholder that

742. Everis, 'Study on data sharing between companies in Europe – Final report', *supra*, p. 93.

743. *Ibid.*, p. iv.

also participates in the pool. One example is the Skywise platform created by Airbus.[744] Launched in 2017, Skywise is a web-based platform on which Airbus and the airlines that purchased Airbus aircraft share aviation data for free among themselves.[745] This allows Airbus to improve its aircraft and the participating airlines to become more performant and efficient, thanks to the access to the pooled aggregated data. Another example is the cloud-based RIO platform, created by MAN, that pools data from a plurality of stakeholders involved in the transport, freight and logistics sector.[746]

Mostly known in the UK, data trusts, on the other hand, are defined by the Open Data Institute as 'a legal structure that provides independent stewardship of data'.[747] Stewardship is about having control over the access to the data, over the purposes and conditions under which data sharing can occur, and over the determination of the beneficiaries of such sharing. In the data trust model, several stakeholders entrust an independent organisation (the trustee) to decide on how the pooled data should be used and shared. This is the main difference with industrial data platforms, as in the later model, the pool is generally managed by a stakeholder that also participates in the pool. Trustees, on the other hand, do not themselves contribute any data to the pool, but only manage the participants' data, to the benefit of the latter. Naturally, the trustees' margin of manoeuvre is limited as they are bound by the predefined rules of the trust and the previously agreed purpose of the data trust.

3.1.1.7 Open Data Platforms

111. The last conceptual model is the Open Data platform, where the data holder chooses to share its data with anybody who wishes to access it, as illustrated in Figure 3.7. This is generally done for free, but it can also entail a small fee covering the reproduction, provision and dissemination costs.

---

744. https://www.airbus.com/aircraft/support-services/skywise.html.
745. Everis, 'Study on data sharing between companies in Europe – Final report', *supra*, p. 66. *See also* Everis, 'Study on data sharing between companies in Europe – Case studies', *supra*, pp. 56-64.
746. https://rio.cloud/fr/. *See* Everis, 'Study on data sharing between companies in Europe – Case studies', *supra*, pp. 64-71.
747. Open Data Institute, 'Data trusts: Lessons from Three Pilots', 2019, available at https://theodi.org/article/odi-data-trusts-report/, p. 6. For examples of such data trusts, *see* pp. 11 et seq.

Figure 3.7 Open Data

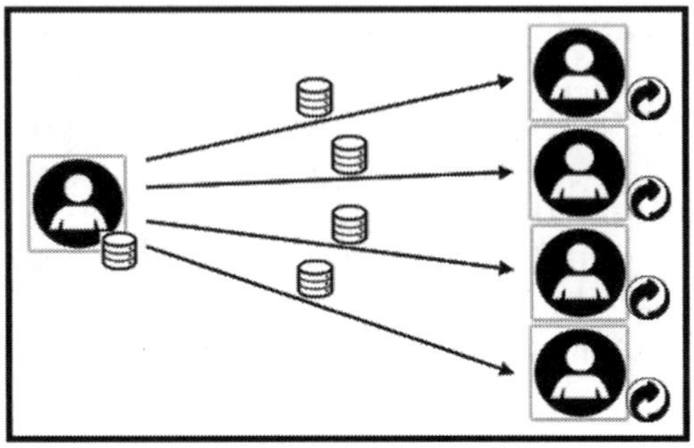

Open Data is mostly used in the G2B context,[748] where public sector data are compiled on Open Data platforms, gathering data from various public sector bodies, such as the national data platforms 'data.gov.be', 'data.gouv.fr', 'data.overheid.nl' or 'data.gov.uk'. Yet, some private undertakings have also started experimenting with this model in a B2B context. For instance, Elering, an electricity and gas system operator from Estonia, has launched the 'Estfeed' data platform, which allows providers of energy applications and consumers to access energy data from various data holders.[749] Another example is the French company Enedis, which has set up a platform providing access to energy distribution and consumption data to recipients active in the (renewable) energy market, or in the smart building/homes sector.[750] Interestingly, both these undertakings started sharing data because of legal obligations and voluntarily went one step further as they realised that Open Data could be a valuable business model.

3.1.2 A Typology of Conceptual Data Sharing Models

112. After having reviewed the most notorious conceptual data sharing models, two main parameters underlying these models emerge, namely whether the sharing is bilateral or multilateral and whether the sharing is intermediated by a platform or not.

3.1.2.1 Bilateral/Multilateral Sharing

113. As data sharing comes into multiple forms and shapes, the number of recipients depends on the conceptual model that is chosen. This parameter is

748. *See* point 3.
749. Everis, 'Study on data sharing between companies in Europe – Case studies', *supra*, pp. 98-103.
750. *Ibid.*, pp. 104-109.

especially important in terms of control, by the data holder, of the shared data. Indeed, if the sharing benefits a single recipient, the control exercised by the data holder on the shared data is much greater than in cases where the data is shared with a large (sometimes even unknown) number of recipients. The greater the number of recipients, the lesser the amount of control on what the data is used for. In this regard, four situations can be identified: single bilateral sharing, multiple bilateral sharing, multilateral sharing with finite users and multilateral sharing with indefinite users.

114. In the case of single bilateral sharing, the sharing takes place in a one-to-one situation. There is a single recipient per act of sharing. This is the situation where the control on the data remains the greatest for the data holder. Bilateral contracts belong to this category, but so does data portability. On the one hand, Article 20.2 of the GDPR, which provides that the data subject has the right to have the personal data transmitted directly from one controller to another, benefits a single recipient, who must nevertheless have obtained the prior consent from the data subject. On the other hand, Article 20.1 of the GDPR, which provides that the data subject has the right to receive the data in a structured, commonly used and machine-readable format and have the right to transmit it to another controller without hindrance from the controller, implies two successive and independent acts of bilateral sharing. The first occurs between the data controller and the data subject, and the second between the data subject and the data recipient.

115. In the case of multiple bilateral sharing, sharing occurs within a network involving multiple actors, but it remains bilateral in nature because each act of sharing within the network requires a form of consent by one of the parties in order to get access to the data. The data holder keeps a strong control over the data as there is still, in this category, a single recipient per act of sharing.

The first model falling within this category is the PIMS. Indeed, though these PIMS create a network involving multiple recipients who get access to (some) of the data subject's data, each individual act of sharing only benefits one recipient. This is because the access, by recipients, to the data subject's data, held by a data holder belonging to the network, is subject to this data subject's consent. Therefore, each act of consent (for instance, to port the data from firm A to firm B) represents an isolated act of sharing, within a wider network, and only benefits a single recipient.

The second model falling within this category is the data clearing house. This is true for both the gateway and the network hub sub-models identified above. In the gateway model, the clearing house acts as the checkpoint through which all recipients have to go in order to access a single database. Thus, even though the clearing house model involves multiple actors (for instance, all the stakeholders having an interest in accessing vehicle data), each individual act of sharing is bilateral and only benefits a single recipient, as the clearing house has to authorise each and every one of them. Similarly, in the network hub model, the data clearing house is the hub of a network involving various data holders and recipients and is at the core of each interaction between two peers of the network. Once again, though multiple actors participate in the network, each individual act of sharing is bilateral and only benefits a single recipient, as the clearing house has to authorise each of them. For instance, though all the Belgian SSIs participate in the CBSS ecosystem, each access request made by one institution to another institution's data requires a prior approval and only benefits a single recipient.

The third model falling within this category is the data marketplace. Here, the third party managing the marketplace provides data holders/data recipients with a platform offering multiple potential buyers/sellers. Yet, each act of data sharing is bilateral, as it is subject to the data holder's approval and only benefits a single recipient.

116. In the case of multilateral sharing with finite users, the data is shared with multiple well-identified recipients. The data holder retains less control over the data as it is shared with a larger number of recipients, but still retains some control as these recipients are, in principle, known in advance. This is typically the case for data pools. Indeed, in both the industrial data platform and the data trust models, the data holders contribute data to the pool, which will benefit multiple recipients, namely all the other participants to the data pool. For instance, when Airbus feeds a data set to its 'Skywise' platform, all the airlines that participate in this data pool get access to this data set. The sharing thus benefits a predetermined and finite number of recipients, i.e., all the members of the pool.

117. In the case of multilateral sharing with indefinite users, the data is shared with an indefinite number of recipients. The 'unknown' factor is what distinguishes this category from the 'multilateral sharing with finite users' category, as in the latter case, the number of recipients is predetermined and finite. The only model falling within this category is the Open Data platform model. Indeed, making the data available in Open Data implies that it can be accessed by anyone. By uploading its data on the platform, the data holder signals that any recipient can access it. The sharing thus benefits an indefinite number of recipients.

3.1.2.2 Intermediated/Non-intermediated Sharing

118. The second main parameter is whether these conceptual data sharing models are intermediated or not. A model is intermediated when the sharing occurs, thanks to a platform that has been set to enable the large-scale and systematic exchange of the data between multiple actors, by providing them with the necessary technical infrastructure for this exchange and by lowering transaction costs.[751]

In fact, only the bilateral contracts and data portability models are non-intermediated. All the other models imply some form of intermediation. Indeed, the Open Data model is usually intermediated by a passive third party (the government having set up the Open Data platform accessible to all) on which the data holder uploads its data, allowing an unlimited number of data recipients to access it. The PIMS model is intermediated by an active third party, as it implies the creation of a personal data platform, from which the access to the data subject's data is managed by the data subject herself or by a trusted third party. Similarly, in the data clearing house model, the clearing house can be considered as a platform through which every access request has to pass. Data marketplaces obviously also qualify as such platforms, whose goal is to match data holders and data suppliers and to technically enable data sharing. Finally, data pools are also intermediated by an active third party that controls the access to the pooled data, whether this platform is managed by one of the participants of the pool (industrial data platforms) or by an independent third party (data trusts).

119. This intermediation parameter is also important because, when dealing with intermediation platforms, it is crucial to distinguish whether the undertaking that set up this intermediation platform also uses the data in order to improve its own business, or whether it solely acts as an intermediate third party that does not make use of the data shared on its platform, but rather acts as a mere sharing facilitator. Indeed, if the sharing platform has been set up by an undertaking which also uses the data, there is a risk that the platform owner might integrate third-party data and, if this leads to a lock-in situation, this might entail a risk for competition.[752] This probably explains why, in its proposal for a Data Governance Act, the European Commission included a provision precluding trusted data intermediaries from using the data, obtained through the operation of an intermediation service, for other purposes than to put them at the disposal of data recipients.[753]

When looking at the outlined data sharing models, it appears that platform owners generally solely act as intermediate third parties not making use of the data in the PIMS, data clearing house, data marketplace, data trust

751. H. Richter and P. Slowinski, 'The Data Sharing Economy: On the Emergence of New Intermediaries', *International Review of Intellectual Property and Competition Law*, 2019, Vol. 50(1), pp. 9-10. *See also* B. Martens, et al., 'Business to Business Data Sharing', *supra*, pp. 25-27.

752. H. Richter and P. Slowinski, 'The Data Sharing Economy: On the Emergence of New Intermediaries', *supra*, p. 15.

753. *See* Article 11.1 of the Proposal for a Regulation of the European Parliament and of the Council on European data governance (Data Governance Act), 25 November 2020, COM(2020) 767 final.

and Open Data platform models. On the contrary, in the industrial data platform model, platform owners not only set up the intermediation platform but also use the data themselves.

120. It is also useful to discuss whether the data sharing model is open or closed. For intermediated data sharing models relying on platforms, the question is whether the platform is open to new participants.[754] A platform is closed if access to it is restricted to a limited number of participants and no other participant can join it in any case whatsoever. A platform is open if the access is open to any party wishing to join it. Having an open platform can imply that some conditions have to be met in order to get access to it. Rather, the open nature comes from the fact that any party is free to meet those conditions. For clarity purposes, it is distinguished below between platforms that are open, provided that some conditions are met, and platforms that are completely open.

Data clearing house-network hub models are generally closed as they are limited to a strict category of participants. For instance, only the Belgian SSIs can participate in the Belgian's CBSS. The data pools (industrial data platforms and data trusts) in which only a strict category of participants is allowed will also generally be considered as closed. This is the case of the 'Skywise' platform, which can only be accessed by Airbus and the airlines having purchased Airbus aircraft.

The PIMS model is open provided that some conditions are met, as any recipient may get access to the platform, provided that it has obtained the data subject's consent and that it respects the other provisions of the GDPR. Moreover, while the data pools (industrial data platforms and data trusts) will generally be closed, some of them might be open if any third party can join the pool. This openness will however often be subject to the fulfilment of some conditions.

By nature, data marketplaces are completely open as their success relies on having as many data holders and data recipients on the platform as possible, in order to generate network effects. Similarly, data clearing house-gateway models are open as any third party is free to file a request to the clearing house in order to get access to the data holder's data. Finally, by essence, Open Data platforms are necessarily completely open, as the aim is to make the data uploaded on the platform available to as many recipients as possible.

As far as the non-intermediated models are concerned, bilateral contracts are completely open because, in principle, any two parties are free to conclude such a contract. Similarly to PIMS, data portability is open provided that some conditions are met, as any data subject and/or data recipient is entitled to rely on Article 20 of the GDPR, provided that this

754. H. Richter and P. Slowinski, 'The Data Sharing Economy: On the Emergence of New Intermediaries', *supra*, pp. 11-12.

provision's conditions are met and that the other provisions of the GDPR are respected.

3.1.2.3 Summary

121. In sum, the conceptual data sharing models reviewed above can be classified into four groups, on the basis of these two main parameters, as illustrated in Figure 3.8. The first group is made of the bilateral contracts and the data portability models, which are single bilateral and non-intermediated. The second group is made of the PIMS, data clearing houses and data marketplace models, which are multiple bilateral and actively intermediated. The third group is made of data pools, which are multilateral for finite users and actively intermediated. The fourth group is made of Open Data platforms, which are multilateral for indefinite users and passively intermediated.

Figure 3.8 Typology of Main Data Sharing Models

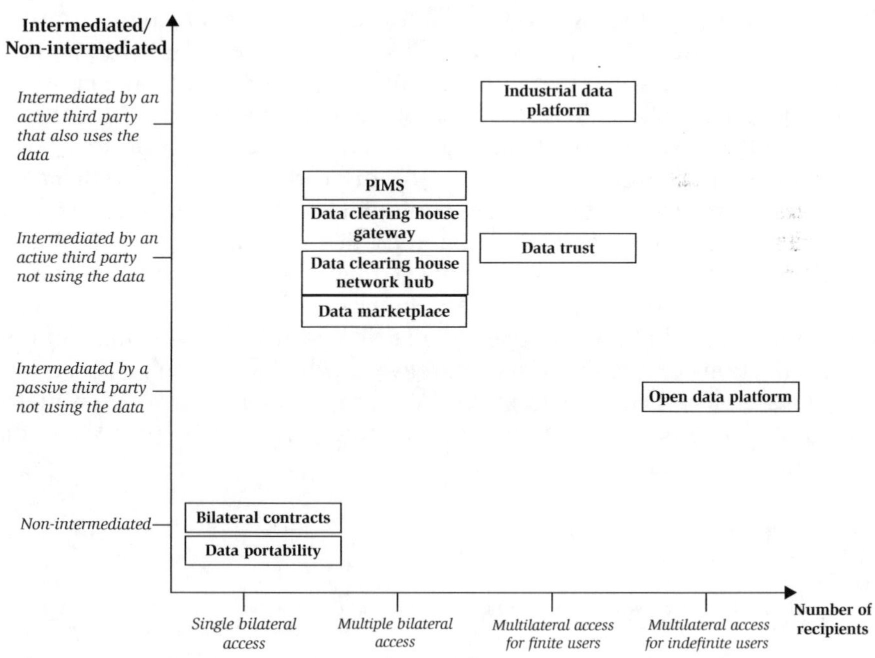

3.1.3 The Typology in the European Legal Framework

122. After having suggested a typology of conceptual data sharing models, it is interesting to briefly depict how the European legal framework approaches these models. In fact, it is striking to observe that the European legislator favours certain models when it comes to adopting binding legislations. On the one hand, for B2B data sharing, the European legislator favours (forms of) data portability models. Indeed, four recent legal instruments rely on (forms of) this conceptual data sharing model.[755] On the other hand, for G2B data sharing, the European legislator favours Open Data models.[756]

123. Referring to the first typology parameter ('Number of recipients'), the European legal framework seems to favour the two 'extreme' categories ('Single bilateral sharing' and 'Multilateral sharing with indefinite users') while neglecting to consider the middle categories ('Multiple bilateral sharing' and 'Multilateral sharing with finite users'). Yet, numerous valuable conceptual data sharing models are located in these middle categories (PIMS, data clearing houses, data marketplaces, data pools) and these could be relevant options as well. Nevertheless, these other types of conceptual data sharing models are mentioned in soft law instruments, such as the European Commission's 'Guidance on sharing private sector data in the European data economy', which underlines that data sharing models may be bilateral or be concluded between multiple parties and which mentions the data marketplace and the data pools models.[757] Moreover, it is apparent from the Commission's *Strategy for data* that it is starting to focus on PIMS and data pools. Indeed, it indicated that it would support the development and roll-out of 'Personal data spaces' in order to empower data subjects by strengthening the control they exercise on their data,[758] and that one of its priorities would be to create an enabling legislative framework for the governance of common European data spaces (data pools), in order to facilitate cross-border data use and to foster standardisation activities and data interoperability.[759] These European data spaces should lead to the availability of large pools of data in strategic economic sectors and domains of public interest,[760] which could be organised in a centralised or distributed way. In fact, the Commission's reflections expressed in its *Strategy for data* have been integrated into a proposal for a Data Governance Act that notably aims at promoting *voluntary* data sharing services by intermediaries through PIMS, data marketplaces and data pools.[761]

---

755. *See* Part II, Chapter 4, Sections 4.1 and 4.2.
756. *See* point 3.
757. Commission Staff Working Document establishing a guidance on sharing private sector data in the European data economy accompanying the Communication '*Towards a Common European Data Space*', Brussels, 25 April 2018, SWD(2018) 125 final, pp. 5-6.
758. Communication from the Commission to the European Parliament, the Council, the European Economic and Social Committee and the Committee of the Regions, '*A European Strategy for Data*', 19 February 2020, COM(2020) 66, p. 20.
759. *Ibid.*, p. 12.
760. *Ibid.*, p. 21. These strategic economic sectors and domains of public interest are listed in the Appendix the 'European strategy for data' (*see* pp. 26-34).
761. *See* the Proposal for a Data Governance Act.

Referring to the second typology parameter (intermediated/non-intermediated), the European legal framework focuses on non-intermediated data sharing models (data portability) and on models intermediated by a passive third party (open data), and somewhat overlooks models intermediated by an active third party. However, as outlined above, the European Commission included in its proposal for a Data Governance Act a provision precluding trusted data intermediaries from using the data, obtained through the operation of an intermediation service, for other purposes than to put them at the disposal of data recipients.[762] Moreover, the Commission has announced in its *Strategy for data* that it would update its Horizontal Cooperation Guidelines[763] in order to provide more guidance on the compatibility of data pooling agreements with EU competition law.[764] Indeed, *voluntary data sharing*, notably through data pooling, could entail competition problems, as it might lead to 'collusion through the exchange of commercially sensitive information among competitors', which is prohibited by Article 101 of the Treaty on the functioning of the European Union[765] (hereinafter 'TFEU').[766] This will be further detailed below.[767]

3.2 TWO DISTINCT CATEGORIES OF COMPULSORY B2B DATA SHARING INITIATIVES

124. Moving away from the conceptual models of data sharing presented in Section 3.1, which focused on how *voluntary data sharing* usually occurs in practice, this Section will take a more abstract approach, by focusing on the underlying objectives pursued by *compulsory B2B data sharing initiatives*.

As outlined in Chapter 2, while the debates at the European level usually focus on economic objectives,[768] societal objectives could also be pursued through the imposition of compulsory B2B data sharing.[769] Furthermore, compulsory data sharing is also increasingly presented as a way to

762. *See* Article 11.1 of the Proposal for a Data Governance Act.
763. Communication from the Commission, Guidelines on the applicability of Article 101 of the Treaty on the Functioning of the European Union to horizontal co-operation agreements, 14 January 2011, 2011/C 11/01.
764. Communication from the Commission, '*A European Strategy for Data*', *supra*, p. 14.
765. Treaty on the functioning of the European Union, *OJ C 326/47*, 26 October 2012.
766. B. Martens, et al., 'Business to Business Data Sharing', *supra*, p. 24.
767. *See* Part III, Chapter 6, Section 6.4.4.
768. *See* Part I, Chapter 2, Section 2.2. *See also* Communication from the Commission, '*A European Strategy for Data*', *supra*, pp. 3, 5, 8 and 14; Communication from the Commission, '*Shaping Europe's Digital Future*', *supra*, p. 8.
769. *See* Part I, Chapter 2, Section 2.3.1. *See also* Communication from the Commission, '*A European Strategy for Data*', *supra*, p. 3. *See also* J. Drexl, 'Data Access and Control in the Era of Connected Devices', *supra*, pp. 6-8; P. Picht, 'Towards an Access Regime for Mobility Data', *supra*, p. 942.

'empower' individuals.[770] Considering these distinct, but possibly also complementary, objectives leads to the identification of two main categories of *compulsory B2B data sharing initiatives,* namely *empowerment initiatives imposing B2B data sharing*, on the one hand, and *economic or societal initiatives imposing B2B data sharing*, on the other hand.

3.2.1 'Empowerment' Initiatives Imposing B2B Data Sharing

125. *Empowerment initiatives imposing B2B data sharing* aim to give more control to individuals on 'their' data.[771] As will be outlined in Part II, these empowerment initiatives can pursue two different types of sub-objectives, namely allowing the exercise of fundamental rights, such as the right to personal data protection and informational self-determination, on the one hand,[772] or addressing specific market failures, on the other hand.[773] A common point between these two types of empowerment initiatives, which explains why their analysis is combined in Part II, is that they are based on the idea that the best way to achieve the objective pursued is to give more control to the individuals on 'their' data, and that the solution thus resides in the sharing of individual-level data. Accordingly, they are mostly built as (forms of) portability rights, of which the right to personal data portability, enshrined in Article 20 of the GDPR, is the prime example.[774] Reverting to the above-suggested typology of conceptual data sharing models and to the European legal framework's approach of these models,[775] it thus becomes apparent that, by focusing on data portability models, and more recently on PIMS models of data sharing,[776] the European legislator has in fact put the accent on these *empowerment initiatives imposing B2B data sharing.*[777]

As hinted above, a core difference with the second category of initiatives that will be presented below, other than the types of objectives pursued, is that the amount of data transferred in this first category is relatively small, as it is limited to the data relating to the specific individual at hand. Naturally, the framework, as a whole, that is created by these initiatives can potentially lead to the sharing of data pertaining to a very large number of individuals, but each act of sharing will relate to a specific

770. *See* Part I, Chapter 2, Section 2.3.2. *See also* Communication from the Commission, '*A European Strategy for Data*', *supra*, p. 10. *See also* pp. 20-21.
771. *See* Part I, Chapter 2, Section 2.3.2.
772. *See* Part II, Chapter 4, Section 4.1.
773. *See* Part II, Chapter 4, Section 4.2.
774. *See* Part II, Chapter 4, Section 4.1.
775. *See* Part I, Chapter 3, Section 3.1.
776. *See* point 172.
777. Communication from the Commission, '*A European Strategy for Data*', *supra*, p. 20. *See also* Recital 23 and Article 9.1.b) of the Proposal for a Data Governance Act. *See also* p. 7 of its 'Explanatory memorandum'.

individual. For instance, a broad use of Article 20 of the GDPR could lead to a situation where one million users request a porting of their data from firm A to firm B. Yet, this would require one million specific and separate acts of sharing, rather than a single act of sharing covering the data of the one million users as a whole. In sum, for *empowerment initiatives imposing B2B data sharing*, a framework, potentially applicable to numerous individuals, is created to facilitate the transfer of individual-level data. Accordingly, while these 'empowerment' initiatives mostly benefit a specific individual, they also have indirect benefits for third parties (such as (potential) competitors of the data holder), which is not surprising as some of these initiatives precisely aim at remedying specific market failures through the mean of individual empowerment.[778]

3.2.2 Economic or Societal Initiatives Imposing B2B Data Sharing

126. The second category of B2B data sharing initiatives I analyse is those pursuing economic or societal objectives.[779] An important common point between these two subtypes of initiatives, which explains why they are analysed together in Part III, is that the focus of these initiatives is not set on the individuals, but rather on broader economic or societal considerations that go beyond individual interests. Accordingly, what will be shared are larger amounts of (aggregated) personal data pertaining to multiple individuals and/or non-personal data, rather than smaller quantities of data linked to a specific individual.

For instance, economic initiatives imposing B2B data sharing, which aim to remedy market failures deriving from a lack of data sharing,[780] would allow a single act of sharing from firm A to firm B, covering the data of the one million users as a whole (likely in an aggregated form), rather than one million separate acts of sharing, each pertaining to a specific individual. The objective would notably be to provide competitors with a sufficient amount of data that allows them to compete, in order to avoid the 'cold start problem'.[781] These initiatives thus mostly benefit third parties, but they also

778. *See* Part II, Chapter 4, Section 4.2.
779. *See* Part III.
780. On these market failures *see* Part I, Chapter 2, Section 2.2.3.3.
781. To be able to offer a quality service, a firm needs a certain amount of data. To collect this data, it needs to attract customers, but the customers will not use its service if the quality is insufficient. Hence the cold start problem, because if the firm does not have enough data to start with, it will be unable to reach a minimal level of quality and will be unable to attract customers. This is also sometimes referred to as the 'chicken and egg problem'. *See*, *inter alia*, V. Fast, D. Schnurr and M. Wohlfarth, 'Data-Driven Market Power: An Overview of Economic Benefits and Competitive Advantages from Big Data Use', July 2019, available at https://ssrn.com/abstract=3427087, p. 10; J. Krämer, P. Senellart and A. de Streel, 'Making Data Portability More Effective for the Digital Economy', *CERRE*

have indirect benefits for the individuals' whose data are shared (usually in an aggregated way). In practice, this is mainly tackled through competition law,[782] with the exception of a sector-specific data sharing legislation in the automotive sector.[783,784]

The compulsory sharing of larger amounts of (aggregated) personal data pertaining to multiple individuals and/or non-personal data could also be justified by broader societal objectives, as highlighted above.[785] An example of such legislation is the Finnish Act on the Secondary Use of Health and Social Data.[786]

127. For this second category of initiatives, it has been opted not to make a distinction between the initiatives pertaining to personal and non-personal data because, as outlined above, the boundary between these two concepts is porous and often difficult to establish in practice,[787] and because what matters are, in fact, the objectives pursued by these categories of compulsory B2B data sharing initiatives. Accordingly, I suggest, for this second category of compulsory B2B data sharing initiatives, to adopt an alternative data typology,[788] following a common holistic approach for both personal and non-personal data,[789] which will nevertheless take the personal data considerations into account when relevant.[790]

128. In conclusion, because these two categories of compulsory B2B data sharing initiatives pursue different objectives, they will be addressed separately. This key distinction will therefore structure the remainder of my contribution. Accordingly, Part II will be dedicated to *Empowerment initiatives imposing B2B data sharing*, while Part III will be dedicated to *Economic or societal initiatives imposing B2B data sharing*.

Report, 2020, available at https://www.cerre.eu/publications/report-making-data-portability-more-effective-digital-economy, p. 64.

782. *See* Part III, Chapter 6.

783. Regulation (EU) 715/2007 of the European Parliament and of the Council of 20 June 2007 on type approval of motor vehicles with respect to emissions from light passenger and commercial vehicles (EUR 5 and EUR 6) and on access to vehicle repair and maintenance information, *OJ L 171/1*, 29 June 2007, Articles 6 and 7; Regulation (EU) 2018/858 of the European Parliament and of the Council of 30 May 2018 on the approval and market surveillance of motor vehicles and their trailers, and of systems, components and separate technical units intended for such vehicles, amending Regulations (EC) No. 715/2007 and (EC) No. 595/2009 and repealing Directive 2007/46/EC, *OJ L 151/1*, 14 June 2018. *See* Articles 61-66, 86 and annexes X and XI.

784. *See* Part III, Chapter 8, Section 8.1.1.

785. *See* Part I, Chapter 2, Section 2.3.1 and Part III, Chapter 9.

786. *See* point 93. For more information on this Act, *see* https://stm.fi/en/secondary-use-of-health-and-social-data.

787. *See* Part I, Chapter 1, Section 1.2.

788. *See* Part I, Chapter 1, Section 1.3.

789. *See* point 21.

790. *See* Part III, Chapter 7.

For both of these Parts, the key underlying economic and/or societal balancing exercises will be studied, and, where relevant, it will be questioned whether these balances need to be adapted for data markets, in light of data's characteristics. Some insights will also be formulated on how these balancing exercises can be addressed.

Finally, it must be clarified from the outset that while these two main categories of compulsory B2B data sharing initiatives pursue different objectives, synergies can be found between them, which explains why they are both addressed here. Indeed, *empowerment initiatives* will only provide more choice for individuals, and/or more control on their data, if a sufficient number of alternatives to their current situation are available. Accordingly, even if the main objective of these initiatives is to empower individuals, this entails the pursuit of a secondary objective, which could be qualified as economic, namely ensuring the presence of a sufficient number of viable competitors on the markets at hand. Reversely, although *economic initiatives* mainly aim at addressing market failures and at fostering more competition, this will have as a secondary consequence to empower individuals, as they will be offered more alternatives to choose from. The same goes for *societal initiatives*, which mainly aim to pursue general purpose goals (healthier environment, smoother mobility, increased access to healthcare, etc.), but which, in doing so, indirectly benefit individuals as well.

Part II

'Empowerment' Initiatives Imposing B2B Data Sharing

129. Part II will be dedicated to *empowerment initiatives imposing B2B data sharing*. As mentioned above, these empowerment initiatives can pursue two different types of sub-objectives.

On the one hand, empowerment initiatives can pursue the objective of allowing the exercise of fundamental rights, such as the right to personal data protection and informational self-determination.[791] The core instrument, adopted at the European level, to pursue this goal is naturally the GDPR,[792] which has replaced the previous Directive 95/46,[793] and which aims to frame the use of personal data in the European internal market. In order to do so, this instrument aims at reaching an equilibrium between the fundamental right of the protection of personal data and the fundamental right of the freedom to conduct a business.[794] Indeed, technological developments and globalisation have transformed the economy, and the GDPR aims at facilitating the free flow of personal data within the EU in order to support the development of the digital economy across the internal market while ensuring a high level of personal data protection and creating the necessary trust.[795] To do so, the GDPR grants to the data subjects[796] a certain number of rights,[797] among which the right to personal data portability, which

791. *See* Part II, Chapter 4, Section 4.1.
792. Regulation (EU) 2016/679 of the European Parliament and of the Council of 27 April 2016 on the protection of natural persons with regard to the processing of personal data and on the free movement of such data, and repealing Directive 95/46/EC (General Data Protection Regulation), *OJ L 119*, 4 May 2016.
793. Directive 95/46/EC of the European Parliament and of the Council of 24 October 1995 on the protection of individuals with regard to the processing of personal data and on the free movement of such data, *OJ L 281*, 23 November 1995.
794. Respectively, Articles 8 and 16 of the Charter of Fundamental Rights of the European Union, *OJ C 326*, 26 October 2012. *See* Recital 4 of the GDPR.
795. Recitals 6 and 7 of the GDPR.
796. 'Any identified or identifiable natural person' (Article 4.1 of the GDPR).
797. Articles 13-22 of the GDPR. *See* point 98.

improves the power of control that the data subjects have on 'their' personal data, and which will be further analysed below.[798]

This 'power of control' that data subjects can (re)claim on their data is fundamental as it will facilitate the exercise of their fundamental rights, as increased access to information will improve their decision-making and will allow them to take fundamental decisions about all aspects of their life.[799] For instance, they can better understand how they are profiled and the influence this has on the media content or news feed that are presented to them, which may notably influence their electoral choices.

Importantly, while the GDPR gives control to the data subjects on 'their' data, it does not, by any means, confer any 'property' rights over personal data.[800] Indeed, although such data are often used as a 'counterpart' in exchange for the use of a 'free' service (such as social networks, video platforms or search engines), the fact remains that the right to personal data protection is a fundamental right that cannot be transferred.[801] However, this debate between the legal principles and the reality of the situation in practice remains lively.[802]

130. On the other hand, empowerment initiatives can be adopted to address specific market failures.[803] The underlying idea of these initiatives is that by giving more control to individuals on 'their' data, this will allow them to multi-home or to switch more easily between service providers as their searching and switching costs are reduced, and this should reduce the market failures deriving from consumer inertia and lock-in effects.[804] Indeed, the aim is to give more autonomy to the individuals by allowing them to optimise the use of their resources, as illustrated by the UK's Open Banking and Smart Data initiatives, which will be further detailed below.[805] In turn, this should facilitate entry and should foster competition on the targeted

---

798. *See* Part II, Chapter 4, Section 4.1.
799. *See* points 39 and 97.
800. For a broader discussion on the 'property of data', *see supra* Part I, Chapter 2, Section 2.2.2.
801. *See* point 62.
802. Communication from the Commission to the European Parliament, the Council, the European Economic and Social Committee and the Committee of the Regions, '*A New Deal for Consumers*', Brussels, 11 April 2018, COM(2018) 183 final, p. 5.
803. *See* Part II, Chapter 4, Section 4.2.
804. *See* point 97.
805. *See* points 161-163 and 169-171. Competition and Markets Authority, 'The Retail Banking Market Investigation Order 2017', 2017, available at https://assets.publis hing.service.gov.uk/media/5893063bed915d06e1000000/retail-bankingmarketinvestigat ionor der-2017.pdf; Competition and Markets Authority, 'Final Approved Roadmap for Open Banking', 14 May 2020, available at https://assets.publishing.service.gov.uk/ government/uploads/system/uploads/attachment_data/file/885537/Notice_of_proposed_ changes_to_the_open_banking_roadmap_-_web_publication_-_cma_gov_uk_---_May_ 2020_-.pdf; HM Government, 'Smart Data: Putting consumers in control of their data and enabling innovation', June 2019,

markets, which should lead to better services, more choice and lower prices for the individuals.

131. Chapter 4 will be dedicated to the main *empowerment initiatives imposing B2B data sharing*, which are, to a large extent, built around (some forms of) data portability rights, whether they aim to allow the exercise of fundamental rights or to address specific market failures.[806] This chapter will also discuss more recent trends, such as the request to introduce a 'continuous portability' right,[807] and the adoption of legislations aiming at empowering specific (small) business users.[808] **Chapter 5** will then focus on the fundamental balancing exercises entailed by such *empowerment initiatives*.

available at https://www.gov.uk/government/consultations/smart-data-putting-consumers-in-control-of-their-data-and-enabling-innovation.

806. *See* Part II, Chapter 4, Sections 4.1 and 4.2.

807. *See* Part II, Chapter 4, Section 4.3.

808. *See* Part II, Chapter 4, Section 4.4.

Chapter 4

Main 'Empowerment' Initiatives Imposing B2B Data Sharing and Recent Trends

132. The most notorious empowerment initiative imposing B2B data sharing is arguably the personal data portability right enshrined in Article 20 of the GDPR.[809] As will be outlined below, this initiative pursues the objective of allowing the exercise of the fundamental rights to personal data protection and to informational self-determination (Section 4.1).

However, as outlined above, not all empowerment initiatives pursue such an objective, and in fact, several initiatives have rather been adopted in order to address specific market failures. These are the data retrieval right enshrined in Article 16.4 of the Digital Content Directive,[810] and the data access and use rights granted in the PSD2[811] and in the Electricity Directive[812] (Section 4.2).

Importantly, it must be underlined that the effectiveness of these data sharing initiatives, and their ability to truly empower individuals, which is their primary aim, is being criticised.[813] Accordingly, the growing call for the

---

809. Regulation (EU) 2016/679 of the European Parliament and of the Council of 27 April 2016 on the protection of natural persons with regard to the processing of personal data and on the free movement of such data, and repealing Directive 95/46 (General Data Protection Regulation), *OJ L 119*, 4 May 2016.

810. Directive 2019/770 of the European Parliament and of the Council of 20 May 2019 on certain aspects concerning contracts for the supply of digital content and digital services, *OJ L 136/1*, 22 May 2019.

811. Directive (EU) 2015/2366 of the European Parliament and of the Council of 25 November 2015 on payment services in the internal market, amending Directives 2002/65/EC, 2009/110/EC and 2013/36/EU and Regulation (EU) No. 1093/2010, and repealing Directive 2007/64/EC, *OJ L 337/35*, 23 December 2015.

812. Directive (EU) 2019/944 of the European Parliament and of the Council of 5 June 2019 on common rules for the internal market for electricity and amending Directive 2012/27/EU, *OJ L 158/125*, 14 June 2019.

813. *See* J. Krämer, P. Senellart and A. de Streel, 'Making Data Portability More Effective for the Digital Economy', *CERRE Report*, 2020, available at https://www.cerre.eu/publications/report-making-data-portability-more-effective-digital-economy.

creation of a 'continuous portability' right will also be presented (Section 4.3).[814]

Then, Section 4.4 will make a brief digression about the more recent phenomenon of regulatory initiatives aiming at empowering specific (small) business users. These represent the beginning of a move from individual empowerment towards small businesses empowerment, which fits in a broader context of extending consumer protection (B2C) towards small businesses protection (B2b).

4.1 'EMPOWERMENT' INITIATIVES IMPOSING B2B DATA SHARING IN ORDER TO ALLOW THE EXERCISE OF FUNDAMENTAL RIGHTS: PERSONAL DATA PORTABILITY IN THE GDPR

133. The main instrument adopted by the European legislator in order to empower individuals through data sharing is, without a shadow of a doubt, the personal data portability right enshrined in Article 20 of the GDPR. This subsection will present this right by focusing on its definition and objectives, on its scope and on some considerations pertaining to its exercise.

4.1.1 Definition and Objectives

134. Article 20 of the GDPR provides that:

1. The data subject shall have the right to receive the personal data concerning him or her, which he or she has provided to a controller, in a structured, commonly used and machine-readable format and have the right to transmit those data to another controller without hindrance from the controller to which the personal data have been provided, where:
   (a) the processing is based on consent pursuant to point (a) of Article 6.1 or point (a) of Article 9.2 or on a contract pursuant to point (b) of Article 6.1; and
   (b) the processing is carried out by automated means.
2. In exercising his or her right to data portability pursuant to paragraph 1, the data subject shall have the right to have the personal data transmitted directly from one controller to another, where technically feasible.
3. The exercise of the right referred to in paragraph 1 of this Article shall be without prejudice to Article 17. That right shall not apply

814. *Ibid. See* Part II, Chapter 4, Section 4.3.

to processing necessary for the performance of a task carried out in the public interest or in the exercise of official authority vested in the controller.

4. The right referred to in paragraph 1 shall not adversely affect the rights and freedoms of others.

While this provision has marked the apparition of the concept of 'portability' in the field of personal data protection law, it is worth mentioning that this concept had already existed for several years in electronic communications law.[815] Indeed, phone number portability had been introduced at the end of the 1990s to facilitate the entry of new operators in the electronic communications market, by allowing subscribers to keep their landline (or mobile) telephone number, if they so requested, when changing providers.[816] The aim was thus to empower the consumers, by encouraging them to switch to cheaper providers without having to worry about the hassle of changing phone number and communicating this new phone number to their family, friends, colleagues, etc.

135. In the same vein, the right to personal data portability aims at strengthening 'data subject empowerment', i.e., the power of control that the data subjects have on 'their' personal data,[817] as this right will enable them to move, copy or transmit personal data easily from one IT environment to another.[818] Indeed, it should 'further improve access of individuals to their personal data'.[819] In reality, this 'data subject empowerment' objective is translated into two sub-objectives.

815. *See* Directive 98/61/EC of the European Parliament and of the Council of 24 September 1998 amending Directive 97/33/EC with regard to operator number portability and carrier pre-selection, *OJ L 268/37*, 3 October 1998, Article 1; Directive 2002/22/EC of the European Parliament and of the Council of 7 March 2002 on universal service and users' rights relating to electronic communications networks and services (Universal Service Directive), *OJ L 108/51*, 24 April 2002, Article 30; Directive (EU) 2018/1972 of the European Parliament and of the Council of 11 December 2018 establishing the European Electronic Communications Code, *OJ L 321/36*, 7 December 2018, Article 106.

816. *See* M. Ledger et T. Tombal, 'Le droit à la portabilité dans les textes européens: droits distincts ou mécanisme multi-facettes ?', *R.D.T.I.*, 2018/3, n°72, pp. 26-27.

817. Recital 68 of the GDPR. *See also* Recital 68 of the Position (EU) No. 6/2016 of the Council at first reading with a view to the adoption of a Regulation of the European Parliament and of the Council on the protection of natural persons with regard to the processing of personal data and on the free movement of such data, and repealing Directive 95/46/EC (General Data Protection Regulation, *OJ C 159/1*, 3 May 2016.

818. Article 29 Working Party, *Guidelines on the right to data portability*, WP 242 rev.01, 13 April 2017, p. 4.

819. Proposal for a Regulation of the European Parliament and of the Council on the protection of individuals with regard to the processing of personal data and on the free movement of such data (General Data Protection Regulation), 25 January 2012, COM/2012/011 final, p. 9.

On the one hand, in a strict conception of the notion of 'data subject empowerment', this right to data portability 'represents an opportunity to "re-balance" the relationship between data subject and data controllers', and this, 'by affirming individuals' personal rights and control over the personal data concerning them'.[820] This objective is transversal in the GDPR and goes beyond the right to data portability.[821]

On the other hand, and in a broader conception of the notion of 'data subject empowerment', this right to data portability should make it easier for the data subject to change service providers.[822] This demonstrates the influence that phone number portability has had on personal data portability. In the first version of its guidelines on the right to data portability, the Article 29 Working Party (today the EDPB) even indicated that this was the 'primary aim' of this new right, as it should facilitate the creation of new services, which is perfectly in line with the strategy of the European legislator to create a digital single market.[823] This echoed the statement made by the Council regarding its position at first reading, where it outlined that the right to portability 'also encourages competition amongst controllers'.[824] However, in what seems to be a move to position this right as a fundamental rights empowerment tool, rather than as a tool aiming to address market failures / competition issues,[825] the indication that this constituted the 'primary aim' of the right was deleted in the revised version of the Article 29 Working Party's guidelines of April 2017, which now state that the main objective of this right is to promote 'data subject empowerment' and that the GDPR aims to regulate the processing of personal data, and not to deal with competition law issues.[826]

Nevertheless, the creation of this new right to portability shows the significant impact that the emergence of social networks has had on the reflections leading to the adoption of the GDPR.[827] It reflects the clear desire

820. *Ibid.*
821. L. Somaini, 'The Right to Data Portability and User Control: Ambitions and Limitations', *MediaLaws – Rivista dir. media*, 2018/3, p. 172.
822. Article 29 Working Party, *Guidelines on the right to data portability*, WP 242 rev.01, 13 April 2017, p. 4.
823. Article 29 Working Party, *Guidelines on the right to data portability*, WP 242, 13 December 2016, p. 4.
824. Statement of the Council's reasons: Position (EU) No. 6/2016 of the Council at first reading with a view to the adoption of a Regulation of the European Parliament and of the Council on the protection of natural persons with regard to the processing of personal data and on the free movement of such data, and repealing Directive 95/46/EC (General Data Protection Regulation, *OJ C 159/83*, 3 May 2016, p. 89.
825. *See* Part II, Chapter 4, Section 4.2 for examples of empowerment initiatives aiming to address such market failures / competition issues.
826. Article 29 Working Party, *Guidelines on the right to data portability*, WP 242 rev.01, 13 April 2017, p. 4.
827. D. de Bot, 'De uitvoering van de algemene verordening gegevensbescherming – enkele bemerkingen bij de Belgische context', *Tijdschrift voor Wetgeving*, 2016/3, p. 221.

to prevent the data subjects from being 'locked-in' by Internet giants such as Facebook or Google, by allowing them to port their personal data to a new alternative online service. Indeed, in the absence of such a right, one could imagine that the data subjects might refrain from using such alternative services, as, for instance, re-uploading all the personal data that they have already uploaded on Facebook (personal information, photos, etc.) would be time-consuming.

136. Accordingly, in order to achieve this 'data subject empowerment', the right to data portability allows the data subject to receive (part of) the personal data concerning her that she has provided to a controller.[828] In this sense, the right to data portability is rather a complement to the right to data access provided in Article 15 of the GDPR, allowing the data subjects to manage and reuse personal data themselves, as these data must be provided to them in a structured, commonly used and machine-readable format.[829] The Article 29 Working Party cites, as an example, the hypothesis in which the data subject wishes to extract her contact list from a Webmail application, in order to build a wedding list.[830]

Although this example is instructive, it must be noted that, in practice, this specific situation, in which the data subject would herself wish to manage and reuse her data, without using a service offered by a third party, will rarely occur. Indeed, a large proportion of the data subjects will not have the necessary technical skills to use these data themselves. For example, if a data subject exercises her data portability right towards Google, in order to receive information that she has provided to this firm, this extensive amount of information will be provided to her in HTML, JSON or OPML format. Although such formats are structured, commonly used and machine-readable, the data is likely to be incomprehensible, as it stands, for the data subject. Indeed, it should not be forgotten that 'machine-readable' data will not necessarily be 'understandable' for an ordinary person, as this might require appropriate technical skills. In light of the above, the right to data portability will thus most likely not be used by data subjects simply in order to receive personal data concerning them, but rather in order to transfer this data from one controller (hereinafter the 'data holder') to another (hereinafter the 'recipient'). The right to data portability provides that this should be possible, without hindrance from the data holder.[831] According to the Article 29 Working Party, such hindrance could derive from 'fees asked for delivering data, lack of interoperability or access to a data format or API or

828. Article 20.1 of the GDPR.
829. It should be noted that these format requirements are not identical than for the right to data access, which merely requires the use of a 'commonly used electronic form' (Article 15.3 of the GDPR).
830. Article 29 Working Party, *Guidelines on the right to data portability*, WP 242 rev.01, 13 April 2017, p. 5.
831. Article 20.1 of the GDPR.

the provided format, excessive delay or complexity to retrieve the full dataset, deliberate obfuscation of the dataset, or specific and undue or excessive sectorial standardisation or accreditation demands'.[832]

In this perspective, the right to data portability goes a step further, in that it allows the data subject not only to manage and reuse personal data concerning her but also to share them with a data recipient, active in the same economic sector, or not, as the original data holder.[833] The underlying idea is to strengthen 'data subject empowerment' by avoiding 'lock-in' situations and by fostering 'opportunities for innovation and sharing of personal data between data controllers in a safe and secure manner, under the control of the data subject'.[834] The challenge arising from Article 20.1 of the GDPR is that its use in practice is dependent on whether the data subjects will dedicate time to such data sharing initiatives, and whether they have the technical understanding and storage capacity to port the data on their own system before transferring it themselves to the data recipient.

137. It might be tempting to say that Article 20.2 of the GDPR circumvents this challenge by providing that the data subject shall have the right to have the personal data transmitted directly, without hindrance, from the data holder to a data recipient (e.g., transferring a playlist from iTunes to Spotify). Interestingly, this possibility of direct transfer had not been envisaged on the Commission's original proposal.[835] Indeed, this was introduced by the Parliament's position at first reading, where, in fact, the Parliament had deleted the specific provision pertaining to data portability, but had instead requalified it as a 'right to obtain data' and had grouped it with the data subject's right of access.[836] The specific provision pertaining to the right to data portability was however reinstated by the Council's position at first reading, and contained the wording of the final versions of Articles 20.1 and 20.2.[837]

---

832. Article 29 Working Party, *Guidelines on the right to data portability*, WP 242 rev.01, 13 April 2017, p. 15.
833. *Ibid.*, p. 5.
834. *Ibid.*
835. Article 18 of the Proposal for a Regulation of the European Parliament and of the Council on the protection of individuals with regard to the processing of personal data and on the free movement of such data (General Data Protection Regulation), 25 January 2012, COM/2012/011 final.
836. Article 15.2a of the European Parliament legislative resolution of 12 March 2014 on the proposal for a regulation of the European Parliament and of the Council on the protection of individuals with regard to the processing of personal data and on the free movement of such data (General Data Protection Regulation), 12 March 2014, *OJ C 378/399*, 9 November 2017.
837. Article 20 of the Position (EU) No. 6/2016 of the Council at first reading with a view to the adoption of a Regulation of the European Parliament and of the Council on the protection of natural persons with regard to the processing of personal data and on the free movement of such data, and repealing Directive 95/46/EC (General Data Protection Regulation, *OJ C 159/1*, 3 May 2016).

However, it must be outlined that such direct transfer can only be required by the data subject 'where technically feasible', which means that the original data holder has no obligation to ensure this technical feasibility. While the Article 29 Working Party does not clarify in its guidelines what should be considered as being 'technically feasible', one could interpret this wording as an implicit reference to the notion of interoperability,[838] which is mentioned in Recital 68, but not in Article 20 of the GDPR, so that the data could only be transmitted directly between two interoperable systems.

In this regard, it should be pointed out that Google, Facebook, Microsoft and Twitter contribute, with other actors, to the *Data Transfer Project*, launched in 2017, which aims at creating an open-source platform allowing the direct portability of data between the participating data controllers.[839] Such a platform would, according to the members of the project, foster interoperability and reduce the infrastructure burden for portability. This project relies on three main components, namely 'Data Models', 'Adapters' and 'Task Management Libraries'. More concretely, 'Data Models are the canonical formats that establish a common understanding of how to transfer data. Adapters provide a method for converting each Provider's proprietary data and authentication formats into a form that is usable by the system. Task Management Library provides the plumbing to power the system.'[840] Importantly, however, it must be underlined that while anyone can contribute to the development of this open-source platform, the ability to make use of it requires an authorisation from the Hosting Entities (Google, Facebook, Microsoft or Twitter, depending on the Host Platform, as it is a decentralised model), as they are the ones responsible for granting the API keys that are necessary to access the system.[841] Therefore, this project might not be as open as it seems, as service providers might have to agree to the terms imposed by these powerful Hosting Entities in order to access the platform. Moreover, it cannot be excluded that these Hosting Entities might refuse to give access to the platform to (potential) competitors.[842] Furthermore, it must be outlined that in order to join the platform, the service

---

838. Interoperability is defined as 'the ability of disparate and diverse organisations to interact towards mutually beneficial and agreed common goals, involving the sharing of information and knowledge between the organisations, through the business processes they support, by means of the exchange of data between their respective ICT systems' (Decision 2015/2240 of the European Parliament and of the Council of 25 November 2015 establishing a programme on interoperability solutions and common frameworks for European public administrations, businesses and citizens (ISA2 programme) as a means for modernising the public sector, *OJ L 318/1*, 4 December 2015, Article 2.1).
839. *See* https://datatransferproject.dev/.
840. *See* https://datatransferproject.dev/documentation. For more information, *see* Data Transfer Project, 'White Paper: Data Transfer Project Overview and Fundamentals', 20 July 2018, available at https://datatransferproject.dev/dtp-overview.pdf.
841. *See* Data Transfer Project, 'White Paper: Data Transfer Project Overview and Fundamentals', *supra*, pp. 12-13.
842. On these competition law issues, *see* Part III, Chapter 6.

providers have to agree to a reciprocity obligation, as in order to be able to import data, they also have to allow the export of their own data.[843] Such a reciprocity obligation is not included in the GDPR, and this might deter service providers from joining the platform as they might not want to provide even more data to the large Hosting Entities.

Another project worth mentioning is the *Solid Project*,[844] initiated by Sir Tim Berners-Lee, founder of the internet, which aims at allowing 'linked data' between different data controllers.[845] In short, *Solid* is a 'fully decentralised space for personal information, with data distributed over multiple personal online data stores (pods) located on different hosts, with a mechanism allowing a user to grant third party applications fine-grained access to specific data items on specific pods'.[846] More concretely, a Solid Server hosts one or more Solid Pods, which are fully compartmentalised from one another and have their own data and access rules.[847] Through the use of open, standard formats and of a linked data model, interoperability is insured and data can be shared between Pods.

However, these are stand-alone small-scale initiatives, which are still in development, and, in practice, this direct transmission between the data holders and the data recipients is rarely technically feasible as the former are often not willing to tackle the costly issues of technical interoperability, standardisation and security that would need to be solved in order to make this transfer technically feasible.

4.1.2 Scope of the Right to Data Portability

138. As apparent from the definition of the right to data portability enshrined in Article 20 of the GDPR, its scope is limited to specific categories of personal data processing and to certain specific categories of personal data.

4.1.2.1 Specific Categories of Personal Data Processing

139. Data subjects can only call upon their data portability right for processing carried out by automated means, and which are based either on the data subjects' consent or are necessary for the performance of a contract.[848] There is thus no general right to data portability since this right

843. *See* Data Transfer Project, 'White Paper: Data Transfer Project Overview and Fundamentals', *supra*, p. 17.
844. *See* https://solidproject.org/.
845. J. Krämer, P. Senellart and A. de Streel, 'Making Data Portability More Effective for the Digital Economy', *supra*, p. 14.
846. *Ibid.*, p. 46.
847. *See* https://solidproject.org/about.
848. Article 20.1 of the GDPR.

does not apply to processing operations necessary for the performance of a task in the public interest vested in the controller, nor to processing operations necessary for the compliance with a legal obligation to which the controller is subject.[849] For instance, a public administration will have no obligation to port personal data that it has collected for its public service mission,[850] and a financial institution will have no obligation to respond to a portability request relating to personal data that has been collected in the context of the compliance with its legal obligation to fight money laundering.[851] Similarly, data subjects will not be able to port data that is processed by the data controller on the basis of 'legitimate interests'.[852] Yet, this can be highly problematic as this legal basis is a 'fall-back' option that, in fact, is widely used by data controllers.

However, even for these categories of processing not covered by the data portability right, the Article 29 Working Party calls on controllers to implement best practices to respond quickly to potential requests for portability, even if they have no obligation to comply with them, citing as an example the creation of a public e-service offered by the tax administrations and allowing the data subjects to easily download all their tax forms.[853]

4.1.2.2 Specific Categories of Personal Data

140. Additionally, data subjects only have the right to receive the personal data concerning them, which they have 'provided' to a controller.[854] The GDPR does not provide further clarification in its Article 20 or in its recitals on the categories of personal data in question, and in particular on what is meant by personal data 'provided' by the data subject. However, the Article 29 Working Party's guidelines shed light on the matter.

4.1.2.2.1 Personal Data Concerning the Data Subject

141. Only personal data are subject to this right to portability, excluding, de facto, non-personal data as well as personal data that have been anonymised.[855] On the contrary, personal data that have simply been

849. Article 20.3 and Recital 68 of the GDPR.
850. This limitation of the scope of the portability right was included in order to avoid burdening public bodies. *See* Opinion of the Committee of the Regions on 'Data protection package', 18 December 2012, *OJ C 391/127*, p. 129.
851. Article 29 Working Party, *Guidelines on the right to data portability*, WP 242 rev.01, 13 April 2017, p. 8.
852. Article 6.1.f) of the GDPR.
853. Article 29 Working Party, *Guidelines on the right to data portability*, WP 242 rev.01, 13 April 2017, p. 8.
854. Article 20.1 of the GDPR.
855. *See* definition at footnote 116.

pseudonymised[856] remain personal data and will be subject to this right to portability.

Yet, the expression 'personal data concerning them' should not be interpreted too strictly.[857] Namely, this expression should not be understood as limiting the scope of the data portability right to personal data 'exclusively pertaining to the data subject', as, in a broad number of cases, personal data will pertain not only to a single individual but also to several data subjects. For example, the Article 29 Working Party refers to the case of telephone records or other interpersonal messaging systems that may include information about third parties with whom the data subject has been in contact. According to the Article 29 Working Party, while it is true that these records may thus contain personal data relating to third parties, this should not be invoked by the data holder in order to refuse to comply with the request for the portability of these records made by the data subject. This echoes one of the key limits of 'empowerment' initiatives imposing B2B data sharing, namely that they must consider and comply with the other data subjects' right to personal data protection.[858] This will be further detailed below.[859]

4.1.2.2.2 Personal Data 'Provided' by the Data Subject

142. The scope of the data portability right is also limited to personal data 'provided' by the data subject.[860] In this regard, the Article 29 Working Party identifies three categories of personal data and considers that only the first two should be considered as data 'provided' by the data subject.[861] These categories have already been outlined above (actively provided, observed and inferred/derived data) and have been integrated into my proposed data typology.[862]

The first category of personal data covered by the right to data portability is 'data actively and knowingly provided by the data subject'.[863] This includes information provided by the data subject in a registration form (email address, user name, age, etc.) or posts on social media. On the contrary, data that has been provided by a third party (e.g., the comments or likes made by a friend on a social media picture) should arguably not be covered, as they are not 'provided by the data subject', but by someone else.

856. Article 4.5 of the GDPR.
857. Article 29 Working Party, *Guidelines on the right to data portability*, WP 242 rev.01, 13 April 2017, p. 9.
858. *Ibid.*, pp. 11-12.
859. *See* Part II, Chapter 5, Section 5.1.2.
860. Article 20.1 of the GDPR.
861. Article 29 Working Party, *Guidelines on the right to data portability*, WP 242 rev.01, 13 April 2017, pp. 9-11.
862. *See* Part I, Chapter 1, Sections 1.2 and 1.3.
863. *See* point 17. Article 29 Working Party, *Guidelines on the right to data portability*, WP 242 rev.01, 13 April 2017, p. 10.

The second category of personal data covered by the right to data portability is 'observed data provided by the data subject by virtue of the use of the service or the device'.[864] Examples of observed data include the data subject's search or web history, or location data generated by the use of a product or service offered by the data controller. This second category of personal data should, according to the Article 29 Working Party, also be considered as being 'provided' by the data subject.[865] However, this is criticised by some members of the European Commission, who consider that this goes beyond what has been envisaged by the European legislator.[866] On the contrary, some argue that there is a strong rationale to include observed data in the scope of the data portability right, as they are 'a valuable input for data-intensive business models in the digital economy'.[867] Indeed, as the markets for several key services (search, social networks) are highly concentrated, only a few firms can observe the individuals' activity across the web, and, as a consequence, 'observed data is not ubiquitously available, and it is also usually neither feasible nor socially desirable to duplicate the collection of the same observed data'.[868]

It should also be pointed out that, while I made a further distinction between first-party and third-party observed data,[869] such a distinction is not made by the Article 29 Working Party. Yet, this distinction is important as the right to data portability might not apply to both types of observed data. In fact, the Article 29 Working Party only seems to consider 'first party observed data', namely data collected *directly* by the controller from its users (e.g., the number of steps walked in a day by the owner of a FitBit bracelet).[870] For these types of data, as they are *directly* collected from the data subject by the controller, it does indeed make sense to consider them as 'provided' by the data subject. However, third-party observed data, on the other hand, are data *indirectly* collected from the users by the data collector, via technologies such as 'cookies' installed on the product or service of a third party (e.g., the data collected by Facebook on third-party websites that

864. *Ibid.*
865. *Ibid.*
866. D. Meyer, 'European Commission Experts Uneasy over WP29 Data Portability Interpretation', 25 April 2017, available at https://iapp.org/news/a/european-commission-experts-uneasy-over-wp29-data-portability-interpretation-1/.
867. J. Krämer, P. Senellart and A. de Streel, 'Making Data Portability More Effective for the Digital Economy', *supra*, p. 55. *See also* R. Feasey and A. de Streel, 'Data Sharing for Digital Market Contestability', *supra*, p. 16.
868. J. Krämer, P. Senellart and A. de Streel, 'Making Data Portability More Effective for the Digital Economy', *supra*, p. 53.
869. *See* Part I, Chapter 1, Section 1.3.
870. OECD, *Consumer Data Rights and Competition – Background note*, June 2020, DAF/COMP(2020)1, available at http://www.oecd.org/daf/competition/consumer-data-rights-and-competition.htm, p. 16.

embed the opportunity to 'like' a content on that website).[871] For these types of data, there is an uncertainty as to whether they should also be considered as being 'provided' by the data subject. Indeed, Article 20.1 of the GDPR seems to solely envisage the possibility for the data subject to exercise her portability right against controllers to which she *directly* provided data.[872] Because third-party observed data are *indirectly* collected by the controller, they might thus fall outside of the scope of the portability right, unless an extensive interpretation of the text is made.[873] This would merit to be clarified, notably because the arguments mentioned in the previous paragraph would also support the inclusion of these third-party observed data in the scope of the data portability right.

The third category of personal data, namely 'inferred data and derived data', will, on the other hand, not be covered by the data portability right.[874] These are essentially a second generation of data, such as user profiles or health recommendations, which are created by the data controller, thanks to the analysis of the data 'provided' (actively or observed) by the data subject.[875] It makes sense to exclude this type of data since they have not strictly speaking been 'provided' by the data subject, but rather 'created' by the controller. Moreover, these types of data will often be the most valuable for data controllers, as this is where the real added-value of their service must be found. This echoes another key balancing exercise underlying 'empowerment' initiatives imposing B2B data sharing, namely the balance between the benefits of sharing for the specific individual and the need to preserve the business interests of the data holder.[876] This balance will also be further detailed below.[877]

While not being mentioned in the Article 29 Working Party's guidelines, a fourth category of personal data, outlined in my proposed data typology, shall be discussed, namely 'acquired data'.[878] These are personal data obtained from third parties on the basis of a voluntary or compulsory data sharing mechanism. These 'acquired data' could either be data actively provided by a data subject to a third party, observed data collected from data

871. *Ibid. See also* V. Robertson, 'Excessive Data Collection: Privacy Considerations and Abuse of Dominance in the Era of Big Data', *Common Market Law Review*, 2020, Vol. 57, p. 162.
872. This could be supported by the fact that Article 20.1 of the GDPR provides that the data should be transmitted 'without hindrance from *the controller to which the personal data have been provided*' (emphasis added).
873. For instance, due to the fact that Article 20.1 mentions data 'provided to *a* controller' (emphasis added).
874. Article 29 Working Party, *Guidelines on the right to data portability*, WP 242 rev.01, 13 April 2017, p. 10.
875. *See* point 17.
876. Article 29 Working Party, *Guidelines on the right to data portability*, WP 242 rev.01, 13 April 2017, pp. 11-12.
877. *See* Part II, Chapter 5, Section 5.1.1.
878. *See* point 17.

subjects by this third party or inferred/derived data created by this third party.[879] For this fourth category of data, which is overlooked by the legal literature dealing with the data portability right, there is an uncertainty on whether they fall within the scope of this right. Or rather, while it seems non-controversial that 'acquired inferred/derived data' shall not be covered, as it has never been 'provided' by the data subject, it is much less certain whether 'acquired actively provided data' and 'acquired observed data' should fall within the scope of the data portability right. This is because these data have been 'provided' by the data subject to a first controller before being acquired by another party. Yet, the GDPR is mute on whether the data subject should only be able to exercise her right against the original controller to whom she provided the data, or whether it can also be used against subsequent 'acquirers' of these 'provided' data. Indeed, Article 20.1 mentions data 'provided to *a* controller' (emphasis added). It is very likely that the European legislator did not consider this hypothesis and solely envisaged the possibility for the data subject to exercise her portability right against the original controller to whom she 'directly' provided the data. This interpretation could be supported by the fact that Article 20.1 of the GDPR provides that the data should be transmitted 'without hindrance from *the controller* to which the personal data have been provided' (emphasis added). However, some doubt remains on whether 'acquired actively provided data' and 'acquired observed data' could fall within the scope of the data portability right. This would also merit to be clarified.

143. Even if this uncertainty around 'acquired data' is set aside, the above-mentioned distinction between the first three categories of personal data (actively provided, observed and inferred/derived data) raises two difficulties in practice. On the one hand, it will not be easy for the controller to technically isolate, in its IT system, the third category of data from the other two, in anticipation of the exercise by a data subject of her portability right. On the other hand, and this further accentuates this technical difficulty, it may not always be clear whether certain data have been 'provided' (actively or observed) by the data subject, or whether, on the contrary, these data have been 'inferred' by the controller. To illustrate this, an overly simplified example can be used: on a timespan of one month, a person does several searches on Google in order to buy blue sports shoes, blue shirts and blue pants, because that person's favourite colour is blue. Based on this search history, Google starts to present her with a majority of advertisements related to blue clothing. To which category of data does the information that this person is only interested in blue clothes correspond to? It is obviously not actively provided data (1st category), as the data subject has never explicitly indicated that she was only looking for blue clothes. It is, however, less clear whether this information falls into the category of 'observed data'

879. *See* point 22.

provided by the data subject through the use of the controller's service (2nd category), or whether this information has been 'inferred' by the controller (3rd category). All of the above shows that even if the scope of the data portability right seems, to a large extent, rather clear from a theoretical point of view, its application in practice will not always be straightforward.

4.1.3 Exercise of the Right to Data Portability

144. I will now turn to some considerations pertaining to the exercise of this right (cost and deadline to respond to a portability request, data format and 'temporality' of the right). Another important consideration pertaining to the exercise of this right is contained in Article 20.4 of the GDPR, which provides that this right to data portability needs to be articulated with the rights and freedoms of others, *in casu* the data holder and other data subjects, that it shall not affect. Such a provision was absent in the Commission's original proposal[880] and was first included in the Council's position at first reading.[881] As these considerations are at the heart of the balances underlying 'empowerment' initiatives imposing B2B data sharing, they will be addressed in a separate Section below.[882]

4.1.3.1 Cost and Deadline to Respond to a Portability Request

145. Like for any other data subject's right contained in the GDPR, the data controller must act on a data portability request without undue delay and in any event within one month of the receipt of the request, except in more complex cases, where the maximum response time is three months.[883] It is important to stress that, in any case, the controller cannot remain silent and will have to react within one month of the receipt, whether to grant the request, to indicate that it refuses the request, or to inform the data subject that her request is complex and that, accordingly, it will need to extend the response deadline by two months. In the latter case, it must provide the reasons for this delay.[884]

880. Proposal for a Regulation of the European Parliament and of the Council on the protection of individuals with regard to the processing of personal data and on the free movement of such data (General Data Protection Regulation), 25 January 2012, COM/2012/011 final.
881. Article 20.4 of Position (EU) No. 6/2016 of the Council at first reading with a view to the adoption of a Regulation of the European Parliament and of the Council on the protection of natural persons with regard to the processing of personal data and on the free movement of such data, and repealing Directive 95/46/EC (General Data Protection Regulation, *OJ C 159/1*, 3 May 2016.
882. *See* Part II, Chapter 5, Section 5.1.
883. Article 12.3 of the GDPR.
884. *Ibid.*

146. Regarding the costs of the right, the controller may not request any payment from the data subject exercising her right to data portability, unless the data subject's request is manifestly unfounded or excessive, in particular because of its repetitive character.[885] For information society services specialised in the automated processing of personal data, this exception should rarely be met, even if the controller is confronted with multiple requests for portability.[886] Indeed, the notion of 'repetitive character' used in Article 12 of the GDPR refers to repeated requests from the same data subject, and not to the total number of requests for portability that the controller could receive from several data subjects. Accordingly, 'the overall system implementation costs should neither be charged to the data subjects, nor be used to justify a refusal to answer portability requests'.[887]

Moreover, the 'repetitive character' of the request should not be interpreted too strictly; otherwise, this right will be deprived of its effectiveness. Thus, the mere fact of renewing the request to port the same data a second time, for example, to forward them to a different recipient, should not be sufficient to conclude that the request is 'repetitive'. In doing so, it will be necessary to make a case-by-case assessment of the repetitive or non-repetitive nature of the request, and therefore of the possibility for the controller to claim payment. Similarly, if the data subject exercises her right to portability again, towards the same controller, in order to port the data that has been updated since the first request (new data, modified data, etc.), this request should not be considered as repetitive as, by assumption, the data concerned will be different from the data ported the first time.

4.1.3.2 Data Format

147. As the objective of the right to data portability is to allow the data subject or a recipient to reuse the ported data, it is essential that the data format allows such reuse. This is why Article 20 of the GDPR states that these data have to be provided in a structured, commonly used and machine-readable format. Interestingly, this latter requirement of a 'machine-readable' format was absent from the Commission's original proposal[888] and was first included in the Council's position at first reading.[889] According to

885. Article 12.5 of the GDPR.
886. Article 29 Working Party, *Guidelines on the right to data portability*, WP 242 rev.01, 13 April 2017, p. 15.
887. *Ibid.*
888. Proposal for a Regulation of the European Parliament and of the Council on the protection of individuals with regard to the processing of personal data and on the free movement of such data (General Data Protection Regulation), 25 January 2012, COM/2012/011 final, p. 9.
889. Article 20.1 of the Position (EU) No. 6/2016 of the Council at first reading with a view to the adoption of a Regulation of the European Parliament and of the Council on the protection of natural persons with regard to the processing of personal data and on the

the Article 29 Working Party, 'the terms structured, commonly used and machine-readable are a set of minimal requirements that should facilitate the interoperability of the data format provided by the data controller. In that way, "structured, commonly used and machine readable" are specifications for the means, whereas interoperability is the desired outcome'.[890] In fact, Recital 68 of the GDPR adds that this format should also be interoperable, although this requirement does not appear in the text of Article 20. This notion of 'interoperability' must not be confused with the notion of 'compatibility', as Recital 68 of the GDPR indicates that the data portability right should not create an obligation for the controllers to adopt or maintain processing systems which are technically compatible. This might seem somewhat contradictory at first sight. Yet, the interoperability is suggested at the 'data format' level, while no compatibility is required at the 'processing systems' level. Said otherwise, each data holder is free to work with the processing systems it prefers (no requirement of compatibility), but they are encouraged to produce, store and share their data in an interoperable format, which can be reused by data recipients, independently of the processing systems they use. Indeed, requiring technical compatibility of processing systems could have limited too strongly the emergence of technological developments.

Beyond these requirements, the GDPR does not impose specific recommendations as to the format to be used. This is left to the discretion of the controllers, who must nevertheless bear in mind that it is desirable that the chosen format should allow interoperability. In doing so, the use of proprietary formats should be avoided, and priority should be given to commonly used open/free formats (such as XML, JSON or CSV).[891]

Additionally, the data controllers should also provide metadata[892] that is as accurate and exhaustive as possible, in order to best describe the meaning of the ported data.[893] This is fully in line with the European legislator's desire to facilitate the reuse of the ported data, as well as with the invitation made to controllers to propose, if possible, several types of formats to the data subject, while clearly explaining to her the consequences of choosing one or the other of these formats.[894]

---

free movement of such data, and repealing Directive 95/46/EC (General Data Protection Regulation, *OJ C 159/1*, 3 May 2016).

890. *Ibid.*, p. 17.

891. Article 29 Working Party, *Guidelines on the right to data portability*, WP 242 rev.01, 13 April 2017, pp. 17-18.

892. 'Metadata is "data information that provides information about other data". Many distinct types of metadata exist, including descriptive metadata, structural metadata, administrative metadata, reference metadata and statistical metadata' (https://en.wikipedia.org/wiki/Metadata).

893. Article 29 Working Party, *Guidelines on the right to data portability*, WP 242 rev.01, 13 April 2017, p. 18.

894. *Ibid.*

Finally, the Article 29 Working Party 'strongly encourages cooperation between industry stakeholders and trade associations to work together on a common set of interoperable standards and formats to deliver the requirements of the right to data portability'.[895] To do so, these stakeholders could find inspiration in the European Interoperability Framework,[896] which establishes a set of common elements in terms of vocabulary, concepts, principles, policies, guidelines, recommendations, standards, specifications and practices.[897] Arguably, this coordination in order to implement these interoperability standards will have a greater chance of success if it is organised at sectoral level, as this makes it possible to have a reasonable number of partners around the table. Standards having a more horizontal application, and based on these sectoral standards, could then be discussed in a second phase.

4.1.3.3 'Temporality' of the Right

148. In recent years, growing discussions have emerged regarding the 'temporality' of the data portability right, i.e., whether Article 20 of the GDPR could be used as a basis to establish a continuous flow of personal data, pertaining to a specific individual, between a data holder and a data recipient, or whether this article only enables 'one-shots'.[898]

In this regard, it is important to specify that the exercise of the right to data portability does not automatically imply an obligation for the controller to erase the ported data.[899] Nevertheless, if the data subject decides to exercise her right to erasure in parallel to her right to data portability,[900] the controller will have to erase it.[901] Reversely, if the data subject exercises her right to erasure without ever having exercised her right to data portability beforehand, she should no longer be able to exercise her right to portability in a post-erasure situation. Indeed, the right to data portability does not impose any obligation on the controller to store the data after their erasure solely for the purpose of the potential future exercise of that right by a data subject.[902]

---

895. *Ibid.*
896. *See* https://ec.europa.eu/isa2/sites/isa/files/eif_brochure_final.pdf.
897. Article 29 Working Party, *Guidelines on the right to data portability*, WP 242 rev.01, 13 April 2017, p. 18.
898. *See* J. Krämer, P. Senellart and A. de Streel, 'Making Data Portability More Effective for the Digital Economy', *supra.*
899. Article 20.3 of the GDPR.
900. For example, a data subject decides to unsubscribe from Facebook and requests to transfer all her personal data to a new social network and, at the same time, to delete all the personal data concerning her held by Facebook.
901. Article 29 Working Party, *Guidelines on the right to data portability*, WP 242 rev.01, 13 April 2017, p. 7.
902. *Ibid.*, p. 6.

Accordingly, when Article 20.1 of the GDPR indicates that the data subject has the right to receive the data, this should be understood as meaning that the data subject has a right to receive a 'copy' of this data, which is implicitly confirmed by the Article 29 Working Party's guidelines.[903] This is because, after the exercise of this portability right, the data subject may, in fact, wish to continue to use and benefit from the services of the data holder to whom she submitted the portability request.[904] The right to data portability can thus be called upon not only to stop using a service in order to join another but also to start using another service by 'recycling' personal data already provided to a first service while continuing to use that first service. In light of the growing possibilities for data subjects to 'multi-home', i.e., to use several similar platforms/services at the same time, it is very likely that the right to data portability will mainly be relied upon in cases where the data subject wishes to continue to use the original controller's services. It can therefore not be excluded that the same data subject might exercise her right to data portability several times towards the same original controller. This right to portability should therefore not be solely seen as a 'one-shot' mechanism.

149. Although the formulation of Article 20 of the GDPR leaves no doubt about the fact that the right to personal data portability is not merely a 'one-shot', it is more obscure whether this article could be used as a basis to establish a continuous portability of personal data, which would imply that data can be constantly transferred between the original holder and the recipient.[905] Indeed, the wording of Article 20.1 merely evokes 'the right to receive the data in a structured, commonly used and machine-readable format', but is mute about the 'temporality' of such porting. Yet, one could argue that nothing prevents a data subject from relying on Article 20.2 of the GDPR to request a continuous flow of the data, pertaining to her, between the data holder and a data recipient 'where technically feasible'. In that perspective, the data holder would then have one month (three if the case is complex) to reply to this request and to set in place the continuous flow of data.[906] That being said, it seems unlikely that the drafters of the GDPR had this continuous porting possibility in mind. This is because this right has been designed to enable switching between service providers rather than to enable data reuse in a wider digital ecosystem.[907] Yet, the fact that such a possibility has likely not been considered by the drafters of the GDPR, nor

903. *Ibid.*, p. 4.
904. *Ibid.*, p. 7.
905. *See* Part II, Chapter 4, Section 4.3. J. Krämer, P. Senellart and A. de Streel, 'Making Data Portability More Effective for the Digital Economy', *supra*, p. 81.
906. Article 12.3 of the GDPR.
907. Communication from the Commission, '*A European Strategy for Data*', *supra*, p. 10.

by the Article 29 Working Party,[908] does not mean that the text of Article 20 could not be read as allowing such continuous portability.

Nevertheless, due to this uncertainty, some authors argue that Article 20, in its current form, does not allow for the continuous porting of personal data; that this makes it highly burdensome for data subjects to use their data portability right as they have to repeat their requests; and that this limits its effectiveness and the potential benefits they can derive from it.[909] As a consequence, there are growing calls for the establishment of such near real-time continuous porting initiatives.[910] This will be further detailed in Section 4.3.

4.2 'EMPOWERMENT' INITIATIVES IMPOSING B2B DATA SHARING IN ORDER TO ADDRESS SPECIFIC MARKET FAILURES

150. While the revised version of the Article 29 Working Party's guidelines on the GDPR's data portability right now states explicitly that the main objective of this right is to promote the exercise of fundamental rights and not to deal with market failure / competition law issues,[911] several other empowerment initiatives have, on the contrary, precisely been adopted in order to address specific market failures, through the strengthening of the individuals' control on their data. Such initiatives, to which I will now turn, are contained in the Digital Content Directive,[912] in the PSD2,[913] and in the Electricity Directive.[914]

---

908. None of the examples provided by the Article 29 Working Party in its guidelines on the right to data portability addresses continuous porting (Article 29 Working Party, *Guidelines on the right to data portability*, WP 242 rev.01, 13 April 2017).
909. *See* J. Krämer, P. Senellart and A. de Streel, 'Making Data Portability More Effective for the Digital Economy', *supra*, p. 13; Communication from the Commission, '*A European Strategy for Data*', *supra*, p. 10.
910. Communication from the Commission, '*A European Strategy for Data*', *supra*, p. 20; J. Krämer, P. Senellart and A. de Streel, 'Making Data Portability More Effective for the Digital Economy', *supra*, p. 81.
911. *See* point 135.
912. Directive 2019/770 of the European Parliament and of the Council of 20 May 2019 on certain aspects concerning contracts for the supply of digital content and digital services, *OJ L 136/1*, 22 May 2019.
913. Directive (EU) 2015/2366 of the European Parliament and of the Council of 25 November 2015 on payment services in the internal market, amending Directives 2002/65/EC, 2009/110/EC and 2013/36/EU and Regulation (EU) No. 1093/2010, and repealing Directive 2007/64/EC, *OJ L 337/35*, 23 December 2015.
914. Directive (EU) 2019/944 of the European Parliament and of the Council of 5 June 2019 on common rules for the internal market for electricity and amending Directive 2012/27/EU, *OJ L 158/125*, 14 June 2019.

4.2.1 Data Retrieval Right in the Digital Content Directive

151. The first 'empowerment' initiative imposing B2B data sharing in order to address a specific market failure is the data retrieval right enshrined in Article 16.4 of the Directive on the supply of digital content and digital services ('Digital Content Directive').[915] This article provides that, in the event of the termination of a contract between a trader[916] and a consumer[917] for the supply of digital content[918] or digital services,[919] the trader shall, at the request of the consumer, make available to the consumer any content other than personal data, which was provided or created by the consumer when using the digital content or digital service supplied by the trader.[920] Furthermore, the consumer shall be entitled to retrieve that digital content free of charge, without hindrance from the trader, within a reasonable time and in a commonly used and machine-readable format.[921]

Article 16.4 thus grants the consumers with a 'data retrieval right', but does not allow the direct transmission of data between two firms, since it only aims to establish the consumer's right to recover the data personally after the termination of the contract.[922] In this sense, it is closer to the right of access contained in the GDPR, which allows a data subject to obtain a copy of her personal data.[923] The trader is thus required to share the data with the consumer, but not with other undertakings. There is thus no equivalent of Article 20.2 of the GDPR in the Digital Content Directive. Naturally, the consumer is, herself, free to share the data she has recovered through the data retrieval right with another content or service provider. The regime created by Article 16.4 of the Digital Content Directive thus diverges from the

915. Directive 2019/770.
916. 'Any natural or legal person, irrespective of whether privately or publicly owned, that is acting, including through any other person acting in that natural or legal person's name or on that person's behalf, for purposes relating to that person's trade, business, craft, or profession, in relation to contracts covered by this Directive' (Article 2.5 of Directive 2019/770).
917. 'Any natural person who, in relation to contracts covered by this Directive, is acting for purposes which are outside that person's trade, business, craft, or profession' (Article 2.6 of Directive 2019/770).
918. 'Data which are produced and supplied in digital form' (Article 2.1 of Directive 2019/770).
919. 'A service that allows the consumer to create, process, store or access data in digital form; or that allows the sharing of or any other interaction with data in digital form uploaded or created by the consumer or other users of that service' (Article 2.2 of Directive 2019/770).
920. Article 16.4, al. 1 of Directive 2019/770.
921. Article 16.4, al. 2 of Directive 2019/770.
922. Article 16.4 of Directive 2019/770; I. Graef, *EU Competition Law, Data Protection and Online Platforms: Data as Essential Facility*, Alphen aan den Rijn, Kluwer, 2016, p. 148.
923. Article 15.3 of the GDPR.

regime created by Article 20 of the GDPR, although they present some similarities.[924]

4.2.1.1 Objectives and Scope of Application

152. The objective of the data retrieval right contained in the Digital Content Directive is to tackle market failures deriving from consumer lock-in on the digital content markets, through the means of consumer empowerment.[925] More concretely, it aims at giving more control to consumers on their data and at making it easier for consumers to change service providers. Indeed, the proposal at the origin of the Directive outlined that, in order to promote competition, it is necessary to ensure that consumers can easily switch content providers, by reducing legal, technical and practical obstacles, such as the inability to recover all the data that the consumer has produced or generated through her use of digital content.[926] This is because the consumer could be deterred from terminating a contract for digital content or a digital service if she cannot recover access to the content in question as a result of such termination.[927]

153. Article 16.4 of the Digital Content Directive applies to 'any content other than personal data, which was provided or created by the consumer when using the digital content or digital service supplied by the trader'.[928] It therefore only applies to non-personal data that the consumer has (actively) provided or created (e.g., data that she has generated through her use of the content or service, i.e., 'observed data' in my typology), but not to inferred/derived data nor to acquired data. Indeed, here, and contrary to Article 20 of the GDPR, the wording of Article 16.4 does not leave room for doubt on the fact that 'acquired provided data' and 'acquired observed data' do not fall in the scope of this article, as it explicitly refers to data provided 'when using the digital content or digital service supplied by the trader',

---

924. For more information on the comparison between this data retrieval right and the data portability right enshrined in Article 20 of the GDPR *see also*: I. Graef, M. Husovec and N. Purtova, 'Data Portability and Data Control: Lessons for an Emerging Concept in EU Law', *German Law Journal*, 2018, Vol. 19(6), pp. 1359-1398; I. Graef, T. Tombal and A. de Streel, 'Limits and Enablers of Data Sharing: An Analytical Framework for EU Competition, Data Protection and Consumer Law', *TILEC Discussion Paper DP 2019-005*, November 2019, available at https://ssrn.com/abstract=2956308; M. Ledger et T. Tombal, 'Le droit à la portabilité dans les textes européens: droits distincts ou mécanisme multi-facettes ?', *R.D.T.I.*, 2018/3, n°72, pp. 25-44.

925. Proposal for a Directive of the European parliament and of the council on certain aspects concerning contracts for the supply of digital content, 9 December 2015, COM(2015) 634 final, p. 3.

926. *Ibid.*, p. 22.

927. Recital 70 of Directive 2019/770.

928. Article 16.4 of Directive 2019/770.

which thus excludes data provided when using a third party's content or service.

Moreover, it does not apply to data that has no utility outside the context of the digital content or digital service supplied by the trader (for instance, the consumer's login and password); to data that only relates to the consumer's activity when using the digital content or digital service supplied by the trader (for instance, data about the fact that the consumer has stopped watching in the middle of the movie, so that when she returns, she can start over from that point and does not have to restart from the beginning); or to data that has been aggregated with other data by the trader and cannot be disaggregated or only with disproportionate efforts (for instance, data that contributed to the identification of viewing or listening trends in a specific country).[929] These exceptions are justified by the fact that, in those cases, the content is of little practical use to the consumer, who therefore has a limited interest in retrieving such data, particularly in view of the fact that requiring such a mechanism would be costly for the trader.[930]

The scope of application of the Directive is thus complementary to that of the right to data portability in the GDPR, which applies to personal data 'provided' by the data subject.[931] This is explicitly stated in the text of the Directive, which provides that the trader remains bound by the obligations of the GDPR,[932] which prevails over this Directive in the event of a conflict of provisions.[933] It therefore seems that the objective of the final text of this Directive was to avoid any overlap with the regime of Article 20 of the GDPR.[934] However, this distinction between personal and non-personal data is problematic in practice. This is because it is difficult to imagine situations in which content provided by the consumer would not qualify as personal data. Indeed, given the GDPR's broad definition of this concept, namely 'any information relating to an identified or identifiable natural person',[935] the vast

929. Article 16.3 of Directive 2019/770.
930. Recital 71 of Directive 2019/770.
931. *See* points 142 and 143.
932. Article 16.2 of Directive 2019/770.
933. Article 3.8 of Directive 2019/770.
934. On the contrary, the proposal at the origin of the Directive targeted 'all content provided by the consumer and any other data produced or generated through the consumer's use of the digital content' (Proposal for a Directive of the European parliament and of the council on certain aspects concerning contracts for the supply of digital content, 9 December 2015, COM(2015) 634 final, Articles 13.2.c) and 16.4.b)). The reference to 'any data' would have thus potentially covered personal data. Accordingly, the wording of this provision seems to have been adapted in order to avoid any overlap with the GDPR and its right to data portability, which would apply in parallel (*see* Recital 38 of Directive 2019/770).
935. Article 4.1 of the GDPR.

majority (if not all) of the data provided or created by the consumer will likely be considered as personal data.[936]

Although the scope of application of the Directive and of the GDPR are complementary, none of these instruments apply to inferred/derived data. This echoes a key balancing exercise underlying 'empowerment' initiatives imposing B2B data sharing, namely between the benefits of sharing for the specific individual and the need to preserve the business interests of the data holder, which will be further detailed below.[937]

4.2.1.2 Exercise of the Right

154. Similarly to Article 20 of the GDPR,[938] the Digital Content Directive also provides that the consumer shall be entitled to retrieve the data free of charge.[939] Regarding the deadline to process the requests, the Directive only provides that the data should be given to the consumer 'within a reasonable time' after the termination of the contract.[940] While the Directive does not provide any further information as to how these terms must be interpreted, the deadline of one month provided in the GDPR (three months for complex cases)[941] could arguably be used to assess this 'reasonable' character.

155. As a welcome development, the format requirements contained in the final text of the Digital Content Directive have been aligned with those contained in the GDPR, as the data must be returned to the consumer 'in a commonly used and machine-readable format'.[942] This was not the case in the proposal at the origin of the Directive, which had less stringent data format requirements than Article 20 of the GDPR, as this initial text provided that the data had to be returned to the consumer in a 'commonly used data format'.[943] In this sense, the proposal was closer to the format requirement for the right of access in the GDPR, according to which the data had to be delivered in a 'commonly used electronic form'.[944] It should however be noted that the requirement for a 'structured format' is not mentioned in the Directive, whereas it appears in Article 20 of the GDPR.[945] Moreover, the

---

936. *See* Part I, Chapter 1, Section 1.2. *See also* N. Purtova, 'The Law of Everything: Broad Concept of Personal Data and Future of EU Data Protection Law', *Law, Innovation and Technology*, 2018, Vol. 10(1), pp. 40-81.
937. *See* Part II, Chapter 5, Section 5.1.1.
938. *See* point 146.
939. Article 16.4 of Directive 2019/770.
940. *Ibid.*
941. *See* point 145.
942. Article 16.4 of Directive 2019/770.
943. Proposal for a Directive of the European parliament and of the council on certain aspects concerning contracts for the supply of digital content, 9 December 2015, COM(2015) 634 final, Articles 13.2.c) and 16.4.b).
944. Article 15.3 of the GDPR.
945. *See* point 147.

Digital Content Directive does not make any reference to the need for interoperability, while Recital 68 of the GDPR adds that the format should also be interoperable (although this requirement does not appear in the text of Article 20).[946]

156. Regarding the influence of the exercise of the right on the data holder's ability to keep using the data, the Digital Content Directive provides that, when the consumer terminates the contract, the trader must refrain from using the non-personal data provided or created by the consumer, and will thus have to erase them.[947] This is a clear difference with the right to personal data portability in the GDPR, which does not automatically imply an obligation for the data holder to stop using the ported data.[948] Indeed, the right to data portability is not limited to 'one-shot' data transfers.[949] The exercise of the data retrieval right, on the other hand, amounts to a 'one-shot' transfer. The difference between the two regimes can be explained by the fact that data can be ported at any time under the GDPR, while the data retrieval right can only be used after the termination of the contract by the consumer.[950]

157. To sum up, the Digital Content Directive creates an 'empowerment' compulsory B2B data sharing mechanism that is analogous, yet non-identical, to Article 20 of the GDPR. Indeed, these mechanisms have complementary scopes of application. Moreover, they are aligned in terms of costs and deadline to process the request, and in terms of format requirements, even if the Digital Content Directive does not mention the 'structured format' requirement. However, these mechanisms diverge when it comes to the objective that they pursue, to the consequences of the exercise of the right and to the temporality of requests. More importantly, Article 16.4 of the Digital Content Directive only requires the trader to share the data with the consumer, but not with other undertakings. There is thus no equivalent of Article 20.2 of the GDPR in the Digital Content Directive, which makes it a much less efficient 'empowerment' compulsory B2B data sharing mechanism.

---

946. *Ibid.*
947. Article 16.3 of Directive 2019/770. The trader can however continue to use some of the data that had been provided or created by the consumer, namely the data that has no use outside the context of the content or service; that only relates to the consumer's activity when using the content or service; that has been aggregated with other data by the trader and cannot be disaggregated or can only be disaggregated with disproportionate effort; or that has been generated jointly by the consumer and other persons who continue to use the content or service (Article 16.3 of Directive 2019/770).
948. Article 20.3 of the GDPR.
949. *See* points 148 and 149.
950. I. Graef, *EU Competition Law, Data Protection and Online Platforms: Data as Essential Facility*, *supra*, p. 148.

4.2.2 PSD2 AND OPEN BANKING

158. The second 'empowerment' initiatives imposing B2B data sharing in order to address a specific market failure are the data access and use rights granted in Articles 65-67 of the PSD2.[951] In the UK, PSD2 has been further refined by the Open Banking initiative,[952] which is worth presenting here as well.

4.2.2.1 Access to and Use of Banking Data in PSD2

159. PSD2 allows the providers of payment initiation services and the providers of account information services[953] to access and use the payment account information[954] of the users of their services (the consumers) if the latter have explicitly consented to it.[955] Thus, thanks to PSD2, a service provider creating a smartphone payment application, for example, called 'Easypay', will be able to obtain access to, and to use, the bank account data of the users of this application who wish to carry out a transaction, in order to ensure that they have sufficient funds and to validate the transaction. However, such access may only be granted if the service provider has obtained the explicit consent of the user of the mobile application (generally via adherence to the services' terms and conditions). Moreover, there is no correlative obligation for the banks to erase or stop processing the data, and the providers of payment initiation services and of account information services shall only process (e.g., access, use and store) personal data

951. Directive (EU) 2015/2366 of the European Parliament and of the Council of 25 November 2015 on payment services in the internal market, amending Directives 2002/65/EC, 2009/110/EC and 2013/36/EU and Regulation (EU) No. 1093/2010, and repealing Directive 2007/64/EC, *OJ L 337/35*, 23 December 2015.

952. Competition and Markets Authority, 'The Retail Banking Market Investigation Order 2017', 2017, available at https://assets.publishing.service.gov.uk/media/5893063bed915d06e1000000/retail-bankingmarketinvestigationor der-2017.pdf; Competition and Markets Authority, 'Final Approved Roadmap for Open Banking', 14 May 2020, available at https://assets.publishing.service.gov.uk/government/uploads/system/uploads/attachment_data/file/885537/Notice_of_proposed_changes_to_the_open_banking_roadmap_-_web_publication_-_cma_gov_uk_---_May_2020_-.pdf.

953. Respectively defined as 'a service to initiate a payment order at the request of the payment service user with respect to a payment account held at another payment service provider' and as 'an online service to provide consolidated information on one or more payment accounts held by the payment service user with either another payment service provider or with more than one payment service provider' (Articles 4.15 and 4.16 of Directive 2015/2366).

954. Defined as 'account held in the name of one or more payment service users which is used for the execution of payment transactions' (Article 4.12 of Directive 2015/2366).

955. Articles 65 to 67 of Directive 2015/2366.

necessary for the provision of their services, in full compliance with the data minimisation principle of the GDPR.[956]

PSD2 notably aims at tackling the consumer lock-in and consumer inertia market failures that have been observed in the banking sector, through the empowerment of these consumers by giving them more control on their banking data and operations, and by providing them with more choice and transparency.[957] Indeed, by allowing the access to, and the use of, the payment account information of the incumbent banks, PSD2 promotes the development of innovative payment services through increased competition on the market, and the consequence should be that consumers are no longer 'locked-in' the services of their traditional bank, as they are provided with alternative choices and better offers of payment services.[958] Moreover, this access and use can give rise to complementary account information services, which the consumers can use in order to have an aggregated view of their accounts (that could be spread out across several banks), and this would allow them to have a clearer visibility on their finances and empowers them to manage them more efficiently.[959]

160. In fact, it is argued that the data access and use rights granted in Articles 65-67 of PSD2 could be seen as a sector-specific complement to Article 20.2 of the GDPR, as it compels the banks (data holders) to make the direct transmission of the data subjects' personal banking information to recipients 'technically feasible'.[960] This is a key difference with Article 20.2 of the GDPR, which contains no such technical feasibility obligation.[961] Another key difference with Article 20 of the GDPR is that PSD2 expressly provides for continuous portability through the use of APIs.[962] Indeed, the European Commission adopted regulatory technical standards, based on a draft of the European Banking Authority, which notably impose the obligation for banks to set in place at least one API to support this data sharing mechanism.[963]

---

956. Article 94.2 of Directive 2015/2366. The data minimisation principle is enshrined in Article 5.1.c) of the GDPR.
957. Recitals 5 and 6 of Directive 2015/2366.
958. Recital 67 of Directive 2015/2366.
959. Recital 28 of Directive 2015/2366.
960. G. Colangelo and O. Borgogno, 'Data, Innovation and Transatlantic Competition in Finance: The Case of the Access to Account Rule', *Stanford-Vienna European Union Law Working Paper No. 35*, 2018, available at https://law.stanford.edu/publications/no-35-data-innovation-and-transatlantic-competition-in-finance-the-case-of-the-access-to-account-rule/, p. 3; S. Vezzoso, 'Fintech, Access to Data, and the Role of Competition Policy', 2018, available at https://papers.ssrn.com/sol3/papers.cfm?abstract_id=3106594, pp. 12-13.
961. *See supra* point 137.
962. J. Krämer, P. Senellart and A. de Streel, 'Making Data Portability More Effective for the Digital Economy', *supra*, p. 32.
963. Commission Delegated Regulation 2018/389 of 27 November 2017 supplementing Directive 2015/2366 of the European Parliament and of the Council with regard to

In light of these two differences, the data sharing mechanism in PSD2[964] might thus, at first sight, seem much more effective than the one contained in Article 20 of the GDPR. Yet, much like for data portability, while Recital 93 of PSD2 provides that the interoperability of the different technological communication solutions should be ensured, none of the articles of PSD2 refer to this necessary interoperability. As a consequence, each banking institution holding these payment account data is free to set up its own API allowing continuous portability. This may lead to interoperability problems if each of these institutions develops a mechanism based on different technical standards.[965] Indeed, while the European Commission's regulatory technical standards mentioned above list minimal technical requirements that must be met by the various APIs (notably in terms of identification and authentication),[966] and provides that the APIs should be based on existing international or European standards,[967] it does not in any way require the various banks to use a single common standard for their APIs. This is why it is relevant here to mention the UK's Open Banking initiative,[968] which went further in this regard than PSD2.

4.2.2.2 The UK's Open Banking Initiative

161. In the UK, as a result of its market investigation in the banking sector,[969] the Competition and Markets Authority required the nine major UK banks to build and ensure the maintenance of common and open APIs, based on common technical standards, to allow data sharing with providers of payment initiation services and of account information services.[970] This avoids the interoperability issue outlined above as the payment initiation

---

regulatory technical standards for strong customer authentication and common and secure open standards of communication, *OJ L 69/23*, 13 March 2018, Articles 30-36.

964. PSD2 can indeed be considered as creating data sharing mechanisms as the payment account information may not only be accessed but also used and stored by the providers of payment initiation services and of account information services (*see* Articles 66.3, g) and 67.2, f) of Directive 2015/2366).
965. G. Colangelo and O. Borgogno, 'Data, Innovation and Transatlantic Competition in Finance', *supra*, p. 25.
966. Articles 30.1 and 30.2 of Commission Delegated Regulation 2018/389.
967. Article 30.3 of Commission Delegated Regulation 2018/389.
968. Competition and Markets Authority, 'The Retail Banking Market Investigation Order 2017', *supra*; Competition and Markets Authority, 'Final Approved Roadmap for Open Banking', *supra*.
969. Competition and Markets Authority, 'Retail Banking Market Investigation – Final Report', 26 February 2016, available at https://www.gov.uk/cma-cases/review-of-banking-for-small-and-medium-sized-businesses-smes-in-the-uk.
970. Competition and Markets Authority, 'The Retail Banking Market Investigation Order 2017', *supra*; Competition and Markets Authority, 'Making Banks Work Harder for You', 9 August 2016, available at http://www.agefi.fr/sites/agefi.fr/files/fichiers/2016/08/cma_overview-of-the-banking-retail-market_9_aout .pdf. *See also* Open Data Institute and Fingleton, 'Open Banking, Preparing for Lift Off: Purpose Progress and

service providers and account information service providers only have to develop specific technical solutions to connect to these common APIs for all nine banks, rather than having to develop a multitude of technical solutions to connect to various non-interoperable APIs (one API per bank).

As for PSD2, the goal behind this common API is to foster the development of new services that will be better tailored to consumer's specific needs, and this should empower them to better manage their finances, notably by being able to manage accounts held in several banks through a single application, by moving funds between their various accounts in order to avoid overdraft charges or higher interest payments, or by being able to make simple, safe and reliable price and service quality comparisons in order to select those that are the best tailored to their financial profile.[971] Indeed, the Competition and Markets Authority's investigation in the banking sector[972] showed that this market was gangrened by 'consumer inertia', as 'more than half of retail banking customers stayed with their bank for more than 10 years and three-quarters of them did not look for more efficient alternatives on the market in the previous year'.[973] The goal is thus to give consumers more control over their banking data by allowing them to securely share it with third parties, in order to be offered better financial services, more choice and lower prices.[974] Consumers are thus empowered to compare services, which should facilitate multi-homing and service switching.[975] They have an active role to play in the digital ecosystem, provided that their searching and switching costs are reduced.[976]

162. More concretely, these nine banks were required to fund, and cooperate with, the Open Banking Implementation Entity (OBIE), which is the independent body responsible for building and maintaining these common and open APIs.[977] In substance, the role of the OBIE is to: '(i) design the specifications for the APIs that banks use to securely provide Open Banking, (ii) support regulated third party providers and banks to use the Open Banking standards, (iii) create security and messaging standards, (iv) manage

---

Potential', 16 July 2019, available at https://www.openbanking.org.uk/wp-content/uploads/open-banking-report-150719.pdf.

971. Competition and Markets Authority, 'Making Banks Work Harder for You', *supra*, pp. 6-8.
972. Competition and Markets Authority, 'Retail Banking Market Investigation – Final Report', *supra*.
973. O. Borgogno and G. Colangelo, 'Consumer Inertia and Competition-Sensitive Data Governance: The Case of Open Banking', 3 January 2020, available at SSRN: https://ssrn.com/abstract=3513514, p. 5.
974. Open Data Institute and Fingleton, 'Open Banking, Preparing for Lift Off', *supra*, p. 6.
975. *Ibid.*, p. 4.
976. O. Borgogno and G. Colangelo, 'Consumer Inertia and Competition-Sensitive Data Governance', *supra*, pp. 4 and 12.
977. J. Krämer, P. Senellart and A. de Streel, 'Making Data Portability More Effective for the Digital Economy', *supra*, p. 32.

the Open Banking Directory which allows regulated participants like banks and third party providers to enrol in Open Banking, (v) produce guidelines for participants in the Open Banking ecosystem and (vi) set out the process for managing disputes and complaints'.[978]

Interestingly, the OBIE followed a 'minimum viable product' approach, through which the APIs were made live as early as possible in order to receive quick user feedback allowing to adapt the APIs through iteration.[979] This approach contributed to the success of the initiative. Another factor that contributed to its success is that recipients have to be authorised by the Financial Conduct Authority (FCA) to get access to the banks' data.[980] The goal is to protect the consumers by ensuring that these entities are secure and that their services and processing activities are legitimate and lawful. There are now 135 entities approved by the FCA to offer services that use Open Banking, and these are listed in the 'Open Banking Directory', which serves the role of a white list.[981]

163. To conclude, it should be mentioned that the Open Banking initiative, similarly to PSD2, is currently limited to banking (accounts) information. However, the aim of some organisations, such as the Open Data Institute, is to expand this initiative to 'Open Finance' (mortgages, pensions, insurances) and to other sectors such as energy and telecoms, as it is argued that this would also empower consumers in these fields by offering them more control on their data in order to be offered more choices.[982] For instance, as outlined by the Open Data Institute, 'if smart meter data was accessible it may make switching easier and enable customers to easily take advantage of cheaper tariffs and off-peak energy pricing'.[983]

4.2.3 Electricity Directive

164. In fact, this expansion towards other sectors has already started as Article 20 of the Directive on common rules for the internal market for electricity ('Electricity Directive') provides that 'it shall be possible for final customers to retrieve their metering data or transmit them to another party at no additional cost and in accordance with their right to data portability'.[984]

---

978. *Ibid.*, pp. 32-33. *See also* Open Data Institute and Fingleton, 'Open Banking, Preparing for Lift Off', *supra*, pp. 22-25.
979. Open Data Institute and Fingleton, 'Open Banking, Preparing for Lift Off', *supra*, p. 4.
980. *Ibid.*, p. 25.
981. *Ibid.*, pp. 24 and 35. *See* pp. 26-32 for a list of Open Banking use cases.
982. Open Data Institute and Fingleton, 'Open Banking, Preparing for Lift Off', *supra*, pp. 4-5.
983. *Ibid.*, p. 5.
984. Directive (EU) 2019/944 of the European Parliament and of the Council of 5 June 2019 on common rules for the internal market for electricity and amending Directive 2012/27/EU, *OJ L 158/125*, 14 June 2019, Article 20, al. 2.

This is a third 'empowerment' initiative imposing B2B data sharing in order to tackle a specific market failure, as its goal is to strengthen competition on the energy market. More specifically, this article provides that 'if final customers request it, data on the electricity they fed into the grid and their electricity consumption data shall be made available to them through a standardised communication interface or through remote access, or to a third party acting on their behalf, in an easily understandable format allowing them to compare offers on a like-for-like basis'.[985] Moreover, 'non-validated near real-time consumption data shall also be made easily and securely available to final customers at no additional cost, through a standardised interface or through remote access, in order to support automated energy efficiency programmes, demand response and other services'.[986]

This Directive also provides that the parties responsible for data management of the final costumer's data (metering and consumption data as well as data required for customer switching, demand response and other services) should provide access to it to any 'eligible party' in a non-discriminatory manner.[987] Surprisingly, while the Commission's proposal provided that 'eligible parties' shall include at least 'customers, suppliers, transmission and distribution system operators, aggregators, energy service companies, and other parties which provide energy or other services to customers',[988] the final text of the Directive does not define this notion, which creates uncertainties as to who can benefit from this access.[989] While these eligible parties can be charged a fee for this access, the access should be free for the final customers.[990] The Member States have a role to play in promoting this data access, as they should ensure efficient and secure data access and exchange, as well as data protection and data security.[991] They should also facilitate the full interoperability of energy services by ensuring that electricity undertakings apply the interoperability requirements and procedures for access to data, which will be adopted by the Commission in implementing acts of the Directive.[992] Moreover, Article 34 of this Directive provides that if smart metering systems[993] have been deployed in a Member

985. Article 20, al.1, e) of Directive 2019/944.
986. Article 20, al.1, a) of Directive 2019/944.
987. Articles 23.1 and 23.2 of Directive 2019/944.
988. Article 23.1 of the Proposal for a Directive of the European Parliament and of the Council on common rules for the internal market in electricity (recast), 30 November 2016, COM/2016/0864 final.
989. *See* C. Ducuing, 'Data as Infrastructure? A Study of Data Sharing Legal Regimes', *Competition and Regulation in Network Industries*, 2020, Vol. 21(2), pp. 124-142.
990. Article 23.5 of Directive 2019/944.
991. Article 23.2 of Directive 2019/944.
992. Article 24 of Directive 2019/944.
993. 'An electronic system that is capable of measuring electricity fed into the grid or electricity consumed from the grid, providing more information than a conventional

State, and that distribution system operators[994] are involved in the management of this smart meter data, this Member State shall ensure that all eligible parties (suppliers and service providers) have non-discriminatory access to this smart meter data under clear and equal terms, in accordance with the relevant data protection rules.

165. The above could be seen as another sector-specific complement to Article 20.2 of the GDPR, aiming at solving market failures through the empowerment of individuals, which creates a form of continuous individual-level data sharing. Indeed, this provides individuals with the tools to participate more actively in the energy market,[995] thanks to accurate and near real-time feedback on their energy consumption,[996] which allows them to better manage their consumption and to benefit from affordable energy through the facilitated possibility to switch for suppliers offering lower tariffs.[997]

4.3 GROWING CALL FOR A NEW 'EMPOWERMENT' INITIATIVE IMPOSING B2B DATA SHARING: 'CONTINUOUS PORTABILITY'

166. So far, I have presented the existing 'empowerment' initiatives imposing B2B data sharing, which either aim to allow the exercise of fundamental rights or to address specific market failures.[998] However, there are growing criticisms about the effectiveness of these initiatives, and about their ability to truly empower individuals.[999] This is, for instance, the case with Article 20 of the GDPR, which fails to impose direct portability,[1000] and which,

meter, and that is capable of transmitting and receiving data for information, monitoring and control purposes, using a form of electronic communication' (Article 2.23 of Directive 2019/944).

994. 'A natural or legal person who is responsible for operating, ensuring the maintenance of and, if necessary, developing the distribution system in a given area and, where applicable, its interconnections with other systems, and for ensuring the long-term ability of the system to meet reasonable demands for the distribution of electricity' (Article 2.29 of Directive 2019/944).
995. Recital 10 of Directive 2019/944.
996. Recital 10 of Directive 2019/944.
997. Recitals 43, 48 and 52 of Directive 2019/944.
998. *See* Part II, Chapter 4, Sections 4.1 and 4.2.
999. J. Krämer, P. Senellart and A. de Streel, 'Making Data Portability More Effective for the Digital Economy', *supra*, p. 79.
1000. Article 20.2 of the GDPR only provides that the data subject has the right to have the personal data transmitted directly from one controller to another *where technically feasible*.

according to some authors, falls short of requiring continuous portability.[1001] This is also the case with Article 16.4 of the Digital Content Directive, which only grants to the consumer a data retrieval right at the termination of the contract with the trader.[1002] Accordingly, there have been calls for the creation of a new 'empowerment' initiative imposing B2B data sharing, namely the introduction of a 'continuous portability' right.[1003] In the UK, this is sometimes referred to as 'Data mobility'.[1004]

'Continuous portability' implies that data can be transferred – usually via application programming interfaces ('APIs')[1005] – in a timely and frequent manner from a data holder to a data recipient, on a constant basis and in (near) real time.[1006] Rather than merely providing for bulk transfers, such continuous portability would allow, with the consent of the individual whose data is shared, for a continuous flow of data between data holders and data recipients. This would allow the individuals to benefit immediately from the services of the recipient, as the latter would receive immediate and continuous access to the data that it needs to offer this service, rather than having to wait for a bulk transfer of data from the data holder or from the individual.[1007]

167. In practice, this could be done either through an extension of Article 20 GDPR[1008] or through the adoption of a new legal instrument. Yet, as a modification of the GDPR seems highly unlikely, in light of the complicated negotiations it entailed and of its recent entry into force, the second option seems more realistic. This second option itself opens an alternative between

---

1001. *See* Part II, Chapter 4, Section 4.1.3.3. I however argue that Article 20.2 of the GDPR could be read as enabling a data subject to request a continuous flow of the data, pertaining to her, between the data holder and a data recipient 'where technically feasible'.
1002. *See* Part II, Chapter 4, Section 4.2.1.
1003. Communication from the Commission, '*A European Strategy for Data*', *supra*, p. 20; J. Krämer, P. Senellart and A. de Streel, 'Making Data Portability More Effective for the Digital Economy', *supra.*
1004. *See* CtrlShift, 'Data Mobility: The Personal Data Portability Growth Opportunity for the UK Economy', 2018, available at https://www.ctrl-shift.co.uk/reports/DCMS_Ctrl-Shift_Data_mobility_report_full.pdf.
1005. 'An application programming interface (API) is an interface or communication protocol between a client and a server intended to simplify the building of client-side software. It has been described as a "contract" between the client and the server, such that if the client makes a request in a specific format, it will always get a response in a specific format or initiate a defined action' (https://en.wikipedia.org/wiki/Application_programming_interface).
1006. J. Krämer, P. Senellart and A. de Streel, 'Making Data Portability More Effective for the Digital Economy', *supra*, p. 81.
1007. *Ibid.*, p. 79.
1008. I however argue that Article 20.2 of the GDPR could already be read as enabling a data subject to request a continuous flow of the data, pertaining to her, between the data holder and a data recipient 'where technically feasible'. *See* Part II, Chapter 4, Section 4.1.3.3.

the adoption of a participative and non-binding approach via the establishment of codes of conducts, on the one hand, and the adoption of a binding regulatory instrument making it compulsory for (certain categories of) data holders to implement the necessary standards and APIs enabling continuous portability.[1009] However, as participative and non-binding approaches are strongly criticised,[1010] while compulsory instruments (such as PSD2, the Open Banking initiative and the Energy Directive) are praised for the empowering effects they have on individuals,[1011] it would be preferable to opt for the latter. In this regard, it is worth underlining that the European Commission's proposal for a Digital Markets Act[1012] provides that 'gatekeepers'[1013] will have to provide tools facilitating continuous portability,[1014] while its inception impact assessment on its future 'Data Act' hints at the fact that certain undertakings, notably those selling smart home appliances, wearables and home assistants, could be required to create technical interfaces allowing real-time portability.[1015]

168. The creation of a continuous portability right would arguably entail benefits for the individual whose data is ported. Indeed, in order to empower individuals by offering them more choice, it is necessary to ensure that large data holders are not the only ones having the most up-to-date data about individuals.[1016] In this perspective, continuous portability, rather than bulk transfers of historic data, could further lower switching costs and facilitate multi-homing, by ensuring that seamless and real-time access to the individuals' data is only one click away, which is necessary to offer truly valuable services.[1017] In turn, this could entail wide-scale switching,[1018] as individuals would be offered alternative options in real time.[1019]

1009. *Ibid.*, pp. 81-82.
1010. *See* below point 177. B. Lundqvist, 'Regulating Competition and Property in the Digital Economy', *supra*, pp. 43-46. *See also* L. Somaini, 'Regulating the Dynamic Concept of Non-personal Data in the EU: From Ownership to Portability', *supra*, pp. 90-93.
1011. *See* Part II, Chapter 4, Sections 4.2.2 and 4.2.3.
1012. Proposal for a Regulation of the European Parliament and of the Council on contestable and fair markets in the digital sector (Digital Markets Act), 15 December 2020, COM(2020) 842 final. For more details on this Digital Markets Act, *see* points 317, 380 and 384-385.
1013. *See* Articles 2.1 and 3 of the Proposal for a Digital Markets Act. For more details on the designation of these gatekeepers, *see* points 384 and 385.
1014. Article 6.1.h) of the Proposal for a Digital Markets Act.
1015. European Commission, Inception Impact Assessment: '*Data Act (including the review of the Directive 96/9/EC on the legal protection of databases)*', May 2021, Ares (2021)3527151, p. 6.
1016. J. Krämer, P. Senellart and A. de Streel, 'Making Data Portability More Effective for the Digital Economy', *supra*, p. 80.
1017. *Ibid.*, pp. 9 and 80; OECD, *Consumer Data Rights and Competition*, *supra*, p. 43. *See also* J. Crémer, Y.-A. de Montjoye and H. Schweitzer, 'Competition Policy for the Digital Era: Final Report', 2019, available at http://ec.europa.eu/competition/publications/reports/ kd0419345enn.pdf.

169. Looking at the example of PSD2 in general, and of the UK's Open Banking initiative in particular, the requirement to build and ensure the maintenance of common and open APIs, based on common technical standards, to allow data sharing with providers of payment initiation services and of account information services, opens the room for continuous portability.[1020] Arguably, this would generate more switching possibilities, would allow consumers to avoid 'loyalty penalties', as they end up paying more for essential services such as banking, energy and telecoms when they do not switch providers.[1021] This is because incumbents often charge higher prices to long-term consumers, due to a combination of behavioural biases, asymmetry of information and lack of bargaining power.[1022]

170. Such continuous portability could also be envisaged in other fields, as illustrated by Article 20 of the Electricity Directive presented above,[1023] or the UK's Smart Data initiative.[1024] The aim of this initiative, which expressly states that it is an extension of the GDPR's data portability right, is to make data about consumers more easily and instantly accessible to them, and to allow them to be able to transfer it securely via APIs to third parties who can use it to provide them with innovative services.[1025] In turn, this would reduce the efforts required from consumers in order to find deals that best suit them.[1026] Indeed, presently, consumers need to engage in significant effort in order to understand if they benefit from the best deals available, and searching for, and switching to, better alternatives is highly time-consuming.[1027] Some therefore call for more proactive approaches in order to incentivise individuals to port their data, as due to strong consumer inertia,[1028] 'simply relying on engaging consumers by providing them with more information has proven to be a rather ineffective approach'.[1029]

171. In this perspective, (continuous) portability could enable third parties to be more proactive and to actively inform the individual about the fact that it

1018. OECD, *Consumer Data Rights and Competition*, *supra*, p. 44. *See also* M. Gal and O. Aviv, 'The Competitive Effects of the GDPR', *Journal of Competition Law and Economics*, September 2020, Vol. 16(3), pp. 349-391.
1019. Open Data Institute and Fingleton, 'Open Banking, Preparing for lift off', *supra*, p. 6.
1020. *See* point 161.
1021. Open Data Institute and Fingleton, 'Open Banking, Preparing for lift off', *supra*, p. 39.
1022. O. Borgogno and G. Colangelo, 'Consumer Inertia and Competition-Sensitive Data Governance', *supra*, pp. 1 and 6.
1023. *See* point 164.
1024. *See* HM Government, 'Smart Data: Putting consumers in control of their data and enabling innovation', *supra*.
1025. *Ibid.*, pp. 9 and 11.
1026. *Ibid.*, p. 11.
1027. *Ibid.*, p. 13.
1028. *See* point 97.
1029. O. Borgogno and G. Colangelo, 'Consumer Inertia and Competition-Sensitive Data Governance', *supra*, p. 2.

is in a position to provide her with a better and/or cheaper product/service, and this could reduce the hassle of switching. Coming back to the example of the Smart Data initiative, it outlines that individuals should be able to use a single product/service developed by a third party, which could monitor their various consumption and/or financial data and, on that basis, could actively suggest to them to switch towards the product/service of an alternative undertaking that better matches their needs and preferences, ideally by proposing 'one click switching' possibilities.[1030] Third parties could even go a step further, by offering automatic switching services 'that enable consumers to set their preferences and let the service switch them automatically if a better deal appears'.[1031] Such automatic switching services are already available in the UK's energy market and they automatically select the best tariffs available for the individual, on the basis of parameters that she has set.[1032] Some argue that this would especially be valuable for vulnerable individuals who, for instance, have difficulties managing their finances.[1033] Naturally, the sharing of the individual's data should be secure and subject to her consent and to the verification of her identity through a secure authentication process, and this could be coupled with the requirement, for data recipients, to obtain an accreditation in order to ensure that their services are legitimate, secure and comply with the personal data protection requirements.[1034] Moreover, it is fundamental to underline that these potential individual short-term gains that are promised to individuals via these 'empowerment' initiatives will have to be balanced with the potential long-term costs and collective costs in terms of control, autonomy and self-determination.[1035]

172. In fact, the third parties mentioned in the previous paragraph could be PIMS,[1036] as these can offer a centralised dashboard for monitoring and controlling the uses of an individual's data,[1037] which can be managed either by the individual herself or by an independent intermediary acting on her

1030. HM Government, 'Smart Data: Putting consumers in control of their data and enabling innovation', *supra*, p. 13.
1031. *Ibid.*
1032. *Ibid.*, p. 16.
1033. *Ibid.*, p. 22.
1034. *Ibid.*, p. 28. On this point *see* Part II, Chapter 5, Section 5.3.3.
1035. *See* Part I, Chapter 2, Section 2.3.2 and Part II, Chapter 5, Section 5.1.3.
1036. For more information on these PIMS, *see* point 107.
1037. *See* J. Krämer, P. Senellart and A. de Streel, 'Making Data Portability More Effective for the Digital Economy', *supra*, p. 13. *See also*, CtrlShift, 'Data Mobility: The Personal Data Portability Growth Opportunity for the UK Economy', *supra*; Competition and Markets Authority, 'Online Platforms and Digital Advertising: Market Study Interim Report – Appendix L: Potential Approaches to Improving Personal Data Mobility', 18 December 2019, available at https://www.gov.uk/cma-cases/online-platforms-and-digital-advertising-market-study.

behalf.[1038] In substance, a PIMS allows an individual to build an integrated view of her data, which is normally spread across different services, in a system that she controls and trusts, via high-performance APIs.[1039] In this regard, the introduction of a continuous portability right could enable the efficient functioning of such PIMS, through seamless and real-time access to the individual's data.

However, caution should be exercised in view of the potential 'centralisation' of personal data that such initiatives may represent. Indeed, it would be inappropriate to gather all the personal data in question in a single database, however secure it may be; otherwise, a 'Single Point of Failure' could be created. It is therefore imperative to consider decentralised data storage models for the technical implementation of these PIMS.[1040] Although these decentralised models heavily rely on the availability of powerful APIs, they are more scalable than centralised models as they do not require as much local storage and computational capacity.[1041] An example of such decentralised PIMS is the *Solid Project* mentioned above.[1042]

The introduction of a continuous portability right enabling seamless and real-time access to the individual's data could boost the prospect of the emergence of such PIMS. However, some have questioned whether the business model of a privately financed PIMS is sustainable.[1043] Indeed, 'privately funded PIMS, which rely on revenue generation from users, from the data controllers or on the data markets, may either not be sustainable or not have a significant impact on the data ecosystem'.[1044] There might thus be a need for publicly funded or non-for-profit open-source PIMS, the creation of which could be facilitated by the setting of common standards, which are currently lacking.[1045] It should however be outlined that, independently of this concern, one of the aims of the European Commission's proposal for a

1038. S. Delacroix and N. Lawrence, 'Bottom-Up Data Trusts: Disturbing the "One Size Fits All" Approach to Data Governance', *International Data Privacy Law*, November 2019, Vol. 9(4), pp. 236-252. *See also* C. Wendehorst, 'Of Elephants in the Room and Paper Tigers: How to Reconcile Data Protection and the Data Economy', *Trading Data in the Digital Economy: Legal Concepts and Tools*, S. Lohsse, R. Schulze and D. Staudenmayer (eds), *Baden-Baden,* Nomos, 2017, pp. 349-353.
1039. *See* J. Krämer, P. Senellart and A. de Streel, 'Making Data Portability More Effective for the Digital Economy', *supra*, pp. 45 and 67.
1040. T. Tombal, 'Les droits de la personne concernée dans le RGPD', *Le Règlement general sur la protection des données (RGPD / GDPR) – Analyse approfondie*, C. De Terwangne et K. Rosier (coord.), Bruxelles, Larcier, 2018, pp. 509-510.
1041. *See* J. Krämer, P. Senellart and A. de Streel, 'Making Data Portability More Effective for the Digital Economy', *supra*, p. 45.
1042. *See* point 137. *See* https://solidproject.org/.
1043. *See* J. Krämer, P. Senellart and A. de Streel, 'Making Data Portability More Effective for the Digital Economy', *supra*, pp. 66-73.
1044. *Ibid.*, p. 72.
1045. *Ibid.*, pp. 67 and 72-73.

Data Governance Act is precisely to stimulate the emergence of such PIMS, by increasing trust in data sharing and by lowering transaction costs.[1046]

4.4 THE RECENT PHENOMENON OF REGULATORY INITIATIVES PERTAINING TO SPECIFIC (SMALL) BUSINESS USERS: FROM INDIVIDUAL EMPOWERMENT TOWARDS SMALL BUSINESSES EMPOWERMENT

173. So far, Sections 4.1 to 4.3 have focused on 'empowerment' initiatives imposing B2B data sharing that aim to empower individuals. It is however necessary to briefly discuss a more recent phenomenon, namely regulatory initiatives aiming at 'empowering' specific (small) business users. These represent the beginning of a move from individual empowerment towards small businesses empowerment, which fits in a broader context of extending consumer protection (B2C) towards small business protection (B2b). At the European level, a clear example of this broader trend is the Directive on unfair trading practices in B2b relationships in the agricultural and food supply chain.[1047] At the national level, Belgium adopted a law on the abuse of economic dependence, abusive clauses and unfair trading practices in B2b relationships.[1048] In the same vein, in the Netherlands, Article 6:235(1) of Civil Code (*Burgerlijk Wetboek*) provides that the list of black and grey unfair clauses for B2C contracts also applies to standard form contracts concluded with SMEs in B2b settings.[1049] Moreover, several Member States

---

1046. *See* Recital 23 and Article 9.1.b) of the Proposal for a Regulation of the European Parliament and of the Council on European data governance (Data Governance Act), 25 November 2020, COM(2020) 767 final. *See also* p. 7 of its 'Explanatory memorandum'.

1047. Directive (EU) 2019/633 of the European Parliament and of the Council of 17 April 2019 on unfair trading practices in business-to-business relationships in the agricultural and food supply chain, *OJ L 111/59*, 25 April 2019.

1048. Loi du 4 avril 2019 modifiant le Code de droit économique en ce qui concerne les abus de dépendance économique, les clauses abusives et les pratiques du marché déloyales entre entreprises, *M.B.*, 24 mai 2019.

1049. G. Sulija, *Standard Contract Terms in Cross-Border Business Transactions – A Comparative Study from the Perspective of European Union Law*, Frankfurt am Main, Peter Lang, 2011, p. 63.

have extended the scope of the Unfair Commercial Practices Directive[1050] to B2b settings.[1051]

Importantly, it should be outlined from the outset that while the word 'empowerment' is used for both individuals and small business users in my analysis, this word should not be understood exactly in the same way in these two situations. Indeed, as outlined above,[1052] 'empowering' individuals means giving them more control over their data, in order for them to be able to take appropriate decisions about *all aspects of their lives*. On the other hand, initiatives 'empowering' small business users should be understood in a narrower way, as a solely *economic empowerment* to operate freely and efficiently on the market, which derives from their freedom to conduct a business. Indeed, as will be shown below, such initiatives mainly attempt to rebalance the strong discrepancies in bargaining power that these small users suffer from against several large actors. Despite this difference, it was nevertheless decided to use the word 'empowerment' in both situations, as both types of 'empowerment' initiatives aim to reinstate some form of *control* for weaker actors (individuals in the first case, small business users in the second). However, for small business users, this is only a form of *economic control*, while, for individuals, this control relates to *all aspects of their lives*, and is thus broader than sole economic control.

In this Section, two recent regulatory initiatives will be briefly presented. These will, however, not be analysed in depth, as they do not create *compulsory* B2b data sharing, on which I focus, but rather either call for the adoption of self-regulatory codes of conduct for the porting of non-personal data (Article 6 of the Regulation on the Free-Flow of Non-personal Data)[1053] or merely impose transparency obligations (but no sharing obligations) in terms of the access to data from and for (small) business users of online

---

1050. Directive 2005/29/EC of the European Parliament and of the Council of 11 May 2005 concerning unfair business-to-consumer commercial practices in the internal market and amending Council Directive 84/450/EEC, Directives 97/7/EC, 98/27/EC and 2002/65/EC of the European Parliament and of the Council and Regulation (EC) No. 2006/2004 of the European Parliament and of the Council ('Unfair Commercial Practices Directive'), *OJ L 149/22*, 11 June 2005.

1051. A. Renda, et al., 'Study on the Legal Framework Covering Business-to-Business Unfair Trading Practices in the Retail Supply Chain – Final report', DG MARKT/2012/049/E, 26 February 2014, available at https://op.europa.eu/en/publication-detail/-/publication/c82dc8c6-ec15-11e5-8a81-01aa75ed71a1/language-en, p. 64; A. de Streel, 'Online Intermediation Platforms and Fairness: An Assessment of the Recent Commission Proposal', September 2018, available at https://papers.ssrn.com/sol3/papers.cfm?abstract_id=3248723, p. 16.

1052. *See* point 97.

1053. Regulation (EU) 2018/1807 of the European Parliament and of the Council of 14 November 2018 on a framework for the free flow of non-personal data in the European Union, *OJ L 303/59*, 28 November 2018.

intermediation services (Article 9 of the Platform to Business Regulation).[1054]

4.4.1 Regulation on the Free-Flow of Non-personal Data

174. The first data initiative pertaining to specific (small) business users is Article 6 ('Porting of data') of the Regulation on the free flow of non-personal data:[1055]

1. The Commission shall encourage and facilitate the development of self-regulatory codes of conduct at Union level ('codes of conduct'), in order to contribute to a competitive data economy, based on the principles of transparency and interoperability and taking due account of open standards, covering, inter alia, the following aspects:
   (a) *best practices for facilitating the switching* of service providers and the porting of data in a structured, commonly used and machine-readable format including open standard formats where required or requested by the service provider receiving the data;
   (b) *minimum information requirements* to ensure that professional users are provided, before a contract for data processing is concluded, with sufficiently detailed, clear and transparent information regarding the processes, technical requirements, timeframes and charges that apply in case a professional user wants to switch to another service provider or port data back to its own IT systems;
   (c) *approaches to certification schemes* that facilitate the comparison of data processing products and services for professional users, taking into account established national or international norms, to facilitate the comparability of those products and services. Such approaches may include, inter alia, quality management, information security management, business continuity management and environmental management;
   (d) *communication roadmaps* taking a multi-disciplinary approach to raise awareness of the codes of conduct among relevant stakeholders (emphasis added).

1054. Regulation (EU) 2019/1150 of the European Parliament and of the Council of 20 June 2019 on promoting fairness and transparency for business users of online intermediation services, *OJ L 186/57*, 11 July 2019.
1055. Regulation (EU) 2018/1807.

The objective of this provision is to tackle cloud service providers' lock-in practices and to empower 'professional users'[1056] of these services by allowing them to switch more easily between service providers.[1057] Indeed, cloud service providers can resort to legal, contractual and technical restrictions in order to hinder or prevent users from porting their data from one service provider to another or back to their own IT systems, even after the termination of the contract.[1058] This is especially true for small business users who have very limited bargaining power – as they are often presented with a 'take it or leave it' alternative –[1059] and who face very high switching costs.[1060] This has led to a lack of competition between cloud service providers, to lock-in issues, and to a serious lack of data mobility.[1061] Yet, the ability to port data without hindrance is a key factor in order to ensure the small business users' choice and to ensure effective competition in the cloud markets.[1062] Small business users should be empowered to make informed choices by comparing the cloud services offered in the market, and more specifically their terms and conditions pertaining to the porting of their data upon the termination of the contract.[1063]

175. The scope of this 'porting right' is limited to non-personal data, which are residually defined as all data other than personal data,[1064] either because they have never been personal data to begin with or because they have been anonymised.[1065] The decision to opt for such a residual definition has been vividly criticised, as, in practice, it will be complex to determine precisely what constitutes personal data, and thus, by exclusion, what constitutes non-personal data.[1066] This could pose serious issues in terms of the determination of the concrete scope of this 'porting right' in practice.

1056. 'A natural or legal person, including a public authority or a body governed by public law, using or requesting a data processing service for purposes related to its trade, business, craft, profession or task' (Article 3.8 of Regulation 2018/1807.
1057. Recitals 2 and 31 of Regulation 2018/1807. *See also* Communication from the Commission to the European Parliament and the Council, '*Guidance on the Regulation on a Framework for the Free Flow of Non-personal Data in the European Union*', *supra,* pp. 16-19.
1058. Recital 5 of Regulation 2018/1807.
1059. L. Somaini, 'Regulating the Dynamic Concept of Non-personal Data in the EU: From Ownership to Portability', *supra*, p. 92; B. Lundqvist, 'Regulating Competition and Property in the Digital Economy', *supra*, p. 10.
1060. B. Lundqvist, 'Regulating Competition and Property in the Digital Economy', *supra*, p. 9.
1061. Recital 6 of Regulation 2018/1807. *See also* B. Lundqvist, 'Regulating Competition and Property in the Digital Economy', *supra*, p. 4.
1062. Recital 29 of Regulation 2018/1807.
1063. Recital 30 of Regulation 2018/1807.
1064. Article 1 of Regulation 2018/1807.
1065. *See* point 18.
1066. *See* points 19 and 20.

176. Importantly, and contrary to what was originally envisaged,[1067] the Regulation falls short of establishing a compulsory portability right for non-personal data. Rather, the European legislator opted to promote the development of self-regulatory codes of conduct to address the relationship between cloud service providers and their (small) business users.[1068] These codes of conduct should enable the porting of these users' non-personal data in order to empower them to switch easier between service providers. In order to ensure a sufficient degree of representativeness of the undertakings collaborating to the creation of these codes of conduct, the European Commission had to ensure that all relevant stakeholders (including associations of SMEs and start-ups, users and cloud service providers) were involved in its creation.[1069] In practice, two codes of conduct (for the Infrastructure as a service (IaaS) and Software as a Service (SaaS) markets) have been developed by the SWIPO (Switching and Porting) industry working group.[1070] Their effects on the competitiveness of the cloud market, through the facilitation of portability they should entail, will be assessed by the European Commission before November 2022.[1071]

177. Some authors have, however, expressed some serious doubts about the efficiency of such a self-regulatory approach relying on non-binding codes of conduct that merely set best practices, and call for the introduction of compulsory sharing obligations instead.[1072] Indeed, the self-regulatory approach echoes the cloud providers' fear that B2B data sharing obligations would hamper innovation,[1073] but such an approach might in fact reinforce the existing network effects to the benefit of large cloud providers, and would thus not be a workable solution to tackle the small business users' lock-in.[1074]

To a certain extent, this is probably due to the fact that, since the aim is to empower (small) business users rather than individual consumers/data subjects, the European legislator is more reluctant to hamper the cloud providers' business interests. The result of the balance between the benefits

1067. Communication from the Commission to the European Parliament, the Council, the European Economic and Social Committee and the Committee of the Regions, '*Building a European Data Economy*', *supra*, pp. 17-18.
1068. S. Vezzoso, 'Competition Policy in Transition: Exploring Data Portability's Roles', *15th ASCOLA (Virtual) Conference*, June 2020, available at https://ssrn.com/abstract=3634736, p. 6.
1069. Article 6.2 of Regulation 2018/1807.
1070. *See* https://swipo.eu/download-section/.
1071. S. Vezzoso, 'Competition Policy in Transition: Exploring Data Portability's Roles', *supra*, pp. 6-7.
1072. *See* B. Lundqvist, 'Regulating Competition and Property in the Digital Economy', *supra*, pp. 43-46. *See also* L. Somaini, 'Regulating the Dynamic Concept of Non-Personal Data in the EU', *supra*, pp. 90-93.
1073. L. Somaini, 'Regulating the Dynamic Concept of Non-personal Data in the EU', *supra*, p. 91.
1074. B. Lundqvist, 'Regulating Competition and Property in the Digital Economy', *supra*, p. 45.

for the (small) business users and the (incentive) costs for the cloud providers thus seems to lean more towards the latter than in situations where the data holders' business interests are weighed against benefits that compulsory B2B data sharing would entail for individuals/data subjects.[1075] However, as a result, strong doubts can be cast on whether this self-regulatory approach can truly empower (small) business users. The European Commission seems to be aware of this issue, as it suggests, in its inception impact assessment on its future 'Data Act', that this act 'could introduce a binding obligation for cloud computing service providers to offer data and application portability (…) for free or against an additional, but modest specified maximum fee'.[1076]

4.4.2 Platform to Business Regulation

178. The second data initiative pertaining to specific (small) business users is Article 9 ('Access to data') of the Platform to Business Regulation:[1077]

> 1. Providers of online intermediation services[1078] shall include in their terms and conditions a description of the technical and contractual access, or absence thereof, of business users[1079] to any personal data or other data, or both, which business users or consumers provide for the use of the online intermediation services concerned or which are generated through the provision of those services.

1075. *See* Part II, Chapter 5, Section 5.1.

1076. European Commission, Inception Impact Assessment: '*Data Act (including the review of the Directive 96/9/EC on the legal protection of databases)*', May 2021, Ares (2021)3527151, p. 6.

1077. Regulation (EU) 2019/1150 of the European Parliament and of the Council of 20 June 2019 on promoting fairness and transparency for business users of online intermediation services, *OJ L 186/57*, 11 July 2019. *See also* European Commission, Guidelines on ranking transparency pursuant to Regulation (EU) 2019/1150 of the European Parliament and of the Council, *OJ C 424/1*, 8 December 2020.

1078. 'Any natural or legal person which provides, or which offers to provide, online intermediation services to business users' (Article 2.3 of Regulation 2019/1150). Online intermediation services are 'services which meet all of the following requirements: (a) they constitute information society services within the meaning of point (b) of Article 1(1) of Directive (EU) 2015/1535 of the European Parliament and of the Council; (b) they allow business users to offer goods or services to consumers, with a view to facilitating the initiating of direct transactions between those business users and consumers, irrespective of where those transactions are ultimately concluded; (c) they are provided to business users on the basis of contractual relationships between the provider of those services and business users which offer goods or services to consumers' (Article 2.2 of Regulation 2019/1150).

1079. 'Any private individual acting in a commercial or professional capacity who, or any legal person which, through online intermediation services offers goods or services to consumers for purposes relating to its trade, business, craft or profession' (Article 2.1 of Regulation 2019/1150).

2. Through the description referred to in paragraph 1, providers of online intermediation services shall adequately inform business users in particular of the following:
   (a) whether the provider of online intermediation services has access to personal data or other data, or both, which business users or consumers provide for the use of those services or which are generated through the provision of those services, and if so, to which categories of such data and under what conditions;
   (b) whether a business user has access to personal data or other data, or both, provided by that business user in connection to the business user's use of the online intermediation services concerned or generated through the provision of those services to that business user and the consumers of the business user's goods or services, and if so, to which categories of such data and under what conditions;
   (c) in addition to point (b), whether a business user has access to personal data or other data, or both, including in aggregated form, provided by or generated through the provision of the online intermediation services to all of the business users and consumers thereof, and if so, to which categories of such data and under what conditions; and
   (d) whether any data under point (a) is provided to third parties, along with, where the provision of such data to third parties is not necessary for the proper functioning of the online intermediation services, information specifying the purpose of such data sharing, as well as possibilities for business users to opt out from that data sharing.

Article 9 of the Platform to Business Regulation thus merely imposes transparency obligations, but no compulsory data sharing obligations, to the benefit of (small) business users of online intermediation services. Indeed, the online intermediation service provider must solely specify if, and to what extent:

- it has access to (personal or non-personal) data provided by the business user or consumers for the use of the service or to data generated through the use of this service (actively provided and observed data);[1080]
- the business user has access to such actively provided and observed data;[1081]

1080. Article 9.2.a) of Regulation 2019/1150.
1081. Article 9.2.b) of Regulation 2019/1150.

– the business user has access to (personal or non-personal) data, including in aggregated form, that has been derived, by the service provider, from the data provided by or generated through the provision of the online intermediation services to all of the business users and consumers thereof (derived data).[1082]

The providers of online intermediation services should also specify whether they offer a preferential access to this data to themselves and/or to business users that they control.[1083] In such case, they shall refer to the main economic, commercial or legal considerations for such differentiated treatment.[1084]

179. This provision addresses the fact that online intermediation services, through strong data-driven indirect network effects, play a crucial role in the success of (small) business users that resort to their services to reach consumers, but this also leads to an increased dependence of these business users, especially SMEs, on their services.[1085] As outlined by Martens:

> Platforms are both a blessing and a curse in the data economy. They are necessary intermediaries to generate benefits from data aggregation, realize data-driven positive network externalities and thereby enable the emergence of new markets that were not feasible prior to the arrival of digital data. At the same time, exclusive control over the data allows gatekeepers to control the ecosystem and generate significant value for their intermediation services. They can impose excessive entry and access conditions, and exclusive dealing rules preventing sellers from promoting their offers outside the gatekeeper's platform.[1086]

Because of this increased dependence, these business users have extremely limited bargaining power and often cannot negotiate the access conditions to the actively provided, observed and derived data mentioned above. Yet, the ability to access and use such data could enable important value creation in the online platform economy.[1087] Accordingly, Article 9 aims at empowering (small) business users by requiring providers of online

1082. Article 9.2.c) of Regulation 2019/1150.
1083. Article 7.3.a) of Regulation 2019/1150. On this issue of 'differentiated treatment', *see* Expert Group for the Observatory on the Online Platform Economy, 'Work stream on Data: Final Report', 26 February 2021, available at https://ec.europa.eu/digital-single-market/en/news/expert-group-eu-observatory-online-platform-economy-final-reports, pp. 39-40; Expert Group for the Observatory on the Online Platform Economy, 'Work stream on Differentiated Treatment: Final Report', 26 February 2021, available at https://ec.europa.eu/digital-single-market/en/news/expert-group-eu-observatory-online-platform-economy-final-reports.
1084. Article 7.1 of Regulation 2019/1150.
1085. Recital 2 of Regulation 2019/1150.
1086. B. Martens, 'An Economic Perspective on Data and Platform Market Power', *supra* p. 13.
1087. Recital 33 of Regulation 2019/1150.

intermediation services to be transparent regarding the scope, nature and conditions of their access to, and use of, the actively provided, observed and derived data mentioned above.[1088] This information should be proportionate and 'should enable business users to understand whether they can use the data to enhance value creation'.[1089] This should, in turn, allow these (small) business users to make an informed decision on whether the conditions offered by this service provider are fair, or whether they should opt for the services of an alternative provider.

180. Yet, while this provision reduces the asymmetry of information between the services providers and the (small) business users,[1090] it might be insufficient, on its own, to tackle the bargaining power asymmetry between the service providers and the (small) business users, and to truly empower the latter. Indeed, even if these service providers are transparent about the scope and conditions of access, this will only empower the business users, who consider these terms as unfair, if they are able to resort to alternative services. Yet, there could be situations in which these online intermediation service providers are the only viable channel through which the business users can reach the consumers (gatekeeping position),[1091] because of entry barriers and because of these providers' strong market power.[1092] In such cases, the business users will have no other choice than to accept these terms – even if they consider them to be unfair – or to resort to competition law in order to establish the illegality of the service providers' practices (abuse of dominant position or abuse of economic dependence).[1093]

The extent to which (small) business users are truly empowered by Article 9 of the Platform to Business Regulation is thus uncertain, as there is no compulsory obligation for the providers of online intermediation services to provide access to business users to the actively provided, observed and derived data mentioned above.[1094] Yet, these providers may very well opt to protect their own business interests, by refusing to provide access to these data to business users that are already competing with them, or that could grow and compete with them in the future.[1095]

1088. *Ibid.*
1089. *Ibid.*
1090. *See* point 78.
1091. European Commission, 'Questions and Answers – Establishing a fair, trusted and innovation driven ecosystem in the Online Platform Economy', 9 July 2020, available at https://ec.europa.eu/digital-single-market/en/business-business-trading-practices, p. 8.
1092. Expert Group for the Observatory on the Online Platform Economy, 'Work stream on Data: Final Report', *supra*, p. 4.
1093. *See* Part III, Chapter 6, Sections 6.1 and 6.2.
1094. Recital 35 of Regulation 2019/1150.
1095. Expert Group for the Observatory on the Online Platform Economy, 'Work stream on Data: Final Report', *supra*, p. 7.

Once again, this makes it apparent that the European legislator is more reluctant to hamper the service providers' business interests in order to empower (small) business users, than in order to empower individual consumers/data subjects.[1096] This leads to stronger claims by (small) business users to implement compulsory B2B data sharing mechanisms, as they argue that they lack access to individualised data about their own business activity and consumers (actively provided and observed data), and to aggregated data that has been derived, by the service provider, from the data provided by or generated through the provision of the online intermediation services to all of the business users and consumers thereof (derived data).[1097]

In fact, these claims seem to have been heard by the European Commission, which recently adopted a proposal for a Digital Markets Act,[1098] which contains the obligation for 'gatekeepers' to share with their business users or with third parties authorised by them, free of charge, the data that has been provided or generated by these business users, or their end users, through their activity on the gatekeeper's core service, in an effective, high-quality, continuous and real-time manner.[1099] 'Gatekeepers' should also allow their business users to continuously port such actively provided and/or observed data, in compliance with personal data protection law.[1100]

1096. *See*, by analogy, point 177.
1097. Expert Group for the Observatory on the Online Platform Economy, 'Work stream on Data: Final Report', *supra*, pp. 29 and 38.
1098. Proposal for a Digital Markets Act. For more details on this Digital Markets Act, *see* points 317, 380 and 384-385.
1099. *See* Recitals 54 and 55 and Article 6.1.i) of the Proposal for a Digital Markets Act.
1100. *See* Article 6.1.h) of the Proposal for a Digital Markets Act. On continuous portability for end users, *see* point 167.

Chapter 5

Key Balancing Exercises Entailed by 'Empowerment' Initiatives Imposing B2B Data Sharing

181. Like any other data sharing initiative, *empowerment initiatives imposing B2B data sharing* entail balancing exercises. First, the benefits that the specific individual will derive from the data sharing must be articulated with the rights and freedoms of others (the data holder and other data subjects) that it shall not adversely affect.[1101] This will be analysed in Sections 5.1.1 and 5.1.2. Second, there is a need to consider the potential long-term and collective costs in terms of control, autonomy and self-determination that such 'empowerment' initiatives could entail.[1102] This will be analysed in Section 5.1.3. Moreover, it will be outlined that the competitive effects of such 'empowerment' initiatives imposing B2B data sharing are ambiguous (Section 5.2). On that basis, some insights on how future similar types of initiatives could be constructed will be formulated (Section 5.3).

5.1 BALANCING THE BENEFITS FROM THESE 'EMPOWERMENT INITIATIVES' WITH THEIR POTENTIAL COSTS

5.1.1 Finding a Balance Between the Benefits for the Specific Individual and the Business Interests of the Data Holder

182. Any 'empowerment' initiative imposing B2B data sharing necessarily implies finding a balance between the benefits that this initiative will entail for the specific individual (empowerment, reduced lock-in, etc.) and the potential negative effects that this could have on the data holder's business interests. Indeed, data sharing may have an economic impact on the data

1101. Article 20.4 of the GDPR.
1102. *See* Part I, Chapter 2, Section 2.3.2 and Part II, Chapter 5, Section 5.1.3.

holder's business strategy.[1103] As will be outlined below, this balance is internally embedded in the existing 'empowerment' initiatives imposing B2B data sharing that have been described above. This is apparent from the fact that the data holders' (IP and trade secret) rights should not be affected, that the scope of the data covered by the data sharing initiatives is limited, and that they can keep using (some of) the data despite the sharing.

5.1.1.1 The Data Holders' (IP and Trade Secret) Rights Should Not Be Affected

183. 'Empowerment' initiatives imposing B2B data sharing, such as the GDPR's data portability right, should not affect the data holder's IP rights or trade secrets.[1104] Indeed, although many of the data held by the data holders will not qualify for any type of IP protection, some of the data may meet the required thresholds of protection.[1105] As outlined above,[1106] while data, as such, cannot be protected by copyright,[1107] it will often be included in databases and could therefore be subject to the sui generis right granted, to the maker of the database, on the content of the database.[1108] Moreover, individual data can benefit from the protection granted to trade secrets if they meet the requirements defined in the Trade Secret Directive.[1109,1110] In substance, individual data (or a data set) will be considered as a trade secret if:[1111]

- it is secret in the sense that it is not generally known among or readily accessible to persons within the circles that normally deal with the kind of information in question;

1103. I. Graef, M. Husovec and N. Purtova, 'Data Portability and Data Control: Lessons for an Emerging Concept in EU Law', *supra*, p. 1375.
1104. *See* Recital 63 of the GDPR.
1105. I. Graef, M. Husovec and N. Purtova, 'Data Portability and Data Control: Lessons for an Emerging Concept in EU Law', *supra*, p. 1377.
1106. *See* points 58-60.
1107. N. Duch-Brown, B. Martens and F. Mueller-Langer, 'The Economics of Ownership, Access and Trade in Digital Data', *Digital Economy Working Paper 2016-10*, JRC Technical Reports, 2016, available at https://papers.ssrn.com/sol3/papers.cfm?abstract_id=2914144, p. 7.
1108. Articles 7-11 of Directive 96/9/EC. I however outlined that the evolution of the European Court of Justice's case law has arguably slipped towards the protection of some individual data in the set, namely those which required a substantial investment to obtain (*see* points 59 and 60).
1109. Directive (EU) 2016/943 of the European Parliament and of the Council of 8 June 2016 on the protection of undisclosed know-how and business information (trade secrets) against their unlawful acquisition, use and disclosure, *OJ L 157*, 15 June 2016.
1110. J. Drexl, 'Designing Competitive Markets for Industrial Data – Between Propertisation and Access', *Max Planck Institute for Innovation & Competition Research Paper No. 16-13*, 31 October 2016, available at https://ssrn.com/abstract=2862975, p. 23.
1111. Article 2.1 of Directive 2016/943.

- it has commercial value because it is secret; and
- it has been subject to reasonable steps under the circumstances, by the person lawfully in control of the information, to keep it secret.

Importantly, this Trade Secret Directive only protects the trade secret holders[1112] against the unlawful acquisition, use and disclosure of trade secrets.[1113] Thus, the protection of trade secrets is constructed as a set of defensive rights, rather than as a right in rem enforceable *erga omnes*. When applied to data, this means that this legislation authorises lawful data access while reassuring trade secret owners by granting them a series of rights in the event of illegal use of their data by third parties, equating to a protection of de facto possession of data rather than to a protection of the 'ownership' of data.[1114] As pointed out by Drexl, this defensive perspective 'can be considered as better suited to serve the purposes of the data economy, by focussing on the particular way in which a third party has in particular acquired access to the data instead of granting exclusive protection against the use of data'.[1115]

184. 'Empowerment' initiatives imposing B2B data sharing can thus not be used to commit unfair commercial practices or to infringe an IP right.[1116] In fact, there are three areas of friction with IP/trade secret rights as data sharing initiatives 'can force disclosure of data that could otherwise be kept away from competitors and thus be preserved as an advantage in the process of competition; can prescribe sharing of data where exclusivity was previously promised as a reward; [and] can undermine revenue that the potential beneficiary expected from her licensing activity and thus broadly innovation incentives'.[1117]

However, the potential risks that this initiative might entail for the data holder's business interests and (IP/trade secret) rights cannot, in and of itself, serve as the basis for a refusal to apply such data sharing initiatives.[1118] Indeed, taking the example of Article 20.4 of the GDPR, Drexl outlines that the mere existence of a sui generis database right of the data controller should not, in and of itself, constitute an obstacle to the right to data

1112. 'Any natural or legal person lawfully controlling a trade secret' (Article 2.2 of Directive 2016/943).
1113. Article 1.1 of Directive 2016/943.
1114. Commission Staff Working Document on the free flow of data and emerging issues of the European data economy accompanying the Communication '*Building a European Data Economy*', Brussels, 10 January 2017, SWD(2017) 2 final, pp. 33-34.
1115. J. Drexl, 'Designing Competitive Markets for Industrial Data' – Between Propertisation and Access', *supra*, p. 24.
1116. *See* Article 29 Working Party, *Guidelines on the right to data portability*, WP 242 rev.01, 13 April 2017, p. 12.
1117. I. Graef, M. Husovec and N. Purtova, 'Data Portability and Data Control: Lessons for an Emerging Concept in EU Law', *supra*, p. 1378.
1118. *See* Article 29 Working Party, *Guidelines on the right to data portability*, WP 242 rev.01, 13 April 2017, p. 12.

portability, as otherwise this would compromise the effectiveness of this right.[1119] Rather, a concrete analysis of the adverse effects that data sharing could entail for the data holders' IP/trade secret rights must therefore be carried out, and some suggest that the standard should be higher than mere 'interference' with these rights.[1120] In this regard, I make the argument that while the adverse effects for the data holder may be extremely small (or even inexistent) regarding data actively provided by the data subject, these effects might be bigger regarding some of the observed data that the data holder has collected. For instance, observed data about the data subjects' behaviour (what content does she consult, how long did she stay on a specific page, what link did she click on, etc.) could be considered as being highly valuable from a commercial point of view (targeted recommendations, targeted advertising, etc.).

If an adverse effect does occur, the Article 29 Working Party (today the EDPB) nevertheless argues that this should not lead to a plain and simple refusal to share, but rather that the data holder shall ensure that (a part of) the data can be transmitted in a form that does not affect these (IP/trade secret) rights.[1121] However, the Article 29 Working Party remained mute on what should be done if the form of the data cannot be adapted and this generates uncertainties that must be addressed by the European legislator.[1122]

185. In this regard, some authors suggest that the possibility to refuse sharing data covered by IP/trade secret rights with the data subject/consumer herself should be extremely limited, while there could be more leeway for data holders to refuse the sharing with third-party recipients.[1123] Indeed, in the latter case, these authors argue that 'a reconciliation of the interests might particularly confine the follow-on use of ported data to [a] specific set of socially justifiable purposes of re-use, possibly with schemes of fair remuneration'.[1124] To do so, the idea of white lists of data recipients, as done in the Open Banking initiative through the 'Open Banking Directory', could be explored.[1125] However, it must be outlined that, in that case, the goal of this list is not to protect the data holder's interests, but rather to protect the

1119. J. Drexl, 'Data Access and Control in the Era of Connected Devices', *supra*, pp. 84-85.
1120. I. Graef, M. Husovec and N. Purtova, 'Data Portability and Data Control: Lessons for an Emerging Concept in EU Law', *supra*, p. 1379.
1121. *See* Article 29 Working Party, *Guidelines on the right to data portability*, WP 242 rev.01, 13 April 2017, p. 12.
1122. I. Graef, 'Paving the Way Forward for Data Governance: A Story of Checks and Balances', *Technology and Regulation,* Special issue: Governing Data as a Resource, 2020, p. 28. *See also* I. Graef, M. Husovec and N. Purtova, 'Data Portability and Data Control: Lessons for an Emerging Concept in EU Law', *supra*, p. 1378.
1123. I. Graef, M. Husovec and N. Purtova, 'Data Portability and Data Control: Lessons for an Emerging Concept in EU Law', *supra*, p. 1379.
1124. *Ibid.*, p. 1359. For more detailed explanations, *see* pp. 1380-1388.
1125. *See* point 162.

consumers by ensuring that these recipients are secure and that their services and processing activities are legitimate and lawful.

This suggestion does not seem to have been picked up, and it is therefore uncertain whether a data holder would be entitled to limit the purposes for which the data pertaining to a specific individual can be reused by third parties, on the grounds of IP/trade secret rights. It can also be questioned whether this would be desirable. Indeed, if given the possibility to limit the purposes of reuse by third parties, the data holder will likely limit the possibility for third parties to develop competing products on the basis of the shared data pertaining to a specific individual. However, this would run contrary to the very essence of these data sharing initiatives, which precisely aim at empowering the individuals by allowing them to share their data in order to be offered better services, and to be able to multi-home and to switch more easily between services. Such possibilities to refuse data sharing should thus be envisaged with great caution.

The uncertainty of this articulation with the (IP and trade secrets) rights of the data holder is however attenuated by the fact that the scope of the data covered by the 'empowerment' initiatives imposing B2B data sharing is limited, and by the fact that the data holder can keep using (some of) the data despite the sharing.

5.1.1.2 Limitation of the Scope of the Data Covered

186. The balance between the benefits for the specific individual and the business interests of the data holder is also embedded in the scope of the data covered by the main data sharing initiatives mentioned above.

Indeed, the personal data portability right of Article 20 GDPR is limited to data 'provided' by the data subject,[1126] namely actively provided and observed data.[1127] While there is a doubt on whether 'acquired actively provided data' and 'acquired observed data' could fall within the scope of this right,[1128] what is certain is that 'inferred data and derived data' created by the data controller on the basis of the data 'provided by the data subject' are not be covered by the data portability right.[1129] Yet, these types of data will often be the most valuable for data holders. Similarly, the data retrieval right of Article 16.4 of the Digital Content Directive only applies to 'any content other than personal data, which was provided or created by the consumer when using the digital content or digital service supplied by the trader'.[1130] It therefore only applies to non-personal data created or provided

1126. Article 20.1 of the GPDR.
1127. *See* Part II, Chapter 4, Section 4.1.2.2.
1128. *See* point 142.
1129. Article 29 Working Party, *Guidelines on the right to data portability*, WP 242 rev.01, 13 April 2017, p. 10.
1130. *See* point 153. Article 16.4 of Directive 2019/770.

by the consumer (actively provided or observed), but not to inferred/derived data nor to acquired data.[1131] The scope of PSD2's data access and use rights granted in Articles 65-67 is, arguably, also limited to actively provided data (the identification data pertaining to the client) and observed data (the amount of funds available on the payment account and the transactions made, which are observed on the basis of the use made of this account by the client), excluding inferred/derived data.[1132] In the same vein, the access right contained in Article 20 of the Electricity Directive is limited to final customers' metering data and to their electricity consumption data.[1133] These are also observed data and not inferred/derived data.

187. It is thus clear from the above that the scope of the data covered by 'empowerment' initiatives imposing B2B data sharing is limited to actively provided and observed data, and excludes inferred/derived data, in order to preserve the business interests of the data holder. Indeed, this prevents potential competitors of the data holders from benefiting from the data subject/consumer profiles in which the data holder invested heavily, as this is where the true value of their services lies, and these competitors will need to create these profiles themselves on the basis of the actively provided/ observed data.[1134] This should stimulate innovation.[1135] Yet, it must be outlined that these competitors could nevertheless try to use this actively provided/observed data in order to reverse-engineer these profiles (inferred data).[1136] This would however be a time-consuming task, and these competitors might actually prefer to create their own profiles. Accordingly, exempting inferred/derived data from the scope of these data sharing initiatives protects the investment and collection incentives of the data holders, and thus provides an appropriate balance between the benefits for the specific individual and the business interests of the data holder.[1137]

188. However, it must be added that providing this inferred/derived data to the individuals would empower them and would enhance their informational self-determination.[1138] This is where the existence of the data access right

1131. Indeed, here, and contrary to Article 20 of the GDPR, the wording of Article 16.4 does not leave room for doubt on the fact that 'acquired provided data' and 'acquired observed data' do not fall in the scope of this article, as it explicitly refers to data provided 'when using the digital content or digital service supplied by the trader', which thus excludes data provided when using a third party's content or service.

1132. *See* point 159.

1133. *See* point 164.

1134. I. Graef, M. Husovec and N. Purtova, 'Data Portability and Data Control: Lessons for an Emerging Concept in EU Law', *supra*, p. 1375.

1135. J. Krämer, P. Senellart and A. de Streel, 'Making Data Portability More Effective for the Digital Economy', *supra*, p. 9.

1136. I. Graef, M. Husovec and N. Purtova, 'Data Portability and Data Control: Lessons for an Emerging Concept in EU Law', *supra*, p. 1384.

1137. OECD, *Consumer Data Rights and Competition*, *supra*, p. 45.

1138. *See* point 97.

contained in Article 15 of the GDPR must be reminded, which now explicitly provides that the data subject has the right to receive a copy of her personal data undergoing processing.[1139] Importantly, the scope of this data access right is broader than the scope of the data sharing initiatives mentioned above, as the data subject can receive a copy of all of the data processed by the data controller, which also includes inferred/derived data.

However, the effect of this data access right on the business interests of the data holder is limited, as it does not provide for the direct transmission of the data to a recipient. Only the data subject will receive a copy of this data. Naturally, the data subject could then be inclined to transfer the received data to a recipient, but the reuse possibilities will likely be limited by the format of such data. Indeed, Article 15.3 of the GDPR provides that the data shall be provided in a commonly used electronic form. Yet, a PDF file will probably be considered as meeting the condition of 'commonly used electronic form', but it will not allow the recipient to easily extract the data contained therein. This is a major difference with the data sharing initiatives mentioned above, which precisely aim at facilitating reuse by imposing the sharing of data in structured, commonly used and machine-readable formats.[1140] The impact of the data access right on the business interests of the data holder is thus limited, as this right mainly aims at enabling data subjects to understand what is done with their data, and not at allowing the technical reuse of such data.

5.1.1.3 Possibility for the Data Holders to Keep Using the Data Despite the Sharing

189. Finally, the balance between the benefits for the specific individual and the business interests of the data holder is also embedded in the possibility for the data holders to keep using the data despite the sharing. Indeed, data are a non-rivalrous resource and this allows, from a technical aspect, data holders to keep using the data for their own business activities, even if they have to share (some of) it.[1141] Their business interests are thus preserved.

In this regard, the data sharing initiatives contained in the GDPR, in PSD2, and in the Electricity Directive do not prevent the data holder from keeping to use the (actively provided/observed data) data pertaining to a specific individual that it has to share.[1142] This is because the obligation to share does not entail a correlative obligation to erase or stop processing the data.[1143]

1139. Article 15.3 of the GDPR.
1140. *See* points 147 and 155.
1141. *See* point 52.
1142. *See* points 148, 159 and 164.
1143. *See,* for example, Article 20.3 of the GDPR.

The situation is slightly different for the data retrieval right contained in the Digital Content Directive. This right is exercised by the consumer at the termination of the contract,[1144] and the Directive provides that, when the consumer terminates the contract, the trader must refrain from using the non-personal data provided or created by the consumer.[1145] However, there are exceptions to this principle, which illustrate the balance analysed here and the consideration for the data holder (trader)'s business interests.[1146]

5.1.2 Considering the Other Data Subjects' Right to Personal Data Protection

190. Any 'empowerment' initiative imposing B2B data sharing also implies considering the 'adverse effects'[1147] that this sharing could have on other data subjects' right to personal data protection. Indeed, although the compulsory B2B data sharing initiative pertains to a specific individual, the data that will be shared as a result of it will often not solely pertain to this individual. This is because this data might also contain information about other individuals. For instance, porting a picture from one social network to another is not problematic if the person requesting the transfer is alone on the picture, but this might be more problematic if other people are tagged on the picture, as their rights might be adversely affected by the transfer. According to the Article 29 Working Party, such an 'adverse effect' would occur if the sharing would prevent these other data subjects 'from exercising their rights as data subjects under the GDPR (such as the rights to information, access, etc.)'.[1148]

Solving this issue is one of the core challenges of 'empowerment' initiatives imposing B2B data sharing, and it is often pointed out as one of the key obstacles to their wider use.[1149] Naturally, the importance of this issue will be particularly exacerbated in social media and communication

1144. Article 16.4 of Directive 2019/770.

1145. Article 16.3 of Directive 2019/770.

1146. Even after the termination of the contract, the trader can continue to use data that has no utility outside the context of the content or service supplied by the trader; that only relates to the consumer's activity when using the content or service; that has been aggregated with other data by the trader and cannot be disaggregated or can only be disaggregated with disproportionate effort; or that has been generated jointly by the consumer and other persons who continue to use the content or service (Article 16.3 of Directive 2019/770).

1147. Article 29 Working Party, *Guidelines on the right to data portability*, WP 242 rev.01, 13 April 2017, p. 11. *See also* Article 20.4 of the GDPR: 'The right [to data portability] shall not *adversely affect* the rights and freedoms of others' (emphasis added).

1148. Article 29 Working Party, *Guidelines on the right to data portability*, WP 242 rev.01, 13 April 2017, p. 11.

1149. *See,* for example, E. Egan, 'Data Portability and Privacy', *Facebook White Paper*, September 2019, available at https://iapp.org/media/pdf/fb_whitepaper_sep_2019.pdf; S. Martinelli, 'Sharing Data and Privacy in the Platform Economy: The Right to Data

services markets where the value of data is, to some extent, determined by the social interactions between data subjects.[1150] Indeed, in those cases, what is valuable is not so much the content of a post or of a message sent by a specific individual, but rather with whom it was shared or to whom it was sent, as this allows to paint the individual's 'social graph'.[1151] On the other hand, this will be less of a problem in markets where the data only concerns a specific individual and where interactions with others are not so important (e.g., music and video streaming preferences and habits).[1152]

191. If the data covered by the 'empowerment' initiatives imposing B2B data sharing also contains data about other data subjects, sharing this data with the individual or with recipients creates tensions with two fundamental principles of the GDPR, namely the purpose limitation[1153] and data minimisation[1154] principles.[1155] Accordingly, these two principles have to be considered when implementing 'empowerment' initiatives imposing B2B data sharing, in order to determine whether the other data subjects' rights might be 'adversely affected' by the transfer.

According to the purpose limitation principle, personal data can only be processed for specified, explicit and legitimate purposes, and cannot be further processed in a manner that is incompatible with those purposes.[1156] This means that other data subjects' personal data that have been collected for a specific purpose cannot be shared with the individual or with recipients if this further processing does not fit within this initial purpose of processing.

According to the data minimisation principle, only the adequate, relevant and necessary data for the fulfilment of the specific purpose of processing shall be processed.[1157] This implies that, in combination with the purpose limitation principle, the categories and amount of data that can be shared with the individual or with recipients should be limited to what is necessary to meet the purpose pursued by the compulsory B2B data sharing

---

Portability and "Porting Rights"', *Regulating New Technologies in Uncertain Times*, L. Reins (ed.), The Hague, T.M.C. Asser Press, 2019, pp. 133-152.

1150. OECD, *Consumer Data Rights and Competition*, *supra*, p. 45. *See also* G. Nicholas and M. Weinberg, 'Data Portability and Platform Competition: Is User Data Exported from Facebook Actually Useful to Competitors?', 2019, available at https://www.law.nyu.edu/centers/engelberg/pubs/2019-11-06-Data-Portability-And-Platform-Competition, p. 3.
1151. *See* G. Nicholas and M. Weinberg, 'Data Portability and Platform Competition: Is User Data Exported from Facebook Actually Useful to Competitors?', *supra*, p. 12.
1152. OECD, *Consumer Data Rights and Competition*, *supra*, p. 45.
1153. Article 5.1.b) of the GDPR.
1154. Article 5.1.c) of the GDPR.
1155. *See* I. Graef, T. Tombal and A. de Streel, 'Limits and Enablers of Data Sharing: An Analytical Framework for EU Competition, Data Protection and Consumer Law', *TILEC Discussion Paper DP 2019-005*, November 2019, available at https://ssrn.com/abstract=2956308, pp. 25-26.
1156. Article 5.1.b) of the GDPR.
1157. Article 5.1.c) of the GDPR.

initiative. If the other data subjects' personal data is not necessary for this purpose, it shall not be transferred.

192. There is thus a necessity to articulate the benefits for the specific individual whose data is shared, with the need to avoid causing 'adverse effects' for other data subjects, and this should be done prior to the sharing. Indeed, while the individual whose data is shared has given her consent to the transfer, this is not the case for the other data subjects whose data could be intertwined with this individual's data. Therefore, this transfer can only take place if the purpose for which the transfer is made is compatible with the data holders' initial purpose of processing.[1158] If the transfer is deemed to be 'incompatible' with the initial purpose for which the data has been collected, it can only be carried out if the other data subjects consented to it or if this transfer is necessary to comply with a legal obligation.[1159] While collecting the consents from all of these other data subjects might be infeasible in practice, the data holder could probably argue that the act of sharing is necessary to comply with a legal obligation, *in casu* the *empowerment initiatives imposing B2B data sharing* (e.g., Article 20 of the GDPR, Articles 65-67 of PSD2 or Article 20 of the Electricity Directive).

However, this is not sufficient in itself, as, according to the principle of separate justification, which provides that 'each transaction in data requires a legal basis at two levels: the level of the supplier of the data and the level of the recipient',[1160] the recipient of the other data subjects' personal data also needs a lawful basis for the further processing of this data. In the context of 'empowerment' initiatives imposing B2B data sharing, this recipient could be either the individual at the origin of the sharing (Article 20.1 of the GDPR) or a recipient with which the individual wants to share the data (Article 20.2 of the GDPR, PSD2 or the Electricity Directive). In the first case, the individual will actually likely process the other data subjects' data for purely personal or household activities, and will thus not have to apply the GDPR.[1161] In the second case, the recipient will need its own specific lawful basis for the processing of the other data subjects' personal data.[1162]

1158. Article 5.1.b) of the GDPR.
1159. Article 6.4 of the GDPR. *See also* C. de Terwangne, 'Article 5. Principles Relating to Processing of Personal Data', *The EU General Data Protection Regulation (GDPR): A Commentary*, C. Kuner, L. Bygrave and C. Docksey (eds), Oxford, Oxford University Press, 2020, p. 316.
1160. C. Wendehorst, 'Of Elephants in the Room and Paper Tigers: How to Reconcile Data Protection and the Data Economy', *Trading Data in the Digital Economy: Legal Concepts and Tools*, S. Lohsse, R. Schulze and D. Staudenmayer (eds), Baden-Baden, Nomos, 2017, pp. 334-337.
1161. Article 2.2.c) of the GDPR.
1162. C. Wendehorst, 'Of Elephants in the Room and Paper Tigers', *supra*, pp. 334-337.

In practice, the recipient will rely either on these other data subjects' consent or on 'legitimate interests'.[1163]

Indeed, the recipient could attempt to argue that processing these other data subjects' personal data is necessary for the purposes of the legitimate interests pursued by the individual at the origin of the sharing, namely 'individual empowerment'.[1164] Indeed, Article 6.1.f) of the GDPR provides that a personal data processing is lawful if it is 'necessary for the purposes of the legitimate interests pursued by the controller *or by a third party*' (emphasis added). In this case, it could be argued that the individual at the origin of the sharing is such a *third party*.

To take an example, an individual uses the compulsory B2B data sharing mechanism contained in PSD2 in order to share some of its payment account information (e.g., the list of the transactions she has made) with a provider of an account information service (the recipient), in order to be empowered to better manage her finances. The data at hand (the list of transactions) will necessarily contain personal data about other data subjects, who were at the other end of some of these transactions. In that case, the recipient could argue that the processing of these other data subjects' personal data is necessary for the purposes of the legitimate interests (i.e., the empowerment goal) pursued by the individual at the origin of the sharing.

However, such a processing will only be lawful if these legitimate interests of the individual at the origin of the sharing are not overridden by the interests or fundamental rights and freedoms of the other data subjects.[1165] A case-by-case assessment of the 'adverse effects' on these other individuals will thus have to be conducted. Coming back to the example mentioned above, the rights and freedoms of the other data subjects appearing on the individual's bank transactions are unlikely to be adversely affected by the sharing of the bank account information with the provider of an account information service.[1166] In such case, the other data subjects' rights should not be an obstacle to the compulsory B2B data sharing mechanism, as the balance between the interests of the individual at the origin of the sharing and the interests of the other data subjects weigh in favour of the former, as the latter are not 'adversely affected' by the sharing. These potential 'adverse effects' should indeed be the key criteria to have in mind when considering this balance.

193. In order to avoid these 'adverse effects', the Article 29 Working Party (today the EDPB) suggests that the processing of these other data subjects' personal data should be authorised only insofar as these data remain under

1163. Article 6.1.f) of the GDPR. *See* Article 29 Working Party, *Guidelines on the right to data portability*, WP 242 rev.01, 13 April 2017, p. 11.
1164. *See* point 181.
1165. Article 6.1.f) of the GDPR.
1166. Article 29 Working Party, *Guidelines on the right to data portability*, WP 242 rev.01, 13 April 2017, p. 11.

the sole control of the individual at the origin of the sharing, and that they should only be processed for the purposes determined by this individual.[1167] In this perspective, if the data is shared with a recipient, this recipient could therefore not process the other data subjects' personal data for purposes that have not been defined by the individual at the origin of the data sharing, such as marketing purposes.[1168] Moreover, the Article 29 Working Party invites both the data holder and the recipient to implement technical tools allowing the individual to select the personal data she wishes to share while excluding, where possible, the personal data of other data subjects.[1169] This would make it possible to avoid, upstream, any 'adverse effect' on the rights of these other data subjects. Yet, it is not unimaginable that some of these other data subjects' personal data may pass through this filter or might necessarily have to be shared. Alternatively, the Article 29 Working Party also invites to reflect on the implementation of consent mechanisms for these other data subjects, in order to facilitate the empowerment initiative imposing B2B data sharing.[1170]

194. Naturally, identifying lawful bases for the processing of these other data subjects' personal data and complying with the purpose limitation principle are only the first steps in order to avoid these 'adverse effects'. Like for any other processing of personal data, the recipient will also have to comply with the general principles of personal data protection.[1171] Namely, it will have to inform the other data subjects about the further processing in a fair and transparent manner.[1172] In this regard, it will notably have to inform the data subjects about the categories of personal data concerned, about the purposes of the processing for which the personal data are intended and about the period for which the personal data will be stored.[1173] Moreover, it will have to ensure that these other data subjects' rights (such as their right to object to the processing[1174]) are given their fullest effect,[1175] and that it has implemented appropriate technical and organisational measures in order to ensure the security of these other data subjects' data.[1176] Finally, it will have to document how it has complied with all of the above-mentioned principles, in light of the accountability principle.[1177]

1167. *Ibid.*, p. 12.
1168. *Ibid.*
1169. *Ibid.*
1170. *Ibid.*
1171. For more details, *see*, by analogy, points 361-366.
1172. Articles 5.1.a) and 12-14 of the GDPR.
1173. Articles 14.1.c) and d) and 14.2.a) of the GDPR.
1174. Article 21 of the GDPR.
1175. Articles 13-22 of the GDPR.
1176. Article 5.1.f) and 32 of the GDPR.
1177. Article 5.2 of the GDPR.

195. In light of the above, it is suggested that the key criterion to have in mind when considering the protection of other data subjects' personal data is the assessment of the potential 'adverse effects' that the *empowerment initiatives imposing B2B data sharing* could have on these other data subjects. Said otherwise, the other data subjects' right to personal data protection should not be an obstacle to the compulsory B2B data sharing mechanism if they are not 'adversely affected' by the sharing. This suggestion could be a way to solve the uncertainty surrounding this issue, which has, for instance, not been sufficiently considered by the European legislator when establishing the data portability right of Article 20 GDPR, and which is often pointed out as one of the key obstacles to a wider use of 'empowerment' initiatives imposing B2B data sharing.[1178]

Finally, it is worth underlining that any 'adverse effect' could potentially be exacerbated by the creation of a continuous portability right,[1179] as it would entail continuous flows of information about other individuals, rather than merely periodic bulk transfers. This thus increases the risks of potential data breaches, abuses and frauds.[1180]

5.1.3 Finding a Balance Between the Potential Individual Short-Term Gains of 'Empowerment' Initiatives and Their Potential Long-Term Costs and Collective Costs in Terms of Control, Autonomy and Self-Determination

196. As it has been extensively explained above,[1181] great caution will have to be exercised in the adoption of *empowerment initiatives imposing data sharing*, as a specific attention will have to be paid to the risks that they could entail in terms of individual's control and autonomy. In fact, if these initiatives are not strictly circumscribed, they might actually entail a severe loss of control for the individuals. This is because, due to strong asymmetries of information, there is a risk that the numerous data that the individuals are asked to divulge, in the name of 'empowerment', could be further disseminated with an important number of actors, thus generating a loss of control on these data,[1182] as they will often not know which data are used by whom

1178. *See,* for example, E. Egan, 'Data Portability and Privacy', *supra.*
1179. *See* Part II, Chapter 4, Section 4.3.
1180. O. Borgogno and G. Colangelo, 'Consumer Inertia and Competition-Sensitive Data Governance', *supra*, p. 10.
1181. This detailed explanation will not be repeated here and the interested reader is invited to consult Part I, Chapter 2, Section 2.3.2.
1182. A. Rouvroy, '"Of Data and Men": Fundamental Rights and Liberties in a World of Big Data', *Report for the Consultative Committee of the Convention for the Protection of Individuals with Regard to Automatic Processing of Personal Data (T-PD)*, T-PD-BUR(2015)09REV, Council of Europe, Strasbourg, 11 January 2016, p. 8; A. Acquisti,

and for which purposes.[1183] Consequently, these data could be used to influence their decision-making without their knowledge, raising serious issues in terms of autonomy and self-determination.[1184] It is thus of paramount importance to see beyond the potential short-term gains that are promised to individuals, and to consider with great care these potential long-term costs.

197. Moreover, it is important to understand the necessary collective approach of autonomy and (informational) self-determination.[1185] Indeed, an individual's decision to share data will create negative externalities, as it also reveals information about other individuals, which potentially did not share any data themselves, as this data could be used to draw correlations about them.[1186] In light of this relational and collective nature of data,[1187] it will also be fundamental to factor these potential collective costs for other individuals, in order to preserve their autonomy.

198. In order to assess these long-term and collective costs that could potentially derive from the adoption of empowerment initiatives imposing B2B data sharing, legislators could engage in a case-by-case risk assessment of the 'systemic risks' that these initiatives could entail, by analogy with the proposal for a Digital Services Act (DSA) that requires very large platforms to manage systemic risks.[1188]

In this regard, legislators should first consider the economic risks that such data sharing initiatives could entail for (other) individuals. To illustrate this, one could imagine a scenario where individuals can consent to the

---

C. Taylor and L. Wagman, 'The Economics of Privacy', *Sloan Foundation Economics Research Paper No. 2580411*, 8 March 2016, available at https://ssrn.com/abstract=2580411, p. 3.

1183. A. Rouvroy and Y. Poullet, 'The Right to Informational Self-Determination and the Value of Self-Development: Reassessing the Importance of Privacy for Democracy', *Reinventing Data Protection: Proceedings of the International Conference (Brussels, 12-13 October 2007)*, Dordrecht, Springer, 2009, p. 68.

1184. A. Acquisti, C. Taylor and L. Wagman, 'The Economics of Privacy', *supra*, p. 44.

1185. *See* point 101.

1186. D. Acemoğlu, et al., 'Too Much Data: Prices and Inefficiencies in Data Markets', *NBER Working Paper No. 26296*, 2019, available at https://www.nber.org/system/files/working_papers/w26296/w26296.pdf, pp. 3 and 36-37; J.A. Fairfield and C. Engel, 'Privacy as a Public Good', *Duke Law Journal*, 2015, Vol. 65(3), pp. 385-457; M. MacCarthy, 'New Directions in Privacy: Disclosure, Unfairness and Externalities', *Journal of Law and Policy for the Information Society*, 2011, Vol. 6, pp. 425-512.

1187. A. Rouvroy, '*Homo juridicus* est-il soluble dans les données ?', *Law, Norms and Freedoms in Cyberspace / Droit, normes et libertés dans le cybermonde: Liber Amicorum Yves Poullet*, E. Degrave, C. de Terwangne, S. Dusollier et R. Queck (dir.), Bruxelles, Larcier, 2018, p. 429.

1188. *See*, by analogy, Articles 25 and 26 and Recital 57 of the Proposal for a Regulation of the European Parliament and of the Council on a Single Market For Digital Services (Digital Services Act) and amending Directive 2000/31/EC, 15 December 2020, COM(2020) 825 final.

collection and sharing of IoT sensor data from their car or from a connected watch, in order to be offered a lower price for their car or health insurance. While this might bring short-term benefits to the consenting individual, this might also create higher costs for the other individuals if the insurers increase the normal premiums in order to compensate for this price reduction. Hence, there is a risk of negative economic consequences for other individuals that must be factored.

In fact, such practices could also lead to broader 'surveillance capitalism' risks,[1189] which will also need to be considered by legislators. Indeed, in a scenario such as the one mentioned above, the other individuals might feel like they have to consent to the use of such IoT devices and to the sharing of their data as well in order to avoid these additional costs, even if they would have preferred not to. As a result, this could lead not only to a broad dissemination with third parties of the data shared by the individual that consented to the sharing but also to increased data sharing that does not accurately represent the individuals' privacy preferences. In turn, this would increase these surveillance capitalism risks, as individuals would become increasingly transparent, and this could lead to their economic manipulation in the future.[1190]

Indeed, it cannot be excluded that the shared data will feed into Artificial Intelligence (AI) systems that could be detrimental to the individuals. In this regard, it is worth underlining here that the European Commission's proposal for an AI Act provides that the placing on the market, putting into service or use of an AI system that deploys subliminal techniques beyond a person's consciousness, or that exploits any of the vulnerabilities of a specific group of people due to their age or (physical or mental) disability, in order to materially distort a person's behaviour, is prohibited if this 'is likely to cause that person or another person *physical or psychological harm*' (emphasis added).[1191] As emphasised, the deployment of AI techniques that could influence the behaviour of individuals, or exploit their vulnerabilities, would only be prohibited if this leads to 'physical or psychological harm'. Reversely, this means that AI techniques, fed with the shared data, could potentially be deployed in order to influence the economic behaviour of individuals, through subliminal manipulation or through the exploitation of vulnerabilities identified via the data sharing. For instance, if an individual shares her financial history data with a payment service provider in order to be offered better prices, there is a risk that this data could be further

---

1189. *See* S. Zuboff, *The Age of Surveillance Capitalism: The Fight for a Human Future at the New Frontier of Power*, New York, PublicAffairs, 2019.

1190. A. Rouvroy and Y. Poullet, 'The Right to Informational Self-Determination and the Value of Self-Development', *supra*, pp. 45-46.

1191. Articles 5.1.a) and 5.1.b) of the Proposal for a Regulation of the European Parliament and of the Council laying down harmonised rules on artificial intelligence (Artificial Intelligence Act) and amending certain Union legislative acts, 21 April 2021, COM(2021) 206 final.

disseminated with advertisers. The latter could then use this data in order to materially distort the individual's behaviour in a matter that causes her to buy things that she might not need because the advertising companies have learned from the data that this person is a reckless spender due to her young age. They could thus exploit this vulnerability and deploy subliminal techniques nudging her to buy more products. It is thus fundamental for legislators to question whether a risk of increased surveillance capitalism is an acceptable price to pay in order to gain a short-term benefit from the data sharing initiative.

Furthermore, legislators will also have to take into consideration the systemic risks that such data sharing initiatives could have on the exercise of fundamental rights by individuals, such as their possibility to take fundamental decisions about their health, their family life or their professional life. Once again, inspiration can be drawn in this regard from the proposal for an AI Act, which lists in its Annex 3 several 'high-risk' AI systems. For instance, AI systems intended to be used to evaluate the creditworthiness of natural persons or establish their credit score are considered as 'high-risk'.[1192] Yet, data shared through empowerment initiatives could contribute to the elaboration of such systems. Indeed, if an individual shares her energy consumption data in order to get better energy prices, this data might be further shared with banks. In turn, this might affect the creditworthiness of this individual if she is deemed to be using much more energy than a 'reasonable' person. As a result, a bank might consider that this person spends too much money on energy and will thus not have enough means to pay back a loan, or more globally that she is not careful and sensible about the management of her financial resources, and is thus not trustworthy. This could thus have an impact on this person's faculty to take fundamental decisions about her private life if the further sharing of her data leads to her inability to buy a house as banks refuse to grant her loans.

Building on the previous example, one could imagine that the energy consumption data, as well as the banking or telecommunications data, that has been shared by the individual in order to get lower prices for these services, might be shared with creditworthiness institutions that, themselves, further share it with educational institutions or recruitment agencies. As a result, such creditworthiness data might be integrated into the AI systems that these educational institutions use in order to determine who can have access to, and register to, their institution (e.g., to ensure that the individual can pay her fees or those of her children), and/or in the AI systems that recruitment agencies use in order to select the appropriate candidate (e.g., a person having a low creditworthiness might be considered as being insufficiently reliable), which are both considered as 'high-risk' AI applications.[1193] Furthermore, in such a scenario, the fact that these educational institutions or

1192. Annex III, point 5.b) of the Proposal for an Artificial Intelligence Act.
1193. Annex III, points 3.a) and 4.a) of the Proposal for an Artificial Intelligence Act.

recruitment agencies do not have any creditworthiness data about a specific individual, because she has refused to share the above-mentioned data, might be used as a criterion to deny access to the institution or to decide not to offer the job opportunity to this person. This is because these institutions / recruitment agencies might consider that there is too much uncertainty regarding this person's profile due to the lack of data, while such information is available about other applicants / candidates that have agreed to share their data, and that it would thus be 'safer' to offer the opportunity to a person from the second category. This illustrates, once again, that the choice of individuals to share data can entail both long-term risks for themselves, as well as collective risks for others, in terms of the ability for individuals to take fundamental decisions about their private life (e.g., education and job opportunities). In assessing these risks, as well as the economic and capitalism surveillance risks mentioned above, particular consideration should thus be given to the potentially rapid and wide dissemination of the data shared by individuals.[1194]

199. On the basis of this risk assessment, legislators should then integrate – into the instrument creating the empowerment initiative – reasonable, proportionate and effective measures aimed at mitigating the specific long-term and collective risks that will have been identified.[1195] An interesting example of such a mitigation measure can be found in a 2020 modification of the Belgian legislation on insurances.[1196] Indeed, the Belgian legislator indicated that, in the context of the conclusion of a life insurance or of a health insurance contract, the refusal, by the insurance candidate, to acquire or use a connected object collecting personal data about her lifestyle or her health may not lead to a refusal to insure the candidate nor to a price increase of the insurance product.[1197] Similarly, the fact that the insurance candidate does not agree to the sharing of her personal data collected by the said connected object may not lead to a refusal to insure the candidate, to a price increase of the insurance product, nor to a reduction of the scope of the insurance coverage.[1198] Hence, such mitigation measures should address the economic risks mentioned above. Moreover, these mitigation measures should also address the capitalism surveillance and fundamental rights risks mentioned above, for example, by providing that the data that has been shared by an individual with a service provider, in order to be offered a better

1194. *See*, by analogy, Article 26.2 of the Proposal for a Digital Services Act.
1195. *See*, by analogy, Article 27 and Recital 58 of the Proposal for a Digital Services Act.
1196. Loi du 10 décembre 2020 modifiant la loi du 4 avril 2014 relative aux assurances en vue d'établir dans le domaine de l'assurance maladie et de l'assurance individuelle sur la vie une restriction de traitement des données à caractère personnel concernant le mode de vie ou la santé issues des objets connectés, *M.B.*, 15 janvier 2021.
1197. Articles 46/1 and 46/2 of the Loi du 4 avril 2014 relative aux assurances, *M.B.*, 30 avril 2014.
1198. Articles 46/3 of the Loi du 4 avril 2014 relative aux assurances, *M.B.*, 30 avril 2014.

price, cannot be further shared with third parties, in order to avoid the loss of control on the data that could lead to the undesirable effects for individuals presented in the previous paragraphs.

200. Finally, the empowerment initiative should also provide that external and independent audits can be conducted in order to verify compliance with these mitigation measures.[1199] To understand why this is important, it can be reverted to the Belgian insurance law mentioned above, as these provisions might be circumvented. Indeed, if instead of raising the insurance price for those who do not want to share data (the prohibited practice), the 'normal' price is raised for everyone, and a 'price reduction' is given to those who share data, the economic effect will, in fact, be the same than if a higher price was charged to those who do not consent to the collection/sharing of their data, as people will pay more if they do not want to share data, and are thus incentivised to share it. Accordingly, including in the empowerment initiative the possibility to conduct external and independent audits that could reveal such practices is fundamental, as it will reduce the risk of circumvention of the mitigation measures adopted by the legislator. Similarly, these audits could reveal practices where the data is further shared with third parties, while this is expressly prohibited by the empowerment initiative.

5.2 THE AMBIGUOUS COMPETITIVE EFFECTS OF 'EMPOWERMENT' INITIATIVES IMPOSING B2B DATA SHARING

201. While 'empowerment' initiatives imposing B2B data sharing primarily aim at empowering the individual whose data is shared, such initiatives should also arguably stimulate competition and innovation by third parties.[1200] This is even an explicit objective of some empowerment initiatives that precisely aim at tackling specific market failures deriving from a lack of competition.[1201] Indeed, they should, in theory, have indirect competition-enhancing effects, as they would stimulate competition and innovation by third parties in order to offer complementary services that compete with those offered by the incumbent data holders, or to offer services on secondary markets.[1202] They should arguably lower individual's switching costs,[1203]

1199. *See*, by analogy, Article 28 and Recitals 60-61 of the Proposal for a Digital Services Act.

1200. S. Vezzoso, 'Competition Policy in Transition: Exploring Data Portability's Roles', *15th ASCOLA (Virtual) Conference*, June 2020, available at https://ssrn.com/abstract=3634736, pp. 9 and 11.

1201. *See* Part II, Chapter 4, Section 4.2.

1202. S. Vezzoso, 'Competition Policy in Transition', *supra*, pp. 9 and 11; J. Krämer, P. Senellart and A. de Streel, 'Making Data Portability More Effective for the Digital Economy', *supra*, p. 13.

which in turn should facilitate market entry by making it easier for new players to collect the necessary (actively provided and observed) data to jump-start their service.[1204] Moreover, they should arguably allow third parties to 'overcome network effects which cause markets to tip'.[1205]

202. Yet, whether the theoretical findings outlined above will be translated in practice 'will also depend on whether consumers actually make use of [these initiatives], and whether data is actually imported by other services'.[1206] Indeed, due to the fact that, in order to ensure a balance with the data holders' business interests, the scope of these initiatives should be limited to actively provided and observed data and should exclude inferred/derived data,[1207] there is a risk that the shared data would provide too little context or would be too closely tied to the incumbent data holder's service design, which might, in turn, make it complex for the recipient to build new products/services that directly compete with the incumbent's.[1208] As outlined by Nicholas and Weinberg, 'trying to use exported user data to reproduce Facebook would be like trying to use furniture to reproduce the office building it came from'.[1209] Rather, these initiatives may better serve the development of complementary services on secondary markets.[1210]

Moreover, third parties might be hesitant to build products/services relying on the continuous porting of data through an incumbent's API[1211] out of fear that the incumbent might 'monitor how competitors use their APIs and potentially use that information to copy them (...) limit or cut off API access to competitors as they see fit, [or] change the data or the structure of

1203. *See* J. Krämer, P. Senellart and A. de Streel, 'Making Data Portability More Effective for the Digital Economy', *supra*, p. 56.
1204. I. Graef, M. Husovec and N. Purtova, 'Data Portability and Data Control: Lessons for an Emerging Concept in EU Law', *supra*, p. 1359. For more detailed explanations, *see* p. 1386.
1205. J. Furman, et al., 'Unlocking Digital Competition', *supra*, p. 57; S. Vezzoso, 'Competition Policy in Transition: Exploring Data Portability's Roles', *supra*, p. 21; G. Nicholas and M. Weinberg, 'Data Portability and Platform Competition: Is User Data Exported from Facebook Actually Useful to Competitors?', *supra*, p. 1.
1206. *See* J. Krämer, P. Senellart and A. de Streel, 'Making Data Portability More Effective for the Digital Economy', *supra*, p. 57. *See also* L. Somaini, 'The Right to Data Portability and User Control: Ambitions and Limitations', *MediaLaws – Rivista dir. Media*, 2018/3, p. 189.
1207. *See* Part II, Chapter 5, Section 5.1.1.2.
1208. G. Nicholas and M. Weinberg, 'Data Portability and Platform Competition: Is User Data Exported from Facebook Actually Useful to Competitors?', *supra*, pp. 2 and 6.
1209. *Ibid.*, p. 2.
1210. G. Nicholas, 'Taking It With You: Platform Barriers to Entry and the Limits of Data Portability', 6 March 2020, available at https://ssrn.com/abstract=3550870, p. 16.
1211. *See* Part II, Chapter 4, Section 4.3.

the data they make available, creating technical overhead or even destroying the business model for competitors'.[1212]

203. Furthermore, the *ratione personae* scope of the 'empowerment' initiatives imposing B2B data sharing could, in fact, potentially generate anticompetitive effects. Indeed, if, similarly to Article 20 of the GDPR, they are applied symmetrically to all data holders, irrespective of their size or of the scale of their processing activities, this might in fact benefit large data holders, who could better sink the compliance costs than smaller players that would be disproportionally burdened.[1213] This could negatively affect competition and consequently harm consumers[1214] if these initiatives are overly burdensome for emerging SMEs.[1215]

Additionally, there is a risk that this might further reinforce the strong market position of large data holders if individuals mostly use them to share data from smaller competitors towards the incumbent, rather than the other way around.[1216] Indeed, this 'may strengthen economies of scope in data aggregation when a major market player manages to leverage portability rights to collect data from smaller and fragmented service providers and aggregate them in a larger data pool that generates efficiencies in service production compared to the original holders of fragmented data sets. In such cases data aggregation may lead to increased market concentration and efficiency losses because of reduced competition'.[1217] This might also increase large data holders' network effects.[1218]

204. Despite this, it could nevertheless still be argued that these 'empowerment' initiatives imposing B2B data sharing would likely mainly benefit smaller competitors than larger data holders, as the marginal benefits that will be derived from the collection of additional data will likely be higher for

1212. G. Nicholas and M. Weinberg, 'Data Portability and Platform Competition: Is User Data Exported from Facebook Actually Useful to Competitors?', *supra*, p. 8; G. Nicholas, 'Taking It With You: Platform Barriers to Entry and the Limits of Data Portability', *supra*, p. 16.
1213. I. Graef, M. Husovec and N. Purtova, 'Data Portability and Data Control: Lessons for an Emerging Concept in EU Law', *supra*, p. 1359. For more detailed explanations, *see* p. 1386. *See also* L. Somaini, 'The Right to Data Portability and User Control', *supra*, p. 181.
1214. OECD, *Consumer Data Rights and Competition*, *supra*, p. 43. *See also* D. Lyons, 'GDPR: Privacy as Europe's Tariff by Other Means?', 3 July 2018, available at https://www.aei.org/technology-and-innovation/gdpr-privacy-as-europes-tariff-by-other-means/; P. Swire and Y. Lagos, 'Why the Right to Data Portability Likely Reduces Consumer Welfare: Antitrust and Privacy Critique', *Maryland Law Review*, 2013, Vol. 72(3), pp. 335-380.
1215. *See* J. Krämer, P. Senellart and A. de Streel, 'Making Data Portability More Effective for the Digital Economy', *supra*, p. 11.
1216. *Ibid.*, p. 13.
1217. B. Martens, et al., 'Business to Business Data Sharing', *supra*, p. 9.
1218. *See* J. Krämer, P. Senellart and A. de Streel, 'Making Data Portability More Effective for the Digital Economy', *supra*, p. 60.

the former (who currently have limited data and could thereby gain access to a substantially larger amount of it) than for the latter (who already have troves of data and might only get little more data out of these initiatives). Moreover, these large data holders often have many consumer facing products/services and can thus easily collect (actively provided and observed) data from individuals without relying on these initiatives, while smaller competitors struggle to collect (actively provided and observed) data from individuals and are deeply in need of such compulsory B2B data sharing initiatives to expand their databases in order to improve their services and to be able to compete with the large data holders.

205. In light of the above, it can be concluded that the competitive effects of 'empowerment' initiatives imposing B2B data sharing are ambiguous. Accordingly, any potential initiative of this kind will have to be carefully tailored and will have to take these considerations into account. Moreover, this finding sheds light on the fact that 'empowerment' initiatives imposing B2B data sharing are therefore probably not the right tool to address market failures linked to data. Rather, other types of data sharing initiatives should be favoured if the main goal is to promote competition, namely economic initiatives imposing B2B data sharing, to which I will turn in Part III.

5.3 INSIGHTS ON HOW POTENTIAL FUTURE 'EMPOWERMENT' INITIATIVE IMPOSING B2B DATA SHARING SHOULD BE CONSTRUCTED

206. In Chapter 4, I presented the existing 'empowerment' initiatives imposing B2B data sharing.[1219] It was also outlined that, because these initiatives present some effectiveness issues (for instance, Article 20 of the GDPR fails to impose direct portability[1220] and, according to some authors, falls short of requiring continuous portability[1221]), there have been calls for the creation of new 'empowerment' initiatives imposing B2B data sharing, for instance, a 'continuous portability' right.[1222] Other than imposing continuous portability, these initiatives could also go a step further in creating the obligation for the data holder to enable direct portability towards the data recipient, at the request of the data subjects, whether in new sectors

1219. *See* Part II, Chapter 4, Sections 4.1 and 4.2.
1220. Article 20.2 of the GDPR only provides that the data subject has the right to have the personal data transmitted directly from one controller to another *where technically feasible*.
1221. *See* point 166.
1222. Communication from the Commission, '*A European Strategy for Data*', *supra*, p. 20; J. Krämer, P. Senellart and A. de Streel, 'Making Data Portability More Effective for the Digital Economy', *supra*.

(other than the banking or the electricity sector) or horizontally across sectors.

In this perspective, the aim of this Section is to draw insights on how such potential future *empowerment initiatives imposing B2B data sharing* should be constructed, in light of the balancing exercises presented in Section 5.1 and of the ambiguous competitive effects of such initiatives outlined in Section 5.2. These insights pertain to the *ratione materiae* (types of data covered) and *ratione personae* (symmetric or asymmetric) scope of the initiative (Section 5.3.1), to remuneration considerations (Section 5.3.2), and to the potential requirement for data recipients to be certified/accredited (Section 5.3.3). Finally, it will be outlined that (continuous) data sharing will not always, in and of itself, be sufficient to empower the individuals to switch services, and that, for some types of services, it will be needed to go further, towards more interoperability (Section 5.3.4).

5.3.1 Scope of the Regulatory Initiative

5.3.1.1 *Ratione Materiae*: Types of Data Covered?

207. A first key element to consider is the determination of the types of data that should be covered by an *empowerment initiative imposing B2B data sharing*. As outlined above,[1223] the *ratione materiae* scope of such an initiative should be limited to actively provided and observed data, and should exclude inferred/derived data.[1224] Indeed, as inferred/derived data will often be the most valuable for the data holder,[1225] this would strike a good balance between safeguarding the data holders' economic interests and the objective of 'individual empowerment' which underlies the adoption of such an initiative. Nevertheless, it must be reminded that inferred/derived data can be obtained by the data subject through her data access right, although in a different format.[1226]

Moreover, it should be made explicit that data holders have the possibility to keep using the data despite the data sharing obligation.[1227] Indeed, due to data's non-rivalrous nature, this allows the data holders and the data recipients to use the data at the same time.[1228] This, in turn, also preserves the data holder's business interests while empowering individuals.

1223. *See* Part II, Chapter 5, Section 5.1.1.2.
1224. *See also* R. Feasey and A. de Streel, 'Data Sharing for Digital Market Contestability' *supra*, pp. 10 and 62-63. *See also*, in this sense, Recitals 54 and 55 and Article 6.1.i) of the Proposal for a Digital Markets Act. *See* point 180.
1225. *See* point 187.
1226. *See* point 188.
1227. *See* point 189.
1228. *See* point 52.

208. So far as possible, the *ratione materiae* scope of such an initiative should also be limited to the data pertaining to the specific individual making the sharing request, and it should only enable an individual to share her data to the extent that this does not 'adversarily affect' other data subjects' right to personal data.[1229] This thus requires to limit the 'adverse effects'[1230] that this sharing could have on other data subjects' right to personal data protection. Such an 'adverse effect' would notably occur if the sharing would prevent these other data subjects from exercising their data subject rights (right of information, access, erasure, opposition, etc.).[1231] In this regard, it must be underlined that the continuous flows of data that might result from the creation of a continuous portability right could potentially intensify the risk of the materialisation of such 'adverse effects'.

5.3.1.2 *Ratione Personae*: Symmetric or Asymmetric Regulatory Initiative?

209. A second key element to consider is the determination of the *ratione personae* scope of the *empowerment initiatives imposing B2B data sharing*, i.e., the determination of the data holders that should be mandated to share data. In this regard, it should be reminded that the competitive effects of such initiatives are ambiguous.[1232] Indeed, they could potentially generate anti-competitive effects if they were to apply symmetrically to all data holders, irrespective of their size or of the scale of their processing activities, as small players could be disproportionally burdened.[1233]

Accordingly, some authors have argued that such initiatives should not apply symmetrically and indistinctively to all data holders processing this individual's data, and that their scope should thus be less extensive than the scope of the GDPR.[1234] In this regard, some argue that it should only apply to large data holders benefitting from strong market power,[1235] while others call for an exemption of SMEs which only have a limited market share

---

1229. *See* Part II, Chapter 5, Section 5.1.2.
1230. Article 29 Working Party, *Guidelines on the right to data portability*, WP 242 rev.01, 13 April 2017, p. 11. *See also* Article 20.4 of the GDPR: 'The right [to data portability] shall not *adversely affect* the rights and freedoms of others' (emphasis added).
1231. Article 29 Working Party, *Guidelines on the right to data portability*, WP 242 rev.01, 13 April 2017, p. 11.
1232. *See* Part II, Chapter 5, Section 5.2.
1233. *See* point 203.
1234. R. Feasey and A. de Streel, 'Data Sharing for Digital Market Contestability', *supra*, pp. 10 and 56.
1235. *See* B. Engels, 'Data Portability Among Online Platforms', *Internet Policy Review*, 2016, Vol. 5(2), available at https://policyreview.info/articles/analysis/data-portability-among-online-platforms.

and/or turnover, in order to avoid overburdening them.[1236] In this perspective, the Open Banking model should be preferred to the GDPR/Electricity Directive model, as the former only creates a B2B data sharing obligation on a specific set of actors (i.e., the nine major UK banks),[1237] while the latter implies B2B data sharing obligations for all data controllers/electricity providers, independently of their size, market share or turnover.[1238]

210. Yet, it would arguably make sense to impose them symmetrically, so the individual can have more control on all of her data, and not just on the data that is held by a limited amount of data holders. Such initiatives should facilitate the individual's ability to switch towards the product/service of an alternative energy provider (gas, electricity, water), bank, insurer, etc., that better matches her needs and preferences, independently of the size or market power of her current service provider. Indeed, even if, for instance, the individual currently uses the services of a smaller energy provider, she should also, from an individual empowerment perspective, be able to (continuously) share her consumption data with a third-party intermediary, which could thereby monitor her consumption and could actively suggest to her to switch towards the product/service of an alternative provider that better matches her needs and preferences.

A clear balance will thus have to be struck between maximising the individuals' empowerment and avoiding the potentially anticompetitive effects mentioned above when determining the *ratione personae* scope of such initiatives (symmetric applications to all data holders or asymmetric application to a limited amount of data holders). When assessing this balance, it is nevertheless important to keep in mind that the core objective of such initiatives is to empower the individuals whose data is shared, and more weight should thus arguably be given to this objective than to competition considerations. Indeed, I argue that other types of data sharing initiatives should be considered if the main goal is to promote competition, namely *economic initiatives imposing B2B data sharing*, as will be apparent from my analysis in Part III.

5.3.2 Remuneration Considerations

211. The third key element to consider is whether the data holder should be compensated for the compulsory sharing. Indeed, data sharing creates

1236. *See* A. Diker Vanberg and M. Ünver, 'The Right to Data Portability in the GDPR and EU Competition Law: Odd Couple or Dynamic Duo?', *European Journal of Law and Technology*, 2017, Vol. 8(1), pp. 1-22; OECD, *Consumer Data Rights and Competition*, *supra*, p. 43.
1237. *See* Part II, Chapter 4, Section 4.2.2.
1238. *See* Part II, Chapter 4, Sections 4.1 and 4.2.3.

(incentive) costs for the data holder.[1239] The question is thus whether the data holder should be remunerated in order to preserve these incentives.

As the aim of *empowerment initiatives imposing B2B data sharing* is to empower individuals, it could be argued that such initiatives should not entail any cost for the individuals, at least in principle, as otherwise this could deter them from invoking them. Such an approach would be consistent with most of the existent 'empowerment' initiatives imposing B2B data sharing. Indeed, the data holder may not request any payment from the data subject exercising her GDPR right to data portability, unless the request is manifestly unfounded or excessive.[1240] Similarly, the Digital Content Directive's data retrieval right also provides that the consumer shall be entitled to retrieve the data free of charge,[1241] and PSD2's data access and use rights do not provide for any type of fee for the data holder either.[1242]

212. Yet, as outlined above,[1243] any *empowerment initiative imposing B2B data sharing* must consider the (IP and trade secret) rights that a data holder might have on the data, and a balance must thus be found between the benefits for the specific individual and the business interests of the data holder. Accordingly, some authors suggest that while the individual should be able to share her data at no cost, the data holders should be entitled to require a fair remuneration from third-party recipients to which the data would be directly transferred if this data is covered by IP/trade secret rights.[1244] In this regard, it is interesting to point out that the Electricity Directive makes such a distinction.[1245] While it provides that final customers should be able to retrieve their metering and consumption data or to transmit them to an 'eligible party' at no additional cost,[1246] these 'eligible parties' (i.e., the data recipients), on the other hand, can be charged a fee for the direct access to the data.[1247]

213. At first sight, this distinction is appealing, as it seems to preserve the interests of both the individual whose data is shared (as she is empowered to share her data by not being charged for the sharing) and the data holder (who can charge a fee to the data recipient in case of direct transfer). Yet, two caveats must be expressed here.

1239. *See* Part I, Chapter 2, Section 2.2.3.5.
1240. Article 12.5 of the GDPR. *See* point 146.
1241. Article 16.4 of Directive 2019/770. *See* point 154.
1242. Articles 65-67 of Directive 2015/2366. *See* points 159 and 160.
1243. *See* Part II, Chapter 5, Section 5.1.1.1.
1244. I. Graef, M. Husovec and N. Purtova, 'Data Portability and Data Control: Lessons for an Emerging Concept in EU Law', *supra*, p. 1359. For more detailed explanations, *see* pp. 1379-1388.
1245. *See* point 164.
1246. Article 20 and 23.5, al. 1 of Directive 2019/944.
1247. Article 23.5, al. 2 of Directive 2019/944.

First, if the data recipient is charged for this access and if the product/service that it offers to the individual whose data is shared implies the payment of a monetary price (utility provider, bank, insurer, etc.), then this recipient will more than likely pass on the cost of this access to the individual, in the price of its product/services. Therefore, in such situations, the sharing will, in fact, entail an indirect cost for the individual, and it can be questioned whether this is a desirable outcome. Indeed, as the aim of such initiatives is to empower individuals, it could be argued that they should not entail any cost for them, even an indirect one, as otherwise this could deter them from relying on such initiatives.

Second, if the data recipient can be charged by the data holder, there is a risk that the data holder might set a high price in order to deter the recipients from building alternative services on the basis of the shared data. In turn, this might prevent such initiatives from truly empowering the individuals, as they might be provided with less switching opportunities than in a situation where recipients are not charged for this access.

One way to limit these caveats would be to limit the fee that can be required by the data holder from the data recipient. For instance, the Electricity Directive provides that the charges for access for 'eligible parties' (i.e., the data recipients) should be 'reasonable and duly justified'.[1248] This could indeed preserve the recipients' incentives to develop alternatives by limiting their cost of data access and this would also avoid that high costs are passed on to the individual whose data is shared. Yet, this would generate a lot of uncertainties on what constitutes a 'reasonable and justified' cost of access. This uncertainty could slow down the apparition of alternative services for the individuals, due to endless disputes between the data holders and the data recipients regarding the 'reasonable and justified' cost of access. Therefore, even 'reasonable and justified' fees might hamper the empowerment objective of such initiatives.

214. Finally, it is important to outline that some authors support, on the contrary, the idea that 'empowerment' initiatives imposing B2B data sharing should not imply any form of payment, even from the data recipient.[1249] This is because these initiatives mainly pursue individual empowerment objectives and because the potential costs that this might entail on the data holders' incentives to collect and process the data will, in fact, be minimal as the volumes of data that will be transferred through such mechanisms are quite low.[1250] Indeed, they only entail the sharing of data pertaining to one specific individual, and not the sharing of aggregated data pertaining to

1248. Article 23.5, al. 3 of Directive 2019/944.

1249. R. Feasey and A. de Streel, 'Data Sharing for Digital Market Contestability', *supra*, pp. 10 and 79-80. *See also*, in this sense, Recitals 54 and 55 and Article 6.1.i) of the Proposal for a Digital Markets Act. *See* point 180.

1250. R. Feasey and A. de Streel, 'Data Sharing for Digital Market Contestability', *supra*, p. 80.

multiple individuals, which, on the other hand, should imply some form of remuneration for the data holder, as it is more likely to affect its business interests.[1251]

215. In light of all of the above, there is a strong argument to be made that 'empowerment' initiatives imposing B2B data sharing, such as a continuous portability right, should not imply any form of payment, neither from the individual whose data is shared nor from a potential data recipient.

5.3.3 Potential Certification of Data Recipients?

216. The fourth key element to consider is whether the individuals should be able to (continuously) share their data with any data recipient whatsoever (the GDPR data portability right model), or whether they should only be able to (continuously) share their data with data recipients that have obtained a 'certification' for the reuse (the Open Banking model).

Indeed, as outlined above,[1252] one of the factors that contributed to the Open Banking initiative's success is that recipients have to obtain an authorisation from the FCA in order to get access to the banks' data.[1253] The goal is to protect the consumers by ensuring that these entities are secure and that their services and processing activities are legitimate and lawful. Similarly, the Smart Data initiative seems to support the requirement, for data recipients, to obtain an accreditation if they want to access 'high risk' data – i.e., 'data where the consequences of loss or misuse are likely to be greatest' – in order to ensure that their services are legitimate, secure and comply with the personal data protection requirements.[1254]

There is thus a case to be made for the inclusion of such a certification/accreditation scheme in potential 'empowerment' initiatives imposing B2B data sharing, as this would protect the individuals' interests. Moreover, this would generate more trust from the individuals whose data is shared, which is fundamental as, absent this trust, these individuals would probably not make use of these initiatives.[1255] While such certification/accreditation

1251. *Ibid.*, pp. 11 and 77-79. *See* Part III, Chapter 8, Section 8.2.4.
1252. *See* point 162.
1253. Open Data Institute and Fingleton, 'Open Banking, Preparing for Lift Off', *supra*, p. 25.
1254. HM Government, 'Smart Data: Putting consumers in control of their data and enabling innovation', *supra*, p. 28. *See also* European Data Protection Board and European Data Protection Supervisor, *Joint Opinion 03/2021 on the Proposal for a regulation of the European Parliament and of the Council on European data governance (Data Governance Act)*, 10 March 2021, available at https://edpb.europa.eu/our-work-tools/our-documents/edpbedps-joint-opinion/edpb-edps-joint-opinion-032021-proposal_fr, p. 34.
1255. R. Feasey and A. de Streel, 'Data Sharing for Digital Market Contestability', *supra*, pp. 59-60.

procedure will necessarily entail some administrative red-tape in order to verify that the recipients present the guarantees mentioned above, this burden should be reduced as much as possible, as otherwise this could deter the recipients from building alternative services on the basis of the shared data. In turn, this would likely prevent these initiatives from truly empowering the individuals, as they would be provided with less switching opportunities if this certification/accreditation procedure is too cumbersome.

In this regard, it is interesting to point out that, in the context of the Smart Data initiative, it is suggested that the accreditation process should be cross-sectoral, in order to avoid unnecessary burdens and duplicative procedures for recipients acting across several sectors.[1256] Following the advocates of this initiative, such an accreditation system would be appropriate and proportionate as 'this would provide reassurance to consumers that [recipients] seeking access to personal data have been vetted, while also simplifying the process for [recipients] that operate across markets'.[1257]

Moreover, it should be outlined that, in the context of its proposal for a Data Governance Act, the European Commission reflected on whether a voluntary or compulsory certification/labelling mechanism should be created for trusted data intermediaries.[1258] The advantage of compulsory certification over voluntary certification is that it would generate more trust in the data sharing process, but the downside is that it could have prohibitive costs on SMEs and start-ups and could thus have a negative effect on their willingness and ability to provide such services.[1259] Interestingly, in order to address this balance, the Commission eventually proposed an intermediary solution, consisting of a 'notification obligation with *ex post* monitoring of compliance with the requirements to exercise the activities by the competent authorities of the Member States'.[1260,1261]

217. Such an intermediary solution could also be proposed in the context of *empowerment initiatives imposing B2B data sharing*, where, in order to be entitled to receive the data, the recipient would be required to notify a

1256. HM Government, 'Smart Data: Putting consumers in control of their data and enabling innovation', *supra*, p. 29.
1257. *Ibid.*
1258. Proposal for a Regulation of the European Parliament and of the Council on European data governance (Data Governance Act), 25 November 2020, COM(2020) 767 final, p. 5. *See also* Commission Staff Working Document, Impact assessment report accompanying the Data Governance Act, *supra*, pp. 25-27, 38-42, 46 and 52-53.
1259. Proposal for a Data Governance Act, p. 5.
1260. The alternative of the creation, at the European level, of a new independent structure with legal personality (similar to the European Data Protection Board) was also suggested, but this was abandoned due to the high costs and the issues of political feasibility that it implied (Proposal for a Data Governance Act, p. 6). *See also* Commission Staff Working Document, Impact assessment report accompanying the Data Governance Act, *supra*, pp. 28-29, 40, 43 and 52-53.
1261. Proposal for a Data Governance Act, p. 6.

description of the product/service that it intends to provide to competent authorities to be appointed in each Member State.[1262] These national authorities would then be competent to assess, *ex post*, the trustworthiness of the recipients and whether they offer sufficient guarantees in terms of privacy and security (in collaboration with the data protection authorities[1263]).[1264] Moreover, such initiatives could impose harmonised requirements/obligations on the recipients for the provision of their products/services, in order to ensure their trustworthiness, to be monitored *ex post* by these competent authorities.[1265] In order to avoid an unnecessary multiplication of regulatory authorities, I suggest that these regulatory authorities should be the same as the ones created in the context of the Data Governance Act in order to monitor trusted data intermediaries.

While such a 'notification obligation with *ex post* monitoring of the compliance' could be perceived, by the data recipients, as being too cumbersome and as delaying the benefits of the data sharing, it is certainly less burdensome than requiring a prior certification for the reuse. On the other hand, the option not to subject the reuse to any prior formality should arguably be excluded, as it is vital to ensure that the data is not shared openly with anyone without any limits, as this could have dramatic consequences in terms of the individuals' personal data protection and informational self-determination.[1266] Moreover, as what is required from the data receiver is a simple notification, and not a request for a prior authorisation, these notification forms could be standardised in order to streamline and simplify the process. Then, it would be up to the data recipient to document appropriately the use that it makes of the data, as well as the steps that it has taken to comply with the above-mentioned harmonised requirements/obligations, in order to be able to demonstrate this *ex post* to the relevant regulatory authorities, by analogy with the 'accountability' principle contained in Article 5.2 of the GDPR.

Following this logic, if the regulatory authorities receive a complaint (from an individual, the data holder or a third party) regarding the fact that a data recipient has provided false information in its notification or that it has breached the requirements/obligations contained in the data sharing initiative, these authorities should be able to request, *ex post*, further information to the data recipient in order to verify this, and should also be able to audit its systems. This could notably lead to sanctions ranging from fines, for minor breaches, to the imposition of the deletion of the data that has been

1262. *See*, by analogy, Article 10.6.f) of the Proposal for a Data Governance Act.
1263. *See*, by analogy, Recitals 28 and 29 and Article 12.3 of the Proposal for a Data Governance Act.
1264. *See*, by analogy, Article 13 of the Proposal for a Data Governance Act. *See also* point 395.
1265. *See*, by analogy, Recitals 22-34 and Articles 9-14 of the Proposal for a Data Governance Act.
1266. *See* Part II, Chapter 5, Section 5.1.3.

received (or of the interruption of the API access to the data holder's data), for the most serious breaches. To be sure, this could give rise to quite 'interventionistic' practices by these authorities, and data recipients might be required to divulge more information about their business model than they would want to, but this is arguably the necessary price to pay in order to generate trust in the data sharing, by both the individuals whose data are shared and the data holders. Furthermore, this is also arguably a necessary price to pay to make sure that the data is not shared openly with anyone without any limits, as that would amount to opening Pandora's box and is thus not a viable solution.

218. Finally, it should be added that, in the same perspective of limiting/controlling the potential recipients, some authors have suggested that, in order to preserve the data holders' business interests, they should be able to 'confine the follow-on use of ported data to [a] specific set of socially justifiable purposes of re-use'.[1267] However, it would arguably be undesirable to enable the data holder to limit the data reuse purposes, as this could potentially limit the alternatives offered to individuals, and thus their empowerment. Great caution should thus be applied before creating such limitations.

5.3.4 Beyond (Continuous) Data Sharing: (Full Protocol) Interoperability

219. Finally, it should be outlined that an 'empowerment' initiative imposing (continuous) B2B data sharing will not always, in and of itself, be sufficient to empower the individuals to switch services. Indeed, while this may be sufficient for services that mainly rely on the individual's own profile and preferences, and where interactions with others are not so important (e.g., utility, banking, insurance or music and video streaming services), this will not be the case for social media and communication services where the ability to interact with other individuals is key. This is because such services are characterised by network effects, which create a coordination problem as their value will directly or indirectly depend on the number of other individuals that also use them.[1268]

Yet, while (continuous) data sharing might reduce individual's switching costs, it does not remedy the lock-in effects deriving from network

1267. *See* point 185. I. Graef, M. Husovec and N. Purtova, 'Data Portability and Data Control: Lessons for an Emerging Concept in EU Law', *supra*, p. 1359. For more detailed explanations, *see* pp. 1380-1388.

1268. *See* J. Krämer, P. Senellart and A. de Streel, 'Making Data Portability More Effective for the Digital Economy', *supra*, p. 58.

effects' coordination problem.[1269] Taking the example of social media, even if an individual has the possibility to request the continuous sharing of her data with another social media, she will only be willing to do so if a sufficient number of other individuals (friends, family, colleagues ...) also switch at the same time.[1270] In this regard, Nicholas suggests the implementation of 'functional group portability', which would allow groups of individuals to coordinate in order to switch, all at once, towards a new service provider.[1271]

Accordingly, several authors have outlined that there is a necessity to move beyond (continuous) data sharing, towards more interoperability, in order to tackle these network effects and to truly empower the individuals to switch services.[1272] More precisely, this would require 'full protocol interoperability', which implies that 'services interoperate to a degree where ultimately users can interact seamlessly albeit being on different networks – like users of different telecom networks can communicate with each other. Then users can switch to a new provider without losing access to the network effect exerted by users who remain with the old provider'.[1273] This is also sometimes qualified as 'content interoperability'.[1274] To give an example, such interoperability would enable a former Facebook user, which decided to switch to a new social network, to continue to view her former Facebook friends' posts and to discuss with them. Figure 5.1 provides a visual representation of what this could look like.

1269. *Ibid. See also* G. Nicholas, 'Taking It With You: Platform Barriers to Entry and the Limits of Data Portability', 6 March 2020, available at https://ssrn.com/abstract=3550870, p. 3.

1270. *See* J. Krämer, P. Senellart and A. de Streel, 'Making Data Portability More Effective for the Digital Economy', *supra*, p. 58.

1271. G. Nicholas, 'Taking It With You: Platform Barriers to Entry and the Limits of Data Portability', *supra*.

1272. J. Crémer, Y.-A. de Montjoye and H. Schweitzer, 'Competition Policy for the Digital Era', *supra*, pp. 58-60 and 83-85; J. Krämer, P. Senellart and A. de Streel, 'Making Data Portability More Effective for the Digital Economy', *supra*, p. 58. *See also* Commission Staff Working Document, Impact assessment report accompanying the Data Governance Act, *supra*, p. 21.

1273. *See* J. Krämer, P. Senellart and A. de Streel, 'Making Data Portability More Effective for the Digital Economy', *supra*, p. 58. *See also*, OECD, *Consumer Data Rights and Competition*, *supra*, p. 45; J. Crémer, Y.-A. de Montjoye and H. Schweitzer, 'Competition Policy for the Digital Era', *supra*, p. 85.

1274. *See* Competition and Markets Authority, 'Online Platforms and Digital Advertising: Market Study Final Report', 1 July 2020, available at https://www.gov.uk/cma-cases/online-platforms-and-digital-advertising-market-study, pp. 372-374.

Figure 5.1 Visual Representation of 'Full Protocol Interoperability'/'Content Interoperability'

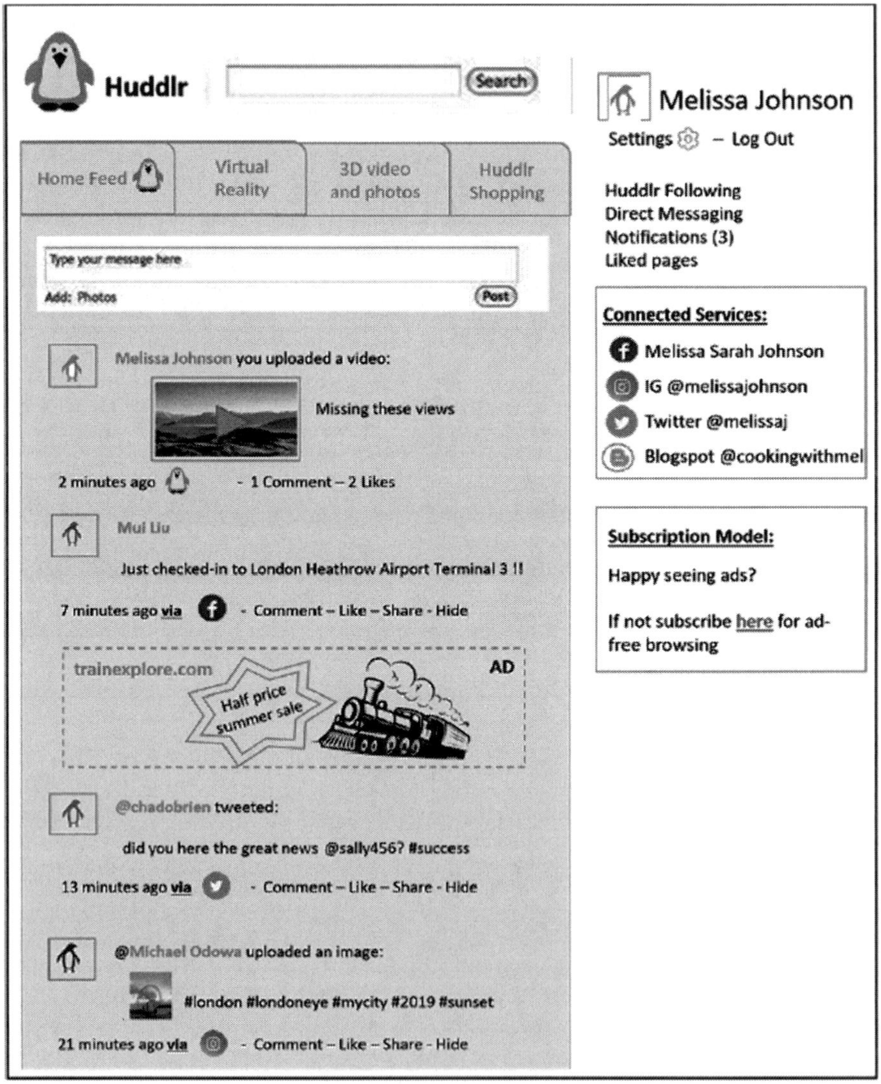

Source: CMA, Final report on online platforms and digital advertising, Figure 8.1.[1275]

However, such 'full protocol interoperability' might entail risks of barriers to innovation, as the various service providers will be constrained by

1275. *Ibid.*, p. 373.

the technical standards selected to implement it.[1276] Moreover, there is the potential risk of being locked in inefficient standards.[1277] Therefore, this requirement for 'full protocol interoperability' should only be considered for service markets where the ability to interact with other individuals is key, as, for those types of services, the benefits of interoperability (the benefits of network effects are shared among competitors and this increases competition in the market) are likely to outweigh its costs (reduced innovation due to strong standardisation, which could in turn weaken or even eliminate competition).[1278]

In this regard, it is worth pointing out that the European Commission indicated that it would explore, in the context of its future 'Data Act' proposal, the possibility to define essential requirements enabling interoperability, notably through the increased use of standardised smart contracts.[1279] Moreover, the European Commission's proposal for a Digital Markets Act[1280] includes obligations for 'gatekeepers' to enable some form of interoperability.[1281] Indeed, according to Article 6.1.c) of the proposal, gatekeepers shall 'allow the installation and effective use of third party software applications or software application stores using, or interoperating with, operating systems of that gatekeeper and allow these software applications or software application stores to be accessed by means other than the core platform services of that gatekeeper. [This should not prevent these gatekeepers] from taking proportionate measures to ensure that third party software applications or software application stores do not endanger the integrity of the hardware or operating system provided by the gatekeeper', while Article 6.1.f) provides that they shall also 'allow business users and providers of ancillary services access to and interoperability with the same operating system, hardware or software features that are available or used in the provision by the gatekeeper of any ancillary services'. It is, however, important to underline that Article 6.1.f) is limited to 'ancillary services', namely services provided in the context of, or together with, core platform services, such as payment, fulfilment, identification or advertising services.[1282] Accordingly, third parties could not rely on this provision in

---

1276. *See* J. Krämer, P. Senellart and A. de Streel, 'Making Data Portability More Effective for the Digital Economy', *supra*, p. 58; J. Crémer, Y.-A. de Montjoye and H. Schweitzer, 'Competition Policy for the Digital Era', *supra*, p. 59.
1277. OECD, *Consumer Data Rights and Competition*, *supra*, p. 46.
1278. J. Crémer, Y.-A. de Montjoye and H. Schweitzer, 'Competition Policy for the Digital Era', *supra*, pp. 59-60; J. Krämer, P. Senellart and A. de Streel, 'Making Data Portability More Effective for the Digital Economy', *supra*, p. 58.
1279. European Commission, Inception Impact Assessment: '*Data Act (including the review of the Directive 96/9/EC on the legal protection of databases)*', May 2021, Ares (2021)3527151, p. 6.
1280. Proposal for a Digital Markets Act. For more details on this Digital Markets Act, *see* points 317, 380 and 384 to 385.
1281. *See* Articles 6.1.c) and 6.1.f) of the Proposal for a Digital Markets Act.
1282. Article 2.14 of the Proposal for a Digital Markets Act.

order to develop a directly competing service, e.g., another social network where it would still be possible for users to interact with their 'friends' on Facebook, as illustrated in Figure 5.1 above.

220. To conclude this Section, the above-mentioned insights regarding the key elements that *empowerment initiatives imposing B2B data sharing* should consider are summarised in Table 5.1.

Table 5.1 Insights on the Key Elements to Consider for 'Empowerment' Initiatives Imposing B2B Data Sharing

	Empowerment Initiatives Imposing B2B Data Sharing
Data holders subject to the sharing obligation	Symmetric application to all data holders.[1283]
Data recipients entitled to benefit from the sharing obligation	Recipient could be required to notify a description of the product/service that it intends to provide.[1284] *Ex post* assessment of the trustworthiness of the recipients and of whether they offer sufficient guarantees in terms of privacy and security.[1285] Imposition of harmonised obligations on the recipients for the provision of their products/services, to be monitored *ex post* as well.[1286]
Types of data covered by the sharing obligation	Only actively provided and observed data (not acquired, nor inferred/derived data).[1287] However, inferred/derived data can be obtained through the exercise of the GDPR data access right.[1288] So far as possible, only the data of the specific individual making the sharing request, and to the extent that this does not 'adversarily affect' other data subjects' right to personal data.[1289]
Remuneration of the data holder as compensation for the sharing obligation	Should, in principle, not imply any form of payment, neither from the individual whose data is shared nor from a potential data recipient.[1290]

1283. *See* Part II, Chapter 5, Section 5.3.1.2.
1284. *See* Part II, Chapter 5, Section 5.3.3.
1285. *See* point 216.
1286. *Ibid.*
1287. *See* Part II, Chapter 5, Section 5.3.1.1.
1288. *See* point 188. Article 15 of the GDPR.
1289. *See* Part II, Chapter 5, Section 5.3.1.1.
1290. *See* Part II, Chapter 5, Section 5.3.2.

Technical implementation of the sharing obligation	Depending on the cases, it could be necessary to move beyond (continuous) data sharing, towards more interoperability, in order to truly empower the individuals to switch services.[1291]

1291. *See* Part II, Chapter 5, Section 5.3.4.

Part III

Economic or Societal Initiatives Imposing B2B Data Sharing

221. While Part II focused on *empowerment initiatives imposing B2B data sharing*, **Part III** will be devoted to *economic or societal initiatives imposing B2B data sharing*. These two types of initiatives are grouped together in this Part, as their focus is not set on the individuals, but rather on broader economic or societal considerations that go beyond individual interests. Therefore, and contrary to the empowerment initiatives presented in Part II, these economic or societal initiatives will not lead to the sharing of small quantities of data linked to a specific individual, but rather to the sharing of larger amounts of (aggregated) personal data pertaining to multiple individuals and/or non-personal data.

Most of the analysis conducted in Part III will be dedicated to economic initiatives imposing B2B data sharing, which aim to remedy market failures deriving from a lack of data sharing (concentrated data markets, high entry barriers and lack of contestability, etc.).[1292] Indeed, a small number of large firms currently hold a significant part of the world's data, and this might diminish the incentives of smaller data-driven firms to emerge, grow and innovate, due to high entry barriers.[1293] The high degree of market power deriving from this 'data advantage' could also affect the contestability of some markets.[1294] Similarly, some platforms have acquired significant scale, effectively allowing them to act as 'private gatekeepers', which might

---

1292. On these market failures *see* Part I, Chapter 2, Section 2.2.3.3. Communication from the Commission to the European Parliament, the Council, the European Economic and Social Committee and the Committee of the Regions, '*A European Strategy for Data*', 19 February 2020, COM(2020) 66, pp. 3, 5, 8 and 14. *See also* Communication from the Commission to the European Parliament, the Council, the European Economic and Social Committee and the Committee of the Regions, '*Shaping Europe's Digital Future*', Brussels, 19 February 2020, COM(2020) 67, p. 8.
1293. Communication from the Commission, '*A European Strategy for Data*', *supra*, p. 3.
1294. *Ibid.*, p. 8.

endanger the fairness and openness of the markets.[1295] Accordingly, compulsory data sharing could be imposed to ensure the contestability of data markets and to level the competitive playing field, by providing competitors with a sufficient amount of data to address the 'cold start problem'.[1296]

At present, these market failures are mainly tackled through competition law, with the exception of a sector-specific data sharing legislation in the automotive sector.[1297,1298] This strong reliance on competition law is explained by the fact that a balance must be found between the benefits and costs of sharing.[1299] In this regard, **Chapter 6** will analyse whether the existing competition law balances pertaining to refusals to share a resource are equally suitable for data, or whether the results of these balancing exercises need to be rethought in light of data's characteristics. Then, **Chapter 7** will shed light on the articulation between competition and data protection law, and will emphasise two core issues that emerge at the intersection of these two fields of law. Finally, **Chapter 8** will move beyond competition law, and will discuss the creation of potential *ex ante* legislations imposing B2B data sharing for economic purposes.

222. While most of the discussions, in the policy and legislative circles, pertaining to compulsory B2B data sharing revolve around economic objectives, compulsory B2B data sharing initiatives could also pursue societal objectives (tackling environmental challenges, contributing to healthier and more sustainable societies, improving mobility, etc.).[1300] For instance, data sharing between navigation technology service providers and freight and logistics businesses can assist the latter in their transition towards more sustainable, efficient and secure transport services.[1301] However, the reflections around the creation of societal initiatives imposing B2B data sharing are still in their infancy. Accordingly, they will be addressed in a

---

1295. Communication from the Commission, '*Shaping Europe's Digital Future*', *supra*, p. 8.
1296. *See* point 126.
1297. Regulation (EU) 715/2007 of the European Parliament and of the Council of 20 June 2007 on type approval of motor vehicles with respect to emissions from light passenger and commercial vehicles (EUR 5 and EUR 6) and on access to vehicle repair and maintenance information, *OJ L 171/1*, 29 June 2007, Articles 6 and 7; Regulation (EU) 2018/858 of the European Parliament and of the Council of 30 May 2018 on the approval and market surveillance of motor vehicles and their trailers, and of systems, components and separate technical units intended for such vehicles, amending Regulations (EC) No. 715/2007 and (EC) No. 595/2009 and repealing Directive 2007/46/EC, *OJ L 151/1*, 14 June 2018. *See* Articles 61-66, 86 and annexes X and XI.
1298. *See* Part III, Chapter 8, Section 8.1.1.
1299. P. Larouche, 'The European Microsoft Case at the Crossroads of Competition Policy and Innovation', *Antitrust Law Journal*, 2008, Vol. 75(3), pp. 933-937. *See* Part I, Chapter 2, Section 2.2.3.5.
1300. *See* Part I, Chapter 2, Section 2.3.1.
1301. Communication from the Commission, '*A European Strategy for Data*', *supra*, p. 28. *See also* https://www.aisin.com/en/product/mobility/cs-s/. For other examples, *see* point 93.

shorter **Chapter 9**, which will not aim for exhaustivity on this growingly important topic, but will rather have as main objective to launch avenues of exploration on why such initiatives could be envisaged and on how they could be constructed in the future.

Chapter 6

Balancing Exercises in Competition Law: Incentivising Innovation *Versus* Maximising Social Welfare Through Large Dissemination

223. The category of B2B data sharing initiatives analysed in Part III mostly focus on economic objectives, and are mainly tackled through competition law. The goal of competition law is to protect consumer welfare by ensuring that competition is not distorted by practices that harm consumers directly, or by practices that are indirectly detrimental to them as they impact the effective structure of competition.[1302] Its goal is thus not to protect competitors, but rather competition in order to ensure that consumers are provided with sufficient choices, notably in terms of price and quality. While digital innovations have entailed profound revolutions in some industries and have given birth to the digital economy, the goals of competition law are still very much relevant and do not need to be changed. However, this digital revolution might require an adaptation of the theories of harm justifying competition law intervention.[1303]

Indeed, the competition law balances applied to 'brick and mortar' industries might not be appropriate to address competitive issues in the digital economy. This is because data have different characteristics than 'traditional resources'.[1304] Indeed, as outlined above, data can be characterised as an 'infrastructural resource', as they are non-rivalrous, capital and general-purpose goods.[1305] Due to data's characteristics, the digital economy

1302. J. Crémer, Y.-A. de Montjoye and H. Schweitzer, 'Competition Policy for the Digital Era: Final Report', 2019, available at http://ec.europa.eu/competition/publications/reports/ kd0419345enn.pdf, p. 40. *See also* Protocol (No. 27) on the internal market and competition annexed to the Treaty on the Functioning of the European Union, *OJ C 115/309*, 9 May 2008.

1303. J. Crémer, Y.-A. de Montjoye and H. Schweitzer, 'Competition Policy for the Digital Era', *supra*, pp. 40-41.

1304. *See* Part I, Chapter 2, Section 2.2.1.

1305. *See* point 52.

is characterised by network effects and by strong economies of scale, scope and speed.[1306] Data therefore plays a prominent role, as being able to use data to develop or improve innovative products or services is a key competitive parameter.[1307] Conversely, these characteristics might create entry barriers, which will make it very difficult to contest the position of incumbent data holders relying on 'data advantages'.[1308] Consequently, data concentration and data conglomeration market failures might appear.[1309] To remedy these market failures, competition intervention imposing B2B data sharing[1310] is increasingly considered in numerous policy reports across the globe.[1311] On the contrary, because they primarily aim at empowering individuals, the 'empowerment' initiatives imposing B2B data sharing, analysed in Part II, cannot solve these market failures.[1312] Finally, it is important to keep in mind that while they can generate competitive benefits, compulsory B2B data sharing remedies entail incentives costs in terms of data collection and processing for both the data holder and the recipients.[1313]

224. Accordingly, from an economic perspective, a balance must be found between the benefits and costs of data sharing, taking into consideration the incentives of the various parties.[1314] Said otherwise, a balance must be found between incentivising innovation (data collection and processing by data holders) and maximising social welfare through large dissemination (data sharing). Therefore, this chapter will question whether the existing competition law balances pertaining to refusals to share a resource – namely abuses of dominant position (i.e., the essential facilities doctrine) (Section 6.1); abuses of economic dependence (Section 6.2); and input foreclosure in vertical integration (Section 6.3) – remain suitable in light of data's

---

1306. *See* Part I, Chapter 2, Section 2.2.3.1. *See* M. Stucke and A. Grunes, *Big Data and Competition Policy*, *supra*, 2016; D. Rubinfeld and M. Gal, 'Access Barriers to Big Data', *supra*, pp. 339-381.
1307. J. Crémer, Y.-A. de Montjoye and H. Schweitzer, 'Competition Policy for the Digital Era', *supra*, pp. 19-24.
1308. *See* Part I, Chapter 2, Section 2.2.3.2. *See* M. Stucke and A. Grunes, *Big Data and Competition Policy*, *supra*; D. Rubinfeld and M. Gal, 'Access Barriers to Big Data', *supra*, pp. 339-381.
1309. *See* Part I, Chapter 2, Section 2.2.3.3. For a broader analysis of all of the potential types of data market failures, *see* references in footnote 19.
1310. Importantly, compulsory B2B data sharing is not the only available remedy to tackle these market failures and other options are suggested in the legal doctrine (*see* point 86). However, as I focus on compulsory B2B data sharing, these alternatives will not be further detailed here.
1311. *See* footnote 62 and Part I, Chapter 2, Section 2.2.3.4.
1312. J. Prüfer, 'Competition Policy and Data Sharing on Data-driven Markets', *Report for the Friedrich-Ebert-Stiftung*, 2020, available at http://library.fes.de/pdf-files/fes/15999.pdf, pp. 8-9.
1313. *See* Part I, Chapter 2, Section 2.2.3.5. B. Martens et al., 'Business to Business Data Sharing', *supra*, p. 5.
1314. P. Larouche, 'The European Microsoft Case at the Crossroads of Competition Policy and Innovation', *supra*, pp. 933-937. *See* Part I, Chapter 2, Section 2.2.3.5.

characteristics, or whether they must be adapted for data markets. This question is important because sharing data may potentially entail more benefits and less (incentive) costs than sharing other resources.[1315]

In fact, this fits in a broader discussion pertaining to the adaptation of competition law to the digital environment. Indeed, the European Commission indicated that it is important for competition rules to remain fit for an increasingly digital world, and that this requires to assess the effectiveness of the current rules, and to potentially review them where necessary.[1316]

As the determination of the concrete data sharing remedy to be imposed implies overarching considerations that are equally relevant for the three types of competition law infringements mentioned above, these will be addressed in a specific separate section (Section 6.4).

Finally, the issue of the time-consuming process of competition intervention will be discussed, as, in digital markets where quick reactions are indispensable, the length of the competitive process serves as a key rationale for complementing competition law intervention with *ex ante* legislations imposing B2B data sharing (Section 6.5).

6.1 ABUSE OF DOMINANT POSITION: ESSENTIAL FACILITIES DOCTRINE

225. As data plays a prominent role in the digital economy, timely access to data may turn out to be essential for a firm's competitiveness.[1317] Accordingly, in order to ensure that the competitive advantage of large data holders remains contestable, it might be necessary to safeguard access by competitors to some of their data, in order to (re)create a form of competitive pressure.[1318] This will especially be the case if a large data holder benefits from a dominant position in a specific data market.

A dominant position refers to 'a position of economic strength enjoyed by an undertaking, which enables it to prevent effective competition being maintained on the relevant market by giving it the power to behave to an

1315. *See* point 90.
1316. Communication from the Commission, '*Shaping Europe's Digital Future*', *supra*, p. 8.
1317. J. Crémer, Y.-A. de Montjoye and H. Schweitzer, 'Competition Policy for the Digital Era', *supra*, p. 73.
1318. German Federal Ministry for Economic Affairs and Energy, 'A New Competition Framework for the Digital Economy: Report by the Commission "Competition Law 4.0" – Executive Summary', 9 September 2019, available at https://www.bmwi.de/Redaktion/EN/Downloads/a/a-new-competition-framework.pdf?__blob=publicationFile&v=2, p. 1. The full report, in German, is available at https://www.wettbewerbsrecht-40.de/KW40/Redaktion/DE/Downloads/bericht-der-kommission-wettbewerbsrecht-4-0.pdf?__blob=publicationFile&v=3.

appreciable extent independently of its competitors, customers and ultimately of its consumers'.[1319] This requires the identification of the relevant product market, which comprises 'all those products and/or services which are regarded as interchangeable or substitutable by the consumer, by reason of the products' characteristics, their prices and their intended use'.[1320] It also requires identifying the relevant geographic market, which comprises 'the area in which the undertakings concerned are involved in the supply and demand of products or services, in which the conditions of competition are sufficiently homogeneous and which can be distinguished from neighbouring areas because the conditions of competition are appreciably different in those area'.[1321] Combined, these constitute the relevant market.[1322]

226. To preserve its dominant position on a relevant data market, a large data holder may refuse to share (some of) its data with its (potential) competitors, and this raises the question of whether this could amount to an abuse of a dominant position, prohibited by Article 102 of the Treaty on the functioning of the EU[1323] (hereinafter 'TFEU').[1324] More specifically, this raises the question of whether refusals to share a resource (or 'refusals to deal') can constitute such an abuse. In the EU, these refusals to deal have been tackled by European Court of Justice, and are traditionally referred to as the 'essential facilities doctrine' case law.[1325] This doctrine has been imported from the US, where it finds its roots in the Supreme Court's *Terminal Railroad* case.[1326,1327] As I focus on the balancing exercises underlying

---

1319. ECJ, *United Brands Company and United Brands Continentaal BV v. Commission*, 14 February 1978, C-27/76, EU:C:1978:22, § 65.
1320. Commission Notice on the definition of relevant market for the purposes of Community competition law, *OJ C 372/5*, 9 December 1997, § 7. This Notice is currently under review: *see* https://ec.europa.eu/info/law/better-regulation/have-your-say/initiatives/12325-Evaluation-of-the-Commission-Notice-on-market-definition-in-EU-competition-law.
1321. *Ibid.*, § 8.
1322. *Ibid.*, § 9.
1323. Treaty on the functioning of the European Union, *OJ C 326/47*, 26 October 2012.
1324. J. Drexl, 'Designing Competitive Markets for Industrial Data – Between Propertisation and Access', *Max Planck Institute for Innovation & Competition Research Paper No. 16-13*, 31 October 2016, available at https://ssrn.com/abstract=2862975, p. 44.
1325. ECJ, *Istituto Chemioterapico Italiano and Commercial Solvents v. Commission*, 6 March 1974, joined cases C-6/73 and C-7/73, EU:C:1974:18; ECJ, *AB Volvo v. Erik Veng (UK) Ltd*, 5 October 1988, C-238/87, EU:C:1988:477; ECJ, *RTE and ITP v. Commission*, 6 April 1995, joined cases C-241/91 and C-242/91, EU:C:1995:98; ECJ, *Bronner*, 26 November 1998, C-7/97, EU:C:1998:569; ECJ, *IMS Health*, 29 April 2004, C-418/01, EU:C:2004:257; CFI, *Microsoft v. Commission*, 17 September 2007, T-201/04, EU:T:2007:289.
1326. Supreme Court of the United States, *United States v. Terminal Railroad Association of St. Louis*, 1912, 224 US 383. *See also* Supreme Court of the United States, *Verizon Communications v. Law Offices of Curtis v. Trinko,* 2004, *LLP*, 540 US 398.
1327. I. Graef, 'Rethinking the Essential Facilities Doctrine for the EU Digital Economy', *Revue juridique Thémis de l'Université de Montréal*, 2019, Vol. 53, p. 39.

compulsory B2B data sharing, I will outline the 'traditional' balance reached by the essential facilities doctrine in the EU (Section 6.1.1) and will assess whether the result of this balancing exercise needs to be adapted for data markets (Section 6.1.2).

6.1.1 The 'Traditional' Essential Facilities Doctrine Balance

227. The first relevant case to mention in the context of the essential facilities doctrine, where the European Court of Justice had to address a refusal to deal, is *Commercial Solvents*.[1328] Commercial Solvent was a company manufacturing and selling nitropropane and aminobutanol, which are both necessary for the manufacture of ethambutol that is used in anti-tuberculosis drugs.[1329] For several years, Commercial Solvents sold aminobutanol to Zoya, which used it for the manufacture of ethambutol-based products, but then stopped this supply after having developed its own ethambutol-based products.[1330] Following a complaint by Zoya, the European Court of Justice ruled that 'an undertaking which has a dominant position in the market in raw materials and which, with the object of reserving such raw material for manufacturing its own derivatives, refuses to supply a customer, which is itself a manufacturer of these derivatives, and therefore risks eliminating all competition on the part of this customer, is abusing its dominant position'.[1331]

228. The second relevant case to mention is *Volvo v. Veng*.[1332] In that case, Volvo, which was the owner of a registered design in respect of body panels for motor vehicles, refused to grant a licence for the import and sale of such panels to Veng, despite the fact that the latter was willing to pay a reasonable royalty.[1333] When asked whether this could amount to an abuse of dominant position, the European Court of Justice outlined that a refusal to grant such a licence could not, in itself, constitute an abuse of dominant position, as otherwise Volvo would be deprived of the substance of its exclusive right on the design.[1334] However, the Court underlined that such a refusal to licence could be subject to a competition law intervention if it involved, on the part of the dominant undertaking, an abusive conduct, such as 'the arbitrary refusal to supply spare parts to independent repairers, the fixing of prices for spare parts at an unfair level or a decision no longer to produce spare parts

1328. ECJ, *Istituto Chemioterapico Italiano and Commercial Solvents v. Commission*, 6 March 1974, joined cases C-6/73 and C-7/73, EU:C:1974:18.
1329. *Ibid.*, 'I. Statement of the facts'.
1330. *Ibid.*
1331. *Ibid.*, § 25.
1332. ECJ, *AB Volvo v. Erik Veng (UK) Ltd*, 5 October 1988, C-238/87, EU:C:1988:477.
1333. *Ibid.*, §§ 1 and 4.
1334. *Ibid.*, § 8.

for a particular model even though many cars of that model are still in circulation, provided that such conduct is liable to affect trade between Member States'.[1335] Yet, the Court considered that, in the case at hand, there was no such abusive conduct and Volvo was thus entitled to refuse to grant a licence to Veng.[1336]

229. The third relevant case to mention is *Magill*.[1337] In this case, three television stations, namely RTE, ITV and the BBC, which each had their own television guide covering exclusively their own programmes, refused to licence these programme listings to Magill, which aimed at publishing a comprehensive weekly television guide that would combine these different listings.[1338] When asked whether this could amount to an abuse of dominant position by the television stations, that were each deemed to have a monopoly on their programme listings,[1339] the European Court of Justice repeated that the refusal by a dominant undertaking to grant a licence cannot in itself constitute an abuse of a dominant position.[1340] However, the Court outlined that, in 'exceptional circumstances', the exercise of such an exclusive right could involve an abusive conduct.[1341] In the case at hand, the Court considered that such 'exceptional circumstances' were met due to the combination of three elements:

(1) The dominant undertakings' refusal to provide their programme listings to Magill prevented the appearance of a new product, *in casu* a comprehensive weekly guide for television programmes, that they did not offer and for which there was a potential consumer demand.[1342]
(2) By denying the access to information that was indispensable in order to compile such a comprehensive weekly guide, the dominant undertakings reserved to themselves the secondary market for comprehensive weekly guides by excluding all competition on that market.[1343]
(3) There was no justification for this refusal.[1344]

1335. *Ibid.*, § 9.
1336. *Ibid.*, § 10.
1337. ECJ, *RTE and ITP v. Commission*, 6 April 1995, joined cases C-241/91 and C-242/91, EU:C:1995:98.
1338. *Ibid.*, §§ 6-10.
1339. *Ibid.*, § 47.
1340. *Ibid.*, § 49.
1341. *Ibid.*, § 50.
1342. *Ibid.*, § 54.
1343. *Ibid.*, §§ 53 and 56.
1344. *Ibid.*, § 55.

230. The fourth relevant case to mention is *Bronner*.[1345] In that case, Bronner, the publisher of the Austrian daily newspaper *Der Standard*, wanted its newspaper to be included in Mediaprint's nationwide home-delivery scheme that it had established for its own newspapers.[1346] Following Mediaprint's refusal to do so, Bronner argued that such a refusal amounted to an abuse of dominant position, as postal delivery did not represent an equivalent alternative to home-delivery, and as, due to its small number of subscribers, it was unable, either alone or in cooperation with other publishers, to operate its own home-delivery scheme in economically reasonable conditions.[1347] Reverting to its decision in Magill, the Court held that such a refusal will only be deemed to be abusive if:[1348]

- the access to the dominant undertaking's resource/service (*in casu* the nationwide home-delivery system) is indispensable to carry a business activity on a secondary market (*in casu* the daily newspaper market), inasmuch as there is no actual or potential substitute;
- this refusal is likely to eliminate all competition on the secondary market; and
- it cannot be objectively justified.

In the case at hand, the Court considered that Mediaprint's nationwide home-delivery system was not indispensable. Importantly, the Court indicated that in order for the indispensability of the facility to be established, there must be technical, legal or even economic obstacles capable of making it impossible, or even unreasonably difficult, for any undertaking other than the dominant undertaking to develop an alternative to the facility, whether alone or in cooperation with others.[1349] In this regard, the Court added that it is not enough to argue that it is not economically viable for the access seeker to develop such an alternative, but rather that it is necessary to establish that it is not economically viable 'for any undertaking other than the dominant undertaking' to create any alternative facility that is comparable to that of the dominant undertaking.[1350] In this perspective, access to a facility will not be indispensable if an alternative (even a less advantageous one) can be developed by any undertaking other than the dominant undertaking.[1351] This is because Article 102 TFEU aims at preventing distortions of competition, rather than at protecting specific competitors.[1352] In reaching

1345. ECJ, *Bronner,* 26 November 1998, C-7/97, EU:C:1998:569.
1346. *Ibid.*, §§ 4-7.
1347. *Ibid.*, §§ 8 and 23.
1348. *Ibid.*, § 41.
1349. *Ibid.*, § 44.
1350. *Ibid.*, §§ 45-46. *See also* Opinion of Advocate General Jacobs in *Bronner* (ECJ), C-7/97, delivered on 28 May 1998, EU:C:1998:264, § 68.
1351. ECJ, *Bronner,* 26 November 1998, C-7/97, EU:C:1998:569, § 43.
1352. Opinion of Advocate General Jacobs in *Bronner* (ECJ), C-7/97, delivered on 28 May 1998, EU:C:1998:264, § 58.

such a conclusion, the Court seems to have strongly relied on Advocate General Jacobs' opinion:

> [The imposition of a duty to deal] can be justified in terms of competition policy only in cases in which the dominant undertaking has a genuine stranglehold on the related market. That might be the case for example where duplication of the facility is impossible or extremely difficult owing to physical, geographical or legal constraints or is highly undesirable for reasons of public policy. It is not sufficient that the undertaking's control over a facility should give it a competitive advantage.
>
> I do not rule out the possibility that the cost of duplicating a facility might alone constitute an insuperable barrier to entry. That might be so particularly in cases in which the creation of the facility took place under non-competitive conditions, for example, partly through public funding. However, the test in my view must be an objective one: in other words, in order for refusal of access to amount to an abuse, it must be extremely difficult not merely for the undertaking demanding access but for any other undertaking to compete. Thus, if the cost of duplicating the facility alone is the barrier to entry, it must be such as to deter any prudent undertaking from entering the market. In that regard it seems to me that it will be necessary to consider all the circumstances, including the extent to which the dominant undertaking, having regard to the degree of amortisation of its investment and the cost of upkeep, must pass on investment or maintenance costs in the prices charged on the related market.[1353]

231. The fifth relevant case to mention is *IMS Health*.[1354] In this case, IMS Health refused to provide access, to its competitor NDC Health, to the '1860 bricks structure' it had developed for the presentation of German regional sales data on pharmaceutical products to pharmacies and doctors.[1355] The problem for NDC, which also offered such services, was that it could not develop an alternative brick structure for the presentation of its data and thus had no other choice than to request a licence to use IMS' structure, which was protected by a database right.[1356] This is because the users (pharmacies and doctors) were unfavourable to the use of an alternative brick structure, as the brick structure developed by IMS had become the normal industry standard.[1357] NDC therefore argued that IMS' refusal to license its brick structure amounted to an abuse of dominant position.[1358] In line with its previous case law, the European Court of Justice held that the refusal, by a dominant undertaking, to license an indispensable resource on which it holds

1353. *Ibid.*, §§ 65-66.
1354. ECJ, *IMS Health*, 29 April 2004, C-418/01, EU:C:2004:257.
1355. *Ibid.*, §§ 2-8.
1356. *Ibid.*, § 21.
1357. *Ibid.*, § 6.
1358. *Ibid.*, § 11.

an IP right (*in casu* the brick structure) constitutes an abuse of dominant position if three conditions are fulfilled:[1359]

(1) The dominant undertakings' refusal to licence prevents the appearance of a new product or service that is not offered by this undertaking and for which there is a potential consumer demand.
(2) By refusing to license its indispensable resource, the dominant undertaking reserves to itself a secondary market by excluding all competition on that market.
(3) There is no objective justification for this refusal.

The Court considered that these conditions were met in this case. Interestingly, the Court provided some additional explanations about some of these conditions. Regarding the condition of indispensability, and building on the reasoning pertaining to this condition that it had developed in *Bronner*,[1360] the Court outlined that the degree of participation by users in the development of IMS' standard brick structure, and the costs linked to it, had to be taken into consideration when determining whether IMS' structure was indispensable for the presentation of regional sales data on pharmaceutical products, as the users had become technically dependent on IMS' structure.[1361] Regarding the condition of the reservation of, and the exclusion of competition on, a secondary market, the Court outlined that it was sufficient to identify a potential or even hypothetical market.[1362] For the Court, 'such is the case where the products or services are indispensable in order to carry on a particular business and where there is an actual demand for them on the part of undertakings which seek to carry on the business for which they are indispensable. Accordingly, it is determinative that two different stages of production may be identified and that they are interconnected, inasmuch as the upstream product is indispensable for the supply of the downstream product'.[1363]

232. The sixth relevant case to mention is *Microsoft*.[1364] In that case, Sun Microsystems complained that Microsoft's refusal to provide it with the necessary information and technology to allow its work group server operating systems to interoperate with Microsoft's client PC operating system (i.e., Windows) constituted an abuse of dominant position.[1365] Coherently with the previous case law of the European Court of Justice, the

1359. *Ibid.*, § 52.
1360. *See supra* point 230. *See* ECJ, *Bronner,* 26 November 1998, C-7/97, EU:C:1998:569, §§ 43-46. *See also* Opinion of Advocate General Jacobs in *Bronner* (ECJ), C-7/97, delivered on 28 May 1998, EU:C:1998:264, § 68.
1361. ECJ, *IMS Health*, 29 April 2004, C-418/01, EU:C:2004:257, §§ 29-30.
1362. *Ibid.*, § 44.
1363. *Ibid.*, §§ 44-45.
1364. CFI, *Microsoft v. Commission*, 17 September 2007, T-201/04, EU:T:2007:289.
1365. *Ibid.*, § 7.

Court of First Instance reminded that the refusal, by a dominant undertaking, to license a product on which it holds an IP right does not, in itself, constitute an abuse of dominant position, but rather that this will only be the case in 'exceptional circumstances'.[1366] According to the Court, such 'exceptional circumstances' are met if:[1367]

- the refusal relates to a product or service indispensable to the exercise of a particular activity on a neighbouring market;
- the refusal is of such a kind as to exclude any effective competition on that neighbouring market; and
- the refusal prevents the appearance of a new product for which there is potential consumer demand.

If such circumstances are present, the dominant undertaking's refusal will be considered as an abuse, unless it can demonstrate an objective justification for the refusal.[1368] In the case at hand, the Court found that these conditions were met and that Microsoft could not rely on an objective justification for its refusal to provide the necessary interoperability information to Sun Microsystems.

233. Importantly, it must be pointed out that, as outlined by Graef, it seems that the Court of First Instance has lowered, in *Microsoft*, the standard for the application of the conditions of the essential facilities doctrine.[1369] First, regarding the indispensability requirement, the Court concluded that access to the interoperability information was indispensable in order for Sun Microsystems to be able to compete 'on an equal footing'.[1370] Yet, this finding is in stark contrast with the European Court of Justice's decision in *Bronner*, where it held that the access to a facility will not be indispensable if a less advantageous alternative can be developed by any undertaking other than the dominant undertaking.[1371]

Second, regarding the condition of the reservation of, and the exclusion of competition on, a secondary market, the Court reminded that 'it is necessary to distinguish two markets, namely, a market constituted by that product or service and on which the undertaking refusing to supply holds a dominant position and a neighbouring market on which the product or service is used in the manufacture of another product or for the supply of another service', and that 'the fact that the indispensable product or service is not marketed separately does not exclude from the outset the possibility of

1366. *Ibid.*, § 331.
1367. *Ibid.*, § 332.
1368. *Ibid.*, § 333.
1369. *See* I. Graef, 'Rethinking the Essential Facilities Doctrine for the EU Digital Economy', *supra*, pp. 45-46.
1370. CFI, *Microsoft v. Commission*, 17 September 2007, T-201/04, EU:T:2007:289, § 421.
1371. ECJ, *Bronner,* 26 November 1998, C-7/97, EU:C:1998:569, § 43.

identifying a separate market'.[1372] This echoes the European Court of Justice's reasoning in *IMS Health.*[1373] Yet, the Court of First Instance departed from this decision by holding that it is not necessary to demonstrate that 'all competition on the market would be eliminated', but rather that it is sufficient to demonstrate that 'the refusal at issue is liable to, or is likely to, eliminate all effective competition on the market'.[1374] In this regard, the Court added that 'the fact that the competitors of the dominant undertaking retain a marginal presence in certain niches on the market cannot suffice to substantiate the existence of such competition'.[1375]

Third, regarding the condition of the prevention of the appearance of a 'new product', the Court of First Instance made two important adaptations. On the one hand, it noted that this condition is only found in the essential facilities case law dealing with an IP right (namely *Magill* and *IMS Health*).[1376] On the other hand, the Court significantly lowered the threshold to meet this condition, as it provided that a refusal to licence will constitute an abuse not only if this prevents the appearance of a 'new product' but also if it prevents the appearance of technical developments.[1377] Once again, such a finding is in stark contrast with the previous case law of the European Court of Justice, in particular its *IMS Health* decision, where the Court held that a refusal to licence will only be abusive if 'the undertaking which requested the license does not intend to limit itself essentially to duplicating the goods or services already offered on the secondary market by the owner of the intellectual property right, but intends to produce new goods or services not offered by the owner of the right and for which there is a potential consumer demand'.[1378] This has led some authors to question whether the 'new product' requirement should still be considered as a condition for the application of the essential facilities doctrine, as virtually anything could be framed as being a 'technical development'.[1379]

To conclude on this *Microsoft* case, it is fundamental to underline that the judgment of the Court of First Instance has not been appealed by Microsoft, and that, consequently, the European Court of Justice did not have the opportunity to rule on whether it agrees or not with the Court of First Instance's lowering of the standards for the application of the essential

---

1372. CFI, *Microsoft v. Commission*, 17 September 2007, T-201/04, EU:T:2007:289, § 335.
1373. *See supra* point 231. ECJ, *IMS Health*, 29 April 2004, C-418/01, EU:C:2004:257, §§ 43-45.
1374. CFI, *Microsoft v. Commission*, 17 September 2007, T-201/04, EU:T:2007:289, § 563.
1375. *Ibid.*
1376. *Ibid.*, § 334.
1377. *Ibid.*, § 647.
1378. ECJ, *IMS Health*, 29 April 2004, C-418/01, EU:C:2004:257, § 49.
1379. E. Elhauge and D. Geradin, *Global Antitrust Law and Economics*, Third Edition, St. Paul, Foundation Press, 2018, pp. 507-508. *See also* I. Graef, 'Rethinking the Essential Facilities Doctrine for the EU Digital Economy', *supra*, p. 46.

facilities doctrine.[1380] It is thus uncertain whether this lowering was a consequence of Microsoft's superdominant position, and should thus not be translated in other cases, or whether this lowering represents an evolution that should be applied to any subsequent case.[1381]

234. Finally, it is important to mention the recent *Slovak Telekom* case.[1382] The starting point of this case is that Slovak Telekom, which is the incumbent and largest telecommunications operator and broadband provider in Slovakia, has been compelled by the Slovak telecommunications' regularity authority to grant all reasonable and justified access requests to its local loop, as it was considered as an operator having a significant power on the wholesale market for unbundled access to the local loop.[1383] To do so, Slovak Telekom published its reference unbundling offer setting out contractual and technical conditions for the access.[1384] However, the European Commission ruled that the conditions of access set by Slovak Telekom, between 12 August 2005 and 31 December 2010, constituted an abuse of dominant position, notably because it had set unfair terms and conditions in its reference unbundling offer and because it applied unfair tariffs 'which did not allow a competitor as efficient as [Slovak Telekom] relying on wholesale access to the unbundled local loops of that operator to replicate the retail broadband services offered by that operator without incurring a loss' (margin squeeze).[1385] This decision was, to a large extent, confirmed by the General Court, although it held that the Commission had failed to prove that Slovak Telekom had engaged in margin squeeze practices between 12 August 2005 and 31 December 2005.[1386]

Slovak Telekom appealed the General Court's decision, arguing that the Commission and the General Court had erred in law by considering that it was not necessary to assess the indispensability of the access to its local loop because it had a regulatory obligation to grant such access.[1387] The Court of Justice ruled that the Commission and the General Court were right to rule that different standards could be applied to outright refusals to deals, such as in the *Bronner* case,[1388] than to constructive refusals to deal (imposition of

1380. I. Graef, 'Rethinking the Essential Facilities Doctrine for the EU Digital Economy', *supra*, p. 46.
1381. *Ibid.*
1382. ECJ, *Slovak Telekom v. Commission*, 25 March 2021, C-165/19 P, EU:C:2021:239.
1383. *Ibid.*, §§ 9-12.
1384. *Ibid.*, § 12.
1385. *Ibid.*, §§ 14-16. *See also* European Commission, *Slovak Telekom*, 15 October 2014, case AT.39523.
1386. *Ibid.*, § 20. *See also* GC, *Slovak Telekom v. Commission*, 13 December 2018, T-851/14, EU:T:2018:929.
1387. *Ibid.*, §§ 21-24 and 31-35.
1388. *See* point 230.

unfair access conditions), such as in the present case.[1389] In substance, the Court held that the demonstration of the indispensable nature of the access to the facility in cases of outright refusals to deal was justified by the fact that forcing the dominant undertaking to provide access, by concluding a contract with a competitor, would be detrimental to its freedom of contract and to conduct a business, and to its right to property.[1390] However, it ruled that 'by contrast, where a dominant undertaking gives access to its infrastructure but makes that access, provision of services or sale of products subject to unfair conditions [constructive refusal to deal], the conditions laid down by the Court of Justice in paragraph 41 of the judgment in Bronner do not apply', and that, accordingly, 'the absence of such an indispensability is not in itself decisive for the purposes of the examination of potentially abusive practices on the part of a dominant undertaking'.[1391]

The Court justifies this distinction by the fact that, in the latter case, the dominant undertaking already provides the access to its infrastructure, and the competition authority would thus not have to force it to give such access.[1392] Therefore, 'the measures that would be taken in such a context will thus be less detrimental to the freedom of contract of the dominant undertaking and to its right to property than forcing it to give access to its infrastructure where it has reserved that infrastructure for the needs of its own business'.[1393] Said otherwise, the result of the balancing exercise between the various rights and interests at hand should be different in cases of outright refusals to deal, than in cases of constructive refusals to deal, where the data holder already provides access or is required to provide access by a regulatory obligation (as in the latter case, the legislator will have factored these rights and interests before adopting the obligation).[1394]

It should however be outlined that, according to some authors, such a distinction between outright refusals to deal, where the indispensability criterion is required, and constructive refusals to deal, such as margin squeeze,[1395] self-preferencing[1396] and tying[1397] practices, where the condition of indispensability does not appear in the legal test, might be problematic in

1389. ECJ, *Slovak Telekom v. Commission*, 25 March 2021, C-165/19 P, EU:C:2021:239, §§ 38-61.
1390. *Ibid.*, § 46.
1391. *Ibid.*, § 50.
1392. *Ibid.*, § 51.
1393. *Ibid.*
1394. *Ibid.*, §§ 54-56.
1395. *See* ECJ, *Konkurrensverket v. TeliaSonera Sverige AB*, 17 February 2011, C-52/09, EU:C:2011:83; GC, *Slovak Telekom v. Commission*, 13 December 2018, T-851/14, EU:T:2018:929; ECJ, *Slovak Telekom v. Commission*, 25 March 2021, C-165/19 P, EU:C:2021:239.
1396. European Commission, *Google Search (Shopping)*, 27 June 2017, AT.39740.
1397. European Commission, *Google Android*, 18 July 2018, AT.40099.

practice.[1398] For instance, knowing that the standard to find an abuse of dominance is higher for outright refusals to deal than for constructive refusals to deal, a dominant undertaking might opt not to provide access at all, rather than to provide access on restricted conditions, in order to protect its competitive position. As a result, this might potentially reduce the incentives for dominant undertakings to provide access (as they will not want to take the risk to 'open the floodgates'), on the one hand, and thus reduce the access possibilities for third parties, on the other hand.

235. To summarise, according to the essential facilities doctrine case law,[1399] the outright refusal by a dominant undertaking on a given market to grant access to another undertaking to a facility (a resource or an IP right) of which it is the owner (de jure or de facto) will constitute an abuse of such dominant position if the following 'exceptional circumstances' are met:[1400]

- Access to the facility is indispensable to enable the undertaking requesting access to operate in a secondary market.
- By refusing the access, the dominant undertaking reserves to itself a secondary market by excluding all competition on that market.
- The refusal prevents the emergence of a new product or service, or of technological developments, which are not offered by the dominant undertaking and for which there is potential consumer demand.
- The refusal cannot be justified by objective considerations.

A refusal to share the access to an essential facility is thus not abusive per se, as otherwise the dominant undertaking would be deprived of the substance of the exclusive (IP) rights it holds on the facility. It will only be so if the above-mentioned 'exceptional circumstances' are met. This is because, as outlined by Advocate General Jacobs in his opinion in *Bronner*,[1401] a dominant undertaking's freedom to contract also entails a freedom not to contract, and any competition intervention interfering with such a

1398. *See*, *inter alia*, P. Ibáñez Colomo, 'Indispensability and Abuse of Dominance: From Commercial Solvents to Slovak Telekom and Google Shopping', 11 December 2019, available at https://ssrn.com/abstract=3502519; D. Geradin, 'Refusal to Supply and Margin Squeeze: A Discussion of Why the "Telefonica Exceptions" Are Wrong', *TILEC Discussion Paper No. 2011-009*, 2011, available at https://ssrn.com/abstract=1762687; H. Auf'mkolk, 'The "Feedback Effect" of Applying EU Competition Law to Regulated Industries: Doctrinal Contamination in the Case of Margin Squeeze', *Journal of European Competition Law & Practice*, 2012, Vol. 3(2), pp. 149-162; A. Azzopardi, 'No Abuse Is an Island: The Case of Margin Squeeze', *European Competition Journal*, 2017, Vol. 13(2-3), pp. 228-248; I. Graef, 'Rethinking the Essential Facilities Doctrine for the EU Digital Economy', *supra*, pp. 56-63.

1399. *See* footnote 1325.

1400. D. Geradin, A. Layne-Farrar and N. Petit, *EU Competition Law and Economics*, Oxford, Oxford University Press, 2012, p. 256.

1401. ECJ, C-7/97, *Bronner*, 26 November 1998, EU:C:1998:569.

freedom requires 'a careful balancing of conflicting considerations',[1402] namely a balance between the costs and the benefits of providing access to the facility presented as 'essential'. Indeed, as the finding of an abuse results in the imposition, on the dominant firm, of a duty to deal with another undertaking, any potential benefits deriving from this forced access to the facility have to be balanced with the 'principles of freedom to contract,[1403] including the right to choose one's trading partners, and freedom to dispose of one's property'.[1404,1405]

This is important because, if the possibility to impose such a duty to deal was not limited to 'exceptional circumstances', this could have serious effects on the dominant undertaking's incentives to create and maintain the essential facility. Indeed, from an innovation perspective, 'while a duty to deal increases short-term competition and innovation complementary to the facility of the dominant firm, it may diminish incentives for competitors as well as dominant firms to develop substitutes for the existing infrastructure in the long term'.[1406] This was also highlighted by the Court of Justice in the *Slovak Telekom* case mentioned above,[1407] where it held that 'while, in the short term, an undertaking being held liable for having abused its dominant position due to a refusal to conclude a contract with a competitor has the consequence of encouraging competition, by contrast, in the long term, it is generally favourable to the development of competition and in the interest of consumers to allow a company to reserve for its own use the facilities that it has developed for the needs of its business. If access to a production, purchasing or distribution facility were allowed too easily, there would be no incentive for competitors to develop competing facilities. In addition, a dominant undertaking would be less inclined to invest in efficient facilities if it could be bound, at the mere request of its competitors, to share with them the benefits deriving from its own investments'.[1408] In doing so, the Court confirmed the point that Advocate General Jacobs had made in his opinion on the *Bronner* case, where he indicated that the essential facilities doctrine is the result of a careful balancing between promoting short-term and long-term competition and innovation.[1409]

1402. Opinion of Advocate General Jacobs in *Bronner* (ECJ), C-7/97, delivered on 28 May 1998, EU:C:1998:264, § 57.
1403. CFI, *Bayer v. Commission*, 26 October 2000, T-41/96, EU:T:2000:242, § 180.
1404. Opinion of Advocate General Jacobs in *Bronner* (ECJ), C-7/97, delivered on 28 May 1998, EU:C:1998:264, § 56.
1405. I. Graef, 'Rethinking the Essential Facilities Doctrine for the EU Digital Economy', *supra*, p. 47.
1406. *Ibid.*
1407. *See* point 234.
1408. ECJ, *Slovak Telekom v. Commission*, 25 March 2021, C-165/19 P, EU:C:2021:239, § 47.
1409. Opinion of Advocate General Jacobs in *Bronner* (ECJ), C-7/97, delivered on 28 May 1998, EU:C:1998:264, § 57.

236. This essential facilities doctrine is also interesting to analyse in the broader perspective of the need to find a balance between competition *in* the market, which favours sustaining innovation (i.e., improvement of an existing product or service that does not affect existing markets), and competition *for* the market, which favours disruptive innovation (i.e., innovation that reshuffles existing markets and leads to the apparition of new markets).[1410] Indeed, the imposition of a duty to deal stimulates competition *in* the market, as competitors will be provided with access to the facility in order to compete on the existing market, while refraining from imposing such access stimulates competition *for* the market, as competitors are rather incentivised to develop alternative products or services that will disrupt the existing market structures from the outside.[1411] Said otherwise, in the former case, competitors are incentivised to develop a similar product/service that is better than the incumbent's, while in latter case, competitors are rather incentivised to create the 'next big thing' that will displace the incumbent through the creation of a new type of product/service ('creative destruction').[1412] The latter approach to competition would arguably lead to a succession of highly dominant (or even monopolistic) positions that would likely persist for a certain period of time, before being displaced by a new highly dominant (or even monopolistic) undertaking in another market that would reshuffle existing markets.[1413] Examples of Facebook's displacement of MySpace and of Google's displacement of Yahoo are often cited in this regard.

Looking at the essential facilities doctrine case law, the European Court of Justice seems inclined to promote competition *in* the market, rather than competition *for* the market, through the imposition of a duty to deal when the above-mentioned 'exceptional circumstances' are met. However, neither the Court nor the European Commission explained why, in such cases, static

---

1410. I. Graef, 'Rethinking the Essential Facilities Doctrine for the EU Digital Economy', *supra*, pp. 47-51. *See also* J. Bower and C. Christensen, 'Disruptive Technologies: Catching the Wave', *Harvard Business Review*, 1995, Vol. 73(1), pp. 43-53; C. Christensen, *The Innovator's Dilemma. When New Technologies Cause Great Firms to Fail*, Boston, Harvard Business School Press, 1997; C. Christensen and M. Raynor, *The Innovator's Solution: Creating and Sustaining Successful Growth*, Boston, Harvard Business School Press, 2003; A. de Streel and P. Larouche, 'Disruptive Innovation and Competition Policy Enforcement', *OECD Working Paper DAF/COMP/GF(2015)7*, 2015, available at https://ssrn.com/abstract=2678890.

1411. I. Graef, 'Rethinking the Essential Facilities Doctrine for the EU Digital Economy', *supra*, p. 49. *See also* D. Evans and R. Schmalensee, 'Some Economic Aspects of Antitrust Analysis in Dynamically Competitive Industries', *Innovation Policy and the Economy*, Vol. 2, A. Jaffe, J. Lerner and S. Stern (eds), Cambridge, MIT Press, 2002, p. 1.

1412. *See* J. Schumpeter, *The Theory of Economic Development: an Inquiry into Profits, Capital, Credit, Interest, and the Business Cycle*, Cambridge, Harvard University Press, 1932.

1413. I. Graef, 'Rethinking the Essential Facilities Doctrine for the EU Digital Economy', *supra*, p. 49.

competition and sustaining innovation should be favoured over dynamic competition and disruptive innovation.[1414] One potential explanation is that the long-term benefits of incentivising competition *for* the market are, in fact, extremely difficult to assess, as they precisely involve long-term considerations about the development of the market which are, by nature, difficult to predict.[1415] On the other hand, short-term benefits of incentivising competition *in* the market are easier to anticipate and can be observed through increased competition in the downstream markets, leading to more choices and lower prices for consumers.[1416] Therefore, it is understandable that, in the above-mentioned 'exceptional circumstances', the competition authorities are willing to impose a duty to deal in order to ensure that a sufficient competitive pressure *in* the market remains in the short term, as it is unsure that a third party will ever be able to engage, in the long term, in disruptive innovation that will displace the incumbent by competing *for* the market. In this regard, serious doubts could be cast on whether large digital players such as Google, Facebook, Amazon, Microsoft or Apple will ever be displaced through disruptive innovation by a third party. This is because these actors have entrenched their strong market positions over the years and have used them to continuously expand their ecosystems.[1417]

6.1.2 Application of the Essential Facilities Doctrine to Data Markets: Adaptation Required?

237. As outlined above, the essential facilities doctrine case law is well established, and it seems to have reached an appropriate balance between the costs and the benefits of providing access to the facility presented as 'essential', at least when this facility is a 'traditional' tangible or intangible resource, in the sense of those that were studied in Part I, Chapter 2, Section 2.1. Yet, I have demonstrated that data has different characteristics than these 'traditional' resources.[1418] Indeed, data is a non-rivalrous and general-purpose good,[1419] which nevertheless remains technically and contractually excludable.[1420]

This raises the question of whether the balance reached by the essential facilities doctrine case law presented above remains appropriate in light of data's characteristics, or whether the result of this balancing exercise needs to be adapted in order to better fit the characteristics of the data markets. Said otherwise, can data be considered as an essential facility, in light of the

1414. *Ibid.*, p. 51.
1415. *Ibid.*
1416. *Ibid.*
1417. *See* points 83-85.
1418. *See* Part I, Chapter 2, Section 2.2.1.
1419. *See* point 52.
1420. *See* point 53.

existing conditions spelled out in the case law? If not, how could these conditions be adapted to better fit the characteristics of the data markets? In fact, the applicability of the essential facilities doctrine to refusals to grant access to data has been the topic of numerous contributions,[1421] and some serious doubts have been cast about its potential application to data markets.[1422] To assess the applicability of this theory to such markets, I will delve further in the suitability of the existing conditions of the essential facilities doctrine for data markets.

6.1.2.1 The 'Indispensability' Condition

238. The first condition for the application of the essential facilities doctrine is that access to the facility must be indispensable to enable the undertaking requesting access to operate in a secondary market.[1423] In this regard, the European Court of Justice held in *Bronner* that access to a facility will not be indispensable if a (less advantageous) alternative can be developed by any undertaking other than the dominant undertaking.[1424] To be precise, the 'indispensability' condition does not require the demonstration of the absence of 'any alternative at all', but rather the absence of 'a sufficient alternative for *any* undertaking' (emphasis added). Indeed, if one takes the example of a port used as the starting point to cross a narrow see, this infrastructure might be considered as an essential facility for ferry operators even if there is another port 500 kilometres away, as this alternative, though existent, might not be considered as 'sufficient for *any* undertaking' (emphasis added) in this context.

While this threshold might have been lowered in *Microsoft*, where the Court of First Instance concluded that the access to Microsoft's interoperability information was indispensable in order for Sun Microsystems to be able to compete 'on an equal footing',[1425] the European Court of Justice did

1421. *See*, *inter alia*, I. Graef, *EU Competition Law, Data Protection and Online Platforms: Data as Essential Facility*, Alphen aan den Rijn, Kluwer, 2016; J. Drexl, 'Designing Competitive Markets for Industrial Data – Between Propertisation and Access', *supra*, pp. 44-55; I. Graef, S. Wahyuningtyas and P. Valcke, 'Assessing Data Access Issues in Online Platforms', *Telecommunications Policy*, 2015, Vol. 39, p. 382; H. Schweitzer, J. Haucap, W. Kerber and R. Welker, *Modernisierung der Missbrauchsaufsicht für marktmächtige Unternehmen*, *supra*; J. Crémer, Y.-A. de Montjoye and H. Schweitzer, 'Competition Policy for the Digital Era', *supra*; J. Furman, et al., 'Unlocking Digital Competition', *supra*.

1422. *See* G. Colangelo and M. Maggiolino, 'Big Data as Misleading Facilities', *European Competition Journal*, 2017, Vol. 2-3(13), pp. 249-281.

1423. *See* point 235.

1424. ECJ, *Bronner*, 26 November 1998, C-7/97, EU:C:1998:569, § 43.

1425. CFI, *Microsoft v. Commission*, 17 September 2007, T-201/04, EU:T:2007:289, § 421.

not have the opportunity to rule on whether it agrees or not with this finding.[1426]

239. When applied to data, the 'indispensability' condition requires demonstrating that 'the data owned by the incumbent is truly unique and that there is no possibility for the competitor to obtain the data that it needs to perform its services'.[1427] If the access is requested to raw (unstructured) data, this requires a case-by-case assessment of whether any alternative raw data set is available to the access seeker, or whether the same raw data could be collected by any undertaking having the same size as the dominant undertaking.[1428] If the access is requested to information deriving from such raw data (i.e., structured data),[1429] this will require a case-by-case assessment of whether the same information is available elsewhere (i.e., whether it could be derived from another raw data set), or whether the same information could be obtained by any undertaking having the same size as the dominant undertaking (potentially on the basis of a similar raw data set).[1430]

According to Colangelo and Maggiolino, if applied to data, the *Bronner* case implies that data that is openly accessible online or can be purchased should never be considered as indispensable, as virtually any undertaking can access it or purchase it from data brokers.[1431] Graef is more nuanced. Although she agrees that data that is truly non-rivalrous may not be considered as being indispensable, she underlines that it should be kept in mind that this same data is excludable and can be made exclusive through contractual or technical means.[1432] This could make some types of data indispensable, notably some types of observed personal data that can, in practice, only be collected by dominant undertakings that benefit from strong network effects.[1433] Moreover, the way in which raw data is structured into information could make it indispensable if this structuring is the consequence

1426. I. Graef, 'Rethinking the Essential Facilities Doctrine for the EU Digital Economy', *supra*, pp. 45-46.
1427. Autorité de la concurrence and Bundeskartellamt, 'Competition Law and Data', 10 May 2016, available at http://www.autoritedelaconcurrence.fr/doc/reportcompetitionlawanddatafinal.pdf, p. 18.
1428. R. Feasey and A. de Streel, 'Data Sharing for Digital Market Contestability', *supra*, p. 36.
1429. *See* point 13.
1430. R. Feasey and A. de Streel, 'Data Sharing for Digital Market Contestability', *supra*, p. 36.
1431. G. Colangelo and M. Maggiolino, 'Big Data as Misleading Facilities', *supra*, pp. 270-271.
1432. I. Graef, *EU Competition Law, Data Protection and Online Platforms: Data as Essential Facility*, *supra*, p. 267. *See also* J. Krämer, P. Senellart and A. de Streel, 'Making Data Portability More Effective for the Digital Economy', *supra*, p. 28.
1433. R. Feasey and A. de Streel, 'Data Sharing for Digital Market Contestability', *supra*, p. 36; J. Krämer, P. Senellart and A. de Streel, 'Making Data Portability More Effective for the Digital Economy', *supra*, p. 53.

of strong network effects leading to a de facto industry standard.[1434] Indeed, it should be reminded that, in *IMS Health*, the Court outlined that the users' degree of participation in the development of IMS' standard brick structure, and the costs linked to it, had to be taken into consideration when determining whether IMS' structure was indispensable for the presentation of regional sales data on pharmaceutical products, as the users had become technically dependent on IMS' structure.[1435]

240. Interestingly, data has already been considered as indispensable, when collected in the context of former public monopolies, in a French (*GDF Suez*)[1436] and a Belgian (*Nationale Loterij*)[1437] case. This echoes Advocate General Jacobs' opinion in *Bronner*, where he indicated that the cost of duplicating a facility created under non-competitive conditions, such as through public funding, might constitute an insuperable barrier to entry rendering the access to this facility indispensable.[1438] In both of these cases, a former public monopolist used a customer list that it had developed when it enjoyed a legal monopoly to promote a new service, and this allowed it 'to compete unfairly through data cross-subsidisation which "un-levels" the playing field between the former monopolist and the new entrants'.[1439] In the French *GDF Suez* case, the French *Autorité de la concurrence* found that the customer list that GDF Suez had developed, thanks to its legal monopoly on the gas market, was not easily replicable by new entrants and that, by refusing to share this indispensable asset with them, GDZ Suez had abused its dominant position in the market for natural gas.[1440] In the Belgian *Nationale Loterij* case, the Belgian Competition Authority found that the access to the customer list that the Nationale Lottery had developed, thanks to its legal monopoly on the Belgian lottery market, was indispensable to compete with the Nationale Lottery on the sports betting market, as this customer list 'could not have been reproduced by competitors in the market

1434. R. Feasey and A. de Streel, 'Data Sharing for Digital Market Contestability', *supra*, p. 36.
1435. ECJ, *IMS Health*, 29 April 2004, C-418/01, EU:C:2004:257, §§ 29-30.
1436. Autorité de la concurrence, Decision n°14-MC-02 (*GDF Suez*), 9 September 2014, available at https://www.autoritedelaconcurrence.fr/sites/default/files/commitments// 14mc02.pdf.
1437. Belgian Competition Authority, Decision n°BMA-2015-P/K-27-AUD, 22 September 2015, available at https://www.abc-bma.be/sites/default/files/content/download/files/ 2015pk27-aud-bma-pub.pdf.
1438. Opinion of Advocate General Jacobs in *Bronner* (ECJ), C-7/97, delivered on 28 May 1998, EU:C:1998:264, §§ 66-67.
1439. R. Feasey and A. de Streel, 'Data Sharing for Digital Market Contestability', *supra*, p. 35.
1440. *Ibid*; I. Graef, *EU Competition Law, Data Protection and Online Platforms: Data as Essential Facility*, *supra*, pp. 271-272.

under reasonable financial conditions and within a reasonable period of time'.[1441]

241. In spite of these two examples, it is important to outline that, even if some data are not accessible to all firms on an equal basis and are not sold by data brokers, this does not necessarily imply that these data are indispensable, as long as it is possible to find substitutes.[1442] This was notably affirmed by the European Commission in the *Facebook/WhatsApp* merger, where it indicated that a wide number of undertakings collect user data for advertising purposes (Google, Facebook, Amazon, eBay, etc.).[1443] In sum, while there might be cases in which a specific data set will be considered as being indispensable, these will likely be exceptional.

In itself, this is not too problematic because the essential facilities doctrine entails a strong interference with the data holder's business interests, which justifies why it should only apply in exceptional circumstances. These circumstances could notably result from the fact that a data holder is the sole source of a specific type of data, the access to which is indispensable for another undertaking evolving on a downstream market.[1444] This could derive from historic national monopolies, as in the *GDF Suez* and *Nationale Loterij* cases presented above,[1445] or from the fact that the collection/production of a certain type of data is the result of a specific type of activity that only a very limited number of actors are able to pursue. Indeed, as outlined by Rubinfeld and Gal, 'unique access points to unique data may lead to situations in which the data cannot be easily replicated', as this would require a two-level entry, which might be unrealistic for a large number of undertakings.[1446] This could notably be the case for data created as the result of interactions on a social network (e.g., data collected by Facebook about how people's emotion affect their conduct), for data collected based on a specific standard (e.g., IMS Health's standard brick structure),[1447] or for data generated as a by-product of a specific production activity (e.g., geological data collected as a by-product of an oil deep-drilling activity).[1448] This could also derive from hypotheses where the incumbent data holder has technically or contractually

1441. R. Feasey and A. de Streel, 'Data Sharing for Digital Market Contestability', *supra*, p. 35.
1442. G. Colangelo and M. Maggiolino, 'Big Data as Misleading Facilities', *supra*, p. 273.
1443. European Commission, *Facebook/WhatsApp*, 3 October 2014, case M.7217, §§ 188-189; G. Colangelo and M. Maggiolino, 'Big Data as Misleading Facilities', *supra*, p. 271.
1444. *See* J. Drexl, 'Data Access and Control in the Era of Connected Devices', *supra*, p. 68.
1445. *See* point 240.
1446. D. Rubinfeld and M. Gal, 'Access Barriers to Big Data', *supra*, p. 351.
1447. *See* point 239.
1448. D. Rubinfeld and M. Gal, 'Access Barriers to Big Data', *supra*, pp. 351 and 357.

excluded the access to a sole source of data,[1449] or where the access to this sole source of data is subject to a very high access price and/or to very strict conditions.[1450] In such cases, the essential facilities doctrine could prove useful to compel the data holder to share the data at hand with several undertakings, provided that the other conditions of the doctrine are met as well.

242. Finally, it is important to remind here that, in light of the European Court of Justice's decision in *Slovak Telekom*, it seems that this indispensability condition would only apply in cases of outright refusals to provide access to the data, and not to constructive refusals to provide access to the data, namely situations in which the data holder already provides (or is compelled by regulation to provide) access to the data, but does so at unfair conditions.[1451] This distinction is important to keep in mind, as arguably this would imply that if a dominant undertaking is compelled by regulation to provide access to some data (*see* the sectoral examples in the banking,[1452] energy[1453] and automotive sector[1454] and the recent proposal for a Digital Markets Act[1455]) but does so at unfair conditions, this could constitute not only an infringement of that regulation but also potentially a constructive refusal to share data that might be considered as an abuse of dominant position, the proof of which will not require the demonstration of the indispensability of the data at hand.

6.1.2.2 The Condition of the Reservation of, and the Exclusion of Competition on, a Secondary Market

243. The second condition for the application of the essential facilities doctrine is that, by refusing to provide access to the facility, the dominant undertaking reserves to itself a secondary market by excluding all competition on that market.[1456] In this regard, the European Court of Justice held in *IMS Health* that it was sufficient to identify a potential or even hypothetical market.[1457]

1449. *See* I. Graef, *EU Competition Law, Data Protection and Online Platforms: Data as Essential Facility*, *supra*, p. 267. *See also* J. Krämer, P. Senellart and A. de Streel, 'Making Data Portability More Effective for the Digital Economy', *supra*, p. 28.
1450. D. Rubinfeld and M. Gal, 'Access Barriers to Big Data', *supra*, p. 362. *See also* B. Lundqvist, 'Regulating Competition and Property in the Digital Economy', *supra*, p. 4.
1451. *See* point 234.
1452. *See* Part II, Chapter 4, Section 4.2.2.
1453. *See* Part II, Chapter 4, Section 4.2.3.
1454. *See* Part III, Chapter 8, Section 8.1.1.
1455. *See* point 380.
1456. *See* point 235.
1457. *See* point 231.

244. The key factor to take into consideration when assessing whether this second condition is fulfilled is thus if 'the dominant firm reserves the downstream market to itself by denying a competitor access to an input'.[1458] This implies that such a condition will only be fulfilled in hypothesis where the dominant undertaking is itself already active on the downstream market, and not in hypotheses where it is not (yet) active on the downstream market. Indeed, in the latter case, a refusal to provide access to an input to third parties wishing to conduct a business on a downstream market would not amount to a reservation, by the dominant undertaking, of that market to itself as it is not active on it.[1459] In the context of the application of the essential facilities doctrine to 'traditional' resources, this is justified by the fact that, in principle, the dominant firm does not have any incentive to refuse access to an input to third parties wishing to conduct a business on a downstream market on which it is not active, as it does not have to protect its position on that market and as charging third parties for the access will in fact provide it with additional revenues.[1460]

245. Yet, if applied to digital markets, this requirement might be highly problematic. This is because 'data advantages' may be leveraged by undertakings active on one market to expand and strengthen their position in *connected markets*, i.e., distinct markets in which the data gathered in the first market turns out to be a valuable input to improve the goods or services offered.[1461] Indeed, as outlined by Drexl, 'a typical feature of the data economy is that data is collected for one purpose but may turn out to be interesting for very different purposes pursued by other firms of very different sectors'.[1462] These connections between markets make the digital economy much more dynamic than the 'brick-and-mortar' economy.[1463]

Therefore, as the dynamic connection between markets is greater in data markets than in traditional markets, a dominant undertaking may, in fact,

1458. I. Graef, 'Differentiated Treatment in Platform-to-Business Relations: EU Competition Law and Economic Dependence', *Yearbook of European Law*, 2019, Vol. 38, p. 452. *See also* ECJ, *RTE and ITP v. Commission*, 6 April 1995, joined cases C-241/91 and C-242/91, EU:C:1995:98, § 56; ECJ, *IMS Health*, 29 April 2004, C-418/01, EU:C:2004:257, § 52.

1459. I. Graef, 'Differentiated Treatment in Platform-to-Business Relations: EU Competition Law and Economic Dependence', *supra*, p. 452.

1460. *Ibid.*, p. 453.

1461. J. Prüfer and C. Schottmüller, 'Competing with Big Data', *TILEC Discussion Paper No. 2017-006 and CentER Discussion Paper No. 2017-007*, February 2017, available at https://pure.uvt.nl/ws/portalfiles/portal/15514029/2017_007.pdf, pp. 2-3; J. Krämer, D. Schnurr and S. Broughton Micova, 'The Role of Data for Digital Markets Contestability', *supra*, p. 56; B. Martens, et al., 'Business to Business Data Sharing', *supra*, p. 19.

1462. J. Drexl, 'Designing Competitive Markets for Industrial Data: Between Propertisation and Access', *supra*, p. 49.

1463. I. Graef, 'Differentiated Treatment in Platform-to-Business Relations: EU Competition Law and Economic Dependence', *supra*, p. 453.

refuse to share data with third parties wishing to conduct a business on a downstream market on which it is not (yet) active 'either because it plans to enter in the downstream market (future offensive leverage) or because it fears that the data seeker will disrupt its business (defensive leverage)'.[1464] Indeed, due to the complex data markets' dynamics, complements to the dominant undertaking's product/service on the upstream market, developed on a downstream market, may, in time, become substitutes to the dominant undertaking's product/service on the upstream market (disruptive innovation).[1465]

246. There is thus a strong argument to be made that this second condition of the essential facilities doctrine should be adapted for digital markets.[1466] More specifically, some authors argue that, since a dominant firm might engage in future offensive or defensive leveraging tactics, 'the fact that it is not active in the downstream market itself should not stand in the way of holding the refusal to deal abusive'.[1467] Accordingly, when applied to refusals to provide access to data, the second condition of the essential facilities doctrine should arguably be adapted and should arguably also apply to hypothesis in which the refusal prevents a third party from operating a business on a downstream market on which the dominant undertaking is not (yet) active.[1468] In this perspective, it should be added that 'the fact that the requested data have not already been traded, which is very often the case in practice, should not be an obstacle to imposing sharing as it suffices that there is demand and that such demand can legally and practically be met'.[1469] This echoes the European Court of Justice finding in *IMS Health* that it is sufficient to identify a potential or even hypothetical market.[1470]

1464. J. Krämer, P. Senellart and A. de Streel, 'Making Data Portability More Effective for the Digital Economy', *supra*, p. 28. *See also* R. Feasey and A. de Streel, 'Data Sharing for Digital Market Contestability', *supra*, pp. 36-37; I. Graef, 'Rethinking the Essential Facilities Doctrine for the EU Digital Economy', *supra*, pp. 67-68.

1465. *See* L. Cabral, et al., 'The EU Digital Markets Act: A Report from a Panel of Economic Experts', *EU Science Hub*, 2021, available at https://ec.europa.eu/jrc/en/publication/eu-digital-markets-act, p. 26.

1466. I. Graef, 'Differentiated Treatment in Platform-to-Business Relations: EU Competition Law and Economic Dependence', *supra*, p. 453.

1467. *Ibid. See also* R. Feasey and A. de Streel, 'Data Sharing for Digital Market Contestability', *supra*, p. 36.

1468. I. Graef, 'Rethinking the Essential Facilities Doctrine for the EU Digital Economy', *supra*, p. 68.

1469. R. Feasey and A. de Streel, 'Data Sharing for Digital Market Contestability', *supra*, p. 36.

1470. ECJ, *IMS Health*, 29 April 2004, C-418/01, EU:C:2004:257, § 44.

6.1.2.3 The 'New Product' Condition

247. The third condition for the application of the essential facilities doctrine is that the refusal to provide access to the facility must prevent the emergence of a new product or service, or of technological developments, which are not offered by the dominant undertaking and for which there is potential consumer demand.[1471] Following the *Microsoft* judgment, this condition has become more difficult to interpret.[1472]

248. If applied to refusals to share data, this 'new product' condition implies that the access seeker will have to demonstrate that the data would allow him to create a sufficiently new product/service – or at least an improved product/service if the reduction of the threshold in *Microsoft* became the norm – compared to that of the dominant undertaking.[1473] In this regard, Drexl outlines that while it can be doubted that the mere generation of new information by the access seeker deriving from the data will be sufficiently innovative to meet this requirement, such information could be used to offer new products/services, or at least technical improvements of an existing product/service, on a secondary market.[1474]

However, as for the second condition of the essential facilities doctrine analysed above,[1475] this third condition requires, in the context of 'traditional' resources, that the dominant undertaking should also be active on the secondary market.[1476] Indeed, the European Court of Justice held in *IMS Health* that the access seeker should not 'limit itself essentially to duplicating the goods or services *already offered on the secondary market* by the [dominant undertaking]' (emphasis added).[1477] Yet, as outlined above, in data markets, the dominant undertaking may in fact not (yet) be active, and may thus not (yet) offer products/services, in the downstream market.[1478] Therefore, some authors have suggested adapting this 'new product' requirement in the context of the application of the essential facilities doctrine to refusals to share data, and to adopt a more general consumer harm approach, that would amount to conducting a balance between the negative consequences

---

1471. *See* point 235.
1472. *See* point 233.
1473. J. Krämer, P. Senellart and A. de Streel, 'Making Data Portability More Effective for the Digital Economy', *supra*, p. 29. *See also* R. Feasey and A. de Streel, 'Data Sharing for Digital Market Contestability', *supra*, p. 37.
1474. J. Drexl, 'Designing Competitive Markets for Industrial Data: Between Propertisation and Access', *supra*, p. 52.
1475. *See* points 243-246.
1476. J. Krämer, P. Senellart and A. de Streel, 'Making Data Portability More Effective for the Digital Economy', *supra*, p. 29. *See also* R. Feasey and A. de Streel, 'Data Sharing for Digital Market Contestability', *supra*, p. 37.
1477. ECJ, *IMS Health*, 29 April 2004, C-418/01, EU:C:2004:257, § 49.
1478. *See* point 245.

that the refusal to share would entail for consumers and the negative consequences that the imposition of a data sharing remedy could entail.[1479]

249. To some extent, adopting such a general consumer harm approach is the aim of Graef's proposal to make the application of the 'new product' condition dependent on whether the upstream market is characterised by external market failures, such as strong network effects.[1480] For her, such an adaptation of the 'new product' requirement 'would bring the essential facilities doctrine more in line with the underlying economic interests and the balance between competition *for* and *in* the market' (emphasis in the text).[1481]

Applying this 'new product' condition strictly in situations where the upstream market is not characterised by external market failures would promote competition *for* the market in such situations, by encouraging investments in innovation by the access seekers.[1482] This would incentivise these access seekers to create disruptive products/services that would displace the dominant undertaking, as they know that the creation of the 'next big thing'[1483] will provide them with a (temporary) monopoly position on the newly created market.[1484] Indeed, as outlined by the Supreme Court of the US in *Trinko*, 'the opportunity to charge monopoly prices – at least for a short period – is what attracts "business acumen" in the first place; it induces risk taking that produces innovation and economic growth'.[1485]

On the other hand, external market failures, such as strong network effects, lock-in situations and high switching costs,[1486] 'may make it commercially unviable for competitors to introduce a new product'.[1487] In such cases, long-term competitive advantages may be established, and this

1479. J. Krämer, P. Senellart and A. de Streel, 'Making Data Portability More Effective for the Digital Economy', *supra*, p. 29. *See also* R. Feasey and A. de Streel, 'Data Sharing for Digital Market Contestability', *supra*, p. 37.

1480. I. Graef, *EU Competition Law, Data Protection and Online Platforms: Data as Essential Facility*, *supra*, p. 275. *See also* I. Graef, 'Rethinking the Essential Facilities Doctrine for the EU Digital Economy', *supra*, pp. 69-72.

1481. *See* point 236. I. Graef, 'Rethinking the Essential Facilities Doctrine for the EU Digital Economy', *supra*, p. 71.

1482. *Ibid.*, p. 70.

1483. *See* J. Schumpeter, *The Theory of Economic Development: An Inquiry into Profits, Capital, Credit, Interest, and the Business Cycle*, *supra*.

1484. I. Graef, 'Rethinking the Essential Facilities Doctrine for the EU Digital Economy', *supra*, p. 52.

1485. Supreme Court of the United States, *Verizon Communications v. Law Offices of Curtis V. Trinko*, 2004, *LLP*, 540 US 398, p. 407.

1486. *See* Part I, Chapter 2, Section 2.2.3.1 and Part I, Chapter 2, Section 2.2.3.2. *See* M. Stucke and A. Grunes, *Big Data and Competition Policy*, *supra*; D. Rubinfeld and M. Gal, 'Access Barriers to Big Data', *Arizona Law Review*, 2017, Vol. 59, pp. 339-381; J. Crémer, Y.-A. de Montjoye and H. Schweitzer, 'Competition Policy for the Digital Era', *supra*, p. 24.

1487. I. Graef, 'Rethinking the Essential Facilities Doctrine for the EU Digital Economy', *supra*, p. 69.

could endanger the contestability of these data-driven markets.[1488] Indeed, as the market power of these dominant undertakings entrenches over time, this could delay, or even prevent, the occurrence of new waves of competition *for* the market by new entrants.[1489] In such cases where external market failures shield the dominant undertakings from sufficient competitive pressure and market contestability, the standard for competition law intervention should be lowered in order to re-establish some level of competition *in* the market.[1490] Accordingly, Graef argues that in the presence of such external market failures, 'the new product condition should be dropped to ensure that access seekers who intend to introduce sustaining innovations or products similar to that of the dominant undertaking are able to gain access to the necessary input so that the process of competition in the market can be (re)launched'.[1491] In turn, this would benefit consumers who would be offered lower prices and more choices/variety.[1492]

In fact, Graef argues that her proposal could find some support in the existing essential facilities doctrine case law. For her, the fact that important external market failures prevented market entry by potential competitors in the *Microsoft* case might explain why the Court of First Instance lowered the standards for the fulfilment of the doctrine's conditions.[1493] In contrast, the higher standards imposed by the European Court of Justice in the other cases presented above[1494] would remain applicable in cases where there are no external market failures preventing entry by potential competitors.[1495]

6.1.2.4 Adaptation to the Characteristics of Data

250. In light of the above, there are strong arguments to support the adaptation of the essential facilities doctrine when it is applied to refusals to share data, as the result of the balancing exercise reached by this doctrine when applied to 'traditional' resources may need to be reconsidered in order to better fit the characteristics of the data markets.[1496]

Indeed, any competition intervention interfering with a dominant undertaking's freedom (not) to contract requires 'a careful balancing of

1488. J. Krämer, D. Schnurr and S. Broughton Micova, 'The Role of Data for Digital Markets Contestability', *supra*, p. 55.
1489. I. Graef, 'Rethinking the Essential Facilities Doctrine for the EU Digital Economy', *supra*, pp. 54-55.
1490. *Ibid.*
1491. *Ibid.*, pp. 69-70.
1492. *Ibid.*, p. 70.
1493. *See* point 232. *Ibid.*, pp. 55 and 70.
1494. *See* especially points 229-231.
1495. I. Graef, 'Rethinking the Essential Facilities Doctrine for the EU Digital Economy', *supra*, p. 55.
1496. *Ibid.*, p. 40; R. Feasey and A. de Streel, 'Data Sharing for Digital Market Contestability', *supra*, pp. 37-38.

conflicting considerations',[1497] namely a balance between the costs and the benefits of providing access to the facility presented as 'essential'. A balance must thus be found between the 'need to protect the dominant firm's investment incentives and the need to ensure that strongly entrenched positions of market power, protected by high barriers of entry, remain contestable'.[1498] Said otherwise, a careful balancing between promoting short-term and long-term competition and innovation must be operated.[1499]

251. If applied to refusals to share data, this means that compulsory data sharing, through the means of a competition law intervention, should only be imposed if the benefits outweigh the costs.[1500] Indeed, data collection and processing, and consequently data sharing, entail costs, and data sharing obligations might create disincentives for data collection and processing by both the dominant undertaking (fear of free-riding) and the access seekers (expectation to free-ride).[1501] On the other hand, compulsory data sharing could allow access seekers to enter (or create) a secondary market, which could lead to more diversity, choice, innovation and competition.[1502] A balance must thus be found. In this regard, it must be reminded that, due to data's characteristics, the benefits of data sharing may arguably be greater than the benefits of sharing other resources.[1503] Moreover, the costs of data sharing may arguably be smaller than the costs of sharing rival resources, as the impact on the dominant undertaking's incentives will be lower in the former than in the latter situation, since the sharing does not prevent the dominant undertaking from keeping to use the data.[1504] This is even more so if the data to be shared has been generated as a by-product of another

1497. Opinion of Advocate General Jacobs in *Bronner* (ECJ), C-7/97, delivered on 28 May 1998, EU:C:1998:264, § 57.

1498. J. Crémer, Y.-A. de Montjoye and H. Schweitzer, 'Competition Policy for the Digital Era', *supra*, p. 98.

1499. Opinion of Advocate General Jacobs in *Bronner* (ECJ), C-7/97, delivered on 28 May 1998, EU:C:1998:264, § 57.

1500. B. Martens, et al., 'Business to Business Data Sharing', *supra*, p. 5; W. Kerber, 'Data Governance in Connected Cars: The Problem of Access to In-Vehicle Data', *Journal of Intellectual Property, Information Technology and E-Commerce Law*, 2018, Vol. 9(3), p. 330; R. Feasey and A. de Streel, 'Data Sharing for Digital Market Contestability', *supra*, p. 37.

1501. *See* point 89.

1502. R. Feasey and A. de Streel, 'Data Sharing for Digital Market Contestability', *supra*, p. 37.

1503. M. Bourreau and A. de Streel, 'Digital Conglomerates and EU Competition Policy', *supra*, p. 31; H. Schweitzer, J. Haucap, W. Kerber and R. Welker, 'Modernising the Law on Abuse of Market Power: Executive Summary', *Report for the German Federal Ministry for Economic Affairs and Energy*, 29 August 2018, available at https://ssrn.com/abstract=3250742, p. 10. *See also* J. Prüfer and C. Schottmüller, 'Competing with Big Data', *supra.*; R. Feasey and A. de Streel, 'Data Sharing for Digital Market Contestability', *supra*, p. 37.

1504. R. Feasey and A. de Streel, 'Data Sharing for Digital Market Contestability', *supra*, p. 37.

business activity,[1505] or if it has been collected in the context of a legal monopoly.[1506,1507]

252. Accordingly, some authors argue that the threshold for imposing the access to data as a remedy to an abuse of a dominant position should be lower than the threshold to impose access to more 'traditional' resources.[1508] In this regard, several policy reports on the adaptation of competition law to the digital environment have also outlined that 'the threshold for finding that a refusal to supply data constitutes an abuse may be somewhat lower than the threshold for finding an abuse in cases of a refusal to grant access to infrastructures or to intellectual property rights.[1509] This is true in particular if and to the extent that the refusal to grant access relates to data which is generated virtually incidentally and without special investment'.[1510] Importantly, this does not mean that there should be no threshold at all, as the benefits of the sharing still need to be balanced with the costs that it entails for the dominant undertaking, but rather that the threshold for imposing the sharing should be lower for data than for more 'traditional' resources.[1511]

253. More concretely, the threshold for the application of the essential facilities doctrine could be reduced, when applied to refusals to share data, through the adaptation of the second (reservation of, and the exclusion of competition on, a secondary market) and third (prevention of the appearance of a 'new product') conditions of the doctrine. As outlined above,[1512] the second condition of the essential facilities doctrine could be adapted in order to also apply to hypotheses in which the refusal prevents a third party from operating a business on a downstream market on which the dominant undertaking is not (yet) active,[1513] while the third condition could be made

1505. *See* the *Magill* case at point 229.
1506. *See* the *GDF Suez* and *Nationale Loterij* cases at point 240.
1507. R. Feasey and A. de Streel, 'Data Sharing for Digital Market Contestability', *supra*, p. 37.
1508. *Ibid.*, p. 38.
1509. In this perspective, the threshold for finding an abuse could thus be higher for data protected by a sui generis right than for data that are not protected by such a right, for instance, because there has been no substantial investment in their obtention, verification or presentation. On this sui generis right, *see* points 58-60.
1510. H. Schweitzer, J. Haucap, W. Kerber and R. Welker, 'Modernising the Law on Abuse of Market Power: Executive Summary', *supra*, p. 10. *See also* J. Furman, et al., 'Unlocking Digital Competition', *supra*, pp. 74-77; J. Crémer, Y.-A. de Montjoye and H. Schweitzer, 'Competition Policy for the Digital Era', *supra*, pp. 98-108.
1511. R. Feasey and A. de Streel, 'Data Sharing for Digital Market Contestability', *supra*, p. 38.
1512. *See* points 243-249.
1513. I. Graef, 'Rethinking the Essential Facilities Doctrine for the EU Digital Economy', *supra*, p. 68; I. Graef, 'Differentiated Treatment in Platform-to-Business Relations: EU Competition Law and Economic Dependence', *supra*, p. 453; R. Feasey and A. de Streel, 'Data Sharing for Digital Market Contestability', *supra*, p. 36.

dependent on whether the upstream market is characterised by external market failures, in which case it could arguably be dropped.[1514]

254. Regarding the first condition of the doctrine (the 'indispensability' condition), it is argued that it should apply to outright refusals to share data, as the imposition of a data sharing remedy in such a scenario would strongly interfere with the data holder's business interests.[1515] On the other hand, it is argued that this condition should not be applied to constructive refusals to share data.[1516] Indeed, as the imposition of a data sharing remedy would require a form of monitoring,[1517] which could be extremely burdensome for competition authorities, this should be limited to exceptional cases, especially because competition authorities may be ill-suited to deal with such issues.[1518] In this regard, opting for more systemic solutions in order to ensure contestability and innovation on the data markets, rather than resorting to case-by-case competition interventions, might be preferable, notably through the creation of potential *ex ante* legislations imposing B2B data sharing.[1519]

255. The fourth condition of the doctrine (the absence of an objective justification for the refusal) should also be briefly pointed out. Indeed, as some (most) of the data that the access seekers wish to obtain may be personal data, dominant undertakings could be tempted to use personal data protection considerations as an objective justification for refusals to share it,[1520] and it might be difficult for competition authorities to evaluate whether such a claim is legitimate, or whether it is a disguise for an anticompetitive conduct.[1521] In this regard, competition authorities should require these

1514. I. Graef, *EU Competition Law, Data Protection and Online Platforms: Data as Essential Facility*, *supra*, p. 275. *See also* I. Graef, 'Rethinking the Essential Facilities Doctrine for the EU Digital Economy', *supra*, pp. 69-72.
1515. *See* points 238-241.
1516. *See* point 242.
1517. P. Ibáñez Colomo, 'Indispensability and Abuse of Dominance: From Commercial Solvents to Slovak Telekom and Google Shopping', 11 December 2019, available at https://ssrn.com/abstract=3502519, p. 35. *See also* R. Feasey and A. de Streel, 'Data Sharing for Digital Market Contestability', *supra*, p. 38.
1518. *See* V. Kathuria and J. Globocnik, 'Exclusionary Conduct in Data-Driven Markets: Limitations of Data Sharing Remedy', *Max Planck Institute for Innovation and Competition Research Paper No. 19-04*, 2019, available at https://ssrn.com/abstract=3337524, pp. 18-19; J. Crémer, Y.-A. de Montjoye and H. Schweitzer, 'Competition Policy for the Digital Era', *supra*, p. 10.
1519. *See* Part III, Chapter 8. *See also* Communication from the Commission, '*Shaping Europe's Digital Future*', *supra*, p. 9; Communication from the Commission, '*A European Strategy for Data*', *supra*, pp. 5 and 14.
1520. *See*, for instance, E. Egan, 'Data Portability and Privacy', *Facebook White Paper*, September 2019, available at https://iapp.org/media/pdf/fb_whitepaper_sep_2019.pdf.
1521. D. Geradin, T. Karanikioti and D. Katsifis, 'GDPR Myopia: How a Well-Intended Regulation Ended Up Favoring Google in Ad Tech', *TILEC Discussion Paper DP 2020-012*, May 2020, available at https://ssrn.com/abstract=3598130, pp. 36-37.

dominant undertakings to lay down and substantiate the data protection concerns they raise in order to refuse data sharing with third parties, and they should cooperate with data protection authorities in order to assess whether the data protection standards imposed on third parties by these dominant undertakings are (suspiciously) high.[1522] As this articulation between personal data protection law and competition law requires an extensive analysis, this will be tackled below in a separate chapter.[1523]

256. To conclude, it should be mentioned here that, as the questions pertaining to the type of data sharing remedy to be imposed are equally relevant for the other types of competition law infringements that will be analysed in the following sections, namely abuses of economic dependence (Section 6.2) and input foreclosure in vertical integration (Section 6.3), they will be addressed in a specific section dedicated to overarching considerations pertaining to compulsory B2B data sharing as a competition law remedy (Section 6.4).

Moreover, it is important to underline that, in any case, the essential facilities doctrine might not often be called upon in practice because the threshold, even if it is lowered in the way suggested above, would remain difficult to reach,[1524] as the doctrine should only apply in 'exceptional circumstances'.[1525] Moreover, it only allows targeting a limited number of undertakings, namely those holding a dominant position in a well-defined market.

Yet, market definition is a complex task in the digital environment, as digital markets are often two-sided and characterised by network externalities that each side imposes on the other.[1526] Moreover, they often imply 'zero' price products/services on one side of the market, generally the consumer side (these products/services are however not 'free', as consumers 'pay' with their personal data to use them[1527]), which are subsidised by the other side of the market.[1528] As a result, the classic 'small but significant non-transitory increase in price' (SSNIP) test is difficult to apply in such markets, and the alternative proposition of resorting to a 'small but significant non-transitory decrease in quality' (SSNDQ) test faces the same

1522. *Ibid.*
1523. *See* Part III, Chapter 7.
1524. R. Feasey and A. de Streel, 'Data Sharing for Digital Market Contestability', *supra*, p. 8.
1525. *See* point 235.
1526. J. Crémer, Y.-A. de Montjoye and H. Schweitzer, 'Competition Policy for the Digital Era', *supra*, pp. 42-43. For a broader analysis of the complexity of market definition in the digital environment, *see* pp. 42-50; I. Graef, 'Market Definition and Market Power in Data: The Case of Online Platforms', *World Competition Law and Economics Review*, 2015, Vol. 38(4), pp. 473-506.
1527. *See* point 129.
1528. J. Crémer, Y.-A. de Montjoye and H. Schweitzer, 'Competition Policy for the Digital Era', *supra*, p. 44.

difficulties of balancing between the two sides of the market than the SSNIP test.[1529] Therefore, there are growing calls to reconsider the way in which digital markets are defined in the digital environment. Traditionally, as outlined by Bourreau and de Streel:

> The determination of market power is done in two steps which are closely related. First, the product market is defined mainly on the basis of demand substitution between existing products and, in a subsidiary way, on the basis of supply substitution when new suppliers can enter in the short term without entailing a significant adjustment of existing tangible and intangible assets.[1530] Then, the market power is determined mainly on the basis of the current market position of the firms and the barriers to entry and expansion and, when relevant, the countervailing buyer power.[1531,1532]

When determining market power on digital multisided markets, the European Commission's expert report on 'Competition Policy for the digital era' suggests, instead, focusing on product/service functionalities as the starting point for determining substitutability relationships, even if this test is not as rigorous as the SSNIP test.[1533] In this perspective, it is suggested that competition policy should analyse all the sides of the market and should consider the way in which they interact.[1534] Indeed, the interdependence between these different sides/markets is crucial in digital markets, and this contrasts with classic market definition which traditionally aims at isolating markets from one another.[1535] Pushing this logic further, some have suggested taking this interdependence into account by focusing on 'ecosystems of products/services',[1536] and to complement this with 'a novel analysis based on capabilities/input markets in order to better reflect the importance, the rate and the uncertainty of innovation and the key role played by

---

1529. *Ibid.*, pp. 44-45.
1530. Commission Notice on the definition of relevant market for the purposes of Community competition law, *OJ C 372/5*, 9 December 1997, §§ 13-23. This Notice is currently under review: *see* https://ec.europa.eu/info/law/better-regulation/have-your-say/initiatives/12325-Evaluation-of-the-Commission-Notice-on-market-definition-in-EU-competition-law.
1531. Communication from the Commission, Guidance on the Commission's enforcement priorities in applying Article 82 of the EC Treaty to abusive exclusionary conduct by dominant undertakings, *OJ C 45/7*, 24 February 2009, §§ 12-18.
1532. M. Bourreau and A. de Streel, 'Digital Conglomerates and EU Competition Policy', *supra*, p. 25.
1533. J. Crémer, Y.-A. de Montjoye and H. Schweitzer, 'Competition Policy for the Digital Era', *supra*, p. 45.
1534. *Ibid.*
1535. *Ibid.*, p. 46.
1536. M. Bourreau and A. de Streel, 'Digital Conglomerates and EU Competition Policy', *supra*, p. 26; *see also* J. Crémer, Y.-A. de Montjoye and H. Schweitzer, 'Competition Policy for the Digital Era', *supra*, pp. 47-48.

innovation capabilities [such as data]'.[1537] In any case, the dynamic nature of the digital environment might entail that it will always be complicated to identify well-defined markets because, as outlined by Crémer et al.:

> Dynamic market environment leads to fluid, quickly-changing relationships of substitutability and possibly partial overlaps of varying significance between different services, sometimes combined with practices of multihoming and/or changing perceptions of consumer needs. (...) In such settings, the determination of substitutability relationships based on the present patterns of choice may turn out to be too narrow in hindsight and lead to 'false positives'. At the same time, inaction in the light of a mere possibility of changing market boundaries may lead to 'false negatives'.[1538]

257. As a result, establishing dominance of large digital firms in such markets will likely remain a complex task.[1539] Accordingly, some have argued that there could be more flexibility in applying the abuse of dominance rules, as 'instead of first defining the relevant market, competition authorities and courts could be allowed to find relevant market power by implication when anti-competitive behaviour is not sufficiently controlled by competition and a subsequent foreclosure effect can be proven'.[1540] In the same vein, others have held that, in digital markets, 'less emphasis should be put on the market definition part of the analysis, and [that] more importance [should be] attributed to the theories of harm and identification of anti-competitive strategies'.[1541]

In this perspective, it is interesting to note that the German experts' report for the modernisation of competition law suggested the introduction, in German competition law, of the possibility for competition authorities to intervene below the threshold of market dominance, in cases where the unilateral behaviour of an undertaking that is not (yet) dominant, but that is active on a market characterised by strong positive network effects, aims at inducing market 'tipping' in its favour, notably through targeted obstruction of multi-homing or switching.[1542] Yet, as outlined

1537. M. Bourreau and A. de Streel, 'Digital Conglomerates and EU Competition Policy', *supra*, p. 27.
1538. J. Crémer, Y.-A. de Montjoye and H. Schweitzer, 'Competition Policy for the Digital Era', *supra*, p. 47.
1539. W. Kerber, 'Updating Competition Policy for the Digital Economy?', *supra*, p. 5.
1540. H. Schweitzer, et al., 'Modernising the Law on Abuse of Market Power: Executive Summary', *supra*, p. 1.
1541. J. Crémer, Y.-A. de Montjoye and H. Schweitzer, 'Competition Policy for the Digital Era', *supra*, p. 46.
1542. H. Schweitzer, et al., 'Modernising the Law on Abuse of Market Power: Executive Summary', *supra*, p. 2; H. Schweitzer, et al., *Modernisierung der Missbrauchsaufsicht für marktmächtige Unternehmen*, *supra*, pp. 59-64. *See also* the Governmental draft bill (GWB-Digitalisierungsgesetz) for the 10th amendment to the Competition Act of 9 September 2020: Gesetzesentwurf der Bundesregierung, Entwurf eines Gesetzes zur Änderung des Gesetzes gegen Wettbewerbsbeschränkungen für ein fokussiertes,

above,[1543] such 'tipping' could be particularly harmful for competition due to its potential irreversibility.[1544] Accordingly, the report suggested the introduction of a new provision in the GWB,[1545] 'which prohibits platform operators in tight oligopolies, or platform operators with superior market power, to obstruct multi-homing or the changing of platforms, insofar as this strategic obstruction is suitable to promote a "tipping" of the market'.[1546] Such a provision has eventually been included in the 10th amendment to the German Competition Act, namely the GWB Digitalisation Act ('GWB-Digitalisierungsgesetz').[1547]

Moreover, the same report also suggested the inclusion of a third form of market power in the GWB, distinct from supplier and buyer power, namely 'intermediation power',[1548] which some large digital actors benefit from due to increasing returns to scale, network externalities and their control on large amounts of data, and which they can leverage in adjacent markets.[1549] Such a provision has also been included in the GWB Digitalisation Act.[1550] As summarised by Kerber, 'the basic idea is that many platforms do not only have market power due to large direct and indirect network effects, and can therefore be gatekeepers to large groups of

---

proaktives und digitales Wettbewerbsrecht 4.0 und anderer wettbewerbsrechtlicher Bestimmungen, available at https://www.bmwi.de/Redaktion/DE/Artikel/Service/Gesetzesvorhaben/gwb-digitalisierungsgesetz.html.

1543. *See* point 79. *See also* J. Prüfer, 'Competition Policy and Data Sharing on Data-Driven Markets', *Report for the Friedrich-Ebert-Stiftung*, 2020, available at http://library.fes.de/pdf-files/fes/15999.pdf, pp. 6-9; J. Prüfer and C. Schottmüller, 'Competing with Big Data', *supra*, p. 2.
1544. W. Kerber, 'Updating Competition Policy for the Digital Economy?', *supra*, p. 6; H. Schweitzer, et al., 'Modernising the Law on Abuse of Market Power: Executive Summary', *supra*, p. 3.
1545. '*Gesetz gegen Wettbewerbsbeschränkungen*' (Act against Restraints of Competition, adopted on 26 August 1998 and lastly amended on 19 January 2021). The official English translation of the GWB is available at http://www.gesetze-im-internet.de/englisch_gwb/englisch_gwb.html#p0066.
1546. H. Schweitzer, J. Haucap, W. Kerber and R. Welker, 'Modernising the Law on Abuse of Market Power: Executive Summary', *supra*, p. 3.
1547. *See* Bundeskartellamt, 'Amendment of the German Act Against Restraints of Competition (Press Release)', 19 January 2021, available at https://www.bundeskartellamt.de/SharedDocs/Meldung/EN/Pressemitteilungen/2021/19_01_2021_GWB%20Novelle.html. The full text, in German, of the GWB-Digitalisierungsgesetz is available at https://www.bgbl.de/xaver/bgbl/start.xav#__bgbl__%2F%2F*%5B%40attr_id%3D%27bgbl121s0002.pdf%27%5D__1612262835179.
1548. H. Schweitzer, et al., 'Modernising the Law on Abuse of Market Power: Executive Summary', *supra*, pp. 3-4. For more information on this concept, *see* H. Schweitzer, et al., *Modernisierung der Missbrauchsaufsicht für marktmächtige Unternehmen*, *supra*, pp. 66 et seq. *See also* the Governmental draft bill (GWB-Digitalisierungsgesetz) for the 10th amendment to the Competition Act of 9 September 2020, *supra*.
1549. J. Crémer, Y.-A. de Montjoye and H. Schweitzer, 'Competition Policy for the Digital Era', *supra*, p. 49.
1550. *See* Bundeskartellamt, 'Amendment of the German Act Against Restraints of Competition (Press release)', *supra*.

customers, but that they are at the same time also information intermediaries, e.g. by offering search functions, rankings and ratings, which implies information asymmetries between the platforms and the users'.[1551] As a result, the German report outlines that 'providers of goods and services may depend for their economic survival on being present on each and any of those platforms, or at least on the majority of them if the same customers cannot be served in a similarly effective way otherwise and if it is essential to reach a large proportion of potential customers. A provider of goods or services may therefore be dependent on a digital platform under similar conditions as – conventionally – on a reseller, such as a food retailer'.[1552] In fact, it should be outlined that the GWB already contains a provision forbidding the abuses of such economic dependence,[1553] which also allows competition authorities to intervene below the threshold of market dominance. I will now turn to the analysis of such provisions forbidding the abuse of economic dependence.

6.2 ABUSE OF ECONOMIC DEPENDENCE[1554]

258. While Article 102 TFEU only allows targeting dominant undertakings, powerful data holders that do not benefit from such a dominant position could also start refusing to share their data with undertakings having a limited bargaining power. For instance, in the USA, Twitter suddenly decided to stop providing access to its 'Firehose' data to PeopleBrowsr, a data analytics company, while this access had been provided freely for years and while PeopleBrowsr had built its business model on this access.[1555] Similarly, after having allowed hiQ's access and use of its data for several years, LinkedIn requested hiQ to stop accessing its data, and used blocking techniques preventing hiQ from doing so, while this access was at the core of hiQ's business model.[1556] In these two cases, while neither Twitter nor LinkedIn was considered as being dominant, both PeopleBrowsr and hiQ

1551. W. Kerber, 'Updating Competition Policy for the Digital Economy?', *supra*, p. 6.
1552. H. Schweitzer, et al., 'Modernising the Law on Abuse of Market Power: Executive Summary', *supra*, pp. 3-4.
1553. *See* § 20 GWB '*Gesetz gegen Wettbewerbsbeschränkungen*' (Act against Restraints of Competition, adopted on 26 August 1998 and lastly amended on 19 January 2021).
1554. This Section is based on T. Tombal, 'Economic Dependence and Data Access', *International Review of Intellectual Property and Competition Law*, 2020, Vol. 51(1), pp. 70-98.
1555. Superior Court of the State of California, *PeopleBrowsr, Inc. et al. v. Twitter, Inc. (PeopleBrowsr)*, No. C-12-6120 EMC, 2013 WL 843032, N. D. Cal., 6 March 2013; I. Graef, *EU Competition Law, Data Protection and Online Platforms: Data as Essential Facility*, Alphen aan den Rijn, Kluwer, 2016, p. 257.
1556. United States District Court, Northern District of California, *hiQ Labs, Inc. v. LinkedIn Corporation*, No. 17-cv-03301-EMC, 14 August 2017, available at https://epic.org/amicus/cfaa/linkedin/2017-08-15-PI-Order.pdf; United States Court of Appeals for the Ninth Circuit, *hiQ Labs, Inc. v. LinkedIn Corporation*, Case No. 17-16783, WL

were arguably dependent on these platforms to operate their business. Indeed, as outlined by the Expert Group for the Observatory on the Online Platform Economy, 'platforms generate value for businesses by providing them with access to demand for their products, or to factors of production such as labour or capital. A business can become to varying extents dependent on (or even "locked in" to) such a platform. This makes the business vulnerable to possible unfair and distortive practices by the platform'.[1557]

These two cases, which will be discussed more extensively further,[1558] raise the question of whether the concept of abuse of economic dependence could prove to be a valuable alternative in order to deal with refusals, by non-dominant undertakings, to share data with undertakings having a weaker bargaining power (Section 6.2.2). In order to be able to answer this question, the 'traditional' balance reached by the application of the concept of abuse of economic dependence to 'traditional' resources must first be analysed (Section 6.2.1).

6.2.1 The 'Traditional' Abuse of Economic Dependence Balance

259. Given that there is no harmonisation of the provisions pertaining to the abuse of economic dependence in the EU, each Member State is free to adopt the rules that it sees fit.[1559] I have been chosen to focus on Belgium, which has adopted such a law on 4 April 2019,[1560] and on Germany and France, which provided inspiration to the Belgian legislator.[1561] In Belgium, the law

---

4251889, 9 September 2019, available at https://law.justia.com/cases/federal/appellate-courts/ca9/17-16783/17-16783-2019-09-09.html; United States District Court, Northern District of California, *hiQ Labs, Inc. v. LinkedIn Corporation*, Case No. 17-CV-03301-EMC, 2020 WL 5408210, 9 September 2020.

1557. Expert Group for the Observatory on the Online Platform Economy, 'Measurement & Economic Indicators: Final Report', 26 February 2021, available at https://ec.europa.eu/digital-single-market/en/news/expert-group-eu-observatory-online-platform-economy-final-reports, p. 17.

1558. *See* point 266.

1559. *See* Article 3.2 of Council Regulation (EC) No. 1/2003 of 16 December 2002 on the implementation of the rules on competition laid down in Articles 81 and 82 of the Treaty Regulation, *OJ L 1*, 4 January 2003. This article allows Member States to adopt and apply on their territory stricter national laws which prohibit or sanction unilateral conduct engaged in by undertakings.

1560. Loi du 4 avril 2019 modifiant le Code de droit économique en ce qui concerne les abus de dépendance économique, les clauses abusives et les pratiques du marché déloyales entre entreprises, *M.B.*, 24 mai 2019.

1561. For an overview of all of the EU Member States that have such provisions against the abuse of economic dependence *see*: College of Europe, 'Study on the impact of national rules on unilateral conduct that diverge from Article 102 of the Treaty on the Functioning of the European Union (TFEU) – Final Report', 21 November 2012, available at https://ec.europa.eu/competition/calls/tenders_closed.html.

of 4 April 2019 has added a new Article IV.2/1 in the 'Code de droit économique' (hereinafter 'CDE'), which provides that:

> The abusive exploitation, by one or more undertaking(s), of the state of economic dependence of one or more dependent undertaking(s) is prohibited, if competition is likely to be affected on the relevant Belgian market or a substantial part of it.[1562]

In Germany, § 20 GWB[1563] provides that:

> (1) § 19(1)[1564] in conjunction with paragraph 2 no. 1 shall also apply to undertakings and associations of undertakings insofar as other undertakings are dependent on them as suppliers or purchasers of a certain type of goods or commercial services, in such a way that there aren't sufficient and reasonable possibilities to switch to third undertakings, and that there is a clear imbalance to the countervailing power of the other undertakings (relative market power).[1565]

While the previous version of § 20 GWB only benefitted small or medium-sized enterprises, this limitation was abolished by the 10th amendment to the German Competition Act, namely the GWB Digitalisation Act ('GWB-Digitalisierungsgesetz'),[1566] as the situation of dependence covered by this provision could also arise for large firms.[1567]

In France, Article L. 420-2, al. 2 of the French 'Code de Commerce' provides that:

> The abuse of the state of economic dependence of a client or supplier by an undertaking or group of undertakings is also prohibited, if it is likely to affect the functioning or structure of competition.[1568]

From these provisions, it appears that two main conditions of application are common to the three Member States, namely the need to show a state of economic dependence and the need to show an abuse of this state of economic dependence.

1562. Author's translation of: 'Est interdit le fait pour une ou plusieurs entreprises d'exploiter de façon abusive une position de dépendance économique dans laquelle se trouvent une ou plusieurs entreprises à son ou à leur égard, dès lors que la concurrence est susceptible d'en être affectée sur le marché belge concerné ou une partie substantielle de celui-ci'.
1563. '*Gesetz gegen Wettbewerbsbeschränkungen*' (Act against Restraints of Competition, adopted on 26 August 1998 and lastly amended on 19 January 2021).
1564. § 19 GWB targets the prohibited conduct of dominant undertakings.
1565. Author's own translation.
1566. *See* Bundeskartellamt, 'Amendment of the German Act Against Restraints of Competition (Press Release)', *supra*.
1567. H. Schweitzer, et al., 'Modernising the Law on Abuse of Market Power: Executive Summary', *supra*, p. 7. For a more extensive discussion of this point, *see* H. Schweitzer, et al., *Modernisierung der Missbrauchsaufsicht für marktmächtige Unternehmen*, *supra*, pp. 56-57.
1568. Official English translation: https://www.legifrance.gouv.fr/Traductions/en-English/Legifrance-translations.

6.2.1.1 State of Economic Dependence

260. The notion of economic dependence can be defined as the absence of 'sufficient and reasonable possibilities' of switching to other undertakings. According to Feteira, '[it] is usually understood that the *sufficiency* of existing alternatives can be assessed on *objective* grounds, whilst the *reasonableness* of resorting to such alternatives necessarily entails a more *subjective* assessment which relies more heavily on the possibilities available to the plaintiff' (emphasis in the original text).[1569]

Although this is the specific wording used in Germany, the test is substantially the same in France and Belgium. Indeed, French law requires to show the absence of an equivalent solution (objective assessment of the sufficiency of alternatives), making it impossible for the plaintiff to resort, within a reasonable time frame,[1570] to another undertaking due to technical or economic reasons[1571] (subjective assessment of the reasonableness to resort to these alternatives). Similarly, Belgian law requires to show the absence of an equivalent alternative (objective assessment of the sufficiency of alternatives) for the dependent undertaking to switch towards another undertaking within a reasonable time frame, on reasonable terms and at reasonable cost[1572] (subjective assessment of the reasonableness to resort to these alternatives).

261. Contrary to the assessment of a position of dominance, which takes place in the context of a given relevant market involving multiple actors, the assessment of a state of economic dependence focuses on a concrete bilateral relationship. This bilateral perspective is at the core of these provisions, as the concern is not whether a dominant undertaking has the market power to behave independently of the other actors on the market, but rather whether an undertaking is dependent on its bilateral relationship with a (non-dominant) undertaking in order to operate.[1573] This is apparent from the four classical case groups of economic dependence, namely: assortment-based

---

1569. L. Feteira, *The Interplay Between European and National Competition Law after Regulation 1/2003*, Alphen aan den Rijn, Kluwer, 2016, p. 150.

1570. Autorité de la concurrence, Decision No.15-A-06, 31 March 2015, § 269.

1571. *Ibid.*, pp. 167-168. *See also* French Cour de Cassation, Case No. 02-14529, 3 March 2004.

1572. Article I.6, 4° CDE. Belgian law requires to show that, due to this lack of reasonably equivalent alternative, the stronger undertaking can impose services or conditions which could not be obtained under normal market circumstances, but this condition is redundant with the definition of the abuse provided for in Belgian law: 'any behaviour that an undertaking can adopt because it holds the dependent undertaking in a situation of economic dependence' (Proposition de loi du 22 février 2019 modifiant le Code de droit économique en ce qui concerne les abus de dépendance économique, les clauses abusives et les pratiques du marché déloyales entre entreprises, *Doc.*, Ch., 2018-2019, no. 3595/001, p. 15 – author's own translation).

1573. *See*, for instance, Autorité de la concurrence, Decision No. 10-D-08, 3 March 2010, § 165.

dependence[1574] (the other party's good is considered as a must-stock good due to its notoriety or popularity); scarcity-based dependence[1575] (the other party is one of the rare sources where the good can be found); dependence arising from a long-lasting business relationship;[1576] and demand-based dependence[1577] (due to the other party's importance in the undertaking's turnover).[1578]

Yet, despite the clear identification of these case groups, situations of economic dependence have rarely been acknowledged by the courts in practice because the requirement of the demonstration of the absence of reasonable alternatives has been restrictively interpreted by the courts.[1579] Indeed, courts require the (allegedly) dependent undertakings to provide in-depth economic and financial evidence to support their claim, and these

1574. *See*, for example, BGH, *Designer Polstermöbel*, 9 May 2000, WuW/DE-R 481; *Depotkosmetik*, 15 May 1998, WuW/DE-R 206; *Reparaturbetrieb*, 23 February 1988, WuW/E BGH 2479; *Cartier*, 10 November 1987, WuW/E BGH 2451; *Adidas*, 30 June 1981, WuW/E BGH 1885; *Rossignol*, 20 November 1975, WuW/E BGH 1391. *See also* French Cour de Cassation, cases No. 91-16988 and 91-17090, 12 October 1993; Autorité de la concurrence, Decisions Nos 87-MC-02, 25 March 1987; 89-D-39, 13 December 1989; 93-D-48, 9 November 1993; 98-D-32, 26 May 1998; and 01-D-49, 31 August 2001.
1575. *See*, for example, Berlin Court of Appeal, *Agip II*, 7 June 1974 and 4 July 1974, WuW/E OLG 1497 and 1499. *See also* French Cour de Cassation, cases No. 91-16988 and 91-17090, 12 October 1993.
1576. *See*, for example, BGH, *Kfz-Vertragshändler*, 21 February 1995, WuW/E BGH 2983; *Herstellerleasing*, 19 January 1993, WuW/E BGH 2875; *Opel Blitz*, 23 February 1988, WuW/E BGH 2491; *Kraftwagenleasing*, 30 September 1971, WuW/E BGH 1211. *See also* Autorité de la concurrence, Decisions Nos 89-D-16, 30 May 1989; 90-D-42, 6 November 1990; 99-D-54, 29 September 1999; and 20-D-04, 16 March 2020.
1577. *See*, for example, BGH, *Konditionenanpassung*, 24 September 2002, WuW/DE-R 948; *Sehhilfen*, 12 May 1976, WuW/E BGH 1423. *See also* French Cour de Cassation, cases No. 91-16988 and 91-17090, 12 October 1993; Autorité de la concurrence, Decisions Nos 91-D-51, 19 November 1991; 94-D-60, 13 December 1994; 96-D-44, 18 June 1996; 03-D-11, 23 February 2003; and 20-D-04, 16 March 2020; Comm. Gand (réf.), 28 octobre 2020, inéd., R.G. n°A/20/02490, commented in B. Gielen and C. Verdonck, 'First Belgian Ruling on Abuse of Economic Dependence', 3 December 2020, available at https://www.lexology.com.
1578. L. Feteira, *The Interplay Between European and National Competition Law after Regulation 1/2003*, *supra*, pp. 151-158 and 170-171.
1579. I. Graef, 'Differentiated Treatment in Platform-to-Business Relations: EU Competition Law and Economic Dependence', *Yearbook of European Law*, 2019, p. 490. *See also* College of Europe, 'Study on the impact of national rules on unilateral conduct that diverge from Article 102 of the Treaty on the Functioning of the European Union (TFEU) – Final Report', *supra*, pp. 51-57. For rare cases where this situation of economic dependence was acknowledged, *see* Comm. Gand (réf.), 28 octobre 2020, inéd., R.G. n°A/20/02490, commented in B. Gielen and C. Verdonck, 'First Belgian ruling on abuse of economic dependence', 3 December 2020, available at https://www.lexology.com; and Autorité de la concurrence, Decision No. 20-D-04, 16 March 2020, pp. 205-209.

undertakings truly struggle to bring such a proof.[1580] Therefore, in light of this high burden of proof, many (allegedly) dependent undertakings refrain from formulating such complaints, as they fear reprisals if they were to be unsuccessful.[1581]

6.2.1.2 Abuse of the Economic Dependence

262. Showing a state of economic dependence is not enough, as it must also be shown that there has been an abuse of this state. This calls for two types of considerations. On the one hand, it is first necessary to discuss the types of conduct that may constitute a potential abuse. On the other hand, the anticompetitive harm deriving from this abuse must be questioned, and there is a need to find a balance between the benefits and the costs of competition law intervention.

6.2.1.2.1 Types of Conduct That May Constitute a Potential Abuse

263. Any behaviour that an undertaking can adopt because it holds the dependent undertaking in a situation of economic dependence may constitute a potential abuse. Therefore, it will be necessary to show that the undertaking has exceeded the reasonable exercise of its economic freedom and that it could not have adopted this behaviour 'but for' the state of economic dependence.[1582] In this regard, Belgian law proves particularly useful as Article IV.2/1 CDE identifies five practices that can be considered as abusive:

> 1° the unlawful refusal of a sale, purchase or other transaction conditions;[1583] 2° the direct or indirect imposition of purchase or sale prices or other unfair trading conditions; 3° the limitation of production, markets or technical development to the detriment of consumers; 4° the application of unequal conditions to equivalent services to economic partners, thereby placing them at a competitive disadvantage;[1584] 5° the subjection of the conclusion of contracts

---

1580. *See* College of Europe, 'Study on the impact of national rules on unilateral conduct that diverge from Article 102 of the Treaty on the Functioning of the European Union (TFEU) – Final Report', *supra*, p. 51.
1581. *Ibid.*, p. 52.
1582. L. Feteira, *The Interplay Between European and National Competition Law after Regulation 1/2003*, *supra*, p. 171; Proposition de loi du 22 février 2019 modifiant le Code de droit économique en ce qui concerne les abus de dépendance économique, les clauses abusives et les pratiques du marché déloyales entre entreprises, *Doc.*, Ch., 2018-2019, n° 3595/001, p. 15.
1583. For an example, *see* Comm. Gand (réf.), 28 octobre 2020, inéd., R.G. n°A/20/02490, commented in B. Gielen and C. Verdonck, 'First Belgian Ruling on Abuse of Economic Dependence', 3 December 2020, available at https://www.lexology.com.
1584. *See* Autorité de la concurrence, Decision No. 20-D-04, 16 March 2020, pp. 209-219, where the *Autorité* ruled that Apple subjected its premium distributors to unfair and unfavourable commercial conditions in comparison with those it imposed to its

to the acceptance, by the economic partners, of additional services which, by their nature or according to commercial usage, are not related to the subject matter of those contracts.[1585]

This list provides some clarity regarding practices that could potentially be considered as abusive, as it is presumed that an undertaking has only been able to adopt them because it holds the dependent undertaking in a situation of economic dependence.

6.2.1.2.2 Anticompetitive Effects

264. As these provisions on the abuse of economic dependence are situated in the realm of competition law, it seems natural that a form of anticompetitive effect must also be demonstrated. Yet, this might seem counter-intuitive as, at first sight, these provisions focus on bilateral relationships and not on a given market. To clarify this, the *ratio legis* of these abuse of economic dependence provisions must be outlined.

In Belgian law, the stated objective is to protect weaker parties against stronger undertakings which act unfairly, by limiting marginally, and in the public interest, their entrepreneurial freedom by sanctioning abusive conducts resulting from positions of economic dependence.[1586] Similarly, abuse of economic dependence provisions were introduced in French law in order to counter the economic power of distribution groups that the rules of abuse of dominance were allegedly not able to address, and in German law in order to tackle concerns over market conditions in the retail market.[1587] This tends to show that the goal of such provisions is twofold, namely protecting weaker

---

network of integrated distributors, and that this differential treatment was not objectively justified. According to the *Autorité*, this constituted an abuse as these premium distributors (mostly SMEs) were discriminated, as they were often deprived of sufficient stock during the launch of new goods and were thus unable to fulfil client orders, while its network of integrated distributors was regularly supplied and thus did not have these problems.

1585. Author's translation of: '1° le refus illicite d'une vente, d'un achat ou d'autres conditions de transaction; 2° l'imposition de façon directe ou indirecte des prix d'achat ou de vente ou d'autres conditions de transaction non équitables; 3° la limitation de la production, des débouchés ou du développement technique au préjudice des consommateurs; 4° le fait d'appliquer à l'égard de partenaires économiques des conditions inégales à des prestations équivalentes, en leur infligeant de ce fait un désavantage dans la concurrence; 5° le fait de subordonner la conclusion de contrats à l'acceptation, par les partenaires économiques, de prestations supplémentaires, qui, par leur nature ou selon les usages commerciaux, n'ont pas de lien avec l'objet de ces contrats'.

1586. Proposition de loi du 22 février 2019 modifiant le Code de droit économique en ce qui concerne les abus de dépendance économique, les clauses abusives et les pratiques du marché déloyales entre entreprises, *Doc.*, Ch., 2018-2019, n° 3595/001, pp. 4-5.

1587. L. Feteira, *The Interplay Between European and National Competition Law after Regulation 1/2003*, *supra*, pp. 144-145 and 165.

parties against stronger undertakings and countering the economic power of some non-dominant undertakings.

This illustrates the core issue at hand when applying legal provisions relating to economic dependence, as they require to reach a careful balancing between 'safeguarding competition in the market, respecting freedom of contract and protecting the freedom of competition of the weaker parties against powerful business partners'.[1588] Indeed, while the non-dominant undertaking has the freedom not to contract (or to bring an end to an existing contract) with the dependent undertaking, this might create anticompetitive effects by restricting the latter's freedom to compete, and more broadly by restricting market access and contestability. On the other hand, protecting smaller competitors could potentially harm consumers if this leads to market inefficiencies resulting in higher prices.[1589] A balance of interest thus has to be conducted, whose aim is to protect the ability of the parties to take part in the process of competition and to ensure that all benefit from an equal opportunity to enter and operate in the market, which illustrates the core underlying balance between the parties' individual interests and the broader institutional interest of protecting the competitive process and market efficiency.[1590]

265. More fundamentally, this illustrates the debate between the different approaches of the economic role of competition law, namely whether competition law's focus should be the efficiency of the market or the protection of the freedom to compete.[1591] Incidentally, this debate is especially important for the effectivity of the French and Belgian provisions, which explicitly state that the abuse has to be likely to affect the functioning or the structure of competition.[1592]

1588. L. Boy, 'Abuse of Market Power: Controlling Dominance or Protecting Competition?', *The Evolution of European Competition Law: Whose Regulation, Which Competition?*, H. Ullrich (ed.), Cheltenham and Northampton, Edward Elgar, 2006, p. 218, cited in M. Bakhoum, 'Abuse without Dominance in Competition Law: Abuse of Economic Dependence and its Interface with Abuse of Dominance', *Max Planck Institute for Innovation & Competition Research Paper No. 15-15*, 2015, available at https://ssrn.com/abstract=2703809, p. 14.

1589. I. Graef, 'Differentiated Treatment in Platform-to-Business Relations: EU Competition Law and Economic Dependence', *supra*, p. 491; College of Europe, 'Study on the impact of national rules on unilateral conduct that diverge from Article 102 of the Treaty on the Functioning of the European Union (TFEU) – Final Report', *supra*, pp. 13-15.

1590. L. Feteira, *The Interplay Between European and National Competition Law after Regulation 1/2003*, *supra*, pp. 161-162; I. Graef, 'Differentiated Treatment in Platform-to-Business Relations: EU Competition Law and Economic Dependence', *supra*, p. 491.

1591. M. Bakhoum, 'Abuse Without Dominance in Competition Law: Abuse of Economic Dependence and Its Interface with Abuse of Dominance', *supra*, p. 14.

1592. Article L. 420-2, al. 2 of the French Code de Commerce; Article IV.2/1 of the Belgian Code de droit économique. Interestingly, this condition was completely omitted by the

Under the 'efficiency approach', the possibility to protect against abuses of economic dependence through competition law is questionable because, as pointed out by Bougette et al., 'at first sight, an abuse of economic dependence involves only a vertical relationship between two partners along a supply chain. It may not affect any relevant markets and inflict harm only on a given undertaking'.[1593] Indeed, given that this issue of economic dependence is assessed in a bilateral relationship and that the stronger undertaking is not required to have a dominant position, but merely a relative market power towards the weaker undertaking, the exclusion, by a non-dominant undertaking's behaviour, of a small dependent undertaking may arguably rarely be likely to affect the functioning or structure of competition under the 'efficiency approach'. This is because showing that the dependent undertaking's mere exclusion from the market is likely to have such an effect is a major hurdle.[1594] For instance, if an aftermarket service provider is dependent on a car manufacturer having a 20% market share, due to a long-lasting business relationship, and that the latter terminates this relationship in an abusive way, the small undertaking may not be able to show that this is likely to affect the efficiency of this aftermarket. Moreover, the competition authorities' reluctance to deal with issues that appear to be more linked to contract law than to competition law explains that cases of abuse of economic dependence have been neglected in their decisional practice.[1595]

President of the Ghent Commercial Court, in one of the rare cases where an abuse of economic dependence was established. *See* Comm. Gand (réf.), 28 octobre 2020, inéd., R.G. n°A/20/02490, commented in B. Gielen and C. Verdonck, 'First Belgian ruling on abuse of economic dependence', 3 December 2020, available at https://www.lexology.com. This condition was however analysed in the French *Apple* case, which is one of the rare French cases where an abuse of economic dependence was established (*see* Autorité de la concurrence, Decision No. 20-D-04, 16 March 2020). In that case, the *Autorité* ruled that Apple subjected its premium distributors to unfair and unfavourable commercial conditions in comparison with those it imposed to its network of integrated distributors, and that this differential treatment was not objectively justified (*see* footnote 1584). For the *Autorité*, this had anticompetitive effects as these practices limited the competitive emulation on, and thus the functioning and the structure of, intra-brand competition for Apple products, which could have led to the emergence of new proximity services for consumers; and as these practices led to the weakening of these premium distributors, and in some cases to their eviction from the market (*see* pp. 219-224).

1593. P. Bougette, O. Budzinski and F. Marty, 'Exploitative Abuse and Abuse of Economic Dependence: What Can We Learn from an Industrial Organization Approach?', *Ilmenau Economics Discussion Papers No. 119*, 2018, available at http://hdl.handle.net/10419/191022, p. 6.

1594. F. De Boüard, *La dépendance économique née d'un contrat*, Paris, LGDJ, 2007, pp. 298-299; L. Feteira, *The Interplay Between European and National Competition Law after Regulation 1/2003*, *supra*, p. 171.

1595. P. Bougette, O. Budzinski and F. Marty, 'Exploitative Abuse and Abuse of Economic Dependence: What Can We Learn from an Industrial Organization Approach?', *supra*, p. 6.

However, under the 'freedom to compete approach', protecting against abuses of economic dependence may be justified in order to protect the market against structural restrictions.[1596] As pointed out by Bougette et al., 'economic dependence related abuses can have significant effects on overall welfare. Ignoring such abuses as potential anticompetitive behaviour per se, violates the fundamental idea of the effects-based approach, namely that actual effects should trump formalistic assertions. Depending on the case in question, consumer welfare and the competition process may be negatively affected by (…) economic dependence abuses in several ways'.[1597] Notably, the competitive process could be harmed if these abuses of economic dependence undermine the undertakings' possibilities to access the market. Accordingly, such abuses should be sanctioned on the basis of competition law in order to protect the freedom to compete.[1598] In this second perspective, the standard for establishing that there is a likely effect on the functioning or the structure of competition is lower as 'intervention is required in order to protect freedom, as an institution, and as an individual economic right'.[1599]

This second approach fits more with the twofold objective of the provisions pertaining to the abuse of economic dependence, as the weaker party is protected not only because it is in a situation of unequal bargaining power but also because this 'protects the competitive process as a whole'[1600] by countering the economic power of some non-dominant undertakings. Indeed, 'preserving market access cannot be seen as a non-economic goal of antitrust legislation which can be criticized for an induced trade-off with economic efficiency. Instead, freedom to access the market (contestability) is considered a necessary condition for efficiency and long-run welfare'.[1601] Therefore, in light of this potential effect on the competitive process and of the potential negative welfare it might entail, abuses of economic

1596. M. Bakhoum, 'Abuse Without Dominance in Competition Law: Abuse of Economic Dependence and Its Interface with Abuse of Dominance', *supra*, p. 17.
1597. P. Bougette, O. Budzinski and F. Marty, 'Exploitative Abuse and Abuse of Economic Dependence: What Can We Learn from an Industrial Organization Approach?', *supra*, p. 7.
1598. *Ibid.*, p. 8.
1599. M. Bakhoum, 'Abuse without Dominance in Competition Law: Abuse of Economic Dependence and Its Interface with Abuse of Dominance', *supra*, p. 17.
1600. W. Kerber, 'Data-Sharing in IoT Ecosystems from a Competition Law Perspective: The Example of Connected Cars', 26 August 2019, available at https://ssrn.com/abstract=3445422, p. 29.
1601. P. Bougette, O. Budzinski and F. Marty, 'Exploitative Abuse and Abuse of Economic Dependence: What Can We Learn from an Industrial Organization Approach?', *supra*, p. 8.

dependence should fall within the scope of competition law.[1602] Of course, the standard should not be so low as to protect free-riding firms.[1603]

6.2.2 Application of Abuses of Economic Dependence to Data Markets?

266. Moving forward, I raise the question of whether the concept of abuse of economic dependence, classically applied to 'traditional' resources, could be translated in data markets. Indeed, this could prove to be a valuable alternative in order to deal with refusals, by non-dominant undertakings, to share data with undertakings having a weaker bargaining power.[1604] To illustrate this, two USA cases can be presented.

The first case is *PeopleBrowsr v. Twitter*.[1605] PeopleBrowsr's business model was to analyse Twitter data in order to resell information to clients about consumer's feedback towards products/services and to identify 'influencers', via its access to the Twitter 'firehose' (all the tweets passing through Twitter on a real-time basis). At one point, Twitter informed PeopleBrowsr, and other third-party developers, that as of 30 November 2012, it would cut the 'firehose' tap and that PeopleBrowsr would have to conclude a contract with one of Twitter's certified data resellers in order to get access to the 'firehose' data.[1606] PeopleBrowsr argued that it was 'dependent' on this access in order to deliver the service it had built, and a San Francisco court issued a temporary restraining order mandating Twitter to temporarily keep providing access to the 'firehose' to PeopleBrowsr. Unfortunately, no decision on the merits of the case followed this preliminary injunction as the parties settled the case in 2013, by agreeing that PeopleBrowsr would retain its access to the 'firehose' until the end of 2013, and would then have to transition towards access via a certified data reseller in 2014.[1607]

The second case is *hiQ v. LinkedIn*.[1608] hiQ's business model was to provide information to businesses about their workforces based on statistical

1602. *Ibid.*, p. 10.
1603. M. Bakhoum, 'Abuse Without Dominance in Competition Law: Abuse of Economic Dependence and Its Interface with Abuse of Dominance', *supra*, p. 17.
1604. *See supra* point 258.
1605. Superior Court of the State of California, *PeopleBrowsr, Inc. et al. v. Twitter, Inc. (PeopleBrowsr)*, No. C-12-6120 EMC, 2013 WL 843032, N. D. Cal., 6 March 2013.
1606. I. Graef, *EU Competition Law, Data Protection and Online Platforms: Data as Essential Facility*, *supra*, p. 257.
1607. *Ibid.*
1608. United States District Court, Northern District of California, *hiQ Labs, Inc. v. LinkedIn Corporation*, No. 17-cv-03301-EMC, 14 August 2017, available at https://epic.org/amicus/cfaa/linkedin/2017-08-15-PI-Order.pdf.

analysis of publicly available LinkedIn data.[1609] Their 'Keeper' product told employers which of their employees presented the greatest risk of being recruited by another company, while their 'Skill Mapper' product provided a summary of the workers' skills. After having allowed hiQ's access and use of its data for several years (from 2012 to 2017), LinkedIn sent, on 23 May 2017, a cease and desist letter requesting hiQ to stop accessing its data, and used blocking techniques preventing hiQ from doing so. hiQ complained and argued that its data analytics business was wholly 'dependent' on the access to that data, and that LinkedIn's decision to block its access to its data had an anticompetitive purpose – namely to monetise this data itself with a competing product – and thus had to be considered as an unfair competition practice. LinkedIn argued that its decision was only motivated by the aim to protect its users' privacy and to preserve their trust, to which hiQ replied that it was only accessing data that users had willingly made public to all. The District Court concluded that hiQ had raised serious questions about whether LinkedIn had unfairly leveraged its power in the professional networking market in order to develop a competing product ('Talent Insights'), and therefore issued a preliminary injunction ordering LinkedIn to stop preventing hiQ's access to the data. This preliminary ruling was confirmed by the Ninth Circuit Court of Appeals, which concluded that hiQ had successfully established that the survival of its business was threatened by LinkedIn's suspension of the access to its data, and that hiQ had thus demonstrated a likelihood of irreparable harm.[1610] However, when ruling on the merits,[1611] the District Court ruled that hiQ had failed to properly define the product market and to adequately allege anticompetitive conduct, but granted hiQ leave to amend its market definition and its anticompetitive claims.[1612]

1609. LinkedIn users can choose to keep their profiles entirely private, or to make them viewable by their direct connections on the site, a broader network of connections, all other LinkedIn members or the entire public (including internet users not registered on LinkedIn). In the case at hand, *hiQ* conducted its business by automatically collecting, harvesting or 'scraping' the data from the latter categories of profiles (publicly available LinkedIn profiles).

1610. United States Court of Appeals for the Ninth Circuit, *hiQ Labs, Inc. v. LinkedIn Corporation*, Case No. 17-16783, WL 4251889, 9 September 2019, available at https://law.justia.com/cases/federal/appellate-courts/ca9/17-16783/17-16783-2019-09-09.html.

1611. United States District Court, Northern District of California, *hiQ Labs, Inc. v. LinkedIn Corporation*, Case No. 17-CV-03301-EMC, 2020 WL 5408210, 9 September 2020.

1612. C. Brennan, et al., 'hiQ Labs, Inc. v. LinkedIn Corp.: Federal Judge Dismisses Antitrust Claims Regarding Access to Data', 1 October 2020, available at https://www.reedsmith.com/en/perspectives/2020/10/hiq-labs-inc-v-linkedin-corp-federal-judge-dismisses-antitrust-claims.

267. In fact, these two cases present some striking similarities with the *Commercial Solvents*[1613] case presented above.[1614] Indeed, the underlying justification for a competition law intervention is similar, as in all three cases an undertaking active in an upstream market suddenly stopped to supply undertakings active on a downstream market, following the development of its own product/service on that downstream market.[1615] Naturally, the biggest difference is that Commercial Solvents was a dominant undertaking and that the case was thus assessed on the basis of Article 102 TFEU.

PeopleBrowsr v. Twitter and *hiQ v. LinkedIn*, on the other hand, raise the question of whether the refusal, by a non-dominant undertaking benefiting from a 'relative or superior market power', to share data with another undertaking, whose commercial activity 'depends' on this access, could amount to an abuse of economic dependence. The above overview of the Belgian, German and French law showed that two main conditions for the application of these provisions are common to the three Member States, namely the need to show a state of economic dependence and the need to show an abuse of this state of economic dependence.

6.2.2.1 Assessment of the State of Economic Dependence

268. The assessment of a state of economic dependence focuses on whether an undertaking is dependent on its bilateral relationship with a non-dominant undertaking in order to operate. Interestingly, such questions of economic dependence have been evoked in two cases that did not imply questions of data sharing, but which nevertheless involved digital platforms.[1616] Indeed, several French publishers and news agencies complained to the *Autorité de la Concurrence* that Google's implementation of the French Law No. 2019-775 of 24 July 2019, creating a neighbouring right for the benefit of several news agencies and publishers, constituted an abuse of dominant position, as well as an abuse of economic dependence.[1617] Unfortunately, as the French Competition Authority ruled that Google was dominant on the French market for generalised search services, it did not assess the existence of such an economic dependence *in casu*.[1618] Similarly, in the context of its

---

1613. ECJ, *Istituto Chemioterapico Italiano and Commercial Solvents v. Commission*, 6 March 1974, joined cases C-6/73 and C-7/73, EU:C:1974:18.
1614. *See* point 227.
1615. *See Istituto Chemioterapico Italiano and Commercial Solvents v. Commission*, 6 March 1974, joined cases C-6/73 and C-7/73, EU:C:1974:18, § 25.
1616. For reflections pertaining to potential cases of 'platform dependence', *see* S. Lee and J. Schißler, 'Platform Dependence and Exploitation', *Paper Presented at the* 14th *ASCOLA Conference*, June 2019, available at https://ssrn.com/abstract=3403002.
1617. Autorité de la concurrence, Decision n°20-MC-01 (*Syndicat des éditeurs de presse v. Google*), 9 April 2020, available at https://www.autoritedelaconcurrence.fr/sites/default/files/integral_texts/2020-04/20mc01.pdf, § 2.
1618. *Ibid.*, § 181.

investigation against Amazon, the *Bundeskartellamt* considered that it could be relevant to assess small seller's dependence on Amazon's relative market power in order to have access to final consumers, but nevertheless did not investigate this question *in casu*.[1619]

Coming back to the topic of data sharing, on which I focus, a two-step assessment must be conducted in order to determine whether an access seeker is dependent, in order to conduct its business, on the access to the data of a non-dominant undertaking having a superior market power. First, an objective assessment of the sufficiency of alternatives for any undertaking is necessary. Second, a subjective assessment of the reasonableness to resort to these alternatives for the access seeker must be conducted.

6.2.2.1.1 Objective Assessment of the Sufficiency of Alternatives for Any Undertaking

269. The first question is thus whether sufficient alternatives to the data held by the undertaking having superior market power are available to any other undertaking. Said otherwise, it must be questioned whether the access seeker could, in theory, collect that data itself or access it via another undertaking. This first objective assessment is rather similar to the 'indispensability' condition of the essential facilities doctrine, which applies to dominant undertakings.[1620] Indeed, according to the French *Autorité de la concurrence* and the German *Bundeskartellamt*, this 'indispensability' condition requires to show that 'the data owned by the incumbent is truly unique and that there is no [other] possibility for the competitor to obtain the data that it needs to perform its services'.[1621]

As a reminder, the 'indispensability' condition does not require the demonstration of the absence of 'any alternative at all', but rather the absence of 'a sufficient alternative for *any* undertaking' (emphasis added).[1622] This finding can be derived from the *Bronner* case, where the European Court of Justice held that access to a facility will not be indispensable if an alternative (even a less advantageous one) can be developed by *any* undertaking other than the dominant undertaking.[1623] In order for the indispensability of the facility (*in casu* a newspapers' nationwide home-delivery system) to be

1619. I. Graef, 'Differentiated Treatment in Platform-to-Business Relations: EU Competition Law and Economic Dependence', *supra*, p. 492; Bundeskartellamt, *Amazon – Online Sales*, 17 July 2019, B2 – 88/18 (case summary available at https://www.bundeskartellamt.de/SharedDocs/Entscheidung/EN/Fallberichte/Missbrauchsaufsicht/2019/B2-88-18.pdf?__blob=publicationFile&v=4).

1620. *See* points 238-242.

1621. Autorité de la concurrence and Bundeskartellamt, 'Competition Law and Data', 10 May 2016, available at http://www.autoritedelaconcurrence.fr/doc/reportcompetitionlawanddatafinal.pdf, p. 18.

1622. *See* point 238.

1623. ECJ, *Bronner*, 26 November 1998, C-7/97, EU:C:1998:569, § 43.

established, the Court ruled that there must be 'obstacles capable of making it impossible, or even unreasonably difficult, for *any* other publisher [to develop a substitute]' (emphasis added).[1624]

270. If it appears from this objective assessment that no sufficient alternatives to the data held by a non-dominant undertaking having superior market power exist for *any* undertaking, it will de facto not be reasonable *for the access seeker* to collect that data itself or to access it via another undertaking (subjective assessment of the reasonableness to resort to these alternatives). Therefore, the state of economic dependence will be established. However, if this objective assessment leads to the finding that the data is not indispensable and that there are, in fact, sufficient alternatives to the data, then it is necessary to move on to the second step and to assess, from a subjective point of view, whether it is reasonable *for the access seeker* to collect that data itself or to access it via another undertaking.

6.2.2.1.2 Subjective Assessment of the Reasonableness to Resort to These Alternatives for the Access Seeker

271. This subjective assessment is one of the key differences between resorting to provisions of abuse of economic dependence and resorting to Article 102 TFEU, as the latter does not provide such a second step (*see* Figure 6.1). This is because Article 102 TFEU requires an absolute indispensability, while the provisions forbidding the abuse of economic dependence only require a relative dependence (e.g., the access to the data set is necessary in order *for the access seeker* to conduct its business, but it might not be necessary for other undertakings).

Figure 6.1 Comparison Between Dependence and Indispensability

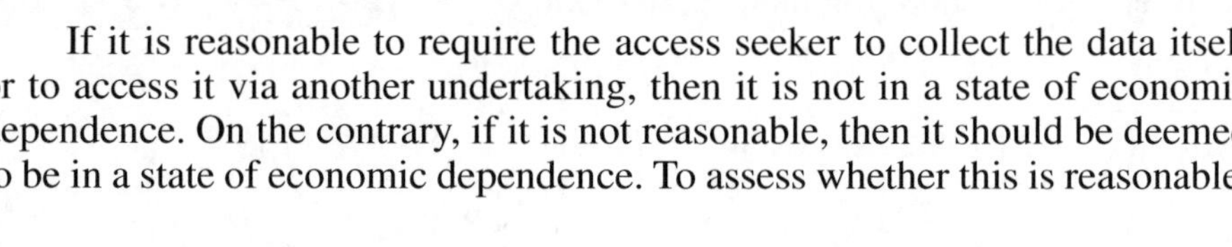

Source: T. Tombal, Economic Dependence and Data Access.[1625]

If it is reasonable to require the access seeker to collect the data itself or to access it via another undertaking, then it is not in a state of economic dependence. On the contrary, if it is not reasonable, then it should be deemed to be in a state of economic dependence. To assess whether this is reasonable,

1624. *Ibid.*, § 44.
1625. T. Tombal, 'Economic Dependence and Data Access', *International Review of Intellectual Property and Competition Law*, 2020, Vol. 51(1), p. 83.

the technical and economic barriers to this alternative should be considered. This means questioning whether this could be done within a reasonable time frame, on reasonable terms and at reasonable cost.

272. Considering such barriers is not new in the realm of competition law. As indicated earlier, the European Court of Justice held in *Bronner* that, in the context of Article 102 TFEU, there must be '*obstacles* capable of making it impossible, or even unreasonably difficult, for *any other publisher* [to develop a substitute]' (emphasis added).[1626] The Court added that 'it is not enough to argue that it is not economically viable by reason of the small circulation of the daily newspaper or newspapers to be distributed. For such access to be capable of being regarded as indispensable, it would be necessary (…) to establish (…) that it is not economically viable to create a second home-delivery scheme (…) with a circulation comparable to (…) the existing scheme'.[1627] This finding could be used to assess the existence of economic barriers creating a situation of economic dependence. Naturally, given that the provisions prohibiting the abuse of economic dependence only require a relative dependence, while Article 102 TFEU requires an absolute indispensability, the standard for recognising such an economic barrier should be lower. Thus, the test could be reformulated as follows: are there economic and technical barriers making it unreasonably difficult for the access seeker (and not for *any* undertaking) to collect the data itself or to access that data via another undertaking? Considering that the assessment of dependence is relative and not absolute, it will be enough to argue that it is not economically viable for the access seeker to do so due to its own limited capacities, rather than having to show that it would not be economically viable for *any* undertaking having the same capacities as the data holder.

273. In the digital economy, such economic and technical barriers could stem from the fact that the undertaking faces high costs to switch away from the non-dominant undertaking towards a substitute.[1628] Such high switching costs can notably derive from the fact that the undertaking has made significant investments to build its technology in a way that complies with the non-dominant undertakings' specifications, and that these investments would be lost ('sunk costs'), implying a need for new investments, if the undertaking wanted to switch to a substitute.[1629] Alternatively, high switching costs can also arise from the fact that any substitute would be far inferior, such as when a non-dominant undertaking is a 'gatekeeper' to a specific

1626. ECJ, *Bronner,* 26 November 1998, C-7/97, EU:C:1998:569, § 44.
1627. *Ibid.*, §§ 45-46.
1628. Expert Group for the Observatory on the Online Platform Economy, 'Measurement & Economic Indicators: Final Report', 26 February 2021, available at https://ec.europa.eu/digital-single-market/en/news/expert-group-eu-observatory-online-platform-economy-final-reports, p. 17.
1629. *Ibid.*

market segment, because there are few other means of reaching that segment.[1630]

More specifically, for data, it should be outlined that access to data relevant for competition is considered as one of the five factors to assess an undertaking's power in a multisided market and network.[1631] Therefore, 'consumer lock-in' and 'network effects' could constitute such economic and technical barriers that make an access seeker dependent on another undertaking having relative or superior market power. Indeed, if the users are locked in the latter's product or service – because no alternative having reached a critical mass of users is available (network effects) – the access seeker will be dependent on this undertaking as it is the only viable connexion to these users. The undertaking having superior market power could thus be a 'gatekeeper' of that user data, as the access seeker would not be able to collect the data itself, or to access that data via another undertaking, within a reasonable time frame, on reasonable terms and at reasonable cost.

274. This 'gatekeeper' situation was arguably present in the *PeopleBrowsr v. Twitter* and *hiQ v. LinkedIn* cases.[1632] Indeed, PeopleBrowsr argued that its business model was dependent on the access to the Twitter 'firehose' in order to deliver the service it had built. Indeed, it argued that Twitter's data was unique and essential as tweets provide unique insight about which members of communities are influential and provide unique feedback regarding consumers' reactions to products and brands, and as other social networking sites, such as Facebook, do not provide the same rich set of public data regarding users' sentiments and influence.[1633] The Superior Court of the State of California validated this argument. Similarly, hiQ argued that its data analytics business was wholly dependent on access to LinkedIn's data, as no

1630. *Ibid.*

1631. § 18, n°3a of the Gesetz gegen Wettbewerbsbeschränkungen (Act against Restraints of Competition); J. Haucap, 'A German Approach to Antitrust for Digital Platforms', in *Digital Platforms and Concentration – Second Annual Antitrust and Competition Conference*, S. Eyler-Driscoll, A. Schechter and C. Patiño (eds), 2018, available at https://promarket.org/wp-content/uploads/2018/04/Digital-Platforms-and-Concentration.pdf, p. 10.

1632. *See* point 266.

1633. Declaration of John David Rich in support of plaintiff's application for a temporary restraining order in the case *PeopleBrowsr v. Twitter* in the Superior Court of the State of California, County of San Francisco, November 2012, paras 4-5, available at http://www.scribd.com/doc/114846303/Rich-Declaration-PB-v-TW-Restraining-Order-28-Nov-12, cited in I. Graef, 'Market Definition and Market Power in Data: The Case of Online Platforms', *World Competition Law and Economics Review*, 2015, Vol. 38(4), p. 499.

viable alternative to LinkedIn's data was available.[1634] Ruling on the preliminary injunction, both the District Court[1635] and the Court of Appeal concurred with hiQ, by holding that there was no equivalent alternative source of data (not even Facebook) and that it would not be reasonable to require hiQ to collect the data itself either, as this would imply a considerable amount of time and expenses for hiQ to fundamentally change the nature of its business.[1636] In light of these examples, it can be argued that, like several other digital platforms, Twitter and LinkedIn might benefit from a form of 'gatekeeper power' as they effectively serve as an infrastructure for their specific market segments because they are in fact 'the only real option', which could allow them to extort and extract better terms from undertakings that depend on their infrastructure.[1637]

275. An additional key factor for this 'assessment of reasonableness' test lies in the access seeker's burden of proof, as it has to convince the competition authorities that it is truly dependent on the access because it cannot reasonably collect the data itself or access that data via another mean. To do so, the access seeker has to provide clear explanations about the product/service that it offers (or intends to offer) and the reasons why that data is necessary for its (current or future) business model. Indeed, requiring these additional explanations would avoid that these provisions on the abuse of economic dependence are used as proxies for free-riding tactics, which would deter innovation. This implies that access should not be granted to undertakings that simply want to copy the data holder's business model. Rather, access to data through the provisions on the abuse of economic dependence should only be granted if the access seeker offers (or wishes to

---

1634. United States Court of Appeals for the Ninth Circuit, *hiQ Labs, Inc. v. LinkedIn Corporation*, Case No. 17-16783, WL 4251889, 9 September 2019, available at https://law.justia.com/cases/federal/appellate-courts/ca9/17-16783/17-16783-2019-09-09.html, p. 13.

1635. United States District Court, Northern District of California, *hiQ Labs, Inc. v. LinkedIn Corporation*, No. 17-cv-03301-EMC, 14 August 2017, available at https://epic.org/amicus/cfaa/linkedin/2017-08-15-PI-Order.pdf.

1636. United States Court of Appeals for the Ninth Circuit, *hiQ Labs, Inc. v. LinkedIn Corporation*, Case No. 17-16783, WL 4251889, 9 September 2019, available at https://law.justia.com/cases/federal/appellate-courts/ca9/17-16783/17-16783-2019-09-09.html, pp. 13-14.

1637. L. Khan, 'What Makes Tech Platforms So Powerful?', *Digital Platforms and Concentration, Second Annual Antitrust and Competition Conference*, S. Eyler-Driscoll, A. Schechter and C. Patiño (eds), 2018, available at https://promarket.org/wp-content/uploads/2018/04/Digital-Platforms-and-Concentration.pdf, pp. 13-14. *See also* P. Bougette, O. Budzinski and F. Marty, 'Exploitative Abuse and Abuse of Economic Dependence: What Can We Learn from an Industrial Organization Approach?', *supra*, p. 14.

offer) a different product/service than the one offered by the data holder, or at least a technical improvement of that product/service.[1638]

Arguably, this requirement was satisfied in the *PeopleBrowsr v. Twitter* and *hiQ v. LinkedIn* cases.[1639] Indeed, PeopleBrowsr's business model was to analyse Twitter data in order to resell information to clients about consumer's feedback towards products/services and to identify 'influencers'. It therefore did not access Twitter's data in order to copy its business model and to create a similar social network, but rather to provide new added-value services on the basis of this data. Similarly, hiQ's business model was to provide information to businesses about their workforces based on statistical analysis of publicly available LinkedIn data, by telling employers which of their employees presented the greatest risk of being recruited by another company and by providing a summary of the workers' skills. Once again, this access to LinkedIn's data was not made to copy its business model and to create a similar professional social network, but rather to provide new added-value services.

6.2.2.2 Assessment of the Abuse

276. After having established that the access seeker is in a state of economic dependence towards the data holder, it will be necessary to determine whether the refusal, by the latter, to provide access to the data constitutes an abuse of such economic dependence. This second condition calls for two types of considerations. On the one hand, it is first necessary to demonstrate a conduct that constitutes a potential abuse. On the other hand, the anticompetitive harm deriving from this abuse must be proven.

6.2.2.2.1 Demonstrating a Conduct That Constitutes a Potential Abuse

277. In Belgian law, Article IV.2/1, 1° CDE explicitly identifies the unlawful refusal to supply as a practice that can be considered as abusive. Similarly, in French law, Article L.420-2, al. 2 of the Code de Commerce provides that a refusal to sell may be abusive. An unlawful refusal to supply/provide access to data to an undertaking which has demonstrated that it is dependent on this access could thus, in certain circumstances, be abusive. The key issue is to determine when such a refusal to share data is 'unlawful'. Two possible sets of cases should be outlined.

278. In the first set of cases, the access seeker has already developed its product/service on the basis of the access to the data holder's data, and the

1638. *See*, by analogy, the 'new product' condition of the essential facilities doctrine: points 247 to 249.
1639. *See* point 266.

latter decides to 'close the tap' and to no longer share this data (termination of an existing business relationship). The question is whether this refusal to keep sharing the data for the future, while access had been provided in the past which allowed the dependent undertaking to build its product/service, constitutes an unlawful restriction of the latter's possibility to compete in the market, amounting to an abuse. In this regard, it should be noted that the European Commission indicates, in its guidance on abusive exclusionary conducts by dominant undertakings, that terminating an existing business relationship is more likely to be abusive than a de novo refusal to supply because of the relationship-specific investments that have already been made.[1640]

Once again, the *PeopleBrowsr v. Twitter* and *hiQ v. LinkedIn* cases could arguably be considered as conducts that constitute a potential abuse.[1641] Indeed, in both these cases, the data holders let another undertaking develop an added-value service on the basis of the free access to its data, creating the impression that they could create a perennial business model via this free access. Yet, once Twitter and LinkedIn realised that these services had added-value and that they were dependent on this access, they decided to terminate the existing business relationship. This conduct could potentially be abusive if it generates anticompetitive effects.[1642]

279. In the second set of cases, the access seeker has no pre-existing business relationship with the data holder, and alleges that it is dependent on the data holder's data to launch a new product/service, which is not a simple copy of the data holder's business model, but rather aims at creating added-value (refusal to supply). Here, there could potentially be an abuse if the undertaking has exceeded the reasonable exercise of its economic freedom and that it could not have refused the access absent the state of economic dependence. To do so, the conduct, *in casu*, of the undertaking having a superior market power towards the dependent undertaking should be compared with the conduct of a similar undertaking operating in a similar market (e.g., in other countries or in markets for similar products/services) where there is no dependence.

1640. Communication from the Commission, Guidance on the Commission's enforcement priorities in applying Article 82 of the EC Treaty to abusive exclusionary conduct by dominant undertakings, *OJ C 45*, 24 February 2009, § 84.

1641. *See* point 266.

1642. On this point, *see* United States Court of Appeals for the Ninth Circuit, *hiQ Labs, Inc. v. LinkedIn Corporation*, Case No. 17-16783, WL 4251889, 9 September 2019, available at https://law.justia.com/cases/federal/appellate-courts/ca9/17-16783/17-16783-2019-09-09.html, pp. 22-23. However, when ruling on the merits, the District Court ruled that hiQ had failed to substantiate this claim, but granted hiQ leave to amend it (United States District Court, Northern District of California, *hiQ Labs, Inc. v. LinkedIn Corporation*, Case No. 17-CV-03301-EMC, 2020 WL 5408210, 9 September 2020; C. Brennan, et al., 'hiQ Labs, Inc. v. LinkedIn Corp.: Federal Judge Dismisses Antitrust Claims Regarding Access to Data', *supra*.).

For instance, Kerber raises the question of whether the refusal, by car manufacturers, to share vehicle data with independent repairers and providers of complementary services (e.g., on-board applications), while it is shared with official distributors or 'certified' service providers, could amount to an abuse of economic dependence.[1643] He points out, in this regard, that 'it can be argued that under certain conditions firms on aftermarkets and in IOT-contexts with several stakeholders that need access to the same data for offering valuable services might claim access to the data that one stakeholder holds exclusively'.[1644] Moreover, and because refusal to share data might not fit perfectly within the four traditional case groups of abuse of economic dependence identified earlier,[1645] Kerber suggests to develop a new case group for situations where data holders have a de facto exclusive control on the access to certain data sources and where they might abuse from the state of economic dependence of other firms who need this access in order to offer products or services to the users.[1646] To support this, Kerber relies on a report for the German Federal Ministry for Economic Affairs and Energy, which indicated that:

> It may be useful to clarify in § 20 para. 1 GWB that a relevant form of dependence may also result from an undertaking being dependent, in order to achieve a substantial value creation within a value creation network, on access to automatically generated machine or service usage data that is exclusively controlled by another company; and *denial of access to data can constitute an unreasonable exclusionary conduct, even if markets for such data do not yet exist* (emphasis added).[1647]

Indeed, the benefit of the protection of § 20 GWB is not limited to undertakings engaged in existing agreements or business relations, but may extend to undertakings willing to enter into such agreements or relations.[1648] Accordingly, the authors of the report saw great potential in a broader application of § 20 GWB, which 'can become an effective instrument for closing persisting gaps in controlling abusive behaviour in view of the

1643. W. Kerber, 'Data Governance in Connected Cars: The Problem of Access to In-Vehicle Data', *supra*, p. 329.
1644. *Ibid.*
1645. *See* point 261.
1646. W. Kerber, 'Data-Sharing in IoT Ecosystems from a Competition Law Perspective', *supra*, p. 32. For a more thorough analysis of how this could be applied to the automotive sector, where the car manufacturers might have such a de facto exclusive control, *see* pp. 28-35.
1647. H. Schweitzer, et al., 'Modernising the Law on Abuse of Market Power: Executive Summary', *supra*, p. 6. For a more extensive discussion of this point, *see* H. Schweitzer, et al., *Modernisierung der Missbrauchsaufsicht für marktmächtige Unternehmen*, *supra*, pp. 47-57 and 156. *See also* the Governmental draft bill (GWB-Digitalisierungsgesetz) for the 10th amendment to the Competition Act of 9 September 2020, *supra*.
1648. L. Feteira, *The Interplay Between European and National Competition Law after Regulation 1/2003*, *supra*, p. 152.

special challenges facing the digital economy'.[1649] As a result of these arguments, the 10th amendment to the German Competition Act, namely the GWB Digitalisation Act ('GWB-Digitalisierungsgesetz'),[1650] included a new paragraph (1a) in § 20 GWB, which provides that:

> A dependency pursuant to paragraph 1 may also result from the fact that a company is dependent on access to data controlled by another company for its own activities. The denial of access to such data for a reasonable fee may constitute an unreasonable impediment under paragraph 1 in conjunction with §19(2)(1). This shall also apply if a business transaction has not yet been opened for this data.[1651]

Once again, the importance of the access seeker's explanations about the product/service that it intends to offer, and about the reasons why that data is necessary to offer that product/service, will be paramount in order to avoid free-riding tactics that would deter innovation.

6.2.2.2.2 Demonstrating the Anticompetitive Harm Deriving from This Abuse

280. Additionally, the anticompetitive harm deriving from this abuse must be proven. As discussed above,[1652] the 'freedom to compete approach' of the economic role of competition law fits more with the twofold objective of the provisions pertaining to the abuse of economic dependence, as the weaker party is protected not only because it is in a situation of unequal bargaining power but also because this 'protects the competitive process as a whole'[1653] by countering the economic power of some non-dominant undertakings. Indeed, 'freedom to access the market (contestability) is considered a necessary condition for efficiency and long-run welfare'.[1654] Abuses of economic dependence might thus be sanctioned in order to protect the freedom to compete, as an institution, and as an individual economic right.[1655]

The first set of conducts outlined above (termination of an existing business relationship) can indeed have anticompetitive effects. To illustrate

---

1649. H. Schweitzer, et al., 'Modernising the Law on Abuse of Market Power: Executive Summary', *supra*, p. 1.
1650. *See* Bundeskartellamt, 'Amendment of the German Act Against Restraints of Competition (Press release)', *supra*.
1651. Author's own translation.
1652. *See supra* points 264 and 265.
1653. W. Kerber, 'Data-Sharing in IoT Ecosystems from a Competition Law Perspective', *supra*, p. 29.
1654. P. Bougette, O. Budzinski and F. Marty, 'Exploitative Abuse and Abuse of Economic Dependence: What Can We Learn from an Industrial Organization Approach?', *supra*, p. 8.
1655. M. Bakhoum, 'Abuse Without Dominance in Competition Law: Abuse of Economic Dependence and Its Interface with Abuse of Dominance', *supra*, p. 17.

this, the *PeopleBrowsr v. Twitter* and *hiQ v. LinkedIn* cases should once again be outlined.[1656] In *PeopleBrowsr*, Twitter's conduct might have been considered as anticompetitive, as it can arguably be defined as a 'leveraging' behaviour by which Twitter intended to foreclose competition in this downstream analysis market to the benefit of its certified resellers.[1657] Additionally, it could also be argued that Twitter's conduct was anticompetitive as it waited for a data recipient, *in casu* PeopleBrowsr, to show the lucrative nature of a market based on the 'firehose' data analysis before reserving that market to its certified data resellers.[1658] Similarly, LinkedIn's conduct does tend to indicate an anticompetitive 'leveraging' behaviour by which it intended to foreclose competition in the downstream analysis market by developing a competing product after having waited for a data recipient, *in casu* hiQ, to show the lucrative nature of a such a data analysis market.[1659] In both of these cases, it seemed necessary to protect the access seekers' freedom to compete.

Similarly, the second set of conducts outlined above (refusal to supply) might also have anticompetitive effects as there might be cases where the refusal to share data unlawfully restricts the access seeker's possibility to compete in the market. In this regard, the European Commission's expert report on 'Competition Policy for the digital era' outlined that:

> [W]here a machine producer enjoys some degree of market power, or even just bilateral power, the bargaining power of a machine user may not suffice. A number of experts and industry participants argue that exclusive control over machine usage data then leads to the foreclosure of secondary markets and *may significantly reduce the contestability of a machine producer's position* on the primary market, *due to a data-driven lock-in of machine users* (emphasis added).[1660]

1656. *See* point 266.

1657. I. Graef, S. Wahyuningtyas and P. Valcke, 'Assessing Data Access Issues in Online Platforms', *Telecommunications Policy*, 2015, Vol. 39, pp. 384-385; I. Graef, *EU Competition Law, Data Protection and Online Platforms: Data as Essential Facility*, *supra*, p. 257.

1658. Z. Abrahamson, 'Essential Data', *The Yale Law Journal*, 2014, Vol. 124(3), p. 874, cited in I. Graef, *EU Competition Law, Data Protection and Online Platforms: Data as Essential Facility*, *supra*, p. 257.

1659. *See* United States Court of Appeals for the Ninth Circuit, *hiQ Labs, Inc. v. LinkedIn Corporation*, Case No. 17-16783, WL 4251889, 9 September 2019, available at https://law.justia.com/cases/federal/appellate-courts/ca9/17-16783/17-16783-2019-09-09.html, pp. 22-23. However, when ruling on the merits, the District Court ruled that hiQ had failed to substantiate this claim, but granted hiQ leave to amend it (*see* footnote 1642).

1660. J. Crémer, Y.-A. de Montjoye and H. Schweitzer, 'Competition Policy for the Digital Era', *supra*, p. 88.

6.2.2.3 Potential Remedy and Potential Adaptation of EU Competition Law

281. If the conditions identified above are fulfilled, the provisions prohibiting the abuse of economic dependence could theoretically be applied to the refusal to share data. Quite logically, a potential remedy would then be to impose on the non-dominant undertaking an obligation to share (some of) its data with the access seeker. This requires determining the categories of data potentially covered by the sharing remedy. Indeed, depending on this scope, the consequences for the non-dominant data holder, and for the data subjects in case personal data are involved, could vary greatly. As the determination of the categories of data that should be covered by such a compulsory B2B data sharing remedy implies overarching considerations equally applicable to the different types of competition law infringements I analyse, these will be addressed in a specific section (Section 6.4).

282. Finally, it is fundamental to underline that the above analysis has been conducted on the basis of the national law of three Member States, as there is no harmonisation of the provisions pertaining to the abuse of economic dependence in the EU.[1661] In order to avoid national law discrepancies on how these issues are handled in the internal market, the European Commission could consider the adoption of an abuse of economic dependence provision at the EU level, that would allow to deal, in specific cases, with refusals by non-dominant undertakings to share data. Together with a lowered threshold of application of the essential facilities doctrine for refusals, by dominant undertakings, to share data,[1662] this could constitute a welcome evolution of the European competition framework in order to tackle one of the two core data market failures presented above, namely data concentration.[1663]

Indeed, adopting an abuse of economic dependence provision at the EU level, and lowering the threshold of the essential facilities doctrine, should not be seen as mutually exclusive evolutions, but rather as complementary initiatives to remedy this data concentration market failure. A competition intervention based on the essential facilities doctrine allows to tackle, through a single action, more systemic market failures in order to benefit a broad number of downstream competitors. On the other hand, competition interventions based on abuse of economic dependence considerations take, by nature, place in more bilateral scenarios, and thus do not enable to remedy

1661. For an overview of all of the EU Member States that have such provisions against the abuse of economic dependence *see*: College of Europe, 'Study on the impact of national rules on unilateral conduct that diverge from Article 102 of the Treaty on the Functioning of the European Union (TFEU) – Final Report', 21 November 2012, available at https://ec.europa.eu/competition/calls/tenders_closed.html.

1662. *See* points 250-256.

1663. *See* points 78-83.

a systemic market failure through a single action. Moreover, the threshold for finding an abuse of economic dependence is easier to meet than the threshold of the essential facilities doctrine, and this provision could potentially be applied to a broader number of undertakings, as the demonstration of a dominant position of the data holder is not required. Accordingly, these two courses of action are complementary, as an adapted essential facilities doctrine could be used to remedy systemic market failures that result from the conduct of a circumscribed number of dominant actors, while competition interventions based on abuse of economic dependence considerations could be used against a broader amount of non-dominant undertakings, in order to remedy more specific market failures deriving from the dependence of certain undertakings on another one. They would thus both contribute to tackling data concentration market failures, but would be resorted to in different scenarios. The other core data market failure, namely data conglomeration and domino effects,[1664] on the other hand, could be addressed through merger regulation, to which I now turn.

6.3 INPUT FORECLOSURE IN VERTICAL MERGERS

283. As outlined above,[1665] network effects and economies of scope, scale and speed in data may not only protect large data holders in their core data-driven markets, but they may also be leveraged by these undertakings to expand and strengthen their position in a *connected market*.[1666] If these connected markets' dynamics are combined with the first-mover advantage outlined above,[1667] this could lead to a *domino effect*, i.e., 'a first mover in market A can leverage its dominant position, which comes with an advantage on user information, to let connected market B tip, too, even if market B is already served by traditional incumbent firms'.[1668] In turn, this could lead to successive market tipping in several connected markets,[1669] and to the establishment of digital conglomerates.[1670]

1664. *See* points 84 and 85.
1665. *See* points 84 and 85.
1666. J. Prüfer and C. Schottmüller, 'Competing with Big Data', *supra*, pp. 2-3; J. Krämer, D. Schnurr and S. Broughton Micova, 'The Role of Data for Digital Markets Contestability', *supra*, p. 56; B. Martens, et al., 'Business to Business Data Sharing', *supra*, p. 19.
1667. *See* points 79 and 80.
1668. J. Prüfer and C. Schottmüller, 'Competing with Big Data', *supra*, pp. 2-3.
1669. J. Krämer, D. Schnurr and S. Broughton Micova, 'The Role of Data for Digital Markets Contestability', *supra*, p. 71.
1670. *See supra* point 84. *See also* T. Eisenmann, G. Parker and M. Van Alstyne, 'Platform Envelopment', *Strategic Management Journal*, 2011, Vol. 32(12), pp. 1270-1285; D. Condorelli and J. Padilla, 'Harnessing Platform Envelopment Through Privacy Policy Tying', December 2019, available at https://ssrn.com/abstract=3504025; M. Bourreau

284. Although these conglomerates could be procompetitive, they could also generate market failures (e.g., raise entry barriers for innovative entrants) and long-term competitive advantages, which could have a negative impact on the contestability of these markets.[1671] Moreover, the conglomerate could also foreclose competition on some of the markets where it is active if these markets depend on the access to a key resource, such as specific types of data, produced on a primary market where the conglomerate is also active and dominant, and if the conglomerate refuses to share this resource with its competitors and reserves its use for itself.[1672] This is where the 'input foreclosure' theory could potentially come into play, in order to prevent vertical mergers from leading to such a situation. The application of this theory to 'traditional' markets will first be briefly presented (Section 6.3.1), before questioning whether it could be applied to 'data foreclosure' (Section 6.3.2). Then, the complex issue of the acquisition of 'nascent innovative players' will be briefly presented (Section 6.3.3).

6.3.1 The Traditional 'Input Foreclosure' Theory

285. While vertical mergers do not lead to the elimination of direct competitors, and might even lead to an improvement of competition in cases where the merged entity's competitors are already vertically integrated, these mergers can nevertheless create foreclosure risks.[1673] One of these risks is downstream foreclosure, namely a situation in which the merged entity decides to no longer supply an important input[1674] to its competitors in the downstream market (or decides to raise the price or reduce the quality of this input for these competitors) – while this input was supplied to them by the merging party operating on the upstream market prior to the merger – in

---

and A. de Streel, 'Digital Conglomerates and EU Competition Policy', *CERRE Report*, March 2019, available at http://www.crid.be/pdf/public/8377.pdf, pp. 4 and 11. For a discussion of the 'killer acquisitions' issue, *see* pp. 21-23.

1671. M. Bourreau and A. de Streel, 'Digital Conglomerates and EU Competition Policy', *supra*, p. 14; J. Krämer, D. Schnurr and S. Broughton Micova, 'The Role of Data for Digital Markets Contestability', *supra*, p. 55.

1672. M. Bourreau and A. de Streel, 'Digital Conglomerates and EU Competition Policy', *supra*, pp. 18-19.

1673. D. Geradin, A. Layne-Farrar and N. Petit, *EU Competition Law and Economics*, Oxford, Oxford University Press, 2012, p. 514.

1674. An input will be important if, for example, it 'represents a significant cost factor relative to the price of the downstream product (…) [or if it is] a critical component without which the downstream product could not be manufactured or effectively sold on the market, or [if it represents] a significant source of product differentiation for the downstream product, [or if] the cost of switching to alternative inputs is relatively high' (European Commission, Guidelines on the assessment of non-horizontal mergers under the Council Regulation on the control of concentrations between undertakings, *OJ C 265/6*, 18 October 2008, § 34).

order to advantage its own downstream operations after the merger.[1675] For instance, in the *TomTom/TeleAtlas* merger,[1676] the Commission expressed concerns that the merged entity would deny supplying downstream competitors in the portable navigation system market with digital maps.[1677]

According to the Commission's guidelines on non-horizontal mergers,[1678] in order to establish such an input foreclosure, it is not needed to demonstrate that any competitor would be forced to leave the market, but rather solely to demonstrate that this would entail higher prices for consumers.[1679] In order to do so, the merged entity's ability to foreclose access to the input (significant degree of market power),[1680] its incentive to foreclose (the foreclosure would be profitable),[1681] and the overall likely impact on effective competition (increased rivals' costs or entry barriers)[1682] must be assessed.[1683] Naturally, likely efficiencies deriving from the merger will also have to be assessed.[1684] A balance will thus have to be found between the market efficiencies and deficiencies that may result from the vertical merger.

For instance, the Commission cleared the *TomTom/TeleAtlas* merger[1685] after concluding that the merged entity would not have been able to limit its competitors' access to the input (the digital maps) nor to increase the costs of the access to the input, due to the presence of an upstream competitor, and that it would have had no incentive to foreclose the access to the input because the additional sales of portable navigation systems would not have compensated the loss of revenue from the sales of digital maps to competitors.[1686]

1675. D. Geradin, A. Layne-Farrar and N. Petit, *EU Competition Law and Economics*, *supra*, p. 514.
1676. European Commission, *TomTom/TeleAtlas*, 14 May 2008, case M.4854.
1677. D. Geradin, A. Layne-Farrar and N. Petit, *EU Competition Law and Economics*, *supra*, p. 500.
1678. European Commission, Guidelines on the assessment of non-horizontal mergers, *supra*.
1679. *Ibid.*, § 31; R. Whish and D. Bailey, *Competition Law*, 7th ed., Oxford, Oxford University Press, 2012, p. 878.
1680. European Commission, Guidelines on the assessment of non-horizontal mergers, *supra*, §§ 33-39.
1681. *Ibid.*, §§ 40-46.
1682. *Ibid.*, §§ 47-51.
1683. R. Whish and D. Bailey, *Competition Law*, *supra*, p. 878.
1684. *Ibid*; European Commission, European Commission, Guidelines on the assessment of non-horizontal mergers, *supra*, §§ 52-57.
1685. European Commission, *TomTom/TeleAtlas*, 14 May 2008, case M.4854.
1686. A. Jones and B. Sufrin, *EU Competition Law: Text, Cases, and Materials*, 4th ed., Oxford, Oxford University Press, 2011, p. 951.

6.3.2 Application to 'Data Foreclosure'?

286. It is worth questioning whether this input foreclosure theory could be applied to data, in situations where a merged entity might have the possibility to decide to no longer provide access to (or to raise the price or reduce the quality of) important data to its competitors in the downstream market after the merger.

287. In order to do so, the merged entity's ability to foreclose access to the data would first have to be demonstrated, in light of the merged entity's 'significant degree of market power' on the upstream market.[1687] In this regard, it must be reminded that the economic characteristics of data benefit large incumbent data holders who have access to more (recent) data than their competitors,[1688] and lead to market concentration.[1689] Indeed, data-driven markets have a natural tendency to tip towards monopolisation.[1690] Moreover, because such situation is persistent once the market has tipped, even in dynamic high-tech markets, there is a strong *first-mover advantage*.[1691] Therefore, if the merged entity has benefited from such first-mover advantage and market tipping dynamics in order to gain a stronghold on the upstream market, it could be considered as benefitting from a 'significant degree of market power'.

Such a finding will, however, be function of the determination of the scope of the data market at hand. Yet, market definition is a complex task in the digital environment.[1692] A key consideration, in this regard, will be to determine whether there are substitutes to the merged entity's data on the upstream market, which could be used by its competitors on the downstream market in case of a foreclosure of access to the upstream data.[1693] Indeed, as

---

1687. European Commission, European Commission, Guidelines on the assessment of non-horizontal mergers, *supra*, §§ 33-39.
1688. J. Crémer, Y.-A. de Montjoye and H. Schweitzer, 'Competition Policy for the Digital Era', *supra*, pp. 3 and 19-24.
1689. *See* Part I, Chapter 2, Section 2.2.3.1. M. Stucke and A. Grunes, *Big Data and Competition Policy*, *supra*, p. 336.
1690. *See* J. Prüfer, 'Competition Policy and Data Sharing on Data-Driven Markets', *Report for the Friedrich-Ebert-Stiftung*, 2020, available at http://library.fes.de/pdf-files/fes/15999.pdf, pp. 6-9; J. Prüfer and C. Schottmüller, 'Competing with Big Data', *TILEC Discussion Paper No. 2017-006 and CentER Discussion Paper No. 2017-007*, February 2017, available at https://pure.uvt.nl/ws/portalfiles/portal/15514029/2017_007.pdf, p. 2.
1691. J. Prüfer and C. Schottmüller, 'Competing with Big Data', *supra*, p. 2.
1692. *See* point 256. On the complexity of market definition in the digital environment, *see also* I. Graef, 'Market Definition and Market Power in Data: The Case of Online Platforms', *World Competition Law and Economics Review*, 2015, Vol. 38(4), pp. 473-506; J. Crémer, Y.-A. de Montjoye and H. Schweitzer, 'Competition Policy for the Digital Era', *supra*, pp. 42-50.
1693. *See*, by analogy, G. Colangelo and M. Maggiolino, 'Big Data as Misleading Facilities', *European Competition Journal*, 2017, Vol. 2-3(13), p. 273.

outlined by the European Commission in the *TomTom/TeleAtlas* merger,[1694] the merged entity will not be able to limit its competitors' access to the input, nor to increase the costs of the access to the input, if there are sufficiently strong upstream competitors that offer a substitutable input.[1695]

Demonstrating the absence of such viable substitute data sources could be a significant hurdle to overcome. For instance, the European Commission has affirmed, in its *Google/DoubleClick* merger decision, that Google and DoubleClicks' competitors could purchase data on users' search and web-browsing behaviour from third parties such as other major web publishers, internet service providers or portals.[1696] Similarly, in its *Facebook/WhatsApp* merger decision, it held that a wide number of undertakings, which are not controlled by Facebook (Google, Apple, Amazon, eBay, Microsoft, Twitter, etc.), collected sizeable amounts of user data that could be used by competitors as alternatives to Facebook's data for targeted advertising purposes.[1697]

Nevertheless, it is interesting to point out that, in its *Microsoft/LinkedIn* decision, the European Commission outlined that, in theory, refusals, by the merged entity, to share data with competitors on the downstream market may 'increase barriers to entry/expansion in the market for actual or potential competitors, which may need this data to operate on this market'.[1698] Yet, when assessing whether this concern was established *in casu*, the European Commission concluded, like in the *Facebook/Whatsapp* case, that several other undertakings collected sizeable amounts of user data that could be used by competitors as alternatives to the merged entity's data for targeted advertising purposes.[1699] The European Commission also reached a similar conclusion in its *Apple/Shazam* merger decision, where it held that 'it would be unlikely that the merged entity would have the ability to foreclose competing providers of digital music streaming apps even if Shazam's data would be integrated into Apple's dataset'.[1700]

On the contrary, in the *Thomson/Reuters* merger case, the European Commission did express concrete concerns that the merging entities'

1694. European Commission, *TomTom/TeleAtlas*, 14 May 2008, case M.4854.
1695. A. Jones and B. Sufrin, *EU Competition Law. Text, Cases, and Materials*, *supra*, p. 951.
1696. European Commission, *Google/DoubleClick*, 11 March 2018, case M.4731, §§ 269-272 and 365; R. Feasey and A. de Streel, 'Data Sharing for Digital Market Contestability', *supra*, p. 38.
1697. European Commission, *Facebook/WhatsApp*, 3 October 2014, case M.7217, §§ 187-190; G. Colangelo and M. Maggiolino, 'Big Data as Misleading Facilities', *supra*, p. 271; R. Feasey and A. de Streel, 'Data Sharing for Digital Market Contestability', *supra*, p. 39.
1698. European Commission, *Microsoft/LinkedIn*, 6 December 2016, case M.8124, § 179; R. Feasey and A. de Streel, 'Data Sharing for Digital Market Contestability', *supra*, p. 39.
1699. European Commission, *Microsoft/LinkedIn*, 6 December 2016, case M.8124, § 180; R. Feasey and A. de Streel, 'Data Sharing for Digital Market Contestability', *supra*, p. 40.
1700. European Commission, *Apple/Shazam*, 6 September 2018, case M.8788, § 340; R. Feasey and A. de Streel, 'Data Sharing for Digital Market Contestability', *supra*, p. 40.

competitors would not have sufficient alternatives to access necessary financial information products after the merger, and that this could significantly reduce competition 'in the markets for the distribution of aftermarket broker research reports, of earning estimates, of fundamental financial data of enterprises and of time series of economic data'.[1701] To alleviate these concerns, the merging parties committed to share copies of the databases containing such financial information products with competitors that would request it.[1702] Similarly, in the *Google/Fitbit* merger, the merging parties committed to maintain access, for software applications, to the users' health and fitness data through the Fitbit Web API, without charges and provided that the users have consented to this.[1703]

According to Hoffmann and Johannsen, the European Commission's decisional practice analysing the merged entity's ability to foreclose access to the data has been too short-sighted, as it has been centred on the overall availability of data post-merger (absolute foreclosure theory of harm), and this explains why, in light of data's non-rivalrous and ubiquitous nature, it rarely expressed competition concerns.[1704] Yet, because data is a general-purpose good,[1705] and because the competitive advantages that the merged entity could derive from the data will not necessarily be limited to one market,[1706] the European Commission should consider the fact that 'additional competition concerns may arise when the accumulation of large piles of data from a huge multitude of sources by digital conglomerates leads to such an advantage that competitors will not be able to match anymore, increasing the likelihood of further anti-competitive strategies (relative foreclosure theory of harm)'.[1707] If the Commission were to adopt such a relative foreclosure theory of harm instead, this could increase the cases in which the merged entity's ability to foreclose access to the data could be established, as it could also encompass cases in which 'the accumulation of data generated by a merger gives the merged entity such a large advantage that regardless of having access to specific information no one will have sufficient incentives to challenge the market(s) in which the merged entity is

---

1701. European Commission, *Thomson Corporation/Reuters Group*, 19 February 2008, case M.4726, §§ 151-156; R. Feasey and A. de Streel, 'Data Sharing for Digital Market Contestability', *supra*, p. 39.
1702. European Commission, *Thomson Corporation/Reuters Group*, 19 February 2008, case M.4726, § 480; R. Feasey and A. de Streel, 'Data Sharing for Digital Market Contestability', *supra*, p. 39.
1703. European Commission, *Google/Fitbit*, 17 December 2020, case M.9660; European Commission, 'Mergers: Commission clears acquisition of Fitbit by Google, subject to conditions', *Press release n° IP/20/2484*, 17 December 2020, available at https://ec.europa.eu/commission/presscorner/detail/en/IP_20_2484.
1704. J. Hoffmann and G. Johannsen, 'EU-Merger Control & Big Data, *supra*, pp. 1 and 7.
1705. *See* point 52.
1706. *See* points 283 and 284.
1707. J. Hoffmann and G. Johannsen, 'EU-Merger Control & Big Data', *supra*, p. 1.

active'.[1708] For Hoffmann and Johannsen, the justification of the need, for the European Commission, to adopt such a 'relative foreclosure theory of harm' in digital markets could be based 'on the assumption that data-induced economic power can generate a greater advantage than it would have generated in a pre-digital era. This advantage is not related to a specific relevant market, but to the whole conglomerate's digital ecosystem'.[1709]

288. Second, the merged entity's incentive to foreclose the access to the data for competitors in the downstream market, as this would be profitable for it, will have to be assessed.[1710] In this regard, it must be reminded that network effects and economies of scope, scale and speed in data, which the merged entity benefits from on the upstream market, may be leveraged by the merged entity to expand and strengthen its position in the downstream market if such data turns out to be a valuable input to improve the goods or services offered on that downstream market (*connected markets* dynamic).[1711] In fact, this could even reinforce the merged entity's position in the upstream market if the data gathered on the downstream market is a valuable input to improve the goods or services offered on the upstream market.[1712] As this would be profitable for the merged entity, it could be argued that it has an incentive to foreclose access to the data for competitors in the downstream market.

289. Third, the overall likely impact of the foreclosure on effective competition must be assessed.[1713] This will require finding an appropriate balance between the procompetitive effects of the merger (notably in terms of the efficiencies that it might entail), and its potential anticompetitive effects. Regarding the latter, it should be reminded that the first-mover advantage, market tipping and connected markets dynamics mentioned above could lead to a *domino effect*. Any efficiencies deriving from the merger will thus have to be balanced with the risks that this could entail.[1714]

290. In light of the above, I argue that the 'input foreclosure' theory could potentially have been applied to Twitter and LinkedIn in the two cases mentioned above in the analysis of the abuse of economic dependence,[1715] had the circumstances of these cases been slightly different. Indeed, had Twitter/LinkedIn merged with a downstream data analytics company, the

1708. *Ibid.*, p. 7. For more details, *see* pp. 7-32.
1709. J. Hoffmann and G. Johannsen, 'EU-Merger Control & Big Data', *supra*, p. 22.
1710. European Commission, European Commission, Guidelines on the assessment of non-horizontal mergers, *supra*, §§ 40-46.
1711. *See* point 283.
1712. J. Prüfer and C. Schottmüller, 'Competing with Big Data', *supra*, pp. 2-3.
1713. European Commission, European Commission, Guidelines on the assessment of non-horizontal mergers, *supra*, §§ 47-51.
1714. R. Whish and D. Bailey, *Competition Law*, 7th ed., Oxford, Oxford University Press, 2012, p. 878; European Commission, European Commission, Guidelines on the assessment of non-horizontal mergers, *supra*, §§ 52-57.
1715. *See* point 266.

issue could have been raised of whether this merger could have led to an input foreclosure if Twitter/LinkedIn had decided to no longer provide access (or to raise the price or reduce the quality of) to its important data[1716] to its competitors in the downstream data analysis market after the merger. In light of the merged entity's ability to foreclose access to the input (significant degree of market power of Twitter/LinkedIn as no viable alternative to Twitter/LinkedIn's data was available),[1717] of its incentive to foreclose (the foreclosure would be profitable as PeopleBrowsr/hiQ had demonstrated the lucrative nature of this downstream market),[1718] and of the overall likely impact on effective competition (increased costs for PeopleBrowsr/hiQ to access the data),[1719] this might have been a potential case of application of the theory.

291. If the conditions of the 'input foreclosure' theory are fulfilled, a potential remedy would then be to subject the validation of the merger to the merging entity's commitment to guarantee that it will share (some of) its important data with competitors in the downstream market at a reasonable price, as in the *Thomson/Reuters* case mentioned above.[1720] Indeed, sharing specific types of data could attenuate the anticompetitive effects of conglomerates by allowing competition to emerge and ensuring market contestability, as 'compulsory access will allow entrants, on the one hand, to enjoy the same economies of scope in product development than the [merged] firm and, on the other hand, to generate demand-side synergies of similar magnitude when integrating the key [data] in their product ecosystems'.[1721] Due to overarching considerations with the two previous Sections, the delineation of the categories of data that should fall within such a commitment to share data will be addressed in Section 6.4.

Nevertheless, it must be kept in mind that, in light of the dynamic nature of data markets, which makes their evolution somewhat unpredictable, it could be difficult for the European Commission to assess whether the proposed data sharing commitment will comprehensively eliminate the competition concerns.[1722] To alleviate this predictability issue, the use of 'conditional remedies' could be envisaged, which are 'remedies which only apply under certain circumstances, i.e. certain events or a certain

1716. *See* footnote 1674.
1717. *See* point 274.
1718. *See* point 280.
1719. *See* point 266.
1720. *See* point 287. *See also* J. Hoffmann and G. Johannsen, 'EU-Merger Control & Big Data', *supra*, pp. 56-62.
1721. M. Bourreau and A. de Streel, 'Digital Conglomerates and EU Competition Policy', *supra*, p. 30.
1722. J. Hoffmann and G. Johannsen, 'EU-Merger Control & Big Data', *supra*, p. 53.

timeframe'.[1723,1724] Indeed, this would ease the complex balancing between under- and over-enforcement in dynamic markets. Obviously, in light of the principle of legal certainty, the conditions in which the (data sharing) remedy would have to be 'activated' will have to be clearly defined from the outset and will have to be as operable as possible.[1725]

Naturally, commitments to share data are not the only available remedies, and other avenues are suggested in the legal doctrine, such as the imposition of non-discrimination obligations, structural breakups or preventing the merged entity from combining the data sets produced on the upstream and downstream markets (data siloing[1726]).[1727] Finally, the competition authority could also decide to block the merger due to the competition concerns that a data combination would entail, but this has never been done so far, at the European level, by the European Commission.[1728] As I focus on compulsory B2B data sharing, these alternatives will not be further detailed here.

6.3.3 The Particular Issue of the Acquisition of 'Nascent Innovative Players'

292. Finally, to conclude this Section pertaining to mergers, the complex issue of the acquisition of 'nascent innovative players'[1729] will be briefly presented. Indeed, in the digital economy, large data holders often acquire such 'nascent innovative players'. For instance, since 2008, Google has acquired 168 undertakings (notably Waze, YouTube or DoubleClick that were potential competitors), Facebook has acquired 71 undertakings (including Instagram and WhatsApp that were also arguably potential competitors),

1723. F. De Bure and L. Bary, 'Disruptive Innovation and Merger Remedies: How to Predict the Unpredictable?', *Concurrences*, 2017, No. 3, Article No. 84407, p. 7.
1724. J. Hoffmann and G. Johannsen, 'EU-Merger Control & Big Data', *supra*, p. 53.
1725. *Ibid.*, p. 55.
1726. *See*, in this regard, the commitments proposed by Google in the *Google/Fitbit* merger: European Commission, *Google/Fitbit*, 17 December 2020, case M.9660; European Commission, 'Mergers: Commission clears acquisition of Fitbit by Google, subject to conditions', *Press release n° IP/20/2484*, 17 December 2020, available at https://ec.europa.eu/commission/presscorner/detail/en/IP_20_2484.
1727. On these alternative remedies, *see* references in footnote 567.
1728. R. Feasey and A. de Streel, 'Data Sharing for Digital Market Contestability', *supra*, p. 38. For such cases of merger blockings in the United States, *see* S. Besen and P. Verveer, 'Competition and Data: Potential Remedies', *supra*, pp. 116-126.
1729. This expression is preferred to the more broadly used expression 'killer acquisition' as, in fact, large data holders rarely simply acquire a potential competitor in order to 'kill' its activities (like in the pharma sector), but rather often develop it in order to reinforce their position on the market or on a neighbouring market, as illustrated by Google's acquisition of YouTube, or by Facebook's acquisitions of Instagram and WhatsApp (*see* Autorité de la concurrence, 'Contribution de l'Autorité de la concurrence au débat sur la politique de concurrence et les enjeux numériques', *supra*, p. 10).

and Amazon has acquired 60 undertakings, which is a respective average of around 15, 6 and 5 acquisitions per year.[1730]

The effects on competition of such acquisitions are challenging to assess.[1731] On the one hand, such acquisitions could pursue legitimate goals, such as acquiring specific human or technical competences that are precious and rare, or acquiring an extensive potential user-base.[1732] Moreover, they might be efficient and beneficial for both parties, as these 'nascent innovative players' might lack the sufficient (human and technical) skills and resources to develop their innovative ideas themselves.[1733] Indeed, an innovative idea created by a 'nascent innovative player' might be dependent on the mobilisation of a large data holder's skills and resources in order to blossom into a product/service that is picked up by a large user-base, and it is possible that the 'nascent innovative player' would have never reached this result on its own. In this regard, some 'nascent innovative players' might even never really intend to bring a new/disruptive product/service on the market themselves, which would compete with the large data holder's product/service, but rather simply aim at being acquired by the said large data holder.[1734]

On the other hand, acquisitions of 'nascent innovative players' could also entail anticompetitive effects if large data holders systematically identify and acquire smaller innovative players, which could become potential rivals in the future.[1735] In fact, it is extremely complex for competition authorities to identify such practices, as such potential rivals will often emerge in niche markets that may not necessarily clearly overlap with the markets on which the acquiring large data holder is active.[1736] Conversely, the troves of data that these large data holders control across several markets in their ecosystem

1730. Autorité de la concurrence, 'Contribution de l'Autorité de la concurrence au débat sur la politique de concurrence et les enjeux numériques', *supra*, p. 9; Lear, 'Ex-post Assessment of Merger Control Decisions in Digital Markets – Final Report', 9 May 2019, available at https://assets.publishing.service.gov.uk/government/uploads/system/uploads/attachment_data/file/803576/CMA_past_digital_mergers_GOV.UK_version.pdf, p. ii.
1731. H. Schweitzer, et al., 'Modernising the Law on Abuse of Market Power: Executive Summary', *supra*, p. 4.
1732. Autorité de la concurrence, 'Contribution de l'Autorité de la concurrence au débat sur la politique de concurrence et les enjeux numériques', *supra*, p. 9; H. Schweitzer, et al., 'Modernising the Law on Abuse of Market Power: Executive Summary', *supra*, p. 4.
1733. M. Bourreau and A. de Streel, 'Digital Conglomerates and EU Competition Policy', *supra*, p. 21.
1734. *Ibid.*
1735. Autorité de la concurrence, 'Contribution de l'Autorité de la concurrence au débat sur la politique de concurrence et les enjeux numériques', *supra*, p. 10; H. Schweitzer, et al., 'Modernising the Law on Abuse of Market Power: Executive Summary', *supra*, p. 4.
1736. H. Schweitzer, et al., 'Modernising the Law on Abuse of Market Power: Executive Summary', *supra*, p. 5.

allow them to identify early on potential threats that might emerge on niche markets.[1737]

293. That being said, such acquisitions will, in practice, only be subject to a competition assessment (for instance, in order to determine whether they could lead to an 'input foreclosure') if they have been notified to a competition authority, which will only occur if certain thresholds are met. As I analyse compulsory B2B data sharing initiatives in the European legal framework, I will focus on the European Union mergers' thresholds enshrined in the 'Merger Regulation'.[1738] In this regard, Article 1.2 of the Merger Regulation provides that a merger has an EU dimension if:

(a) the combined aggregate worldwide turnover of all the undertakings concerned is more than EUR 5 000 million; and
(b) the aggregate Community-wide turnover of each of at least two of the undertakings concerned is more than EUR 250 million,

unless each of the undertakings concerned achieves more than two-thirds of its aggregate Community-wide turnover within one and the same Member State.

Article 1.3 of the Merger Regulation adds that a merger that does not meet the thresholds contained in Article 1.2 will nevertheless have an EU dimension if:

(a) the combined aggregate worldwide turnover of all the undertakings concerned is more than EUR 2 500 million;
(b) in each of at least three Member States, the combined aggregate turnover of all the undertakings concerned is more than EUR 100 million;
(c) in each of at least three Member States included for the purpose of point (b), the aggregate turnover of each of at least two of the undertakings concerned is more than EUR 25 million; and
(d) the aggregate Community-wide turnover of each of at least two of the undertakings concerned is more than EUR 100 million,

unless each of the undertakings concerned achieves more than two-thirds of its aggregate Community-wide turnover within one and the same Member State.

294. Therefore, only the acquisitions that meet these 'EU dimension' thresholds will have to be notified to the European Commission prior to their implementation.[1739] Yet, quite often, the 'nascent innovative players' that are

---

1737. M. Bourreau and A. de Streel, 'Digital Conglomerates and EU Competition Policy', *supra*, p. 21.
1738. Council Regulation (EC) No. 139/2004 of 20 January 2004 on the control of concentrations between undertakings, *OJ L 24/1*, 29 January 2004.
1739. Article 4 of Council Regulation 139/2004.

acquired by large data holders have not yet monetised their innovation, and, in such cases, the value of the target company is not reflected by the turnover it achieves and the notification thresholds are usually not reached.[1740] This is because, in such digital markets, 'nascent innovative players' often prioritise the growth of their user-base, in order to be the first to reap network effects and to attempt to make the (niche) market tip in their favour, rather than the growth of their turnover and profit.[1741]

As a result, only a handful of these acquisitions have been substantially scrutinised by competition authorities,[1742] while some others, which might have a significant impact on competition, have escaped review by competition authorities, in particular in the digital sector.[1743] For instance, Facebook's USD 19 billion acquisition of Whatsapp was only notified to the European Commission[1744] because market share thresholds were met in several Member States (Spain, Cyprus, UK), in which the transaction was notifiable and for which the competition authorities accepted to refer the case to the European Commission.[1745]

295. Accordingly, growing calls for the adaptation of these notification thresholds have been made, and several alternatives have been suggested. For instance, the French *Autorité de la Concurrence* has suggested 'the introduction of an obligation to inform the Commission and/or the competition authorities concerned of *all concentrations* implemented on European territory *by "structuring" undertakings*' (emphasis added).[1746] These are defined as undertakings 'which hold considerable market power on the market in which they are mainly active but also on neighbouring markets, due to their "gatekeeper" status'.[1747] The European Commission and/or national competition authorities could then require the structuring undertaking to formally notify the acquisition for merger control review if they consider that it might present competitive risks (such as risks of input foreclosure).[1748] A similar suggestion has been made in the Furman Report, which recommended that the UK Competition and Markets Authority should be informed of all intended acquisitions by an undertaking having 'strategic

1740. Autorité de la concurrence, 'Contribution de l'Autorité de la concurrence au débat sur la politique de concurrence et les enjeux numériques', *supra*, p. 9.
1741. M. Bourreau and A. de Streel, 'Digital Conglomerates and EU Competition Policy', *supra*, p. 32.
1742. J. Furman, et al., 'Unlocking Digital Competition', *supra*, p. 12.
1743. Communication from the Commission, Guidance on the application of the referral mechanism set out in Article 22 of the Merger Regulation to certain categories of cases, Brussels, 26 March 2021, C(2021) 1959 final, p. 3.
1744. European Commission, *Facebook/WhatsApp*, 3 October 2014, case M.7217.
1745. Autorité de la concurrence, 'Contribution de l'Autorité de la concurrence au débat sur la politique de concurrence et les enjeux numériques', *supra*, p. 12.
1746. *Ibid.*, p. 13. Author's own translation.
1747. *Ibid.*, p. 5. Author's own translation.
1748. *Ibid.*, p. 13.

market status'.[1749] These are the undertakings that are 'in a position to exercise market power over a gateway or bottleneck in a digital market, where they control others' market access'.[1750] While starting from the same perspective, the Stigler Committee report went a step further, as it not only recommended that the Federal Trade Commission (FTC) should be informed of every acquisition made by an undertaking having 'bottleneck power'[1751] but rather suggested that all of these acquisitions should be formally notified to the FTC and receive a pre-clearance.[1752]

Another potential adaptation that has been suggested would be to include the value of the acquisition as an alternative threshold in the Merger Regulation, as is currently done in Austria and Germany.[1753] This would allow the European Commission 'to determine whether the high transaction price reflects the important future revenues expected from the innovative target (which is welfare enhancing) or reflects the insurance premium for market stability and monopoly rent when the acquired innovation will be killed (which is welfare detrimental)'.[1754]

Alternatively, the German experts' report for the modernisation of competition law suggested the inclusion of a broader provision in German competition law which would aim at keeping markets open and contestable, independently of the meeting of a particular threshold, and which would allow 'the competition authority to consider, when assessing the existence of a significant impediment to effective competition, the existence of an overall strategy of a dominant company to systematically acquire fast-growing companies with a recognizable and considerable potential to become competitors in the dominated market in the future'.[1755] In the same

---

1749. J. Furman, et al., 'Unlocking Digital Competition', *supra*, p. 95; S. Ennis and A. Fletcher, 'Developing International Perspectives on Digital Competition Policy', *supra*, p. 4.
1750. J. Furman, et al., 'Unlocking Digital Competition', *supra*, p. 55.
1751. Bottleneck power 'describes a situation where consumers primarily single-home and rely upon a single service provider, which makes obtaining access to those consumers for the relevant activity by other service providers prohibitively costly' (Stigler Committee on Digital Platforms, 'Final Report', *supra*, p. 32).
1752. Stigler Committee on Digital Platforms, 'Final Report', *supra*, p. 111; S. Ennis and A. Fletcher, 'Developing International Perspectives on Digital Competition Policy', *supra*, p. 4.
1753. M. Bourreau and A. de Streel, 'Digital Conglomerates and EU Competition Policy', *supra*, p. 32. *See* Bundeskartellamt and Bundeswettbewerbsbehörde, 'Guidance on Transaction Value Thresholds for Mandatory Pre-Merger Notification (Section 35(1a) GWB and Section 9(4) KartG)', July 2018, available at https://www.bundeskartellamt.de/SharedDocs/Publikation/EN/Leitfaden/Leitfaden_Transaktionsschwelle.pdf?__blob=publicationFile&v=2.
1754. M. Bourreau and A. de Streel, 'Digital Conglomerates and EU Competition Policy', *supra*, p. 32.
1755. H. Schweitzer, et al., 'Modernising the Law on Abuse of Market Power: Executive Summary', *supra*, p. 5. *See also* Bundeskartellamt, 'Amendment of the German Act Against Restraints of Competition (Press Release)', *supra*.

perspective, the European Commission's expert report on 'Competition Policy for the digital era' outlined that 'where an acquisition plausibly is part of such a strategy, the burden of proof [should be] on the notifying parties to show that the adverse effects on competition are offset by merger-specific efficiencies'.[1756]

In any case, the implementation of any of these alternatives would require a modification of the existing European legal framework applicable to mergers.[1757] In this regard, it is worth mentioning that the European Commission's proposal for a Digital Markets Act[1758] provides that 'gatekeepers'[1759] offering 'core platform services'[1760] will have to 'inform the Commission of any intended concentration within the meaning of Article 3 of Regulation (EC) No 139/2004 involving another provider of core platform services or of any other services provided in the digital sector irrespective of whether it is notifiable to a Union competition authority under Regulation (EC) No 139/2004 or to a competent national competition authority under national merger rules'.[1761] This notification will notably have to specify the number of yearly active business users and of monthly active end users of the acquisition target, and the rationale for the merger.[1762]

Finally, it must be underlined that the European Commission has indicated in its guidance on the application of the referral mechanism (by national competition authorities to the Commission), set out in Article 22 of the Merger Regulation, that this mechanism could be used for 'transactions where the turnover of at least one of the undertakings concerned does not reflect its actual or future competitive potential. This would include, for example, cases where the undertaking: (1) is a start-up or recent entrant with significant competitive potential that has yet to develop or implement a business model generating significant revenues (or is still in the initial phase of implementing such business model); (2) is an important innovator or is conducting potentially important research; (3) is an actual or potential important competitive force; (4) has access to competitively significant assets (such as for instance raw materials, infrastructure, data or intellectual property rights); and/or (5) provides products or services that are key

1756. J. Crémer, Y.-A. de Montjoye and H. Schweitzer, 'Competition Policy for the Digital Era', *supra*, p. 124. On this point, *see also* Stigler Committee on Digital Platforms, 'Final Report', *supra*, p. 98; and S. Ennis and A. Fletcher, 'Developing International Perspectives on Digital Competition Policy', *supra*, p. 3.
1757. On the broader discussion pertaining to the potential need to adapt competition law in order to better fit the digital environment, *see* the references mentioned in footnote 62.
1758. Proposal for a Digital Markets Act. For more details on this Digital Markets Act, *see* points 317, 380 and 384-385.
1759. *See* Articles 2.1 and 3 of the Proposal for a Digital Markets Act. For more details on the designation of these gatekeepers, *see* points 384 and 385.
1760. *See* Article 1.2 of the Proposal for a Digital Markets Act. For a definition of these services, *see* Articles 2.2 and 2.5 to 2.11 of the Proposal.
1761. Article 12.1 of the Proposal for a Digital Markets Act.
1762. Article 12.2 of the Proposal for a Digital Markets Act.

inputs/components for other industries. In its assessment, the Commission may also take into account whether the value of the consideration received by the seller is particularly high compared to the current turnover of the target'.[1763] According to the Commission, such referrals could even be made for transactions that have already been closed, although the referral of mergers that have been implemented for more than six months would only be considered as appropriate in exceptional circumstances, for instance, due to 'the magnitude of the potential competition concerns and of the potential detrimental effect on consumers'.[1764] It should however be outlined that both the national competition authorities and the Commission respectively retain a considerable margin of discretion in deciding whether to refer cases or to accept such referrals.[1765] While this guidance introduces some flexibility in an attempt to address the phenomenon of the acquisition of 'nascent innovative players', its application could generate legal uncertainties, notably in terms of the possibility to refer transactions that have already been completed.

6.4 OVERARCHING CONSIDERATIONS PERTAINING TO COMPULSORY B2B DATA SHARING AS A COMPETITION LAW REMEDY

296. Through Sections 6.1 to 6.3, I have demonstrated that refusals to share data could lead to three types of competition law infringements, namely abuses of a dominant position, abuses of economic dependence and input foreclosure in vertical mergers, if the conditions of application of these theories are met. For each of these infringements, a potential remedy could be to impose on the large data holder[1766] an obligation to share (some of) its data with several third parties. Naturally, other remedies (data siloing, structural breakups, non-discrimination obligations, etc.) could also be envisaged.[1767] However, as I focus on compulsory B2B data sharing, these alternatives will not be further detailed here.

In order to impose such a compulsory B2B data sharing remedy on a large data holder, it is necessary to identify the third parties that will be entitled to benefit from the access to the data (Section 6.4.1), to determine the

---

1763. Communication from the Commission, Guidance on the application of the referral mechanism set out in Article 22 of the Merger Regulation to certain categories of cases, *supra*, p. 5.

1764. *Ibid.*

1765. *Ibid.*, p. 1.

1766. In the context of this Section, this expression relates to a 'dominant undertaking' in cases of an abuse of a dominant position, to a 'non-dominant undertaking with relative market power' in cases of an abuse of economic dependence, and to a 'merged entity having significant market power' in cases of input foreclosure in vertical mergers.

1767. On these alternative remedies, *see* references in footnote 567.

categories of data that should be shared (Section 6.4.2), and to consider a potential remuneration for the large data holder (Section 6.4.3). Finally, the potential anticompetitive effects of such a data sharing remedy will need to be considered (Section 6.4.4).

6.4.1 Identification of the Third Parties That Will Be Entitled to Benefit from the Data Sharing Remedy

297. Imposing a compulsory B2B data sharing remedy on a large data holder first requires identifying the third parties that should benefit from the access to such data. Indeed, as the aim of the remedy is to restore competition on the markets at hand, the remedy should not create *erga omnes* rights of access, but should only grant access rights to certain well-identified undertakings. In this regard, and as outlined respectively in Sections 6.1 to 6.3, in the case of a refusal to share data leading to an abuse of dominant position, the data sharing remedy should only benefit third parties for whom the access to the dominant undertaking's data is indispensable to operate a business on a downstream market.[1768] In the case of a refusal to share data leading to an abuse of economic dependence, the data sharing remedy should only benefit third parties that are dependent on the non-dominant undertaking's data in order to operate a business on a downstream market.[1769] Finally, in the case of input foreclosure by a merged entity, the shared data should only benefit third parties that would be unable to operate on the downstream market if they were foreclosed from accessing the merged entity's data.[1770]

What is thus common, in all three cases, is that an access seeker will have to demonstrate that it cannot collect the data itself, nor access it via another undertaking, and that it needs it to operate on a downstream market. However, the threshold for demonstrating such an absence of alternative is different in the three cases, as, for instance, the threshold for demonstrating the indispensability of a data set implies an objective assessment and is much higher than the threshold for demonstrating the dependence on the access to a data set, which requires both an objective and a subjective assessment.[1771]

In light of the above, it is thus apparent that this requirement of the identification of the third parties benefitting from the data sharing remedy is inextricably linked with the requirement to determine the categories of data that should be shared by the large data holder, to which I now turn.

1768. *See* points 238-242. However, this indispensability condition should arguably not apply to constructive refusals to share data (*see* point 234).
1769. *See* points 268-275.
1770. *See* points 287-289.
1771. *See* points 238-242, 268-275 and 287-289.

6.4.2 Determination of the Categories of Data That Should Be Shared

298. Imposing a compulsory B2B data sharing remedy on a large data holder also requires determining the categories of data that should be shared. As the primary purpose of such a data sharing remedy is to tackle market failures[1772] deriving from a lack of data sharing,[1773] I argue that the remedy should cover larger amounts of (aggregated) personal data pertaining to multiple individuals and/or non-personal data, rather than smaller quantities of data linked to a specific individual.[1774] It should be outlined from the outset that this will require a careful articulation between personal data protection law and competition law, which will be tackled below in a separate Section.[1775]

In order to determine the concrete categories of data that should be covered by the remedy, I suggest to consider the data typology that has been proposed in Part I, Chapter 1, Section 1.3. As a reminder, I suggested a common holistic approach for both personal and non-personal data, which is composed of four categories of data, namely actively provided data, observed data, inferred/derived data and acquired data.

299. The third category of data ('acquired data') should arguably be excluded from the scope of the remedy as, in principle, if the large data holder has been able to acquire the said data from a third party, the access seeker should normally also be able to acquire the same data from such third party. In such a scenario, there would be no reason to compel the large data holder to share such data with the access seeker.

300. Instead, the key question is to determine whether the data sharing remedy should only cover the large data holder's actively provided and observed data or whether it should also extend to its inferred/derived data. When answering this question, it should be kept in mind that while a data sharing remedy would entail benefits for the access seeker, this could also entail potential negative effects on the data holder's business interests. Indeed, data sharing generates costs for the data holder, which must be balanced with the potential benefits deriving from the sharing.[1776]

301. In this perspective, there are strong arguments to be made that the large data holder's actively provided and observed data should fall within the

---

1772. On these market failures *see* Part I, Chapter 2, Section 2.2.3.3.
1773. Communication from the Commission to the European Parliament, the Council, the European Economic and Social Committee and the Committee of the Regions, '*A European Strategy for Data*', 19 February 2020, COM(2020) 66, pp. 3, 5, 8 and 14. *See also* Communication from the Commission to the European Parliament, the Council, the European Economic and Social Committee and the Committee of the Regions, '*Shaping Europe's Digital Future*', Brussels, 19 February 2020, COM(2020) 67, p. 8.
1774. *See* Part I, Chapter 3, Section 3.2.
1775. *See* Part III, Chapter 7, Section 7.2.
1776. *See* Part I, Chapter 2, Section 2.2.3.5.

scope of the data sharing remedy. Indeed, the true value of data does not generally stem from its mere collection, but rather from the information and knowledge that can be derived and inferred from this primary data.[1777] These actively provided and observed data are thus 'a valuable input for data-intensive business models in the digital economy'.[1778] Yet, in markets which are highly concentrated and where only a handful of undertakings can observe the individuals' activity, 'observed data is not ubiquitously available, and it is also usually neither feasible nor socially desirable to duplicate the collection of the same observed data'.[1779] This explains why, in practice, access requests are frequently targeted at 'observed data, which often cannot be replicated, and at [actively provided] data that would take a significant amount of effort to volunteer again'.[1780]

302. The justification for the inclusion of these actively provided and observed data in the scope of the data sharing remedy will arguably even be stronger if these have been collected as a by-product of the large data holder's core economic activity, rather than as the object of its core economic activity.[1781] This is notably due to the fact that data that are collected as a by-product of a core economic activity are difficult to replicate by another firm that is interested in this data rather than in the core economic activity (drilling oil, selling grocery goods, providing health services, etc.).[1782] This might create 'a two-level entry problem that may erect high entry barriers in the data-collection market'.[1783] Moreover, the (incentive) costs of sharing this data in both scenarios are arguably different. Indeed, requiring the sharing of data collected as a by-product will arguably generate lower incentives costs for the large data holder than requiring the sharing of data collected as the object of its core economic activity because, in the former case, data are not collected for the sake of a data-centric business, but rather in order to facilitate the pursuit of the undertaking's core economic activity for which data are a mean and not a goal. Therefore, the large data holder has

1777. D. Rubinfeld and M. Gal, 'Access Barriers to Big Data', *Arizona Law Review*, 2017, Vol. 59, p. 342. *See also* C. Argenton and J. Prüfer, 'Search Engine Competition with Network Externalities', *Journal of Competition Law and Economics*, 2012, Vol. 8(1), p. 73; V. Mayer-Schönberger and Y. Padova, 'Regime Change? Enabling Big Data Through Europe's New Data Protection Regulation', *supra*, p. 320.

1778. J. Krämer, P. Senellart and A. de Streel, 'Making Data Portability More Effective for the Digital Economy', *CERRE Report*, 2020, available at https://www.cerre.eu/publications/report-making-data-portability-more-effective-digital-economy, p. 55. *See also* R. Feasey and A. de Streel, 'Data Sharing for Digital Market Contestability', *supra*, p. 16.

1779. J. Krämer, P. Senellart and A. de Streel, 'Making Data Portability More Effective for the Digital Economy', *supra*, p. 53.

1780. J. Crémer, Y.-A. de Montjoye and H. Schweitzer, 'Competition Policy for the Digital Era', *supra*, p. 101.

1781. On this distinction, *see* point 12.

1782. D. Rubinfeld and M. Gal, 'Access Barriers to Big Data', *supra*, p. 357.

1783. *Ibid.*, p. 377.

to collect these data in any case for the pursuit of its core economic activity, and its incentive to collect the data will thus only be marginally affected by a data sharing obligation.

To be sure, this does not mean that requiring the sharing does not entail any costs at all in terms of innovation and incentives to collect the data, but rather that these costs will be lower. This has to be balanced with the fact that these data generated as a by-product could be reused for other purposes, potentially not linked to the undertaking's core activity, thus generating additional value for society. To give an example, one could think of data collected by sensors on machines in an assembly line, which could be used for other purposes. Indeed, these data are not collected and structured as a goal in itself, but as a by-product of the core economic activity, e.g., assembling cars in a factory, as a means to increase the efficiency of production.

Additionally, taking this factor into consideration is in line with the analogous discussions pertaining to the 'spin-off effect' for the sui generis database right, according to which it is questioned whether databases that are by-products ('spin-offs') of a main or other activity of the data producer should also be protected by the sui generis database right.[1784] Indeed, in some cases, protecting these spin-off databases could give rise to absolute or unwanted natural monopolies.[1785]

303. Nevertheless, while this distinction could have merit when assessing the balance between the benefits and the costs of imposing the data sharing remedy, it must be underlined that, in practice, it might be extremely difficult to determine whether a specific data set has been collected as a by-product or as the object of the large data holder's core economic activity. Indeed, this notion of 'core economic activity' is evolutive.[1786] In many cases, firms will first start to collect data passively, as a by-product of their core economic

1784. On this 'spin-off effect' theory, *see, inter alia*, E. Derclaye, 'Databases Sui Generis Right: Should I Adopt the Spin Off Theory?', *European Intellectual Property Review*, 2004, Issue 26(9), pp. 402-413; B. Hugenholtz, 'Program Schedules, Event Data and Telephone Subscriber Listings under the Database Directive – The "Spin-Off" Doctrine in the Netherlands and Elsewhere in Europe', *Paper Presented at 11th Annual Conference on International Intellectual Property Law and Policy, Fordham University School of Law, New York, April 14-25*, 2003, available at https://www.ivir.nl/publicaties/download/spinofffordham.pdf.

1785. E. Derclaye, 'Databases Sui Generis Right: Should I Adopt the Spin Off Theory?', *supra*, p. 412; B. Hugenholtz, 'Program Schedules, Event Data and Telephone Subscriber Listings under the Database Directive – The "Spin-Off" Doctrine in the Netherlands and Elsewhere in Europe', *supra*, p. 7.

1786. *See* point 12.

activity, but once they realise the value that such data can have, they will tend to move towards more active data collection approaches.[1787]

304. On the other hand, I argue that, in order to preserve the business interests of the data holder, its inferred/derived data should not be covered by the data sharing remedy. This is because these types of data will often be the most valuable for data holders, as this is where the real added-value of their product/service must be found.[1788] Indeed, as outlined by Krämer et al., 'such data is the result of innovation efforts (e.g. in data analytics) with the intent to derive actionable insights that are then the basis for competition in digital markets'.[1789] Accordingly, excluding such categories of data from the scope of the remedy would prevent potential competitors of the data holders from benefiting from these actionable insights in which the data holders have heavily invested, and would incentivise them to derive such actionable insights themselves on the basis of the actively provided/observed data that they would obtain through the remedy. Indeed, inferred/derived data should arguably be seen as 'the basis for competition between data-intensive firms, whereas [actively provided] data and observed data are the "raw data" inputs'.[1790] As the focus of competition is shifted from collection to analysis considerations, this is also likely to stimulate innovation.[1791]

305. To conclude on the determination of the categories of data that should be shared, two additional remarks must be formulated. First, I argue that the concrete categories of personal and non-personal data covered by the remedy should not be *all of* the large data holder's actively provided and observed data, but rather only a *specific subset* of these actively provided and observed data, which will need to be determined on a case-by-case basis. This is because the requirement to identify the scope of the data covered by the remedy is inextricably linked with the above-mentioned requirement of the identification of the third parties benefitting from the data sharing remedy. More specifically, the remedy should be limited to the actively provided and observed data that are considered as indispensable to operate a business on a downstream market, in the case of an abuse of dominant position;[1792] to the non-dominant undertaking's actively provided and observed data on which the access seeker is dependent in order to operate a business on a

1787. OECD, *Consumer Data Rights and Competition*, *supra*, pp. 15-16. For an example in the retail business, *see* J. Turow, *The Aisles Have Eyes: How Retailers Track Your Shopping, Strip Your Privacy, and Define Your Power*, New Haven, Yale University Press, 2017.

1788. *See* point 17.

1789. J. Krämer, D. Schnurr and S. Broughton Micova, 'The Role of Data for Digital Markets Contestability', *supra*, p. 93.

1790. *Ibid.*, p. 17.

1791. J. Krämer, P. Senellart and A. de Streel, 'Making Data Portability More Effective for the Digital Economy', *supra*, p. 9.

1792. *See* points 238-242.

downstream market, in the case of an abuse of economic dependence;[1793] or to the merged entity's important actively provided and observed data, without which the access seeker would be unable to operate on a downstream market, in the case of input foreclosures in vertical mergers.[1794]

Second, in order to ensure that its data sharing remedy will efficiently tackle the anticompetitive practice that it aims to address, the competition authority will also have to determine whether the data sharing remedy should be static or dynamic. Indeed, in certain situations, it might not be sufficient to impose the static sharing of data through a one-shot (or periodic) bulk data transfer(s). Rather, due to the digital economy's dynamic nature, it might be necessary to consider the imposition of a more dynamic data sharing remedy that would guarantee that the access seeker has access to the large data holder's relevant actively provided and observed data, via APIs,[1795] on a constant basis and in (near) real time. As the latter type of remedy will entail higher implementation costs for the large data holder, it should however only be imposed when the benefits of such dynamic real-time access trump its costs. This will thus require a case-by-case assessment by the competition authority.

6.4.3 Remuneration of the Large Data Holder

306. One way to attenuate the costs of the sharing for the large data holder would be to provide for a potential remuneration. Indeed, this would counterbalance the possible stifling effects that such a duty to share (aggregated) personal data pertaining to multiple individuals and/or non-personal data could have on these data holder's business incentives.

As, due to the Arrow information paradox,[1796] the value of data is difficult to assess, it is advisable for the competition authority not to impose a specific price for the sharing, but rather to 'rely on more open terms provided they are sufficiently precise for the data owner to determine with enough legal certainty the price to charge'.[1797] In this perspective, the competition authority could require the large data holder to propose a FRAND (Fair Reasonable And Non-Discriminatory) price for the sharing, by analogy with the licensing-fee requirements used in the context of the Standard Essential Patents (SEPs).[1798] While this would be more comfortable for competition authorities than setting the concrete price themselves, it is important to outline that there are also a significant number of uncertainties

1793. *See* points 268-275.
1794. *See* points 287-289.
1795. *See* definition at footnote 1005.
1796. *See* point 109.
1797. R. Feasey and A. de Streel, 'Data Sharing for Digital Market Contestability', *supra*, p. 38.
1798. D. Rubinfeld and M. Gal, 'Access Barriers to Big Data', *supra*, p. 373.

in determining what constitutes a FRAND price, as illustrated by the numerous discussions around this term in the realm of SEPs.[1799]

In this regard, Drexl points out that the *Huawei*[1800] judgment of the European Court of Justice, where the Court created a negotiation framework for the licensing of SEPs,[1801] could provide inspiration to deal with data sharing cases and could assist the parties to reach an agreement on the data sharing price.[1802] This negotiation framework, applied to data, could be the following:

- Once the access seeker has expressed its willingness to pay a FRAND remuneration for the data, the data holder must present a specific written offer specifying the price and the way in which it is to be calculated.
- It is then for the access seeker to respond diligently to that offer in good faith and without delaying tactics.
- Should the access seeker not accept the offer made to it, it has to submit to the data holder, promptly and in writing, a specific counter-offer that corresponds to FRAND remuneration.
- Where no agreement is reached on the details of the FRAND remuneration following the counter-offer, the parties should, by common agreement, request that the price be determined by an independent third party. To set this price, I argue that the independent third party could, for instance, rely on the 'baseball arbitration' mechanism, originally used in the USA for baseball salary negotiations.[1803] According to this mechanism, each party proposes a price to the third party, who is tasked with choosing the price that appears to be the most 'reasonable' under the circumstances of the cases. This forces each party to restrain themselves from proposing unreasonable

1799. *See*, for instance, D. Geradin, A. Layne-Farrar and N. Petit, *EU Competition Law and Economics*, Oxford, Oxford University Press, 2012, p. 457; D. Geradin, 'Ten Years of DG Competition Effort to Provide Guidance on the Application of Competition Rules to the Licensing of Standard-Essential Patents: Where Do We Stand?', 21 January 2013, available at https://ssrn.com/abstract=2204359, pp. 7-8; C. Graham and J. Morton, 'Latest Developments in Standards, Patents and FRAND licensing', *European Intellectual Property Review*, 2014, Vol. 36(11), pp. 700-706; R. Stern, 'What Are Reasonable and Non-discriminatory Terms for licensing a Standard-essential Patent?', *European Intellectual Property Review*, 2015, Vol. 37(9), pp. 549-557; J. Drexl, 'Designing Competitive Markets for Industrial Data – Between Propertisation and Access', *Max Planck Institute for Innovation & Competition Research Paper No. 16-13*, 31 October 2016, available at https://ssrn.com/abstract=2862975, p. 55; ECJ, *Huawei*, 16 July 2015, C-170/13, EU:C:2015:477.
1800. ECJ, *Huawei*, 16 July 2015, C-170/13, EU:C:2015:477.
1801. *Ibid.*, §§ 60-69.
1802. J. Drexl, 'Designing Competitive Markets for Industrial Data – Between Propertisation and Access', *supra*, p. 55. *See also* H. Richter and P. Slowinski, 'The Data Sharing Economy: On the Emergence of New Intermediaries', *supra*, pp. 4-29.
1803. *See* http://www.arbitration.com/articles/what-is-baseball-arbitration.aspx.

prices, as they know that if they suggest an extravagant price, while the other party suggests a more 'reasonable' one, the independent third party will pick the other party's price. A variant form is the 'night baseball arbitration', where the independent third party first decides itself what could be a reasonable price and then looks at the party's proposals and chooses whichever is the closest to the price it first considered.

307. The independent third party mentioned above could be one of the national authorities that the European Commission's proposal for a Data Governance Act suggests to appoint in order to supervise *voluntary* B2B data sharing with trusted data intermediaries.[1804] Indeed, these national authorities will arguably be in a good position to assess the appropriateness of the proposed price for the data sharing, due to their expertise with *voluntary* data sharing. It could thus also be resorted to them in the context of *compulsory* data sharing imposed by a competition law remedy. Moreover, if technical experts are appointed within these authorities, they will arguably also be in a better position to determine the technical means of the sharing (one-shot data transfer; daily/weekly/monthly transfers of bulks of data; real-time access[1805] via APIs, etc.) if the parties do not find an agreement in this regard. This would relieve the competition authorities from assuming this role for which they are ill-suited.[1806] This is especially so in cases where the sharing needs to be continuous, for instance, in order to ensure interoperability, as the competition authorities are not well equipped to deal with these issues.[1807] To fulfil these tasks, these national authorities could be assisted by the Support Centre for Data Sharing, created in 2019, which has been tasked with collecting the best practices and existing model contract terms for *voluntary* data sharing agreements,[1808] and which could thus provide valuable insights.[1809] Moreover, they could be assisted by the future European Data

1804. *See* Recitals 22-34 and Articles 13 and 2-25 of the Proposal for a Regulation of the European Parliament and of the Council on European data governance (Data Governance Act), 25 November 2020, COM(2020) 767 final.

1805. The 'freshness' and 'up-to-dateness' of the data can indeed be of the utmost importance for certain business models. *See* V. Kathuria and J. Globocnik, 'Exclusionary Conduct in Data-Driven Markets', *supra*, pp. 18-19.

1806. *Ibid.*, p. 17.

1807. J. Crémer, Y.-A. de Montjoye and H. Schweitzer, 'Competition Policy for the Digital Era', *supra*, p. 10.

1808. Commission Staff Working Document establishing a guidance on sharing private sector data in the European data economy accompanying the Communication '*Towards a common European data space*', Brussels, 25 April 2018, SWD(2018) 125 final, p. 6.

1809. *See* Commission Staff Working Document, Impact assessment report accompanying the document '*Proposal for a Regulation of the European Parliament and of the Council on European data governance: An enabling framework for common European data spaces (Data Governance Act)*', Brussels, 25 November 2020, SWD(2020) 295 final, p. 55.

Innovation Board, which is a formal expert group that the European Commission suggests to create in order to implement the future horizontal governance framework for *voluntary* data sharing, and which should support the European Commission's work on technical standardisation and interoperability to facilitate data sharing.[1810]

308. Independently of the determination of the body that should monitor this negotiation process, I argue that several factors should, in any case, be taken into consideration when determining the price of the sharing remedy. On the one hand, in cases where a refusal to share data leads to the termination of an existing business relation, the price of the sharing should arguably remain the same as the one that existed prior to the termination, for a reasonable period of time to be determined on a case-by-case basis. For instance, this reasonable period of time could correspond to the above-mentioned negotiation period. Indeed, although there might be an objective justification for a price increase, 'freezing' the price during this reasonable period should ensure that the access seeker will be put in a more comfortable bargaining position during this negotiation period. Accordingly, if the data was shared for free prior to the refusal to keep sharing the data in the future, like in the *PeopleBrowsr v. Twitter* and *hiQ v. LinkedIn* cases mentioned above,[1811] the sharing should arguably remain free during this negotiation period.

On the other hand, and provided that such a difference can be established in practice,[1812] the sharing price for data generated as a by-product of a core economic activity should, arguably, be lower than the sharing price for data whose collection, structuration and analysis is the core economic activity of the large data holder. This is because sharing data collected as a by-product will arguably generate lower incentives costs for the large data holder than sharing data collected as part of the data holder's core economic activity.[1813]

6.4.4 Factoring the Potential Anticompetitive Effects of the Data Sharing Remedy

309. Last but not least, the data sharing remedy will have to be carefully designed in order to avoid the creation of potential anticompetitive effects. This would notably be the case if the large data holder and the specific third parties receiving the data (i.e., the data recipients) decided to use the shared data in order to enter into anticompetitive agreements, prohibited by Article

1810. *See* Recitals 40 and 41 and Articles 26 and 27 of the Proposal for a Data Governance Act. *See also* Commission Staff Working Document, Impact assessment report accompanying the Data Governance Act, *supra*, p. 54.
1811. *See* point 266.
1812. *See* points 12 and 303.
1813. *See* point 302.

101 of the TFEU.[1814] Indeed, 'Article 101 TFEU can stand in the way of data sharing in situations where the exchange of information among competitors gives rise to collusion under Article 101(1) TFEU and the resulting restriction of competition cannot be justified under Article 101(3) TFEU by showing that the procompetitive effects outweigh the anticompetitive effects.'[1815]

Arguably, this collusion risk might not materialise if the competition authority solely compels the large data holder to share the data with specific data recipients, but does not provide for a reciprocal data flow from the recipients towards the data holder, nor for data sharing between the various recipients. This is especially so because, in order to preserve the business interests of the data holder, only actively provided and observed data will be shared with the data recipients, and not the large data holder's inferred/derived data, which are the most commercially sensitive.[1816]

On the other hand, this collusion risk must be factored if the competition authority envisages imposing to the large data holder the obligation to pool some of its data with other data held by the specific third parties 'receiving' the data. Indeed, in such a scenario, there is a risk that the procompetitive goal of the data sharing remedy could be misused by the participants to the data pooling agreement, for instance, to fix prices, limit production or share markets or sources of supply.[1817] Therefore, if the competition authority wishes to impose such a data pooling remedy, it will need to ensure that the procompetitive effects of the data pool outweigh its potential anticompetitive effects.

However, at this point in time, this might be difficult to assess for the competition authority, as there is some uncertainty on the way in which Article 101 TFEU should be applied to data pooling arrangements.[1818] Indeed, while the Commission's Guidelines on Horizontal Agreements outline several factors that must be taken into consideration in order to weigh these anticompetitive risks – such as 'the strategic nature of the information,

1814. On this issue, *see* B. Lundqvist, 'Competition and Data Pools', *Journal of European Consumer and Market Law*, 2018, Vol. 7(4), pp. 146-154; J. Crémer, Y.-A. de Montjoye and H. Schweitzer, 'Competition Policy for the Digital Era', *supra*, pp. 92-98; I. Graef, T. Tombal and A. de Streel, 'Limits and Enablers of Data Sharing: An Analytical Framework for EU Competition, Data Protection and Consumer Law', *TILEC Discussion Paper DP 2019-005*, November 2019, available at https://ssrn.com/abstract=2956308, pp. 7-8; H. Richter and P. Slowinski, 'The Data Sharing Economy: On the Emergence of New Intermediaries', *International Review of Intellectual Property and Competition Law*, 2019, Vol. 50(1), pp. 22-23; B. Martens, et al., 'Business to Business Data Sharing', *supra*, p. 24.

1815. I. Graef, T. Tombal and A. de Streel, 'Limits and Enablers of Data Sharing', *supra*, p. 7.

1816. *See* Part III, Chapter 6, Section 6.4.2.

1817. Article 101.1, a)-c) of the TFEU.

1818. I. Graef, T. Tombal and A. de Streel, 'Limits and Enablers of Data Sharing', *supra*, p. 7.

the market coverage of the firms involved, the individualised or aggregated nature of the company information exchanged, the age of the data, the frequency of the information exchange, the public or non-public nature of the information, and whether the exchange of information is public or non-public'[1819] – competition issues entailed by data pooling are still relatively new and under-researched, and several voices have been raised regarding the need for more legal clarity on these issues.[1820] In fact, this is one of the goals of the current revision process of these Guidelines, which will likely be concluded in the beginning of 2022. In the meantime, it can be recommended to competition authorities to exercise caution and restraint regarding the imposition of data pooling as a remedy, until more clarity is provided on the matter.

310. However, if, despite this existing uncertainty, a competition authority wants to impose a data pooling remedy, it will, at the very least, have to ensure that the pool will not lead to the foreclosing of competitors from the market, due to a denial of access to the pool, or to the granting of the access to the pool on less favourable terms.[1821] In this regard, the competition authority could take inspiration from past cases. For instance, in the *Asnef-Equifax* case, the European Court of Justice assessed the compatibility with Article 101 TFEU of a register that allowed Spanish financial institutions to share solvency and credit information data about their clients in order to evaluate the risks of non-repayment of loans.[1822] In that case, the Court held that such an information sharing practice would be less likely to restrict competition if the relevant market is not highly concentrated and if the access to the information sharing tool is accessible in a non-discriminatory manner to all the actors active in the relevant market.[1823] Similarly, it should be highlighted that the European Commission has recently sent a Statement of Objections to Insurance Ireland, which is an association of companies active in the insurance sector in Ireland covering over 90% of the Irish motor

1819. *Ibid*; Communication from the Commission, Guidelines on the applicability of Article 101 of the Treaty on the Functioning of the European Union to horizontal co-operation agreements, 14 January 2011, 2011/C 11/01, §§ 86-94.

1820. *See*, *inter alia*, Commission Staff Working Document, Evaluation of the Horizontal Block Exemption Regulation, Brussels, 6 May 2021, SWD(2021) 103 final, pp. 29, 43, 57 and 68; J. Crémer, Y.-A. de Montjoye and H. Schweitzer, 'Competition Policy for the Digital Era', *supra*, pp. 9 and 92-98; B. Lundqvist, 'Competition and Data Pools', *supra*, p. 153.

1821. Commission Staff Working Document, Evaluation of the Horizontal Block Exemption Regulation, *supra*, p. 29; J. Crémer, Y.-A. de Montjoye and H. Schweitzer, 'Competition Policy for the Digital Era', *supra*, pp. 9 and 92-93 and 97-98.

1822. ECJ, *Asnef Equifax and Administración des Estado*, 23 November 2006, C-238/05, EU:C:2006:734.

1823. *Ibid.*, §§ 58-61; I. Graef, T. Tombal and A. de Streel, 'Limits and Enablers of Data Sharing', *supra*, p. 7.

vehicle insurance market.[1824] This is because the Commission considers that Insurance Ireland has infringed competition law by denying access to its 'Insurance Link' data sharing platform (which comprises a non-life insurance claims data pool) to certain insurers and their agents, as this puts the latter at a competitive disadvantage.

Moreover, the competition authority will need to ensure that the pooling remedy will not discourage the participants in the pool from differentiating and improving their own data collection and analytics processes (which would hamper innovation), and that it will not lead to an anticompetitive information exchange of competitively sensitive information (although, as outlined above, this risk should be quite limited as only actively provided and observed data will be shared, and not inferred/derived data, which are the most sensitive and valuable).[1825] Regarding the latter concern, competition authorities could build on the valuable insights provided by Lundqvist:

> [A]s a rule of thumb, pools where the parties share relevant strategic and competitive information, such as pricelists, future output prediction and new innovations, should be considered at risk of being anticompetitive, according to Article 101(1) TFEU, while still possibly being available for an exemption under Article 101(3) TFEU. On the other end of the spectrum, data pools containing technical information for the development of new products and services could be regarded as benign research or technical developments cooperations, and should be judged in analogy with R&D collaborations, standard-setting efforts or, to some extent, patent pools. We could add to this latter group also the data pools facilitating interoperability between devices and products, such as connected cars.[1826]

311. In light of the above, if a competition authority envisages imposing a data pooling remedy, it will need to carefully balance the potential procompetitive and anticompetitive effects of this option. As there is much uncertainty pertaining to this question, competition authorities might be better off imposing, for the time being, 'unilateral' data sharing remedies on large data holders (which do not imply a reciprocal sharing of data from the data recipients nor any form of data exchange between the data recipients), at least until the Commission has completed the revision of its Guidelines on Horizontal Agreements.

1824. European Commission, 'Antitrust: Commission sends Statement of Objections to Insurance Ireland', *Press release n° IP/21/3081*, 18 June 2021, available at https://ec.europa.eu/commission/presscorner/detail/en/ip_21_3081.

1825. Commission Staff Working Document, Evaluation of the Horizontal Block Exemption Regulation, *supra*, p. 29; J. Crémer, Y.-A. de Montjoye and H. Schweitzer, 'Competition Policy for the Digital Era', *supra*, pp. 9 and 92-93 and 96-97.

1826. B. Lundqvist, 'Competition and Data Pools', *supra*, p. 150.

312. To conclude this Section, the above-mentioned overarching considerations pertaining to compulsory B2B data sharing as a competition law remedy are summarised in Table 6.1.

Table 6.1 Overarching Considerations Pertaining to Compulsory B2B Data Sharing as a Competition Law Remedy

	Compulsory B2B Data Sharing as a Competition Law Remedy
Data holders subject to the sharing obligation	Undertakings abusing their dominant position (essential facilities doctrine).[1827] Undertakings abusing their 'relative market power' (abuse of economic dependence).[1828] Merged entities having 'significant market power' and foreclosing the access to an important input (input foreclosure in vertical mergers).[1829]
Data recipients entitled to benefit from the sharing obligation	Only those:[1830] – for whom the access to the dominant undertaking's data is 'indispensable';[1831] – that are 'dependent' on the 'non-dominant undertaking' data; or – that need access to the 'important data' of the merged entity; in order to operate on a downstream market.
Types of data covered by the sharing obligation	Only actively provided and observed data (not acquired, nor inferred/derived data).[1832] Not all of the large data holder's actively provided and observed data, but rather only a specific subset of these actively provided and observed data, which will need to be determined on a case-by-case basis.[1833] Personal data should only be shared to the extent that this complies with the GDPR's principles and that there are lawful basis of processing allowing the sharing.[1834]

1827. *See* Part III, Chapter 6, Section 6.1.
1828. *See* Part III, Chapter 6, Section 6.2.
1829. *See* Part III, Chapter 6, Section 6.3.
1830. *See* Part III, Chapter 6, Section 6.4.1.
1831. However, this indispensability condition should arguably not apply to constructive refusals to share data (*see* points 234 and 238-242).
1832. *See* Part III, Chapter 6, Section 6.4.2.
1833. *See* point 305.
1834. *See* Part III, Chapter 7, Section 7.2.

Remuneration of the data holder as compensation for the sharing obligation	FRAND remuneration (lower price for data generated as by-product than as core economic activity of the data holder).[1835] If the data holder(s) and data recipient(s) fail to agree on the data sharing price, price could be determined by an independent third party.[1836]
Technical implementation of the sharing obligation	Depending on the case, could be a static or dynamic data sharing remedy. The latter should only be imposed when the benefits of real-time access trump its costs.[1837] An independent third party could also determine the technical means of the sharing if the parties do not agree on them.[1838] If a data pooling remedy is envisaged, the potential procompetitive and anticompetitive effects of this option will need to be balanced[1839]

6.5 THE ISSUE OF THE TIME-CONSUMING PROCESS OF COMPETITION INTERVENTION

313. In order for the B2B data sharing remedy imposed by the competition authority to be truly efficient, this competition intervention must also be timely. Indeed, if a long period of time elapses before the competition authority is able to establish the competition law infringement resulting from a refusal to share data, and to determine the appropriate data sharing remedy,[1840] such a remedy may come too late for the access seeker. As outlined by Bourreau and de Streel, 'the timing of antitrust decisions is often too slow and not aligned with the timing of market evolutions. This time lag is particularly harmful in the digital sector because, on the one hand, antitrust actions often take more time than average as new and complex technical and legal issues are raised while, on the other hand, markets are evolving more quickly than average due to rapid technological progress'.[1841] As a result, the downstream market on which the access seeker wishes to operate, but for which it needs the access to the large data holder's data to do so, might tip in favour of the latter due to strong network effects. Consequently, the access seeker might be driven out of such market, due to the large data holder's

1835. *See* Part III, Chapter 6, Section 6.4.3.
1836. *See* points 306 and 307.
1837. *See* Part III, Chapter 6, Section 6.4.2.
1838. *See* Part III, Chapter 6, Section 6.4.3.
1839. *See* Part III, Chapter 6, Section 6.4.4.
1840. *See* Part III, Chapter 6, Sections 6.4.1 to 6.4.4.
1841. M. Bourreau and A. de Streel, 'Digital Conglomerates and EU Competition Policy', *supra*, p. 33.

refusal to share, before the competition intervention process is completed. Accordingly, there have been growing calls to speed up this competition process in order to better match these rapid digital market evolutions.[1842]

6.5.1 Exploring the Use of Interim Measures and Market Investigations

314. In substance, three evolutions have been suggested in order to tackle the above-mentioned issue. The first suggestion, which I will simply briefly mention, is to create, like in Spain, deadlines for antitrust cases, similarly to what currently exists for merger cases, in order to ensure that these cases do not drag on for lengthy periods of time.[1843] Naturally, the imposition of such deadlines should be accompanied by safeguards in order to 'alleviate adverse case selection and to ensure that the agencies will not focus merely on the easy cases that can be decided quickly and ignore the hard cases that can be more useful for the agencies and for the markets'.[1844]

315. The second suggestion is that competition authorities should more frequently rely, in digital markets, on interim measures, which could be imposed on the large data holder, pending the outcome of the investigation, and which would be accompanied by financial penalties in cases of non-compliance.[1845] Indeed, Article 8 of Council Regulation on the implementation of Articles 101 and 102 of the TFEU provides that:

1. In cases of urgency due to the risk of serious and irreparable damage to competition, the Commission, acting on its own initiative may by decision, on the basis of a prima facie finding of infringement, order interim measures.
2. A decision under paragraph 1 shall apply for a specified period of time and may be renewed in so far this is necessary and appropriate.[1846]

1842. *See* footnote 62 for an overview.
1843. M. Bourreau and A. de Streel, 'Digital Conglomerates and EU Competition Policy', *supra*, p. 34.
1844. *Ibid.*
1845. *See* H. Schweitzer, et al., 'A New Competition Framework for the Digital Economy', *supra*, pp. 71-73; Competition and Markets Authority, 'Online Platforms and Digital Advertising: Market Study Final Report', 1 July 2020, available at https://www.gov.uk/cma-cases/online-platforms-and-digital-advertising-market-study, p. 348; Autorité de la concurrence, 'Contribution de l'Autorité de la concurrence au débat sur la politique de concurrence et les enjeux numériques', *supra*, pp. 2 and 6; M. Bourreau and A. de Streel, 'Digital Conglomerates and EU Competition Policy', *supra*, p. 33; P. Picht, 'Towards an Access Regime for Mobility Data', *supra*, p. 961.
1846. Council Regulation (EC) No. 1/2003 of 16 December 2002 on the implementation of the rules on competition laid down in Articles 81 and 82 of the Treaty, *OJ L 1/1*, 4 January 2003.

Yet, these interim measures have rarely been used by the European Commission in the past 20 years, notably because the interim measure that it had imposed in the *IMS Health* case in 2001[1847] – by which it had required IMS Health to license its brick structure, considered as being indispensable, to NDC Health[1848] – had been suspended by the Court of First Instance.[1849] Moreover, such interim measures entail high procedural requirements for the European Commission, which could delay the decision in the main proceedings, and the European Court of Justice has a wide leeway in deciding whether to suspend these measures during annulment proceedings brought before it.[1850]

However, it has to be pointed out that the European Commission has renewed with the use of such interim measures in its *Broadcom* decision of October 2019.[1851] This could be an encouraging sign that it is intending to rely more on such tools in the future, and this could reduce the time lag between competition law procedures and the rapid evolution of the digital markets 'without sacrificing the due process and the quality of the final decision'.[1852] Importantly, when assessing whether to impose such measures in the future, the European Commission will need to weigh the interests of all of the parties concerned, namely the 'interest in the protection of competition and the interest of the companies affected by the interim measure; and (…) [i]n the case of high risks to competition, serious doubts as to the legality of the conduct may suffice to order interim measures, particularly in the earliest stages of examination'.[1853] Yet, while these high risks to competition may indeed exist, in some circumstances, in the digital sector due to dynamic market evolutions and the risks of fast market tipping, it might be more tricky to raise serious doubts regarding the legality of the conduct at hand, as such conducts often raise new technical and legal issues.[1854]

1847. European Commission, *NDC Health/IMS Health: Interim measures*, 3 July 2001, COMP D3/38.044, *OJ L 59/18*.
1848. R. Feasey and A. de Streel, 'Data Sharing for Digital Market Contestability', *supra*, p. 58.
1849. CFI, *IMS Health, Inc. v. Commission of the European Communities*, 10 March 2005, T-184/01, EU:T:2005:95; H. Schweitzer, et al., 'A New Competition Framework for the Digital Economy', *supra*, p. 71.
1850. H. Schweitzer, et al., 'A New Competition Framework for the Digital Economy', *supra*, p. 71.
1851. European Commission, *Broadcom*, 16 October 2019, AT.40608; H. Schweitzer, M. Schalbruch, A. Wambach, et al., 'A New Competition Framework for the Digital Economy', *supra*, p. 71.
1852. M. Bourreau and A. de Streel, 'Digital Conglomerates and EU Competition Policy', *supra*, p. 33.
1853. H. Schweitzer, et al., 'A New Competition Framework for the Digital Economy', *supra*, pp. 71-72.
1854. M. Bourreau and A. de Streel, 'Digital Conglomerates and EU Competition Policy', *supra*, p. 33.

316. The third suggestion was the creation of a 'New Competition Tool', which would have allowed the European Commission to conduct market investigations in order to address structural market failures in a timely and effective manner, similar to what the Competition and Markets Authority can do in the UK.[1855] This is yet another measure that aims at ensuring that competition rules remain fit for an increasingly digital world.[1856] Indeed, to justify the creation of such a tool, the European Commission argued that there is a growing body of economic evidence suggesting the existence of structural competition problems that cannot be tackled under existing competition law rules (e.g., monopolisation strategies by non-dominant undertakings with market power) or, at least, not in the most effective manner (e.g., parallel leveraging strategies by dominant companies into multiple adjacent markets), and that this results in inefficient market outcomes.[1857] Indeed, as outlined by the European Commission's inception impact assessment of this 'New Competition Tool':

> A few large platforms have become gatekeepers for many digital and non-digital products and services. Underlying this development are market characteristics such as extreme economies of scale and scope, strong network effects, zero pricing and data dependency, as well as market dynamics favouring sudden and radical decreases in competition ('tipping') and 'winner-takes-most' scenarios. (…) [T]hese characteristics can make a position of market power or dominance, once acquired, difficult to contest.[1858]

For the European Commission, these structural competition problems are twofold.[1859] On the one hand, there are 'structural risks for competition', which are scenarios in which certain market characteristics (network effects, economies of scale and scope, lock-in effects, etc.) and the conduct of several undertakings operating in these markets (e.g., unilateral strategies by non-dominant companies to monopolise a market through anticompetitive means) create a threat for competition (e.g., risks of market tipping), which could be prevented through early intervention. On the other hand, there are 'structural lacks of competition', which are scenarios in which the structure

---

1855. European Commission, Inception Impact Assessment: '*New Competition Tool ("NCT")*', June 2020, Ares(2020)2836004, p. 1; S. Vezzoso, 'Competition Policy in Transition: Exploring Data Portability's Roles', *15th ASCOLA (Virtual) Conference*, June 2020, available at https://ssrn.com/abstract=3634736, pp. 18-19. For a criticism of this proposition, notably of its effectivity and of its ability to foster timelier competition intervention, *see* Freshfields Bruckhaus Deringer, 'New Competition Tool: Observations in the context of the Commission's Public Consultation', 8 September 2020, available at https://passle-net.s3.amazonaws.com/Passle/5832ca6d3d94760e8057a1b6/MediaLibrary/Document/2020-09-09-14-52-58-669-FreshfieldsSubmissionNewCT.pdf.
1856. Communication from the Commission, '*Shaping Europe's Digital Future*', *supra*, p. 8.
1857. European Commission, Inception Impact Assessment: '*New Competition Tool ("NCT")*', June 2020, Ares(2020)2836004, pp. 1-2.
1858. *Ibid.*, p. 1.
1859. *Ibid.*, p. 2.

of the market prevents it from working well and from delivering competitive outcomes due to systemic failures (high concentration and barriers of entry, lack of access to data, lock-ins, etc.).

In order to tackle these structural competition problems and to restore undistorted competition on these markets, the European Commission argued that it needed new tools at its disposal that would allow it to intervene in a timelier fashion, and that would provide it with more intervention powers than 'sector inquiries', which only empower it to request information from undertakings but not to impose remedies outside the scope of individual infringement procedures.[1860] Concretely, what was proposed was to adapt the EU competition law framework in order to allow the Commission, in close cooperation with national competition authorities, to conduct market investigations in order to 'intervene when a structural risk for competition or a structural lack of competition prevents the internal market from functioning properly. The tool would enable the Commission to impose behavioural and, where appropriate, structural remedies. The Commission could also recommend legislative action to improve the functioning of the market concerned. (...) [However] there would be no finding of an infringement, no fines and no damage claims'.[1861] Naturally, these market investigations would have to respect the rights of defence of the undertakings concerned.[1862] Such market investigations could be particularly useful to address systemic market tipping issues. Indeed, as outlined by Prüfer:

> Market tipping occurs in data-driven markets even if the [undertaking]'s conduct is flawless as it depends on data-driven indirect network effects, which are an unavoidable (and potentially very efficient) economic characteristic of such markets. Moreover, if a market is found to be data-driven, tipping can be predicted. [Anti-competitive behaviour] is not necessary to tip the market or to discourage competitors from innovating heavily. Therefore, what is needed is the option to intervene in such markets ex ante, that is, before the market has tipped and the [undertaking] can be accused of abusing its position (which perhaps it has not). Moreover, in order to avoid the cumbersome and lengthy process of repetitive legal cases, a quicker and more flexible tool that allows competition authorities to intervene in markets without invoking [a competition law infringement] is needed.[1863]

Four options were considered for the design of such a tool, as it could have applied either to competition concerns raised by dominant undertakings

1860. *Ibid.*, p. 3.
1861. *Ibid.*
1862. *Ibid.*, p. 4.
1863. J. Prüfer, 'Competition Policy and Data Sharing on Data-driven Markets', *Report for the Friedrich-Ebert-Stiftung*, 2020, available at http://library.fes.de/pdf-files/fes/15999.pdf, p. 9.

only or also to competition concerns raised by non-dominant undertakings, and either to some specific sectors only or horizontally to all sectors.[1864]

317. Eventually, the possibility to conduct market investigations has been included in the European Commission's proposal for a Digital Markets Act.[1865] However, it has been somewhat 'downgraded' compared to the initial proposal mentioned above, following concerns raised by the 'Regulatory scrutiny board', i.e., the European Commission's internal review panel.[1866]

According to this proposal, the European Commission can first conduct a market investigation in order to examine whether a provider of 'core platform services'[1867] should be designated as a 'gatekeeper'.[1868,1869] This can be done on its own initiative, or if three or more Member States request it and if there are reasonable grounds to open such an investigation.[1870] The Commission will have to communicate its preliminary findings within 6 months of the opening of the investigation and will have to close the investigation within 12 months of its opening.[1871] If the Commission designates as a gatekeeper a large data holder that does not yet benefit from an entrenched and durable position in its operations,[1872] but that it is foreseeable that it will enjoy such a position in the near future (likeliness of the market to tip), only the obligations that are appropriate and necessary to prevent this data holder from entrenching its position through unfair means shall be declared applicable to it.[1873]

Second, the European Commission can conduct a market investigation to determine whether a 'gatekeeper' 'has systematically infringed the obligations laid down in Articles 5 and 6 and has further strengthened or

1864. European Commission, Inception Impact Assessment: '*New Competition Tool ("NCT")*', June 2020, Ares(2020)2836004, p. 3.
1865. *See* Articles 14-17 of the Proposal for a Digital Markets Act.
1866. *See* S. Stolton, 'Blacklist Prohibitions to Be "Very Limited" to Large Platforms, Commission Says', 9 December 2020, available at https://www.euractiv.com/section/digital/news/blacklist-prohibitions-to-be-very-limited-to-large-platforms-commission-says/. *See also* Commission Staff Working Document, Impact assessment report accompanying the document '*Proposal for a Regulation of the European Parliament and of the Council on contestable and fair markets in the digital sector (Digital Markets Act)*', Brussels, 15 December 2020, SWD(2020) 363 final, pp. 77-78.
1867. *See* Article 1.2 of the Proposal for a Digital Markets Act. For a definition of these services, *see* Articles 2.2 and 2.5-2.11 of the Proposal.
1868. *See* Articles 2.1 and 3 of the Proposal for a Digital Markets Act. For more details on the designation of these gatekeepers, *see* points 384 and 385.
1869. Article 15 of the Proposal for a Digital Markets Act.
1870. Article 33 of the Proposal for a Digital Markets Act.
1871. Articles 15.1 and 15.2 of the Proposal for a Digital Markets Act.
1872. *See* Article 3.1.c) of the Proposal for a Digital Markets Act.
1873. Article 15.4 of the Proposal for a Digital Markets Act. In this regard, only the obligations provided at Article 5.b) and Article 6.1.e), f), h) and i) can be declared applicable.

extended its gatekeeper position'.[1874] A 'gatekeeper' shall be deemed to have engaged in a systematic non-compliance if it has been the subject of at least three non-compliance or fining decisions issued by the Commission[1875] within a period of five years prior to the decision opening the market investigation.[1876] It shall be deemed to have further strengthened or extended its gatekeeper position if 'its impact on the internal market has further increased, its importance as a gateway for business users to reach end users has further increased or [if] the gatekeeper enjoys a further entrenched and durable position in its operations'.[1877] In such cases, the Commission can impose any behavioural or structural remedies on the 'gatekeeper', which are proportionate to the infringement and are necessary to ensure compliance with the Digital Markets Act.[1878] However, structural remedies may only be imposed 'either where there is no equally effective behavioural remedy or where any equally effective behavioural remedy would be more burdensome for the gatekeeper concerned than the structural remedy'.[1879] Moreover, the Commission may order interim measures against a 'gatekeeper', in case of urgency due to risks of serious and irreparable damage for business users or end users, on the basis of a prima facie finding of an infringement of Articles 5 and/or 6.[1880] Finally, the 'gatekeeper' can offer commitments to ensure compliance with the Digital Markets Act.[1881] The Commission will have to communicate its objections to the 'gatekeeper' within 6 months of the opening of the investigation and will have to close the investigation within 12 months of its opening.[1882] The Commission may however extend these deadlines, up to 6 months, if it is justified on objective grounds and proportionate.[1883]

Third, the European Commission 'may conduct a market investigation with the purpose of examining whether one or more services within the digital sector should be added to the list of core platform services or to detect types of practices that may limit the contestability of core platform services or may be unfair and which are not effectively addressed by [the Digital Markets Act]'.[1884] In such cases, it will have to issue a public report within 24 months from the opening of the investigation, which shall, where appropriate, be accompanied by proposals to amend the list of 'core platform

1874. Article 16.1 of the Proposal for a Digital Markets Act.
1875. *See* Articles 25 and 26 of the Proposal for a Digital Markets Act.
1876. Article 16.3 of the Proposal for a Digital Markets Act.
1877. Article 16.4 of the Proposal for a Digital Markets Act.
1878. Article 16.1 of the Proposal for a Digital Markets Act.
1879. Article 16.2 of the Proposal for a Digital Markets Act.
1880. Article 22 of the Proposal for a Digital Markets Act.
1881. Article 23 of the Proposal for a Digital Markets Act.
1882. Articles 16.1 and 16.5 of the Proposal for a Digital Markets Act.
1883. Article 16.6 of the Proposal for a Digital Markets Act.
1884. Article 17.1 of the Proposal for a Digital Markets Act.

services' and by delegated acts amending the obligations laid down in Articles 5 and 6 of the Digital Markets Act.[1885]

6.5.2 Competition Law May Not Be Sufficient on Itself: Growing Call for *Ex Ante* Legislations Imposing Data Sharing

318. While the three suggestions presented above could indeed reduce, to some extent, the time-consuming process of competition intervention and could allow competition authorities to better tackle systemic competition problems, it is increasingly argued that 'competition policy alone cannot address all the systemic problems (…) [and that] additional rules may be needed to ensure contestability, fairness and innovation and the possibility of market entry'.[1886] Indeed, even if the competition process is sped up through the above-mentioned suggestions, competition law intervention would still require substantial amounts of time to be implemented. In digital markets where quick reactions are indispensable, this serves as a key rationale for complementing competition law intervention with *ex ante* legislations imposing B2B data sharing, which would, notably, aim at avoiding the apparition of such systemic problems in the first place.[1887]

In fact, as outlined by Ennis and Fletcher, several reports pertaining to the modernisation of competition law echo the proposition that *ex ante* legislations could be a valuable complement to competition law.[1888] For instance, the European Commission's expert report on 'Competition Policy for the digital era' suggests there are areas in which *ex ante* legislations might be appropriate to compliment competition law, in particular, 'where similar issues arise continuously and intervention may be needed on an ongoing basis',[1889] and where 'competition law enforcement may be overburdened to deal with the implementation and oversight of interoperability mandates imposed on dominant players'.[1890] In the same vein, the Furman report outlines that, in order to spur competition and innovation, *ex ante* obligations, to be monitored by a 'Digital Markets Unit', should be imposed on

1885. Articles 17.1 and 17.2 of the Proposal for a Digital Markets Act.
1886. Communication from the Commission, '*Shaping Europe's Digital Future*', *supra*, p. 9. *See also* Communication from the Commission, '*A European Strategy for Data*', *supra*, p. 14; L. Cabral, et al., 'The EU Digital Markets Act: A Report from a Panel of Economic Experts', *EU Science Hub*, 2021, available at https://ec.europa.eu/jrc/en/publication/eu-digital-markets-act, p. 6.
1887. R. Feasey and A. de Streel, 'Data Sharing for Digital Market Contestability', *supra*, p. 58.
1888. S. Ennis and A. Fletcher, 'Developing International Perspectives on Digital Competition Policy', *supra*, pp. 5-6.
1889. J. Crémer, Y.-A. de Montjoye and H. Schweitzer, 'Competition Policy for the Digital Era', *supra*, p. 70.
1890. *Ibid.*, p. 126.

undertakings having a 'strategic market status',[1891] in order to complement competition enforcement that 'moves too slowly and, intentionally, resolves only issues narrowly focused on a specific case'.[1892] Similarly, the Stigler Committee report provides that *ex ante* obligations, to be monitored by a 'Digital Authority', could be imposed on undertakings having 'bottleneck power',[1893] in order to complement competition enforcement.[1894] Finally, as outlined by Kerber, the German experts' report for the modernisation of competition law also stresses that the imposition of *ex ante* data sharing obligations might be more suitable than competition law intervention to address specific problems, such as issues of interoperability and of lack of (real-time) access to data.[1895]

In light of the above, a bicephalous approach to the systemic problems that might emerge on digital markets due to their characteristics[1896] is therefore recommended, whereby an adaptation of competition law rules to the digital environment should be complemented by the creation of *ex ante* legislations imposing B2B data sharing.[1897] These legislations[1898] will be further addressed in Chapter 8.

1891. Undertakings that are 'in a position to exercise market power over a gateway or bottleneck in a digital market, where they control others' market access' (J. Furman, et al., 'Unlocking Digital Competition', *supra*, p. 55).

1892. *Ibid. See also* Competition and Markets Authority, 'Online Platforms and Digital Advertising: Market Study Final Report', *supra*, pp. 322-323.

1893. Bottleneck power 'describes a situation where consumers primarily single-home and rely upon a single service provider, which makes obtaining access to those consumers for the relevant activity by other service providers prohibitively costly' (Stigler Committee on Digital Platforms, 'Final Report', *supra*, p. 32).

1894. *Ibid.*, pp. 100-101.

1895. W. Kerber, 'Updating Competition Policy for the Digital Economy?', *supra*, pp. 38-39; H. Schweitzer, et al., 'Modernising the Law on Abuse of Market Power: Executive Summary', *supra*, p. 10.

1896. *See* Part I, Chapter 2, Section 2.2.3.

1897. *See* Communication from the Commission, '*A European Strategy for Data*', *supra*, pp. 5 and 13-14; European Parliament resolution of 20 October 2020 with recommendations to the Commission on the Digital Services Act: Improving the functioning of the Single Market (2020/2018(INL)), P9_TA-PROV(2020)0272, available at https://www.europarl.europa.eu/doceo/document/TA-9-2020-0272_EN.html, p. 10.

1898. *See*, for instance, the Proposal for a Digital Markets Act.

Chapter 7

Articulation Between Data Protection and Competition Law

319. In the previous chapter, it has been outlined that refusals to share data could lead to three types of competition law infringements,[1899] and that, for each of these infringements, a potential remedy could be to impose on the large data holder an obligation to share (some of) its data with several third parties.[1900] Yet, as the data sharing remedy will likely cover personal data pertaining to multiple individuals, the personal data protection rules will need to be considered.[1901] Therefore, this chapter will analyse how a competition authority's decision imposing to share personal data with a third party can be compatible with the 'GDPR'[1902] (Section 7.2).

Prior to delving into such analysis, this chapter will set the focus on another important friction point emerging from the articulation between competition and data protection law, namely the fact that several authors have started to put the spotlight on the potential anticompetitive effects of the GDPR, as this regulation might increase concentration in personal data and data-related markets (Section 7.1).[1903]

1899. *See* Part III, Chapter 6, Sections 6.1 to 6.3.

1900. *See* Part III, Chapter 6, Section 6.4.

1901. J. Haucap, 'A German Approach to Antitrust for Digital Platforms', in *Digital Platforms and Concentration – Second Annual Antitrust and Competition Conference*, S. Eyler-Driscoll, A. Schechter and C. Patiño (eds), 2018, available at https://promarket.org/wp-content/uploads/2018/04/Digital-Platforms-and-Concentration.pdf, p. 12.

1902. Regulation (EU) 2016/679 of the European Parliament and of the Council of 27 April 2016 on the protection of natural persons with regard to the processing of personal data and on the free movement of such data, and repealing Directive 95/46 (General Data Protection Regulation), *OJ L 119*, 4 May 2016.

1903. M. Gal and O. Aviv, 'The Competitive Effects of the GDPR', *Journal of Competition Law and Economics*, September 2020, Vol. 16(3), pp. 349-391; T. Zarsky, 'Incompatible: The GDPR in the Age of Big Data', *Seton Hall Law Review*, 2017, Vol. 47, No. 4(2), pp. 995-1020; T. Zarsky, 'The Privacy–Innovation Conundrum', *supra*, pp. 115-168; D. Geradin, T. Karanikioti and D. Katsifis, 'GDPR Myopia: How a Well-Intended Regulation Ended Up Favoring Google in Ad Tech', *TILEC Discussion*

7.1 DATA PROTECTION AND COMPETITION LAW: FRIENDS OR FOES REGARDING DATA SHARING?

320. Even if it generates benefits, data sharing is not cost-free.[1904] On the one hand, it might entail economic costs. Indeed, data collection and processing, and consequently data sharing, entails costs for the data holder, and data sharing obligations might create disincentives for data collection and processing.[1905] The efficiency gains stemming from sharing (increased competition and innovation from third parties) shall be carefully weighed against the efficiency gains stemming from the data holder's data-driven network effects and economies of scope, scale and speed.[1906]

On the other hand, it might entail societal costs. Indeed, data sharing might create tensions with the GDPR, which aims to frame the use of personal data in the European internal market. In order to do so, this instrument aims at reaching an equilibrium between the fundamental right of the protection of personal data, on the one hand, and the fundamental right of the freedom to conduct a business, on the other hand.[1907] As technological developments and globalisation have transformed the economy, one of the aims of the GDPR is to facilitate the free flow of personal data within the EU in order to support the development of the digital economy across the internal market.[1908] In this sense, the GDPR supports data sharing. However, the GDPR also aims at ensuring a high level of personal data protection and creating the necessary trust, by providing more control to the data subjects on 'their' data.[1909] It is this second objective that might generate tensions with data sharing. Indeed, data sharing will often cover both personal[1910] and

Paper DP 2020-012, May 2020, available at https://ssrn.com/abstract=3598130; G. Johnson and S. Shriver, 'Privacy & Market Concentration' *supra*.

1904. B. Martens, et al., 'Business to Business Data Sharing: An Economic and Legal Analysis', *EU Science Hub*, 2020, available at https://ssrn.com/abstract=3658100, p. 5.
1905. J. Crémer, Y.-A. de Montjoye and H. Schweitzer, 'Competition Policy for the Digital Era: Final Report', 2019, available at http://ec.europa.eu/competition/publications/reports/ kd0419345enn.pdf, pp. 76-77; P. Larouche, 'The European Microsoft Case at the Crossroads of Competition Policy and Innovation', *Antitrust Law Journal*, 2008, Vol. 75(3), pp. 933-937; B. Martens, et al., 'Business to Business Data Sharing', *supra*, p. 5.
1906. J. Krämer, D. Schnurr and S. Broughton Micova, 'The Role of Data for Digital Markets Contestability' *supra*, p. 75.
1907. Recital 4 of the GDPR.
1908. Recital 6 of the GDPR.
1909. Recital 7 of the GDPR.
1910. 'Any information relating to an identified or identifiable natural person ("data subject")' (Article 4.1 of the GDPR).

non-personal data mixed in the same data set,[1911] and favouring data sharing might lead to the broader dissemination of such personal data and to a loss of control by the data subjects.

Perhaps unsurprisingly, large data holders have started to use data protection considerations to justify refusals to share data with third parties,[1912] and it is difficult to evaluate the legitimacy of such claims (dynamic nature of the notion of personal data, compliance with the purpose limitation principle, etc.).[1913] To some extent, this is echoed by the EDPS, which calls 'for cautious approach towards initiatives aimed at compulsory access to personal data in the competition context, i.e. access to personal data held by the incumbent undertaking by its competitors. Such sharing and access to data among competitors must be balanced against other policy concerns, especially data protection'.[1914] These large data holders' behaviour has led to growing concerns, detailed in Section 7.1.1, that the GDPR might limit competition and increase concentration on the data markets.

7.1.1 Growing Concern That the GDPR Limits Competition and Increases Concentration

321. According to several authors, this use of data protection considerations by large data holders to justify refusals to share data with third parties, combined with the fact that these undertakings can better sink the large implementation costs of the GDPR than smaller competitors that are disproportionally burdened by this instrument, could create some serious competition issues.[1915] Indeed, this creates the paradoxical situation in which

1911. I. Graef, R. Gellert and M. Husovec, 'Towards a Holistic Regulatory Approach for the European Data Economy: Why the Illusive Notion of Non-personal Data Is Counter-productive to Data Innovation', *TILEC Discussion Paper No. 2018-028*, September 2018, available at http://ssrn.com/abstract=3256189; C. Wendehorst, 'Of Elephants in the Room and Paper Tigers: How to Reconcile Data Protection and the Data Economy', *Trading Data in the Digital Economy: Legal Concepts and Tools*, S. Lohsse, R. Schulze and D. Staudenmayer (eds), Baden-Baden, Nomos, 2017, pp. 329-330.
1912. *See* point 253. *See*, for instance, E. Egan, 'Data Portability and Privacy', *Facebook White Paper*, September 2019, available at https://iapp.org/media/pdf/fb_white paper_sep_2019.pdf.
1913. I. Graef, R. Gellert and M. Husovec, 'Towards a Holistic Regulatory Approach for the European Data Economy' *supra*, pp. 10-11.
1914. European Data Protection Supervisor, *Opinion 3/2020 on the European strategy for data*, 16 June 2020, available at https://edps.europa.eu/sites/edp/files/publication/20-06-16_opinion_data_strategy_en.pdf, p. 12.
1915. *See* J. Crémer, Y.-A. de Montjoye and H. Schweitzer, 'Competition Policy for the Digital Era', *supra*, p. 99. *See also* M. Gal and O. Aviv, 'The Competitive Effects of the GDPR', *supra*, pp. 349-391; D. Geradin, T. Karanikioti and D. Katsifis, 'GDPR Myopia', *supra*; J. Campbell, A. Goldfarb and C. Tucker, 'Privacy Regulation and Market Structure', *Journal of Economics & Management Strategy*, 2015, Vol. 24(1), pp. 47-73; J. Jia, G. Zhe Jin and L. Wagman, 'The Short-Run Effects of GDPR on

a tool that was adopted to empower individuals by providing them more control on 'their' data,[1916] and consequently aimed at restricting the data controllers' power on data, is actually used (although sometimes possibly as a pretext to justify controversial strategies)[1917] by large data holders in order to raise entry barriers on the data market vis-à-vis third parties. For example, taking the example of Google, Geradin et al. outline that:

> Google has used the GDPR – or privacy concerns more generally – as an excuse to engage in practices that have strengthened its control on the ad tech ecosystem to the detriment of advertisers, publishers and smaller rivals. This could be referred to as the 'weaponization' of the GDPR, i.e. the use of the GDPR by Google as a strategic tool to strengthen its grip on the ad tech market. Because of its market power, Google has become a de facto privacy regulator[1918] able to dictate to rival advertisers, publishers and rival ad tech players its interpretation of the GDPR and other privacy legislation, which is a worrying trend that needs to be countenanced.[1919]

For Gal and Aviv, the GDPR thus 'limits competition and increases concentration in data and data-related markets, and potentially strengthens large data holders. It also further reinforces the already existing barriers to data sharing in the EU, thereby potentially reducing data synergies that might

---

Technology Venture Investment', November 2019, available at https://papers.ssrn.com/abstract=32789128; T. Zarsky, 'Incompatible: The GDPR in the Age of Big Data', *supra*, pp. 995-1020; T. Zarsky, 'The Privacy–Innovation Conundrum', *supra*, pp. 115-168. For empirical evidence of this increased concentration, *see* G. Johnson and S. Shriver, 'Privacy & Market Concentration', *supra*.

1916. Recital 7 of the GDPR provides that 'natural persons should have control of their own personal data'.

1917. For examples of cases in which Google potentially used data protection rationales as a pretext to justify controversial strategies, *see* D. Geradin, T. Karanikioti and D. Katsifis, 'GDPR Myopia', *supra*, pp. 27-35. *See also* the UK Competition and Markets Authority's formal investigation into Google's 'Privacy Sandbox' project, which 'would disable third party cookies on the Chrome browser and Chromium browser engine and replace them with a new set of tools for targeting advertising and other functionality that they say will protect consumers' privacy to a greater extent' (Competition and Markets Authority, 'CMA to investigate Google's "Privacy Sandbox" browser changes', 8 January 2021, available at https://www.gov.uk/government/news/cma-to-investigate-google-s-privacy-sandbox-browser-changes).

1918. It should be outlined here that this situation derives from the principle of accountability of the GDPR (Article 5.2) and is, as such, not specific to large data holders. Indeed, according to this accountability principle, any data controller is responsible for the application of, and should demonstrate compliance with, the GDPR. As such, any data controller could thus be seen as its own 'first line *de facto* privacy regulator', while data protection authorities (the 'official' regulators) come as a second line. However, the fact that large data holders, such as Google, hold troves of data and are capable of having an unprecedented impact on the individuals explains why the focus is set on these actors, as the results of their 'first line *de facto* privacy regulation' can be significantly more problematic than that of a small data controller.

1919. D. Geradin, T. Karanikioti and D. Katsifis, 'GDPR Myopia', *supra*, p. 6.

result from combining different data sets controlled by separate entities'.[1920] These authors notably argue that while sharing data with third parties often entails high hurdles, data can circulate much more easily within the broad ecosystems of large data holders,[1921] which they have constituted through market expansion and through mergers and acquisitions.[1922] In personal data protection terms, it could be argued that the data controller is the same throughout the whole ecosystem, namely the large data holder (Google, Facebook, Amazon, etc.), as it is very likely that this large data holder will determine the purposes and means of the processing of the personal data in the different products/services of the ecosystem.[1923] Hypothesis of joint controllership is nevertheless also possible.[1924]

322. These critiques fit in the broader line of academic work arguing that these large data holders engage in 'envelopment' tactics, in order to strengthen their position in the data markets.[1925] These envelopment tactics are often relied upon in data-driven markets, and have notably been used by Google, Microsoft, LinkedIn or eBay.[1926] Some of these large undertakings have even engaged in 'envelopment strategies through privacy policy tying',[1927] which is a strategy through which 'the enveloper requests consumers to grant their consent to combining their data in both [the] origin and target market[s]'.[1928] In short, if a user wants to use one of the services offered by the enveloper, she must consent to the circulation of her data

1920. M. Gal and O. Aviv, 'The Competitive Effects of the GDPR', *supra*, p. 352.
1921. *Ibid.*, pp. 361-369.
1922. For instance, since 2008, Google has acquired 168 undertakings (notably Waze, YouTube or DoubleClick that were potential competitors), Facebook has acquired 71 undertakings (including Instagram and WhatsApp that were also arguably potential competitors), and Amazon has acquired 60 undertakings, which is a respective average of around 15, 6 and 5 acquisitions per year (Autorité de la concurrence, 'Contribution de l'Autorité de la concurrence au débat sur la politique de concurrence et les enjeux numériques', 19 February 2020, available at https://www.autoritedelaconcurrence.fr/sites/default/files/2020-02/2020.02.19_contribution_adlc_enjeux_numeriques_vf.pdf, p. 9; Lear, 'Ex-post Assessment of Merger Control Decisions in Digital Markets – Final Report', 9 May 2019, available at https://assets.publishing.service.gov.uk/government/uploads/system/uploads/attachment_data/file/803576/CMA_past_digital_mergers_GOV.UK_version.pdf, p. ii).
1923. Article 4.7 of the GDPR.
1924. Article 26 of the GDPR. *See also* European Data Protection Board, *Guidelines 07/2020 on the concepts of controller and processor in the GDPR*, Version 1.0, 2 September 2020, available at https://edpb.europa.eu/sites/edpb/files/consultation/edpb_guidelines_202007_controllerprocessor_en.pdf.
1925. *See* point 84. T. Eisenmann, G. Parker and M. Van Alstyne, 'Platform Envelopment', *Strategic Management Journal*, 2011, Vol. 32(12), p. 1270; D. Geradin, T. Karanikioti and D. Katsifis, 'GDPR Myopia', *supra*, pp. 25-26.
1926. T. Eisenmann, G. Parker and M. Van Alstyne, 'Platform Envelopment', *supra*, p. 1271.
1927. D. Condorelli and J. Padilla, 'Harnessing Platform Envelopment Through Privacy Policy Tying', December 2019, available at https://ssrn.com/abstract=3504025.
1928. *Ibid.*, p. 1.

across the entirety of the enveloper's ecosystem of services. This data combination allows the enveloper to entrench its dominant position in the origin market and to expand it in the other markets, as it can monetise data from each of its services in all of its other services.[1929]

This 'envelopment through privacy policy tying' also leads to problematic 'internal data free-for-all' situations, as large data holders active on separate markets thereby consolidate their various privacy policies, in order to combine the data collected across these various services and to create 'unique user super-profiles', which represents a major threat not only for privacy but also for competition.[1930] Indeed, from a competition perspective, 'this form of envelopment may involve a potential exploitative abuse – the coercive tying of privacy policies – and a possible exclusionary abuse – the monopolization of the target market and the entrenchment of the dominant position in the origin market'.[1931] Yet, as will be outlined below, regulatory authorities have been reluctant to address the legality of these 'internal data free-for-all' practices.[1932]

323. While the above findings raise troubling concerns about the effect of the GDPR on competition, they seem to rely on the double premise that: (i) the GDPR is more lenient towards personal data reuse within the ecosystem of these large data holders than it is towards the sharing of this personal data with third parties;[1933] and (ii) the way in which these large data holders reuse this data within their ecosystem complies with data protection law.[1934] Section 7.1.2 will assess whether these premises are accurate.

7.1.2 Challengeable Nature of the Premises on Which This Concern Relies

324. In fact, these two premises can be challenged from a theoretical point of view. On the one hand, the same data protection principles and standards apply, whether data is shared internally in an ecosystem or with third parties. On the other hand, it is questionable whether these large data holders use personal data within their ecosystem in a way that complies with data protection law.

1929. *Ibid.*, p. 5.
1930. D. Geradin, T. Karanikioti and D. Katsifis, 'GDPR Myopia', *supra*, pp. 24-26.
1931. D. Condorelli and J. Padilla, 'Harnessing Platform Envelopment Through Privacy Policy Tying', *supra*, p. 39.
1932. D. Geradin, T. Karanikioti and D. Katsifis, 'GDPR Myopia', *supra*, p. 1.
1933. M. Gal and O. Aviv, 'The Competitive Effects of the GDPR', *supra*, pp. 361-369.
1934. There is indeed a form of 'trust' in the fact that these large data holders will use the data within their ecosystem in a way that complies with data protection law (D. Geradin, T. Karanikioti and D. Katsifis, 'GDPR Myopia', *supra*, p. 16).

7.1.2.1 Premise 1: The GDPR Is More Lenient Towards Personal Data Reuse Within the Ecosystem of Large Data Holders Than It Is Towards the Sharing of Personal Data with Third Parties

325. While it is true that, as mentioned above, large actors can better sink the large implementation costs of the GDPR than smaller competitors that are disproportionally burdened by this instrument, this does not imply that the GDPR is more lenient towards personal data reuse within the ecosystem of large data holders than it is towards the sharing of personal data with third parties. Indeed, in both these scenarios, the core principles of the GDPR, listed in Article 5, must be respected.

More specifically, according to the purpose limitation principle, data that has been collected for a specific purpose may not be shared with third parties, nor be reused internally within the ecosystem of large data holders, if this further processing does not fit within this initial purpose of processing.[1935] The initial purpose of processing must thus be sufficiently detailed in order for the data subject to be able to determine the kinds of processing included, or not, within the specified purpose.[1936] Accordingly, the principle of purpose limitation limits the possibility for large data holders to use data for any contingent purpose, as they cannot rely on broadly defined purposes as a justification to circulate their users' personal data within their ecosystem.[1937]

Rather, both internal reuse and sharing with third parties constitute further processing. If this further processing does not fit within this initial purpose of processing, this amounts to a new processing activity, distinct from the initial one, which requires a new lawful basis of processing, unless this new processing is compatible with the initial purpose[1938] (although this

---

1935. Article 5.1.b) of the GDPR.

1936. Article 29 Working Party, *Opinion 03/2013 on purpose limitation*, WP 203, 2 April 2013, available at https://ec.europa.eu/justice/article-29/documentation/opinion-recommendation/files/2013/wp203_en.pdf, p. 15. *See also* I. Hahn, 'Purpose Limitation in the Time of Data Power: Is There a Way Forward?', *European Data Protection Law Review*, 2021, Vol. 7(1), pp. 31-44.

1937. S. Ranchordás and G. De Gregorio, 'Breaking Down Information Silos with Big Data: A Legal Analysis of Data Sharing', *University of Groningen Faculty of Law Research Paper Series No. 44/2019*, September 2019, available at https://ssrn.com/abstract=3466313, p. 24. *See also* I. Hahn, 'Purpose Limitation in the Time of Data Power: Is There a Way Forward?', *supra*; Brave, 'Inside the Black Box: A Glimpse of Google's Internal Data Free-for-All', 2020, available at https://brave.com/wp-content/uploads/2020/03/Inside-the-Black-Box.pdf.

1938. To be clear, this does not mean that this 'compatible' new processing will not require a lawful basis of processing *at all*. Indeed, every processing needs to rely on a lawful basis of processing (Article 6.1 of the GDPR). Rather, what this means is that this 'compatible' new processing will not require a *new* lawful basis of processing, distinct from the one that serves as the basis for the initial processing, because it fits within this

latter point is controversial[1939]).[1940] If the further processing is deemed to be 'incompatible' with the initial purpose for which the data has been collected, this further processing may only be carried out if the data subjects have consented to it or if it is necessary to comply with a legal obligation.[1941]

326. It could be tempting to rely on this last point to argue that large data holders can collect such consents for internal data reuse, serving as a lawful basis of processing for the incompatible further reuse, more easily than other actors wishing to collect consents for data sharing, as the data subjects are already using the large data holders' services and ecosystem. Yet, it is interesting to point out that the European Commission's proposal for a Digital Markets Act[1942] provides that 'gatekeepers' shall not make the obtaining of this consent more burdensome for third parties than for its own services.[1943] Moreover, this raises the question of the quality of the consents collected by these large data holders in order to justify their 'internal data free-for-all'.

Indeed, consent must be 'freely given, specific, informed and unambiguous'.[1944] First, consent must be *informed and unambiguous*, which implies that the data holder must be completely transparent towards the processing operations to which the data subjects consent. To do so, they shall take appropriate measures to provide any information referred to in Articles 13 and 14 of the GDPR to the data subjects in a concise, transparent, intelligible and easily accessible form, using clear and plain language.[1945] Second, consent must be *specific*, which implies that it has to be sufficiently granular and that the data subjects must understand the specific purposes to

---

initial processing. This 'compatible' new processing thus, in fact, relies on a lawful basis of processing, namely the *same one* as the one that serves as a basis for the initial processing.

1939. C. Wendehorst, 'Of Elephants in the Room and Paper Tigers', *supra*, pp. 335-336.

1940. Article 6.4 and Recital 50 of the GDPR. On these matters, *see* C. de Terwangne, 'Article 5. Principles Relating to Processing of Personal Data', *The EU General Data Protection Regulation (GDPR): A Commentary*, C. Kuner, L. Bygrave and C. Docksey (eds), Oxford, Oxford University Press, 2020, pp. 309-320.

1941. Article 6.4 of the GDPR. *See also* C. de Terwangne, 'Article 5. Principles Relating to Processing of Personal Data', *supra*, p. 316.

1942. Proposal for a Digital Markets Act. For more details on this Digital Markets Act, *see* points 317, 380 and 384-385.

1943. Article 11.2 of the Proposal for a Digital Markets Act.

1944. Article 4.11 of the GDPR. *See also* Article 7 of the GDPR.

1945. Article 12.1 of the GDPR. *See also* Article 29 Working Party, *Guidelines on transparency under Regulation 2016/679*, WP 260 rev.01, 11 April 2018, available at https://ec.europa.eu/newsroom/article29/item-detail.cfm?item_id=622227; R. Polčák, 'Article 12: Transparent Information, Communication and Modalities for the Exercise of the Rights of the Data Subject', *The EU General Data Protection Regulation (GDPR): A Commentary*, C. Kuner, L. Bygrave and C. Docksey (eds), Oxford, Oxford University Press, 2020, pp. 398-412.

which they separately consent.[1946] Third, and perhaps more importantly, when it comes to internal reuse by large data holders, consent must be *freely given*. In this regard, the GDPR outlines that 'consent should not be regarded as freely given if the data subject has no genuine or free choice or is unable to refuse or withdraw consent without detriment'.[1947] This will especially be the case if there is a clear imbalance between the data controller and the data subject, and if the controller 'does not allow separate consent to be given to different personal data processing operations despite it being appropriate in the individual case, or if the performance of a contract, including the provision of a service, is dependent on the consent despite such consent not being necessary for such performance'.[1948] These are the requirements of granularity and of absence of conditionality.[1949] Therefore, if the data holder bundles the data subjects' consent with the acceptance of its terms of services, or if it ties the provision of a contract/service to the requirement to consent to unnecessary processing for the performance of that contract/ service, consent will not be deemed to be freely given and will thus not be valid.[1950] In this perspective, if a data subject is required to consent to the circulation of her data throughout the whole ecosystem of the large data holder in order to simply use one of the many services offered by the latter, such a consent should not be considered as being *freely given*. Accordingly, and contrary to what the first premise might suggest, large data holders cannot rely on consents obtained in bulk, and which do not provide sufficient information regarding all of the specific data processing purposes that they are supposed to cover, as a justification to freely circulate their users' personal data within their ecosystem ('internal data free-for-all'). This has been confirmed by the Norwegian Data Protection Authority in its *Grindr* case, where it ruled that, since *Grindr* bundled the data subject's consent to the sharing of her personal data with advertisers with the acceptance of the privacy policy as a whole, such consent was in breach of the granularity

---

1946. European Data Protection Board, *Guidelines 05/2020 on consent under Regulation 2016/679*, Version 1.1, May 2020, available at https://edpb.europa.eu/sites/edpb/files/files/file1/edpb_guidelines_202005_consent_en.pdf, p. 14. On consent, *see also* L. Bygrave and L. Tosoni, 'Article 4(11). Consent', *The EU General Data Protection Regulation (GDPR): A Commentary*, C. Kuner, L. Bygrave and C. Docksey (eds), Oxford, Oxford University Press, 2020, pp. 174-187; E. Kosta, 'Article 7: Conditions for Consent', *The EU General Data Protection Regulation (GDPR): A Commentary*, C. Kuner, L. Bygrave and C. Docksey (eds), Oxford, Oxford University Press, 2020, pp. 345-354.
1947. Recital 42 of the GDPR.
1948. Recital 43 of the GDPR.
1949. *See* European Data Protection Board, *Guidelines 05/2020 on consent under Regulation 2016/679*, *supra*, pp. 10-12.
1950. *Ibid.*, p. 10.

requirement.[1951] Consequently, the consent was deemed invalid, as it was not *freely given* and thus deprived the data subjects of real control.[1952]

327. Moreover, the large data holders will also have to comply with the data minimisation principle, according to which only the adequate, relevant and necessary data for the fulfilment of the specific purpose of processing shall be processed.[1953] This implies that, in combination with the purpose limitation principle, the categories and amount of data that may be processed (for each internal reuse or for data sharing with third parties) should be limited to what is necessary to meet this purpose. Therefore, even if large data holders have collected troves of personal data from their users in the context of a first purpose of processing, they will not necessarily be allowed to reuse any/all of this data for a further purpose of processing. Rather, they shall only process the data that is adequate, relevant and necessary for this reuse. On the other hand, data within their ecosystem that would merely be useful, but not necessary, should not be reused, as 'this necessity requirement not only refers to the quantity, but also to the quality of personal data'.[1954]

328. In light of the above, the argument can be made that the GDPR is *not* more lenient towards personal data reuse within the ecosystem of these large data holders than it is towards the sharing of this personal data with third parties. Indeed, as outlined in a joint statement of the UK competition and data protection authorities, 'neither competition nor data protection regulation allows for a "rule of thumb" approach, where intra-group transfers of personal data are permitted while extra-group transfers are not. Under both data protection law and competition law, a careful case-by-case assessment is needed'.[1955] This first premise is thus questionable.

7.1.2.2 Premise 2: The Way in Which Large Data Holders Reuse This Data Within Their Ecosystem Complies with Data Protection Law

329. The second premise is that there is a form of 'trust' in the fact that these large data holders will use the data within their ecosystem in a way that

1951. Norwegian Data Protection Authority, *Grindr LLC* (Advance notification), 24 January 2021, Decision No. 20/02136-5, available at https://www.datatilsynet.no/contentassets/da7652d0c072493c84a4c7af506cf293/advance-notification-of-an-administrative-fine.pdf, pp. 9-10.
1952. *Ibid.*, pp. 10-12.
1953. Article 5.1.c) of the GDPR.
1954. C. de Terwangne, 'Article 5: Principles Relating to Processing of Personal Data', *supra*, p. 317.
1955. Competition and Markets Authority and Information Commissioner's Office, 'Competition and data protection in digital markets: A joint statement between the CMA and the ICO', 19 May 2021, available at https://ico.org.uk/media/about-the-ico/documents/2619797/cma-ico-public-statement-20210518.pdf, p. 26.

complies with data protection law. According to Geradin et al., this trust derives from three assumptions, namely that large data holders have the necessary resources to comply with the GDPR; that they must be compliant as they will be closely monitored by data protection authorities in light of their structural importance; and that they will be compliant because, as their business model is based on data collection and processing, a data protection scandal could greatly impact their profits.[1956] While the first assumption seems established, the other two can be challenged.[1957]

330. Regarding the third assumption, it can be questioned to what extent a potential data protection scandal would truly impact these large data holders' business model, especially if the data subjects are locked in their services and face important switching costs, due to these large data holders' network effects and economies of scale, scope and speed.[1958] Indeed, in such situations, viable alternatives to the services offered by these large data holders may not exist, and data subjects may thus not be able to exercise control on 'their' data by 'penalising' (repeated) violations of their right to personal data protection committed by these large data holders. Arguably, this might explain why Facebook did not lose many users after the 'Cambridge Analytica' scandal, despite the fact that it faces civil class-action lawsuits,[1959] and that was fined EUR 1 million by the *Garante per la protezione dei dati personali* (Italian Data Protection Authority) and GBP 500,000 by the *Information Commissioner's Office* (UK's Data Protection Authority) for allowing Cambridge Analytica to collect and use data from its users.[1960]

331. Regarding the second assumption, it is questionable whether these large data holders process their users' data within their ecosystem in a way that complies with data protection law. Indeed, coming back to the purpose limitation principle outlined above,[1961] it can be questioned whether the vague purposes mentioned by large data holders in their privacy policies ('provide our services', 'improve our services', 'develop new services') are specific enough to comply with the purpose limitation principle, as these

1956. D. Geradin, T. Karanikioti and D. Katsifis, 'GDPR Myopia', *supra*, p. 16.
1957. *Ibid.*, pp. 14-16.
1958. *See* M. Stucke and A. Grunes, *Big Data and Competition Policy*, *supra*; D. Rubinfeld and M. Gal, 'Access Barriers to Big Data', *supra*, pp. 339-381.
1959. *See* https://www.mydataismine.com/. *See also* S. Bodoni, 'Facebook Targeted in the U.K. Legal Action Over Cambridge Analytica', *Bloomberg*, 28 October 2020, available at https://www.bloomberg.com/news/articles/2020-10-28/facebook-targeted-in-u-k-legal-action-over-cambridge-analytica.
1960. Garante per la protezione dei dati personali, *Facebook*, 14 June 2019, Decision No. 9121486, available at https://perma.cc/LHV7-2THY; Information Commissioner's Office, 'Facebook Ireland and Facebook Inc', 24 October 2018, available at https://ico.org.uk/media/action-weve-taken/mpns/2260051/r-facebook-mpn-20181024.pdf.
1961. *See* point 325. Article 5.1.b) of the GDPR.

purposes are not clear, specified and explicit.[1962] This is supported by the fact that the Article 29 Working Party (today the EDPB) expressly stated that vague or general-purposes will usually not meet this specificity requirement,[1963] which has been confirmed by the Norwegian Data Protection Authority in its *Grindr* case.[1964] Moreover, these vague purposes, leading to 'internal data free-for-all' practices by these large data holders, could also be seen as contradicting with the proportionality principle enshrined in the Modernised Convention 108, as this arguably creates an excessive interference with the rights and interests of the data subjects.[1965] Furthermore, this lack of specificity can also be linked to another issue, namely the compliance with the transparency requirement mentioned above.[1966] Indeed, large data holders' ecosystems are complex and obscure to the data subjects, and it is highly doubtful whether the vague and general information provided in their terms of services meets the thresholds of the transparency requirement.[1967] In fact, in its *Grindr* case, the Norwegian Data Protection Authority ruled that such requirement would not be met if the consent request appeared among all other information in a long privacy policy, as such request should be highlighted.[1968]

Additionally, the validity of the consent collected by large data holders through 'privacy policy tying', leading to 'internal data free-for-all' situations, can be questioned.[1969] Indeed, the *informed and unambiguous* nature of data subjects' consent can be challenged, as privacy policies are drafted in such a way that 'regular people' do not understand them (if they even read them, which is often not the case) and as data controllers often resort to dark patterns.[1970] These dark patterns can make it more difficult to reject some terms of the privacy policy rather than to accept them all, or can prevent the

1962. D. Geradin, T. Karanikioti and D. Katsifis, 'GDPR Myopia', *supra*, p. 25. *See also* I. Hahn, 'Purpose Limitation in the Time of Data Power: Is There a Way Forward?', *supra.*; Brave, 'Inside the Black Box: A Glimpse of Google's Internal Data Free-for-All', *supra*.
1963. Article 29 Working Party, *Opinion 03/2013 on purpose limitation*, WP 203, 2 April 2013, available at https://ec.europa.eu/justice/article-29/documentation/opinion-recommendation/files/2013/wp203_en.pdf, p. 16.
1964. Norwegian Data Protection Authority, *Grindr LLC*, 24 January 2021, *supra*, p. 13.
1965. Modernised Convention for the Protection of Individuals with Regard to the Processing of Personal Data, 17-18 May 2018, CM/Inf(2018)15-final, Article 5.1: 'Data processing shall be proportionate in relation to the legitimate purpose pursued and reflect at all stages of the processing a fair balance between all interests concerned, whether public or private, and the rights and freedoms at stake.'
1966. *See* point 326.
1967. D. Geradin, T. Karanikioti and D. Katsifis, 'GDPR Myopia', *supra*, p. 25.
1968. Norwegian Data Protection Authority, *Grindr LLC*, 24 January 2021, *supra*, p. 14.
1969. On the GDPR requirements for consent, *see* point 326.
1970. On these dark patterns, *see* M. Nouwens, et al., 'Dark Patterns after the GDPR: Scraping Consent Pop-Ups and Demonstrating Their Influence', *CHI Conference on Human Factors in Computing Systems*, April 2020, available at https://arxiv.org/abs/2001.02479.

data subject from using the service if she does not consent to all the terms.[1971] This has been confirmed by the Norwegian Data Protection Authority in its *Grindr* case.[1972] Moreover, because the data subject often has no other choice than to consent to the totality of the terms of services in order to use the service, this consent may be deemed as not being *freely given* if the large data holder is dominant on a specific market and no realistic alternatives are available for the data subject.[1973] Indeed, if a data subject is required to consent to the circulation of her data throughout the whole ecosystem of the large data holder in order to simply use one of the many services offered by the latter (but for which there are no realistic alternatives), such a consent should not be considered as being *freely given*. However, such practices are applied, and this allows these large data holders to expand their market power across data markets, as, in order to use the dominant's firm service, data subjects are usually required to consent to the collection, processing and combination of data for other services of the large data holders' ecosystem as well.[1974]

332. The above critiques of the legality of personal data processing within these ecosystems are not merely theoretical, as large data holders have been fined by data protection authorities for infringing personal data protection legislation.[1975] For instance, on 9 December 2020, the Irish *Data Protection Commission* fined Twitter EUR 450,000 following a bug that had as a consequence that some users' private tweets were made public.[1976] On 9 April 2021, the *Autoriteit Persoonsgegevens* (the Dutch Data Protection

1971. D. Condorelli and J. Padilla, 'Harnessing Platform Envelopment Through Privacy Policy Tying', *supra*, p. 26. *See also* M. Botta and K. Wiedemann, 'The Interaction of EU Competition, Consumer, and Data Protection Law in the Digital Economy: The Regulatory Dilemma in the Facebook Odyssey', *Antitrust Bulletin,* 2019, Vol. 64(3), pp. 428-446.
1972. Norwegian Data Protection Authority, *Grindr LLC*, 24 January 2021, *supra*, pp. 9-12 and 15-16.
1973. D. Condorelli and J. Padilla, 'Harnessing Platform Envelopment Through Privacy Policy Tying', *supra*, p. 26. *See also* D. Clifford, I. Graef and P. Valcke, 'Pre-formulated Declarations of Data Subject Consent: Citizen-Consumer Empowerment and the Alignment of Data, Consumer and Competition Law Protections', *CiTiP Working Paper 33/2017*, February 2018, available at https://ssrn.com/abstract=3126706, pp. 34-44; K. Wiedemann, 'A Matter of Choice: The German Federal Supreme Court's Interim Decision in the Abuse-of-Dominance Proceedings Bundeskartellamt v. Facebook (Case KVR 69/19)', *International Review of Intellectual Property and Competition Law*, 2020, Vol. 51(9), pp. 1177-1178.
1974. D. Condorelli and J. Padilla, 'Harnessing Platform Envelopment Through Privacy Policy Tying', *supra*, p. 34.
1975. *See* https://www.enforcementtracker.com/ and points 326, 330 and 332-335.
1976. Data Protection Commission, *Twitter International Company*, 9 December 2020, Decision No. IN-19-1-1, available at https://edpb.europa.eu/sites/edpb/files/decisions/final_decision_-_in-19-1-1_9.12.2020.pdf. *See also* on this case: European Data Protection Board, Decision 01/2020 on the dispute arisen on the draft decision of the Irish Supervisory Authority regarding Twitter International Company under Article

Authority) fined TikTok EUR 750,000 for a breach of its transparency obligations under the GDPR (Article 12.1), as the company did not provide a privacy policy in Dutch to its users – of which an important part are children – but only provided one in English.[1977] On 10 March 2020, the *Datainspektionen* (the Swedish Data Protection Authority) fined Google EUR 7 million for a breach of data subject's right to erasure.[1978] Similarly, on 14 July 2020, the *Autorité de Protection des Données* (the Belgian Data Protection Authority) fined Google EUR 600,000 for the breach of a data subject's right to erasure, and for a breach of the principle of transparency, as Google did not explain sufficiently clearly the motives of its refusal to erase the data subject's data.[1979] In fact, it is interesting to point out that, in this decision, the Belgian Data Protection Authority outlined that large data holders such as Google have a 'special responsibility' in applying the GDPR, as their duty to comply with the GDPR should be proportionate with their large turnover and with the broad use of their products/services by data subjects.[1980] This is a clear call for more scrutiny and a stricter enforcement of the GDPR against these large data holders.

333. More notoriously, on 21 January 2019, the *Commission Nationale de l'Informatique et des Libertés* (CNIL – the French Data Protection Authority) has fined Google EUR 50 million for a lack of transparency and of accessibility of information, as well as for a lack of appropriate lawful basis of processing (the consent it had collected from its users was not valid in light of the lack of transparency and information).[1981] The CNIL's decision was confirmed by the French Conseil d'État on 19 June 2020, following an appeal by Google.[1982]

In substance, the CNIL found that Google's privacy policy and terms of services did not meet the transparency requirement of Article 12 of the GDPR, as there was an overall lack of accessibility to the information, due

---

65(1)(a) GDPR, 9 November 2020, available at https://edpb.europa.eu/sites/edpb/files/files/file1/edpb_bindingdecision01_2020_en.pdf.

1977. Autoriteit Persoonsgegevens, *TikTok Inc.*, 9 April 2021 (confidential reference), available at https://autoriteitpersoonsgegevens.nl/sites/default/files/atoms/files/decision_to_impose_a_fine_on_tiktok.pdf.

1978. Datainspektionen, *Google LLC*, 10 March 2020, Decision No. DI-2018-9274, available at https://www.datainspektionen.se/globalassets/dokument/beslut/2020-03-11-beslut-google.pdf.

1979. Autorité de Protection des Données, *X c/ Google*, 14 July 2020, Decision No. 37/2020, available at https://www.autoriteprotectiondonnees.be/publications/decision-quant-au-fond-n-37-2020.pdf.

1980. Autorité de Protection des Données, *X c/ Google*, 14 July 2020, § 175 (vii).

1981. CNIL, *Google*, 21 January 2019, Deliberation of the Restricted Committee SAN-2019-001, available at https://www.cnil.fr/sites/default/files/atoms/files/san-2019-001.pdf.

1982. Conseil d'État, *Société Google LLC*, 19 June 2020, Case No. 430810, available at https://www.legifrance.gouv.fr/ceta/id/CETATEXT000042040546/.

to the multilayer architecture of Google's information provision,[1983] which is excessively spread out across multiple documents.[1984] Moreover, the CNIL held that the information was not clear and intelligible, as it did not allow data subjects to sufficiently understand the various purposes of processing, which were too generic, imprecise and incomplete.[1985] This was considered as being especially problematic in light of the very large amount of data processed,[1986] including some very intimate categories of data.[1987] Regarding the validity of the consents collected by Google from its users, the CNIL ruled that the deficiencies in terms of transparency and information outlined above led to the conclusion that the data subjects' consents were not sufficiently *informed*.[1988] Finally, the CNIL found that the data subjects' consents were not *unambiguous*, as they were not given through a positive act, because the option of giving specific consent for each purpose should have been given before the options 'Accept all' or 'Refuse all', and should not have been subject to the necessity for data subjects to perform any particular action, such as clicking on 'More options'.[1989] This also echoes the need to have a stricter application of the data protection by design principle.[1990] Indeed, these large data holders increasingly resort to 'nudging techniques' in order to ensure that data subjects act in a way that best meets their own interests, rather than the data subjects' interests.[1991] A clear example is dark patterns used to collect consent, as the data subjects are often presented with a first alternative between 'Agree to all' and 'More options',

1983. In this regard, it is worth making a small digression in order to suggest that another type of multilayer approach could be further investigated to solve this transparency issue. Indeed, the transparency requirement is complex to meet, as a fine line must be found between providing too much or too little information. This is because providing too little and vague information might not be specific enough, while providing too much information might make the privacy policy unreasonably long and might discourage (even further) people from reading it. To solve this issue, a three-layered approach, inspired from the Creative Commons Licences, could be adopted (*see* https://creativecommons.org/about/cclicenses/). The first layer would be composed of standardised icons, easily understandable by the data subjects, as envisaged in Article 12.7 of the GDPR. The second layer would be composed of a 'shortened privacy policy', explaining in clear and intelligible terms the main aspects of the processing (types of data collected, purposes, lawful basis, etc.). The third layer would contain the full privacy policy, with all of the detailed information.

1984. CNIL, *Google*, 21 January 2019, §§ 96-103.

1985. *Ibid.*, §§ 104-128.

1986. Arguably, this finding can be linked to the Belgian Data Protection Authority's finding that large data holders have a 'special responsibility' in applying the GDPR (*see* point 332), as this special responsibility would also derive from the fact that they process very large amounts of data.

1987. CNIL, *Google*, 21 January 2019, § 109.

1988. *Ibid.*, §§ 141-148.

1989. *Ibid.*, §§ 149-167.

1990. Article 25 of the GDPR.

1991. M. Nouwens, et al., 'Dark Patterns after the GDPR: Scraping Consent Pop-Ups and Demonstrating Their Influence', *supra*.

which requires extra efforts from the data subjects as they can only express their preferences on a second screen (where the boxes are even sometimes pre-ticked).[1992] This discourages the data subjects from voicing their true privacy preferences, especially when a nudging message appears saying that they will lose functionality if they do not consent to all/some of the processing.[1993]

334. Recently, on 7 December 2020, the CNIL fined Google EUR 100 million, notably for having placed advertising cookies on the computers of users of www.google.fr, residing in France, without prior consent or satisfactory information.[1994] In substance, the CNIL ruled that the information provided by Google, both in the banner and in the pop-up window, did not allow users residing in France, when they arrived on www.google.fr, to be clearly informed beforehand of the existence of processing allowing the access to information contained in their terminal and allowing the writing of such information (cookies).[1995] Consequently, the information provided by Google did not allow these users to be clearly informed beforehand about the purpose of this processing and of the means made available to them in order to oppose their use.[1996] Moreover, it ruled that since four out of the seven cookies written on the users' terminal pursued an advertising purpose, Google should have obtained the users' explicit consent before putting them on their terminal.[1997] This is because these cookies do not have, as exclusive purpose, the enabling or facilitation of communication by electronic means and they are not strictly necessary for the provision of an online communication service at the express request of the user.[1998]

On the same day, the CNIL also fined Amazon EUR 35 million for substantially the same reasons.[1999] Here as well, it ruled that since more than 40 cookies written on the users' terminal pursued an advertising purpose, Amazon should have obtained the users' explicit consent before putting them

1992. M. Nouwens, et al., 'Dark Patterns after the GDPR: Scraping Consent Pop-Ups and Demonstrating Their Influence', *supra*, pp. 5-6.

1993. *Ibid.*, p. 9.

1994. CNIL, *Google LLC and Google Ireland Limited*, 7 December 2020, Deliberation of the Restricted Committee SAN-2020-012, available at https://www.legifrance.gouv.fr/cnil/id/CNILTEXT000042635706.

1995. *Ibid.*, § 82.

1996. *Ibid.* In this regard, it is worth pointing out that even if Google took steps, during the procedure, to provide more information beforehand, the CNIL considered that this information was still too imprecise, as it still did not enable the users to understand the purposes of processing nor the means made available to them in order to oppose to their use (*see* §§ 86-94).

1997. *Ibid.*, § 100.

1998. *Ibid.* The CNIL however acknowledged that Google had solved this issue during the procedure (*see* § 102).

1999. CNIL, *Amazon Europe Core*, 7 December 2020, Deliberation of the Restricted Committee SAN-2020-013, available at https://www.legifrance.gouv.fr/cnil/id/CNILTEXT000042635729.

on their terminal,[2000] as they did not exclusively aim to enable or facilitate communication by electronic means, and as they were not strictly necessary for the provision of an online communication service.[2001] Moreover, it held that the information, relating to the cookies, provided by Amazon to the users was either incomplete or inexistent.[2002] Indeed, it ruled that the information banner shown on the homepage of www.amazon.fr only contained a general and approximative description of the purpose of the cookies, and that it did not provide any information on the means made available to the users in order to oppose their use.[2003] The CNIL further held that the breach of the information requirement was even more flagrant for users arriving on www.amazon.fr through an advertisement published on the website of a third party as, in that case, no information at all was provided to the users regarding these cookies.[2004]

335. One must however acknowledge that these interventions by data protection authorities have been sporadic and that the fines imposed are quite derisory in comparison with these large data holders' turnovers.[2005] A slight exception to this is the Irish *Data Protection Commission*'s EUR 225 million fine imposed on WhatsApp for a breach of its transparency obligations.[2006] Indeed, the DPC found that WhatsApp has breached its transparency obligations, contained in Articles 12-14 of the GDPR, by providing insufficient information about its personal data processing operations to both non-users[2007] and users[2008] of its services. It also found that WhatsApp has failed to comply with its transparency obligations in relation to how it works and shares data with the other companies of the Facebook ecosystem.[2009] This is notably because the information at hand 'is spread out across a wide range of texts and a significant amount of the information provided is so high

2000. *Ibid.*, §§ 87-90.
2001. *Ibid.*, § 88.
2002. *Ibid.*, § 92.
2003. *Ibid.*, §§ 94-95.
2004. *Ibid.*, §§ 96-97.
2005. For instance, Google LLC had a turnover of more than 160 billion dollars in 2019, Google Ireland Ltd had a turnover of more than 38 billion euros in 2018, and Amazon Europe had a turnover of approximately EUR 7.7 billion in 2019. *See* CNIL, *Google LLC and Google Ireland Limited*, 7 December 2020, §§ 2 and 3; *Amazon Europe Core*, 7 December 2020, § 1.
2006. Data Protection Commission, *WhatsApp Ireland Limited*, 20 August 2021, Decision No. IN-18-12-2, available at https://edpb.europa.eu/system/files/2021-09/dpc_final_decision_redacted_for_issue_to_edpb_01-09-21_en.pdf. *See also* on this case: European Data Protection Board, Binding decision 1/2021 on the dispute arisen on the draft decision of the Irish Supervisory Authority regarding WhatsApp Ireland under Article 65(1)(a) GDPR, 28 July 2021, available at https://edpb.europa.eu/system/files/2021-09/edpb_bindingdecision_202101_ie_sa_whatsapp_redacted_en.pdf.
2007. Data Protection Commission, *WhatsApp Ireland Limited*, § 177.
2008. *Ibid.*, §§ 399; 416; 434; 457; 476; 496 and 520.
2009. *Ibid.*, §§ 591-592.

level as to be meaningless'.[2010] Indeed, according to the DPC, 'there is an over-supply of very high level, generalised information at the sacrifice of a more concise and meaningful delivery of the essential information'.[2011] As a result, it considers the information to be 'unnecessarily confusing and ill-defined'.[2012] Moreover, the DPC found that the information providing that WhatsApp shares personal data with Facebook for safety and security purposes is misleading, as no such processing has ever taken place and its commencement is not imminent.[2013] Finally, it is worth noting that, in addition to the administrative fine, the DPC required WhatsApp to bring its processing operations in compliance with the GDPR, by taking a series of remedial actions.[2014]

A more notable exception is the Luxembourg's *National Data Protection Commission* decision to impose a EUR 746 million fine on Amazon for a lack of valid consent as basis for its targeted advertising purposes, which has been issued on 15 July 2021.[2015] While these decisions could mark the beginning of a new trend of more drastic interventions against Big Tech actors, they could also remain remarkably exceptional islands in a sea of restrained intervention by data protection authorities.

Indeed, up to now, and with the exception of these last two decisions, there has been a form of impunity of the conduct of such data holders, which arguably continue to rely on 'internal data free-for-all' practices and to ignore the core principles of the GDPR, and this allows them to obtain a considerable competitive advantage over GDPR-compliant competitors.[2016] In this perspective, it can be questioned whether these large data holders have solely acquired their strong market position through competition on the merits, or whether this position was, at least partly, acquired through dubious practices in a pre-GDPR era where there was less global awareness about these personal data protection issues, and where there was, in fact, uncertainty as to whether these non-European actors were bound by the rules of

---

2010. *Ibid.*, § 588.
2011. *Ibid.*, § 590.
2012. *Ibid.*
2013. *Ibid.*, § 589.
2014. *Ibid.*, § 888 and Appendix C.
2015. *See* S. Bodoni, 'Amazon Gets Record $888 Million EU Fine Over Data Violations', 30 July 2021, available at https://www.bloomberg.com/news/articles/2021-07-30/amazon-given-record-888-million-eu-fine-for-data-privacy-breach; L. Adam, 'RGPD: Amazon écope d'une amende record à 746 millions d'euros', 30 July 2021, available at https://www.zdnet.fr/actualites/rgpd-amazon-ecope-d-une-amende-record-a-746-millions-d-euros-39926965.htm. Unfortunately, the DPC decided not to publish the decision due to professional secrecy concerns (*see* https://cnpd.public.lu/en/actualites/international/2021/08/decision-amazon-2.html).
2016. D. Geradin, T. Karanikioti and D. Katsifis, 'GDPR Myopia', *supra*, p. 25.

the Data Protection Directive.[2017] In any case, the data advantage that these large data holders have acquired now makes it practically impossible for third parties, in a post-GDPR era, to contest their position while respecting the data protection legislation.

Indeed, despite growing calls for taking personal data protection considerations into account in competition law assessments,[2018] these considerations have often been set aside in light of the premise that large/dominant data holders would be GDPR-compliant as they would be closely monitored by data protection authorities.[2019] As a result, competition authorities have often been encouraged to keep off the data protection authorities' grass. This has been expressly stated by the European Court of Justice in the *Asnef-Equifax* case, where it held that 'any possible issues relating to the sensitivity of personal data are not, *as such*, a matter for competition law, as they may be resolved on the basis of the relevant provisions governing data protection' (emphasis added).[2020] This has also been confirmed by the European Commission in its *Google/DoubleClick* merger decision,[2021] and later in its *Facebook/Whatsapp* merger decision, where it stated that 'any privacy related concerns flowing from the increased concentration of data within the control of Facebook as a result of the transaction do not fall within the scope of the EU competition law rules but within the scope of the data protection rules'.[2022,2023] It also followed a similar approach in the *Microsoft/LinkedIn* merger decision.[2024] Yet, as data

2017. Indeed, this uncertainty was only resolved through the European Court of Justice's decision in the *Google Spain* case (ECJ, *Google Spain and Google*, 13 May 2014, case C-131/12, EU:C:2014:317).
2018. *See*, for instance, W. Kerber, 'Digital Markets, Data, and Privacy: Competition Law, Consumer Law, and Data Protection', *MAGKS Joint Discussion Paper Series in Economics No. 14-2016*, February 2016, available at https://www.econstor.eu/bitstream/10419/144679/1/850599016.pdf; M. Stucke and A. Grunes, *Big Data and Competition Policy*, *supra*; Autorité de la concurrence and Bundeskartellamt, 'Competition Law and Data', 10 May 2016, available at http://www.autoritedelaconcurrence.fr/doc/reportcompetitionlawanddatafinal.pdf; A. Ezrachi and V. Robertson, 'Competition, Market Power and Third-Party Tracking', *World Competition: Law and Economics Review*, 2019, Vol. 42(1), pp. 5-19; G. Colangelo and M. Maggiolino, 'Data Protection in Attention Markets: Protecting Privacy Through Competition?', *Bocconi Legal Studies Research Paper No. 2945085*, 2 April 2017, available at https://ssrn.com/abstract=2945085, pp. 7-9. On the contrary, some argue that data protection and competition law should be kept apart: *see* G. Colangelo and M. Maggiolino, 'Data Protection in Attention Markets', *supra*, pp. 9-11.
2019. *See* OECD, *Consumer Data Rights and Competition*, *supra*, pp. 24-41.
2020. ECJ, *Asnef Equifax and Administración des Estado*, 23 November 2006, C-238/05, EU:C:2006:734, § 63.
2021. European Commission, *Google/DoubleClick*, 11 March 2018, case M.4731, § 368.
2022. European Commission, *Facebook/WhatsApp*, 3 October 2014, case M.7217, § 164.
2023. G. Colangelo and M. Maggiolino, 'Data Protection in Attention Markets', *supra*, p. 5.
2024. European Commission, *Microsoft/LinkedIn*, 6 December 2016, case M.8124, §§ 177-179; G. Colangelo and M. Maggiolino, 'Data Protection in Attention Markets', *supra*, p. 5.

protection authorities failed to properly monitor these large data holders, the latter have arguably been able to consolidate their strong position in the various data markets through questionable practices in terms of data protection law.

336. Therefore, a lack of data protection enforcement has arguably led to a lack of competition enforcement, and has comforted these large data holders in their 'internal data free-for-all' practices. One of the few exceptions to this lack of regulatory intervention is the notorious *Bundeskartellamt*'s case (the German Competition Authority) against Facebook.[2025] In that case, the German Competition Authority found, in interim proceedings, that the firm had abused its dominant position on the German social network market by making it compulsory for users, wishing to use its social network, to consent to the collection, by Facebook, of user data from third-party websites[2026] and from other Facebook-owned services (e.g., Instagram and WhatsApp), and to consent to the combination of such data with the user data stemming from the social network.[2027]

Indeed, the *Bundeskartellamt* found, on the one hand, that the inclusion of such a requirement in Facebook's terms of service constituted an exploitative abuse to the detriment of users, as it was the result of an unlawful data processing in breach of the principle of transparency and of the requirements for valid consent under the GDPR (Articles 5.1.a), 6.1.a) and 7). On the other hand, it found that this conduct impeded competition, as it unlawfully allowed Facebook to acquire a further competitive data advantage over its competitors, thus elevating entry barriers and strengthening Facebook's market power.[2028] Although the *Bundeskartellamt*'s decision was based on Section 19(1) of the German Act against Restraints of Competition ('GWB'),[2029] some argue that Article 102 TFEU could also be used to

---

2025. Bundeskartellamt (6th Division), *Facebook*, 6 February 2019, B6-22/16, available at https://www.bundeskartellamt.de/SharedDocs/Entscheidung/EN/Entscheidungen/Missbrauchsaufsicht/2019/B6-22-16.pdf. *See also* Bundeskartellamt, 'Bundeskartellamt Prohibits Facebook from Combining User Data from Different Sources', 7 February 2019, available at https://www.bundeskartellamt.de/SharedDocs/Meldung/EN/Pressemitteilungen/2019/07_02_2019_Facebook.html.
2026. For more details on the potential impact of third-party tracking on competition and market power, *see* A. Ezrachi and V. Robertson, 'Competition, Market Power and Third-Party Tracking', *supra*, pp. 5-19.
2027. D. Geradin, T. Karanikioti and D. Katsifis, 'GDPR Myopia', *supra*, p. 26. *See also* W. Wils, 'The Obligation for the Competition Authorities of the EU Member States to apply EU Antitrust Law and the Facebook Decision of the Bundeskartellamt', *Concurrences*, 2019, No. 3, pp. 58-66; K. Wiedemann, 'A Matter of Choice', *supra*, pp. 1169-1170.
2028. W. Wils, 'The Obligation for the Competition Authorities of the EU Member States to Apply EU Antitrust Law and the Facebook Decision of the Bundeskartellamt', *supra*, p. 61.
2029. 'Gesetz gegen Wettbewerbsbeschränkungen' (Act against Restraints of Competition, adopted on 26 August 1998 and lastly amended on 19 January 2021).

sanction the imposition of unfair terms infringing data protection law.[2030] Indeed, it derives from the case law of the European Court of Justice that the 'fairness' of trading conditions (Article 102(a) of the TFEU) can be assessed on the basis of principles such as necessity, proportionality or transparency,[2031] which are fundamental data protection law principles.[2032] These personal data principles could thus be used as a benchmark to assess the existence of an exploitative abuse under Article 102 TFEU, but this does not imply that any infringement of data protection law will automatically lead to a competition law infringement, as this will be a function of the specific circumstances of the case.[2033] Yet, as pointed out by Wils:

> In the Facebook Decision, the Bundeskartellamt conducts such an examination. In doing so, it finds not only that Facebook's terms of service constitute exploitative business terms to the detriment of consumers, but also that Facebook's conduct impedes competitors in that it gives Facebook access to a large number of further data sources, thus giving Facebook a further competitive edge over its competitors and reinforcing market entry barriers, which in turn strengthen Facebook's market power vis-à-vis consumers. The Facebook decision thus goes well beyond a mere 'recycling' of a finding of infringement of data protection law.[2034]

337. Yet, Wils' enthusiasm was not shared by all, and some have strongly criticised the *Bundeskartellamt*'s decision,[2035] notably in light of the Dusseldorf Higher Regional Court's decision to suspend the effects of the *Bundeskartellamt*'s ruling,[2036] as it believed that the competition authority had failed to establish concrete anticompetitive effects and had rather derived them automatically from a violation of the GDPR.[2037] Indeed, the Court held

2030. W. Wils, 'The Obligation for the Competition Authorities of the EU Member States to Apply EU Antitrust Law and the Facebook Decision of the Bundeskartellamt', *supra*, p. 63.
2031. ECJ, *BRT and SABAM*, 21 March 1974, C-127/73, EU:C:1974:25; ECJ, *Der Grüne Punkt – Duales System Deutschland v. Commission*, 16 July 2009, C-385/07 P, EU:C:2009:456, § 142; ECJ, *AstraZeneca v. Commission*, 6 December 2012, C-457/10 P, EU:C:2012:770, § 93.
2032. W. Wils, 'The Obligation for the Competition Authorities of the EU Member States to Apply EU Antitrust Law and the Facebook Decision of the Bundeskartellamt', *supra*, p. 63.
2033. *Ibid. See also* J. Hoffmann and G. Johannsen, 'EU-Merger Control & Big Data, *supra*, pp. 33-41.
2034. W. Wils, 'The Obligation for the Competition Authorities of the EU Member States to Apply EU Antitrust Law and the Facebook Decision of the Bundeskartellamt', *supra*, p. 63.
2035. *See*, for instance, P. Këllezi, 'Data Protection and Competition Law: Non-compliance as Abuse of Dominant Position', *Sui-generis*, 2019, pp. 343-359.
2036. Dusseldorf Higher Regional Court, *Facebook/Bunderskartellamt*, 26 August 2019, VI-Kart 1/19.
2037. P. Këllezi, 'Data protection and competition law: non-compliance as abuse of dominant position', *supra*, p. 344.

that the competition authority had not established causality between Facebook's market dominance and the content of its terms of services, because 'other companies were using similar conditions and the "abusive" terms of service were thus not deemed a result of market dominance'.[2038] Moreover, the Court was of the opinion that Facebook users were free to refuse to consent to the terms of service, that Facebook had committed no exploitative abuse as competitors could collect the same data from users, and that the *Bundeskartellamt* had failed to demonstrate that Facebook's practices damaged competition, as users did not suffer any financial loss.[2039]

338. However, this decision of the Dusseldorf Higher Regional Court has been overturned by thc *Bundesgerichtshof* (German Federal Court of Justice), which confirmed the *Bundeskartellamt*'s approach.[2040] Indeed, the *Bundesgerichtshof* held that there is no serious doubt about Facebook's dominant position in the German social networking market, nor that Facebook is abusing this dominant position through the terms of service sanctioned by the *Bundeskartellamt.*[2041] In reaching such a verdict, the *Bundeskartellamt* focused on competition policy considerations, rather than on personal data protection concerns.[2042] Indeed, according to the *Bundesgerichtshof*, the decisive factor outlined by the *Bundeskartellamt* to find such an abuse is not that Facebook's data processing infringes the rules of the GDPR, but rather that Facebook's terms of services are abusive because the users have no other choice but to accept the processing of data from third-party websites and from other Facebook-owned services (e.g., Instagram and WhatsApp), in order to use Facebook's social network.[2043] For the *Bundesgerichtshof*, 'the fact that Facebook does not provide a less "data-intensive" option indicates that it can act on the market irrespective of user preferences, which in turn implies an abuse of dominance'.[2044] This lack of choice constitutes an exploitative abuse of the users, as Facebook's access to a considerably larger amount of data than its competitors leads to lock-in effects and switching costs, which are relevant under competition law because competition can no longer effectively exercise its control function

2038. K. Wiedemann, 'A Matter of Choice', *supra*, p. 1170.
2039. *Ibid*; OECD, *Consumer Data Rights and Competition*, *supra*, p. 30.
2040. BGH, *Facebook*, 23 June 2020, KVR 69/19, no. 080/2020. For a comment of this decision, *see* K. Wiedemann, 'A Matter of Choice', *supra*, pp. 1168-1181.
2041. *See* Bundesgerichtshof, 'Bundesgerichtshof bestätigt vorläufig den Vorwurf der missbräuchlichen Ausnutzung einer marktbeherrschenden Stellung durch Facebook,' 23 June 2020, available at https://www.bundesgerichtshof.de/SharedDocs/Pressemitteilungen/DE/2020/2020080.html.
2042. K. Wiedemann, 'A Matter of Choice', *supra*, p. 1170. For more details, *see* pp. 1170-1178.
2043. *See* Bundesgerichtshof, 'Bundesgerichtshof bestätigt vorläufig den Vorwurf der missbräuchlichen Ausnutzung einer marktbeherrschenden Stellung durch Facebook,' *supra*.
2044. K. Wiedemann, 'A Matter of Choice', *supra*, p. 1172.

due to Facebook's dominant position.[2045] Indeed, it is much more difficult for Facebook's (potential) competitors to compete, as Facebook's strong network effects create high entry barriers, and as competitors are unable to collect as much quantitative and qualitative data about the users, and thus to compete for advertising contracts.[2046]

On the issue of causality, the *Bundesgerichtshof* relied on a normative approach, traditionally applied to exclusionary abuses[2047] rather than to exploitative abuses, to argue that it was Facebook's market dominance that allowed it to adopt terms of services that were detrimental not only to users but also to competition.[2048] As summarised by Wiedemann, for the *Bundesgerichtshof*, 'it does not matter if other, non-market-dominant companies would be factually able to impose the same terms of service on their users, as long as the damage to competition results from the market dominance of the company in question'.[2049]

Finally, the *Bundesgerichtshof* outlined that the fact that the lack of choice for Facebook users also (potentially) affected their right to informational self-determination[2050] and to personal data protection[2051] needed to be factored in the balancing of all the interests involved *in casu*.[2052] Indeed, even if Facebook is not directly bound by human rights because it is a private entity, these users' rights 'must be protected from an overly far-reaching commercial exploitation of their personal data'.[2053]

Since the *Bundesgerichtshof*'s decision was also rendered in interim proceedings, it remains to be seen whether a different ruling will be made in the main proceedings.[2054] It is also worth pointing out that Facebook has been sanctioned for a similar behaviour by the *Autorità Garante della*

2045. *See* Bundesgerichtshof, 'Bundesgerichtshof bestätigt vorläufig den Vorwurf der missbräuchlichen Ausnutzung einer marktbeherrschenden Stellung durch Facebook,' *supra*.
2046. K. Wiedemann, 'A Matter of Choice', *supra*, pp. 1171-1173.
2047. *See* ECJ, *Europemballage Corporation and Continental Can Company v. Commission*, 21 February 1973, C-6/72, EU:C:1973:22, §§ 26-27; and ECJ, *Hoffmann-Laroche v. Commission*, 13 February 1979, C-85/76, EU:C:1979:36, § 91.
2048. K. Wiedemann 'A Matter of Choice', *supra*, p. 1172.
2049. *Ibid.*
2050. *See* German Federal Constitutional Court, *Volkszählungsurteil*, 15 December 1983, 1 BvR 209/83 et al., 65 BVerfGE 1. On informational self-determination, *see* Part I, Chapter 2, Section 2.3.2.
2051. However, the *Bundesgerichtshof* did not rule on whether the consent collected by Facebook constituted a 'valid consent' in the sense of Article 6.1.a) of the GDPR.
2052. K. Wiedemann, 'A Matter of Choice', *supra*, p. 1173.
2053. *Ibid.*, p. 1174.
2054. It must be outlined here that, on 24 March 2021, the Dusseldorf Higher Regional Court has considered that it needed a clarification from the European Court of Justice in order to rule on the matter. *See* S. Stolton, 'German Legal Dispute over Facebook Data Use Sent to European Court of Justice', 24 March 2021, available at https://www.euractiv.com/section/data-protection/news/german-legal-dispute-over-facebook-data-use-sent-to-european-court-of-justice/.

Concorrenza e del Mercato (the Italian Competition Authority),[2055] although on the grounds of consumer law.[2056]

339. In light of the above, and as for the first premise, the second premise, according to which large data holders allegedly reuse personal data within their ecosystem in a data protection law compliant manner, can also be challenged. Therefore, large data holders should, in theory, not be able to apply 'double standards' when it comes to personal data protection rules. Said otherwise, they should not be able to apply low personal data protection standards to themselves in order to gain competitive advantages from (potentially unlawful) 'internal data free-for-all' practices while applying stricter data protection requirements to third parties wishing to reuse (some of) their data (which could potentially be seen as an anticompetitive way of raising entry barriers and strengthening their competitive/dominant position on the data markets).[2057]

However, even if these premises are challengeable from a theoretical point of view, large data holders do apply 'double standards' in practice. Indeed, they adopt a very restrictive approach towards data sharing with third parties while massively circulating their users' data internally. One of the potential explanations for this is that there is less visibility (and also scrutiny) on internal data circulation than on data sharing with third parties. On the one hand, this allows the large data holders to claim that they are fully compliant with the data protection requirements, while this may not be true, as outlined by the cases mentioned above.[2058] On the other hand, it allows them to require 'equivalent compliance' from third parties, who are asked to match the high level of compliance that large data holders claim to have achieved internally. Another potential explanation is that these large data holders fear losing control over the data shared with third parties, as illustrated in the 'Facebook / Cambridge Analytica' scandal mentioned above.[2059] Unfortunately, this 'double standard' practice does not seem to be addressed appropriately by the controlling authorities, which have more often opted to intervene harshly against smaller actors instead.[2060] Section 7.1.3 will attempt to shed light on why this is the case.

2055. Autorità Garante della Concorrenza e del Mercato, *Facebook*, 29 November 2018, Decision No. 27432 available at https://www.agcm.it/dotcmsdoc/allegati-news/PS11112_scorr_sanz.pdf.

2056. *See* M. Botta and K. Wiedemann, 'The Interaction of EU Competition, Consumer, and Data Protection Law in the Digital Economy: The Regulatory Dilemma in the Facebook Odyssey', *Antitrust Bulletin,* 2019, Vol. 64(3), pp. 428-446.

2057. D. Geradin, T. Karanikioti and D. Katsifis, 'GDPR Myopia', *supra*, pp. 27-35.

2058. *See* points 332-336.

2059. *See* point 330.

2060. D. Geradin, T. Karanikioti and D. Katsifis, 'GDPR Myopia', *supra*, p. 1.

7.1.3 Failure of Controlling Authorities to Address the 'Double Standards' Applied by Large Data Holders

340. As outlined above, although some large data holders, such as Google and Facebook, have been fined by data protection authorities for infringing personal data protection legislations,[2061] these interventions have been quite rare and the amount of the fines were quite small in comparison with these large data holders' turnovers. Accordingly, and despite numerous complaints,[2062] there is a form of impunity in the conduct of such data holders.[2063] This is arguably the result of a combination of two factors.

341. On the one hand, data protection authorities only have very limited financial resources and man-power, especially when compared to those of large data holders, to address these highly complex issues. Indeed, the combined budget of the EU's 45 data protection authorities is only EUR 326 million a year; half of them have a budget lower than EUR 10 million a year (the UK *Information Commissioner's Office*'s budget is the highest with EUR 61 million a year); they only have a combined total of 305 tech specialists; and half of them only have five or fewer tech specialists.[2064] This might explain why they sometimes refrain from engaging in such complex and resource-consuming investigations, or why these investigations take a lot of time once initiated.

2061. *See* points 334-337.

2062. *See*, for instance, Privacy International, 'Regulatory complaint against Google and other "ad tech" companies under Europe's GDPR by Johnny Ryan, Jim Killock, and Michael Veale', 12 September 2018, available at https://privacyinternational.org/examples/2983/regulatory-complaint-against-google-and-other-ad-tech-companies-under-europes-gdpr; Privacy International, 'Panoptykon Foundation files complaint against Google and other "ad tech" companies with the with the Polish Data Protection Authority', 28 January 2019, available at https://privacyinternational.org/examples/2982/panoptykon-foundation-files-complaint-against-googleand-other-ad-tech-companies; Privacy International, 'Ad Tech GDPR complaint is extended to four more European regulators', 20 May 2019, available at https://privacyinternational.org/examples/2992/ad-tech-gdpr-complaint-extended-four-more-european-regulators; J. Ryan, 'Formal GDPR Complaint Against Google's Internal Data Free-for-All', 16 March 2020, available at https://brave.com/google-internal-data-free-for-all/.

2063. D. Geradin, T. Karanikioti and D. Katsifis, 'GDPR Myopia', *supra*, p. 19; N. Vinocur, '"We Have a Huge Problem": European Tech Regulator Despairs over Lack of Enforcement', *Politico*, 27 December 2019, available at https://www.politico.com/news/2019/12/27/europe-gdpr-technology-regulation-089605.

2064. Brave, 'Europe's Governments Are Failing the GDPR: Brave's 2020 Report on the Enforcement Capacity of Data Protection Authorities', April 2020, available at https://brave.com/wp-content/uploads/2020/04/Brave-2020-DPA-Report.pdf, pp. 3-6; Access Now, 'Three Years under the EU GDPR: An Implementation Progress Report', 2021, available at https://www.accessnow.org/cms/assets/uploads/2021/05/Three-Years-Under-GDPR-report.pdf, pp. 10-12.

342. On the other hand, the fact that these large data holders are active globally also has a strong impact on enforcement. Indeed, the GDPR designates a lead supervisory authority for the investigation of cross-border processing, namely the data protection authority of the main establishment or of the single establishment of the controller/processor in the EU.[2065] Accordingly, the other national data protection authorities will, in principle,[2066] only be able to investigate cases that relate to an establishment in their Member State, or that substantially affect data subjects only in their Member State.[2067] Yet, there are substantial issues with this mechanism, due to the use of inadequate communication tools between the data protection authorities, to the potential incompatibility of their national procedures, to the lengthiness of the cooperation process and to the difficulties in identifying the lead authority.[2068] Moreover, this leads to a 'forum shopping' scenario, as large data holders, who are active globally and carry cross-border processing, have an incentive to locate their main establishment in countries where the national data protection authorities are less active. As outlined by Geradin et al., this one-stop-shop system 'creates serious bottlenecks which, coupled with the reluctancy of certain [data protection authorities] to intervene, results in tech giants escaping close monitoring and liability, despite regularly engaging in dubious practices'.[2069]

Indeed, in the tech sector, most large data holders, such as Google and Facebook, have located their main establishment, on the territory of the Union, in Ireland and Luxembourg, notably for fiscal reasons.[2070] Accordingly, the Irish *Data Protection Commission* and Luxembourg's *National Data Protection Commission* have a key role to play in the enforcement of the GDPR against these large data holders, and their 'ability and willingness to investigate and sanction these companies therefore determines whether these companies will be able to get away with questionable data processing activities or will be held to account'.[2071] While Luxembourg's *National Data Protection Commission* seems to start realising the importance of its regulatory role,[2072] the Irish *Data Protection Commission*, which is the lead authority for tech firms such as Google or Facebook, has been reluctant to

2065. Article 56.1 of the GDPR.
2066. *See*, however, Opinion of Advocate General Bobek in *Facebook v. Gegevensbeschermingsautoriteit* (ECJ), C-645/19, delivered on 13 January 2021, EU:C:2021:5; and ECJ, *Facebook v. Gegevensbeschermingsautoriteit*, 15 June 2021, C-645/19, EU:C:2021:483, § 96.
2067. Article 56.2 of the GDPR.
2068. Access Now, 'Three Years under the EU GDPR', *supra*, pp. 15-19.
2069. D. Geradin, T. Karanikioti and D. Katsifis, 'GDPR Myopia', *supra*, p. 18. *See also* N. Vinocur, '"We Have a Huge Problem": European Tech Regulator Despairs over Lack of Enforcement', *supra*.
2070. *See* N. Vinocur, '"We Have a Huge Problem": European Tech Regulator Despairs over Lack of Enforcement', *supra*.
2071. D. Geradin, T. Karanikioti and D. Katsifis, 'GDPR Myopia', *supra*, p. 13.
2072. *See* point 335.

intervene strongly against these large data holders, although it has recently issued a large fine against WhatsApp.[2073] This is notably due to the fact that it has a very limited budget (EUR 16.9 million per year, the 6th in Europe)[2074] and staff (140 investigators, lawyers and technologists)[2075] to deal with an extreme case load. Indeed, since the entry into force of the GDPR on 25 May 2018, the Irish *Data Protection Commission* has received more than 8,800 complaints, 9,600 data breach notifications and 593 cross-border processing complaints through the one-stop-shop system.[2076] Moreover, from a political perspective, the Irish *Data Protection Commission* is in an uncomfortable position as Ireland is strongly dependent on these large data holders, such as Google and Facebook, and this might explain why it has not been more active in investigating these actors.[2077] Unsurprisingly, this is generating a lot of criticism against the Irish *Data Protection Commission* from other European data protection authorities and from members of the European Parliament.[2078]

343. However, it would be too simplistic to reject all of the faults on the Irish *Data Protection Commission* and on Luxembourg's *National Data Protection Commission*. Rather, they are the flagships of the worrying observation that data protection authorities across Europe do not have sufficient resources to fulfil their duties and do not sufficiently cooperate, leading to a lack of data protection enforcement.[2079] In turn, this leads to a lack of competition enforcement because data protection considerations have often been set aside in competition law assessments,[2080] in light of the erroneous premise that

2073. *Ibid.*
2074. A. Satariano, 'Europe's Privacy Law Hasn't Shown Its Teeth, Frustrating Advocates', *The New York Times*, 27 April 2020, available at https://www.nytimes.com/2020/04/27/technology/GDPR-privacy-law-europe.html.
2075. Brave, 'Europe's governments are failing the GDPR: Brave's 2020 report on the enforcement capacity of data protection authorities', *supra*, p. 7.
2076. *See* (Irish) Data Protection Commission, 'Annual Report: 25 May – 31 December 2018', 2019, available at https://www.dataprotection.ie/sites/default/files/uploads/2019-02/DPC%20Annual%20Report%2025%20May%20-%2031%20December%202018.pdf; (Irish) Data Protection Commission, 'Annual Report: 1 January – 31 December 2019', 2020, available at https://www.dataprotection.ie/sites/default/files/uploads/2020-02/DPC%20Annual%20Report%202019.pdf; D. Geradin, T. Karanikioti and D. Katsifis, 'GDPR Myopia', *supra*, p. 20.
2077. D. Geradin, T. Karanikioti and D. Katsifis, 'GDPR Myopia', *supra*, p. 20.
2078. *See* V. Manancourt, 'Irish Data Regulator Pulls Out of "Perverse" MEP Hearing as Tensions Boil Over', 18 March 2021, available at https://pro.politico.eu/news/irish-data-regulator-pulls-out-of-perverse-mep-hearing-as-tensions-boil-over; S. Stolton, 'MEPs Rue Lack of GDPR Sanctions Issued by Irish Data Authority', 26 March 2021, available at https://www.euractiv.com/section/data-protection/news/meps-rue-lack-of-gdpr-sanctions-issued-by-irish-data-authority/.
2079. *See* N. Vinocur, '"We Have a Huge Problem": European Tech Regulator Despairs over Lack of Enforcement', *supra*; Access Now, 'Three Years under the EU GDPR', *supra*.
2080. *See* references in footnote 2018.

large/dominant data holders would be GDPR-compliant as they would be closely monitored by data protection authorities.[2081] As data protection authorities failed to monitor these large data holders, they have been able to consolidate their strong position in the various data markets through questionable practices in terms of data protection law. In turn, this also reduces personal data protection.

344. Finally, it should be added that while a lack of enforcement might arguably be the main cause of the above-mentioned problems, another potential cause is the over-reliance on the fact that data subjects are able to make informed decisions when it comes to the processing of their data,[2082] and that they will actually make use of the rights that are granted to them by the GDPR if they stumble upon unlawful processing.[2083]

7.1.4 Crucial Need for More Enforcement by Controlling Authorities

345. It thus stems from the above that while the growing concern that the GDPR limits competition and increases concentration relies on two premises that are challengeable in theory (the GDPR is *not* more lenient towards personal data reuse within the ecosystem of these large data holders than it is towards the sharing of this personal data with third parties; and the way in which these large data holders reuse personal data within their ecosystem *might arguably not* comply with data protection law), large data holders do apply 'double standards' in practice. Indeed, they adopt a very restrictive approach towards data sharing with third parties while massively circulating their users' data internally. This is mainly the result of a lack of data protection enforcement, which led, in turn, to a lack of competition enforcement.

Therefore, to solve this 'double standards' issue, there is a crucial need for more enforcement of the existing rules by data protection authorities. For instance, there should be an increased scrutiny of the large data holders'

2081. *See* OECD, *Consumer Data Rights and Competition*, *supra*, pp. 24-41; G. Colangelo and M. Maggiolino, 'Data Protection in Attention Markets', *supra*.

2082. For a strong criticism of the 'notice and consent paradigm', *see* E. Okoyomon, et al., 'On The Ridiculousness of Notice and Consent: Contradictions in App Privacy Policies', *The Workshop on Technology and Consumer Protection*, 2019, available at https://blues.cs.berkeley.edu/blog/2019/05/10/on-the-ridiculousness-of-notice-and-consent-contradictions-in-app-privacy-policies-conpro-19/.

2083. *See* N. Vinocur, '"We Have a Huge Problem": European Tech Regulator Despairs over Lack of Enforcement', *supra*. For more information on consumers' attitude towards privacy, notably the fact that they have heterogeneous preferences and behavioural biases, *see* OECD, *Consumer Data Rights and Competition*, *supra*, pp. 35-37.

'internal data free-for-all' practices,[2084] as has been done by the French *CNIL* in its cases against Google, where it imposed a EUR 50 million fine and a EUR 100 million fine, and in its case against Amazon, where it imposed a EUR 35 million fine.[2085]

346. To ensure more enforcement, the lead authority mechanism might need to be rethought in order to avoid the bureaucratic logjam and the bottlenecks mentioned above, as these might end up having a chilling effect on data subjects seeking to assert their rights against these large data platforms.[2086] In this perspective, the personal data protection legislation could be adapted, in order to enable lead authorities to delegate some cases to other data protection authorities.[2087] At the very least, cooperation between the various data protection authorities, through sharing not only of legal insights but also of resources, needs to be increased. Indeed, data protection authorities, and especially those dealing with the majority of 'tech cases', need more (financial and staff) support to tackle these complex cases. In this regard, it is interesting to point out that the European Parliament has asked the European Commission 'to ensure that Member States provide national supervisory authorities with the adequate financial means and human resources and enforcement powers to carry out their functions effectively and to contribute to their respective work'.[2088] In order to do so, some authors have suggested creating a 'specialised "tech" unit' at the EU level, potentially within the EDPB, which could help the data protection authorities to deal with the technical aspects of their investigations, by providing them with supporting technical experts.[2089] Others have suggested that 'an EU authority (e.g., the Commission [or the EDPB]) could be put in charge in cases involving a large platform with pan-European systemic importance'.[2090] Whatever form this support might take, it is urgent to relieve some of the data protection authorities' burden and to ensure swifter enforcement, for the benefit of all.

2084. On this point, *see* I. Graef and S. Van Berlo, 'Towards Smarter Regulation in the Areas of Competition, Data Protection and Consumer Law: Why Greater Power Should Come with Greater Responsibility', *European Journal of Risk Regulation*, November 2020, available at https://doi.org/10.1017/err.2020.92.
2085. *See* points 333 and 334.
2086. *See* N. Vinocur, '"We Have a Huge Problem": European Tech Regulator Despairs over Lack of Enforcement', *supra*.
2087. J. Krämer, D. Schnurr and S. Broughton Micova, 'The Role of Data for Digital Markets Contestability' *supra*, p. 84.
2088. European Parliament resolution of 20 October 2020 with recommendations to the Commission on the Digital Services Act: Improving the functioning of the Single Market (2020/2018(INL)), P9_TA-PROV(2020)0272, available at https://www.europarl.europa.eu/doceo/document/TA-9-2020-0272_EN.html, p. 20.
2089. D. Geradin, T. Karanikioti and D. Katsifis, 'GDPR Myopia', *supra*, p. 39.
2090. J. Krämer, D. Schnurr and S. Broughton Micova, 'The Role of Data for Digital Markets Contestability', *supra*, p. 84.

Through this increased enforcement, additional scrutiny should be put on the large data holders, notably in light of the 'special responsibility' they have in applying the GDPR.[2091] In this regard, some have suggested to increase the data protection standards that these large data holders must meet, notably through a strengthening of the consent requirements[2092] or through a limitation of their ability to combine user data across their various services (data silos).[2093] In this perspective, it is interesting to outline that, in its *Facebook* case,[2094] the *Bundeskartellamt* ordered, for the first time, an 'internal unbundling of data held by a dominant platform'.[2095] In fact, it seems that the European Commission has piggy-backed on this idea, as it has included, in its proposal for a Digital Markets Act,[2096] a provision restricting certain forms of personal data combination by 'gatekeepers'.[2097] Indeed, these 'gatekeepers' shall refrain from combining personal data originating from their core services with personal data from any other services they offer or with personal data from third-party services, as well as from signing in users to other services they offer in order to combine personal data, unless the users have been presented with this specific choice and have explicitly consented to it.[2098] In the same vein, these 'gatekeepers' shall refrain from requiring their users to subscribe or register to any other services they offer as a condition to access, sign up or register to their core service.[2099]

347. Moreover, a stronger data protection enforcement would also be beneficial for competition, as GDPR-compliance could become a competitive factor leading to the appearance of new competitors. Indeed, a stricter data protection enforcement against these large data holders would shed

2091. *See* point 332. *See also* I. Graef and S. Van Berlo, 'Towards Smarter Regulation in the Areas of Competition, Data Protection and Consumer Law: Why Greater Power Should Come with Greater Responsibility', *supra*.
2092. There should, for instance, be an increased scrutiny regarding the fact that it should be as easy for data subjects to refuse to consent rather than to provide consent, and that these alternatives should be clearly displayed at the same place and with the same emphasis being put on each option. Yet, nowadays, it often requires more steps for data subjects to signal that they do not consent, or that they only consent to some of the processing, than to consent to all the processing (*see* point 333).
2093. D. Condorelli and J. Padilla, 'Harnessing Platform Envelopment Through Privacy Policy Tying', *supra*, pp. 43-44; J. Krämer, D. Schnurr and S. Broughton Micova, 'The Role of Data for Digital Markets Contestability', *supra*, pp. 82-84.
2094. Bundeskartellamt (6th Division), *Facebook*, 6 February 2019, B6-22/16, available at https://www.bundeskartellamt.de/SharedDocs/Entscheidung/EN/Entscheidungen/Missbrauchsaufsicht/2019/B6-22-16.pdf.
2095. D. Geradin, T. Karanikioti and D. Katsifis, 'GDPR Myopia', *supra*, p. 26. *See also* Bundeskartellamt, 'Bundeskartellamt Prohibits Facebook from Combining User Data from Different Sources', *supra*.
2096. Proposal for a Digital Markets Act. For more details on this Digital Markets Act, *see* points 317, 380 and 384 to 385.
2097. Article 5.a) of the Proposal for a Digital Markets Act.
2098. Article 5.a) of the Proposal for a Digital Markets Act.
2099. Article 5.f) of the Proposal for a Digital Markets Act.

more light on some of their dubious practices, which in turn could reduce their trustworthiness and could pave the way for the emergence of more GDPR-compliant and trustworthy competitors. This in turn would increase data protection standards and the control that data subjects can exercise on 'their' data as well, as being GDPR-compliant would become a competitive argument. There is thus an urgent need to move away from the *vicious circle* mentioned above (a lack of data protection enforcement leads to a lack of competition enforcement, which increases data markets' concentration and reduces personal data protection standards and control by data subjects) towards a *virtuous circle* (more data protection enforcement increases data protection standards, which also increases competition, which in turn increases data protection standards and control by data subjects, etc.). Data protection, which might presently be somewhat of a foe to competition in light of the 'double standards' situation, could become a friend if enforced with more pugnacity against large data holders, as it would not only reinforce the protection of data subjects but also ensure the existence of a healthier competitive environment. As summarised by Kerber, 'the basic idea is that a better privacy / data protection law that gives the consumers more control of their data might also lead to less market power of the large digital platforms'.[2100]

348. Finally, to truly address the 'double standards' situation, the other side of the coin must also be tackled, namely that large data holders should not be able to raise data protection requirements as a pretext to justify controversial strategies in order to raise entry barriers on the data markets vis-à-vis third parties and to strengthen their competitive position by refusing to share (some of) their data.[2101] In this regard, it is no longer the data protection authorities but the competition authorities that must increase their scrutiny against such allegations, in order to determine whether such data protection defence is truly genuine or whether it is a 'smokescreen for anti-competitive conduct'.[2102] To do so, the competition authorities should require these large data holders to lay down and substantiate the data protection concerns they raise in order to refuse data sharing with third parties, and they should cooperate with data protection authorities in order to assess whether the data protection standards imposed on third parties by these large firms are (suspiciously) higher than the ones they apply to themselves.[2103]

2100. W. Kerber, 'Updating Competition Policy for the Digital Economy? An Analysis of Recent Reports in Germany, UK, EU, and Australia', September 2019, available at https://ssrn.com/abstract=3469624, p. 40.

2101. *See* D. Geradin, T. Karanikioti and D. Katsifis, 'GDPR Myopia', *supra*, pp. 27-35.

2102. *Ibid.*, pp. 36-37.

2103. *Ibid.*

In fact, an analogy can be made with the European Court of Justice's reasoning in the *Hilti*[2104] and the *Tetra Pak*[2105] cases, in which dominant undertakings invoked consumer safety and health considerations as an objective justification for their tying practices. In *Hilti*, the Court of First Instance held that 'there are laws attaching penalties to the sale of dangerous products and to the use of misleading claims as to the characteristics of any product. There are also authorities vested with powers to enforce those laws. In those circumstances it is clearly not the task of an undertaking in a dominant position to take steps on its own initiative to eliminate products which, rightly or wrongly, it regards as dangerous or at least as inferior in quality to its own products'.[2106] This decision was confirmed by the European Court of Justice.[2107] This finding was repeated by the Court of First Instance in *Tetra Pak,*[2108] whose decision was, once again, confirmed by the European Court of Justice.[2109] Accordingly, if these decisions were to be applied, by analogy, to refusals by large data holders to share data with third parties on the basis of personal data protection considerations, it could be argued that it is not for these large data holders to decide on the level of data protection and security that should be offered by third parties, as the protection of personal data is guaranteed by a separate set of legislations, and as specific authorities are in charge of enforcing them.[2110]

Naturally, the strength of this argument will be function of the effective level of enforcement of personal data protection rules by the data protection authorities. Indeed, this argument will have little weight if data protection authorities fail to adequately enforce personal data protection rules in practice, which they are blamed for at the moment. Therefore, in order to address the two aspects of the 'double standards' issue, it will be crucial for personal data protection authorities to strengthen their enforcement practice

2104. CFI, *Hilti AG v. Commission of the European Communities*, 12 December 1991, T-30/89, EU:T:1991:70; ECJ, *Hilti AG v. Commission of the European Communities*, 2 March 1994, C-53/92 P, EU:C:1994:77.

2105. CFI, *Tetra Pak International SA v. Commission of the European Communities*, 6 October 1994, T-83/91, EU:T:1994:246; ECJ, *Tetra Pak International SA v. Commission of the European Communities*, 14 November 1996, C-333/94 P, EU:C:1996:436.

2106. CFI, *Hilti AG v. Commission of the European Communities*, 12 December 1991, T-30/89, EU:T:1991:70, § 118.

2107. ECJ, *Hilti AG v. Commission of the European Communities*, 2 March 1994, C-53/92 P, EU:C:1994:77, §§ 11-16; I. Graef, 'Differentiated Treatment in Platform-to-Business Relations: EU Competition Law and Economic Dependence', *Yearbook of European Law*, 2019, p. 487.

2108. CFI, *Tetra Pak International SA v. Commission of the European Communities*, 6 October 1994, T-83/91, EU:T:1994:246, § 138.

2109. ECJ, *Tetra Pak International SA v. Commission of the European Communities*, 14 November 1996, C-333/94 P, EU:C:1996:436; I. Graef, 'Differentiated Treatment in Platform-to-Business Relations: EU Competition Law and Economic Dependence', *supra*, p. 488.

2110. *See* I. Graef, 'Differentiated Treatment in Platform-to-Business Relations: EU Competition Law and Economic Dependence', *supra*, pp. 487-488.

against large data holders. On the one hand, this should lead to a limitation/reduction of these large data holders' 'internal data free-for-all' practices. On the other hand, this should limit the cases in which large data holders should be able to justify the refusal to share data with third parties on the basis of personal data protection considerations.

7.2 DATA SHARING AS A COMPETITION LAW REMEDY: ARTICULATION WITH THE GDPR[2111]

349. In light of the previous Section, it appears that while large data holders might attempt to objectively justify refusals to share data on the basis of personal data protection considerations, they might be overstepping their role in doing so and, in fact, this might conceal anticompetitive tactics.[2112] As a consequence, some undertakings may not be able to access certain data at all.[2113] Yet, under EU competition law, if an undertaking holding a dominant position refuses to share (some of) its data with another undertaking, this could potentially lead to the application of the essential facilities doctrine case law[2114] and to an abuse precluded by Article 102 TFEU.[2115] Moreover, such a refusal to share data might also, in certain circumstances, amount to an abuse of economic dependence[2116] or to input foreclosure in vertical mergers.[2117]

As outlined above,[2118] for each of these infringements, a potential procompetitive remedy could be to impose on the large data holder an obligation to share (some of) its data with several third parties. This is because the digital economy is characterised by extreme returns to scale, network externalities and the prominent role of data as a key competitive parameter.[2119] These characteristics lead to strong economies of scope which

---

2111. This Section is partly based on T. Tombal, 'The GDPR: A Shield to a Competition Authority's Data Sharing Remedy?', *Deep Diving into Data Protection*, J. Herveg (coord.), Bruxelles, Larcier, 2021, pp. 67-94.
2112. *See* point 348. D. Geradin, T. Karanikioti and D. Katsifis, 'GDPR Myopia', *supra*, pp. 36-37.
2113. M. Barbero, et al., 'Study on Emerging Issues of Data Ownership, Interoperability, (Re-)usability and Access to Data, and Liability', 25 April 2018, available at https://ec.europa.eu/digital-single-market/en/news/study-emerging-issues-data-ownership-interoperability-re-usability-and-access-data-and, pp. 92-93.
2114. *See* footnote 1325.
2115. *See* Part III, Chapter 6, Section 6.1.
2116. *See* Part III, Chapter 6, Section 6.2.
2117. *See* Part III, Chapter 6, Section 6.3.
2118. *See* Part III, Chapter 6, Section 6.4.
2119. J. Crémer, Y.-A. de Montjoye and H. Schweitzer, 'Competition Policy for the Digital Era', *supra*, pp. 19-24.

benefit large data holders who have access to more (recent) data than their competitors, making it complicated to dislodge them.[2120]

350. Yet, as the data sharing remedy will likely cover personal data pertaining to multiple individuals, some tensions might emerge between competition law and personal data protection law.[2121] Indeed, while competition law might require the sharing of personal data in order to stimulate innovation and to ensure a level playing field between large data holders and undertakings which need access to these data, the GDPR subjects the processing of personal data to the principles of purpose limitation and data minimisation.[2122] According to the purpose limitation principle, data that has been collected for a specific purpose cannot be shared with third parties if this act of sharing does not fit within this initial purpose. According to the data minimisation principle, the categories and amount of data that can be shared should be limited to what is necessary to meet this purpose. This outlines the importance of clearly defining the specific purpose of the data sharing remedy, as the GDPR prevents 'over-sharing', i.e., sharing more data than what is relevant and necessary for the purpose of the processing.

However, competition law and personal data protection law considerations are not necessarily incompatible, and sharing personal data can be beneficial for society, governments, undertakings and individuals.[2123] The challenge is thus not whether one should prevail over the other, but rather to determine how they can be reconciled.[2124] To shed some light on how competition law and personal data protection law can be reconciled on this matter, this Section will analyse how a competition authority's decision imposing to share personal data with a third party can be compatible with the GDPR.

2120. *Ibid.*, pp. 3 and 24.

2121. J. Haucap, 'A German Approach to Antitrust for Digital Platforms', in *Digital Platforms and Concentration – Second Annual Antitrust and Competition Conference*, S. Eyler-Driscoll, A. Schechter and C. Patiño (eds), 2018, available at https://promarket.org/wp-content/uploads/2018/04/Digital-Platforms-and-Concentration.pdf, p. 12. On the articulation between competition law, personal data protection law and consumer law: *see* I. Graef, T. Tombal and A. de Streel, 'Limits and Enablers of Data Sharing: An Analytical Framework for EU Competition, Data Protection and Consumer Law', *TILEC Discussion Paper DP 2019-005*, November 2019, available at https://ssrn.com/abstract=2956308.

2122. Article 5.1.b) and c) of the GDPR.

2123. For a 'Code of practice' on *voluntary* data sharing, which aims at serving as a guide for businesses wishing to share personal data in a privacy-compliant way, *see* Information Commissioner's Office, 'Data sharing code of practice', 17 December 2020, available at https://ico.org.uk/for-organisations/data-sharing-a-code-of-practice/.

2124. K. Muralidhar, R. Sarathy and H. Li, '"To Share or Not to Share. That Is Not the Question" – A Privacy Preserving Procedure for Sharing Linked Data', 3 July 2014, https://ssrn.com/abstract=2462152, p. 2.

351. As a preliminary consideration, it should be outlined that one way to circumvent the application of the GDPR would be to anonymise the personal data before sharing it. While this might be possible in some cases (e.g., search data), there are other cases where this might reduce the value of the data set and, in any case, truly effective anonymisation[2125] is difficult to achieve.[2126] This is especially true in light of the constant development of *Big Data*[2127] analytics, which increase the risk of reidentification of the data subjects. This failure to effectively anonymise personal data has been demonstrated several times in the literature,[2128] leading to the conclusion that what is often presented as anonymisation techniques are, in fact, merely pseudonymisation[2129] techniques. Yet, pseudonymised data remain personal data covered by the GDPR, given that the data subject can still be re-identified.

In the vast majority of cases, the data will thus remain personal and the data sharing remedy will therefore have to comply with the rules of the GDPR. This requires, on the one hand, to have a lawful basis for the data sharing,[2130] and, on the other hand, to comply with the general principles of personal data protection.[2131] Moreover, competition and data protection authorities will need to cooperate in order to define and implement this remedy.

7.2.1 Lawful Basis for the Data Sharing

352. A remedy imposing data sharing would require a lawful basis at two levels, namely at the level of the undertaking that transfers the data and at the level of the undertaking that will receive the data, although these two lawful

2125. *See* definition at footnote 116.

2126. J. Drexl, 'Legal Challenges of the Changing Role of Personal and Non-Personal Data in the Data Economy', *Max Planck Institute for Innovation & Competition Research Paper No. 18-23*, 31 October 2018, available at https://ssrn.com/abstract=3274519, p. 4. *See also* I. Graef, R. Gellert and M. Husovec, 'Towards a Holistic Regulatory Approach for the European Data Economy' *supra*, p. 6; and C. Wendehorst, 'Of Elephants in the Room and Paper Tigers: How to Reconcile Data Protection and the Data Economy', *Trading Data in the Digital Economy: Legal Concepts and Tools*, S. Lohsse, R. Schulze and D. Staudenmayer (eds), Baden-Baden, Nomos, 2017, pp. 330-331.

2127. '"Big data" is a field that treats ways to analyze, systematically extract information from, or otherwise deal with data sets that are too large or complex to be dealt with by traditional data-processing application software' (https://en.wikipedia.org/wiki/Big_data).

2128. *See* point 20.

2129. Article 4.5 of the GDPR.

2130. Article 6 of the GDPR.

2131. Article 5 of the GDPR.

bases do not need to be the same.[2132] Therefore, I will first address the potential lawful bases for the data holder before turning to the potential lawful bases for the data recipient.

7.2.1.1 Lawful Basis for the Data Holder

353. Transferring data to a third party as a consequence of a data sharing remedy imposed by a competition authority amounts to a new processing[2133] for the data holder and is therefore in need of a lawful basis.[2134] This raises a first preliminary question, namely whether a new separate lawful basis is necessary in order for the data sharing to be GDPR-compliant. Indeed, according to Article 6.4 and Recital 50 of the GDPR, a separate lawful basis is not necessary if the new purpose (*in casu* the data sharing as a remedy) is 'compatible' with the initial purpose for which the data has been collected.[2135] The question is thus whether imposing data sharing as a remedy could be considered as being compatible with the purpose of the initial data processing. To assess this compatibility, the following elements should be considered:[2136]

- Any link between the initial purpose and the purpose of the intended further processing.
- The context in which the personal data have been collected, in particular the reasonable expectations of data subjects based on their relationship with the controller as to their further use.
- The nature of the personal data.
- The consequences of the intended further processing for data subjects.
- The existence of appropriate safeguards in both the original and intended further processing operations.

A key consideration here will be whether the data subjects could reasonably expect that the data holder might have to share the personal data it holds with another undertaking as a result of a competition law remedy.

2132. C. Wendehorst, 'Of Elephants in the Room and Paper Tigers', *supra*, pp. 334-337.
2133. Processing means 'any operation or set of operations which is performed on personal data or on sets of personal data, whether or not by automated means, such as collection, recording, organisation, structuring, storage, adaptation or alteration, retrieval, consultation, use, disclosure by transmission, dissemination or otherwise making available, alignment or combination, restriction, erasure or destruction' (Article 4.2 of the GDPR).
2134. C. Wendehorst, 'Of Elephants in the Room and Paper Tigers', *supra*, pp. 334-335.
2135. This is however contested by some authors, who argue that the final text of the GDPR fails to reflect the agreement that was reached during the negotiations (*see* C. Wendehorst, 'Of Elephants in the Room and Paper Tigers', *supra*, pp. 335-336 and references cited in footnote 25 of that paper).
2136. Article 6.4 and Recital 50 of the GDPR.

Can it be said that if a data subject provides its data to Facebook or Google, she can reasonably expect that these firms might abuse their dominant position and that, as a consequence, they will have to share the personal data they hold with competitors? In conducting this assessment, the types of services that the competitors intend to offer and the potential safeguards that they would set in place, such as pseudonymisation mechanisms, should be considered. Moreover, this assessment of the compatibility of the purposes from a data protection perspective is interesting to compare with the assessment of the reuse purpose from a competition law perspective, as they might actually lead to contradictory findings. Indeed, from a data protection perspective, if the recipient intends to use the data for another type of service, this will likely not be considered as a compatible purpose. In contrast, from a competition law perspective, it will be easier to force a data holder to share its data with a recipient wishing to offer 'new' types of services.[2137]

354. Ruling that the transfer is compatible with the initial purpose of processing would spare the necessity of identifying a separate lawful basis for the data holder and would thus facilitate the implementation of the data sharing remedy. If, on the other hand, the further processing deriving from the remedy imposing data sharing is deemed to be 'incompatible' with the initial purpose for which the data has been collected (and this will likely always be the case), this further processing can only be carried out if the data subjects have consented to it or if it is mandated by a legal obligation.[2138] Indeed, only two of the six lawful bases listed in Article 6.1 of the GDPR can be relied upon to legitimise an incompatible further processing. This is the result of a compromise reached between the European Commission, the Working Party 29 (today the EDPB) and the European Parliament during the negotiations of the final text of the GDPR.[2139] While the Commission only wanted to exclude the possibility to rely on the 'legitimate interests' legal basis[2140] for incompatible further processing,[2141] the Working Party 29 and the European Parliament wanted to exclude the possibility to rely on any lawful basis at all because, by essence, such an incompatible further

2137. *See* Part III, Chapter 6, Section 6.1.
2138. Article 6.4 of the GDPR.
2139. *See* C. de Terwangne, 'Article 5: Principles Relating to Processing of Personal Data', *The EU General Data Protection Regulation (GDPR): A Commentary*, C. Kuner, L. Bygrave and C. Docksey (eds), Oxford, Oxford University Press, 2020, p. 316.
2140. Article 6.1.f) of the GDPR.
2141. *See* Proposal for a Regulation of the European Parliament and of the Council on the protection of individuals with regard to the processing of personal data and on the free movement of such data (General Data Protection Regulation), 25 January 2012, COM/2012/011 final, Article 6.4: 'Where the purpose of further processing is not compatible with the one for which the personal data have been collected, the processing must have a legal basis at least in one of the grounds referred to in points (a) to (e) of paragraph 1'.

processing would be unlawful and therefore prohibited.[2142] Indeed, according to the Working Party 29, 'legalising an otherwise incompatible data processing activity simply by changing the terms of a contract with the data subject, or by identifying an additional legitimate interest of the controller, would go against the spirit of the purpose limitation principle and remove its substance'.[2143] Yet, such a drastic position would have been highly problematic in the perspective of *Big Data* and *Open Data*. Accordingly, a compromise was reached,[2144] having in mind that the key concern of the GDPR is to provide control to the data subjects on what happens with 'their' data. In order to avoid opacity towards incompatible further processing and to ensure transparency, it was thus decided that incompatible processing could only be carried out if the data subjects had consented to them or if they were mandated by a legal obligation.[2145]

In light of the above, two lawful bases could potentially be used for the transfer of the personal data covered by the competition law remedy, namely consent and the necessary processing for the compliance with a legal obligation to which the data holder is subject.[2146]

7.2.1.1.1 Consent

355. The first possibility for the data holder would be to obtain the explicit freely given, specific, informed and unambiguous consent of the data subjects at hand *after* the competition authority's decision.[2147] Indeed, obtaining a general consent *before* the decision will lack the specificity and explicitness required for the consent to be compliant with the GDPR.[2148] The

2142. European Parliament legislative resolution of 12 March 2014 on the proposal for a regulation of the European Parliament and of the Council on the protection of individuals with regard to the processing of personal data and on the free movement of such data (General Data Protection Regulation), 12 March 2014, *OJ C 378/399*, 9 November 2017, p. 428 (where Article 6.4 of the Commission's proposal is deleted); Article 29 Working Party, *Opinion 03/2013 on purpose limitation*, WP 203, 2 April 2013, available at https://ec.europa.eu/justice/article-29/documentation/opinion-recommendation/files/2013/wp203_en.pdf, pp. 36-37; F. Gaullier, 'Le principe de finalité dans le RGPD: beaucoup d'ancien et un peu de nouveau', *Communication commerce électronique,* 2018/4, p. 51.
2143. Article 29 Working Party, *Opinion 03/2013 on purpose limitation*, *supra*, p. 36.
2144. Article 6.4 of the Position (EU) No. 6/2016 of the Council at first reading with a view to the adoption of a Regulation of the European Parliament and of the Council on the protection of natural persons with regard to the processing of personal data and on the free movement of such data, and repealing Directive 95/46/EC (General Data Protection Regulation), *OJ C 159/1*, 3 May 2016.
2145. F. Gaullier, 'Le principe de finalité dans le RGPD: beaucoup d'ancien et un peu de nouveau', *supra*, p. 51.
2146. Articles 6.1.a) and c) of the GDPR.
2147. Articles 4.11 and 6.1.a) of the GDPR.
2148. V. Kathuria and J. Globocnik, 'Exclusionary Conduct in Data-Driven Markets', *supra*, pp. 27-28.

data holder will therefore have to seek the consent to share the data with one or several specific recipients identified in the competition authority's decision.[2149] In this context, the data holder should request some basic information from the various data recipients (such as the purpose for which they will process the data or the types of data they will process[2150]) in order to provide the data subjects with sufficient information allowing them to make a specific and informed choice about whether to consent to the transfer or not. However, it might be extremely complex and burdensome to do so in practice.

The French *GDF Suez*[2151] case has been mentioned by several authors to illustrate this point.[2152] In that case, the French *Autorité de la concurrence* (French Competition Authority) found that GDF Suez had abused its dominant position in the market for natural gas and required GDF Suez to share certain customer information data with its competitors.[2153] More precisely, the *Autorité*, after having consulted the *CNIL* (the French data protection authority), ordered GDF Suez to inform the data subjects about the sharing of their data with their competitors and to give them the possibility to object to this transfer.[2154] Some authors have argued that this remedy relied on an 'opt-out consent', as, at the time, the Data Protection Directive[2155] was still in force and this legislation was silent about whether such an opt-out solution was admissible.[2156] Yet, such an interpretation is

2149. *Ibid.*, p. 28.

2150. The data recipient could, for instance, produce a short form that would be filled by the recipients and that would be presented to the data subjects when asking for their consent.

2151. Autorité de la concurrence, Decision n°14-MC-02 (*GDF Suez*), 9 September 2014, available at https://www.autoritedelaconcurrence.fr/sites/default/files/commitments// 14mc02.pdf.

2152. *See* I. Graef, *EU Competition Law, Data Protection and Online Platforms: Data as Essential Facility*, *supra*, pp. 271-272; V. Kathuria and J. Globocnik, 'Exclusionary Conduct in Data-Driven Markets', *supra*, p. 28.

2153. Autorité de la concurrence, Decision n°14-MC-02 (*GDF Suez*), 9 September 2014, p. 52, Article 1.

2154. *Ibid.*, pp. 52-53, Articles 5 and 6. The following information had to be sent to the clients: 'The Competition Authority ordered GDF Suez, by decision No. 14-MC-02 of 9 September 2014, to give access to its competitors to certain data contained in the files of the clients having a supply contract at the regulated gas sales tariff, in order to re-establish the conditions for effective competition (…). If you do not want your data to be transmitted for commercial prospecting purposes to suppliers who have requested access to the GDF SUEZ customer database, please return this form by ticking the box below. If you do not object within the next 30 days, your data will automatically be made available to these suppliers' (author's translation).

2155. Directive 95/46/EC of the European Parliament and of the Council of 24 October 1995 on the protection of individuals with regard to the processing of personal data and on the free movement of such data, *OJ L 281*, 23 November 1995.

2156. V. Kathuria and J. Globocnik, 'Exclusionary Conduct in Data-Driven Markets', *supra*, p. 28. It should however be underlined that according to some authors, consent under the Directive still required an (explicit) action from the data subject and could not be

erroneous, as the *Autorité* did not subject the sharing to an 'opt-out consent', but rather held that GDF Suez had to inform the data subjects about the sharing with competitors, in order for them to be able to exercise their right to object to the processing[2157] (i.e., the sharing).[2158] Therefore, it seems that, in this case, the lawful basis for the sharing was not consent, but rather that the transfer was necessary for the compliance with a legal obligation to which GDF Suez was subject, namely the *Autorité*'s decision.[2159]

What can be inferred from the above is that, while reliance on consent as a lawful basis is possible in theory, this will arguably be unrealistic in practice. This is especially the case now that the GDPR is in force, as requiring the data subjects to opt out of the transfer, rather than to opt in to the transfer, would not be GDPR-compliant, as, according to Article 4.11 of the GDPR, the data subject has to explicitly consent to the transfer.[2160] The necessity of an explicit consent has been confirmed by the European Court of Justice[2161] and this makes it much more cumbersome for the data holder and will surely affect the efficiency in practice of the data sharing remedy if the data holder relies on consent as a lawful basis for the transfer, as it is very likely that there will be fewer data subjects who opt in than data subjects who do not opt out.[2162] The intended remedy's goal might therefore not be reached if only a few of the data subjects effectively consent.[2163] Additionally, relying on consent might also weaken this remedy as, according to Article 7.3 of the GDPR, the data subjects are free to withdraw their consent at any time.

7.2.1.1.2 Necessary for the Compliance with a Legal Obligation to Which the Data Holder Is Subject

356. The second possibility for the data holder would be to demonstrate that the transfer is necessary for the compliance with a legal obligation to which

inferred from a lack of action (*see* E. Kosta, 'Construing the Meaning of "Opt-Out": An Analysis of the European, U.K. and German Data Protection Legislation', *European Data Protection Law Review*, 2015, Vol. 1, pp. 16-31).

2157. Article 21 of the GDPR.

2158. Autorité de la concurrence, Decision n°14-MC-02 (*GDF Suez*), 9 September 2014, pp. 52-53, Articles 5 and 6.

2159. On this lawful basis, *see* point 356.

2160. V. Kathuria and J. Globocnik, 'Exclusionary Conduct in Data-Driven Markets', *supra*, p. 28.

2161. ECJ, *Planet 49*, 1 October 2019, C-673/17, EU:C:2019:801.

2162. V. Kathuria and J. Globocnik, 'Exclusionary Conduct in Data-Driven Markets', *supra*, pp. 28-29. *See also* J. Campbell, A. Goldfarb and C. Tucker, 'Privacy Regulation and Market Structure', *Journal of Economics & Management Strategy*, Vol. 24(1), 2015, pp. 47-73.

2163. V. Kathuria and J. Globocnik, 'Exclusionary Conduct in Data-Driven Markets', *supra*, p. 28.

it is subject.[2164] The issue is whether a decision by a competition authority could qualify as such a legal obligation. Here, different views are expressed. While Graef indicates that a data sharing remedy imposed by a competition authority would amount to such a legal obligation,[2165] Kathuria and Globocnik argue, on the contrary, that a competition authority's decision will not qualify as a legal obligation for the data sharing because this term presupposes the existence of an underlying generally applicable law.[2166]

Article 5.3 GDPR indeed provides that the basis for the processing shall be laid down in Union law or Member State law. However, the word 'law' is not defined anywhere in the GDPR. In that regard, the interpretation, by the European Court of Human Rights, of the requirement of the legality of an interference with a fundamental right[2167] should be reminded. The Court consistently holds that the term 'law' must not be given a 'formal interpretation', which would necessarily imply the existence of a written statute having a legislative value, but rather a 'material interpretation',[2168] which covers not only the written statutes but all the legal rules in force.[2169] Indeed, the European Court of Human Rights has, at the outset, recognised that in countries having a *Common Law* legal tradition, unwritten rules of law could be considered as satisfying the requirement of legality of interference in a fundamental right.[2170] Importantly, the Court then also subsequently recognised a wider margin of manoeuvre for countries having a *Continental Law* legal tradition as to what should be incorporated under the term 'law'.[2171] In particular, the Court acknowledged that decisions, regulations or unwritten rules of law, such as case law decisions, could satisfy the requirement of legality.[2172] Arguably, a similar interpretation could be given to the words 'law' and 'legal obligation' in the GDPR. In fact, it seems that this is the approach that has been taken by the French *Autorité de la concurrence*, although not explicitly, in the French *GDF Suez* case mentioned above.[2173]

2164. Article 6.1.c) of the GDPR.
2165. I. Graef, *EU Competition Law, Data Protection and Online Platforms: Data as Essential Facility*, *supra*, p. 319.
2166. V. Kathuria and J. Globocnik, 'Exclusionary Conduct in Data-Driven Markets', *supra*, pp. 21-22.
2167. *In casu* Article 8 of the European Convention on Human Rights (Right to respect for private and family life), in which personal data protection is rooted.
2168. E. Degrave, *L'E-Gouvernement et la protection de la vie privée. Légalité, transparence et contrôle*, Bruxelles, Larcier – Collection du CRIDS, 2014, p. 144.
2169. R. Ergec, *Protection européenne et internationale des droits de l'homme*, Bruxelles, Larcier, 2014, p. 232.
2170. ECtHR, *Sunday Times v. United Kingdom*, 26 April 1979, App. No. 6538/74, §§ 46-53.
2171. ECtHR, *Hüvig v. France*, 24 April 1990, App. No. 11105/84, § 28; and ECtHR, *Kruslin v. France*, 24 April 1990, App. No. 11801/85, § 29. *See* P. De Hert, 'Artikel 8. Recht op privacy', *Handboek EVRM, Deel 2. Artikelsgewijze commentaar*, J. Vande Lanotte and Y. Haeck (eds), Antwerp, Intersentia, 2004, p. 716.
2172. P. De Hert, 'Artikel 8. Recht Op Privacy', *supra*, p. 716.
2173. *See* point 355.

This interpretation is supported by the fact that Recital 41 of the GDPR provides that 'where this Regulation refers to a legal basis or a legislative measure, this does not necessarily require a legislative act adopted by a parliament, without prejudice to requirements pursuant to the constitutional order of the Member State concerned'.

However, Recital 41 of the GDPR also provides, in accordance with the case law of the European Court of Human Rights and the European Court of Justice, that this 'law' must be formulated in clear and precise terms, and be sufficiently predictable and accessible.[2174] The requirement of predictability implies that anyone must be able to foresee, with a reasonable degree of certainty, the potential effects of this 'law'.[2175] This is where difficulties might emerge from a *Continental Law* perspective, as this would require for the case law on data sharing as a competition law remedy to be well established, so that it has become clear and predictable. Yet, in practice, such case law is scarce and it might therefore be argued that the 'law' is not sufficiently predictable at this point. Nevertheless, with time, such case law could develop more clearly and systematically, rendering it 'predictable' and, as a consequence, a competition authority's decision imposing to provide access to data could qualify as a 'legal obligation'. As this is a key issue for the future, a clarification by the EDPB and/or the EDPS on the matter would be highly welcomed.

In any case, in order to be GDPR-compliant, the data sharing remedy imposed by the competition authority will have to be specific enough. Indeed, Article 5.3 of the GDPR provides that the legal obligation should[2176] specify the purpose for which the data is shared (e.g., to remedy a specific competition issue), the undertakings with whom the data is shared, and the types of data and the data subjects concerned by the data sharing remedy. Moreover, Article 5.3 of the GDPR adds that this legal obligation should meet an objective of public interest (*in casu* ensuring a competitive environment that will benefit the consumers) and be proportionate to the legitimate aim pursued. In this regard, the competition authority must ensure that its decision does not disproportionally affect the data subjects' interests and rights.[2177]

2174. *See also* R. Ergec, *Protection européenne et internationale des droits de l'homme*, *supra*, p. 232.

2175. *Ibid.*

2176. Article 5.3 of the GDPR uses the word 'may' but, in light of the decision of the European Court of Human Rights in the *Rotaru* (ECtHR, *Rotaru v. Romania*, 4 May 2000, App. No. 28341/95) and *Shimolovos* (ECtHR, *Shimovolos v. Russia*, 21 June 2011, App. No. 30194/09) cases, I argue that the appropriate word should be 'should'.

2177. On this issue, *see* point 360.

7.2.1.2 Lawful Basis for the Data Recipient

357. While the data holder has to have a lawful basis for transferring the data towards the recipient, this recipient also needs its own specific lawful basis for the processing of the data that will be done once it has received the data covered by the data sharing remedy.[2178] As for the data holder, this raises a first preliminary question, namely whether a new separate lawful basis is necessary in order for the data sharing to be GDPR-compliant. In this regard, the data recipient could attempt to demonstrate that it will reuse the data for scientific research[2179] or statistical[2180] purposes, as, in those cases, the further processing is considered as compatible with the initial purpose of processing and no separate lawful basis is necessary.[2181] In such cases, appropriate technical and organisational safeguards, such as pseudonymisation, would, however, have to be set.[2182] As pointed out by Mayer-Schönberger and Padova, this could notably be possible for some *Big Data* applications.[2183]

358. If the data recipient is not able to rely on the above-mentioned exemption for scientific research or statistical purposes, it will have to rely on a new lawful basis of processing. However, contrary to the data holder,[2184] it will have the ability to rely on any of the six lawful bases contained in Article 6.1 of the GDPR. This is because the potential incompatibility of purposes will have arguably been 'purged' either by the consent or the legal obligation that has been used as a lawful basis for the transfer of the data from the holder to the recipient. In practice, the data recipient will rely either on consent or on 'legitimate interests' for further processing. Indeed, contrary to the data holder, the recipient should not be able to argue that this further processing is necessary for compliance with a legal obligation to which it is subject. This is because, while the competition authority's decision to impose a data sharing remedy could be considered as a legal obligation for the data

---

2178. C. Wendehorst, 'Of Elephants in the Room and Paper Tigers', *supra*, pp. 334-337.

2179. According to Recital 159 of the GDPR, scientific research purposes 'should be interpreted in a broad manner including for example technological development and demonstration, fundamental research, applied research and privately funded research (…) [and] should also include studies conducted in the public interest in the area of public health'.

2180. Statistical purposes mean 'any operation of collection and the processing of personal data necessary for statistical surveys or for the production of statistical results. Those statistical results may further be used for different purposes, including a scientific research purpose. The statistical purpose implies that (…) the personal data are not used in support of measures or decisions regarding any particular natural person' (Recital 162 of the GDPR).

2181. Article 5.1.b) and Recital 50 of the GDPR.

2182. Article 89.1 of the GDPR.

2183. V. Mayer-Schönberger and Y. Padova, 'Regime Change? Enabling Big Data Through Europe's New Data Protection Regulation', *supra*.

2184. *See supra* point 354.

holder that must comply with this decision,[2185] this decision does not impose any obligation on the data recipient to process the shared data. Therefore, the recipient cannot argue that it must necessarily process the data as a result of the competition authority's decision.

7.2.1.2.1 Consent

359. The first lawful basis for the data recipient could thus be the obtaining of the explicit freely given, specific, informed and unambiguous consent of the data subjects at hand *after* the competition authority's decision.[2186] In this regard, the data recipient will have to be very specific about the purpose for which it will use this data, as the data subject's consent should be asked for a well-defined purpose and should not remain general.[2187] While data subjects might not see the added-value of consenting to the processing of their personal data by a data recipient that would offer them a service that is similar to (or a copy of) the data holder's service (unless it is offered at better conditions, notably in terms of data protection), they might have more incentives to consent to the processing of their personal data by a data recipient that would offer them a 'new' type of service or an alternative service that interoperates with the data holder's service.[2188] In this perspective, the objectives of data protection are aligned with the objectives of competition law, as competition authorities will be more reluctant to force a data holder to share its data with a recipient wishing to offer similar services than to force a data holder to share its data with a recipient wishing to offer 'new' types of services.[2189]

However, and as for the data holder, it might be too troublesome to do so in practice and the intended remedy's goal might therefore not be reached if only a few of the data subjects effectively consent.[2190]

7.2.1.2.2 Necessary for the Purposes of the Legitimate Interests Pursued by the Data Recipient

360. The other possibility for the data recipient would be to argue that the data processing is necessary for the purposes of the legitimate interests that it pursues, and that these interests are not overridden by the interests or

2185. *See supra* point 356.
2186. Articles 4.11 and 6.1.a) of the GDPR.
2187. Article 6.1.a) and 8.2 of the GDPR.
2188. On the necessity to go further than data portability and the necessity to ensure interoperability between services, *see* J. Crémer, Y.-A. de Montjoye and H. Schweitzer, 'Competition Policy for the Digital Era', *supra*, pp. 58-60.
2189. *See* Part III, Chapter 6, Section 6.1.
2190. *See* point 355.

fundamental rights and freedoms of the data subjects.[2191] This requires to identify legitimate interests for the data recipient, to demonstrate that the data processing resulting from the data sharing remedy is necessary to fulfil these legitimate interests, and to strike a balance between the interests of the data recipient, on the one hand, and the interests of the data subjects, on the other hand.

For the data recipient, the legitimate interests of the access would be the opportunity to offer (privacy-oriented) alternative products or services to the consumers, to restore competition on the market where the data holder has committed an abuse, and to reduce the latter's competitive advantage.[2192] Moreover, processing the data covered by the remedy would arguably be necessary for the data recipient in order to fulfil these legitimate interests, as, in principle, the competition authority will have ordered the data sharing precisely because there was no other remedy to achieve these interests in light of the competition law infringement committed by the data holder (i.e., the data sharing remedy is imposed because it is the only way to reduce the data holder's competitive advantage and to restore competition, and the recipient has to use this data if it wants to be able to offer alternative products or services).[2193]

The key question is therefore whether the data recipient's legitimate interests outweigh the data subjects' interests. At first glance, the data sharing deriving from the competition authority's decision might look like it will always risk affecting the data subjects' rights, as more undertakings will get access to their personal data, thus potentially reducing the data subjects' privacy. Moreover, it might also arguably increase the risks of de-anonymisation of other data.[2194] Accordingly, there might be some cases where the data subjects will be worse off because of this data sharing. In such cases, the legitimate interests of the data recipient should not prevail over the data subjects' interests, and Article 6.1.f) of the GDPR should not be considered as a viable lawful basis.

However, there are other cases where this data sharing might allow competitors to create (privacy-oriented) alternatives to existing services, which would benefit the data subjects in the long term. Indeed, the development of competitive alternatives is necessary to prevent data subjects from being 'locked in' the services of the existing providers, as more switching possibilities would allow the data subjects to resort to services offering more guarantees in terms of personal data protection. To support this

2191. Article 6.1.f) of the GDPR.
2192. V. Kathuria and J. Globocnik, 'Exclusionary Conduct in Data-Driven Markets', *supra*, p. 25.
2193. *See* Part III, Chapter 6, Sections 6.4.1 to 6.4.3.
2194. V. Kathuria and J. Globocnik, 'Exclusionary Conduct in Data-Driven Markets', *supra*, pp. 26 and 32.

argument, the 'About Data About Us' report should be mentioned.[2195] It is the result of a collaboration in the UK between the Open Data Institute, Luminate, and the Royal Society for the encouragement of Arts, Manufactures and Commerce. These institutions explored, via focus groups and a workshop, how UK citizens feel about 'their' data and about the (lack of) control and protection they experience.[2196] The report outlines that people have much more awareness and understanding about these issues than what they are traditionally given credit for by politicians and in the press (where they are traditionally painted as naïve or ignorant), and that people do have clear expectations on how 'their' data should be protected.[2197] They desire more transparency, more control, more fairness and more compliance with personal data protection principles from the undertakings that process their data.[2198] Therefore, if the data recipients were to offer (more privacy-oriented) alternatives to the data holder's services, the legitimate interests of the data recipients could prevail over the data subjects' interests – and might actually be aligned with these interests – and accordingly the data could be shared on the basis of Article 6.1.f) of the GDPR.

In order to achieve the above-mentioned balancing exercise between the interests of the data recipient and those of the data subjects, the data recipient will need to be very specific about the use it will make of the shared data (e.g., which products or services it intends to offer thanks to the data, whether they are privacy-oriented or not, etc.), as this will allow to determine if this further processing would be harmful, or on the contrary beneficial, to the data subjects. Naturally, the data subjects will remain free to oppose this processing, on the basis of Article 21.1 of the GDPR, if they disagree with the outcome of the balance of interests.

7.2.2 Compliance with the General Principles of Personal Data Protection

361. In order for data sharing as a remedy to be compatible with the data protection rules, the data holder and the data recipient must not only rely on a lawful basis for the processing (respectively for the transfer and for the further processing of the data) but also comply with the general principles of personal data protection.

362. First, both the data holder and the data recipient will have to inform the data subjects about the personal data processing deriving from this data

2195. R. Samson, K. Gibbon and A. Scott, 'About Data About Us,' September 2019, available at https://www.thersa.org/globalassets/pdfs/reports/data-about-us-final-report.pdf.
2196. *Ibid.*, p. 3.
2197. *Ibid.*, p. 39.
2198. *Ibid.*, pp. 36-38.

sharing remedy, in a fair and transparent manner.[2199] On the one hand, the data holder will have to inform the data subjects that it has been compelled by a competition authority to make some of the personal data concerning them available to a third party as a remedy to an abuse.[2200] On the other hand, the data recipient will have to inform the data subjects about the further processing it will conduct thanks to the data covered by the remedy.[2201] In this regard, the data recipient will notably have to inform the data subjects about the categories of personal data concerned, about the purposes of the processing for which the personal data are intended and about the period for which the personal data will be stored.[2202]

The data recipient will have to provide this information within a reasonable period after obtaining the personal data. This period should be determined by considering the specific circumstances in which the personal data are processed, and should, in any case, never be longer than one month.[2203] Nevertheless, if these personal data are used by the data recipient to communicate with the data subjects, this information will have to be provided at the latest at the time of the first communication.[2204] According to the Article 29 Working Party (today the EDPB), this does not preclude the one-month time limit mentioned above, and therefore the data recipient will have to provide the information at the time of the first communication (if it takes place less than one month after having obtained the data) or at the latest one month after having obtained the data.[2205]

However, there are situations where this information duty will not apply. On the one hand, it will not apply if the data subject already has the information.[2206] A data recipient might thus be tempted to say that the data subjects have already been informed by the data holder. Nevertheless, this will rarely be the case because the data holder will have provided information about the *transfer* but not about the *further processing* done by the data recipient (the former might allegedly not even be aware of the concrete processing that will be accomplished by the latter). On the other hand, this information duty will not apply if the provision of such information proves impossible or would involve a disproportionate effort.[2207] Here, it should be mentioned that it will not always be easy for the data recipient to identify all

2199. Articles 5.1.a) and 12-14 of the GDPR.
2200. *See* the example of the *GDF Suez* case at point 355 (Autorité de la concurrence, Decision n°14-MC-02 (*GDF Suez*), 9 September 2014, available at https://www.autoritedelaconcurrence.fr/sites/default/files/commitments//14mc02.pdf).
2201. Article 14 of the GDPR.
2202. Articles 14.1.c) and d) and 14.2.a) of the GDPR.
2203. Article 14.3.a) of the GDPR.
2204. Article 14.3.b) of the GDPR.
2205. Article 29 Working Party, *Opinion 03/2013 on purpose limitation*, WP 203, 2 April 2013, available at https://ec.europa.eu/justice/article-29/documentation/opinion-recommendation/files/2013/wp203_en.pdf, p. 16.
2206. Article 14.5.a) of the GDPR.
2207. Article 14.5.b) of the GDPR.

the data subjects concerned by the data sharing, as the shared data should arguably be pseudonymised or aggregated personal data that cannot be immediately linked to well-identified data subjects. In this context, it can be questioned whether the recipient has a duty to make sure that the data holder will pass on the necessary contact details of the data subjects, as this would likely conflict with the data minimisation principle,[2208] because this would entail the sharing of more data than is necessary for the purpose of the processing.[2209] In fact, Article 11.1 of the GDPR provides that data that is not necessary for the purpose of the processing should not be processed for the sole purpose of complying with the GDPR. Accordingly, additional data should not be transferred solely in order to be able to inform the data subjects about the sharing. Therefore, if, in light of the above, these details are not passed on, it might be impossible or disproportionate for the data recipient to inform the data subjects.

363. Second, both the data holder and the data recipient will have to comply with the purpose limitation principle.[2210] For the data holder, the purpose of the sharing will be compliance with the competition authority's decision. For the data recipient, it will be important to define in advice, and ideally already in the competition authority's decision, for which specific purpose the data will be processed (e.g., which products or services does the data recipient intend to offer thanks to the shared data).

364. Third, the data holder and the data recipient will have to comply with the data minimisation principle, and only the necessary data for the fulfilment of the specific purpose justifying the data sharing shall be transferred by the data holder and processed by the data recipient.[2211] To facilitate the compliance with this principle, the use of pseudonymised data and of privacy-preserving techniques should be encouraged. Once again, this outlines the importance of defining in advance, and ideally already in the competition authority's decision, the specific purpose of the processing, in order for the data sharing remedy to cover only the data that is necessary to fulfil it. In the same vein, the accuracy of the shared data should be ensured and it should be stored by the data recipient for no longer than is necessary for this specific purpose.[2212]

365. Fourth, the data holder and the data recipient will have to ensure that the data subjects' rights, such as their right to object to the processing,[2213] are

2208. Article 5.1.c) of the GDPR.
2209. C. Wendehorst, 'Of Elephants in the Room and Paper Tigers', *supra*, pp. 340-341.
2210. Article 5.1.b) of the GDPR.
2211. Article 5.1.c) of the GDPR.
2212. Article 5.1.d) and e) of the GDPR.
2213. Article 21 of the GDPR. *See* the example of the *GDF Suez* case at point 355 (Autorité de la concurrence, Decision n°14-MC-02 (*GDF Suez*), 9 September 2014, available at https://www.autoritedelaconcurrence.fr/sites/default/files/commitments//14mc02.pdf).

given their fullest effect.[2214] Accordingly, if a data holder receives, from a data subject, a valid request for rectification or erasure[2215] of some of the personal data covered by the data sharing remedy, it will have to notify it to the data recipient so that the data is also rectified or erased in the latter's data set as well.[2216]

366. Finally, the data holder and the data recipient will have to implement appropriate technical and organisational measures in order to ensure the security of the data during the transfer and during the further processing,[2217] and they will have to document how the implementation of the data sharing remedy complies with all of the above-mentioned principles, in light of the accountability principle.[2218]

7.2.3 Need for Competition and Data Protection Authorities to Cooperate

367. It stems from the above analysis that, while some tensions might emerge between competition law and personal data protection law, they are not incompatible, and they can be reconciled by making a competition law duty to share data compliant with data protection principles. Yet, this is no easy task and it might be quite complex in certain specific situations. In practice, this implies the need for competition and data protection authorities to cooperate on this matter. Indeed, a competition authority might not be the best suited to handle these personal data protection aspects alone.[2219] Accordingly, the competition authorities should solicit the help of data protection authorities in defining the appropriate data sharing remedy, as the French *Autorité de la concurrence* has done in the *GDF Suez* case,[2220] where it consulted the *CNIL*. The data protection authority could then be put in charge of supervising the correct implementation of the remedy from a personal data protection perspective. This might however create practical challenges, such as overlaps between the powers of the competition and personal data protection authorities. One way to address these challenges would be to organise regular meetings between these authorities, in order to follow up on the implementation of the remedies and to deal with potential overlaps in a concerted way. Finally, this implies the need to interpret data protection law and competition law provisions in a coherent manner, in order

2214. Articles 13-22 of the GDPR.
2215. Articles 16 and 17 of the GDPR.
2216. Article 19 of the GDPR.
2217. Article 5.1.f) and 32 of the GDPR.
2218. Article 5.2 of the GDPR.
2219. *See* the discussions pertaining to the *Bundeskartellamt*'s (the German competition authority) decision in the *Facebook* case, summarised at point 336.
2220. *See* point 355.

to minimise conflicts and to maximise complementarity between these regimes.[2221]

7.2.4 Articulating a Competition Law Data Sharing Remedy with the GDPR: No Incompatibility but Risk of Inefficiency

368. It derives from the above analysis that the effectivity of a competition remedy imposing data sharing might, in fact, be highly uncertain. Indeed, on the one hand, the data holder might arguably not be able to rely on the 'legal obligation' lawful basis for the transfer of the data as long as the case law is not sufficiently clear and predictable. On the other hand, the data recipient might not always be able to rely on 'legitimate interests' for its further processing, as there might be cases where its legitimate interests should not prevail over the data subjects' interests. Therefore, the effectivity of a competition remedy imposing data sharing might ultimately depend on the data subjects' consent. Yet, it might be illusory to obtain such consent and the competition remedy's aim might therefore not be achieved if only a handful of the data subjects effectively consent. Such a finding further supports the argument, made above,[2222] according to which *ex post* competition law intervention might not, on itself, be sufficient to address efficiently the systemic market failures deriving from insufficient data sharing.[2223] This finding also supports the argument that 'additional rules may be needed to ensure contestability, fairness and innovation and the possibility of market entry, as well as public interests that go beyond competition or economic considerations'.[2224]

369. Accordingly, I recommend a bicephalous approach, whereby *ex ante* legislations imposing B2B data sharing should complement competition law rules that have been adapted to the characteristics of the digital markets.[2225] These *ex ante* legislations will be further discussed in the next chapter.

2221. I. Graef, T. Tombal and A. de Streel, 'Limits and Enablers of Data Sharing: An Analytical Framework for EU Competition, Data Protection and Consumer Law', *supra*, p. 31.

2222. *See* Part III, Chapter 6, Section 6.5.2.

2223. Communication from the Commission to the European Parliament, the Council, the European Economic and Social Committee and the Committee of the Regions, '*Shaping Europe's Digital Future*', Brussels, 19 February 2020, COM(2020) 67, p. 9.

2224. *Ibid.*

2225. *See* Communication from the Commission to the European Parliament, the Council, the European Economic and Social Committee and the Committee of the Regions, '*A European Strategy for Data*', Brussels, 19 February 2020, COM(2020) 66, pp. 5 and 13-14; European Parliament resolution of 20 October 2020 with recommendations to the Commission on the Digital Services Act: Improving the functioning of the Single Market (2020/2018(INL)), P9_TA-PROV(2020)0272, available at https://www.europarl.europa.eu/doceo/document/TA-9-2020-0272_EN.html, p. 10.

Chapter 8

Towards More *Ex Ante* Legislations Imposing B2B Data Sharing for Economic Purposes

370. This third chapter will be dedicated to considerations pertaining to *ex ante legislations imposing B2B data sharing for economic purposes.* As outlined by the European Commission, such legislations could promote a wider sharing and availability of data, in order to ensure that markets stay open and fair.[2226] In essence, such *ex ante* legislations could be sectoral (Section 8.1) or could have a more general horizontal scope (Section 8.2). Each of these options, which are not necessarily exclusive from one another, entail their own balancing exercises, which I aim to analyse.

8.1 'EX ANTE' SECTORAL LEGISLATIONS IMPOSING B2B DATA SHARING FOR ECONOMIC PURPOSES

371. The first option is thus to adopt *ex ante* sectoral legislations imposing B2B data sharing. In fact, to this day, the EU's regulatory initiatives pertaining to compulsory B2B data sharing have mostly been sectoral. Compulsory data sharing legislations have notably been adopted in the banking and in the energy sector.[2227] However, these initiatives are classified, in the context of my analysis, in the *empowerment initiatives imposing B2B*

2226. Communication from the Commission, '*A European Strategy for Data*', *supra*, pp. 5 and 14.

2227. Directive (EU) 2015/2366 of the European Parliament and of the Council of 25 November 2015 on payment services in the internal market, amending Directives 2002/65/EC, 2009/110/EC and 2013/36/EU and Regulation (EU) No. 1093/2010, and repealing Directive 2007/64/EC, *OJ L 337/35*, 23 December 2015; Directive (EU) 2019/944 of the European Parliament and of the Council of 5 June 2019 on common rules for the internal market for electricity and amending Directive 2012/27/EU, *OJ L 158/125*, 14 June 2019.

data sharing,[2228] as they could be seen as sector-specific complements to the personal data portability right contained in Article 20 of the GDPR, aiming at addressing specific market failures through the sharing of individual-level data.[2229] On the other hand, in terms of *economic initiatives imposing B2B data sharing,* a sector-specific data sharing legislation has been adopted in the automotive sector,[2230] which will be presented below. Moreover, in the agricultural sector, the European Commission supported the creation, by stakeholders from the sector, of the EU Code of conduct on agricultural data sharing by contractual agreement which can be joined by agribusinesses on a voluntary basis and sets some non-binding principles, notably in terms of data access, control and portability.[2231] However, as this instrument does not impose any data sharing obligation, it will not be further analysed here.

8.1.1 The Current Strong Reliance on Sectoral Legislations

372. In practice, most of the data sharing takes place within a single business sector, rather than in a horizontal way (across sectors). One of the reasons for this is that the European legislative framework itself favours sectoral approaches when it comes to data sharing.[2232] This was already apparent from the Communication 'Towards a European Data Economy', where the European Commission indicated that it had stemmed from the stakeholder dialogue that it was too early for any form of horizontal legislation on data

2228. *See* Part II, Chapter 4, Sections 4.2.2 and 4.2.3.
2229. *See* G. Colangelo and O. Borgogno, 'Data, Innovation and Transatlantic Competition in Finance: The Case of the Access to Account Rule', *Stanford-Vienna European Union Law Working Paper No. 35*, 2018, available at https://law.stanford.edu/publications/no-35-data-innovation-and-transatlantic-competition-in-finance-the-case-of-the-access-to-account-rule/, p. 3; S. Vezzoso, 'Fintech, Access to Data, and the Role of Competition Policy', 2018, available at https://papers.ssrn.com/sol3/papers.cfm?abstract_id=3106594, pp. 12-13.
2230. Regulation (EU) 715/2007 of the European Parliament and of the Council of 20 June 2007 on type approval of motor vehicles with respect to emissions from light passenger and commercial vehicles (EUR 5 and EUR 6) and on access to vehicle repair and maintenance information, *OJ L 171/1*, 29 June 2007, Articles 6 and 7; Regulation (EU) 2018/858 of the European Parliament and of the Council of 30 May 2018 on the approval and market surveillance of motor vehicles and their trailers, and of systems, components and separate technical units intended for such vehicles, amending Regulations (EC) No. 715/2007 and (EC) No. 595/2009 and repealing Directive 2007/46/EC, *OJ L 151/1*, 14 June 2018. *See* Articles 61-66, 86 and annexes X and XI.
2231. *See* https://copa-cogeca.eu/img/user/files/EU%20CODE/EU_Code_2018_web_version.pdf.
2232. *See* point 371.

sharing.[2233] Accordingly, the Commission has chosen to let the data market self-regulate itself and to rely on contractual freedom while nevertheless proposing key principles for the undertakings wishing to engage in *voluntary* B2B data sharing agreements.[2234] Nevertheless, the Commission indicated it that would continue to assess whether such key principles prove to be sufficient in order to maintain fair and open markets, and that it would address the situation, if necessary, 'by taking appropriate action and *sector-specific measures*' (emphasis added).[2235] As outlined by several legal scholars, the advantage of resorting to sector-specific legislation is that they are much more targeted and adapted to the sector's needs, characteristics and data standardisation challenges.[2236] Moreover, in terms of personal data protection, it will be easier to comply with the requirement according to which the legislation serving as the lawful basis of the processing must be clearly formulated and must be sufficiently precise (for instance, regarding the determination of the purposes of processing and of the categories of data that can be processed)[2237] if this legislation addresses a specific sectoral issue. In fact, the European Commission has confirmed this sectoral approach in its 'Data Strategy', where it indicated that, through the means of a 'Data Act' to be adopted in 2021, sector-specific data sharing could be made compulsory when 'specific circumstances' dictate it.[2238]

373. As outlined by the European Commission, 'specific circumstances' justifying the adoption of such a compulsory data sharing legislation would notably be established in situations where a (systemic) market failure (data concentration, data conglomeration, etc.)[2239] is identified or can be foreseen

2233. Communication from the Commission to the European Parliament, the Council, the European Economic and Social Committee and the Committee of the Regions, '*Towards a Common European Data Space*', Brussels, 25 April 2018, COM(2018) 232 final, p. 9.
2234. *Ibid.*, pp. 6-8. *See* points 64 and 65.
2235. *Ibid.*, pp. 10-11.
2236. J. Drexl, et al., 'Position Statement of the Max Planck Institute for Innovation and Competition of 26 April 2017 on the European Commission's "Public Consultation on Building the European Data Economy"', *Max Planck Institute for Innovation and Competition Research Paper No. 17-08*, 2017, available at https://ssrn.com/abstract=2959924, pp. 12-16; J. Drexl, 'Data Access and Control in the Era of Connected Devices', *supra*, p. 159; J. Crémer, Y.-A. de Montjoye and H. Schweitzer, 'Competition Policy for the Digital Era', *supra*, p. 74; W. Kerber, 'From (Horizontal and Sectoral) Data Access Solutions Towards Data Governance Systems', *Joint Discussion Paper Series in Economics No. 40-2020*, 26 August 2020, available at https://ssrn.com/abstract=3681263, pp. 15-16.
2237. Article 6.3 of the GDPR.
2238. Communication from the Commission, '*A European Strategy for Data*', *supra*, p. 13, footnote 39. *See also* European Commission, Inception Impact Assessment: '*Data Act (including the review of the Directive 96/9/EC on the legal protection of databases)*', May 2021, Ares (2021)3527151, pp. 1 and 4.
2239. *See* Part I, Chapter 2, Section 2.2.3.3.

in a specific sector, and cannot be (efficiently) remedied by competition law intervention alone.[2240,2241]

In fact, such 'specific circumstances' have been observed in the automotive sector, which led, already in 2007, to the adoption of Regulation 715/2007 that notably compelled car manufacturers to share the vehicle repair and maintenance information that they hold with independent operators.[2242] In 2018, this data sharing obligation has been removed from Regulation 715/2007 and has been included in a new Regulation 2018/858[2243] that is applicable since 1 September 2020.[2244] This sectoral intervention is justified by the potential market failure that would arise on the aftermarkets for vehicle 'on-board diagnostics' information[2245] services, and for vehicle repair and maintenance information[2246] services, if car manufacturers[2247] refused to share such data with independent

2240. *See* Part III, Chapter 6, Section 6.5.2.
2241. Communication from the Commission, '*A European Strategy for Data*', *supra*, p. 13, footnote 39.
2242. Regulation (EU) 715/2007 of the European Parliament and of the Council of 20 June 2007 on type approval of motor vehicles with respect to emissions from light passenger and commercial vehicles (EUR 5 and EUR 6) and on access to vehicle repair and maintenance information, *OJ L 171/1*, 29 June 2007, Articles 6 and 7.
2243. Regulation (EU) 2018/858 of the European Parliament and of the Council of 30 May 2018 on the approval and market surveillance of motor vehicles and their trailers, and of systems, components and separate technical units intended for such vehicles, amending Regulations (EC) No. 715/2007 and (EC) No. 595/2009 and repealing Directive 2007/46/EC, *OJ L 151/1*, 14 June 2018. *See* Articles 61-66, 86 and annexes X and XI.
2244. Article 91 of Regulation 2018/858. For a comment on the data sharing aspects of this Regulation, *see* W. Kerber and D. Gill, 'Access to Data in Connected Cars and the Recent Reform of the Motor Vehicle Type Approval Regulation', *Journal of Intellectual Property, Information Technology and E-Commerce Law*, 2019, Vol. 10(2), pp. 244-256.
2245. 'The information generated by a system that is on board a vehicle or that is connected to an engine, and that is capable of detecting a malfunction, and, where applicable, is capable of signalling its occurrence by means of an alert system, is capable of identifying the likely area of malfunction by means of information stored in a computer memory, and is capable of communicating that information off-board' (Article 3.49 of Regulation 2018/858).
2246. 'All information, including all subsequent amendments and supplements thereto, that is required for diagnosing, servicing and inspecting a vehicle, preparing it for road worthiness testing, repairing, re-programming or re-initialising of a vehicle, or that is required for the remote diagnostic support of a vehicle or for the fitting on a vehicle of parts and equipment, and that is provided by the manufacturer to his authorised partners, dealers and repairers or is used by the manufacturer for the repair and maintenance purposes' (Article 3.48 of Regulation 2018/858).
2247. 'A natural or legal person who is responsible for all aspects of the type-approval of a vehicle, system, component or separate technical unit, or the individual vehicle approval, or the authorisation process for parts and equipment, for ensuring conformity of production and for market surveillance matters regarding that vehicle, system, component, separate technical unit, part and equipment produced, irrespective of

operators[2248] active on those markets while using it themselves and/or sharing it with authorised dealers or repairers[2249] active on those markets.[2250] Accordingly, such a data sharing obligation aims at ensuring effective competition on these aftermarkets, by allowing independent operators to compete with the car manufacturers themselves and/or authorised dealers or repairers.[2251] As the main objective is to promote competition on these aftermarkets, this justifies that I qualify Regulation 2018/858 as an *economic initiative imposing B2B data sharing.*

More concretely, Regulation 2018/858 imposes on car manufacturers the obligation to share vehicle 'on-board diagnostics' and repair and maintenance information with independent operators in an unrestricted, standardised, non-discriminatory and easily accessible manner, in the form of machine-readable and electronically processable data sets.[2252] Such sharing is, however, not free of charge, as manufacturers may charge reasonable and proportionate fees, which can be transaction-based or duration-based.[2253] Nevertheless, fees that discourage the sharing, because they fail to consider the extent to which the independent operator uses the information, will be considered unreasonable or disproportionate.[2254] Moreover, the details of the technical requirements for the sharing, notably the technical specifications on how the vehicle repair and maintenance information are to be provided, are laid down in Annex X of the Regulation.[2255]

---

whether or not that person is directly involved in all stages of the design and construction of that vehicle, system, component or separate technical unit concerned' (Article 3.40 of Regulation 2018/858).

2248. 'A natural or legal person, other than an authorised dealer or repairer, who is directly or indirectly involved in the repair and maintenance of vehicles, and include repairers, manufacturers or distributors of repair equipment, tools or spare parts, as well as publishers of technical information, automobile clubs, roadside assistance operators, operators offering inspection and testing services, operators offering training for installers, manufacturers and repairers of equipment for alternative-fuel vehicles; it also means authorised repairers, dealers and distributors within the distribution system of a given vehicle manufacturer to the extent that they provide repair and maintenance services for vehicles in respect of which they are not members of the vehicle manufacturer's distribution system (Article 3.45 of Regulation 2018/858). An independent repairer "means a natural or legal person who provides repair and maintenance services for vehicles and who does not operate within the manufacturer's distribution system"' (Article 3.47 of Regulation 2018/858).

2249. Authorised repairer 'means a natural or legal person who provides repair and maintenance services for vehicles and who operates within the manufacturer's distribution system' (Article 3.46 of Regulation 2018/858).

2250. Recital 52 of Regulation 2018/858.

2251. *Ibid. See also* W. Kerber and D. Gill, 'Access to Data in Connected Cars and the Recent Reform of the Motor Vehicle Type Approval Regulation', *supra*, pp. 245-247.

2252. Article 61.1 of Regulation 2018/858.

2253. Article 63.2 of Regulation 2018/858.

2254. Article 63.1 of Regulation 2018/858.

2255. Article 61.4 of Regulation 2018/858.

374. Yet, with the advent of connected (automated) cars, the scope of this Regulation could be considered as being quite limited. Indeed, vehicles (will) increasingly generate a huge amount of data that are valuable not only for the car manufacturers, authorised dealers/repairers and independent operators involved in the repair and maintenance of vehicles but also for a wide array of stakeholders who have an interest in accessing these in-vehicle data to provide additional services.[2256] These competing interests raise controversial questions about the control/sharing of these in-vehicle data.[2257] As explained by Kerber and Frank, three models of control/sharing can potentially be rolled out:[2258]

(1) the 'extended vehicle' model, in which all in-vehicle data are transferred to central servers, outside of the car, controlled by the car manufacturers. In this model, the recipients access the data on those remote servers (one for each car manufacturer), rather than directly in the car;
(2) an adapted version of the 'extended vehicle' model in which, instead of having one server for each car manufacturer, all the in-vehicle data would be transferred to a 'shared server', controlled by a neutral party or a consortium rather than by the car manufacturers. In this model, while the recipients would still have to access the data on this remote server, it is a neutral third party that would decide whether these recipients can get access to the car manufacturers' data;
(3) the 'on-board application platform' model, in which the data is not transferred on an external server, but rather remains in the vehicle that itself becomes the platform through which the recipients can access and use the in-vehicle data. The main difference with the two previous options is that it is now the car owner (or driver) that is in control of the access and that decides whether the recipients can get access to this data.

In practice, tensions arise from the fact that car manufacturers wish to opt for the 'extended vehicle' model, giving them exclusive (almost

2256. *See* W. Kerber, 'Data Governance in Connected Cars: The Problem of Access to In-Vehicle Data', *supra*, pp. 310-331.
2257. *See*, for instance, D. Geradin, 'Access to In-Vehicle Data by Third-Party Service Providers: Is There a Market Failure and, If So, How Should it Be Addressed?', January 2020, available at https://ssrn.com/abstract=3545817; W. Kerber, 'Data Governance in Connected Cars: The Problem of Access to In-Vehicle Data', *supra*, pp. 310-331; W. Kerber and D. Gill, 'Access to Data in Connected Cars and the Recent Reform of the Motor Vehicle Type Approval Regulation', *supra*, pp. 244-256; P. Picht, 'Towards an Access Regime for Mobility Data', *supra*, pp. 940-976.
2258. W. Kerber and J. Franck, 'Data Governance Regimes in the Digital Economy: The Example of Connected Cars', 3 November 2017, available at https://ssrn.com/abstract=3064794.

monopolistic) control over these in-vehicle data. As explained by Kerber, repairers and independent service providers see this privileged position of manufacturers as a risk of competitive problems, and therefore call for regulatory initiatives imposing the sharing of such data, with a view to ensuring fair and undistorted competition.[2259] More specifically, they demand that the 'extended vehicle' model be abandoned in favour of the 'on-board application platform' model. On the one hand, this would allow these independent repairers and service providers to have access to data directly on the vehicle, in real time, rather than having to access the data via an external server controlled by the manufacturers, which necessarily implies a latency time. On the other hand, this solution makes it possible to break the manufacturers' de facto monopoly on this information, by entrusting the control of the access to the in-vehicle data to the vehicle owner (since the access terminal is located on board the vehicle), and no longer to the manufacturers, which is the case when the terminal is an external server located outside of the vehicle. Car manufacturers, on the other hand, are opposed to the adoption of such a model of 'on-board application platform' for safety reasons. The argument often put forward in this respect is that by allowing access to data directly in the vehicle, rather than via an external server, this creates the risk that the vehicle could be hacked and that these hackings could potentially cause accidents. However, a report drafted by TRL for the European Commission demonstrated that an 'on-board application platform' could be developed in such a way that a high and adequate level of security is ensured.[2260]

Although the European Commission is aware of these heated debates, it has indicated that it will, for the time being, limit itself to adopting a non-binding recommendation to improve access and reuse of mobility and vehicle data for commercial and non-commercial purposes. However, it indicated that it would continue to monitor developments and would stand ready to intervene, if necessary, to establish a more binding framework for in-vehicle data sharing in order to ensure fair competition.[2261] As outlined by Geradin, such an intervention would have to be based on the establishment of a market failure as this could create severe compliance costs for the car

2259. *See* W. Kerber, 'Data Governance in Connected Cars: The Problem of Access to In-Vehicle Data', *supra*, pp. 310-331.

2260. TRL, 'Access to In-Vehicle Data and Resources – Final Report', *Study for the European Commission*, May 2017, available at https://ec.europa.eu/transport/sites/transport/files/2017-05-access-to-in-vehicle-data-and-resources.pdf, pp. 77-79.

2261. Communication from the Commission to the European Parliament, the Council, the European Economic and Social Committee and the Committee of the Regions, '*On the Road to Automated Mobility: An EU Strategy for Mobility of the Future*', Brussels, 17 May 2018, COM(2018) 283, p. 13.

manufacturers.[2262] It would also have to precisely define (for instance, by relying on market power considerations) the scope of the undertakings (manufacturers) that would be subject to such a data sharing obligation.[2263]

The automotive sector example provided above thus shows that the 'specific circumstances' justifying the adoption of a compulsory data sharing legislation could be established in situations where a market failure is identified, or can be foreseen, in a specific sector, and cannot be (efficiently) remedied by competition law intervention alone.[2264]

8.1.2 Balancing Exercises to Be Considered When Adopting Sectoral Legislations

375. Importantly, the advantages offered by sectoral legislations, described above, must be balanced with the fact that sector-specific data sharing regimes might actually backfire and be more beneficial to large data holders than to small competitors, and could thus fail to make markets open and fair.[2265]

On the one hand, there is a risk that the sector-specific legislation might be more beneficial to the existing large data holders active in the sector. Indeed, as outlined by Kerber, such sector-specific legislations create a risk of 'regulatory capture', namely that 'important stakeholders in the sector might use their closeness to policy-makers to influence the regulation in favour of their own interests (rent-seeking behaviour), leading to wrong regulations that do not achieve (sufficiently) the intended policy objectives of more competition and innovation (regulatory failure)'.[2266]

On the other hand, there is a risk that the sector-specific legislation might be more beneficial to large data holders active across sectors. This can be illustrated by the PSD2,[2267] presented above.[2268] Indeed, although it

2262. D. Geradin, 'Access to In-Vehicle Data by Third-Party Service Providers', *supra*, pp. 9-10. *See also* P. Picht, 'Towards an Access Regime for Mobility Data', *supra*, pp. 947-948.
2263. P. Picht, 'Towards an Access Regime for Mobility Data', *supra*, p. 963.
2264. Communication from the Commission, '*A European Strategy for Data*', *supra*, p. 13, footnote 39.
2265. *See* M. de la Mano and J. Padilla, 'Big Tech Banking', *Journal of Competition Law & Economics*, 2018, Vol. 14(4), pp. 494-526; F. Di Porto and G. Ghidini, '"I Access Your Data You Access Mine". Setting a Reciprocity Clause for the "Access to Account Rule" in the Payment Services Market', 2019, available at https://ssrn.com/abstract=3407294, p. 23. *See also* European Data Protection Supervisor, *Opinion 3/2020 on the European strategy for data*, 16 June 2020, available at https://edps.europa.eu/sites/edp/files/publication/20-06-16_opinion_data_strategy_en.pdf, p. 8.
2266. *See* W. Kerber, 'From (Horizontal and Sectoral) Data Access Solutions Towards Data Governance Systems', *supra*, p. 16.
2267. Directive (EU) 2015/2366 of the European Parliament and of the Council of 25 November 2015 on payment services in the internal market, amending Directives

mainly aims at empowering consumers by giving them more control over their banking data and operations, and by providing them with more choice and transparency,[2269] its secondary aim is to boost the emergence of (European) small FinTechs.[2270] Yet, as outlined by de la Mano and Padilla, such an instrument might arguably eventually be more beneficial to the existing (American) large data holders for which PSD2 has opened the gate of the payment service market.[2271] For instance, Apple has launched an 'Apple Pay' service.[2272] Indeed, a sector-specific data sharing regime like PSD2 benefits these large data holders in two ways. First, they can leverage all the non-banking data they already have about consumers to further refine the banking data they obtain via PSD2, in order to provide better payment services than the small FinTechs and than the traditional banks. Second, they can use this banking data to improve all their other data-driven services and strengthen their position on all the other data-driven markets in which they are active. This is because the value of data does not only come from the scale of data but also from the scope of data, and these large data holders have a 360° view on the consumers' preferences. In short, such a sector-specific instrument might have the unwanted effect of making large data holders operating across sectors stronger, while exposing the data holders burdened with a sectoral data sharing obligation to fierce competition on their core business, and while potentially missing the original aim, namely boosting small competitors. This is mainly because these large data holders, operating horizontally across markets, have, so far, no comparable *ex ante* data sharing obligation.[2273]

Importantly, this analysis is not only applicable to the banking sector but also can be extended to any sector in which the European legislator would consider adopting a sector-specific legislation imposing B2B data sharing. For instance, if one reverts to the above discussions pertaining to the control/sharing of in-vehicle data,[2274] the same risk might appear, in the

---

2002/65/EC, 2009/110/EC and 2013/36/EU and Regulation (EU) No. 1093/2010, and repealing Directive 2007/64/EC, *OJ L 337/35*, 23 December 2015.

2268. *See* Part II, Chapter 4, Section 4.2.2.1.

2269. *See* Recitals 5, 6, 28 and 67 of Directive 2015/2366.

2270. *See* Recital 67 of Directive 2015/2366.

2271. *See* M. de la Mano and J. Padilla, 'Big Tech Banking', *supra*, pp. 494-526. *See also* Netherlands Authority for Consumers and Markets, 'Big Techs in the Payment System', 16 November 2020, available at https://www.acm.nl/en/publications/acm-study-big-techs-dutch-payment-system, specifically pp. 37-38 and 41-48.

2272. *See* https://www.apple.com/befr/apple-pay/; Netherlands Authority for Consumers and Markets, 'Big Techs in the Payment System', *supra*, pp. 21-24 (*see* pp. 24-31 for explanations on the Google Pay, Amazon Pay and Facebook Pay services). It should be noted that the European Commission has opened, in June 2020, a formal antitrust investigation into Apple's conduct in connection with Apple Pay (*see* https://ec.europa.eu/commission/presscorner/detail/en/ip_20_1075).

2273. *See* however Part III, Chapter 8, Section 8.2.

2274. *See* point 374.

sense that a data sharing legislation imposing an obligation, on car manufacturers, to share such in-vehicle data with independent service providers might arguably be more beneficial for large data holders, who would thereby be offered the possibility to enter such markets, than for small independent service providers. Indeed, whatever the sector, large data holders can leverage all the non-sectoral data they already have about consumers to further refine the sectoral data they obtain, in order to provide better services than the small sectoral competitors. Moreover, they can use this sectoral data to improve all their other data-driven services.

376. One way to alleviate this risk and to solve this balance would be to exclude the large data holders from the benefit of such sector-specific compulsory data sharing legislations. However, this might be difficult to justify because this could arguably lead to an unlawful discrimination against these large data holders. Indeed, when entering the market, they will likely be small competitors like all the others. In this perspective, it might not be objectively justifiable to refuse to share data with them merely on the basis of the 'potentiality' of the advantage that they could gain from data leveraging practices. Indeed, they might end up developing a product/service that is not as good as the one developed by a smaller actor in the specific (niche) market, and completely denying them the opportunity to compete could be seen as excessive.

Alternatively, Di Porto and Ghidini suggest another way to alleviate this risk and to solve this balance, namely adding a reciprocity clause in the sector-specific legislation, according to which large data holders[2275] relying on this legislation to get access to the sectoral data should provide the undertakings that are compelled to share data with a reciprocal right to access some of their data (such as behavioural data), provided that the individuals consented to this.[2276] However, it must be pointed out that such a reciprocity clause would not address the totality of this issue, as it would only benefit the undertakings that are subject to the sector-specific data sharing legislation, but not the smaller service providers trying to compete with these undertakings and with the large data holders.

377. Moreover, the advantages of resorting to sector-specific data sharing must be balanced with the fact that data is a non-rivalrous and general-purpose resource that could be reused for completely different purposes in another sector.[2277] In fact, a study by Deloitte has estimated that 24% to 36%

2275. Di Porto and Ghidini refer to 'digital conglomerates'.

2276. F. Di Porto and G. Ghidini, '"I Access Your Data You Access Mine". Setting a Reciprocity Clause for the "Access to Account Rule" in the Payment Services Market', *supra*, p. 23.

2277. *See* point 52.

of the benefits of data sharing will derive from cross-sectoral data sharing.[2278] Such cross-sectoral reuse could indeed generate additional economic value (one could think of data collected by sensors on machines in a car assembly line, which could be reused for other purposes in other sectors). Accordingly, limiting the scope of the compulsory data sharing legislation to reuses within a single sector would not enable the generation of such additional economic value.

8.2 CREATION OF HORIZONTAL 'EX ANTE' LEGISLATIONS IMPOSING B2B DATA SHARING FOR ECONOMIC PURPOSES: NECESSARY BALANCING EXERCISES

378. As demonstrated in the previous Section, while sectoral legislations imposing data sharing present advantages, they also entail some risks and they present some limitations. Therefore, in parallel to these sectoral approaches, *ex ante* compulsory B2B data sharing initiatives having a more horizontal scope could be pursued.[2279] Indeed, these two approaches are not mutually exclusive, as these horizontal legislations could be seen as a subsidiary form of intervention, providing for a minimal level playing field across sectors and in sectors where no sector-specific legislation exists.[2280] They could also be used to address economic concerns that extend beyond specific sectors.

379. Yet, like any other initiative imposing B2B data sharing, such horizontal *ex ante* legislations will entail balancing exercises. In substance, the economic benefits deriving from the wider data sharing that such legislations would entail would have to be balanced with the data holder's business interests. Indeed, data sharing might deter innovation by the data holder that is compelled to share its data, as it might no longer want to invest in data

2278. Deloitte, 'Realising the Economic Potential of Machine-Generated, Non-personal Data in the EU', *Report for Vodaphone Group*, July 2018, available at https://www.vodafone.com/content/dam/vodcom/files/public-policy/Realising_the_potential_of_IoT_data_report_for_Vodafone.pdf, p. 32. *See also* Commission Staff Working Document, Impact assessment report accompanying the document '*Proposal for a Regulation of the European Parliament and of the Council on European data governance: An enabling framework for common European data spaces (Data Governance Act)*', Brussels, 25 November 2020, SWD(2020) 295 final, p. 15.

2279. J. Drexl, 'Data Access and Control in the Era of Connected Devices', *supra*, pp. 159-161.

2280. *Ibid.*, p. 160. *See also* W. Kerber, 'From (Horizontal and Sectoral) Data Access Solutions towards Data Governance Systems', *supra*, p. 16; European Commission, Inception Impact Assessment: '*Data Act (including the review of the Directive 96/9/EC on the legal protection of databases)*', May 2021, Ares (2021)3527151, p. 5.

collection that used to provide him with a competitive advantage, as it fears free-riding.[2281] Moreover, it should also be factored that imposing data sharing for economic purposes (addressing data market failures)[2282] might also deter innovation by third parties (expectation to free-ride). Additionally, these horizontal legislations will have to comply with the personal data protection rules.[2283]

380. One way to address these issues would be to consider, by analogy with what has been said for sectoral legislations,[2284] that such horizontal *ex ante* legislations imposing B2B data sharing should only be created when 'specific circumstances' justify it. Indeed, such legislations should only be adopted if they are proportional and necessary to address these 'specific circumstances', in order to achieve an optimal balance with the data holder's freedom to conduct a business.

From an economic perspective, such 'specific circumstances' would notably be established in situations where a (systemic) market failure[2285] is identified or can be foreseen, and cannot be (efficiently) remedied by competition law intervention alone.[2286,2287] In this regard, the European Commission had announced, in the past, that it would consider the adoption of a horizontal *ex ante* regulation to address systemic issues related to platforms and data.[2288]

More recently, the European Commission has proposed the adoption of a 'Digital Markets Act'[2289] in the context of its DSA package.[2290] This Act is

2281. D. Rubinfeld and M. Gal, 'Access Barriers to Big Data', *supra*, p. 374.
2282. *See* Part I, Chapter 2, Section 2.2.3.3.
2283. *See* points 91 and 96 and Part III, Chapter 7 and Chapter 8, Section 8.2.
2284. *See* points 372 and 373.
2285. *See* Part I, Chapter 2, Section 2.2.3.3.
2286. *See* Part III, Chapter 6, Section 6.5.2.
2287. Communication from the Commission, '*A European Strategy for Data*', *supra*, p. 13, footnote 39.
2288. *Ibid.*, p. 14. *See also* Communication from the Commission, '*Shaping Europe's Digital Future*', *supra*, p. 9.
2289. Proposal for a Regulation of the European Parliament and of the Council on contestable and fair markets in the digital sector (Digital Markets Act), 15 December 2020, COM(2020) 842 final. *See also* Commission Staff Working Document, Impact assessment report accompanying the document '*Proposal for a Regulation of the European Parliament and of the Council on contestable and fair markets in the digital sector (Digital Markets Act)*', Brussels, 15 December 2020, SWD(2020) 363 final.
2290. For recommendations and comments pertaining to this DMA proposal, *see* A. de Streel, et al., 'Digital Markets Act: Making Economic Regulation of Platforms Fit for the Digital Age', *CERRE Recommendations Paper*, November 2020, available at https://cerre.eu/publications/digital-markets-act-economic-regulation-platforms-digital-age/; A. de Streel, et al., 'The European Proposal for a Digital Markets Act: A First Assessment', *CERRE Assessment Paper*, January 2021, available at https://cerre.eu/publications/the-european-proposal-for-a-digital-markets-act-a-first-assessment/; L. Cabral, et al., 'The EU Digital Markets Act: A Report from a Panel of Economic Experts', *EU Science Hub*, 2021, available at https://ec.europa.eu/jrc/en/publication/

an '*ex ante* regulatory instrument for large online platforms with significant network effects acting as gatekeepers[2291] in the European Union's internal market'.[2292] According to the European Commission, the 'specific circumstances' justifying the adoption of such a regulation are that these gatekeepers benefit from strong network effects due to their large user base and that, as a result, they 'exercise control over whole platform ecosystems in the digital economy and are structurally extremely difficult to challenge or contest by existing or new market operators, irrespective of how innovative and efficient these may be'.[2293] Moreover, due to these gatekeepers' ability to leverage their data advantage from their core market to adjacent markets, there is a risk that these adjacent markets could also tip in favour of these gatekeepers, to the detriment of consumer choice and innovation.[2294] There is thus a risk that innovative new actors (SMEs, start-ups, etc.) could be unfairly excluded from entry.[2295]

In order to tackle (or even prevent) these market failures, the proposal for a Digital Markets Act suggests that the European Commission should be empowered to determine whether a specific data holder offering a 'core platform service'[2296] meets the 'gatekeeper' threshold.[2297] In this regard, it shall work in close cooperation and coordination with the Member States,[2298] and it shall be assisted by the Digital Markets Advisory Committee,[2299]

---

eu-digital-markets-act; A. de Streel and P. Larouche, 'The European Digital Markets Act Proposal: How to Improve a Regulatory Revolution', *Concurrences*, 2021, No. 2, pp. 46-63.

2291. *See* Articles 2.1 and 3 of the Proposal for a Digital Markets Act. For more details on the designation of these gatekeepers, *see* points 384 and 385.
2292. European Commission, Inception Impact Assessment: '*Digital Services Act package: Ex ante regulatory instrument for large online platforms with significant network effects acting as gate-keepers in the European Union's internal market*', June 2020, Ares(2020)2836174, p. 1.
2293. Recital 3 of the Proposal for a Digital Markets Act.
2294. Recitals 25 and 26 of the Proposal for a Digital Markets Act. *See also* European Commission, Inception Impact Assessment: '*Digital Services Act package*', *supra*, p. 2.
2295. Recitals 3, 36 and 56 of the Proposal for a Digital Markets Act. *See also* pp. 1-3 of the Explanatory memorandum of this Proposal; European Parliament resolution of 20 October 2020 with recommendations to the Commission on the Digital Services Act: Improving the functioning of the Single Market (2020/2018(INL)), P9_TA-PROV(2020)0272, available at https://www.europarl.europa.eu/doceo/document/TA-9-2020-0272_EN.html, p. 35.
2296. *See* Article 1.2 of the Proposal for a Digital Markets Act. For a definition of these services, *see* Articles 2.2 and 2.5-2.11 of the Proposal. For more information on why these services are considered as 'core platform services', *see* Commission Staff Working Document, Impact assessment report accompanying the document '*Proposal for a Regulation of the European Parliament and of the Council on contestable and fair markets in the digital sector (Digital Markets Act)*', Brussels, 15 December 2020, SWD(2020) 363 final, pp. 37-45, 64-78, 82, 85 and 96-120.
2297. *See* points 384 and 385.
2298. Articles 1.7 and 19.6 of the Proposal for a Digital Markets Act.
2299. Article 32 of the Proposal for a Digital Markets Act.

composed of Member States' representatives having an expertise in the platform economy.[2300] If a large data holder is designated as a 'gatekeeper', it will have to comply, within six months of its inclusion in the 'list of gatekeepers',[2301] with Articles 5 and 6 of the proposal for a Digital Markets Act, which contain a series of obligations, as well as prohibited practices that limit contestability or that are unfair.[2302] For instance, 'gatekeepers' will have to ensure specific types of data sharing, as they will notably have to provide 'to any third party providers of online search engines, upon their request, access on fair, reasonable and non-discriminatory terms to ranking, query, click and view data in relation to free and paid search generated by end users on online search engines of the gatekeeper, subject to anonymisation for the query, click and view data that constitutes personal data'.[2303] This would ensure that the markets impacted by such gatekeepers would remain fair and contestable,[2304] by potentially arousing the entrance of innovative new actors, and would thereby promote consumer choice and drive innovation beyond what can be achieved on the sole basis of competition law enforcement.[2305] The measures implemented by the 'gatekeeper' to comply with these obligations and to abstain from adopting such prohibited practices will have to be effective and proportionate, and can be specified by the Commission if need be.[2306] The Commission will monitor the effective implementation and compliance with these provisions, and it may issue non-compliance or fining decisions in case of breach of these provisions.[2307]

2300. Proposal for a Digital Markets Act, p. 9.
2301. Articles 3.7 and 4.3 of the Proposal for a Digital Markets Act.
2302. Article 3.8 of the Proposal for a Digital Markets Act. Gatekeepers are, for example, prohibited from engaging in some forms of personal data combination (Article 5.a)), of tying of ancillary services (Articles 5.e) and f)), and of self-preferencing (Articles 6.1.a) and d)); and from adopting most-favoured-nation clauses (Article 5.b)). Moreover, they will have to allow specific types of data sharing (Articles 6.1.h), i) and j)) and of interoperability (Articles 6.1.c) and f)). On the rationale for the inclusion of these obligations and prohibited practices in the Proposal, *see* Commission Staff Working Document, Impact assessment report accompanying the document '*Proposal for a Regulation of the European Parliament and of the Council on Contestable and Fair Markets in the Digital Sector (Digital Markets Act)*', Brussels, 15 December 2020, SWD(2020) 363 final, pp. 50-60, 64-78, 82, 85 and 96-120. For an assessment of these obligations and prohibitions, *see* A. de Streel, et al., 'The European Proposal for a Digital Markets Act: A First Assessment', *supra*, pp. 6-7 and 16-23.
2303. Article 6.1.j) of the Proposal for a Digital Markets Act. *See also* the data sharing obligations contained in Article 6.1.h), presented at point 167, and Article 6.1.i), presented at point 180. *See also* Recitals 54-56.
2304. European Commission, Inception Impact Assessment: '*Digital Services Act package*', *supra*, p. 1.
2305. European Parliament resolution of 20 October 2020 with recommendations to the Commission on the Digital Services Act: Improving the functioning of the Single Market (2020/2018(INL)), P9_TA-PROV(2020)0272, available at https://www.europarl.europa.eu/doceo/document/TA-9-2020-0272_EN.html, p. 19.
2306. Article 7 of the Proposal for a Digital Markets Act.
2307. *See* Articles 24-26 of the Proposal for a Digital Markets Act.

The 'gatekeeper' can also offer commitments to ensure compliance with the Digital Markets Act.[2308] This list of obligations and prohibited practices can be updated by the Commission, on the basis of delegated acts, in order to address new practices that might emerge and that might be unfair or limit the contestability of data markets.[2309] According to Article 10.2 of the Proposal, a practice should be considered as unfair or as limiting the contestability of data markets if: '(a) there is an imbalance of rights and obligations on business users and the gatekeeper is obtaining an advantage from business users that is disproportionate to the service provided by the gatekeeper to business users; or (b) the contestability of markets is weakened as a consequence of such a practice engaged in by gatekeepers'.

381. If such 'specific circumstances' justify the adoption of horizontal *ex ante* legislations imposing B2B data sharing for economic purposes, the provisions of such legislations will nevertheless need to find a balance between the economic benefits of the sharing and the costs on the data holder's business interests, and they will need to comply with the individuals' right to privacy and to personal data protection. This will require tackling fundamental questions such as: who will have to share data and who can receive the data? To which types of data would this apply? Should this be remunerated? How could this be implemented technically? How will these legislations be enforced?

In this regard, it should be outlined from the outset that there is no 'one size fits all' answer to these questions. Instead, the balancing exercises underlying each of these questions should be factored, on a case-by-case basis, when creating a specific horizontal *ex ante* legislation.[2310]

8.2.1 Who Will Have to Share Data?

382. First, the data holders that will be subject to the horizontal *ex ante* legislations imposing B2B data sharing for economic purposes have to be identified. Indeed, as such compulsory sharing will entail costs for these data holders, it is fundamental to ensure that it will only apply to the data holders whose data is considered as necessary to achieve the economic objectives underlying the legislation.

383. If the 'specific circumstances' justifying the adoption of these legislations are economic – namely that (systemic) market failures (data concentration, data conglomeration, etc.)[2311] are identified or can be foreseen, and

2308. Article 23 of the Proposal for a Digital Markets Act.
2309. Articles 10 and 34 of the Proposal for a Digital Markets Act.
2310. On this point, *see* W. Kerber, 'From (Horizontal and Sectoral) Data Access Solutions Towards Data Governance Systems', *supra*.
2311. *See* Part I, Chapter 2, Section 2.2.3.3.

cannot be (efficiently) remedied by competition law intervention alone[2312] – legal scholars seem to agree on the fact that the data sharing obligation should only be imposed to a specific subset of data holders.[2313] In this regard, it is worth reminding[2314] that the European Commission has proposed the adoption of a 'Digital Markets Act',[2315] which should empower the European Commission to determine whether a specific data holder meets the 'gatekeeper' threshold,[2316] in which case it will have to ensure some forms of data sharing.[2317] In the same vein, the Furman report outlines that, in order to spur competition and innovation, *ex ante* data sharing obligations, to be monitored by a 'Digital Markets Unit', should be imposed on undertakings having a

---

2312. *See* Part III, Chapter 6, Section 6.5.2; Communication from the Commission, '*A European Strategy for Data*', *supra*, p. 13, footnote 39.
2313. *See* R. Feasey and A. de Streel, 'Data Sharing for Digital Market Contestability' *supra*, pp. 56-68; A. de Streel, et al., 'Digital Markets Act: Making Economic Regulation of Platforms Fit for the Digital Age', *supra*; J. Crémer, Y.-A. de Montjoye and H. Schweitzer, 'Competition Policy for the Digital Era', *supra*, p. 49; J. Furman, et al., 'Unlocking Digital Competition', *supra*, p. 55; S. Vezzoso, 'Competition Policy in Transition: Exploring Data Portability's Roles', *15th ASCOLA (Virtual) Conference*, June 2020, available at https://ssrn.com/abstract=3634736, p. 20; Stigler Committee on Digital Platforms, 'Final Report', *supra*, p. 32; Autorité de la concurrence, 'Contribution de l'Autorité de la concurrence au débat sur la politique de concurrence et les enjeux numériques', 19 February 2020, available at https://www.autoritedelaconcurrence.fr/sites/default/files/2020-02/2020.02.19_contribution_adlc_enjeux_numeriques_vf.pdf, pp. 5 and 13; V. Mayer-Schonberger and T. Ramge, *Re-inventing Capitalism in the Age of Big Data*, *supra*, pp. 167-169; Unofficial translation of the Draft Bill for the Reform of the German Competition Act, 24 January 2020, available at https://www.d-kart.de/wp-content/uploads/2020/02/GWB10-Engl-Translation-2020-02-21.pdf, p. 3; European Commission, Inception Impact Assessment: '*Digital Services Act package: Ex ante regulatory instrument for large online platforms with significant network effects acting as gate-keepers in the European Union's internal market*', June 2020, Ares(2020)2836174, pp. 3-4; European Parliament resolution of 20 October 2020 with recommendations to the Commission on the Digital Services Act: Improving the functioning of the Single Market (2020/2018(INL)), P9_TA-PROV(2020)0272, available at https://www.europarl.europa.eu/doceo/document/TA-9-2020-0272_EN.html, pp. 25 and 36.
2314. *See* point 380.
2315. Proposal for a Digital Markets Act.
2316. *See* Articles 2.1 and 3 of the Proposal for a Digital Markets Act. For more details on the determination of this threshold, *see* points 384 and 385.
2317. For instance, according to Article 6.1.j) of the Proposal for a Digital Markets Act, a gatekeeper shall 'provide to any third party providers of online search engines, upon their request, with access on fair, reasonable and non-discriminatory terms to ranking, query, click and view data in relation to free and paid search generated by end users on online search engines of the gatekeeper, subject to anonymisation for the query, click and view data that constitutes personal data'. *See also* Article 6.1.h), presented at point 167, and Article 6.1.i), presented at point 180. *See also* Recitals 54-56.

'strategic market status'.[2318,2319] Similarly, the Stigler Committee report provides that *ex ante* data sharing obligations, to be monitored by a 'Digital Authority', could be imposed on undertakings having 'bottleneck power'.[2320,2321]

One of the key common points between these propositions is that they are limited to a specific subset of data holders meeting a certain threshold ('gatekeepers'; undertakings with 'strategic market status'; undertakings having 'bottleneck power'; undertakings of 'paramount significance';[2322] 'unavoidable trading partners';[2323] 'structuring undertakings';[2324] 'large gatekeeper platforms';[2325] etc.[2326]). As outlined by the European Parliament in its resolution pertaining to the Commission's Digital Services Act Package, such regulatory interventions must contain a set of clear indicators allowing the European Commission to decide whether a large data holder must be considered as a 'gatekeeper' or not, such as 'whether the undertaking is active to a significant extent on multi-sided markets or has the ability to lock-in users and consumers, the size of its network (number of users), and the presence of network effects; barriers to entry, its financial strength, the ability to access data, the accumulation and the combination of data from different sources; vertical integration and its role as an unavoidable partner and the importance of its activity for third parties' access to supply and markets, etc'.[2327] Importantly, this would thus imply that the scope of

2318. Undertakings that are 'in a position to exercise market power over a gateway or bottleneck in a digital market, where they control others' market access' (J. Furman, et al., 'Unlocking Digital Competition', *supra*, p. 55).

2319. *Ibid. See also* Competition and Markets Authority, 'Online Platforms and Digital Advertising: Market Study Final Report', 1 July 2020, available at https://www.gov.uk/cma-cases/online-platforms-and-digital-advertising-market-study, pp. 322-323.

2320. Bottleneck power 'describes a situation where consumers primarily single-home and rely upon a single service provider, which makes obtaining access to those consumers for the relevant activity by other service providers prohibitively costly' (Stigler Committee on Digital Platforms, 'Final Report', *supra*, p. 32).

2321. *Ibid.*, pp. 100-101.

2322. *See* the unofficial translation of the Draft Bill for the Reform of the German Competition Act, 24 January 2020, available at https://www.d-kart.de/wp-content/uploads/2020/02/GWB10-Engl-Translation-2020-02-21.pdf, p. 3.

2323. J. Crémer, Y.-A. de Montjoye and H. Schweitzer, 'Competition Policy for the Digital Era', *supra*, p. 49.

2324. Autorité de la concurrence, 'Contribution de l'Autorité de la concurrence au débat sur la politique de concurrence et les enjeux numériques', *supra*, pp. 5 and 13.

2325. A. de Streel, et al., 'Digital Markets Act: Making Economic Regulation of Platforms Fit for the Digital Age', *supra*, p. 4.

2326. In the same perspective, see the suggestion to create a 'progressive data sharing obligation', which would kick in once the market share of a data holder has reached a certain threshold, and according to which the amount of data to be shared by a specific data holder should be function of its market share (V. Mayer-Schonberger and T. Ramge, *Re-inventing Capitalism in the Age of Big Data*, *supra*, pp. 167-169).

2327. European Parliament resolution of 20 October 2020 with recommendations to the Commission on the Digital Services Act: Improving the functioning of the Single

application of the horizontal *ex ante* legislations should be broad enough in order to cover all types of data holders[2328] that may be considered as such 'gatekeepers', even if the concrete obligations contained in the legislations would only have to be respected by those that the European Commission deems to be 'gatekeepers', in light of the indicators contained in the legislations.[2329]

384. Regarding the indicators to be used by the European Commission, the proposal for a Digital Markets Act provides that a large data holder offering a 'core platform service' will meet the 'gatekeeper' threshold if: '(a) it has a significant impact on the internal market; (b) it operates a core platform service which serves as an important gateway for business users to reach end users; and (c) it enjoys an entrenched and durable position in its operations or it is foreseeable that it will enjoy such a position in the near future'.[2330] These criteria are thus cumulative, and three quantitative 'presumption thresholds' have been set in order to streamline the assessment of the existence of a 'gatekeeper' position.[2331]

First, the significant impact on the internal market will be presumed if the large data holder 'achieves an annual EEA turnover equal to or above EUR 6.5 billion in the last three financial years, or where the average market capitalisation or the equivalent fair market value of the undertaking to which it belongs amounted to at least EUR 65 billion in the last financial year, and

Market (2020/2018(INL)), P9_TA-PROV(2020)0272, available at https://www.europarl.europa.eu/doceo/document/TA-9-2020-0272_EN.html, pp. 25 and 36. On these indicators, *see also* European Commission, Inception Impact Assessment: '*Digital Services Act Package*', *supra*, p. 2; and A. de Streel, et al., 'Digital Markets Act: Making Economic Regulation of Platforms Fit for the Digital Age', *supra*, pp. 11-12.

2328. Contrary, for example, to the Platform-to-Business Regulation that only applies to certain types of online intermediation services and to online search engines (Articles 2.2 and 2.5 of Regulation (EU) 2019/1150 of the European Parliament and of the Council of 20 June 2019 on promoting fairness and transparency for business users of online intermediation services, *OJ L 186/57*, 11 July 2019). On this Regulation, *see* points 178-180.

2329. A. de Streel, et al., 'Digital Markets Act: Making Economic Regulation of Platforms Fit for the Digital Age', *supra*, p. 10.

2330. Article 3.1 of the Proposal for a Digital Markets Act. On the different policy options that were considered, *see* Commission Staff Working Document, Impact assessment report accompanying the document '*Proposal for a Regulation of the European Parliament and of the Council on contestable and fair markets in the digital sector (Digital Markets Act)*', Brussels, 15 December 2020, SWD(2020) 363 final, pp. 46-50, 64-78, 82, 85 and 96-120.

2331. Article 3.2 of the Proposal for a Digital Markets Act. According to some authors, a fourth 'ecosystem criterion' could have been added as well, relating to the fact that the large data holder provides several digital services within its ecosystem (A. de Streel, et al., 'The European Proposal for a Digital Markets Act: A First Assessment', *CERRE Assessment Paper*, January 2021, available at https://cerre.eu/publications/the-european-proposal-for-a-digital-markets-act-a-first-assessment/, pp. 6 and 15).

it provides a core platform service in at least three Member States'.[2332] Second, the fact that the large data holder operates an important gateway for business users to reach end users will be presumed if it provides a core platform service[2333] that 'has more than 45 million monthly active end users[2334] established or located in the Union and more than 10 000 yearly active business users established in the Union in the last financial year'.[2335] Third, the large data holder will be presumed to have an entrenched and durable position if the 'users threshold' mentioned above were met in each of the last three financial years.[2336]

Importantly, the European Commission would be empowered to adopt delegated acts to specify the methodology used for assessing whether these

---

2332. Article 3.2.a) of the Proposal for a Digital Markets Act. In order to narrow the scope of the Digital Markets Act on a smaller number of undertakings, namely those that play 'an unquestionable role as gatekeepers due to their size and their impact on the internal market', the European Parliament's 'Draft report' on this Act suggests to raise these thresholds to EUR 10 billion and EUR 100 billion, respectively (*see* Committee on the Internal Market and Consumer Protection of the European Parliament, Draft report on the proposal for a regulation of the European Parliament and of the Council Contestable and fair markets in the digital sector (Digital Markets Act) (COM(2020)0842 – C9-0419/2020 – 2020/0374(COD)), 1 June 2021, 2020/0374(COD), available at https://www.europarl.europa.eu/doceo/document/IMCO-PR-692792_EN.pdf, pp. 32 and 79).

2333. The European Parliament's 'Draft report' on this Act suggests adding another requirement, namely that the gatekeeper must provide at least two core platform services – each of which having more than 45 million monthly active end users established or located in the Union and more than 10,000 yearly active business users established in the Union in the last financial year – in order to take into account the role of 'ecosystems of services' more explicitly (Committee on the Internal Market and Consumer Protection of the European Parliament, Draft report on the proposal for a regulation of the European Parliament and of the Council Contestable and fair markets in the digital sector, *supra*, p. 33 and 79). This echoes a similar call made by some authors and policymakers (*see* French Ministry of the Economy, Finance and the Recovery, German Federal Ministry for Economic Affairs and Energy and Dutch Ministry of Economic Affairs and Climate Policy, 'Strengthening the Digital Markets Act and Its Enforcement', May 2021, available at https://www.economie.gouv.fr/files/2021-05/1055%20-%20Strengthening%20the%20Digital%20Markets%20Act%20and%20Its%20Enforcement.pdf, p. 1; A. de Streel, et al., 'Digital Markets Act: Making Economic Regulation of Platforms Fit for the Digital Age', *supra*, p. 12).

2334. 'Monthly active end users shall refer to the average number of monthly active end users throughout the largest part of the last financial year' (Article 3.2.b), al.2 of the Proposal for a Digital Markets Act).

2335. Article 3.2.b), al.1 of the Proposal for a Digital Markets Act. The European Parliament's 'Draft report' on this Act suggests to add an Annex containing a list of indicators pertaining to the establishment of the number of monthly active end-users and yearly active business users (Committee on the Internal Market and Consumer Protection of the European Parliament, Draft report on the proposal for a regulation of the European Parliament and of the Council Contestable and fair markets in the digital sector, *supra*, pp. 71-77 and 79).

2336. Article 3.2.c) of the Proposal for a Digital Markets Act.

three quantitative 'presumption thresholds' are met, as well as to adjust them to market and technological developments where necessary.[2337] Such a delegated act, which could take the form of guidelines, would have the merit to enhance legal certainty and predictability on this new issue of 'gatekeeper' identification.[2338]

If a large data holder meets all of these three quantitative 'presumption thresholds', it will have to notify the European Commission thereof,[2339] as the latter is in charge of designating those that meet the 'gatekeeper' threshold.[2340] However, in its notification, the large data holder can attempt to rebut this 'gatekeeper' presumption (i.e., that it does not meet the 'gatekeeper' threshold of Article 3.1 even if it meets the three quantitative 'presumption thresholds' of Article 3.2) by presenting sufficiently substantiated arguments relying on qualitative indicators such as low entry barriers or the lack of user lock-in due to multi-homing possibilities.[2341] If the large data holder presents sufficiently substantiated arguments to rebut this 'gatekeeper' presumption, the European Commission shall rely instead on qualitative indicators to demonstrate that the large data holder meets the 'gatekeeper' threshold of Article 3.1.[2342] These are: '(a) the size, including turnover and market capitalisation, operations and position of the provider of core platform services; (b) the number of business users depending on the core platform service to reach end users and the number of end users; (c) entry barriers derived from network effects and data driven advantages, in particular in relation to the provider's access to and collection of personal and non-personal data or analytics capabilities; (d) scale and scope effects the provider benefits from, including with regard to data; (e) business user or end user lock-in; (f) other structural market characteristics'.[2343]

Moreover, the European Commission can also decide, on the basis of a market investigation procedure mentioned above,[2344] that a large data holder meets the 'gatekeeper' threshold even if it does not satisfy each of the three quantitative 'presumption thresholds'.[2345] In doing so, it should consider the qualitative indicators mentioned above. In conducting this assessment, the Commission should consider foreseeable developments of these elements.[2346]

2337. Articles 3.5 and 37 of the Proposal for a Digital Markets Act.
2338. A. de Streel, et al., 'The European Proposal for a Digital Markets Act: A First Assessment', *supra*, pp. 6 and 15.
2339. Article 3.3 of the Proposal for a Digital Markets Act.
2340. Article 3.4, al. 1 of the Proposal for a Digital Markets Act.
2341. Article 3.4, al. 1 of the Proposal for a Digital Markets Act.
2342. Article 3.4, al. 2 of the Proposal for a Digital Markets Act.
2343. Article 3.6, al. 2 of the Proposal for a Digital Markets Act.
2344. *See* point 317. *See* Article 15 of the Proposal for a Digital Markets Act.
2345. Article 3.6, al.1 of the Proposal for a Digital Markets Act.
2346. Article 3.6, al.3 of the Proposal for a Digital Markets Act.

Finally, as data markets are dynamic and evolutive, the European Commission will have to regularly review, at least every two years, whether the 'gatekeepers' that it has listed still meet the threshold mentioned above, as well as whether new large data holders have come to meet it.[2347] In this regard, the Commission can, upon request or on its own initiative, adapt or repeal a decision following which a large data holder meets the 'gatekeeper' threshold if 'there has been a substantial change in any of the facts on which the decision was based', or if 'the decision was based on incomplete, incorrect or misleading information provided by the undertakings'.[2348]

385. In light of the above, there thus seems to be a strong consensus that horizontal *ex ante* legislations imposing B2B data sharing, whose adoption is justified by economic 'specific circumstances', should be asymmetric and limited to a specific subset of data holders. In this regard, the determination of whether a data holder falls within the scope of the data sharing obligation could be based on a set of clear quantitative and qualitative indicators contained in the legislations, to be assessed on a case-by-case basis by the controlling authority. Indeed, if other horizontal *ex ante* legislations were to be adopted, for example, to impose additional data sharing obligations than those contained in the Digital Markets Act,[2349] a semi-flexible approach could be taken, where quantitative indicators (e.g., annual turnover or number of customers) could serve as 'rebuttable presumptions' that specific data holders fall within the scope of the initiative. These could be complemented by qualitative indicators (e.g., barriers to entry or user lock-in) that could be used to make other data holders fall within the scope of the initiative, in situations where the presumptions are rebutted or where the quantitative thresholds are not met. This would require a case-by-case analysis, based on the markets and context at hand, as the legislations should merely provide these indicators, while the concrete list of data holders falling within the scope of the initiative will, by nature, be evolutive and dynamic.[2350] Therefore, these indicators must be 'sufficiently flexible to adapt to different business models as well as technology and market evolution which evolve rapidly and can be unpredictable in the digital economy (…)

2347. Article 4.2 of the Proposal for a Digital Markets Act. For some authors, this two-year cycle is too short and should be extended to five years, in order to reduce the logistical and fact-finding pressure (A. de Streel, et al., 'The European Proposal for a Digital Markets Act: A First Assessment', *supra*, p. 15).

2348. Article 4.1 of the Proposal for a Digital Markets Act.

2349. This Act indeed only contains a certain number of specific data sharing obligations, to the benefit of third-party providers of online search engines (Article 6.1.j) – *see* point 380), of business users of these gatekeepers' services (Article 6.1.i) – *see* point 180), and to individuals (Article 6.1.h) – *see* point 167). However, data sharing obligations could also be created to the benefit of other actors, such as competitors of these gatekeepers or undertakings developing complementary services.

2350. R. Feasey and A. de Streel, 'Data Sharing for Digital Market Contestability', *supra*, pp. 12 and 56-58.

[and] should also be sufficiently clear and easy to implement to ensure legal predictability and not be subject to long and complex procedures'.[2351] Moreover, the regulatory authority's decisions that certain data holders fall within the scope of the data sharing obligation would have to be reassessed at regular intervals, in order to take into account the evolution of the market at hand, as the data holders might no longer fulfil these indicators, or as the market failures justifying the intervention might disappear over time.[2352]

Such a limitation of the scope of application of the legislations is justified by the fact that the costs implied by the data sharing obligation on the data holder's business interests should only be imposed to a specific subset of data holders, namely those that are considered as playing a central role in the (systemic) market failure(s) that led to the legislative intervention.[2353] Indeed, as the aim of these interventions is to enhance competition by levelling the competitive playing field and by ensuring the contestability of data markets, it is preferable to opt for an asymmetric approach,[2354] which would only burden this subset of data holders, and not other market actors. This is, according to us, a key difference with empowerment initiatives imposing B2B data sharing.[2355]

8.2.2 Who Can Receive the Data?

386. Second, the horizontal *ex ante* legislations imposing B2B data sharing for economic purposes will have to determine whether any recipient whatsoever should be entitled to access the data holder's data, or whether only some of them should be entitled to such access. Indeed, an *erga omnes* entitlement to access the data would potentially maximise the economic benefits pursued by the legislations, in light of the non-rivalrous nature of data. On the other hand, the greater the number of potential recipients, the greater the risks for the data holder's business interests and for the privacy and personal data protection of the multiple individuals whose data would be shared in an aggregated way.[2356] Any horizontal compulsory B2B data sharing legislation would thus have to consider this necessary balance.

2351. A. de Streel, et al., 'Digital Markets Act: Making Economic Regulation of Platforms Fit for the Digital Age', *supra*, p. 11.
2352. R. Feasey and A. de Streel, 'Data Sharing for Digital Market Contestability', *supra*, p. 83.
2353. *Ibid.*, p. 58.
2354. *See* J. Prüfer, 'Competition Policy and Data Sharing on Data-driven Markets', *Report for the Friedrich-Ebert-Stiftung*, 2020, available at http://library.fes.de/pdf-files/fes/15999.pdf, p. 12.
2355. *See* points 209 and 210.
2356. *See* R. Feasey and A. de Streel, 'Data Sharing for Digital Market Contestability', *supra*, pp. 9 and 60.

387. In this regard, some guidance could be sought in the principles for B2G data sharing.[2357] Accordingly, the legislations could provide that recipients would have to demonstrate that the purposes they would pursue, thanks to the shared data, would lead to clear economic benefits.[2358] Moreover, the legislations could provide that the sharing with a specific recipient should only be mandated if the costs for data holders and the potential individuals whose data would be shared are reasonable and proportionate to the economic objectives pursued.[2359]

In support of such an idea, Drexl argues that the horizontal B2B compulsory data sharing legislations could provide that only the recipients that pursue a legitimate economic interest should benefit from an access to the data.[2360] Naturally, the core issue here would be to determine what these legitimate interests are. Attempting to draft an extensive list of these interests in the legislations might not be the best solution, as it would risk not being exhaustive. Rather, the legislations could list several criteria to be considered in the determination of these legitimate interests (such as the demonstration of a clear economic benefit for society or of a significant contribution to research in a specific field, which would derive from the recipients processing of the data). Then, a specific regulatory body/authority could be appointed in order to assess, on a case-by-case basis, the legitimacy of the recipient's economic interests in light of these criteria, and to assess whether this recipient presents sufficient guarantees in terms of privacy and security, in order to protect the rights of the multiple individuals whose data would be transferred in an aggregated way.[2361] In this regard, the EDPS underlined that some type of formal 'vetting' of the data recipients might be warranted to address the risks mentioned above,[2362] for example, in the form of a clearing house.[2363]

388. Accordingly, the inclusion of a certification/accreditation scheme for data recipients in these horizontal legislations might be justified, as this

2357. *See* High-Level Expert Group on Business-to-Government Data Sharing, 'Towards a European strategy on business-to-government data sharing for public interests – Final report', 2020, available at https://ec.europa.eu/digital-single-market/en/news/experts-say-privately-held-data-available-european-union-should-be-used-better-and-more; H. Richter, 'The Law and Policy of Government Access to Private Sector Data ("B2G Data Sharing")', *Max Planck Institute for Innovation and Competition Research Paper No. 20-06*, 2020, available at https://ssrn.com/abstract=3594109.

2358. High-Level Expert Group on Business-to-Government Data Sharing, 'Towards a European strategy on business-to-government data sharing for public interests – Final report', *supra*, p. 81.

2359. *Ibid.*, p. 80.

2360. J. Drexl, 'Data Access and Control in the Era of Connected Devices', *supra*, p. 164.

2361. R. Feasey and A. de Streel, 'Data Sharing for Digital Market Contestability', *supra*, p. 9.

2362. *See* point 386.

2363. European Data Protection Supervisor, *Opinion 3/2020 on the European strategy for data*, *supra*, p. 13.

would generate more trust in the whole sharing process.[2364] In light of the analogous developments made above regarding the relevance to include such schemes in 'empowerment' initiatives imposing data sharing,[2365] which will not be repeated here, I argue that in order to be entitled to receive the data, the data recipient could be required to notify a description of the specific economic purpose that it intends to pursue to competent authorities to be appointed in each Member State.[2366] These authorities, which could be the same as those created by the Data Governance Act in order to avoid a multiplication of regulatory bodies,[2367] could then assess, *ex post*, the legitimacy of the recipients' economic interests and whether they offer sufficient guarantees in terms of privacy and security (in collaboration with the data protection authorities[2368]).[2369] Indeed, as outlined earlier, while such a 'notification obligation with *ex post* monitoring of the compliance' could be quite cumbersome, it is the most pragmatic solution.[2370]

389. Moreover, the horizontal legislations could impose harmonised obligations on the recipients, to be monitored *ex post* as well, in order to ensure their trustworthiness.[2371] Indeed, as outlined by Feasey and de Streel, such legislations should 'devote as much attention to the oversight of those firms that obtain access to the data as to regulating the firms that are obliged to provide access'.[2372] This is an advantage of *ex ante* regulatory initiatives over competition law intervention, as the latter is not really suited to impose obligations on the beneficiaries of the intervention.[2373] For instance, one of the guiding principles for B2G data sharing could be imported in this context,[2374] and these legislations could provide that the recipients shall be prevented from reusing the data for other purposes than the economic purpose(s) that they have notified, except for compatible purposes to the extent necessary and proportionate,[2375] in full compliance with the GDPR

2364. R. Feasey and A. de Streel, 'Data Sharing for Digital Market Contestability', *supra*, pp. 59-60.
2365. *See* Part II, Chapter 5, Section 5.3.3.
2366. *See*, by analogy, Article 17.4.h) of the Proposal for a Data Governance Act.
2367. *See* point 216.
2368. *See*, by analogy, Recitals 28 and 29 and Article 12.3 of the Proposal for a Data Governance Act.
2369. *See*, by analogy, Article 13 of the Proposal for a Data Governance Act. *See also* point 395.
2370. *See* point 217.
2371. *See*, by analogy, Recitals 22-34 and Articles 9-14 of the Proposal for a Data Governance Act.
2372. R. Feasey and A. de Streel, 'Data Sharing for Digital Market Contestability', *supra*, p. 60.
2373. *Ibid.*
2374. High-Level Expert Group on Business-to-Government Data Sharing, 'Towards a European strategy on business-to-government data sharing for public interests – Final report', *supra*, p. 81.
2375. *See*, by analogy, Article 11.1 and 11.2 of the Proposal for a Data Governance Act.

where applicable.[2376] The recipient should, however, not be prevented from combining the data with other data sources in order to achieve its initial purpose(s). Another example is that these legislations could provide that it is forbidden for data recipients to reidentify the individuals whose data have been aggregated and pseudonymised in order to enable the sharing.[2377] In case of a breach of an obligation imposed by the legislations, or if the data recipient has provided false information in its notification, the competent national authorities mentioned above could also be empowered to impose fines and/or to request the cessation of the unlawful processing.[2378]

8.2.3 To Which Types of Data Would This Apply?

390. Third, the horizontal *ex ante* legislations imposing B2B data sharing for economic purposes will have to determine the scope of the data to be covered by the sharing obligation. On the one hand, the greater the scope of the data covered, the greater the potential economic benefits for recipients and society. On the other hand, the greater the scope of the data covered, the greater the risks for the data holder's business interests, as data sharing entails (incentive) costs for the holder.[2379] Moreover, the greater the scope of the data covered, the greater the risks for the privacy and personal data protection of the multiple individuals whose data would be shared in an aggregated way. Any horizontal compulsory B2B data sharing legislation would thus have to consider these balancing exercises.

8.2.3.1 Balance with the Data Holder's Business Interests

391. If the 'specific circumstances' justifying the adoption of these legislations are economic, the determination of the scope of the data to be covered by the legislations can arguably take inspiration from the determination of the scope of the data to be covered by compulsory B2B data sharing competition law remedies.[2380] Based on that reasoning, which will not be repeated here, the scope of *economic initiatives imposing B2B data sharing* should arguably also be limited to actively provided and observed data, excluding inferred/derived data.[2381] Indeed, by analogy with the rules

2376. *See* Article 6.4 of the GDPR.
2377. *See* J. Prüfer, 'Competition Policy and Data Sharing on Data-Driven Markets', *supra*, p. 12.
2378. *See* point 217. *See*, by analogy, Article 13.3-13.5 of the Proposal for a Data Governance Act.
2379. *See* Part I, Chapter 2, Section 2.2.3.5.
2380. *See* Part III, Chapter 6, Section 6.4.2.
2381. *See* points 300-304.

imposing G2B data sharing,[2382] excluding inferred/derived data would amount to excluding the data holder's most commercially sensitive data, and this would address both the data holder's fear of free-riding and the data recipients' potential expectation to free-ride, which are factors that could deter innovation.[2383] Moreover, acquired data should also be excluded from the scope of such legislations, as otherwise this would impose disproportionate and unnecessary costs on the data holders, since this data can be obtained elsewhere through *voluntary* data sharing.[2384]

392. Furthermore, while the legislations should specify the types of data covered by their scope of application, this does not mean that all of the data holder's data potentially falling within this scope (e.g., all of the data holder's actively provided and observed data) will have to be shared. Rather, by analogy with the principles for B2G data sharing,[2385] only the data that are necessary, relevant and proportionate for the economic objectives pursued by the legislations should be shared. This will have to be determined on a case-by-case basis. If there is a disagreement between the data holder and the data recipient in this regard, this could be settled by a regulatory authority.[2386]

Additionally, and similarly than for G2B data sharing,[2387] these legislations could provide that the data holder is compelled to license, under objective, proportionate and non-discriminatory conditions, any potential database right that it may have on the data.[2388] These legislations could also provide that the conditions of these licences should not restrict competition nor reuse possibilities, but that, in exchange, the data holder should be entitled to a remuneration.[2389]

Finally, in order to be truly efficient and sustainable, the legislations should cover not only the data holder's historical data but also present and future data.[2390] Indeed, to reach the economic objectives pursued, the

---

2382. *See* Directive (EU) 2019/1024 of the European Parliament and of the Council of 20 June 2019 on open data and the re-use of public sector information, *OJ L 172/56*, 26 June 2019, Article 1.2.b).

2383. *See* point 89.

2384. *See* point 299.

2385. High-Level Expert Group on Business-to-Government Data Sharing, 'Towards a European strategy on business-to-government data sharing for public interests – Final report', *supra*, p. 80.

2386. R. Feasey and A. de Streel, 'Data Sharing for Digital Market Contestability', *supra*, p. 70.

2387. Articles 6 and 8 of Directive 2019/1024. On this point, *see* H. Richter, 'Exposing the Public Interest Dimension of the Digital Single Market: Public Undertakings as a Model for Regulating Data Sharing', *Max Planck Institute for Innovation and Competition Research Paper No. 20-03*, 2020, available at https://ssrn.com/abstract=3565762, p. 18.

2388. J. Drexl, 'Data Access and Control in the Era of Connected Devices', *supra*, p. 164.

2389. On this remuneration, *see* Part III, Chapter 8, Section 8.2.4.

2390. Stigler Committee on Digital Platforms, 'Final Report', *supra*, p. 117.

imposition of static data sharing might not be sufficient, and dynamic data sharing might be necessary. However, as this would entail more implementation costs for the data holders, such a dynamic real-time data sharing should only be imposed when its benefits trump its costs. Moreover, once again by analogy with G2B data sharing, these legislations could provide that the data holder should not be bound to create, collect or adapt data merely to enable the reuse by data recipients if this would involve disproportionate efforts.[2391] The legislations could also provide that the data holder would not be obliged to further collect and process data that it no longer needs, simply because a recipient relies on it for its activities.[2392] In the latter case, these legislations could nevertheless require that the data holder should make such decisions publicly known in a timely fashion.[2393]

8.2.3.2 Compliance with the Privacy and Personal Data Protection of the Multiple Individuals Whose Data Would Be Shared in an Aggregated Way

393. Horizontal *ex ante* legislations imposing B2B compulsory data sharing will also have to take the rules of personal data protection into account. Indeed, even if I suggest to follow a common holistic approach for both personal and non-personal data in order to determine the categories of data that should be covered by these legislations,[2394] it is nevertheless of paramount importance to take personal data protection considerations into account when relevant.[2395] Yet, as the legislations will likely cover personal data pertaining to multiple individuals, some tensions might emerge with personal data protection law. Accordingly, and as in G2B data sharing legislations,[2396] B2B legislations should make it explicit that they shall not affect the individuals' protection of their personal data.[2397]

394. To bypass the application of the GDPR, the aggregated personal data pertaining to multiple individuals could be anonymised (e.g., with a sufficient level of granularity) before sharing it. To encourage such anonymisation, the horizontal data sharing legislations could even provide, similarly to G2B data sharing legislations, that if the data holder anonymises the personal data

---

2391. Recital 33 and Articles 5.3 and 5.7 of Directive 2019/1024.
2392. Articles 5.4 and 5.7 of Directive 2019/1024.
2393. Recital 45 of Directive 2019/1024.
2394. *See* point 21.
2395. *See*, for example, Part III, Chapter 7. 'Articulation Between Data Protection and Competition Law'.
2396. Recital 52 and Article 1.4 of Directive 2019/1024.
2397. For a 'Code of practice' on *voluntary* data sharing, which aims at serving as a guide for businesses wishing to share personal data in a privacy-compliant way, *see* Information Commissioner's Office, 'Data sharing code of practice', 17 December 2020, available at https://ico.org.uk/for-organisations/data-sharing-a-code-of-practice/.

before sharing it, it could charge the marginal costs incurred for the anonymisation to the recipients.[2398] However, as outlined above, what is presented as anonymisation will, in fact, be mere pseudonymisation, and the rules of the GDPR will thus have to be applied.[2399]

Accordingly, these legislations should provide that aggregated personal data pertaining to multiple individuals should only be shared to the extent that this complies with the GDPR's principles (lawfulness, fairness and transparency; purpose limitation;[2400] data minimisation; data accuracy; storage limitation; integrity and confidentiality; and accountability)[2401] and that there is a lawful basis of processing allowing the sharing.[2402]

395. As far as the data holder is concerned, it should, in principle, be able to argue that the transfer is necessary for compliance with a legal obligation to which it is subject (i.e., the data sharing obligation contained in the horizontal legislation).[2403] However, Recital 41 of the GDPR provides that this legal obligation must be clear, precise, predictable and accessible.[2404] Therefore, the horizontal legislation imposing the data sharing will have to meet an objective of public interest (*in casu* the economic objective) and be proportionate to the legitimate aim pursued, and it will have to specify the purposes and the recipients of the sharing, as well as the types of data and the data subjects concerned by the data sharing.[2405]

Data recipients, on the other hand, could attempt to rely on the explicit freely given, specific, informed and unambiguous consent of the multiple individuals whose data is shared,[2406] or could attempt to argue that the reuse is necessary for the purposes of their 'legitimate interests', and that these economic interests are not overridden by the interests or fundamental rights and freedoms of the data subjects.[2407] In fact, such a demonstration could be requested in the context of the notification obligation mentioned above.[2408] One way for the recipient to demonstrate that the balance tips in its favour would be to show that it relies on the use of privacy-enhancing technologies

2398. Article 6.1 of Directive 2019/1024.
2399. *See* point 351.
2400. *See*, for instance, Recitals 54 and 55 and Article 6.1.i) of the Proposal for a Digital Markets Act.
2401. Articles 5 of the GDPR. For a more detailed analysis of this articulation, *see*, by analogy, Part III, Chapter 7, Section 7.2.2.
2402. Articles 6 of the GDPR. For a more detailed analysis of this articulation, *see*, by analogy, Part III, Chapter 7, Section 7.2.1.
2403. Article 6.1.c) of the GDPR.
2404. *See also* R. Ergec, *Protection européenne et internationale des droits de l'homme*, Bruxelles, Larcier, 2014, p. 232.
2405. *See* point 356.
2406. Article 6.1.a) of the GDPR. *See* Part III, Chapter 7, Section 7.2.1.2.1, for more information on the limits of resorting to this lawful basis.
2407. Article 6.1.f) of the GDPR. *See* Part III, Chapter 7, Section 7.2.1.2.2, for more information on the possibility, for a recipient, to rely on this lawful basis.
2408. *See* point 388.

in order to limit the risks for the data subjects.[2409] Indeed, if, for instance, the aggregated personal data pertaining to multiple individuals that it receives is pseudonymised, this reduces the risks that the reuse could entail for the data subjects. In fact, this could be combined with a limitation of the risks embedded in the horizontal legislations if the latter contained a provision forbidding data recipients from reidentifying the multiple individuals whose data have been aggregated and pseudonymised prior to the sharing.[2410]

8.2.4 Should This Be Remunerated?

396. Horizontal *ex ante* legislations imposing B2B data sharing could arguably provide for a remuneration in exchange for the sharing, as this would be a way to protect the data holders' business interests, in return for the expected benefits of these legislations.[2411] This would indeed compensate the data collection costs incurred by the data holder, and would preserve its data collection incentives, as well as those of the recipients.[2412]

As the value of data is difficult to assess, it is advisable for the legislations not to impose a specific price for the sharing, but rather to set a sufficiently precise criteria to determine this price.[2413] One possibility would be to take inspiration from the PSI Directive (G2B data sharing), as these legislations could provide that the price should cover the costs of data collection, production, reproduction, dissemination and storage incurred by the data holder, as well as a reasonable return on investment for the holder.[2414] While this price calculation method presents the advantage of being relatively simple, it might however not reflect appropriately the value of the data and the incentive costs of the sharing for the holder. Indeed, data will not necessarily be valuable for a data holder because it was expensive to collect or produce, but rather because it is one of the few actors that has collected it (e.g., it is not, as such, expensive for Google to collect search data, but rather the value of search data for Google derives from the fact that most of the users use its search engine, and it is thus able to draw data

2409. *See* Recital 6 of the Proposal for a Data Governance Act. *See also* Commission Staff Working Document, Impact assessment report accompanying the Data Governance Act, *supra*, p. 13.
2410. *See* J. Prüfer, 'Competition Policy and Data Sharing on Data-Driven Markets', *supra*, p. 12.
2411. *See* R. Feasey and A. de Streel, 'Data Sharing for Digital Market Contestability', *supra*, pp. 11 and 77-80. Some however argue that the data holders should not be entitled to a remuneration: *see* J. Prüfer, 'Competition Policy and Data Sharing on Data-Driven Markets', *supra*, p. 14.
2412. *See* R. Feasey and A. de Streel, 'Data Sharing for Digital Market Contestability', *supra*, pp. 11 and 77-80.
2413. *Ibid.*, p. 38.
2414. *See*, by analogy, Article 6.1 of Directive 2019/1024.

advantages from this).[2415] This loss of 'data power' is important to factor in the sharing price in B2B scenarios, while it is less of a concern in G2B scenarios, where the objective is precisely to break the monopoly that public authorities might have on some data, which are seen as highly valuable resources.[2416] Accordingly, it might not be advisable to import this price calculation method from G2B data sharing to B2B data sharing.

397. Alternatively, the horizontal legislations could provide that this remuneration should be proportionate.[2417] This would imply that the price of sharing should be lower in cases where the incentives costs of sharing are low and where the potential benefits of sharing are high; and that this price should be higher in cases where the incentives costs of sharing are high and where the potential benefits of sharing are low.[2418] Determining such a proportionate remuneration would thus, once again, require a case-by-case analysis. To guide and facilitate this case-by-case assessment of the 'proportionality' of the remuneration, the legislations could outline several factors to be taken into consideration. For instance, the remuneration could be a function of the volume of data being shared.[2419] Moreover, and to the extent that this would be possible in practice,[2420] the price for data generated as a by-product should, arguably, be lower than the price for data generated as the core economic activity of the data holder.[2421] Similarly, the price could be higher if (some of) the shared data is covered by an IP right (e.g., by a sui generis database right).[2422] Furthermore, the price could be higher if the data is shared with a direct competitor, than if the data is shared with a data recipient offering complementary products or services.

398. However, relying on an open formula such as 'proportionate remuneration', even if the legislations outline several factors to be taken into consideration, might lead to uncertainties in the determination of the concrete remuneration, as illustrated by the numerous discussions around the notion of FRAND licensing fees for SEPs.[2423,2424] Nevertheless, several authors have suggested that the negotiation framework created by the European Court of

---

2415. *See* Part I, Chapter 2, Section 2.2.3.
2416. *See* Recitals, 3, 7, and 11 of Directive 2019/1024.
2417. *See*, by analogy, High-Level Expert Group on Business-to-Government Data Sharing, 'Towards a European strategy on business-to-government data sharing for public interests – Final report', *supra*, p. 83.
2418. *See* R. Feasey and A. de Streel, 'Data Sharing for Digital Market Contestability', *supra*, pp. 77-80.
2419. *Ibid.*, p. 11.
2420. *See* point 303.
2421. *See* point 302.
2422. On this right, *see* points 58-60.
2423. *See* references mentioned in footnote 1799.
2424. R. Feasey and A. de Streel, 'Data Sharing for Digital Market Contestability', *supra*, p. 80.

Justice in its *Huawei*[2425] judgment could provide inspiration and could assist the parties to reach an agreement on the data sharing price.[2426] If no agreement is reached between the parties on the determination of this 'proportional remuneration', the price could be determined by an independent third party. By analogy with what has been outlined above regarding the remuneration of the data holder in the context of a competition data sharing remedy,[2427] I argue that this could be done by the national authorities whose appointment is suggested in the European Commission's proposal for a Data Governance Act,[2428] with the assistance of the Support Centre for Data Sharing and of the future European Data Innovation Board.[2429]

While this might be perceived by data holders as being a significant intervention by third parties / regulatory authorities in their business activities, this is probably the most pragmatic solution that can be designed. Indeed, while it would be much simpler to set a price in advance in the legislation, this does not appear to be realistic nor appropriate in B2B scenarios.[2430] On the other hand, the alternative of not providing for any remuneration at all is even more undesirable for the interests of the data holders. Moreover, it must be reminded that these economic initiatives imposing B2B data sharing should only be warranted when specific circumstances dictate it. Hence, if the legislator decides to intervene, this means that it has identified a (significant) problem that must be solved, which explains while some constraints could justifiably be imposed on a specific subset of data holders, namely those that are considered as playing a central role in the (systemic) market failure(s) that provoked the regulatory intervention.[2431]

To be sure, relying on an open formula such as 'proportionate remuneration' and on the above-mentioned negotiation framework would generate a certain amount of red-tape that could delay and complicate the implementation of the data sharing initiative. Indeed, if long negotiations are necessary in order to agree on the determination of what constitutes a 'proportionate' price for the data sharing, the implementation of the data sharing initiative might not be as timely as originally desired. To mitigate this risk, the initiative could set binding deadlines for this negotiation period. In this regard, the initiative could, for instance, provide that the data holders and the data recipients have one month to agree on a 'proportionate' price, and

2425. ECJ, *Huawei,* 16 July 2015, C-170/13, EU:C:2015:477, §§ 60-69.
2426. *See* point 306.
2427. *See* point 307.
2428. *See* Recitals 22-34 and Articles 13 and 23-25 of the Proposal for a Data Governance Act.
2429. *See* Recitals 40 and 41 and Articles 26 and 27 of the Proposal for a Data Governance Act. *See also* Commission Staff Working Document, Impact assessment report accompanying the Data Governance Act, *supra*, p. 54.
2430. *See* point 396.
2431. *See* Part III, Chapter 8, Section 8.2.1.

that if they do not manage to come to an agreement within that period, the parties will have to refer the issue to the designated independent third party, which will itself then have one month to determine the price of the sharing. Moreover, the initiative could provide that the designated independent third party will have to draft guidelines, at regular intervals, aiming at providing more contextual information about the above-mentioned factors that have to be taken into consideration on a case-by-case basis to determine this 'proportionate' remuneration (volume of data shared; by-product or not; covered by an IP right or not; sharing with a direct competitor or not).[2432] These guidelines could also suggest the addition of new factors that would be worth taking into consideration. This could then assist future negotiations between data holders and data recipients, especially if these guidelines are illustrated with relevant examples and success cases.

399. Finally, remunerating the data holder could also contribute to the personal data protection of the multiple individuals whose data would be shared. Indeed, as for G2B data sharing, the horizontal *ex ante* legislations could provide that the data holder can charge the marginal costs incurred for the anonymisation of the aggregated data (e.g., the costs incurred in order to reach a sufficient level of granularity) to the data recipients.[2433] This would incentivise the data holders to resort to such anonymisation techniques prior to the sharing, and would thus reduce the risks for the multiple individuals whose data would be shared.

8.2.5 How Could This Be Implemented Technically?

400. Another important issue to consider for the horizontal *ex ante* legislations imposing B2B data sharing for economic purposes is to determine how the data sharing should be implemented technically. Indeed, there are various technical ways in which such sharing could take place,[2434] and they each entail their own benefits and costs. As I focus on legal considerations rather than on technical considerations, I will not delve extensively into this point. Rather, the objective of this subsection is to point out that determining the appropriate technical approach will require a balancing exercise.

401. An important number of scientific contributions make the argument that, in order for the horizontal *ex ante* legislations imposing B2B data sharing to be truly efficient, they should require the data holders to share their data in

2432. *See* point 397.
2433. Article 6.1 of Directive 2019/1024.
2434. *See*, for instance, the various conceptual models of data sharing presented in Part I, Chapter 3, Section 3.1.

(near) real time and on a constant basis via APIs,[2435] and to ensure the interoperability of their data formats.[2436] Indeed, in certain situations, it might be necessary to consider the imposition of dynamic data sharing obligations in order to reach the economic objectives of the horizontal legislations.

This would however require the adoption of common technical standards for APIs and data interoperability, and would thus entail higher implementation costs for the data holders.[2437] This could have a substantial impact on their business interests. To limit this impact, large data holders could be tempted to influence the standard-setting process with the objective that their own proprietary standard be chosen as the common technical standard.[2438] This, in turn, could entail high costs for the data recipients and could affect their ability to develop their own products/services. As a result, the economic objectives of the horizontal legislations might not be achieved. Accordingly, in order to ensure that the interests of all of the parties are fairly balanced and taken into consideration in the determination of these standards, while ensuring that the process remains manageable, an appropriate representation of all the different interests should be ensured in the standardisation process.[2439]

Yet, the above would entail substantial costs in terms of resources and time for both the data holders and the data recipients. It is thus important to keep in mind that standardisation and interoperability will not always necessarily entail a positive effect on competition and innovation.[2440] Moreover, the direct continuous and interoperable sharing between data holders and data recipients could increase the risks for the individuals' personal data protection, as well as security risks.[2441] Therefore, the European legislator should carefully consider these costs when pondering

2435. *See* definition at footnote 1005.

2436. *See*, for instance, J. Furman, et al., 'Unlocking Digital Competition', *supra*, pp. 71-74; Stigler Committee on Digital Platforms, 'Final Report', *supra*, pp. 113 and 117-118; S. Ennis and A. Fletcher, 'Developing International Perspectives on Digital Competition Policy', *supra*, p. 7; J. Hoffmann and G. Johannsen, 'EU-Merger Control & Big Data', *supra*, p. 64; J. Prüfer, 'Competition Policy and Data Sharing on Data-Driven Markets', *supra*, p. 1; J. Crémer, Y.-A. de Montjoye and H. Schweitzer, 'Competition Policy for the Digital Era', *supra*, p. 71; European Parliament resolution of 20 October 2020 with recommendations to the Commission on the Digital Services Act: Improving the functioning of the Single Market (2020/2018(INL)), P9_TA-PROV(2020)0272, available at https://www.europarl.europa.eu/doceo/document/TA-9-2020-0272_EN.html, pp. 20 and 36; W. Kerber, 'From (Horizontal and Sectoral) Data Access Solutions Towards Data Governance Systems', *supra*, pp. 28-29.

2437. R. Feasey and A. de Streel, 'Data Sharing for Digital Market Contestability', *supra*, pp. 9 and 71.

2438. *Ibid.*, p. 72.

2439. *Ibid.*

2440. W. Kerber, 'From (Horizontal and Sectoral) Data Access Solutions Towards Data Governance Systems', *supra*, p. 29.

2441. *Ibid.*, pp. 29-31.

whether horizontal legislations imposing B2B data sharing should require the adoption of common technical standards for APIs and data interoperability, and should arguably only impose it when the expected economic benefits trump these important costs.

402. It should also be outlined that this technical approach of the direct sharing of the data between the data holders and the recipients, via APIs and common technical standards, is criticised due to its impracticability, as it would require hundreds of holder-recipient relations.[2442] Moreover, the volume of data directly received by the recipients could be overwhelming and many of the (smaller) recipients could have difficulties to store and process such data.[2443] Therefore, Prüfer suggests to rely on trustworthy data intermediaries[2444] (data trustees) rather than on direct sharing between the holders and the recipients.[2445] In this technical approach, the data holder's data would be shared with an intermediary instead of with the recipient, and the latter would only be entitled to execute its algorithms in the intermediary's database, without receiving any of the shared data itself.[2446] As for B2G data sharing, the intermediaries' databases could constitute a form of 'testing environments ("sandboxes") for pilot testing ("pilots") to help assess the potential value of data for new situations in which a product or service could potentially be used ("use cases")'.[2447] As a result, only the trained algorithms, but not the data originally shared by the data holders, would then be transferred by the intermediaries to the recipients.[2448]

The advantage of resorting to such intermediaries is that this could reduce the risks for the multiple individuals whose data could be shared, as these intermediaries could, for instance, ensure the anonymisation of the data before it is accessed by the data recipients to train their algorithms.[2449] Moreover, these risks for the individuals are further reduced if only the algorithms, but not the training data, are transferred to the recipients. On the other hand, this technical approach makes it much more cumbersome for the data recipients to conduct their activities, and it would require an enormous

2442. J. Prüfer, 'Competition Policy and Data Sharing on Data-Driven Markets', *supra*, p. 15.
2443. R. Feasey and A. de Streel, 'Data Sharing for Digital Market Contestability', *supra*, p. 69.
2444. It is interesting to point out that the European Commission's proposal for a Data Governance Act addresses the activities of such 'trusted data intermediaries' in the context of *voluntary* B2B data sharing (*see* Recitals 22-34 and Articles 9-14 of the Proposal for a Data Governance Act).
2445. J. Prüfer, 'Competition Policy and Data Sharing on Data-Driven Markets', *supra*, pp. 12 and 15.
2446. *Ibid.*
2447. High-Level Expert Group on Business-to-Government Data Sharing, 'Towards a European strategy on business-to-government data sharing for public interests – Final report', *supra*, p. 7.
2448. J. Prüfer, 'Competition Policy and Data Sharing on Data-Driven Markets', *supra*, p. 12.
2449. *Ibid.*

infrastructure for the intermediary, in order to process the data (continuously) in any meaningful way.[2450] As a result, the economic objectives of the horizontal legislations might not be achieved to their full extent.

403. In light of all of the above, it appears that determining how the data sharing should be implemented technically will require finding a balance between the benefits and costs of various technical approaches. As the result of this balance will largely be function of the circumstances of the cases at hand, the horizontal legislations themselves may not be the best place to address this issue. However, it would be advisable for these legislations to charge regulatory bodies to define the technical modalities of the sharing in cases where the data holders and recipients (and potentially the trusted data intermediaries) do not agree on them. In such a case, it will be important for these regulatory bodies to be aware of the potential anticompetitive effects of the data sharing obligation, notably if they envisage to resort to the creation of a data pool for the technical implementation of the data sharing.[2451]

These regulatory bodies could be the national authorities to be appointed in the context of the Data Governance Act.[2452] Indeed, the knowledge of the technical experts that could be appointed within these authorities could be precious to suggest concrete technical sharing means in the absence of an agreement between the data holder and the data recipient, as the technical mechanisms used for *voluntary* data sharing are equally relevant for *compulsory* data sharing imposed by horizontal legislations. These national authorities could be assisted by the future European Data Innovation Board.[2453]

8.2.6 How Will These Legislations Be Enforced?

404. Finally, it is essential to ensure an appropriate enforcement of the above-mentioned rules, in order for the horizontal *ex ante* legislations imposing compulsory B2B data sharing for economic purposes to be truly efficient and to reach the aims pursued. Indeed, a lack of (timely) enforcement can affect the full deployment of the legal framework's effects. For instance, it has been outlined that the time-consuming process of competition intervention is not aligned with the timing of market evolutions and that, as a result, enforcement might come too late, when the damage is already irreparable.[2454] Moreover, it has been outlined that even if the GDPR has

---

2450. J. Krämer, D. Schnurr and S. Broughton Micova, 'The Role of Data for Digital Markets Contestability', *supra*, p. 97.
2451. On this issue, *see* Part III, Chapter 6, Section 6.4.4.
2452. *See* Recitals 22-34 and Articles 13 and 23-25 of the Proposal for a Data Governance Act.
2453. Recitals 40 and 41 and Articles 26 and 27 of the Proposal for a Data Governance Act.
2454. *See* Part III, Chapter 6, Section 6.5.

created a strict legal framework for the processing of personal data, the enforcement of the GDPR by data protection authorities is sporadic (largely due to a lack of sufficient resources), leading to negative effects not only on the individuals' right to personal data protection but also on competition.[2455]

Accordingly, it is fundamental for the horizontal *ex ante* legislations imposing compulsory B2B data sharing to ensure that the rules they enshrine will be respected and adequately enforced. Moreover, as outlined throughout this subsection, many concrete issues will need to be determined on a case-by-case basis. Therefore, while these horizontal legislations will need to determine the 'rules of the game' for compulsory data sharing, one or several regulatory bodies will need to be appointed in order to apply these rules on a case-by-case basis, and to enforce them. In substance, two avenues can be pursued.

405. On the one hand, a (new) regulatory body could be appointed at the European level, in order to ensure a harmonised, consistent and coherent application and enforcement of these horizontal *ex ante* legislations imposing B2B data sharing for economic purposes.[2456] Another advantage of resorting to a single authority appointed at the European level is that it would quickly develop the appropriate expertise since it would be the sole body to apply the 'rules of the game'. In this regard, it should be reminded that the proposal for a 'Digital Markets Act' provides that the compliance with this legislation should be monitored by the European Commission,[2457] and that similar proposals of appointing a single authority have also been made in the UK and in the US.[2458] Interestingly, the European Commission's proposal for a Data Governance Act also considered the creation, at the European level, of a single new independent structure with legal personality (similar to the EDPB) to oversee the implementation of this legislation, but this idea was abandoned due to the high costs and the issues of political feasibility that it implied.[2459]

406. On the other hand, instead of appointing a (new) regulatory body at the European level, competent authorities could be appointed in each Member State. In fact, this is the approach that was taken by the European

2455. *See* Part III, Chapter 7, Section 7.1.3.

2456. *See* P. Alexiadis and A. de Streel, 'Designing an EU Intervention Standard for Digital Platforms', *Robert Schuman Centre for Advanced Studies Research Paper No. 2020/14*, 26 February 2020, available at https://ssrn.com/abstract=3544694, pp. 46-47; A. de Streel, et al., 'Digital Markets Act: Making Economic Regulation of Platforms Fit for the Digital Age', *supra*, pp. 17-19.

2457. *See* Articles 3-7 and 18-33 of the Proposal for a Digital Markets Act.

2458. *See* points 383-385.

2459. Proposal for a Data Governance Act, p. 6. *See also* Commission Staff Working Document, Impact assessment report accompanying the Data Governance Act, *supra*, pp. 28-29, 40, 43 and 52-53.

Commission in its proposal for a Data Governance Act.[2460] To ensure an effective enforcement of these legislations, these national authorities will have to cooperate and assist each other where necessary,[2461] notably through the exchange of information and best practices.[2462] This should be facilitated by the Support Centre for Data Sharing and the European Data Innovation Board.[2463] Moreover, they will have to be impartial, transparent, consistent and reliable and they will need to intervene in a timely manner.[2464] If this second option is taken, I argue that, in order to avoid an unnecessary multiplication of regulatory bodies, the same authorities should be appointed to monitor the horizontal *ex ante* legislations pertaining to both *voluntary* and *compulsory* data sharing.

407. Independently of the option taken, such authority will have an important role to play. Indeed, it could first be charged with determining whether a (large) data holder falls within the scope of the data sharing obligation.[2465] Second, it could be tasked with receiving the compulsory notification of activities from the data recipients,[2466] in order to assess the legitimacy of their activities and whether they offer sufficient guarantees, notably in terms of personal data protection,[2467] and it could be empowered to impose fines and/or other remedies of this is not the case.[2468] Third, it could be charged with identifying the data that are necessary, relevant, and proportionate for the recipient's purposes, and with determining the 'proportionate remuneration' and the technical modalities for the sharing, in the absence of an agreement between the data holders and the data recipients on these matters.[2469]

408. Finally, as the monitoring and enforcement of the *ex ante* legislations would imply a substantial workload, it will have to be ensured that these regulatory authorities have adequate financial and human resources, as well as the necessary technical knowledge and resources, to carry out these

2460. Articles 13 and 23 to 25 of the Proposal for a Data Governance Act.
2461. Articles 13.6 and 23.6 of the Proposal for a Data Governance Act.
2462. *See*, by analogy, European Parliament resolution of 20 October 2020 with recommendations to the Commission on the Digital Services Act: Improving the functioning of the Single Market (2020/2018(INL)), P9_TA-PROV(2020)0272, available at https://www.europarl.europa.eu/doceo/document/TA-9-2020-0272_EN.html, p. 20.
2463. *See* Recitals 40 and 41 and Articles 26 and 27 of the Proposal for a Data Governance Act. *See also* Commission Staff Working Document, Impact assessment report accompanying the Data Governance Act, *supra*, pp. 54-55.
2464. Article 23.2 of the Proposal for a Data Governance Act.
2465. *See* point 385.
2466. *See* point 388.
2467. *See*, by analogy, Article 13 of the Proposal for a Data Governance Act. *See also* point 395.
2468. *See*, by analogy, Article 13.3-13.5 of the Proposal for a Data Governance Act.
2469. *See* points 392, 398 and 403.

missions.[2470] Moreover, to ensure an efficient and harmonised enforcement across the Digital Single Market, it will be fundamental for these regulatory authorities to cooperate with, and assist, each other and to be coherent in their decisional practice.[2471] Additionally, they will need to cooperate with the data protection and competition authorities, as well as with other relevant sectoral authorities, as some overlapping issues may have to be tackled by different regulatory authorities.[2472]

To be sure, the multiplication of regulatory authorities can lead to several issues that could hamper the swift enforcement of these compulsory data sharing initiatives. Indeed, if, as suggested, regulatory authorities are appointed in each Member State, there is a risk that this could lead to different degrees of enforcement across the Union, as well as to diverging or even contradicting case law, if there is insufficient cooperation and exchange of information and good practices between the different authorities. The cooperation issues that have become apparent in the context of the enforcement of the GDPR are a clear illustration of this problem.[2473] Moreover, even if the data sharing initiatives could require these authorities to cooperate with other types of authorities, such as data protection and competition authorities, one should be aware of the risks of overlapping 'enforcement competences', and of the ensuing 'regulator wars' that could occur in order to handle specific types of cases that could be dealt with on the basis of different regulatory approaches (compulsory data sharing initiatives, competition law, data protection law, consumer protection law, etc.). This could lead to a dilution of the application of these norms, generating significant levels of legal insecurity and thus hampering the accomplishment of the objectives pursued by the data sharing initiatives. Although these 'enforcement design' considerations will not be further detailed nor analysed here, as they fall outside of the scope of my analysis, it is important to underline that further research on the matter is indispensable in order to identify concrete proposals that would allow to solve these issues, as without proper and efficient enforcement, it might be missed out on the numerous benefits that should result from these compulsory data sharing initiatives.

409. To conclude this chapter, the above-mentioned insights regarding the key elements that horizontal *ex ante* legislations imposing B2B data sharing for economic purposes should consider are summarised in Table 8.1.

2470. *See*, by analogy, Article 23.5 of the Proposal for a Data Governance Act.
2471. Articles 13.6 and 23.6 of the Proposal for a Data Governance Act.
2472. *See* Recitals 28 and 29 and Article 12.3 of the Proposal for a Data Governance Act.
2473. *See* Part III, Chapter 7, Section 7.1.4.

Table 8.1 Insights on the Key Elements to Consider for Horizontal Ex Ante *Legislations Imposing B2B Data Sharing for Economic Purposes*

	'Ex Ante' *Legislations Imposing B2B Data Sharing for Economic Purposes*
Data holders subject to the sharing obligation	Asymmetric application to a specific subset of data holders.[2474] Determination based on a set of clear quantitative and qualitative indicators contained in the legislations, which would allow the regulatory authority to decide, on a case-by-case basis, whether a specific data holder falls within the scope of the initiative.[2475]
Data recipients entitled to benefit from the sharing obligation	Recipient could be required to notify a description of the economic purposes that it intends to pursue.[2476] *Ex post* assessment of the legitimacy of the recipients' interests and of whether they offer sufficient guarantees in terms of privacy and security.[2477] Imposition of harmonised obligations on the recipients for the provision of their products/services, to be monitored *ex post* as well.[2478]
Types of data covered by the sharing obligation	Only actively provided and observed data (not acquired, nor inferred/derived data).[2479] Only the data that are necessary, relevant and proportionate, in terms of detail (e.g., type of data, granularity, quantity, frequency of access).[2480] Not only historical data but also present and future data.[2481] Personal data should only be shared to the extent that this complies with the GDPR's principles and that there is a lawful basis of processing allowing the sharing.[2482] Legislations could contain a provision forbidding data recipients from reidentifying the multiple individuals whose data have been aggregated and pseudonymised prior to the sharing.[2483]

2474. *See* Part III, Chapter 8, Section 8.2.1.
2475. *See* points 383-385.
2476. *See* Part III, Chapter 8, Section 8.2.2.
2477. *See* point 388.
2478. *See* point 389.
2479. *See* Part III, Chapter 8, Section 8.2.3.1.
2480. *See* Part III, Chapter 8, Section 8.2.3.1.
2481. *See* point 392.
2482. *See* Part III, Chapter 8, Section 8.2.3.2.
2483. *See* point 395. *See* J. Prüfer, 'Competition Policy and Data Sharing on Data-Driven Markets', *supra*, p. 12.

	'Ex Ante' *Legislations Imposing B2B Data Sharing for Economic Purposes*
Remuneration of the data holder as compensation for the sharing obligation	Proportionate remuneration (legislations could outline several factors to be taken into consideration: volume of data; by-product v. core economic activity of the data holder; data covered by an IP right or not; data shared with a direct competitor or not).[2484] If the data holder(s) and data recipient(s) fail to agree on the data sharing price, this price could be determined by an independent third party.[2485] To mitigate the risk of lengthy negotiations, the legislations could set binding deadlines to speed up the process. Data holder can charge the marginal costs incurred for the anonymisation of the aggregated data (e.g., the costs incurred in order to reach a sufficient level of granularity) to the data recipients.[2486]
Technical implementation of the sharing obligation	The horizontal legislations themselves may not be the best place to address this issue.[2487] Rather, it would be advisable for these legislations to charge regulatory bodies to define the technical modalities of the sharing in cases where the data holders and recipients do not agree on them.

2484. *See* Part III, Chapter 8, Section 8.2.4.
2485. *See* point 398.
2486. *See* point 399.
2487. *See* Part III, Chapter 8, Section 8.2.5.

Chapter 9

Societal Initiatives Imposing B2B Data Sharing

410. Coincidentally to the creation of economic initiatives imposing B2B data sharing, one could also consider the adoption of compulsory B2B data sharing initiatives pursuing societal objectives. As outlined in the European Commission's *Strategy for data,* 'making more data available and improving the way in which data is used is essential for tackling societal, climate and environment-related challenges, contributing to healthier, more prosperous and more sustainable societies'.[2488] Indeed, as it is apparent from the numerous examples provided in Part I, not only public sector data but also private sector data can make a significant contribution to the common good.[2489]

Yet, one must acknowledge that the policy and legislative discussions pertaining to the creation of societal initiatives imposing B2B data sharing are scarce. Indeed, while some societal initiatives pertaining to (compulsory) data sharing are being proposed in the B2G field,[2490] the same cannot be said about societal initiatives imposing B2B data sharing. Therefore, this chapter will aim at developing some prospective reflections on why they might make sense and on how they could be constructed in the future, in the hope to spur further discussions on this topic. The aim is thus not to be exhaustive but rather to set some foundations on which future research could build.

2488. Communication from the Commission, '*A European Strategy for Data*', *supra*, p. 3.
2489. *See* Part I, Chapter 2, Section 2.3.1, particularly point 93.
2490. *See*, for instance, Articles 15-22 of the Proposal for a Data Governance Act; European Commission, Inception Impact Assessment: '*Data Act (including the review of the Directive 96/9/EC on the legal protection of databases)*', May 2021, Ares (2021)3527151, pp. 2 and 5.

9.1 CONTEXTUALISATION

411. Like any other initiative imposing B2B data sharing, societal initiatives will entail balancing exercises. In substance, the broader societal benefits deriving from the wider data sharing that such initiatives would entail[2491] would have to be balanced with the data holder's business interests, as compulsory data sharing might deter the data holder's incentive to further collect data, due to the fear of free-riding.[2492] However, I argue that, in light of the fact that the B2B data sharing initiative would pursue societal objectives, the data holder's costs may weigh less heavily in the balance, as they are opposed to fundamental societal objectives that could be viewed as superseding 'mere' economic considerations. Additionally, these horizontal legislations will have to comply with the personal data protection rules.[2493]

412. One way to address these balancing exercises would be to consider, by analogy with what has been said for economic initiatives,[2494] that such societal initiatives imposing B2B data sharing should only be created when 'specific circumstances' dictate it. Indeed, such legislations should only be adopted if they are proportional and necessary to address these 'specific circumstances', in order to achieve an optimal balance with the data holder's freedom to conduct a business. Accordingly, this would entail that such compulsory data sharing should only be imposed if less stringent alternatives, such as the stimulation of *voluntary* data sharing for societal purposes/the common good,[2495] turn out to be insufficient to achieve the desired societal objectives, or if it is highly important and/or urgent to achieve these objectives.

'Specific circumstances' justifying the adoption of a compulsory data sharing legislation could, arguably, be established in situations where a just, fair and equal access to (some) data would be necessary to tackle societal challenges.[2496] For instance, one could consider whether B2B data sharing could be imposed in order to tackle global pandemics, in cases where pharmaceutical companies refuse to share data about their research aiming at developing the appropriate vaccine or medication, thus slowing down the global cure-finding process to the detriment of the general interest. In such a scenario, it might be justified to make it compulsory for pharmaceutical companies to share, with private healthcare and/or research institutions, data

2491. *See* Part I, Chapter 2, Section 2.3.1, particularly point 93.
2492. D. Rubinfeld and M. Gal, 'Access Barriers to Big Data', *supra*, p. 374.
2493. *See* points 91 and 96 and Part III, Chapter 7 and Chapter 8, Section 8.2.
2494. *See* point 380.
2495. *See*, in this regard, Articles 15-22 of the Proposal for a Regulation of the European Parliament and of the Council on European data governance (Data Governance Act), 25 November 2020, COM(2020) 767 final.
2496. J. Shkabatur, 'The Global Commons of Data', *Stanford Technology Law Review*, 2019, Vol. 22, pp. 401-402. *See* Part I, Chapter 2, Section 2.3.1.

pertaining to vaccine/medication trial results, in order to rapidly identify the trials that lead to unsatisfactory results and those that lead to more promising results, in order to address such global healthcare challenges caused by pandemics as fast as possible.

Other important societal objectives such as avoiding food waste or limiting mankind's environmental footprint could also be deemed as justifying compulsory B2B data sharing in 'specific circumstances'. To illustrate this, it can be reminded that, as mentioned above,[2497] farmers increasingly resort to 'smart farming', notably in order to monitor the health of crops and to detect plant diseases at an early stage (crop sensors). As this data is usually collected through sensors integrated into farming equipment sold by specialised manufacturers, it is the latter who often have control over the data, and they might not be eager to share it. Yet, one could reflect on whether it would be justified, in some specific situations, to compel these farming equipment manufacturers to share such data in order to prevent food waste. For instance, these manufacturers could be forced to share data about the apparition of a disease (inferred from the observation of crop sensor data they have received from one/several farms) with farmers active in the same territory on a very short notice, in order to enable the farmers to address the issue rapidly and to limit the loss of crops. In the same vein, these manufacturers could be forced to share data about the efficiency of a certain type of pesticide and the appropriate dose to be sprayed, in order to reduce the environmental damage caused by such products. Indeed, as these manufacturers could financially benefit from 'over-spraying' as it implies that they will sell more products, they might not be willing to share such data on a voluntary basis. Yet, this could lead to highly detrimental environmental consequences, and could therefore potentially justify the adoption of compulsory B2B data sharing initiatives.

9.2 PROSPECTIVE THOUGHTS ON HOW THESE SOCIETAL INITIATIVES IMPOSING B2B DATA SHARING COULD BE CONSTRUCTED

413. Similarly to economic initiatives, societal initiatives imposing B2B data sharing could either be sectoral or could have a more general horizontal scope. As mentioned above,[2498] while sector-specific legislations have the advantage of being much more targeted and adapted to the sector's needs, this must be balanced with the non-rivalrous and general-purpose nature of data, which implies that it could be reused for completely different purposes

2497. *See* point 93.
2498. *See* Part III, Chapter 8, Section 8.1.

in another sector.[2499] In fact, such a sectoral limitation seems especially unwarranted if the data sharing legislation pursues societal objectives, as cross-sectoral reuse could generate significant societal value.[2500] For instance, an energy provider's research data pertaining to its decarbonisation initiatives could also be useful for other actors active in other sectors, such as transport, to reduce their environmental footprint. Similarly, air pollution data collected by sensors located on buses operated by a ride-sharing service provider could be highly useful for farmers that are active in the same territory, as such data about the air quality could enable them to relocate their cattle to less polluted places. Therefore, limiting the scope of the compulsory data sharing legislation to reuses within a single sector would not enable the generation of such additional societal value. Accordingly, horizontal initiatives imposing B2B data sharing for societal purposes might have to be favoured.

414. Furthermore, even if 'specific circumstances' justify the adoption of societal initiatives imposing B2B data sharing, the concrete provisions of such legislations will nevertheless need to find a balance between the societal benefits of the sharing and the costs on the data holder's business interests, and they will need to comply with the individuals' right to privacy and to personal data protection. This will require tackling the same fundamental questions as the ones raised in the analysis pertaining to economic initiatives imposing data sharing,[2501] namely: who will have to share data and who can receive the data? To which types of data would this apply? Should this be remunerated? How could this be implemented technically? How will these legislations be enforced?

Once again, it should be made clear from the outset that there is no 'one size fits all' answer to these questions, and that the result of the balancing exercises underlying each of these questions will necessarily be case specific. As many of the reflections pertaining to these questions are, to a large extent, similar to those developed in the context of the analysis of economic initiatives imposing B2B data sharing, the structure of this chapter will mirror the structure of Chapter 8, Section 8.2, and I will solely focus here on developments that are specifically relevant for societal initiatives, while reverting, for the rest, to the corresponding developments in Chapter 8.

9.2.1 Who Will Have to Share Data?

415. Because compulsory B2B data sharing entails costs for data holders, it is important to ensure that this obligation will only apply to the data holders

2499. *See* points 52 and 377.
2500. *See* Part I, Chapter 2, Section 2.3.1.
2501. *See* Part III, Chapter 8, Section 8.2.

whose data is considered as necessary to achieve the societal objectives pursued by the initiative. However, arguably, it could be conceivable to apply the data sharing obligation to a broader amount of data holders if the purpose is societal, rather than economic.[2502] Indeed, by analogy with what has been said above about *empowerment initiatives imposing data sharing*, it would make sense to impose such obligations symmetrically.[2503] This is because not only large data holders but also smaller actors may hold data that is considered as being valuable in order to fulfil these societal objectives.

Yet, the risk of applying such data sharing obligations symmetrically is that it could disproportionally burden smaller undertakings, and that this could negatively affect competition if it has an impact on their capacity to innovate, notably in a situation where they would have to dedicate an important share of their resources to the compliance with societal initiatives imposing data sharing. Accordingly, to limit this risk, it could be envisaged to include, in such legislations, an exemption for smaller actors that have a limited number of financial and human resources and/or a small turnover, in order to avoid overburdening them.[2504] In this perspective, and as suggested by Mayer-Schonberger and Ramge, the legislations could create 'progressive data sharing obligations', which would kick in once the data holder has reached a certain size or turnover, and according to which the amount of data to be shared by a specific data holder should be function of its size / turnover.[2505] The bigger its size or turnover, the more data it has to share. This determination of whether a data holder meets this minimal threshold and of the amount of data to be shared could be made on a case-by-case basis, by regulatory authorities. In order to avoid an unnecessary multiplication of regulatory authorities, these regulatory authorities could be the same as those that will be created in the context of the Data Governance Act.[2506]

However, it must be considered that such an exemption and progressive sharing mechanism would potentially limit the societal benefits to be expected from the legislations imposing the compulsory data sharing, compared to a situation in which the sharing obligation would apply in full

2502. On this point for economic initiatives imposing B2B data sharing, *see* Part III, Chapter 8, Section 8.2.1.

2503. *See* points 209 and 210.

2504. *See*, by analogy, A. Diker Vanberg and M. Ünver, 'The Right to Data Portability in the GDPR and EU Competition Law: Odd Couple or Dynamic Duo?', *European Journal of Law and Technology*, 2017, Vol. 8(1), pp. 1-22; OECD, *Consumer Data Rights and Competition – Background note*, June 2020, DAF/COMP(2020)1, available at http://www.oecd.org/daf/competition/consumer-data-rights-and-competition.htm, p. 43.

2505. V. Mayer-Schonberger and T. Ramge, *Re-inventing Capitalism in the Age of Big Data*, *supra*, pp. 167-169.

2506. *See* Articles 13 and 23-25 of the Proposal for a Data Governance Act.

to all data holders. Yet, as these benefits must be balanced with the costs that such a sharing imposes on the data holders, it could be argued that the costs that would be imposed on smaller actors would be too important to justify such an obligation, while they would weigh less heavily in the balance when they are applied to larger data holders, which can absorb them more easily.

9.2.2 Who Can Receive the Data?

416. When considering the creation of a societal initiative imposing B2B data sharing, it should also be reflected on whether any recipient whatsoever should be entitled to access the data holder's data, or whether only some of them should be entitled to such access. The former option would potentially maximise the societal benefits pursued by the initiative, in light of the non-rivalrous nature of data. However, the greater the number of potential recipients, the greater the risks for the data holder's business interests and for the privacy and personal data protection of the multiple individuals whose data would be shared in an aggregated way.[2507]

Accordingly, the second option might be preferable, and, by analogy with the principles for B2G data sharing,[2508] the compulsory B2B data sharing initiative could provide that only the recipients that can demonstrate that their reuse will contribute to the societal objective underlying the initiative should benefit from an access to the data.[2509]

By analogy with what has been said in this regard for empowerment initiatives and for economic initiatives,[2510] which will not be repeated here, I argue that in order to be entitled to receive the data, the data recipient could be required to notify a description of the specific societal purpose that it intends to pursue to supervisory authorities.[2511] These authorities, which could be the same as those created by the Data Governance Act,[2512] could then assess, *ex post*, the legitimacy of the recipients' societal interests and whether they offer sufficient guarantees in terms of privacy and security (in

2507. *See* R. Feasey and A. de Streel, 'Data Sharing for Digital Market Contestability', *supra*, pp. 9 and 60.
2508. High-Level Expert Group on Business-to-Government Data Sharing, 'Towards a European strategy on business-to-government data sharing for public interests – Final report', *supra*, p. 81.
2509. J. Drexl, 'Data Access and Control in the Era of Connected Devices', *supra*, p. 164.
2510. *See* Part II, Chapter 5, Section 5.3.3; and Part III, Chapter 8, Section 8.2.2.
2511. *See*, by analogy, Article 17.4.h) of the Proposal for a Data Governance Act.
2512. *See* point 216.

collaboration with the data protection authorities[2513]).[2514] Moreover, harmonised obligations could be imposed on the recipients in order to ensure their trustworthiness, which could be monitored *ex post* as well.[2515]

9.2.3 To Which Types of Data Would This Apply?

417. Societal initiatives imposing B2B data sharing will also have to determine the scope of the data to be covered by the sharing obligation. This implies another key balancing exercise, as opting for a broad scope of data would increase the potential societal benefits for recipients and society, but would imply greater costs for the data holder's business interests, as well as greater the risks for the privacy and personal data protection of the multiple individuals whose data would be shared in an aggregated way.

418. By analogy with what has been said above regarding economic initiatives,[2516] which will not be repeated here, actively provided and observed data should be included in the scope of societal initiatives imposing B2B data sharing. For instance, car manufacturers, navigation system providers, fleet managers and parking operators could be compelled to share location and parking availability data (i.e., observed data) in order to enable 'smart parking' services, which would limit the pollution deriving from CO2 car emissions and would reduce the number of cars on the network.[2517] Similarly, in the context of a global pandemic, private healthcare institutions could be compelled to share data pertaining to their intensive care units' bed occupation rate (i.e., observed data), in order to better distribute the arrival of new patients and to address sanitary concerns.[2518]

Moreover, in light of the societal objectives pursued by these initiatives, one could reflect on whether the scope of the data covered should also include, in some circumstances, some of the data holder's inferred/derived data, as these could contain highly valuable information. Indeed, if socially valuable inferred/derived data are held (exclusively) by some data holders, including these types of data in the scope of these legislations could generate immense societal benefits.[2519] For instance, coming back to the examples

---

2513. *See*, by analogy, Recitals 28 and 29 and Article 12.3 of the Proposal for a Data Governance Act.
2514. *See*, by analogy, Article 13 of the Proposal for a Data Governance Act. *See also* point 395.
2515. *See*, by analogy, Recitals 22-34 and Articles 9-14 of the Proposal for a Data Governance Act.
2516. *See* Part III, Chapter 8, Section 8.2.3.1.
2517. *See* point 93.
2518. *Ibid.*
2519. J. Shkabatur, 'The Global Commons of Data', *Stanford Technology Law Review*, 2019, Vol. 22, p. 383.

mentioned earlier in this chapter,[2520] it might be justified to make it compulsory for pharmaceutical companies to share, with private healthcare and/or research institutions, inferred/derived data pertaining to vaccine/medication trial results; or to make it compulsory for farming equipment manufacturers to share inferred/derived data about the apparition of a disease with farmers active in the same territory, or inferred/derived data about the efficiency of a certain type of pesticide and the appropriate dose to be sprayed.

Yet, these societal benefits would have to be carefully balanced with the costs that this would warrant for the data holder, notably due to the fact that such derived/inferred data might be covered by IP rights.[2521] This might however be justified in circumstances where it is highly important and/or urgent to achieve these societal objectives. Moreover, if, as suggested above,[2522] these legislations pursuing societal objectives are constructed around 'progressive data sharing obligations',[2523] data holders having smaller sizes or turnovers could be exempted from the obligation to share inferred/derived data.

419. For the rest, and by analogy with what has been said above regarding economic initiatives,[2524] which will not be repeated here, only the data that are necessary, relevant and proportionate for the societal objectives pursued by the initiative should be shared – although this could cover not only historical but also present and future data – and these societal initiatives imposing B2B data sharing could provide that the data holder is compelled to license, under objective, proportionate and non-discriminatory conditions, any potential database right that it may have on the data.

Finally, these initiatives should provide that aggregated personal data pertaining to multiple individuals should only be shared to the extent that this complies with the GDPR's principles (lawfulness, fairness and transparency; purpose limitation; data minimisation; data accuracy; storage limitation; integrity and confidentiality; and accountability)[2525] and that there is a lawful basis of processing allowing the sharing.[2526]

2520. *See* point 412.
2521. *See* Part I, Chapter 2, Section 2.2.2.1.
2522. *See* point 415.
2523. *See* V. Mayer-Schonberger and T. Ramge, *Re-inventing Capitalism in the Age of Big Data*, *supra*, pp. 167-169.
2524. *See* Part III, Chapter 8, Section 8.2.3.1.
2525. Articles 5 of the GDPR. For a more detailed analysis of this articulation, *see*, by analogy, Part III, Chapter 7, Section 7.2.2.
2526. Articles 6 of the GDPR. For a more detailed analysis of this articulation, *see*, by analogy, Part III, Chapter 7, Section 7.2.1; and Part III, Chapter 8, Section 8.2.3.2.

9.2.4 Should This Be Remunerated?

420. Similar to economic initiatives,[2527] societal initiatives imposing B2B data sharing could also provide that the data holder should be remunerated in exchange for the data sharing, as this would be a way to protect his business interests, in return for the expected benefits of these initiatives.[2528]

In this regard, and contrary to what has been said regarding economic initiatives, the price calculation method contained in the PSI Directive might be preferable than an open formula such as a 'proportionate remuneration'.[2529] Indeed, contrary to economic initiatives, the fact that such a method does not take appropriately into account the loss of 'data advantage' or of 'data power' for the data holder deriving from the sharing is not as problematic, as in this context the data is shared for societal purposes, and not for economic purposes with competitors. The sharing of the data, in such circumstances, is thus less likely to affect the data holders' 'data advantage', especially if the recipients have to demonstrate that their reuse will contribute to the societal objective underlying the initiative.[2530] Moreover, in light of the importance of achieving the societal objectives in a timely manner, using a more concrete price calculation method, such as the one contained in the PSI Directive, would arguably make the process faster, as it will not be hampered by discussions pertaining to what should be considered as a 'proportionate remuneration', which is the downside of a more open formula.[2531]

Accordingly, societal initiatives imposing B2B data sharing could provide that the price should cover the costs of data collection, production, reproduction, dissemination and storage incurred by the data holder, as well as a reasonable return on investment for the holder.[2532] Indeed, this price calculation method presents the advantage of being relatively simple, especially if the initiatives define what constitutes a 'reasonable' return on investment.[2533] Furthermore, they could provide, as for G2B data sharing, that the data holder can charge the marginal costs incurred for the

2527. *See* Part III, Chapter 8, Section 8.2.4.

2528. *See* R. Feasey and A. de Streel, 'Data Sharing for Digital Market Contestability', *supra*, pp. 11 and 77-80. Some however argue that the data holders should not be entitled to a remuneration: *see* J. Prüfer, 'Competition Policy and Data Sharing on Data-Driven Markets', *supra*, p. 14.

2529. *See* points 396-398.

2530. *See* point 416.

2531. *See* point 398.

2532. *See*, by analogy, Article 6.1 of Directive 2019/1024.

2533. *See*, by analogy, Article 2.16 of Directive 2019/1024: '"reasonable return on investment" means a percentage of the overall charge, in addition to that needed to recover the eligible costs, not exceeding 5 percentage points above the fixed interest rate of the ECB'.

anonymisation of the aggregated data (e.g., the costs incurred in order to reach a sufficient level of granularity) to the data recipients.[2534]

9.2.5 How Could This Be Implemented Technically and How Will This Be Enforced?

421. Finally, when reflecting on the creation of a societal initiative imposing B2B data sharing, matters of technical implementation and of enforcement should also be considered. As the above analysis of these matters conducted in the context of economic initiatives is equally applicable to societal initiatives imposing B2B data sharing, they will not be repeated here.[2535] It will simply be reminded that, if a 'progressive data sharing obligation' is adopted, supervisory authorities will have an important role to play, as they could be charged with determining whether a small data holder can be exempted from the sharing obligation, or whether it could at least be exempted from sharing its inferred/derived data.[2536]

422. To conclude this chapter, the above-mentioned insights regarding the key elements that societal initiatives imposing B2B data sharing should consider are summarised in Table 9.1.

Table 9.1 Insights on the Key Elements to Consider for Societal Initiatives Imposing B2B Data Sharing

	Societal Initiatives Imposing B2B Data Sharing
Data holders subject to the sharing obligation	Symmetric application to all data holders but exemption for smaller actors which only have a limited size and/or turnover, in order to avoid overburdening them (consideration of a 'progressive data sharing obligation').[2537]
Data recipients entitled to benefit from the sharing obligation	Recipient could be required to notify a description of the societal purposes that it intends to pursue.[2538] *Ex post* assessment of the legitimacy of the recipients' interests and of whether they offer sufficient guarantees in terms of privacy and security.[2539] Imposition of harmonised obligations on the recipients for the provision of their products/services, to be monitored *ex post* as well.[2540]

2534. Article 6.1 of Directive 2019/1024.
2535. *See* Part III, Chapter 8, Sections 8.2.5 and 8.2.6.
2536. *See* points 415 and 418.
2537. *See* Part III, Chapter 9, Section 9.2.1.
2538. *See* Part III, Chapter 9, Section 9.2.2.
2539. *Ibid.*

Types of data covered by the sharing obligation	Actively provided and observed data + potentially also inferred/derived data (notably in circumstances where it is highly important and/or urgent to achieve these societal objectives), following a 'progressive data sharing obligation' approach: data holders having smaller sizes and/or turnovers could be exempted from the obligation to share inferred/derived data.[2541] Only the data that are necessary, relevant and proportionate, in terms of detail (e.g., type of data, granularity, quantity, frequency of access). Not only historical data but also present and future data.[2542] Personal data should only be shared to the extent that this complies with the GDPR's principles and that there is a lawful basis of processing allowing the sharing.[2543] Legislations could contain a provision forbidding data recipients from reidentifying the multiple individuals whose data have been aggregated and pseudonymised prior to the sharing.[2544]
Remuneration of the data holder as compensation for the sharing obligation	Remuneration covering the costs of data collection, production, reproduction, dissemination and storage incurred by the data holder, as well as a reasonable return on investment for the holder.[2545] Data holder can charge the marginal costs incurred for the anonymisation of the aggregated data (e.g., the costs incurred in order to reach a sufficient level of granularity) to the data recipients.[2546]
Technical implementation of the sharing obligation	The societal initiatives themselves may not be the best place to address this issue. Rather, it would be advisable for these legislations to charge regulatory bodies to define the technical modalities of the sharing in cases where the data holders and recipients do not agree on them.[2547]

2540. *Ibid.*
2541. Part III, Chapter 9, Section 9.2.3.
2542. *Ibid.*
2543. *Ibid.*
2544. *Ibid. See* J. Prüfer, 'Competition Policy and Data Sharing on Data-Driven Markets', *supra*, p. 12.
2545. Part III, Chapter 9, Section 9.2.4.
2546. *Ibid.*
2547. *See* Part III, Chapter 9, Section 9.2.5 and Part III, Chapter 8, Section 8.2.5.

Conclusion

423. The aim of my contribution was to answer the following research question: 'What are the economic and societal balancing exercises underlying compulsory B2B data sharing?'

To answer this question, the concept of data (what?) was first specified.[2548] Data was defined in a broad sense, as any digital representation of acts, facts or information and any compilation of such acts, facts or information, including in the form of sound, visual or audiovisual recording.[2549]

While the European legal framework and the legal literature traditionally distinguish personal from non-personal data, I opted to follow a common holistic approach for both categories of data because the boundary between these two concepts is porous and often difficult to establish in practice. Nevertheless, personal data considerations were taken into account when relevant. This led to the establishment of an alternative data typology composed of four categories of data, namely actively provided data, observed data, inferred/derived data and acquired data.[2550] In fact, this typology can be reduced to three broader categories of data, namely: (i) primary data, (ii) inferred/derived data, and (iii) acquired data. Indeed, actively provided and observed data can be classified in a common group of primary data. Inferred/derived data are a second generation of data drawn, by the data holder itself, from the analysis of this first generation of primary data. The data holder could also opt not to create/collect primary data or to generate inferred/derived data itself, but rather to acquire data from third parties, such as data brokers.

Although a common holistic approach for both personal and non-personal data was followed, I focused more on behavioural/consumer data than on non-personal IoT data. This is mainly because the two gaps that my analysis aimed to fill through a normative approach precisely pertain to such

2548. *See* Part I, Chapter 1.
2549. This definition is based on Article 2.1 of the Proposal for a Data Governance Act; Article 2.19 of the Proposal for a Digital Markets Act.
2550. *See* Part I, Chapter 1, Section 1.3.

behavioural/consumer data.[2551] Moreover, most of the European policy discussions pertaining to compulsory B2B data sharing relate to large data actors that draw a 'data advantage' from their privileged access to, and control of, consumer/behavioural data.[2552] On the other hand, IoT non-personal data have received much less policy attention, especially since the option to create a 'data producers right' on non-personal machine-generated data has been abandoned.[2553] While this could change in the future with the growth of the IoT, notably in the context of societal initiatives imposing B2B data sharing,[2554] this also explains why my focus was mostly set on consumer/behavioural data, rather than on IoT non-personal data.

424. Then, I focused on the rationale for (data) sharing (why?).[2555] In order to do so, I first reverted to the more standard discussions on whether a resource should be shared.[2556] Indeed, finding a balance between granting exclusive ownership/property rights to the few, on the one hand, and providing access to and sharing resources with the many, on the other hand, has also always been a challenge, whether this related to tangible or intangible resources. Regarding intangible resources, it was outlined that the free-rider dilemma that underlies the creation of IP rights, which were established in order to avoid an information underproduction problem, is also a key concern in discussions pertaining to whether data sharing should be made compulsory in certain circumstances. Indeed, the prospect of free-riders may discourage the creators/inventors from producing intangible resources, in light of their potential inability to generate returns on investments, and it may also discourage, for the same reasons, data holders from investing in data collection and/or analysis.

In fact, the European Commission itself reflected on whether an 'IP-like' right on data should be granted to data producers, in order to stimulate data production, in light of this free-rider dilemma.[2557] However, a large majority of legal scholars argued that there was no economic justification to support such a proposal, as there is no evidence that the absence of such a right creates a lack of incentives for the production, analysis or marketing of data (i.e., there is no data underproduction problem). Moreover, the creation of such a right could have led to disruptive juxtapositions and delimitation problems with existing IP rights, and it could have strengthened entry barriers that, consequently, would have increased the market power of

2551. *See* point 5.

2552. *See* Part I, Chapter 2, Section 2.2.3; Part II, Chapter 4; Part III, Chapters 6 and 8. *See*, for instance, the Proposal for a Regulation of the European Parliament and of the Council on contestable and fair markets in the digital sector (Digital Markets Act), 15 December 2020, COM(2020) 842 final.

2553. On this topic, *see* Part I, Chapter 2, Section 2.2.2.2.

2554. *See* Part I, Chapter 2, Section 2.3.1; and Part III, Chapter 9.

2555. *See* Part I, Chapter 2.

2556. *See* Part I, Chapter 2, Section 2.1.

2557. *See* Part I, Chapter 2, Section 2.2.2.2.

large data holders. Accordingly, the policy debates have moved away from the idea of creating an IP-like right on data, towards legal reflections revolving around data reservation (i.e., the fact that data holders have a de facto exclusive control on their data and can decide on whether, and to whom, they provide access to it).[2558] This explains why these IP rights considerations were less relied on in the remainder of my contribution, and that the focus was rather set on competition considerations linked to data control and access.

425. It was, however, outlined that even if the Commission has moved away from (intellectual) property on data towards data reservation, it has not moved away from the dominant approach in our Western societies, namely that exclusive ownership or exclusive property is generally the default model (*in casu* data is exclusively reserved through contractual and technical means), while models based on sharing/access are less common.[2559] Yet, I made the argument that concepts such as property or ownership, and sharing or commons, should not be opposed so strongly. Indeed, commons can be subject to ownership and can thus be subject to a form of appropriation or reservation, but, importantly, this does not lead to the exclusion of others. Rather, commons are a form of ownership that organise the collective and shared use of a resource. To some extent, they reflect a form of inclusive property, as opposed to exclusive property. Commons, and other forms of sharing, are thus situated somewhere along a continuum between absolute exclusive property/ownership, on the one hand, and the absence of any form of property/ownership (public good/free-for-all), on the other hand. While a (data) commons approach could be a fertile ground to move away from the traditional conception of exclusive property towards more generative forms of rights, based on collective access and usage rights, I did not further investigate this approach, because it is based on voluntary efforts, within a diffused community of actors, to govern a resource and to share it. It thus relies on *voluntary* (data) sharing in the context of the exercise of collective rights on commons. Yet, I instead focused on hypotheses of *compulsory* data sharing, which do not fit in this commons approach.

Indeed, as outlined in the introduction, legal instruments promoting *voluntary* data sharing tend to focus more on data governance and technical issues (standardisation, interoperability, etc.), in order to create more favourable conditions for the market actors to share data. The underlying idea behind these instruments is that it is preferable to first attempt to create a clear framework to incentivise the market actors to share data on their own initiative, rather than to compel them to do so. Yet, such *voluntary* data sharing initiatives may not always be sufficient, and legislators could be tempted to go a step further, by imposing *compulsory* data sharing. That

---

2558. *See* Part I, Chapter 2, Sections 2.2.1 and 2.2.2.
2559. *See* Part I, Chapter 2, Section 2.2.2.3.

being said, *voluntary* and *compulsory* data sharing should not be seen as two extremes on the regulatory intervention scale. Rather, there are links to be made between these two approaches, which complement each other. Indeed, if the step has to be taken from *voluntary* to *compulsory* data sharing regulatory initiatives, the latter should build on the former, as the data governance principles and technical provisions contained in the former are equally relevant for the latter. Despite this complementarity, I chose to focus on *compulsory* B2B data sharing regulatory initiatives because if the legislator decides to force the sharing, this will require the prior consideration of a certain number of fundamental economic and societal balancing exercises. Highlighting the nature of these balancing exercises was my core objective.

426. Building on the above-mentioned discussions, I then delved into the analysis of the rationale for data sharing.[2560] In this regard, it was emphasised that, in light of the data's characteristics, a growing call for compulsory data sharing is being made.[2561] Yet, compulsory B2B data sharing is not a goal in itself, and it should only be used in specific circumstances as a way to achieve determined objectives. In fact, three types of rationale can be called upon to support compulsory B2B data sharing, namely economic, societal, and empowerment considerations.

427. To get a better grasp of the economic rationale for data sharing, the economics of data were presented.[2562] The digital economy is characterised by network effects and by strong economies of scale, scope and speed. Data therefore plays a prominent role, and the ability to use data to develop or improve innovative products or services is a key competitive parameter. Looking at it from the other side of the coin, these characteristics might lead to techno-economic entry barriers (uniqueness of the data collected by the incumbent data holder or unique gateway to it; economies of scale, scope and speed; network effects; lock-in and switching costs). Consequently, several market failures may appear. First, the economics of data favour concentration. Indeed, data-driven markets have a natural tendency to tip towards monopolisation as there is a strong first-mover advantage. Due to these first-mover advantage and market tipping dynamics, data concentration might increase entry barriers for new firms and strengthen the market power of data aggregators, leading to diminishing incentives for innovation. Such concentration may also establish long-term competitive advantages and this could endanger the contestability of these data-driven markets. Second, these network effects and economies of scope, scale and speed may also be leveraged by an incumbent data holder to expand and strengthen its position in adjacent connected markets. Accordingly, there are clear incentives for

2560. *See* Part I, Chapter 2, Sections 2.2 and 2.3.
2561. *See* Part I, Chapter 2, Section 2.2.3.
2562. *Ibid.*

data-driven firms to expand their activities in as many markets as possible and to build conglomerates. In light of the above, compulsory B2B data sharing is increasingly being proposed in order to remedy these market failures.

At present, this is mainly tackled through competition law,[2563] with the exception of a sector-specific data sharing legislation in the automotive sector.[2564] However, as competition intervention is a time-consuming process, it is increasingly argued that competition law rules should be adapted to the digital environment (e.g., by adapting the traditional balances to digital markets, or by increasing the use of interim measures or of market investigations) and that they should be complemented by the creation of potential *ex ante* legislations imposing B2B data sharing.[2565]

428. Compulsory B2B data sharing could also be justified by societal objectives.[2566] Indeed, increased data sharing could prove to be essential for tackling societal, environmental, health and mobility challenges.[2567] The underlying idea is that not only public sector data but also private sector data can be used to support societal goals. In contrast, this implies that a lack of data sharing, deriving from data concentration and conglomeration, will create not only economic challenges but also societal challenges. As the societal value of the data held (exclusively) by some incumbent data holders is enormous, allowing (some) third parties to use this data could generate immense scientific benefits and could be used to address these societal challenges.

Yet, I outlined that while the policy and legislative discussions pertaining to the creation of societal initiatives imposing data sharing are emerging in the B2G field, the same cannot be said about societal initiatives imposing B2B data sharing. Accordingly, I developed some prospective reflections on why such initiatives might make sense and on how they could be constructed in the future, in the hope to spur further discussions on this topic. The aim was thus not to be exhaustive, but rather to set some foundations on which future research could build.

429. Third, data sharing is also increasingly presented as a way to empower individuals, by giving them more control over their data through tools that allow them to decide at a much more granular level what can be done with it.[2568] In fact, I outlined that these empowerment initiatives can pursue two different types of sub-objectives.

2563. *See* Part III, Chapter 6.
2564. *See* Part III, Chapter 8, Section 8.1.1.
2565. *See* Part III, Chapter 6, Section 6.5 and Chapter 8.
2566. *See* Part I, Chapter 2, Section 2.3.1.
2567. *See* the numerous examples mentioned at point 93; and Part III, Chapter 9.
2568. *See* Part I, Chapter 2, Section 2.3.2.

On the one hand, empowerment initiatives can pursue the objective of allowing the exercise of fundamental rights, such as the right to personal data protection and informational self-determination.[2569] This 'power of control' that data subjects can (re)claim on their data is fundamental as it will facilitate the exercise of their fundamental rights, as increased access to information will improve their decision-making and will allow them to take fundamental decisions about all aspects of their life.[2570]

On the other hand, empowerment initiatives can be adopted to address specific market failures.[2571] The underlying idea of these initiatives is that by giving more control to individuals on 'their' data, this will allow them to multi-home or to switch more easily between service providers as their searching and switching costs are reduced, and this should reduce the market failures deriving from consumer inertia and lock-in effects.[2572] Indeed, the aim is to give more autonomy to the individuals by allowing them to optimise the use of their resources. In turn, this should facilitate entry and should foster competition on the targeted markets, which should lead to better services, more choice and lower prices for the individuals.

At present, both types of empowerment initiatives imposing data sharing are essentially structured around (some forms of) data portability rights.[2573] However, the effectiveness of these existing initiatives and their ability to truly empower individuals are being criticised, and as a result, a growing call for the creation of a continuous portability right has emerged.[2574]

430. These distinct but possibly also complementary objectives[2575] led to the identification of two main categories of *compulsory B2B data sharing initiatives* that guided my analysis, namely *empowerment initiatives imposing B2B data sharing*, on the one hand, and *economic or societal initiatives imposing B2B data sharing*, on the other hand.[2576] A core difference between these two categories, other than the types of objectives pursued, is the amount of data transferred. Indeed, in this first category of initiatives, the amount of data transferred is relatively small as it is limited to the data relating to the specific individual at hand. Of course, the framework created as a whole by these initiatives can potentially lead to the sharing of data pertaining to a very large number of individuals, but each act of sharing will relate to a specific individual. Accordingly, while these empowerment initiatives mostly benefit a specific individual, they also have indirect

2569. *See* Part II, Chapter 4, Section 4.1.
2570. *See* point 97.
2571. *See* Part II, Chapter 4, Section 4.2.
2572. *See* point 97.
2573. *See* Part II, Chapter 4, Sections 4.1 and 4.2.
2574. *See* Part II, Chapter 4, Section 4.3.
2575. *See* point 128.
2576. *See* Part I, Chapter 3, Section 3.2.

benefits for third parties (such as (potential) competitors of the data holder). On the other hand, what will be shared in the second category of initiatives are larger amounts of (aggregated) personal data pertaining to multiple individuals and/or non-personal data rather than smaller quantities of data linked to a specific individual. These initiatives thus mostly benefit third parties but they also have indirect benefits for the individuals whose data are shared.

431. An important finding is that, independently of the objectives that it pursues, any compulsory B2B data sharing initiative must consider a certain number of fundamental economic and societal balancing exercises. Maximising data sharing should thus not be seen as an objective in its own right, and data sharing obligations should only be imposed if the benefits created trump the economic and societal costs. More concretely, I focused on three balancing exercises,[2577] namely the need to balance the benefits stemming from compulsory B2B data sharing initiatives with: (i) the economic interests of the data holder; (ii) personal data protection considerations; and (iii) the long-term and collective costs that (some of) these initiatives could entail in terms of individual autonomy.

Indeed, the economic, societal or individual empowerment benefits deriving from data sharing have to be balanced with the data holder's business interests.[2578] This is because data collection and processing and consequently data sharing entails costs for the data holder, as although data use by multiple parties does not affect its existence, it may affect its value. Therefore, data sharing obligations might create disincentives for data collection and processing as sharing could deter innovation by the data holder who might no longer want to invest in data collection if it no longer provides him with a competitive advantage, due to the fear of free-riding that derives from the non-rivalrous nature of data. Moreover, a data sharing obligation might also create reputational costs for the data holder, for instance, if it is required to reveal data showing that its activity is highly polluting. If the data sharing initiative pursues economic objectives, it should also be factored that imposing data sharing might also deter innovation by third parties who will no longer see the point in innovating in order to collect the data themselves, as they will receive it from the data holder (expectation to free-ride).[2579] On the other hand, if the data sharing initiative pursues individual empowerment or societal objectives, the data holder's costs may weigh less heavily in the balance, as they are opposed to fundamental societal objectives that could be viewed as superseding mere economic considerations.[2580] In light of the above, my first ambition was to adopt an analytical approach, in order to shed more light on how these economic

2577. *See* point 5 for more details.
2578. *See* Part I, Chapter 2, Section 2.2.3.5; and Part I, Chapter 2, Section 2.3.
2579. *See* Part I, Chapter 2, Section 2.2.3.5.
2580. *See* Part I, Chapter 2, Section 2.3.

interests of the data holders are factored in the existing compulsory B2B data sharing initiatives, and to provide some insights on how these interests could be factored in future initiatives.[2581]

Additionally, whether they pursue economic, societal or empowerment objectives, reaping the potential benefits deriving from these data sharing initiatives will only be acceptable if this is done in compliance with the right to privacy and to personal data protection of the (other) individuals whose data would be shared.[2582] As it quickly appeared that this articulation was insufficiently addressed by legislators and policymakers, my second ambition was to adopt a normative approach in order to fill this gap, by attempting to clarify the core elements that must be factored in this balancing exercise, and by attempting to provide insights on how this delicate articulation can be solved.[2583]

Moreover, *empowerment initiatives imposing B2B data sharing* imply another fundamental balancing exercise, namely that the potential individual short-term gains that are promised to individuals will have to be balanced with the potential long-term costs and collective costs that these initiatives might entail in terms of control, autonomy and self-determination. As this balancing exercise seems to be broadly overlooked by policymakers and legislators, my third ambition was, once again, to adopt a normative approach in order to fill this gap, by attempting to raise awareness about the crucial need to take these risks into consideration, and by attempting to provide insights on how this delicate balance can be addressed.[2584]

Indeed, empowering individuals by offering them more choice will not necessarily increase their control, autonomy and (informational) self-determination. In fact, if these empowerment initiatives are not strictly delineated, they might actually entail a high price and a loss of control for the individuals.[2585] This is because, due to strong asymmetries of information, individuals rarely have a clear understanding of what is done exactly with their data by the data holder, and do not have a clear view on whether the latter processes the data in the way it has announced. They are thus not fully aware of the consequences of sharing and the impact this could have on their privacy. Indeed, this data could be used to influence their future decision-making in covert, subtle and targeted manners, raising concerns in terms of their autonomy and self-determination. As a result, it must be factored that data that has been shared by individuals in exchange for short-term gains

2581. *See*, *inter alia*, Part I, Chapter 2, Section 2.2.3.5; Part II, Chapter 5, Section 5.1.1; Part II, Chapter 5, Section 5.3; Part III, Chapter 6; Part III, Chapter 8, Section 8.2; and Part III, Chapter 9, Section 9.1.

2582. *See* Part II, Chapter 5, Section 5.1.2; Part III, Chapter 7; Part III, Chapter 8, Section 8.2; and Part III, Chapter 9.

2583. *See*, *inter alia*, Part II, Chapter 5, Section 5.1.2; Part II, Chapter 5, Section 5.3; Part III, Chapter 7; Part III, Chapter 8, Section 8.2; and Part III, Chapter 9, Section 9.1.

2584. *See* Part I, Chapter 2, Section 2.3.2 and Part II, Chapter 5, Section 5.1.3.

2585. *See* point 196.

might, in the long term, be broadly disseminated and/or be used against them, potentially leading to a loss of control and autonomy. Furthermore, it is important to acknowledge that an individual's decision to share data will have an impact not only on her own autonomy and self-determination but also on those of others.[2586] Indeed, data sharing by an individual creates negative externalities, as it also reveals information about other individuals whose information is correlated with those of others, even if they themselves did not share any data. In light of this relational and collective nature of data, it is also fundamental to balance the individual's potential gains from data sharing with the potential collective costs for other individuals in terms of control, autonomy and self-determination.

In order to assess these long-term and collective costs, I argued that legislators could engage in a case-by-case risk assessment of the 'systemic risks' that the empowerment initiatives could entail.[2587] In this context, legislators should consider the economic risks that such data sharing initiatives could entail for (other) individuals, as well as the 'surveillance capitalism' risks that might derive from such practices. Moreover, legislators will also have to take into consideration the systemic risks that such data sharing initiatives could have on the exercise of fundamental rights by individuals, such as their possibility to take fundamental decisions about their health, their family life or their professional life. In assessing these risks, particular consideration should be given to the potentially rapid and wide dissemination of the data shared by individuals. On the basis of this risk assessment, legislators should then integrate – in the instrument creating the empowerment initiative – reasonable, proportionate and effective measures aimed at mitigating the specific long-term and collective risks that will have been identified. Furthermore, the empowerment initiative should also provide that external and independent audits can be conducted in order to verify the compliance with these mitigation measures.

432. Another core finding is that there is no one-size-fits-all answer to how the balancing exercises outlined above should be solved. Rather, the objective pursued by the compulsory data sharing initiative (economic, societal or empowerment) should be a key starting point when addressing these fundamental balancing exercises. It should indeed arguably have an impact on the determination of the *ratione personae* (data holders subject to the sharing obligation and data recipients that can access the data) and *ratione materiae* (types of data covered) scopes of these compulsory data sharing initiatives, as well as on considerations pertaining to the remuneration of the data holder and to the technical implementation of the data sharing initiatives.

2586. *See* point 197.
2587. *See* points 198-200.

In terms of the *ratione personae* scope of the initiatives,[2588] I argued that *empowerment initiatives imposing B2B data sharing* should preferably apply symmetrically to all data holders. Indeed, since the core objective of such initiatives is to empower the individuals whose data is shared, it would make sense to impose them symmetrically so individuals can have more control over all their data, and not just on the data that is held by a limited number of data holders. Arguably, such a symmetric approach could also be adopted for *societal initiatives imposing B2B data sharing*, in order to maximise the potential social benefits, although there could be exemptions for smaller actors which only have a limited number of financial and human resources and/or a small turnover, in order to avoid overburdening them. This could, for instance, be done through a progressive data sharing obligation. On the other hand, there seems to be a strong consensus that *economic initiatives imposing B2B data sharing* should be asymmetric and limited to a specific subset of data holders. In this regard, the determination of whether a data holder falls within the scope of the data sharing obligation could be based on a set of clear quantitative and qualitative indicators contained in the legislations, to be assessed on a case-by-case basis by the controlling authority. Arguably, such a limitation of the scope of application of these initiatives is justified by the fact that the costs implied by the data sharing obligation on the data holder's business interests should only be imposed to a specific subset of data holders, namely those that are considered as playing a central role in the (systemic) market failure(s) that provoked the regulatory intervention.

Regarding the determination of the data recipients, it has been suggested that for all types of compulsory B2B data sharing initiatives that the recipient could be required to notify a description of the product/service it intends to provide, or of the economic/societal purposes that it intends to pursue.[2589] This would enable an *ex post* assessment of the trustworthiness and legitimacy of the recipients' activities, and of whether they offer sufficient guarantees in terms of privacy and security. While such a 'notification obligation with *ex post* monitoring of the compliance' could be perceived, by the data recipients, as being too cumbersome and as delaying the benefits of the data sharing, it is certainly less burdensome than requiring a prior certification for the reuse. On the other hand, the option not to subject the reuse to any prior formality should arguably be excluded, as it is vital to ensure that the data is not shared openly with anyone without any limits, as this could have dramatic consequences in terms of the individuals' personal

2588. *See* Part II, Chapter 5, Section 5.3.1.2; Part III, Chapter 8, Section 8.2.1; and Part III, Chapter 9, Section 9.2.1.

2589. *See* Part II, Chapter 5, Section 5.3.3; Part III, Chapter 8, Section 8.2.2; and Part III, Chapter 9, Section 9.2.2.

data protection and informational self-determination.[2590] Additionally, harmonised obligations could also be imposed on these recipients, to be monitored *ex post* as well. In case of a breach of an obligation imposed by the legislations, or if the data recipient has provided false information in its notification, the competent regulatory authorities could also be empowered to impose fines and/or to request the cessation of the unlawful processing.[2591]

Turning to the *ratione materiae* scope of these initiatives,[2592] I argued that *empowerment initiatives imposing B2B data sharing* should only apply to actively provided and observed data but not to inferred/derived data, which are the most valuable for the data holder, or to acquired data. However, it was emphasised that inferred/derived data can be obtained through the exercise of the GDPR data access right. Moreover, it should be made explicit that data holders have the possibility to keep using the data despite the data sharing obligation, and that such sharing should not adversely affect other data subjects' right to personal data. The scope of *economic initiatives imposing B2B data sharing* should arguably also be limited to actively provided and observed data, excluding inferred/derived and acquired data. *Societal initiatives imposing B2B data sharing* on the other hand could potentially apply to inferred/derived data as well, notably in circumstances where it is highly important and/or urgent to achieve these societal objectives. However, if, as outlined above, a progressive data sharing obligation is implemented, smaller data holders could be exempted from having to share such inferred/derived data. Moreover, for both *economic and societal initiatives imposing B2B data sharing*, it was underlined that only the data that are necessary, relevant and proportionate for the fulfilment of these objectives should be shared, although this should not be limited to historical data, but could also include present and future data. Importantly, personal data should only be shared to the extent that this complies with the GDPR's principles and that there is a lawful basis of processing allowing the sharing. In this regard, the legislations could contain a provision forbidding data recipients from reidentifying the multiple individuals whose data have been aggregated and pseudonymised prior to the sharing.

Remuneration considerations were also taken into account.[2593] In this regard, I argued that *empowerment initiatives imposing B2B data sharing* should in principle not imply any form of payment, neither from the individual whose data is shared nor from a potential data recipient. This is because the potential costs that such initiatives might entail on the data holders' incentives to collect and process the data will, in fact, be minimal as

2590. *See* point 217.
2591. *See* points 217 and 389.
2592. *See* Part II, Chapter 5, Section 5.3.1.1; Part III, Chapter 8, Section 8.2.3; and Part III, Chapter 9, Section 9.2.3.
2593. *See* Part II, Chapter 5, Section 5.3.2; Part III, Chapter 8, Section 8.2.4; and Part III, Chapter 9, Section 9.2.4.

the volumes of data that will be transferred through such mechanisms are quite low, as they relate to a specific individual. On the other hand, some form of remuneration could be envisaged for *economic and societal initiatives imposing B2B data sharing*. For *economic initiatives*, it was argued that a 'proportionate remuneration' could be imposed, which would have to be determined on a case-by-case basis. To facilitate this contextual assessment, the legislations could outline several factors to be taken into consideration, such as: (i) the volume of data being shared; (ii) whether the shared data has been generated as a by-product or as the core economic activity of the data holder; (iii) whether the shared data is covered by an IP right; or (iv) whether the data is shared with a direct competitor or not. Additionally, it was highlighted that, if the data holder(s) and data recipient(s) fail to agree on the data sharing price, this price could be determined by an independent third party. To mitigate the risk of lengthy negotiations, the initiative could set binding deadlines for this negotiation period. Moreover, the initiative could provide that the designated independent third party will have to draft guidelines aiming at providing more contextual information about the above-mentioned factors. These guidelines could also suggest the addition of new factors that would be worth taking into consideration. For *societal initiatives*, it was argued that the price should cover the costs of data collection, production, reproduction, dissemination and storage incurred by the data holder, as well as a reasonable return on investment for the holder. Furthermore, for both *economic and societal initiatives imposing B2B data sharing*, I suggested that data holders could charge the marginal costs incurred for the anonymisation of the aggregated data (e.g., the costs incurred in order to reach a sufficient level of granularity) to the data recipients.

I also addressed the technical implementation of the data sharing initiatives.[2594] Regarding *empowerment initiatives imposing B2B data sharing*, depending on the cases it could be necessary to move beyond (continuous) data sharing, towards more interoperability, in order to truly empower the individuals, as (continuous) data sharing by itself does not remedy the lock-in effects deriving from network effects' coordination problem. Concerning *economic and societal initiatives imposing B2B data sharing*, it was outlined that the legislations themselves may not be the best place to address these technical issues. Rather, it would be advisable for these legislations to ask regulatory bodies to define the technical modalities of the sharing in cases where the data holders and recipients fail to agree on them.

433. Finally, and independently of the objectives pursued by the compulsory B2B data sharing initiatives, I emphasised that a timely enforcement of these initiatives will be of paramount significance. Indeed, a lack of (timely)

2594. *See* Part II, Chapter 5, Section 5.3.4; Part III, Chapter 8, Section 8.2.5; and Part III, Chapter 9, Section 9.2.5.

enforcement can affect the full deployment of the legal framework's effects. For instance, it has been outlined that the time-consuming process of competition intervention is not aligned with the timing of market evolutions and that, as a result, enforcement might come too late, when the damage is already irreparable.[2595] Moreover, even if the GDPR has created a strict legal framework for the processing of personal data, the enforcement of the GDPR by data protection authorities is sporadic (largely due to a lack of sufficient resources), leading to negative effects not only on the individuals' right to personal data protection but also on competition.[2596]

Therefore, while these compulsory B2B data sharing initiatives will need to determine very clear rules of the game on how to address the fundamental balancing exercises mentioned above, specific regulatory bodies will need to be appointed to apply and enforce these rules on a case-by-case basis.[2597] As this will imply a substantial workload, they will need adequate financial and human resources, as well as the necessary technical knowledge and resources, to carry out these missions. Furthermore, to ensure an efficient and harmonised enforcement across the Digital Single Market, it will be fundamental for these regulatory authorities to cooperate with, and assist, each other and to be coherent in their decisional practice. Additionally, they will need to cooperate with the data protection and competition authorities, as well as with other relevant sectoral authorities, as some overlapping issues may have to be tackled by different regulatory authorities. To be sure, the multiplication of regulatory authorities can lead to several issues that could hamper the swift enforcement of these compulsory data sharing initiatives (different degrees of enforcement; diverging or even contradicting case law; risks of overlapping 'enforcement competences' and of the ensuing 'regulator wars'; dilution of the application of the norms; etc.).[2598] Accordingly, further research on these 'enforcement design' considerations would be highly welcomed in order to identify concrete proposals that would allow to solve these issues, as without proper and efficient enforcement, it might be missed out on the numerous benefits that should result from these compulsory data sharing initiatives.

434. In conclusion, I aimed to demonstrate that compulsory B2B data sharing initiatives imply fundamental economic and societal balancing exercises, which cannot be solved once and for all in the adoption process of these initiatives. Rather, addressing these balancing exercises will require formulating the rules of these initiatives in such a way that they allow recurring checks and balances, on a case-by-case basis, in order to factor the impact

2595. *See* Part III, Chapter 6, Section 6.5.
2596. *See* Part III, Chapter 7, Section 7.1.3.
2597. *See* Part III, Chapter 8, Section 8.2.6; and Part III, Chapter 9, Section 9.2.5.
2598. *See* point 408.

that the specific circumstances of the case, the passing of time and the development of technological innovations will have on the solution to be given to these balancing exercises. The tale of the economic and societal balances underlying compulsory B2B data sharing initiatives will thus not be a short novel, but rather a continuously evolving story.

References

Books

Adler, M.J., *A Guidebook to Learning: For a Lifelong Pursuit of Wisdom*, London, Macmillan, 1986.

Benkler, Y., *The Wealth of Networks: How Social Production Transforms Markets and Freedom*, New Haven, Yale University Press, 2003.

Blackstone, W., *Commentaries on the Laws of England*, Book 2, Chapter 1, Oxford, Oxford University Press, 1771, available at https://avalon.law.yale.edu/18th_century/blackstone_bk2ch1.asp.

Bollier, D. and Helfrich, S., *Free, Fair and Alive. The Insurgent Power of the Commons*, Gabriola Island, New Society Publishers, 2019.

Bonnecase, J., *Précis de droit civil*, 2e éd., Paris, Rousseau, 1938, t. I.

Catala, P., *Le droit à l'épreuve du numérique. Jus ex machina*, Paris, PUF, 1998.

Christensen, C., *The Innovator's Dilemma: When New Technologies Cause Great Firms to Fail*, Boston, Harvard Business School Press, 1997.

Christensen, C. and Raynor, M., *The Innovator's Solution: Creating and Sustaining Successful Growth*, Boston, Harvard Business School Press, 2003.

De Boüard, F., *La dépendance économique née d'un contrat*, Paris, LGDJ, 2007.

Degrave, E., *L'E-Gouvernement et la protection de la vie privée. Légalité, transparence et contrôle*, Bruxelles, Larcier – Collection du CRIDS, 2014.

Dubuisson, F., *Existe-t-il un principe general d'appriopriation de l'information?*, Thèse de doctorat, Université Libre de Bruxelles, 2005.

Durant, I., *Droit des biens*, Bruxelles, Larcier, 2017.

Dworkin, G., *The Theory and Practice of Autonomy*, Cambridge, Cambridge University Press, 1988.

Ehrlich, P., *The Population Bomb*, New York, Ballantine Books, 1968.

Elhauge, E. and Geradin, D., *Global Antitrust Law and Economics*, 3rd ed., St. Paul, Foundation Press, 2018.

Elkin-Koren, N. and Salzberger, E., *The Law and Economics of Intellectual Property in the Digital Age: The Limits of the Analysis*, London, Routledge, 2013.

Ergec, R., *Protection européenne et internationale des droits de l'homme*, Bruxelles, Larcier, 2014.

Feteira, L., *The Interplay Between European and National Competition Law after Regulation 1/2003*, Alphen aan den Rijn, Kluwer, 2016.

Fisher, M., *Fundamentals of Patent Law: Interpretation and Scope of Protection*, Oxford, Hart Publishing, 2007.

Floridi, L., *Information: A Very Short Guide*, Oxford, Oxford University Press, 2010.

Frischmann, B., *Infrastructure: The Social Value of Shared Resources*, Oxford, Oxford University Press, 2012.

Gansey, P., *Thinking about Property: From Antiquity to the Age of Revolution*, Cambridge, Cambridge University Press, 2007.

Geradin, D., Layne-Farrar, A. and Petit, N., *EU Competition Law and Economics*, Oxford, Oxford University Press, 2012.

Graef, I., *EU Competition Law, Data Protection and Online Platforms: Data as Essential Facility*, Alphen aan den Rijn, Kluwer, 2016.

Grotius, H., *De Iure Belli ac Pacis*, 1625.

Halbert, D., *Intellectual Property in the Information Age: The Politics of Expanding Ownership Rights*, Westport, Quorum books, 1999.

Hobbes, T., *Leviathan or The Matter, Forme and Power of a Commonwealth Ecclesiasticall and Civil*, London, George Routledge and Sons, 1651.

Jones, A. and Sufrin, B., *EU Competition Law: Text, Cases, and Materials*, 4th ed., Oxford, Oxford University Press, 2011.

Kitchin, R., *The Data Revolution: Big Data, Open Data, Data Infrastructures & Their Consequences*, London, Sage Publications, 2014.

Kohn, A., *Punished by Rewards: The Trouble with Gold Stars, Incentive Plans, A's, Praise, and Other Bribes*, Boston, Houghton Mifflin, 1999.

Kramer, M., *John Locke and the Origins of Private Property*, Cambridge, Cambridge University Press, 1997.

Locke, J., *Two Treatises of Government: In the Former, The False Principles, and Foundation of Sir Robert Filmer, and His Followers, Are Detected and Overthrown. The Latter Is an Essay Concerning The True Original,*

Extent, and End of Civil Government, London, Awnsham Churchill, 1690.

Mattei, U. and Quarta, A., *The Turning Point in Private Law. Ecology, Technology and the Commons*, Cheltenham, Edward Elgar, 2019.

Mattei, U., Reviglio, E. and Rodotà, S. (eds), *I beni pubblici. Dal governo democratico dell'economia alla riforma del codice civile*, Rome, Accademia Nazionale dei Lincei, 2010.

Mattei, U., Reviglio, E. and Rodotà, S. (eds), *Invertire la rotta. Idee per una riforma della proprietà pubblica*, Bologna, Il Mulino, 2007.

Mayer-Schonberger, V. and Ramge, T., *Re-inventing Capitalism in the Age of Big Data*, New York, Basic Books, 2018.

OECD, *Enhancing Access to and Sharing of Data: Reconciling Risks and Benefits for Data Re-use across Societies*, Paris, OECD Publishing, 2019, available at https://www.oecd.org/publications/enhancing-access-to-and-sharing-of-data-276aaca8-en.htm.

OECD, *Data-Driven Innovation: Big Data for Growth and Well-Being*, Paris, OECD Publications, 2015, available at https://www.oecd.org/sti/data-driven-innovation-9789264229358-en.htm.

Olson, M., *The Logic of Collective Action: Public Goods and the Theory of Groups*, Cambridge, Harvard University Press, 1965.

Ostrom, E., *Governing the Commons: The Evolution of Institutions for Collective Action*, Cambridge, Cambridge University Press, 1990.

Pasquale, F., *The Black Box Society. The Secret Algorithms That Control Money and Information*, Cambridge, Harvard University Press, 2015.

Posner, R., *Economic Analysis of Law*, Boston, Little Brown, 1973.

Schlatter, R., *Private Property: The History of an Idea*, New Brunswick, Rutgers University Press, 1951.

Schumpeter, J., *The Theory of Economic Development: An Inquiry into Profits, Capital, Credit, Interest, and the Business Cycle*, Cambridge, Harvard University Press, 1932.

Smith, A., *An Inquiry into the Nature and Causes of the Wealth of Nations*, London, Longman and Co., 1776.

Stucke, M. and Grunes, A., *Big Data and Competition Policy*, Oxford, Oxford University Press, 2016.

Sulija, G., *Standard Contract Terms in Cross-Border Business Transactions: A Comparative Study from the Perspective of European Union Law*, Frankfurt am Main, Peter Lang, 2011.

Sunstein, C., *Why Societies Need Dissent*, Cambridge, Harvard University Press, 2003.

Turow, J., *The Aisles Have Eyes: How Retailers Track Your Shopping, Strip Your Privacy, and Define Your Power*, New Haven, Yale University Press, 2017.

von Baeyer, H., *Information: The New Language of Science*, Cambridge, Harvard University Press, 2003.

Weinberger, D., *Too Big to Know*, New York, Basic Books, 2011.

Whish, R. and Bailey, D., *Competition Law*, 7th ed., Oxford, Oxford University Press, 2012.

Windscheid, B., *Lehrbuch des Pandektenrechts*, 3 volumes, Frankfurt am Mein, Rutten & Loening, 1891.

Zuboff, S., *The Age of Surveillance Capitalism: The Fight for a Human Future at the New Frontier of Power*, New York, PublicAffairs, 2019.

Book Chapters

Aplin, T., 'Subject Matter', *Research Handbook on the Future of EU Copyright*, E. Derclaye (ed.), Cheltenham, Edward Elgar, 2009, pp. 49-76.

Arrow, K., 'Economic Welfare and the Allocation of Resources for Invention', *The Rate and Direction of Inventive Activity: Economic and Social Factors*, National Bureau of Economic Research (ed.), Princeton, Princeton University Press, 1962, pp. 609-626.

Bart, J., 'Res communes omnium, res nullius, res publicae, res universatis', *Dictionnaire des biens communs*, M. Cornu, F. Orsi et J. Rochfeld (dir.), Paris, Presses universitaires de France, 2017, pp. 1052-1054.

Boy, L., 'Abuse of Market Power: Controlling Dominance or Protecting Competition?', *The Evolution of European Competition Law: Whose Regulation, Which Competition?*, H. Ullrich (ed.), Cheltenham and Northampton, Edward Elgar, 2006, pp. 201-223.

Bygrave, L. and Tosoni, L., 'Article 4(11). Consent', *The EU General Data Protection Regulation (GDPR): A Commentary*, C. Kuner, L. Bygrave and C. Docksey (eds), Oxford, Oxford University Press, 2020, pp. 174-187.

Carrier, M.A., 'Limiting Copyright Through Property', *Concepts of Property in Intellectual Property Law*, H.R. Howe and J. Griffiths (eds), Cambridge, Cambridge University Press, 2013, pp. 185-204.

Chaigneau, A., 'Propriété collective', *Dictionnaire des biens communs*, M. Cornu, F. Orsi et J. Rochfeld (dir.), Paris, Presses universitaires de France, 2017, pp. 954-957.

Chrocziel, P. and Prinz zu Waldeck und Pyrmont, W., 'Introduction', *Intellectual Property and Competition Law*, P. Chrocziel, M. Lorenz and W. Prinz zu Waldeck und Pyrmont (eds), Alphen aan den Rijn, Kluwer, 2016, pp. 1-32.

Cortese, F., 'What Are Common Goods (beni comuni)? Pictures from the Italian Debate', *Revista da Faculdade de Direito da UFMG – N° Especial 2nd Conference Brazil-Italy*, 2017, pp. 121-146.

De Hert, P., 'Artikel 8. Recht op privacy', *Handboek EVRM, Deel 2. Artikelsgewijze commentaar*, J. Vande Lanotte and Y. Haeck (eds), Antwerp, Intersentia, 2004, pp. 705-788.

de Terwangne, C., 'Article 5. Principles Relating to Processing of Personal Data', *The EU General Data Protection Regulation (GDPR): A Commentary*, C. Kuner, L. Bygrave and C. Docksey (eds), Oxford, Oxford University Press, 2020, pp. 309-320.

de Terwangne, C., 'Droit à la vie privée: un droit sur l'information et un droit à l'information', *Law, Norms and Freedoms in Cyberspace / Droit, normes et libertés dans le cybermonde: Liber Amicorum Yves Poullet*, E. Degrave, C. de Terwangne, S. Dusollier et R. Queck (dir.), Bruxelles, Larcier, 2018, pp. 555-579.

de Terwangne, C., 'Définitions clés et champ d'application du RGPD', *Le Règlement general sur la protection des données (RGPD / GDPR) – Analyse approfondie*, C. De Terwangne et K. Rosier (coord.), Bruxelles, Larcier, 2018, pp. 59-84.

Derclaye, E., 'Introduction', *Research Handbook on the Future of EU Copyright*, E. Derclaye (ed.), Cheltenham, Edward Elgar, 2009, pp. 1-11.

Dreier, T., 'How Much "Property" Is There in Intellectual Property? The German Civil Law Perspective', *Concepts of Property in Intellectual Property Law*, H.R. Howe and J. Griffiths (eds), Cambridge, Cambridge University Press, 2013, pp. 116-136.

Dusollier, S., 'Du commun de l'intelligence artificielle', *Penser le droit de la pensée. Mélanges en l'honneur de Michel Vivant*, Paris, Dalloz, 2020, pp. 107-120.

Dusollier, S. et Rochfeld, J., 'Propriété inclusive ou inclusivité', *Dictionnaire des biens communs*, M. Cornu, F. Orsi et J. Rochfeld (dir.), Paris, Presses universitaires de France, 2017, pp. 983-987.

Dusollier, S., 'The Commons as a Reverse Intellectual Property: From Exclusivity to Inclusivity', *Concepts of Property in Intellectual Property Law*, H.R. Howe and J. Griffiths (eds), Cambridge, Cambridge University Press, 2013, pp. 258-281.

Emerich, Y., 'Propriété exclusive ou exclusivité', *Dictionnaire des biens communs*, M. Cornu, F. Orsi et J. Rochfeld (dir.), Paris, Presses universitaires de France, 2017, pp. 979-983.

Evans, D. and Schmalensee, R., 'Some Economic Aspects of Antitrust Analysis in Dynamically Competitive Industries', *Innovation Policy and the Economy*, Volume 2, A. Jaffe, J. Lerner and S. Stern (eds), Cambridge, MIT Press, 2002, pp. 1-49.

Flanagan, A. and Montagnani, M., 'Intellectual Property Law: Economic and Social Justice Perspectives: Introduction', *Intellectual Property Law: Economic and Social Justice Perspectives*, A. Flanagan and M. Montagnani (eds), Cheltenham, Edward Elgar, 2010, pp. x-xviii.

Gutwirth, S. et Gonzalez Fuster, G., 'L'éternel retour de la propriété des données: de l'insistance d'un mot d'ordre', *Law, norms and freedom in cyberspace – Liber Amicorum Yves Poullet*, E. Degrave, C. de Terwangne, S. Dusollier and R. Queck (ed.), Bruxelles, Larcier, 2018, pp. 117-140.

Haucap, J., 'A German Approach to Antitrust for Digital Platforms', *Digital Platforms and Concentration, Second Annual Antitrust and Competition Conference*, S. Eyler-Driscoll, A. Schechter and C. Patiño (eds), 2018, available at https://promarket.org/wp-content/uploads/2018/04/Digital-Platforms-and-Concentration.pdf, pp. 8-13.

Helfer, L., 'Mapping the Interface Between Human Rights and Intellectual Property', *Research Handbook on Human Rights and Intellectual Property*, C. Geiger (ed.), Cheltenham, Edward Elgar, 2015, pp. 6-15.

Hugenholtz, B., 'Data Property in the System of Intellectual Property Law: Welcome Guest or Misfit?', *Trading Data in the Digital Economy: Legal Concepts and Tools*, S. Lohsse, R. Schulze and D. Staudenmayer (eds), Baden-Baden, Nomos, 2017, pp. 75-99.

Kerber, W., 'Rights on Data: The EU Communication "Building a European Data Economy" from an Economic Perspective', *Trading Data in the Digital Economy: Legal Concepts and Tools*, S. Lohsse, R. Schulze and D. Staudenmayer (eds), Baden-Baden, Nomos, 2017, pp. 109-133.

Khan, L., 'What Makes Tech Platforms So Powerful?', *Digital Platforms and Concentration, Second Annual Antitrust and Competition Conference*, S. Eyler-Driscoll, A. Schechter and C. Patiño (eds), 2018, available at https://promarket.org/wp-content/uploads/2018/04/Digital-Platforms-and-Concentration.pdf, p. 14-17.

Knockaert, M. and Tombal, T., 'Quels droits sur les données?', *Actualites en droit du numerique*, H. Jacquemin and B. Michaux (eds), Limal, Anthémis, 2019, pp. 53-97.

Kosta, E., 'Article 7. Conditions for Consent', *The EU General Data Protection Regulation (GDPR): A Commentary*, C. Kuner, L. Bygrave and C. Docksey (eds), Oxford, Oxford University Press, 2020, pp. 345-354.

Lametti, D., 'The Concept of the Anticommons: Useful, or Ubiquitous and Unnecessary?', *Concepts of Property in Intellectual Property Law*, H.R. Howe and J. Griffiths (eds), Cambridge, Cambridge University Press, 2013, pp. 232-257.

Leclercq, P., 'Essai sur le statut juridique des informations', *Les flux transfrontières de données: vers une économie internationale de l'information?*, A. Madec (ed.), Paris, La Documentation française, 1982, pp. 119-150.

Lomfeld, B., 'Fondements de la propriété (Théories de la propriété)', *Dictionnaire des biens communs*, M. Cornu, F. Orsi et J. Rochfeld (dir.), Paris, Presses universitaires de France, 2017, pp. 566-569.

Martinelli, S., 'Sharing Data and Privacy in the Platform Economy: The Right to Data Portability and "Porting Rights"', *Regulating New Technologies in Uncertain Times*, L. Reins (ed.), The Hague, T.M.C. Asser Press, 2019, pp. 133-152.

Morando, F., 'Copyright Default Rule: Reconciling Efficiency and Fairness', *Intellectual Property Law: Economic and Social Justice Perspectives*, A. Flanagan and M. Montagnani (eds), Cheltenham, Edward Elgar, 2010, pp. 24-43.

Polčák, R., 'Article 12. Transparent Information, Communication and Modalities for the Exercise of the Rights of the Data Subject', *The EU General Data Protection Regulation (GDPR): A Commentary*, C. Kuner, L. Bygrave and C. Docksey (eds), Oxford, Oxford University Press, 2020, pp. 398-412.

Pothier, R.J., 'Traité de la propriété', *Œuvres de R.-J. Pothier*, D. Ainé (ed.), tome V, Bruxelles, Tarlier, 1831.

Ramello, G., 'Intellectual Property, Social Justice and Economic Efficiency: Insights from Law and Economics', *Intellectual Property Law: Economic and Social Justice Perspectives*, A. Flanagan and M. Montagnani (eds), Cheltenham, Edward Elgar, 2010, pp. 1-23.

Régibeau, P. and Rockett, K., 'The Relationship Between Intellectual Property Law and Competition Law: An Economic Approach', *The Interface Between Intellectual Property Rights and Competition Policy*, S. Anderman (ed.), Cambridge, Cambridge University Press, 2007, pp. 505-552.

Rouvroy, A., '*Homo juridicus* est-il soluble dans les données?', *Law, Norms and Freedoms in Cyberspace / Droit, normes et libertés dans le cybermonde: Liber Amicorum Yves Poullet*, E. Degrave, C. de Terwangne, S. Dusollier et R. Queck (dir.), Bruxelles, Larcier, 2018, pp. 417-444.

Rouvroy, A. and Poullet, Y., 'The Right to Informational Self-Determination and the Value of Self-Development: Reassessing the Importance of Privacy for Democracy', *Reinventing Data Protection: Proceedings of the International Conference (Brussels, 12-13 October 2007)*, Dordrecht, Springer, 2009, pp. 45-76.

Salord, G., 'Propriété commune', *Dictionnaire des biens communs*, M. Cornu, F. Orsi et J. Rochfeld (dir.), Paris, Presses universitaires de France, 2017, pp. 960-964.

Sandeen, S., 'The Value of Irrationality in the IP Equation', *Intellectual Property Law: Economic and Social Justice Perspectives*, A. Flanagan and M. Montagnani (eds), Cheltenham, Edward Elgar, 2010, pp. 44-65.

Strowel, A., 'Big Data and Data Appropriation in the EU', Research Handbook on Intellectual Property and Digital Technologies*, T. Aplin (ed.),* Camberley, Edward Elgar, 2020, pp. 107-135.

Tombal, T., 'The GDPR: A Shield to a Competition Authority's Data Sharing Remedy?', *Deep Diving into Data Protection*, J. Herveg (coord.), Bruxelles, Larcier, 2021, pp. 67-94.

Tombal, T., 'Les droits de la personne concernée dans le RGPD', *Le Règlement general sur la protection des données (RGPD / GDPR) – Analyse approfondie*, C. De Terwangne et K. Rosier (coord.), Bruxelles, Larcier, 2018, pp. 407-558.

Van Overwalle, G., 'Inventing Inclusive Patents: From Old to New Open Innovation', *Kritika: Essays on Intellectual Property*, Volume 1, P. Drahos, G. Ghidini and H. Ullrich (eds), Cheltenham, Edward Elgar, 2015, pp. 206-277.

Voorhoof, D., 'Freedom of Expression and the Right to Information: Implications for Copyright', *Research Handbook on Human Rights and Intellectual Property*, C. Geiger (ed.), Cheltenham, Edward Elgar, 2015, pp. 331-353.

Wendehorst, C., 'Of Elephants in the Room and Paper Tigers: How to Reconcile Data Protection and the Data Economy', *Trading Data in the Digital Economy: Legal Concepts and Tools*, S. Lohsse, R. Schulze and D. Staudenmayer (eds), Baden-Baden, Nomos, 2017, pp. 327-355.

Zech, H., 'Data as Tradeable Commodity', *European Contract Law and the Digital Single Market*, A. De Franceschi (ed.), Cambridge, Intersentia, 2016, pp. 51-79.

Papers in Scientific Journals

Abrahamson, Z., 'Essential Data', *The Yale Law Journal*, 2014, Vol. 124(3), pp. 867-881.

Argenton, C. and Prüfer, J., 'Search Engine Competition with Network Externalities', *Journal of Competition Law and Economics*, 2012, Vol. 8(1), pp. 73-105.

Auf'mkolk, H., 'The "Feedback Effect" of Applying EU Competition Law to Regulated Industries: Doctrinal Contamination in the Case of Margin Squeeze', *Journal of European Competition Law & Practice*, 2012, Vol. 3(2), pp. 149-162.

Azzopardi, A., 'No Abuse Is an Island: The Case of Margin Squeeze', *European Competition Journal*, 2017, Vol. 13(2-3), pp. 228-248.

Bagnoli, V., 'Digital Platforms as Public Utilities', *International Review of Intellectual Property and Competition Law*, 2020, Vol. 51(8), pp. 903-905.

Ben-Shahar, O., 'Data Pollution', *Journal of Legal Analysis*, 2019, Vol. 11, pp. 104-159.

Besen, S. and Verveer, P., 'Competition and Data: Potential Remedies', *Wake Forest Journal of Business and Intellectual Property Law*, 2021, Vol. 21(2), pp. 103-143.

Botta, M. and Wiedemann K., 'The Interaction of EU Competition, Consumer, and Data Protection Law in the Digital Economy: The Regulatory Dilemma in the Facebook Odyssey', *Antitrust Bulletin,* 2019, Vol. 64(3), pp. 428-446.

Bower J. and Christensen, C., 'Disruptive Technologies: Catching the Wave', *Harvard Business Review*, 1995, Vol. 73(1), pp. 43-53.

Cabral, L., et al., 'The EU Digital Markets Act: A Report from a Panel of Economic Experts', *EU Science Hub*, 2021, available at https://ec.europa.eu/jrc/en/publication/eu-digital-markets-act.

Calo, R., 'Digital Market Manipulation', *George Washington Law Review*, 2014, Vol. 82(4), pp. 995-1051.

Campbell, J., Goldfarb, A. and Tucker, C. 'Privacy Regulation and Market Structure', *Journal of Economics & Management Strategy*, 2015, Vol. 24(1), pp. 47-73.

Carbonell, I., 'The Ethics of Big Data in Big Agriculture', *Internet Policy Review*, 2016, Vol. 5(1), pp. 1-13, available at https://policyreview.info/articles/analysis/ethics-big-data-big-agriculture.

Colangelo, G. and Maggiolino, M., 'Big Data as Misleading Facilities', *European Competition Journal*, 2017, Vol. 2-3(13), pp. 249-281.

Dawes, R.M., 'The Commons Dilemma Game: An N-Person Mixed Motive Game with a Dominating Strategy for Defection', *Oregon Research Institute Research Bulletin*, 1973, Vol. 13(2), pp. 1-12.

De Bot, D., 'De uitvoering van de algemene verordening gegevensbescherming – enkele bemerkingen bij de Belgische context', *Tijdschrift voor Wetgeving*, 2016/3, pp. 218-234.

De Bure, F. and Bary, L., 'Disruptive Innovation and Merger Remedies: How to Predict the Unpredictable?', *Concurrences*, 2017, No. 3, Art. No. 84407.

de la Mano, M. and Padilla, J., 'Big Tech Banking', *Journal of Competition Law & Economics*, 2018, Vol. 14(4), pp. 494-526.

de Montjoye, Y.-A., et al., 'Comment: On the Privacy-Conscientious Use of Mobile Phone Data', *Scientific Data*, 2018, Issue 5, available at https://www.nature.com/articles/sdata2018286.

de Streel, A. and Larouche, P., 'The European Digital Markets Act Proposal: How to Improve a Regulatory Revolution', *Concurrences*, 2021, No. 2, pp. 46-63.

Deci, E., Koestner, R. and Ryan, R., 'A Meta-Analytic Review of Experiments Examining the Effects of Extrinsic Rewards on Intrinsic Motivation', *Psychological Bulletin*, 1999, Vol. 125(6), pp. 627-668.

Delacroix, S. and Lawrence, N., 'Bottom-Up Data Trusts: Disturbing the "One Size Fits All" Approach to Data Governance', *International Data Privacy Law*, November 2019, Vol. 9(4), pp. 236-252.

Derclaye, E., 'Databases Sui Generis Right: Should I Adopt the Spin Off Theory?', *European Intellectual Property Review*, 2004, Vol. 26(9), pp. 402-413.

Diker Vanberg, A. and Ünver, M., 'The Right to Data Portability in the GDPR and EU Competition Law: Odd Couple or Dynamic Duo?', *European Journal of Law and Technology*, 2017, Vol. 8(1), pp. 1-22.

Ducuing, C., 'Data as Infrastructure? A Study of Data Sharing Legal Regimes', *Competition and Regulation in Network Industries*, Vol. 21(2), pp. 124-142.

Eisenmann, T., Parker, G. and Van Alstyne, M., 'Platform Envelopment', *Strategic Management Journal*, 2011, Vol. 32(12), pp. 1270-1285.

Engels, B., 'Data Portability Among Online Platforms', *Internet Policy Review*, 2016, Vol. 5(2), available at https://policyreview.info/articles/analysis/data-portability-among-online-platforms.

Ezrachi, A. and Robertson, V., 'Competition, Market Power and Third-Party Tracking', *World Competition: Law and Economics Review*, 2019, Vol. 42(1), pp. 5-19.

Fairfield, J.A. and Engel, C., 'Privacy as a Public Good', *Duke Law Journal*, 2015, Vol. 65(3), pp. 385-457.

Feeny, D., Berkes, F., McCay, B. and Acheson, J., 'The Tragedy of the Commons. Twenty-Two Years Later', *Human Ecology*, 1990, Vol. 18(1), pp. 1-19.

Frischmann, B., Marciano, A. and Ramello, G., 'Retrospectives: Tragedy of the Commons After 50 Years', *Journal of Economic Perspectives*, 2019, Vol. 33(4), pp. 211-228.

Gal, M. and Aviv, O., 'The Competitive Effects of the GDPR', *Journal of Competition Law and Economics*, September 2020, Vol. 16(3), pp. 349-391.

Gal, M. and Rubinfeld, D. 'Data Standardization', *New York University Law Review*, 2019, Vol. 94(4), pp. 737-770.

Gaullier, F., 'Le principe de finalité dans le RGPD: beaucoup d'ancien et un peu de nouveau', *Communication commerce électronique*, 2018/4, pp. 45-52.

Graef, I., 'Paving the Way Forward for Data Governance: A Story of Checks and Balances', *Technology and Regulation,* Special issue: Governing Data as a Resource, 2020, pp. 24-28.

Graef, I., 'Rethinking the Essential Facilities Doctrine for the EU Digital Economy', *Revue juridique Thémis de l'Université de Montréal*, 2019, Vol. 53, p. 33-72.

Graef, I., 'Differentiated Treatment in Platform-to-Business Relations: EU Competition Law and Economic Dependence', *Yearbook of European Law*, 2019, Vol. 38, pp. 448–499.

Graef, I., 'Market Definition and Market Power in Data: The Case of Online Platforms', *World Competition Law and Economics Review*, 2015, Vol. 38(4), pp. 473-506.

Graef, I. and Van Berlo, S., 'Towards Smarter Regulation in the Areas of Competition, Data Protection and Consumer Law: Why Greater Power Should Come with Greater Responsibility', *European Journal of Risk Regulation*, November 2020, available at https://doi.org/10.1017/err.2020.92.

Graef, I., Husovec, M. and Purtova, N., 'Data Portability and Data Control: Lessons for an Emerging Concept in EU Law', *German Law Journal*, 2018, Vol. 19(6), pp. 1359-1398.

Graef, I., Wahyuningtyas, S. and Valcke, P., 'Assessing Data Access Issues in Online Platforms', *Telecommunications Policy*, 2015, Vol. 39, pp. 375-387.

Graham, C. and Morton, J., 'Latest Developments in Standards, Patents and FRAND Licensing', *European Intellectual Property Review*, 2014, Vol. 36(11), pp. 700-706.

Hahn, I., 'Purpose Limitation in the Time of Data Power: Is There a Way Forward?', *European Data Protection Law Review*, 2021, Vol. 7(1), pp. 31-44.

Hardin, G., 'The Tragedy of the Commons', *Science*, December 1968, Vol. 162(3859), pp. 1243-1248.

Heller, M., 'The Tragedy of the Anticommons: Property in the Transition from Marx to Markets', *Harvard Law Review*, January 1998, Vol. 111(3), pp. 621-688.

Hoeren, T., 'A New Approach to Data Property?', *Tijdschrift voor Auteurs-, Media- en Informatierecht*, 2018/2, pp. 58-60.

Hoeren, T. and Bitter, P., 'Data Ownership Is Dead: Long Live Data Ownership', *European Intellectual Property Review,* 2018, 40(6), pp. 347-348.

Këllezi, P., 'Data Protection and Competition Law: Non-compliance as Abuse of Dominant Position', *Sui-generis*, 2019, pp. 343-359.

Kerber, W., 'Data Governance in Connected Cars: The Problem of Access to In-Vehicle Data', *Journal of Intellectual Property, Information Technology and E-Commerce Law*, 2018, Vol. 9(3), pp. 310-331.

Kerber, W., 'Governance of Data: Exclusive Property vs. Access', *International Review of Intellectual Property and Competition Law*, 2016, Vol. 47(7), pp. 759-762.

Kerber, W. and Gill, D., 'Access to Data in Connected Cars and the Recent Reform of the Motor Vehicle Type Approval Regulation', *Journal of Intellectual Property, Information Technology and E-Commerce Law*, 2019, Vol. 10(2), pp. 244-256.

Kim, D., 'No One's Ownership as the Status Quo and a Possible Way Forward: A Note on the Public Consultation on Building a European Data Economy', *Journal of Intellectual Property Law & Practice*, 2018, Vol. 13(2), pp. 154-165.

Kosta, E., 'Construing the Meaning of "Opt-Out": An Analysis of the European, U.K. and German Data Protection Legislation', *European Data Protection Law Review*, 2015, Vol. 1, pp. 16-31.

Krämer, J., Schnurr, D. and Wohlfarth, M., 'Winners, Losers, and Facebook: The Role of Social Logins in the Online Advertising Ecosystem', *Management Science*, 2019, Vol. 65(4), pp. 1678-1699.

Larouche, P., 'The European Microsoft Case at the Crossroads of Competition Policy and Innovation', *Antitrust Law Journal*, 2008, Vol. 75(3), pp. 933-964.

Ledger, M. and Tombal, T., 'Le droit à la portabilité dans les textes européens: droits distincts ou mécanisme multi-facettes?', *R.D.T.I.*, 2018/3, n°72, pp. 25-44.

Lundqvist, B., 'Competition and Data Pools', *Journal of European Consumer and Market Law*, 2018, Vol. 7(4), pp. 146-154.

MacCarthy, M., 'New Directions in Privacy: Disclosure, Unfairness and Externalities', *Journal of Law and Policy for the Information Society*, 2011, Vol. 6, pp. 425-512.

Madison, M., 'Tools for Data Governance', *Technology and Regulation*, 2020, Vol. 1, pp. 29-43.

Martens, B., et al., 'Business to Business Data Sharing: An Economic and Legal Analysis', *EU Science Hub*, 2020, available at https://ssrn.com/abstract=3658100.

Masson, A., 'Creation of Database or Creation of Data: Crucial Choices in the Matter of Database Protection', *European Intellectual Property Review*, 2006, Vol. 28(5), pp. 261-267.

Mayer-Schönberger, V. and Padova, Y., 'Regime Change? Enabling Big Data Through Europe's New Data Protection Regulation', C*olumbia Science & Technology Law Review*, 2016, Vol. XVII, pp. 315-335.

Merrill, T., 'Property and the Right to Exclude', *Nebraska Law Review*, 1998, Vol. 77(4), pp. 730-755.

Michaux, B., 'La Cour de justice favorise-t-elle l'appropriation des données par celui qui les a traitées?', note sous C.J.U.E., 29 octobre 2015, C-490/14, *Auteurs et Média*, 2017, Issue 1, pp. 28-34.

Miller, A. and Tucker, C., 'Health Information Exchange, System Size and Information Silos', *Journal of Health Economics*, 2014, Vol. 33(2), pp. 28-42.

Mousseron, J.-M. et Vivant, M., 'Les mécanismes de réservation et leur dalectique: Le "terrain" occupé par le droit', *Semaine Juridique, Cahiers de Droit de l'Entreprise*, 1989/1, pp. 2-4.

Ohm, P., 'Broken Promises of Privacy: Responding to the Surprising Failure of Anonymization', *UCLA Law Review*, 2010, Vol. 57, pp. 1701-1777.

Picht, P., 'Towards an Access Regime for Mobility Data', *International Review of Intellectual Property and Competition Law*, 2020, Vol. 51(8), pp. 940-976.

Purtova, N., 'The Law of Everything: Broad Concept of Personal Data and Future of EU Data Protection Law', *Law, Innovation and Technology*, 2018, Vol. 10(1), pp. 40-81.

Richter, H. and Slowinski, P. 'The Data Sharing Economy: On the Emergence of New Intermediaries', *International Review of Intellectual Property and Competition Law*, 2019, Vol. 50(1), pp. 4-29.

Robertson, V., 'Excessive Data Collection: Privacy Considerations and Abuse of Dominance in the Era of Big Data', *Common Market Law Review*, 2020, Vol. 57, pp. 161-189.

Rocher, L., Hendrickx, J. and de Montjoye, Y.-A., 'Estimating the Success of Re-identifications in Incomplete Datasets Using Generative Models', *Nature Communications*, 2019, Vol. 10(3069), available at https://www.nature.com/articles/s41467-019-10933-3.

Rouvroy, A. et Berns, T., 'Gouvernementalité algorithmique et perspectives d'émancipation. Le disparate comme condition d'individuation par la relation?', *Réseaux*, 2013, Vol. 177(1), pp. 163-196.

Rubinfeld, D. and Gal, M., 'Access Barriers to Big Data', *Arizona Law Review*, 2017, Vol. 59, pp. 339-381.

Shkabatur, J., 'The Global Commons of Data', *Stanford Technology Law Review*, 2019, Vol. 22, pp. 354-411.

Spina Ali, G., 'Intellectual Property and Human Rights: A Taxonomy of Their Interactions', *International Review of Intellectual Property and Competition Law*, 2020, Vol. 51(4), pp. 411-445.

Somaini, L., 'Regulating the Dynamic Concept of Non-personal Data in the EU: From Ownership to Portability', *European Data Protection Law Review*, 2020/1, pp. 84-93.

Somaini, L., 'The Right to Data Portability and User Control: Ambitions and Limitations', *MediaLaws – Rivista dir. media*, 2018/3, pp. 164-190.

Stern, R., 'What Are Reasonable and Non-discriminatory Terms for Licensing a Standard-Essential Patent?', *European Intellectual Property Review*, 2015, Vol. 37(9), pp. 549-557.

Sweeney, L., 'Weaving Technology and Policy Together to Maintain Confidentiality', *Journal of Law, Medicine & Ethics*, 1997, Vol. 25(2 & 3), pp. 98-110.

Swire, P. and Lagos, Y., 'Why the Right to Data Portability Likely Reduces Consumer Welfare: Antitrust and Privacy Critique', *Maryland Law Review*, 2013, Vol. 72/3, pp. 335-380.

Thomas, L. and Leiponen, A., 'Big Data Commercialization', *IEEE Engineering Management Review,* 2016, Vol. 44(2), pp. 74-90.

Tombal, T., 'Economic Dependence and Data Access', *International Review of Intellectual Property and Competition Law*, 2020, Vol. 51(1), pp. 70-98.

Waldron, J., 'From Authors to Copiers: Individual Rights and Social Values in Intellectual Property', *Chicago-Kent Law Review*, 1993, Vol. 68, pp. 841-887.

Weibe, A., 'Protection of Industrial Data – a New Property Right for the Digital Economy?', *Journal of Intellectual Property Law & Practice*, 2017, Vol. 12(1), pp. 62-71.

Wiedemann, K., 'A Matter of Choice: The German Federal Supreme Court's Interim Decision in the Abuse-of-Dominance Proceedings Bundeskartellamt v. Facebook (Case KVR 69/19)', *International Review of Intellectual Property and Competition Law*, 2020, Vol. 51(9), pp. 1168-1181.

Wils, W., 'The Obligation for the Competition Authorities of the EU Member States to Apply EU Antitrust Law and the Facebook Decision of the Bundeskartellamt', *Concurrences*, 2019, No. 3, pp. 58-66.

Zarsky, T., 'Incompatible: The GDPR in the Age of Big Data', *Seton Hall Law Review*, 2017, Vol. 47, No. 4(2), pp. 995-1020.

Zarsky, T., 'The Privacy–Innovation Conundrum', *Lewis & Clark Law Review*, 2015, Vol. 19(1), pp. 115-168.

Zelany, M., 'Management Support Systems: Towards Integrated Knowledge Management', *Human Systems Management*, 1987, Vol. 7, pp. 59-70.

Conference Papers

Hugenholtz, B., 'Program Schedules, Event Data and Telephone Subscriber Listings under the Database Directive – The "Spin-Off" Doctrine in the Netherlands and Elsewhere in Europe', *Paper Presented at 11th Annual Conference on International Intellectual Property Law and Policy, Fordham University School of Law, New York, April 14-25*, 2003, available at https://www.ivir.nl/publicaties/download/spinofffordham.pdf.

Lee, S. and Schißler, J., 'Platform Dependence and Exploitation', *Paper Presented at the 14th ASCOLA Conference*, June 2019, available at https://ssrn.com/abstract=3403002.

Nouwens, M., et al., 'Dark Patterns after the GDPR: Scraping Consent Pop-Ups and Demonstrating Their Influence', *CHI Conference on Human Factors in Computing Systems*, April 2020, available at https://arxiv.org/abs/2001.02479.

Okoyomon, E., et al., 'On the Ridiculousness of Notice and Consent: Contradictions in App Privacy Policies', *The Workshop on Technology and Consumer Protection*, 2019, available at https://blues.cs.berkeley.edu/blog/2019/05/10/on-the-ridiculousness-of-notice-and-consent-contradictions-in-app-privacy-policies-conpro-19/.

Vezzoso, S., 'Competition Policy in Transition: Exploring Data Portability's Roles', *15th ASCOLA (Virtual) Conference*, June 2020, available at https://ssrn.com/abstract=3634736.

Research Papers

Acemoğlu, D., et al., 'Too Much Data: Prices and Inefficiencies in Data Markets', *NBER Working Paper No. 26296*, 2019, available at https://www.nber.org/system/files/working_papers/w26296/w26296.pdf.

Acquisti, A., Taylor, C. and Wagman, L., 'The Economics of Privacy', *Sloan Foundation Economics Research Paper No. 2580411*, 8 March 2016, available at https://ssrn.com/abstract=2580411.

Alexiadis, P. and de Streel, A., 'Designing an EU Intervention Standard for Digital Platforms', *Robert Schuman Centre for Advanced Studies Research Paper No. 2020/14*, 26 February 2020, available at https://ssrn.com/abstract=3544694.

Bakhoum, M., 'Abuse Without Dominance in Competition Law: Abuse of Economic Dependence and Its Interface with Abuse of Dominance', *Max Planck Institute for Innovation & Competition Research Paper No. 15-15*, 2015, available at https://ssrn.com/abstract=27038094.

Borgogno, O. and Colangelo, G., 'Consumer Inertia and Competition-Sensitive Data Governance: The Case of Open Banking', 3 January 2020, available at SSRN: https://ssrn.com/abstract=3513514.

Bougette, P., Budzinski, O. and Marty, F., 'Exploitative Abuse and Abuse of Economic Dependence: What Can We Learn from an Industrial Organization Approach?', *Ilmenau Economics Discussion Papers No. 119*, 2018, available at http://hdl.handle.net/10419/191022.

Clifford, D., Graef, I. and Valcke, P. 'Pre-formulated Declarations of Data Subject Consent – Citizen-Consumer Empowerment and the Alignment of Data, Consumer and Competition Law Protections', *CiTiP Working Paper 33/2017*, February 2018, available at https://ssrn.com/abstract=3126706.

Colangelo, G. and Borgogno, O. 'Data, Innovation and Transatlantic Competition in Finance: The Case of the Access to Account Rule', *Stanford-Vienna European Union Law Working Paper No. 35*, 2018, available at https://law.stanford.edu/publications/no-35-data-innovation-and-transatlantic-competition-in-finance-the-case-of-the-access-to-account-rule/.

Colangelo, G. and Maggiolino, M., 'Data Protection in Attention Markets: Protecting Privacy Through Competition?', *Bocconi Legal Studies Research Paper No. 2945085*, 2 April 2017, available at https://ssrn.com/abstract=2945085.

Condorelli, D. and Padilla, J., 'Harnessing Platform Envelopment Through Privacy Policy Tying', December 2019, available at https://ssrn.com/abstract=3504025.

de Streel, A. 'Online Intermediation Platforms and Fairness: An Assessment of the Recent Commission Proposal', September 2018, available at https://papers.ssrn.com/sol3/papers.cfm?abstract_id=3248723.

de Streel, A. and Larouche, P., 'Disruptive Innovation and Competition Policy Enforcement', *OECD Working Paper DAF/COMP/GF(2015)7*, 2015, available at https://ssrn.com/abstract=2678890.

Di Porto, F. and Ghidini, G., '"I Access Your Data You Access Mine". Setting a Reciprocity Clause for the "Access to Account Rule" in the Payment Services Market', 2019, available at https://ssrn.com/abstract=3407294.

Drexl, J., 'Legal Challenges of the Changing Role of Personal and Non-Personal Data in the Data Economy', *Max Planck Institute for Innovation & Competition Research Paper No. 18-23*, 31 October 2018, available at https://ssrn.com/abstract=3274519.

Drexl, J., et al., 'Position Statement of the Max Planck Institute for Innovation and Competition of 26 April 2017 on the European Commission's "Public Consultation on Building the European Data Economy"', *Max Planck Institute for Innovation and Competition Research Paper No. 17-08*, 2017, available at https://ssrn.com/abstract=2959924.

Drexl, J., 'Designing Competitive Markets for Industrial Data – Between Propertisation and Access', *Max Planck Institute for Innovation & Competition Research Paper No. 16-13*, 31 October 2016, available at https://ssrn.com/abstract=2862975.

Duch-Brown, N., Martens, B. and Mueller-Langer, F., 'The Economics of Ownership, Access and Trade in Digital Data', *Digital Economy Working Paper 2016-10*, JRC Technical Reports, 2016, available at https://papers.ssrn.com/sol3/papers.cfm?abstract_id=2914144.

Ennis, S. and Fletcher, A., 'Developing International Perspectives on Digital Competition Policy', 31 March 2020, available at https://ssrn.com/abstract=3565491.

Fast, F., Schnurr, D. and Wohlfarth, M., 'Data-Driven Market Power: An Overview of Economic Benefits and Competitive Advantages from Big Data Use', July 2019, available at https://ssrn.com/abstract=3427087.

Geradin, D., 'Access to In-Vehicle Data by Third-Party Service Providers: Is There a Market Failure and, If So, How Should it Be Addressed?', January 2020, available at https://ssrn.com/abstract=3545817.

Geradin, D., 'Ten Years of DG Competition Effort to Provide Guidance on the Application of Competition Rules to the Licensing of Standard-Essential Patents: Where Do We Stand?', 21 January 2013, available at https://ssrn.com/abstract=2204359.

Geradin, D., 'Refusal to Supply and Margin Squeeze: A Discussion of Why the "Telefonica Exceptions" Are Wrong', *TILEC Discussion Paper No. 2011-009*, 2011, available at https://ssrn.com/abstract=1762687.

Geradin, D., Karanikioti, T. and Katsifis, D., 'GDPR Myopia: How a Well-Intended Regulation Ended Up Favoring Google in Ad Tech', *TILEC Discussion Paper DP 2020-012*, May 2020, available at https://ssrn.com/abstract=3598130.

Graef, I., Tombal, T. and de Streel, A., 'Limits and Enablers of Data Sharing: An Analytical Framework for EU Competition, Data Protection and Consumer Law', *TILEC Discussion Paper DP 2019-005*, November 2019, available at https://ssrn.com/abstract=2956308.

Graef, I., Husovec, M. and van den Boom, J., 'Spill-Overs in Data Governance: The Relationship Between the GDPR's Right to Data Portability and EU Sector-Specific Data Access Regimes', *TILEC Discussion Paper DP 2019-024*, 8 April 2019, available at https://ssrn.com/abstract=3369509.

Graef, I., Gellert, R. and Husovec, M., 'Towards a Holistic Regulatory Approach for the European Data Economy: Why the Illusive Notion of Non-personal Data Is Counterproductive to Data Innovation', *TILEC Discussion Paper No. 2018-028*, 27 September 2018, available at http://ssrn.com/abstract=3256189.

Hoffmann, J. and Johannsen, G., 'EU-Merger Control & Big Data: On Data-Specific Theories of Harm and Remedies', *Max Planck Institute for Innovation and Competition Research Paper No. 19-05*, 31 May 2019, available at https://ssrn.com/abstract=3364792.

Ibáñez Colomo, P., 'Indispensability and Abuse of Dominance: From Commercial Solvents to Slovak Telekom and Google Shopping', 11 December 2019, available at https://ssrn.com/abstract=3502519.

Jia, J., Zhe Jin, G. and Wagman, L., 'The Short-Run Effects of GDPR on Technology Venture Investment', November 2019, available at https://papers.ssrn.com/abstract=32789128.

Johnson, G. and Shriver, S., 'Privacy & Market Concentration: Intended & Unintended Consequences of the GDPR', March 2020, available at https://ssrn.com/abstract=3477686.

Kathuria, V. and Globocnik, J., 'Exclusionary Conduct in Data-Driven Markets: Limitations of Data Sharing Remedy', *Max Planck Institute for Innovation and Competition Research Paper No. 19-04*, 2019, available at https://ssrn.com/abstract=3337524.

Kerber, W., 'From (Horizontal and Sectoral) Data Access Solutions Towards Data Governance Systems', *Joint Discussion Paper Series in Economics No. 40-2020*, 26 August 2020, available at https://ssrn.com/abstract=3681263.

Kerber, W., 'Updating Competition Policy for the Digital Economy? An Analysis of Recent Reports in Germany, UK, EU, and Australia', September 2019, available at https://ssrn.com/abstract=3469624.

Kerber, W., 'Data-Sharing in IoT Ecosystems from a Competition Law Perspective: The Example of Connected Cars', 26 August 2019, available at https://ssrn.com/abstract=3445422.

Kerber, W., 'Digital Markets, Data, and Privacy: Competition Law, Consumer Law, and Data Protection', *MAGKS Joint Discussion Paper Series in Economics No. 14-2016*, February 2016, available at https://www.econstor.eu/bitstream/10419/144679/1/850599016.pdf.

Kerber, W. and Frank, J., 'Data Governance Regimes in the Digital Economy: The Example of Connected Cars', 3 November 2017, available at https://ssrn.com/abstract=3064794.

Lerner, A., 'The Role of "Big Data" in Online Platform Competition', 26 August 2014, available at SSRN http://dx.doi.org/10.2139/ssrn.2482780.

Lundqvist, B., 'Regulating Competition and Property in the Digital Economy – The Interface Between Data, Privacy, Intellectual Property, Fairness and Competition Law', *Stockholm Faculty of Law Research Paper Series No. 54*, 2018, available at https://ssrn.com/abstract=3103870.

Madison, M., Strandburg, K. and Frischmann, B., 'Knowledge Commons', *Legal Studies Research Paper Series: Working Paper No. 2018-39*, December 2018, available at http://ssrn.com/abstract=3300348.

Martens, B., 'An Economic Perspective on Data and Platform Market Power', *JRC Digital Economy Working Paper 2020-09*, February 2021, available at https://www.researchgate.net/publication/349179464.

Muralidhar, K., Sarathy, R. and Li, H., '"To Share or Not to Share. That Is Not the Question" – A Privacy Preserving Procedure for Sharing Linked Data', 3 July 2014, https://ssrn.com/abstract=2462152.

Nicholas, G., 'Taking It With You: Platform Barriers to Entry and the Limits of Data Portability', 6 March 2020, available at https://ssrn.com/abstract=3550870.

Nicholas, G. and Weinberg, M., 'Data Portability and Platform Competition: Is User Data Exported from Facebook Actually Useful to Competitors?', 2019, available at https://www.law.nyu.edu/centers/engelberg/pubs/2019-11-06-Data-Portability-And-Platform-Competition.

Parker, G., Petropoulos, G. and Van Alstyne, M., 'Digital Platforms and Antitrust', May 2020, available at https://ssrn.com/abstract=3608397.

Priego, L., Osimo, D. and Wareham, J., 'Data Sharing Practices in Big Data Ecosystems', *ESADE Working Paper 273*, 2019, available at https://ssrn.com/abstract=3355696.

Prüfer, J. and Schottmüller, C., 'Competing with Big Data', *TILEC Discussion Paper No. 2017-006 and CentER Discussion Paper No. 2017-007*, February 2017, available at https://pure.uvt.nl/ws/portalfiles/portal/15514029/2017_007.pdf.

Ranchordás, S. and De Gregorio, G., 'Breaking Down Information Silos with Big Data: A Legal Analysis of Data Sharing', *University of Groningen Faculty of Law Research Paper Series No. 44/2019*, September 2019, available at https://ssrn.com/abstract=3466313.

Richter, H., 'The Law and Policy of Government Access to Private Sector Data ("B2G Data Sharing")', *Max Planck Institute for Innovation and Competition Research Paper No. 20-06*, 2020, available at https://ssrn.com/abstract=3594109.

Richter, H., 'Exposing the Public Interest Dimension of the Digital Single Market: Public Undertakings as a Model for Regulating Data Sharing', *Max Planck Institute for Innovation and Competition Research Paper No. 20-03*, 2020, available at https://ssrn.com/abstract=3565762.

Taylor, L., 'Hacking a Path Through the Personal Data Ecosystem', December 2013, available at https://linnettaylor.wordpress.com/2013/12/12/hacking-a-path-through-the-personal-data-ecosystem/.

Vezzoso, S., 'Fintech, Access to Data, and the Role of Competition Policy', 2018, available at https://papers.ssrn.com/sol3/papers.cfm?abstract_id=3106594.

Guidelines and Opinions

Article 29 Working Party, *Guidelines on Automated Individual Decision-Making and Profiling for the Purposes of Regulation 2016/679*, WP 251 rev.01, 6 February 2018, available at https://ec.europa.eu/newsroom/article29/item-detail.cfm?item_id=612053.

Article 29 Working Party, *Guidelines on Transparency under Regulation 2016/679*, WP 260 rev.01, 11 April 2018, available at https://ec.europa.eu/newsroom/article29/item-detail.cfm?item_id=622227.

Article 29 Working Party, *Guidelines on the Right to Data Portability*, WP 242 rev.01, 5 April 2017, available at https://ec.europa.eu/newsroom/article29/item-detail.cfm?item_id=611233.

Article 29 Working Party, *Guidelines on the Right to Data Portability*, WP 242, 13 December 2016, available at https://ec.europa.eu/information_society/newsroom/image/document/2016-51/wp242_en_40852.pdf.

Article 29 Working Party, *Opinion 8/2014 on the Recent Developments on the Internet of Things*, WP 223, 16 September 2014, available at https://ec.europa.eu/justice/article-29/documentation/opinion-recommendation/files/2014/wp223_en.pdf.

Article 29 Working Party, *Opinion 05/2014 on Anonymisation Techniques*, WP 216, 10 April 2014, available at https://www.pdpjournals.com/docs/88197.pdf.

Article 29 Working Party, *Opinion 03/2013 on Purpose Limitation*, WP 203, 2 April 2013, available at https://ec.europa.eu/justice/article-29/documentation/opinion-recommendation/files/2013/wp203_en.pdf.

Article 29 Working Party, *Opinion 4/2007 on the Concept of Personal Data*, WP 136, 20 June 2007, available at https://ec.europa.eu/justice/article-29/documentation/opinion-recommendation/files/2007/wp136_en.pdf.

Bundeskartellamt and Bundeswettbewerbsbehörde, 'Guidance on Transaction Value Thresholds for Mandatory Pre-merger Notification (Section 35(1a) GWB and Section 9(4) KartG)', July 2018, available at https://www.bundeskartellamt.de/SharedDocs/Publikation/EN/Leitfaden/Leitfaden_Transaktionsschwelle.pdf?__blob=publicationFile&v=2.

European Data Protection Board and European Data Protection Supervisor, *Joint Opinion 03/2021 on the Proposal for a Regulation of the European Parliament and of the Council on European Data Governance (Data Governance Act)*, 10 March 2021, available at https://edpb.europa.eu/our-work-tools/our-documents/edpbedps-joint-opinion/edpb-edps-joint-opinion-032021-proposal_fr.

European Data Protection Board, *Guidelines 07/2020 on the Concepts of Controller and Processor in the GDPR*, Version 1.0, 2 September 2020, available at https://edpb.europa.eu/sites/edpb/files/consultation/edpb_guidelines_202007_contro llerprocessor_en.pdf.

European Data Protection Board, *Guidelines 05/2020 on Consent under Regulation 2016/679*, Version 1.1, May 2020, available at https://edpb.europa.eu/sites/edpb/files/files/file1/edpb_guidelines_202005_consent_en.pdf.

European Data Protection Supervisor, *Opinion 3/2020 on the European Strategy for Data*, 16 June 2020, available at https://edps.europa.eu/sites/edp/files/publication/20-06-16_opinion_data_strategy_en.pdf.

European Data Protection Supervisor, *Opinion 8/2018 on the Legislative Package 'A New Deal for Consumers'*, 5 October 2018, available at https://edps.europa.eu/sites/edp/files/publication/18-10-05_opinion_co nsumer_law_en.pdf.

European Data Protection Supervisor, *Opinion 4/2017 on the Proposal for a Directive on Certain Aspects Concerning Contracts for the Supply of Digital Content*, 14 March 2017, available at https://edps.europa.eu/sites/edp/files/publication/17-03-14_opinion_digital_content_en.pdf.

Reports, Position Papers and Studies

Access Now, 'Three Years under the EU GDPR: An Implementation Progress Report', 2021, available at https://www.accessnow.org/cms/assets/uploads/2021/05/Three-Years-Under-GDPR-report.pdf.

Autorité de la concurrence, 'Contribution de l'Autorité de la concurrence au débat sur la politique de concurrence et les enjeux numériques', 19 February 2020, available at https://www.autoritedelaconcurrence.fr/sites/default/files/2020-02/2020.02.19_contribution_adlc_enjeux_nume riques_vf.pdf.

Autorité de la concurrence and Bundeskartellamt, 'Competition Law and Data', 10 May 2016, available at http://www.autoritedelaconcu rrence.fr/doc/reportcompetitionlawanddatafinal.pdf.

Australian Competition and Consumer Commission, 'Digital Platforms Inquiry – Final Report', 26 July 2019, available at https://www.accc.gov.au/publications/digital-platforms-inquiry-final-report.

Barbero, M., et al., 'Study on Emerging Issues of Data Ownership, Interoperability, (Re-)usability and Access to Data, and Liability', 25 April 2018, available at https://ec.europa.eu/digital-single-market/en/news/study-emerging-issues-data-ownership-interoperability-re-usabili ty-and-access-data-and.

Bourreau, M. and de Streel, A., 'Digital Conglomerates and EU Competition Policy', *CERRE Report*, March 2019, available at http://www.crid.be/pdf/public/8377.pdf.

Bourreau, M., de Streel, A. and Graef, I., 'Big Data and Competition Policy: Market Power, Personalised Pricing and Advertising', *CERRE Report*, 2017, available at http://www.cerre.eu/publications/big-data-and-competition-policy.

Brave, 'Europe's Governments Are Failing the GDPR: Brave's 2020 Report on the Enforcement Capacity of Data Protection Authorities', April 2020, available at https://brave.com/wp-content/uploads/2020/04/Brave-2020-DPA-Report.pdf.

College of Europe, 'Study on the Impact of National Rules on Unilateral Conduct that Diverge from Article 102 of the Treaty on the Functioning of the European Union (TFEU) – Final Report', 21 November 2012, available at https://ec.europa.eu/competition/calls/tenders_closed.html.

Competition and Markets Authority, 'Online Platforms and Digital Advertising: Market Study Final Report', 1 July 2020, available at https://www.gov.uk/cma-cases/online-platforms-and-digital-advertising-market-study.

Competition and Markets Authority, 'Final Approved Roadmap for Open Banking', 14 May 2020, available at https://assets.publishing.service.gov.uk/government/uploads/system/uploads/attachment_data/file/885537/Notice_of_proposed_changes_to_the_open_banking_roadmap_-_web_publication_-_cma_gov_uk_---_May_2020_-.pdf.

Competition and Markets Authority, 'Online Platforms and Digital Advertising: Market Study Interim Report – Appendix L: Potential Approaches to Improving Personal Data Mobility', 18 December 2019, available at https://www.gov.uk/cma-cases/online-platforms-and-digital-advertising-market-study.

Competition and Markets Authority, 'The Retail Banking Market Investigation Order 2017', 2017, available at https://assets.publishing.service.gov.uk/media/5893063bed915d06e1000000/retail-bankingmarketinvestigationor der-2017.pdf.

Competition and Markets Authority, 'Making Banks Work Harder for You', 9 August 2016, available at http://www.agefi.fr/sites/agefi.fr/files/fichiers/2016/08/cma_overview-of-the-banking-retail-market_9_aout.pdf.

Competition and Markets Authority, 'Retail Banking Market Investigation – Final Report', 26 February 2016, available at https://www.gov.uk/cma-cases/review-of-banking-for-small-and-medium-sized-businesses-smes-in-the-uk.

Competition and Markets Authority and Information Commissioner's Office, 'Competition and Data Protection in Digital Markets: A Joint Statement Between the CMA and the ICO', 19 May 2021, available at https://ico.org.uk/media/about-the-ico/documents/2619797/cma-ico-public-statement-20210518.pdf.

Council of Europe, 'Explanatory Report to the Protocol amending the Convention for the Protection of Individuals with Regard to Automatic Processing of Personal Data', *Council of Europe Treaty Series n° 223*, Strasbourg, 10 October 2018, available at https://rm.coe.int/cets-223-explanatory-report-to-the-protocol-amending-the-convention-fo/16808ac91a.

Crémer, J., de Montjoye, Y.-A. and Schweitzer, H., 'Competition Policy for the Digital Era – Final Report', 2019, available at http://ec.europa.eu/competition/publications/reports/ kd0419345enn.pdf.

CtrlShift, 'Data Mobility: The Personal Data Portability Growth Opportunity for the UK Economy', 2018, available at https://www.ctrl-shift.co.uk/reports/DCMS_Ctrl-Shift_Data_mobility_report_full.pdf.

(Irish) Data Protection Commission, 'Annual Report: 1 January – 31 December 2019', 2020, available at https://www.dataprotection.ie/sites/default/files/uploads/2020-02/DPC%20Annual%20Report%202019.pdf.

(Irish) Data Protection Commission, 'Annual Report: 25 May – 31 December 2018', 2019, available at https://www.dataprotection.ie/sites/default/files/uploads/2019-02/DPC%20Annual%20Report%2025%20May%20-%2031%20December%202018.pdf.

Data Transfer Project, 'White Paper: Data Transfer Project Overview and Fundamentals', 20 July 2018, available at https://datatransferproject.dev/dtp-overview.pdf.

de Streel, A., et al., 'The European Proposal for a Digital Markets Act: A First Assessment', *CERRE Assessment Paper*, January 2021, available at https://cerre.eu/publications/the-european-proposal-for-a-digital-markets-act-a-first-assessment/.

de Streel, A., et al., 'Digital Markets Act: Making Economic Regulation of Platforms Fit for the Digital Age', *CERRE Recommendations Paper*, November 2020, available at https://cerre.eu/publications/digital-markets-act-economic-regulation-platforms-digital-age/.

Deloitte, 'Realising the Economic Potential of Machine-Generated, Non-personal Data in the EU', *Report for Vodaphone Group*, July 2018, available at https://www.vodafone.com/content/dam/vodcom/files/

public-policy/Realising_the_potential_of_IoT_data_report_for_Vodafone.pdf.

Drexl, J., 'Data Access and Control in the Era of Connected Devices', *Study on Behalf of the European Consumer Organisation (BEUC)*, 2019, available at https://www.beuc.eu/publications/beuc-x-2018 121_data_access_and_control_in_the_area_of _connected_devices.pdf.

Egan, E., 'Data Portability and Privacy', *Facebook White Paper*, September 2019, available at https://iapp.org/media/pdf/fb_whitepaper_sep_2019.pdf.

Everis, 'Study on data sharing between companies in Europe – Final report', *Study for the European Commission*, 2018, available at https://publications.europa.eu/en/publication-detail/-/publication/8b8776ff-4834-11e8-be1d-01aa75ed71a1/language-en.

Everis, 'Study on data sharing between companies in Europe – Case studies', *Study for the European Commission*, 2018, available at https://publications.europa.eu/en/publication-detail/-/publication/8b8776ff-4834-11e8-be1d-01aa75ed71a1/language-en.

Expert Group for the Observatory on the Online Platform Economy, 'Work Stream on Data: Final Report', 26 February 2021, available at https://ec.europa.eu/digital-single-market/en/news/expert-group-eu-observatory-online-platform-economy-final-reports.

Expert Group for the Observatory on the Online Platform Economy, 'Measurement & Economic Indicators: Final Report', 26 February 2021, available at https://ec.europa.eu/digital-single-market/en/news/expert-group-eu-observatory-online-platform-economy-final-reports.

Expert Group for the Observatory on the Online Platform Economy, 'Work Stream on Differentiated Treatment: Final Report', 26 February 2021, available at https://ec.europa.eu/digital-single-market/en/news/expert-group-eu-observatory-online-platform-economy-final-reports.

Feasey, R. and de Streel, A., 'Data Sharing for Digital Market Contestability: Towards a Governance Framework', *CERRE Report*, September 2020, available at https://cerre.eu/publications/data-sharing-digital-markets-competition-governance/.

French Ministry of the Economy, Finance and the Recovery, German Federal Ministry for Economic Affairs and Energy and Dutch Ministry of Economic Affairs and Climate Policy, 'Strengthening the Digital Markets Act and Its Enforcement', May 2021, available at https://www.economie.gouv.fr/files/2021-05/1055%20-%20Strengthening%20the%20Digital%20Markets%20Act%20and%20Its%20Enforcement.pdf.

Freshfields Bruckhaus Deringer, 'New Competition Tool: Observations in the Context of the Commission's Public Consultation', 8 September 2020, available at https://passle-net.s3.amazonaws.com/Passle/5832ca6d3d94760e8057a1b6/MediaLibrary/Document/2020-09-09-14-52-58-669-FreshfieldsSubmissionNewCT.pdf.

Furman, J., et al., 'Unlocking Digital Competition', *Report of the Digital Competition Expert Panel for the British Chancellor of the Exchequer and Secretary of State for Business, Energy and Industrial Strategy*, 2019, available at https://www.gov.uk/government/publications/unlocking-digital-competition-report-of-the-digital-competition-expert-panel.

German Federal Ministry for Economic Affairs and Energy, 'A New Competition Framework for the Digital Economy: Report by the Commission "Competition Law 4.0" – Executive Summary', 9 September 2019, available at https://www.bmwi.de/Redaktion/EN/Downloads/a/a-new-competition-framework.pdf?__blob=publicationFile&v=2.

High-Level Expert Group on Business-to-Government Data Sharing, 'Towards a European Strategy on Business-to-Government Data Sharing for Public Interests – Final Report', 2020, available at https://ec.europa.eu/digital-single-market/en/news/experts-say-privately-held-data-available-european-union-should-be-used-better-and-more.

HM Government, 'Smart Data: Putting Consumers in Control of Their Data and Enabling Innovation', June 2019, available at https://www.gov.uk/government/consultations/smart-data-putting-consumers-in-control-of-their-data-and-enabling-innovation.

Information Commissioner's Office, 'Data Sharing Code of Practice', 17 December 2020, available at https://ico.org.uk/for-organisations/data-sharing-a-code-of-practice/.

Information Commissioner's Office, 'Big Data, Artificial Intelligence, Machine Learning and Data Protection', 4 September 2017, available at https://ico.org.uk/media/for-organisations/documents/2013559/big-data-ai-ml-and-data-protection.pdf.

International Data Corporation and the Lisbon Council, 'The European Data Market Study Monitoring Tool – Final Study Report', June 2020, SMART 2016/0063, available at http://datalandscape.eu/.

Jiip, T. Bently, L. and Derclaye, E., 'Study in Support of the Evaluation of Directive 96/9/EC on the Legal Protection of Databases – Final Report', 2018, available at https://ec.europa.eu/digital-single-market/en/news/study-support-evaluation-database-directive.

Kemp, R., 'Legal Aspects of Managing Data (White Paper)', October 2019, available at http://www.kempitlaw.com/legal-aspects-of-managing-data/.

Krämer, J., Schnurr, D. and Broughton Micova, S., 'The Role of Data for Digital Markets Contestability: Case Studies and Data Access Remedies', *CERRE Report*, September 2020, available at https://cerre.eu/publications/data-digital-markets-contestability-case-studies-and-data-access-remedies/.

Krämer, J., Senellart, P. and de Streel, A., 'Making Data Portability More Effective for the Digital Economy', *CERRE Report*, 2020, available at https://www.cerre.eu/publications/report-making-data-portability-more-effective-digital-economy.

Langford, J., et al. (eds), 'Understanding MyData Operators', *MyData Global Report*, 29 April 2020, available at https://mydata.org/wp-content/uploads/sites/5/2020/04/Understanding-Mydata-Operators-pages.pdf.

Lear, 'Ex-post Assessment of Merger Control Decisions in Digital Markets – Final Report', 9 May 2019, available at https://assets.publishing.service.gov.uk/government/uploads/system/uploads/attachment_data/file/803576/CMA_past_digital_mergers_GOV.UK_version.pdf.

Netherlands Authority for Consumers and Markets, 'Big Techs in the Payment System', 16 November 2020, available at https://www.acm.nl/en/publications/acm-study-big-techs-dutch-payment-system.

OECD, *Consumer Data Rights and Competition – Background note*, June 2020, DAF/COMP(2020)1, available at http://www.oecd.org/daf/competition/consumer-data-rights-and-competition.htm.

OECD, 'Lines of Business Restrictions – Background note', 8 June 2020, DAF/COMP/WP2(2020)1, available at https://one.oecd.org/document/DAF/COMP/WP2(2020)1/en/pdf.

Open Data Institute, 'Sharing Data to Create Value in the Private Sector', 2020, available at https://theodi.org/article/report-sharing-data-to-create-value-in-the-private-sector/.

Open Data Institute, 'Data Trusts: Lessons from Three Pilots', 2019, available at https://theodi.org/article/odi-data-trusts-report/.

Open Data Institute and Fingleton, 'Open Banking, Preparing for Lift Off: Purpose Progress and Potential', 16 July 2019, available at https://www.openbanking.org.uk/wp-content/uploads/open-banking-report-150719.pdf.

Prüfer, J., 'Competition Policy and Data Sharing on Data-driven Markets', *Report for the Friedrich-Ebert-Stiftung*, 2020, available at http://library.fes.de/pdf-files/fes/15999.pdf.

Renda, A., et al., 'Study on the Legal Framework Covering Business-to-Business Unfair Trading Practices in the Retail Supply Chain – Final Report', DG MARKT/2012/049/E, 26 February 2014, available at https://op.europa.eu/en/publication-detail/-/publication/c82dc8c6-ec15-11e5-8a81-01aa75ed71a1/language-en.

Rouvroy, A., '"Of Data and Men": Fundamental Rights and Liberties in a World of Big Data', *Report for the Consultative Committee of the Convention for the Protection of Individuals with Regard to Automatic Processing of Personal Data (T-PD)*, T-PD-BUR(2015)09REV, Council of Europe, Strasbourg, 11 January 2016.

Samson, R., Gibbon, K. and Scott, A., 'About Data About Us,' September 2019, available at https://www.thersa.org/globalassets/pdfs/reports/data-about-us-final-report.pdf.

Schweitzer, H., et al., 'A New Competition Framework for the Digital Economy', *Report by the Commission 'Competition Law 4.0' for the German Federal Ministry for Economic Affairs and Energy*, 2019, available at https://www.bmwi.de/Redaktion/EN/Downloads/a/a-new-competition-framework.pdf?__blob=publicationFile&v=2.

Schweitzer, H., et al., *Modernisierung der Missbrauchsaufsicht für marktmächtige Unternehmen*, Baden-Baden, Nomos, 2018 (also available at https://www.bmwi.de/Redaktion/DE/Publikationen/Wirtschaft/modernisierung-der-missbrauchsaufsicht-fuer-marktmaechtigeunternehmen.html (an executive summary in English is available at https://ssrn.com/abstract=3250742)).

Schweitzer, H., Haucap, J., Kerber, W. and Welker, R., 'Modernising the Law on Abuse of Market Power: Executive Summary', *Report for the German Federal Ministry for Economic Affairs and Energy*, 29 August 2018, available at https://ssrn.com/abstract=3250742.

Steenbergen, J., Snoep, M. and Barthelmé, P., 'Joint Memorandum of the Belgian, Dutch and Luxembourg Competition Authorities on Challenges Faced by Competition Authorities in a Digital World', 2 October 2019, available at https://www.belgiancompetition.be/en/about-us/publications/joint-memorandum-belgian-dutch-and-luxembourg-competition-authorities.

Stigler Committee on Digital Platforms, 'Final Report', September 2019, available at https://research.chicagobooth.edu/stigler/media/news/committee-on-digital-platforms-final-report.

Support Centre for Data Sharing, 'B.2 – Analytical Report on EU Law Applicable to Sharing of Non-personal Data', SMART 2018/2019, 24 January 2020, available at https://eudatasharing.eu/fr/legal-aspects.

Support Centre for Data Sharing, 'B.1 – Report on Collected Model Contract Terms', SMART 2018/2019, 26 July 2019, available at https://eudatasharing.eu/fr/legal-aspects.

TRL, 'Access to In-Vehicle Data and Resources – Final Report', *Study for the European Commission*, May 2017, available at https://ec.europa.eu/transport/sites/transport/files/2017-05-access-to-in-vehicle-data-and-resources.pdf.

United States House of Representatives Committee on the Judiciary, 'Investigation of Competition in Digital Markets – Majority Staff Report and Recommendations', 2020, available at https://judiciary.house.gov/uploadedfiles/competition_in_digital_markets.pdf.

Van Asbroeck, B., Debussche, J. and César, J., 'White Paper – Data Ownership in the Context of the European Data Economy: Proposal for a New Right', 2017, available at https://www.twobirds.com/en/news/articles/2017/global/data-ownership-in-the-context-of-the-european-data-economy.

Blogs, News and Press Releases

Acemoğlu, D., et al., 'Can We Have Too Much Data?', 18 November 2019, available at https://voxeu.org/article/can-we-have-too-much-data.

Adam, L., 'RGPD: Amazon écope d'une amende record à 746 millions d'euros', 30 July 2021, available at https://www.zdnet.fr/actualites/rgpd-amazon-ecope-d-une-amende-record-a-746-millions-d-euros-399 26965.htm.

Aszendorf, Z. and Pratt, G., 'CJEU Narrows Protection Afforded to Database Right in the EU', 9 June 2021, available at https://www.lexology.com/library/detail.aspx?g=f399c5bb-58ac-4162-b2c8-b8a53297f800&utm_source=Lexology+Daily+Newsfeed&utm_medium=HTML+email+-+Body+-+General+section&utm_campaign=Lexology+subscriber+daily+feed&utm_content=Lexology+Daily+Newsfeed+2021-06-11&utm_term=.

Barbaro, M. and Zeller, T., 'A Face Is Exposed for AOL Searcher No. 4417749', *The New York Times*, 9 August 2006, available at https://www.nytimes.com/2006/08/09/technology/09aol.html.

Bertuzzi, L., 'Irish Watchdog Given One Month to Finalise Whatsapp Privacy Ruling', 29 July 2021, available at https://www.euractiv.com/

section/data-protection/news/irish-watchdog-given-one-month-to-final ise-whatsapp-privacy-ruling/.

Bodoni, S., 'Amazon Gets Record $888 Million EU Fine Over Data Violations', 30 July 2021, available at https://www.bloomberg.com/news/articles/2021-07-30/amazon-given-record-888-million-eu-fine-for-data-privacy-breach.

Bodoni, S., 'Facebook Targeted in the U.K. Legal Action Over Cambridge Analytica', *Bloomberg*, 28 October 2020, available at https://www.bloomberg.com/news/articles/2020-10-28/facebook-targeted-in-u-k-legal-action-over-cambridge-analytica.

Brave, 'Inside the Black Box: A Glimpse of Google's Internal Data Free-for-All', 2020, available at https://brave.com/wp-content/uploads/2020/03/Inside-the-Black-Box.pdf.

Brennan, C., et al., 'hiQ Labs, Inc. v. LinkedIn Corp.: Federal Judge Dismisses Antitrust Claims Regarding Access to Data', 1 October 2020, available at https://www.reedsmith.com/en/perspectives/2020/10/hiq-labs-inc-v-linkedin-corp-federal-judge-dismisses-antitrust-claims.

Bundesgerichtshof, 'Bundesgerichtshof bestätigt vorläufig den Vorwurf der missbräuchlichen Ausnutzung einer marktbeherrschenden Stellung durch Facebook,' 23 June 2020, available at https://www.bundesgerichtshof.de/SharedDocs/Pressemitteilungen/DE/2020/2020080.html.

Bundeskartellamt, 'Amendment of the German Act Against Restraints of Competition (Press Release)', 19 January 2021, available at https://www.bundeskartellamt.de/SharedDocs/Meldung/EN/Pressemitteilungen/2021/19_01_2021_GWB%20Novelle.html.

Bundeskartellamt, 'Bundeskartellamt Prohibits Facebook from Combining User Data from Different Sources', 7 February 2019, available at https://www.bundeskartellamt.de/SharedDocs/Meldung/EN/Pressemitteilungen/2019/07_02_2019_Facebook.html.

Chang, A., 'The Facebook and Cambridge Analytica Scandal, Explained with a Simple Diagram', 2 May 2018, available at https://www.vox.com/policy-and-politics/2018/3/23/17151916/facebook-cambridge-analytica-trump-diagram.

Competition and Markets Authority, 'CMA to Investigate Google's "Privacy Sandbox" Browser Changes', 8 January 2021, available at https://www.gov.uk/government/news/cma-to-investigate-google-s-privacy-sandbox-browser-changes.

European Commission, 'Antitrust: Commission sends Statement of Objections to Insurance Ireland', *Press release n° IP/21/3081,* 18 June 2021, available at https://ec.europa.eu/commission/presscorner/detail/en/ip_21_3081.

European Commission, 'Mergers: Commission clears acquisition of Fitbit by Google, subject to conditions', *Press release n° IP/20/2484*, 17 December 2020, available at https://ec.europa.eu/commission/presscorner/detail/en/IP_20_2484.

European Commission, 'Questions and Answers – Establishing a fair, trusted and innovation driven ecosystem in the Online Platform Economy', 9 July 2020, available at https://ec.europa.eu/digital-single-market/en/business-business-trading-practices.

European Data Protection Board, 'EDPB Adopts Art. 65 Decision Regarding WhatsApp Ireland', 28 July 2021, available at https://edpb.europa.eu/news/news/2021/edpb-adopts-art-65-decision-regarding-whatsapp-ireland_en.

Gielen, B. and Verdonck, C., 'First Belgian Ruling on Abuse of Economic Dependence', 3 December 2020, available at https://www.lexology.com.

Granville, K., 'Facebook and Cambridge Analytica: What You Need to Know as Fallout Widens', *New York Times*, 19 March 2018, available at https://www.nytimes.com/2018/03/19/technology/facebook-cambridge-analytica-explained.html.

Lyons, D., 'GDPR: Privacy as Europe's Tariff by Other Means?', 3 July 2018, available at https://www.aei.org/technology-and-innovation/gdpr-privacy-as-europes-tariff-by-other-means/.

Manancourt, V., 'Irish Data Regulator Pulls Out of "Perverse" MEP Hearing as Tensions Boil Over', 18 March 2021, available at https://pro.politico.eu/news/irish-data-regulator-pulls-out-of-perverse-mep-hearing-as-tensions-boil-over.

McCandless, D., 'Data, Information, Knowledge, Wisdom', 29 November 2010, available at http://www.informationisbeautiful.net/2010/data-information-knowledge-wisdom/.

McClelland, J., Grimes, S. and Murphy, S., 'EU Trade Secrets Directive: What Are "Reasonable Steps"?', 7 February 2019, available at https://www.lexology.com/library/detail.aspx?g=b59572d9-5e29-44e4-b4fe-67c5559bcf32&filterId=c6af7021-82de-49f8-96af-884381b2f7d6.

Meyer, D., 'European Commission Experts Uneasy over WP29 Data Portability Interpretation', 25 April 2017, available at https://iapp.org/news/a/european-commission-experts-uneasy-over-wp29-data-portability-interpretation-1/.

Open Data Institute, 'Data Access Map', available at https://theodi.org/project/the-data-access-map/#1565707571855-6d70b0a0-3243.

Pearson, J., 'Yahoo's Gigantic "Anonymized" User Dataset Isn't All That Anonymous', 14 January 2016, available at https://www.vice.com/en/article/yp3d8v/yahoos-gigantic-anonymized-user-dataset-isnt-all-that-anonymous.

Privacy International, 'Ad Tech GDPR Complaint Is Extended to Four More European Regulators', 20 May 2019, available at https://privacyinternational.org/examples/2992/ad-tech-gdpr-complaint-extended-four-more-european-regulators.

Privacy International, 'Panoptykon Foundation Files Complaint Against Google and Other "Ad Tech" Companies with the with the Polish Data Protection Authority', 28 January 2019, available at https://privacyinternational.org/examples/2982/panoptykon-foundation-files-complaint-against-googleand-other-ad-tech-companies.

Privacy International, 'Regulatory Complaint Against Google and Other "Ad Tech" Companies under Europe's GDPR by Johnny Ryan, Jim Killock, and Michael Veale', 12 September 2018, available at https://privacyinternational.org/examples/2983/regulatory-complaint-against-google-and-other-ad-tech-companies-under-europes-gdpr.

Ryan, J., 'Formal GDPR Complaint Against Google's Internal Data Free-for-All', 16 March 2020, available at https://brave.com/google-internal-data-free-for-all/.

Satariano, A., 'Europe's Privacy Law Hasn't Shown Its Teeth, Frustrating Advocates', *The New York Times*, 27 April 2020, available at https://www.nytimes.com/2020/04/27/technology/GDPR-privacy-law-europe.html.

Stolton, S., 'MEPs Rue Lack of GDPR Sanctions Issued by Irish Data Authority', 26 March 2021, available at https://www.euractiv.com/section/data-protection/news/meps-rue-lack-of-gdpr-sanctions-issued-by-irish-data-authority/.

Stolton, S., 'German Legal Dispute over Facebook Data Use Sent to European Court of Justice', 24 March 2021, available at https:// www.euractiv.com/section/data-protection/news/german-legal-dispute-over-facebook-data-use-sent-to-european-court-of-justice/.

Stolton, S., 'Blacklist Prohibitions to Be "Very Limited" to Large Platforms, Commission Says', 9 December 2020, available at https://www.euractiv.com/section/digital/news/blacklist-prohibitions-to-be-very-limited-to-large-platforms-commission-says/.

Vinocur, N., '"We Have a Huge Problem": European Tech Regulator Despairs over Lack of Enforcement', *Politico*, 27 December 2019, available at https://www.politico.com/news/2019/12/27/europe-gdpr-technology-regulation-089605.

INFORMATION LAW SERIES

1. Egbert J. Dommering & P. Bernt Hugenholtz, *Protecting Works of Fact: Copyright, Freedom of Expression and Information Law,* 1991 (ISBN 90-654-4567-6).
2. Willem F. Korthals Altes, Egbert J. Dommering, P. Bernt Hugenholtz & Jan J.C. Kabel, *Information Law Towards the 21st Century,* 1992 (ISBN 90-654-4627-3).
3. Jacqueline M.B. Seignette, *Challenges to the Creator Doctrine: Authorship, Copyright Ownership and the Exploitation of Creative Works in the Netherlands, Germany and The United States,* 1994 (ISBN 90-654-4876-4).
4. P. Bernt Hugenholtz, *The Future of Copyright in a Digital Environment, Proceedings of the Royal Academy Colloquium,* 1996 (ISBN 90-411-0267-1).
5. Julius C.S. Pinckaers, *From Privacy Toward a New Intellectual Property Right in Persona,* 1996 (ISBN 90-411-0355-4).
6. Jan J.C. Kabel & Gerard J.H.M. Mom, *Intellectual Property and Information Law: Essays in Honour of Herman Cohen Jehoram,* 1998 (ISBN 90-411-9702-8).
7. Ysolde Gendreau, Axel Nordemann & Rainer Oesch, *Copyright and Photographs: An International Survey,* 1999 (ISBN 90-411-9722-2).
8. P. Bernt Hugenholtz, *Copyright and Electronic Commerce: Legal Aspects of Electronic Copyright Management,* 2000 (ISBN 90-411-9785-0).
9. Lucie M.C.R. Guibault, *Copyright Limitations and Contracts: An Analysis of the Contractual Overridability of Limitations on Copyright,* 2002 (ISBN 90-411-9867-9).
10. Lee A. Bygrave, *Data Protection Law: Approaching its Rationale, Logic and Limits,* 2002 (ISBN 90-411-9870-9).
11. Niva Elkin-Koren & Neil Weinstock Netanel, *The Commodification of Information,* 2002 (ISBN 90-411-9876-8).
12. Mireille M.M. van Eechoud, *Choice of Law in Copyright and Related Rights: Alternatives to the Lex Protectionis,* 2003 (ISBN 90-411-2071-8).
13. Martin Senftleben, *Copyright, Limitations and the Three-Step Test: An Analysis of the Three-Step Test in International and EC Copyright Law,* 2004 (ISBN 90-411-2267-2).
14. Paul L.C. Torremans, *Copyright and Human Rights: Freedom of Expression – Intellectual Property – Privacy,* 2004 (ISBN 90-411-2278-8).
15. Natali Helberger, *Controlling Access to Content: Regulating Conditional Access in Digital Broadcasting,* 2005 (ISBN 90-411-2345-8).
16. Lucie M.C.R. Guibault & P. Bernt Hugenholtz, *The Future of the Public Domain: Identifying the Commons in Information Law,* 2006 (ISBN 978-90-411-2435-7).

17. Irini Katsirea, *Public Broadcasting and European Law: A Comparative Examination of Public Service Obligations in Six Member States,* 2008 (ISBN 978-90-411-2500-2).
18. Paul L.C. Torremans, *Intellectual Property and Human Rights: Enhanced Edition of Copyright and Human Rights,* 2008 (ISBN 978-90-411-2653-5).
19. Mireille van Eechoud, P. Bernt Hugenholtz, Stef van Gompel, Lucie Guibault & Natali Helberger, *Harmonizing European Copyright Law: The Challenges of Better Lawmaking,* 2009 (ISBN 978-90-411-3130-0).
20. Ashwin van Rooijen, *The Software Interface between Copyright and Competition Law: A Legal Analysis of Interoperability in Computer Programs,* 2010 (ISBN 978-90-411-3193-5).
21. Irini A. Stamatoudi, *Copyright Enforcement and the Internet,* 2010 (ISBN 978-90-411-3346-5).
22. Wolfgang Sakulin, *Trademark Protection and Freedom of Expression: An Inquiry into the Conflict between Trademark Rights and Freedom of Expression under European Law,* 2011 (ISBN 978-90-411-3415-8).
23. Stef van Gompel, *Formalities in Copyright Law: An Analysis of their History, Rationales and Possible Future,* 2011 (ISBN 978-90-411-3418-9).
24. Nadezhda Purtova, *Property Rights in Personal Data: A European Perspective,* 2012 (ISBN 978-90-411-3802-6).
25. Brad Sherman & Leanne Wiseman, *Copyright and the Challenge of the New,* 2012 (ISBN 978-90-411-3669-5).
26. Ewa Komorek, *Media Pluralism and European Law*, 2012 (ISBN 978-90-411-3894-1).
27. Joris van Hoboken, *Search Engine Freedom: On the Implications of the Right to Freedom of Expression for the Legal Governance of Web Search Engines,* 2012 (ISBN 978-90-411-4128-6).
28. Natali Helberger, Lucie Guibault, Marco Loos, Chantal Mak, Lodewijk Pessers & Bart van der Sloot, *Digital Consumers and the Law: Towards a Cohesive European Framework*, 2012 (ISBN 978-90-411-4049-4).
29. Tatiana-Eleni Synodinou, *Codification of European Copyright Law: Challenges and Perspectives,* 2012 (ISBN 978-90-411-4145-3).
30. Heather Ann Forrest, *Protection of Geographic Names in International Law and Domain Name System Policy*, Second Edition, 2017 (ISBN 978-90-411-8839-7).
31. Sari Depreeuw, *The Variable Scope of the Exclusive Economic Rights in Copyright*, 2014 (ISBN 978-90-411-4915-2).
32. Vikrant Narayan Vasudeva, *Open Source Software and Intellectual Property Rights*, 2014 (ISBN 978-90-411-5228-2).
33. Frederik J. Zuiderveen Borgesius, *Improving Privacy Protection in the Area of Behavioural Targeting*, 2015 (ISBN 978-90-411-5990-8).
34. Paul L.C. Torremans, *Intellectual Property Law and Human Rights*, Fourth Edition, 2020 (ISBN 978-94-035-1304-1).

35. Irini A. Stamatoudi, *New Developments in EU and International Copyright Law*, 2016 (ISBN 978-90-411-5991-5).
36. Lodewijk W.P. Pessers, *The Inventiveness Requirement in Patent Law: An Exploration of Its Foundations and Functioning*, 2016 (ISBN 978-90-411-6731-6).
37. Susy Frankel & Daniel Gervais, *The Internet and the Emerging Importance of New Forms of Intellectual Property*, 2016 (ISBN 978-90-411-6789-7).
38. Axel M. Arnbak, *Securing Private Communications: Protecting Private Communications Security in EU Law – Fundamental Rights, Functional Value Chains, and Market Incentives*, 2016 (ISBN 978-90-411-6737-8).
39. Christina Angelopoulos, *European Intermediary Liability in Copyright: A Tort-Based Analysis*, 2017 (ISBN 978-90-411-6835-1).
40. João Pedro Quintais, *Copyright in the Age of Online Access: Alternative Compensation Systems in EU Law*, 2017 (ISBN 978-90-411-8667-6).
41. P. Bernt Hugenholtz, *Copyright Reconstructed: Rethinking Copyright's Economic Rights in a Time of Highly Dynamic Technological and Economic Change*, 2018 (ISBN 978-90-411-9103-8).
42. Manon Oostveen, *Protecting Individuals Against the Negative Impact of Big Data: Potential and Limitations of the Privacy and Data Protection Law Approach*, 2018 (ISBN 978-94-035-0131-4).
43. Tatiana Eleni Synodinou (ed.), *Pluralism or Universalism in International Copyright Law*, 2019 (ISBN 978-94-035-0355-4).
44. Martin Senftleben, *The Copyright/Trademark Interface: How the Expansion of Trademark Protection Is Stifling Cultural Creativity*, 2021 (ISBN 978-94-035-2370-5).
45. Tito Rendas, *Exceptions in EU Copyright Law: In Search of a Balance Between Flexibility and Legal Certainty*, 2021 (ISBN 978-94-035-2395-8).
46. Martin Senftleben, Joost Poort, Mireille van Eechoud, Stef van Gompel & Natalie Helberger (eds), *Intellectual Property and Sports: Essays in Honour of P. Bernt Hugenholtz*, 2021 (ISBN 978-94-035-3733-7).
47. Marijn Sax, *Between Empowerment and Manipulation: The Ethics and Regulation of For-Profit Health Apps*, 2021 (ISBN 978-94-035-3791-7).
48. Thomas Tombal, *Imposing Data Sharing among Private Actors: A Tale of Evolving Balances*, 2022 (ISBN 978-94-035-4160-0).